COLONIAL CAROLINE

A History of
Caroline County, Virginia

BY

T. E. CAMPBELL

THE DIETZ PRESS, INCORPORATED
RICHMOND, VIRGINIA

Please direct all correspondence and orders to:

www.southernhistoricalpress.com
or
SOUTHERN HISTORICAL PRESS, Inc.
PO BOX 1267
375 West Broad Street
Greenville, SC   29601
southernhistoricalpress@gmail.com

Originally published: Richmond 1954
Reprinted by:
Southern Historical Press, Inc.
Greenville, SC
ISBN #0-89308-905-2
All rights Reserved.
Printed in the United States of America

Caroline of Ansbach

(DEDICATION)

THIS history of Caroline County, Virginia, I dedicate to Caroline of Ansbach for whom the county was named. So far as I can learn this is the first attempt of a resident of the county to honor this lady, which is unfortunate because she was a remarkable person.

Caroline was born in 1683, the elder daughter of the second wife of the Margrave of Ansbach, a small principality in central Germany. When she was three her father died, and two years later her mother married again; this time to the Elector of Saxony, and she went to live with her mother and step-father at the Saxon Court in Leipzig. Here she remained for seven years, and until both parent and step-parent died, when she moved on to the Prussian-Brandenburg Court in Berlin to be with her god-mother, the Electress of Brandenburg and Queen of Prussia.

In Berlin she received an excellent education, her god-mother who was a rabid feminist saw to that, and grew up to be what was considered by the standards of the time, a great beauty; flaxen hair, blue eyes, flawless complexion and a short plump figure, which today (1953) would be classed as dumpy. When she was eighteen she entertained her first beau. He was Charles of Hapsburg, pretender to the throne of Spain and heir to the crown of Austria, and considered in royal circles as the greatest catch in Europe. At first Caroline was dazzled, but soon she began to quarrel with her suitor over religion. She was a Protestant, he a Catholic, and it was necessary for her to become a Catholic to be queen of either Spain or Austria. Charles expected her to change her faith as a matter of course. Customarily princesses made the switch to gain a throne without a moment's hesitation, but Caroline was obstinate. She refused to change, unless she was converted. To humor her Charles sent some of the most learned Catholic theologians of the day to Berlin as her teachers, but instead of meekly accepting their instructions, she argued with them until they left her in a huff. This went on until Charles withdrew his suit in disgust. There was no woman worth jeopardizing his inheritance.

In latter years Caroline capitalized on this incident. She battled to place her husband, George II, with the slogan "We want Caroline for Queen. Caroline who scorned two mighty empires for sweet religion's sake."

Friedrich Wilhelm, crown prince of Prussia, was Caroline's next suitor. She regarded him as a barbaric lout, goose-footing about with a phalanx of soldiers over six foot tall. But to get rid of him without giving offense was a delicate matter since he was the son of her patroness, the Queen Electress. In the end to ease out of this unfortunate position, she left Berlin to pay a long visit to her half-brother, who had succeeded her father as the Margrave of Ansbach.

While Caroline was in Ansbach, George Augustus, son of the Elector of Hanover, heard of her, and sent a courtier to see if she was as beautiful as rumored. The courtier reported that she was, but George Augustus still was not satisfied, and went to Ansbach to find out for himself. What he saw evidently pleased him because shortly thereafter, as soon as the necessary formalities were completed, he and Caroline were married, and she went with him to live in Hanover.

When Caroline reached Hanover her troubles began. She had to live in the castle with her father-in-law, the cantankerous Elector of Hanover, who was in time to become George I of England. The Elector hated all women but his mistresses, he tormented his mother, the dowager electress Sophia, to death, and kept his wife Dorothy of Celle, in jail for thirteen years. Caroline was the only woman in his family whom he never conquered, although he tried every means at his command to break her will.

Sophia, the dowager-electress, in a measure acted as a buffer between her son and granddaughter-in-law, but when she died, and the family moved to England to become the royal family of that country, upon the death of Queen Anne, the feud burst into the open. Caroline and George I, now had something to fight about and there was no longer anyone to stand in the way of their fighting. Caroline wanted the family to become anglicized since they now ruled England, and George I wanted them to remain German. In the end she won and her heirs still hold the British crown, but she did not win until after a hard struggle.

George I spoke no English and was determined to keep his court a bit of Germany in the heart of London. When Caroline learned the new tongue and began to cultivate friends among the native nobility, George I drove her and her husband, who was too lazy to learn English but took her side, from St. James Palace. The king did this in a most gruesome manner. He aroused his son and daughter-in-law during the night, and after snatching their children from them, forced them to leave with only the clothes on their backs as their possessions, and without any means for their support. Caroline's child, who was a baby at the time, died a few days later because of neglect after being deprived of its mother. George I placed the older children in the hands of German governesses and tutors to be reared stolid Germans.

Caroline's newly made English friends supported her and her husband until George I due to pressure from Parliament, granted the pair a small stipend for their living expenses. Caroline used this money to set up a rival "court" at Leister House. This "court" was unofficial but it was English and stood out in striking contrast to the royal court at St. James, which had become known as the court of the "Turks and Germans." To Leister House came the great men of London, Newton, Swift and Pope, although they knew to visit Caroline was to be barred from St. James. Caroline assiduously cultivated Sir Robert Walpole and Lord Townshend, leader of the Whig majority in Parliament, whom George I tolerated as unavoidable evils.

These acts widened the breach in the royal family. As George I grew older and realized the end of his reign was near, he tried desperately to arrange to have the crown pass directly at his death to his eldest grandson, and Caroline's eldest son, Frederick, who had spent practically all of his life in Germany and was as thorough a German as his grandsire. But these plans fell through. When the old king died Caroline was ready. After a bitter struggle between the German and English parties, the English party, which she headed, won and she mounted the throne as the consort of her husband the new king, George II. The English masses quickly recognized that she and not George was their real ruler; and in their pubs and music halls sang:

> *"You may strut dapper George*
> *But 'twill be in vain,*
> *We know 'tis Queen Caroline*
> *And not you who reign."*

CONTENTS

CONTENTS (*Cont.*) xiii

INDUSTRY 403
   a. The Grist Mills 404
      Artisans 406

CREDIT 407
   a. Bankers and Money Lenders- 407
      Poor Debtors who Surrendered their Property and
      Took the Pauper's Oath in Caroline County . . . 408

SOCIAL LIFE 410
   1. The Taverns 410
   2. Gambling 415
   3. Horse-racing 417
      Race-tracks 419
   4. Hunting 420
   5. Other Amusements 420

DOMESTIC RELATIONS 420
   1. Marriage 420
   2. Adultery 424
   3. Separate Maintenance 425
   4. Suits for Dower 426
   5. Unwanted Suitors 426
   6. Rape 427
   7. Bastards 427

THE CHURCH 431
   1. Parishes 431
   2. The Churches 431
   3. Ministers 432
   4. Wardens and Vestry 432
   5. The Dissenters 434
   6. Persecutions 434

WELFARE 437

EDUCATION 441

APPRENTICES 444

HEALTH 449
   1. The Physicians 449
   2. Insanity 451

Maps

INTRODUCTION

CAROLINE was the third most populous and affluent county in Virginia during the Revolution. The descendants of its early families contributed, perhaps as much as any other county in America, to the building of the United States. Unfortunately its history has been largely neglected.

This history was based on the Order Books of the Caroline court, the only complete records of the county in existence. They begin in 1732 and form an unbroken log of what happened. Their use presented certain handicaps. They are unindexed and the spelling is far from uniform. The author read them verbatim and made copious notes. He compiled the tables in the encyclopedia of this history from these notes unless exceptions are noted and other sources designated. The author was unable to work out a system to correct spelling. It is obvious that the recording magistrate meant "a chest and three chairs" when he wrote "a chist and three cheers" but deviations in the spelling of proper names present greater difficulties. The recording magistrates either did not know, or did not care, how people spelled their names, and most of the spelling in the Order Books is phonetic. In many instances proper names are spelled as they are pronounced rather than as they are spelled today. For example Acors is often Acuss, Boulware, Bowler and Campbell, Campble or Camel. The author has made a few corrections as an aid to identification, but his corrections are far from uniform.

The author has attempted to write a full history with as much emphasis on the Negro slaves, indentured servants, artisans and smaller freeholders as on the large land grant aristocrats. He has refused to glorify families to feed the ego of their descendants, which is a mistake made by many county historians. Instead he has tried to portray people as they were and let their progenity draw their own conclusions as to the type of stock from which they sprang. While he has traced no family he feels that any person of colonial stock can determine the personality and position of their ancestors by a study of this volume and its accompanying tables.

Colonial Caroline

Indians
In the Year 1610 of
CAROLINE COUNTY

Legend
PRESENT COUNTY LINE ----1953
INDIAN TERITORIAL LINE ——1610

MILES

SECOBEC

Secobec Town

Anostramia

NANTANGTACUND

Checopessawa

Nantangtacund Town

DOGUE

Dogue Town

MATTAPONY

Paussauncack
Unlenstack

YOUNGTAMUND

PAMUNKEY

Cattachipkce

Gnyghtunkpassu

SOUIAN (Nomads)

Indian fishing

Mllng ad masle

Indian Villyage

Chief Indian

Paddling Canoe
Rqse Corn
not Falls wlth
Young Corn

COLONIAL CAROLINE

The Indians

WHEN the English settled at Jamestown in 1607 seven Indian Tribes held land in territory that is now Caroline County. The Pamunkeys, Mattaponys and Youngtamunds occupied the York River basin from the county's eastern boundary to the present day (1953) route of U. S. Highway No. 1 with the exception of a small area around Milford which the Dogues controlled. The Secobecs lived along the south side of the Rappahannock eastward from Snow Creek, the Nantangtacunds on the upper shores of Portobago Bay, and the Manohocs west of Route 1. Seats of government for both the Pamunkeys and the Mattaponys were in present-day King William, and the seat of government for the Youngtamunds was in present-day Hanover. The Mannohocs were nomads and their seat of government was wherever they happened to camp. The chief of the Dogues lived in a village on the creek between Milford and the Devil's Three Jumps, the chief of the Secobecs in a village near Corbin, and the chief of the Nantangtacunds in a village on the north side of Portobago Bay.

Besides the three tribal seats there were at least six other Indian villages in Caroline. The Nantangtacunds had outlying settlements on the lands to become Gaymont called Checopessewa, and near the mouth of Mount Creek called Anastrania. The Mattaponys had villages on the Mattapony; Untenstack on the north bank above the mouth of Marocossic Creek, and Paussaunkack, on the so-called Dick Campbell land, where to this day an "Indian" cave remains. There were two Pamunkey villages in Caroline, Myghtuckpassu, back of the present site of Bethel M. E. Church, and Cattachiptice, astride the river at the confluence of the North and South Anna to make up the Pamunkey with the Caroline portion of the settlement anchored in North Wales. The Youngtamunds were a small tribe, who used their land along the

North Anna from Morris Bridge to Oxford only for hunting.
The Dogues were the segment of a tribe split by civil war.
Originally they lived in the vicinity of Dogue Post Office
in present-day King George. But about fifty years before the
English reached Jamestown their chief died and several braves
tried to take his place. A bloody struggle ensued, which was
not settled until the tribe split into three parts. One of these
subdivisions retained the old hunting grounds, another moved
northward along the Potomac and made a new home on the
stream to become known as Dogue Run, and the third crossed
the Rappahannock and found its way to the Mattapony Valley
around Milford. This subdivision was too small to need more
than one town. The Secobecs recently defeated in battle by
the savage Mannohocs, were lucky to be able to maintain one
town, and their enemy, the Monohocs, were too barbaric to
set up a permanent place of abode.

The seven tribes who lived at least in part of Caroline did
not give the area to be the country of a large Indian population.
Experts on Indian lore have fixed the population of Nantangtacund at seven hundred and fifty, of the Secobec and Doguetown at two hundred and fifty each, and of the average
nontribal seat village at one hundred. According to these
estimates the total number of inhabitants in the area to become
the county was under two thousand in 1607, and the chances
are that this estimate is too large.

The Pamunkeys, Mattaponys, Youngtamunds, Secobecs and
Nantangtacunds were all Algonquian and ruled by the great
chief Powhatan while the Mannohocs were Souian and the
Powhatans' enemies. The two groups were constantly at war.

Around the middle of the sixteenth century Souian Indians
crossed the Allegheny Mountains and pushed their way eastward towards the sea. The Algonquian tribes, who inhabited
this area regarded these newcomers as barbarians, since they
were nomads without fixed places of abode. But the old tribes
were powerless to halt the advance of the new until Powhatan
appeared on the scene.

Powhatan was one of the great leaders of all time. Through
conquest and alliances he increased the number of tribes over

which he ruled from six to thirty-two and extended his domain from the valleys of the York and James to all the area about the Chesapeake Bay. He was never able to drive the Souian invaders back but he did manage to stabilize a frontier with them which ran along the fall line from the Potomac to the Appomattox.

The Pamunkeys, Mattaponys and Youngtamunds were three of his six original tribes. The Nantangtacunds were among the first people he conquered since they were notoriously peaceful and their lands lay adjacent to his domain. The Secobecs came to him for protection, after the Mannohocs destroyed their chief town at the falls of the Rappahannock, drove them from their lands about the site of Fredericksburg and threatened them with extinction. Powhatan accommodated them. He gave them the western portion of the Nantangtacunds land and sent his braves to defend them from further Mannohoc attacks. The Dogues put themselves under the protection of the Mattaponys after they settled near Milford to save themselves from destruction by the Mannohocs and thus indirectly acknowledged the overlordship of Powhatan.

The Explorers

Captain John Smith was the first white man to reach the territory which became Caroline County. He explored the waterways of this area rather thoroughly between 1607 and 1609. He mapped the country he visited and placed large crosses on his map at the furthest point he ascended each river with a key in the map's corner, "to the cross has been discovered, what is beyond is by relation." His maps are remarkably accurate and there is no doubt that he visited the area, as he claimed, since at the time there were no existing maps of the interior of Tidewater Virginia for him to copy. On the rivers which drain Caroline, crosses appear on the South Anna in Western Hanover of the Pamunkey system, on the Mattapony near Milford and on the Rappahannock at its fall at the site of Fredericksburg. When he explored the South

Anna-Pamunkey and the Rappahannock is a matter of record but when he came up the Mattapony to Milford is conjecture.

Captain Smith moved down the South Anna-Pamunkey in the late Fall of 1607. He was a prisoner of the Indians. The Youngtamunds captured him in upper Hanover after they killed the two companions with whom he explored the head waters of the Chickahominy, and took him before their local chief at Youngtamundtown, on the South Anna, for judgment. But to mete out punishment for so important a personage as a white man was too much of a responsibility for the local chief, so he sent the prisoner down stream to face his overlord, Opechancanough, chief of the Pamunkeys and first lord lieutenant of Powhatan's realm. On this journey Captain Smith entered the territorial limits of Caroline at the junction of the North and South Anna. When he reached Cattachiptice on North Wales, the white man had reached Caroline for the first time.

When Smith arrived in Pamunkeytown, Opechancanough decreed for him, a grand tour of many tribal seats before he reached Powhatan's imperial residence in Gloucester for final judgment. The purpose of this tour was to let as many Indians as possible see a white man in the flesh in an attempt to convince them that the whites were neither gods nor supermen as some Indians, who had come in contact with the Jamestown settlers, reported. Captain Smith carefully records the names and sites of all the villages he visited on this trip but he fails to state either his itinerary, or his manner of travel. If he visited the villages in the order listed the most direct route using the most practical means of transportation, when he visited Nantangtacund in Caroline he came up the Mattapony River from Mattaponytown by canoe to Beverly Run, and up Beverly Run to its headwaters, with a short portage to the headwaters of Mill Creek, and down Mill Creek to the Rappahannock, and along the Rappahannock to Portobago Bay and Nantangtacund town. While this is conjecture, there is no doubt however, about the fact that he did visit the Nantangtacunds, whom he describes as a friendly docile people.

Powhatan was not so fierce as his deputy, Opechancanough

and when John Smith reached Gloucester, instead of putting him to death, sent him with an escort of honor back to Jamestown. Back in the colonial capital, Smith immediately began plans for new trips of exploration. He persuaded the colony's council to let him lead an expedition in search of the Northwest Passage. This expedition left Jamestown in the late Spring of 1608. It first ascended the Potomac and then the Rappahannock to their falls. As it passed up the Rappahannock, it explored a section of Caroline County and visited the natives. Captain John Smith in his journal states that the residents of Nantangtacund, Checopessewa, Anastrania and Secobec were friendly, but after the party crossed over into what is now Spotsylvania, it ran into trouble. When the falls blocked their way members of the expedition seized Amoroleck, of the warlike Souian Mannohoc tribe, which had forced the Secobecs to abandon their traditional hunting grounds about the site of Fredericksburg, to show them the way around that obstacle. Amoroleck was a brother of Hassinga, chief of the Mannohocs and that night while the English slept, on the shore near the falls, he attacked their camp. The explorers managed to get back to their ship but they failed to stop the Indians, who followed shooting arrows from their canoes as the white man's boat made its way down the Rappahannock. The battle continued throughout the night, for sixteen miles down stream, well into Caroline waters.

In the morning the English agreed to release Amoroleck and he made a truce by signaling between his captors and his brother. After he debarked the explorers put their ship in a cove near Moss Neck to repair the damages of the battle. One of the party, a man named Featherstone, was seriously wounded and here he died despite the attention of the party's physician, Anthony Bagnalle. The explorers buried him in the river and fired a volley of shots in his honor.

The Pamunkeys

The first English settlers came into Caroline through the back door. Although its Pamunkey valley section lies within sixty miles of Jamestown, settlement did not begin there. Instead it began on the far side along the Rappahannock since Indians, who lived in the Pamunkey valley, blocked the white man's path.

The Pamunkeys were the most powerful tribe over whom Powhatan ruled. They formed the keystone of his empire and occupied in his domain a position similar to that of Prussia in Germany from 1870-1945. When Powhatan died in 1618 his half brother, Opechancanough, who was already chief of the Pamunkeys, became grand sachem of the whole realm. Powhatan had tried appeasement with the English but Opechancanough had different ideas. He believed that an offense was the best defense and in 1622 lead his braves on the bloodiest uprising in the history of the colony. His followers sacked Jamestown and to get rid of the savages the colonist signed an agreement that no white man was to settle on the north side of the Pamunkey River. To put this agreement in effect the House of Burgesses passed an act which imposed the death penalty on any white man who took up residence in this area. This act remained a law in Virginia until 1646.

It was Opechancanough, however, and not the English who violated the treaty. In 1644 his braves went on the warpath and killed off most of the settlers who dared settle along the south bank of the Pamunkey. After this outrage the House of Burgesses repealed the enforcement act attached to the treaty.

Voiding the law did not open the way for settlers to move into Caroline. The Pamunkeys were as strong as ever. Opechancanough died about this time but Totopotomoi, who succeeded him, proved an able chief and continued to block the white man's attempts to settle beyond the Pamunkey. In the long run it was the Iroquois Indians and Nathaniel Bacon, Jr., who opened the road for settlement. The royal government for Virginia never succeeded in doing it on its own power.

The Seneca and Tuscarora tribes of the Iroquois began making raids into eastern Virginia around 1650. These attacks were hit-and-run. They appeared out of nowhere, sacked a village, killed off the men and sped away with the women and children that fell into their clutches. Since the Pamunkeys were a settled tribe, Totopotomoi and his warriors were unable to follow the raiders and destroy them without abandoning their lands and habitations. As an alternative, he, along with many other chiefs of tribes on the colonial frontier, decided to move his people towards the east. This enraged English settlers but they were powerless to act since their governor, William Berkeley, personally profited from a lucrative trade with red men and did not wish to attack them. That is, the settlers were powerless to act until Nathaniel Bacon, Jr. appeared to lead them.

Nathaniel Bacon, Jr. was a fearless as well as an educated young man. He came to Virginia about 1673 and settled in Henrico County. His uncle, Nathaniel Bacon, Sr. was one of the richest men in the colony and being childless, he had made Bacon Jr. his heir. But Bacon Jr. was unwilling to sit around and wait for the old man to die, he took out land himself, and when his neighbors sent him to the House of Burgesses, he immediately espoused the cause of the frontiersmen. When the royal governor refused to defend them he undertook their defense himself. At the head of a band of volunteers he defeated the Indians on all fronts. His defeat of the Pamunkeys came somewhere close to the site of West Point. After the Indians went down in battle, he relentlessly pursued them, destroyed their chief town at Romancoke, and followed them up the peninsula between the Pamunkey and Mattaponi Rivers into Caroline. A threat to Bacon's rear only saved the Pamunkeys from complete destruction. After he got to Caroline he heard that Governor Berkeley had mobilized a large army in Gloucester to destroy him and upon the receipt of this news he did an abrupt about face, leaving the Indians to polish off later, and marched to meet the governor. When Berkeley heard that Bacon was on the way, he abandoned his forces and fled across the Chesapeake to Accomac. Bacon destroyed the royal army but he died in Gloucester before he had the chance to get back to Caroline and finish off the Indians.

When the royal government returned to Jamestown it took advantage of the weakened condition of the Pamunkeys to open the Pamunkey and Mattapony valleys for settlement. In 1678 the colonial council authorized the building of Fort Mattapony on the upper reaches of the river of that name, well within the territorial limits of present-day Caroline, to keep the Indians under control and to encourage settlement.

William Meridaye built Fort Mattapony and Nathaniel Bacon, Sr. garrisoned it and was its first commander. Evidently after the fort was built the council was dissatisfied with the whole project because both Meridaye and Bacon had a hard time collecting for their services. In 1682 Bacon sent a bill to the president of the council for 2,000 pounds of tobacco for transporting soldiers to garrison the fort on the Mattapony in 1679, for horses lost at the Mattapony garrison and for the salaries he advanced Indian interpreters. As late as 1697 the heirs of William Meridaye were dunning the council for an eighteen-year-old bill for their father's work as carpenter at the fort. Whether either Bacon or Meridaye were ever paid the record fails to disclose. It only shows that they sent their bills in, with regularity and with emphasis.

Political Genesis

When the English settlers built Fort Mattapony its site was located in New Kent County. At that time all of Caroline's Mattapony and Pamunkey valleys' lands were in New Kent and its Rappahannock lands were in Rappahannock, a county long since extinct.

The political genesis of Caroline is as complicated as the genealogies of many of its leading families, but if a lucid history of the county is to be recorded it must be set out here. From the time Captain John Smith first explored its rivers in 1607-08 until 1634 its area remained, so far as the white man was concerned, Indian country. When the Virginia House of

Burgesses divided the colony into its eight original political subdivisions in 1634 it became, nominally at least, along with all the other land north of the watershed between the James and the York basins, a part of the shire of Charles River. Eight years later the Burgesses changed the name of Charles River to York without changing its boundaries and Caroline became a part of York.

All of Caroline remained in York until 1648 when the Burgesses cut off the Potomac and Rappahannock valleys from that county and formed a new county which they called at first Chickacoan, and a short time later Northumberland. This division placed the lands that were to become Caroline in two political subdivisions; its lands along the Pamunkey and the Mattapony remained in York while its lands along the Rappahannock went to Northumberland. This split lasted for seventy-nine years, which is almost one quarter of Caroline's total recorded history. The two sections were not reunited under the same local government until the Burgesses established Caroline, as a county, in 1727.

The Rappahannock Valley was not long a part of Northumberland. In 1652 the Burgesses separated it from the Potomac Valley and put it in a new county which they called Lancaster. This new county they split four years later along the north and south line which now divides Lancaster from Richmond County, and Middlesex from Essex. The area to the east remained Lancaster and the area to the west became Rappahannock. The Rappahannock Valley section of Caroline was a part of Rappahannock County for thirty-six years, that is until 1692 when the Burgesses obliterated that county and placed its lands north of the Rappahannock River in Richmond and its lands south of the river in Essex. From 1692 until Caroline was established as a county in 1727, Caroline's Rappahannock River valley was a part of Essex.

Caroline south of the Rappahannock-Mattapony watershed was a part of York until the House of Burgesses organized New Kent in 1654 and fixed its boundaries as extending from Scimino Creek on the east to the headwaters of the Pamunkey and the Mattapony on the west. This act placed a portion of

Caroline in a political subdivision by metes and bounds for the first time.

New Kent retained its original limits for thirty-seven years. In 1691 the Burgesses split it along the Pamunkey and established King and Queen County north of the river. This division put all of Caroline between the Mattapony-Rappahannock watershed and the Pamunkey River in King and Queen. Here the lands north of the Mattapony remained for thirty-six years, but the lands south of the river became a part of King William ten years later when the Burgesses created that county from King and Queen's land between the Pamunkey and the Mattapony.

This was the last change in territorial jurisdiction before the Burgesses reunited the three narrow strips, which were at the time the heads of Essex, King and Queen and King William, and set up Caroline. The first English settlers came to Caroline, when the area, that was to become the county, was split between Rappahannock and New Kent. The white man claimed title to over ninety per cent of its area while it was still divided between Essex, King and Queen and King William. To write a complete history of Caroline the research student must carefully study the papers concerning these five counties, which record events that happened before Caroline was organized, because as Minerva sprang full grown from the head of Jove so Caroline sprang full grown from the heads of Essex, King and Queen and King William.

First Settlers Along the Mattapony

Before the colonists built Fort Mattapony a few white men had already taken up land in the upper Mattapony Valley. As early as 1655 Major William Lewis patented 2,000 acres "on the northeast side of the Mattapony River lying near the head of the said river." This tract appears to be Millwood, since to this day there are ancient tombstones of the Lewis family on this place and its location fits the descriptions in the original grant. Before the Revolution Virginians classed the Mattapony a river only to its principal fork. Above this point they called both branches, swamps. Millwood is only a short distance from the fork of the Mattapony as the crow flies.

Further evidence that the Lewis tract was Millwood, is found in the fact that in 1667 John Hoomes patented 3,000 acres on a swamp leading to the northeast bank of the Mattapony a short distance below the lands of Major William Lewis. This tract was to become known first as the Bowling Green, and at a later date as the Old Mansion and was to continue through the years as one of the best known landmarks in the area which is Caroline County. The old land books show two large grants for the Hoomes family in 1661 but a complete description of them reveals that they were located in what is now King and Queen since they extended by metes and bounds from the Mattapony to the headwaters of the Dragoon. From other grants and purchases it is evident that the Hoomes added to the Old Mansion tract piecemeal but the records also show that the acquisition was begun in 1667.

The third grant of land to a white man in Caroline's Mattapony Valley shows conclusively that the colonist considered the upper Mattapony River a swamp. In 1672 Col. Augustine Warner patented 1,400 acres "lying part in New Kent and part in Rappahannock counties, being on the north side of the main swamp of the Mattapony and extending inland from said swamp right opposite the lands of Robert Taliaferro and Lawrence Smith, the said lands of the said Taliaferro and Smith being lands which extend to the south bank of the Rappahannock River at the point twelve miles below the falls of the said river."

The first three grants in the Mattapony Valley were all on the northeast side of the river. Across the river was Indian country and so it remained until the last decade of the seventeenth century. The English curbed the Pamunkeys but they did not break the Indians' power. For half a century the peninsula between the Mattapony and Pamunkey was known as Pamunkey Neck. Captain Lawrence Smith was so bold as to try to take up land in this section as early as 1764 when he patented 4,600 acres on the south bank of the Mattapony which extended inland on both sides of Reedy Swamp. His original grant provided that he must settle this land within two years to hold his title and immediately before his time limit expired he wrote Sir William Berkeley, governor of the colony, asking for a seven-year extension setting forth in the letter that the grant was in a section so remote from the habitations of other white men and in a country so full of hostile Indians that it was not a safe place for him to bring his family.

As late as 1689 a settler named Arnold petitioned the Colonial Council to let him swap his grant along the south side of the Mattapony for land along the north side of that stream to get away from the Indians.

If the first grantees settled their land before the building of Fort Mattapony the chances are that they built private forts for their protection. The building of private forts in that area remained a common practice so long as the Indians were a power. As late as 1707 Robert Beverly wrote the Hon. Ed. Jennings, president of the council. "We are strongly alarmed in upper King and Queen (Caroline) for fear of an Indian War. I shall take my neighbors for shelter in my fort. I pray ye send me arms for their protection."

The fact that all the original patentees in the upper Mattapony Valley, Major Lewis, Major Hoomes, Colonel Warner, and Captain Smith were military men, suggest that only a military man was able to settle in such a remote area at the time, since the settlers must know how to cope with the Indians, by building and commanding private forts, as well as how to develop the country by turning the wilderness into tillable acres.

George Morris followed Lawrence Smith in claiming land along the Mattapony in the Reedy Creek section. In 1774 he laid claim to 3,000 acres along the north bank of the river opposite the mouth of that creek.

It was, however, farther down stream and along the north bank that the English attempted any mass scale settlement in Caroline's Mattapony Valley before Nathaniel Bacon, Jr. defeated the Indians. These settlements were a mere pushing up stream of the settlements already established in what is now King and Queen. In 1673 Thomas Hall and John Pigg patented 3,831 acres on the northeast side of the Mattapony "above the tides flowing" and John (Bagbee) Bagby and William Herndon took out 2,600 acres with Herndon taking out 430 acres in his own name above the lands of Hall and Pigg on the river. The next year Joshua Storey, William Morris and Thomas Wyatt took out 3,200 acres upstream from the Herndon-Bagby grant. Since all this land was on the north side of the river and "above the tides flowing" a simple study of geography determines that these grants extended well into what is now Caroline County. In 1676 they were on the frontier while the lands of Smith, Hoomes, Lewis and Warner were above the frontier and it was these lands with their settlers that Bacon was primarily interested in defending when he defeated the Indians in the section.

First Settlement Along the Rappahannock

Caroline's Rappahannock Valley filled with white settlers much more rapidly than its land along the Mattapony although ironically the first grant of land to a white man (Major William Lewis in 1655) was on the Mattapony rather than on the Rappahannock.

The first Rappahannock grant came in 1666 and this was for speculation rather than settlement. Robert Taliaferro and Lawrence Smith took out 6,300 acres "in ye freshes and on the south side of the river, lying on the east side of a creek called Snow Creek." The two grantees hoped a town to be located near the head of navigation on the Rappahannock was going to be built on this site. They missed their guess and the town was built on lands John Buckner claimed in 1672 on the south side of the river at its falls. Lawrence Smith settled in this town when it was built and was the first commander of the military stationed here. Robert Taliaferro at a latter date established commercial enterprises on land he patented down stream at the mouth of Peumandsend (Mill Creek).

The first mass scale settlement of Caroline's Rappahannock took place in the area in which Taliaferro in time built his commercial establishments. It extended from the Golden Vale on the west to the present Caroline-Essex boundary on the east and was an extension of the settlements already made in what is now Essex. Prior to 1665 one Thomas Hawkins appears to have gotten a color of title in some way to an extensive tract of land around Portobago Bay, although no record of any such grant appears in the land books. Reference to such a grant however is made in the descriptions of latter grantees, including the Buckners, Beverleys, Wormleys and Taliaferros who were engaged in a series of disputes and lawsuits with Hawkins and his heirs over the title to this land.

A dubious title to the land and pirates appear to have held up settlement along the Rappahannock rather than the Indians. The Nantangtacunds were notoriously peaceful and the Secobees too depleted from wars to offer opposition. Pirates were a different matter. Charles Campbell in his history of *Colonial Virginia* states that they were Dutch privateers rather than pirates, and harrassed the Virginia coast and inland waters at the time in the interest of Holland, which was at war with England.

The only pirate whose name may be identified today was Peuman. If tradition is right the settlers chased him up a branch of Mill Creek and killed him on a small stream which after that time became known as Peumansend. If this is true settlers from what is now Essex and, not from what is now Caroline, killed the pirate because there were no white men in that part of Caroline County at the time. In the fourth grant of Caroline land (the third along the Rappahannock) a stream called Powmandsend (Peumansend) appears in the description. This was a grant on April 17, 1667 to John Meders and Henry Peters which reads "4200 acres on the south side of the river about three miles from the river on the main run of a creek called Powmandsend."

Apparently, although Peuman was dead, other pirates gave the first white settlers in Caroline's Rappahannock Valley trouble, because, it is interesting to note that, all but one of the early grants were back from the river on small streams where the settlers might more easily defend themselves from marauders who came by water.

Here are the earliest patents with dates and descriptions:

1. April 17, 1667, the Meders-Peters tract above mentioned.

2. March 20, 1667, Major General Robert Smith, 1,900 acres "in the freshes on the south side of the river about one mile from the river on the bayside of Portobago."

3. 1667—Alexander Fleming, 2,750 acres two miles from the Rappahannock up Peumandsend Creek.

4. 1667—Henry Corbin, 5.776 acres on the Rappahannock eastward from the mouth of Ware Creek.

5. 7678, Thomas Gouldman, 1,200 acres beyond the land of Major General Robert Smith.

6. In 1671 to Francis Farmer, 150 acres adjacent to the land of Major General Robert Smith.

7. In 1671 to Thomas Bowler (Boulware) 1,460 acres of land "some three miles in the woods, two miles above Portobago Indian town (Nantangtacund).

8. Sept. 19, 1671, to John Buckner, Robert Bryan and Thomas Royston, 3,553½ acres "in the freshes of said river on the south side called the Golden Vale."

9. May 25, 1671, to Anthony Buckner and Major Lawrence Smith, 4,972 acres "on the south side of the river in the freshes near Portobago Bay."

10. March 17, 1673, Robert Taliaferro, the son of Robert Taliaferro, 739 acres on the south side of the Rappahannock River on both sides of the mouth of a creek known as Peumansend. (Evidently at this time all of Mill Creek was called Peumansend.)

11. Nov. 5, 1673, Simon Miller, 817 acres "in the county of Rappahannock in the freshes thereof, on the south side of the river, at the head of Peumansend."

12. Nov. 5, 1673, to Rollins, 650 acres in the back country adjacent to the land granted Simon Miller that day.

A plot of the Taliaferro tract is still in existence. It shows warehouses and wharf located on the south bank of the Rappahannock at the mouth of the Peumansend (Mill Creek).

Robert Taliaferro braved shakey title and pillaging pirates to build his establishments on open water naviable for ocean-going vessels and took advantage of the opportunity for lucrative trade, which the rapidly growing section offered.

Not only were the twelve original patentees in the area, but some, at least, of the first twelve had already divided their holdings with more recently arrived settlers. In 1673 James Kay sold part of his land to Francis and Anthony Thornton. Since there is no record of a grant to a Kay along the Rappahannock prior to this time, the records for original grants are complete, it is evident that he bought his land from one of the original patentees before he sold a portion of it to the Thorntons.

Although the land between the Golden Vale and the present-day Caroline-Essex line and the land along the north side of the Mattapony westward from the mouth of Marocossic Creek was filling rapidly with English settlers before Bacon's Rebellion, the white man showed little inclination to take up land elsewhere in the area to be Caroline. Besides the patents of Smith and Taliaferro at Snow Creek and Henry Corbin eastward from Ware Creek and the Lewis, Warner and Hoomes grants in the upper Mattapony Valley there were only two other grants prior to 1676. In 1672 Col. Thomas Goodrich patented 2,200 acres on Tuckahoe Creek and Francis and Anthony Thornton took up 2,740 acres on the north side of the Mattapony above the stream's major fork. The Thornton brothers, Francis and Anthony, were born in Virginia and used to pioneer life. In the back country they prospered, and in time their grant became Ormesby, which for many years was a famous seat of the Thornton family in Caroline County.

Aftermath of Bacon's Rebellion

The deeds of Nathaniel Bacon, Jr., influenced the development of Caroline County's history more than the acts of any one man in the 17th century. His defeat of the Indians opened the frontier for settlement and at that time the area which is now Caroline was on the frontier. His tragic death at the moment of his greatest triumph gave rise to a new group of favorites from among the men who remained loyal to Sir William Berkeley, the royal governor, during the trouble and brought disgrace for the colonist who dared side with the great rebel leader. The new favorites demanded land as a reward for their services after the restoration of royal government and ironically the land which they demanded was the land which Bacon made fit for settlement when he defeated the Indians along the frontier. Governor Berkeley, upon his return to Jamestown, lost no time in punishing the men who opposed him. He seized their land and sometimes took their lives.

Since the area which is Caroline was on the frontier, most of the settlers were rebels. At least five of these men lost their land, and of the five, two lost both land and lives. These losers were Thomas Goodrich, who lost 2,220 acres on Tuckahoe Creek to Bryan Smith, John Patterson, a homesteader, who lost 500 acres in the Golden Vale to Richard Buckner, the son of John Buckner (the Buckners already had extensive holdings in the Golden Vale), John Godfrey, another homesteader who lost 300 acres to Cornelous Reynolds in the freshies of the Mattapony, Thomas Mott's orphans, who lost land to William and George Morris, and the heirs of Robinson (Clara Robinson, Elizabeth Robinson Hazelwood, Ann Robinson Hazelwood and Benjamin Robinson) who lost 3,400 acres in the vicinity of Port Royal to John Catlett.

From these records it appears that Thomas Mott and Robinson lost their lives during the rebellion either as battle casualties or the hangings in Jamestown after royal government was restored. What happened to Thomas Mott's orphans is unknown, but Robinson's heirs remained in Caroline to play an important part in the development of the county.

Not all Caroline people were rebels. From the statements above it appears that the Buckners and the Morrises at least were royalist, and this is further borne out by the fact that in the period immediately following the end of the rebellion both of these families received grants in their own names along and jointly with fellow royalists from the settlement to the east, whom evidently they brought into the area, to become Caroline, as new settlers. These grants include: a grant in 1677 to John Lewis, Lt. Col. John Smith, Philip Lightfoot and Thomas Royston, of 10,050 acres lying on the watershed of the Mattapony and the Rappahannock in what was at the time New Kent

and Rappahannock counties and extending into the Rappahannock flats in the vicinity of present-day Port Royal. Lewis
as well as Buckner was a Caroline resident. Smith, Lightfoot
and Royston were newcomers, and Lightfoot and Royston's
heirs at least became important citizens of Caroline County.

How the grantees divided this huge patent is not known
because the records are lost. However, it is not the last grant
within the territorial limits of Caroline in which the Buckners
were interested. In 1702 John Buckner patented 3,080 acres
more in the back country of what is now Port Royal District,
(A. P. Hill Military Reservation) in 1722 his son, Richard,
took up 4,500 acres along the Mattapony-Rappahannock watershed, and after Caroline became a county 1,100 acres adjacent
to this tract.

In addition to the Mott land which George Morris got
through escheat at the end of Bacon's Rebellion, he took out
in 1690 as a reward for his services two large patents of 3,000
and 1,190 acres respectively south of the Mattapony-Rappahannock watershed in the vicinity of Tuckahoe swamp.

Besides the Buckners, Morrises and Lewises there were
other Caroline royalists, and they, too, were well paid in land
for their services. The most prominent of these was Captain
Joshua Storey. He got a grant of 11,620 acres in Caroline's
lower Mattapony Valley in his own name, and using the same
system employed by John Buckner of bringing fellow royalists
home with him from the rebellion secured jointly with Col.
James Taylor and Jahnathan Fisher 9,150 acres, "beginning
by ye head of a small branch of Marocossic Creek." Col.
Taylor in time became one of the section's most noted citizens.

Of other families resident in the area to become Caroline in
1676 the Wyatts sided with the royal governor during the
rebellion since they too profited through large grants of land.
The position the Hoomes, Millers and Taliaferros took is not
known since from the records they neither gained nor lost. But
it is a known fact that the Thorntons were notorious partisans
of Bacon, although in some manner they managed to come out
of the rebellion without losing their lives and to keep their
vast holdings intact.

The three men who profited most in Caroline land for siding with Sir William Berkeley, the royal governor, during Bacon's Rebellion, never maintained a residence within the territorial limits of the county. They were Robert Beverley, the soldier, who lived in Middlesex, Lawrence Smith, who skipped over Caroline when he jumped his domicile from Gloucester to the south side of the Rappahannock at the river's falls, and Ralph Wormley, of Middlesex. All three of these men had large holdings of land elsewhere in the colony and the section to become Caroline was not their chief interest, yet each of them played an important part in the development of the county.

Robert Beverley was the prime favorite of the lot. He was a friend of Berkeley's before Bacon rebelled and during the rebellion the governor's staunchest supporter. He not only admired Berkeley but he hated Bacon, whom he considered an upstart and a radical who dared arouse the masses in an attempt to overthrow existing order. He was almost constantly with the governor during the rebellion and fled with him across the Chesapeake to Accomac in the face of Bacon's advance into Gloucester. After they reached the Eastern Shore when Berkeley thought that his cause was totally lost he sent Beverley, as his most trusted aid, back across the bay to accept Bacon's terms for surrender. Luckily for Berkeley and Beverley, Bacon died while Beverley was on the way, and when he reached Gloucester he was able to rally the royalist and cause the rebels, badly demoralized from the loss of their leader, to disband. This paved the way for Berkeley's return to Jamestown and to restore his rule over Virginia.

Beverley never let Berkeley forget this. In payment for his services he demanded land and more land, land for himself, for his family and his friends. He secured grants in every section of the colony and in time became Virginia's third largest landowner. (Lord Fairfax was landowner number one and King Carter landowner number two. Fairfax never owned any Caroline land and Carter's Caroline holdings were comparatively slight.) Beverley's Caroline land was a mere fraction of his total acreage but it was enough to form a nucleus to make his son the largest owner of Caroline land in the county's history. Before Bacon rebelled he already had considerable land in the area. After the rebellion collapsed he patented a huge tract extending from the east side of Marocossic Creek eastward into what is now Essex.

Lawrence Smith made several attempts to settle in the territory that was to become Caroline but he never made the grade. With Robert Taliaferro he had patented land to the east of Snow Creek on the Rappahannock in 1666 in hopes that there was to be built a town. In 1671 he patented with John Buckner 716 acres further down the Rappahannock in the vicinity of Port Royal and in 1673 he took out 4,600 acres of Reedy Creek, which, when Bacon rebelled, he was trying desperately to hold without going there to live.

The collapse of the rebellion affected his fortunes materially. He sided with Governor Berkeley and although, one of the leading military men of the colony, he let the colonial militia under his command suffer an ignoble defeat in Gloucester by an untrained band of rebels under Ingram, Bacon's Chief Lieutenant, the royal governor rewarded him for his loyalty. He got his Reedy Creek land with no strings attached and 6,500 acres nearby jointly with Robert Beverley. Besides he got other large tracts of land for himself and tracts to be held in trust for his young sons, William and Augustine, in the area that was to be Caroline and elsewhere throughout the colony. Finally he got the job he wanted most, the command of the garrison stationed at the new fort at the falls of the Rappahannock on the site of Fredericksburg.

Ralph Wormely, or Sir Ralph Wormely as he is sometimes called, although his title has never been authenticated, was a favorite of the royal governors in Jamestown. For his part in supporting the royalists during Bacon's Rebellion he received a grant of 2,000 acres south of Portobago Bay on the present Caroline-Essex boundary. He built a residence on this land and spent a portion of each year at least in the back country. From his original holdings he began an expansion campaign which involved cringing for favors at the colonial capital, arguing with Thomas Hawkins and his heirs in the back country, and persecuting the docile Nantangtacund Indians until he succeeded by 1695 in annexing to his domain 19,420 acres, giving him 21,420 acres all told and making him the largest landowner in the area. All of this land however was not in the area to be included in Caroline, a good part of it with Sir Ralph's manor house was located in what is now Essex.

Wormely was an important man in the colony but he was not, by present-day standards, a good citizen. Since he had far more land than he was able to work with the supply of labor available, he tried to enslave the Nantangtacund Indians and force them to cultivate his acreage. The Indians' chief town Nansiatico (Nantangtacund town) was located on his original 2,000 acres and he regarded the redskins, who lived there as much a part of his property as the land on which they dwelt. When his attempts to enslave the Indians were unsuccessful, he denied them the privilege to hunt, destroyed their crops and tried to starve them into submission. John Fontaine, who visited the section towards the end of the 17th century was indignant at his conduct and castigates him in the journal he wrote about the journey.

In 1705, after all means failed to subdue the Indians and make them work for the white man's profit, Wormely threw the remaining redskins in the abandoned jail of defunct Rappahannock County near Caret and notified the Colonial Council that he was keeping them there until the Council had them transported. This was illegal. Wormely had no right to jail the Indians. Unfortunately the Council's reply is lost.

When the Indians refused to work Wormely brought in Negro slaves to till his acres. This is the first record of Negroes being brought as slaves into the section in which Caroline is located. Evidently Wormely treated his Negroes no better than he treated the Indians. As early as 1695 he was summoned before the Colonial Council for mutilating his Negro slave, Mingo. Again as concerning the jailed Nantangtacunds, what action the Council took remains a mystery.

Not all the outsiders who got land in Caroline for siding with Governor Berkeley during Bacon's Rebellion were speculators. Many of them established residences on their grants, and became the section's most substantial citizens. Three of

these new settlers were army officers. They were Captain
Martin Palmer with a grant of 1,500 acres, Captain Jacob
Tompkins with a grant of 565 acres and Captain Thomas
Terry with a grant of 1,000 acres. All this land was located
on Caroline's upper Rappahannock-Mattapony watershed with
the major portion of it extending towards the Mattapony. Its
location suggests that since these three men were army officers
they got the land more to be in a position to keep the Indians
quiet than as a reward for their services.

Palmer and Tompkins established seats along the north bank
of the upper Mattapony but in a short time Terry crossed the
river and went to live among the Indians, who occupied the
"Indian Neck" between that stream and the North Anna-
Pamunkey. Here he was quite successful and after the settlers
put the Indians of this section to flight in the second decade of
the 18th century and organized St. Margaret's Parish he
became church warden for the new parish.

One of the most interesting men the opening of the frontier
brought into Caroline was Cornelius Vaughan. Between 1677
and 1685 the royal government granted him at least six different tracts of land within the territorial limits of the county.
Few of these grants were to him alone, but jointly with one or
more of the section's largest landowners. They were never
large and varied from 288 to 500 acres. What Vaughan was
up to is a matter of conjecture. The pattern of his grants were
certainly different from any other patentees. It is not known
if he and his co-owner held on to all the tracts at the same time.
The chances are that he and his partners were turning sections
of the wilderness into partially developed farms which they
sold to new settlers for a profit.

Royal governors, who followed Berkeley, continued to grant
large tracts to their friends. These new favorites included
Edwin Conway in 1681 with 1,200 acres westward along the
Rappahannock from the mouth of Prosser's Run and in the
freshies of Snow Creek, Edward Thacker in 1687 with 1,563
acres on the upper reaches of Tuckahoe Swamp and 2,634
acres more in 1697 on the path leading from Tuckahoe Swamp
to Portobago Bay, Thomas Todd in 1688 with 2,828 acres

along the Mattapony-Rappahannock watershed, and Alexander
McKenny in 1689 with 790 acres in the same section.

There were also, during this period, the last quarter of the
17th century, many patentees of small grants in the area to
become Caroline. These men were often in a better position
to prosper than the large landlords since the labor supply was
limited and a man only needed as much land as he was able to
clear and to farm himself. Some of these small landholders
became among the most affluent residents in the new county.
After their original homesteads were in good shape they
often added the adjacent land through additional grants and
purchases.

Among these small holders was Robert Terrell who took out
170 acres north of the Mattapony in 1682. When the Indians
were driven from the land across the river in the first decade
of the seventeen hundred he transferred his residence to the
south side of the stream, where his descendants in time became
among the most influential and prosperous citizens of Caroline's Reedy Church and Madison magisterial districts.

That same year the first Thomas Blanton came to Caroline.
He had at first 200 acres but five years later patented the
adjacent 266 acres to raise his holdings to 466 acres.

In 1687 the progenitor of another well known name in
Caroline took up land in the area that was to become the
county. This was Thomas Pitts with 376 acres in the basin
of Marocossic Creek.

Records also prove that Kays and Gatewoods were living
in the area to become Caroline as early as 1687. Although the
land books record no patents for these two families, they
reveal that they had land adjacent to other grants.

William Byrd, the Frontiersman

In politics the early settlers in the Mattapony Valley were a
fiercely, independent lot. They cared little for England and
less for the English monarch. In 1702 they elected and sent to
the House of Burgesses, a man who refused to take the oath

of allegiance to Ann, and new Queen of England and England's Virginia Colony, and when the Burgesses under pressure from the Royal Governor and Council, expelled him from membership in their body, the backwoodsmen received him as a hero when he returned to his home in the wilderness, although, he left Williamsburg in disgrace.

This man was William Byrd, or Bird, known as William Byrd, the Frontiersman, to distinguish him from his contemporaries, the William Byrds of Westover, who lived in elegance along the James. From the records it seems that Byrd, the Frontiersman, and the Byrds of Westover were no kin. But they knew each other and were bitter enemies. The Byrds of Westover were rich, well educated leaders among the aristocrats and members of the Governor's Council, on which they served as did all its members at the pleasure of the Royal Governor, the alter ego of the English monarch in Virginia. While Byrd, the Frontiersman, had little schooling and limited means, he was a leader of the common people and as a member of the House of Burgesses believed that he was primarily responsible to his own constituents rather than to a sovereign ruling from beyond the seas.

The clash between the Byrds arose over this issue. When William Byrd, the Frontiersman, arrived in Williamsburg to take his seat in the House of Burgesses, tales followed from his home community that he made anti-royalist speeches to rally the frontiersmen to his support during the election campaign. These rumors shocked the Westover Byrds. They were angry that the people dared elect a man against whom there was even a suspicion of holding such radical notions and persuaded the Council, which they dominated, to have Col. William Leigh, commander of the militia in King and Queen, which included all the Mattapony Valley north of that stream at the time, to investigate.

Since Col. Leigh held this appointment upon recommendation of the Council to the Crown, and there was no way for the people to get rid of him short of revolution, it is hard to evaluate the fairness of the report which he filed with both the Council and the House of Burgesses in a short time, charging "that one William Byrd, a Burgessee from the county of King and Queen did publish and spread abroad, seditious and scandalous reports, highly reflecting on her Majesty, the Queen, the Royal Governor in Virginia, his Council, and the House of Burgesses, tending to raise sedition in the minds of her loving subjects."

When the Burgesses, who had sole jurisdiction in the case because the accused was a member of their body procrastinated and failed to act, the Council became impatient, and abetted by the Royal Governor sent a note to the lower house which demanded the immediate punishment of Byrd, the Frontiersman, "to vindicate the honor of the Governor, to quiet the minds of Her Majesty's subjects, and to prevent the spreading of such dangerous and seditious reports in the future."

The Burgesses yielded to this pressure but the punishment they imposed was mild. They merely ordered Byrd to take the oath of allegiance to the Queen and promise to stop criticizing the Royal Government. But Byrd refused to take either the oath or promise and the Burgesses in exasperation expelled him from their membership.

While many colonists dismissed Byrd, the Frontiersman, as a crackpot for these antics, to the Byrds of Westover and other arch royalists, he remained a dangerous man. When he returned to his home in the wilderness along the Mattapony they sent agents to keep him under surveillance and when he rashly continued to make disparaging remarks about the Queen and her government in Virginia, they frequently summoned him to Williamsburg to answer charges. So far as the records show all these hearings came to naught because there is no evidence that Byrd was either fined or imprisoned.

For four years the matter simmered until 1706 when Byrd brought it to a head himself. That year in conjunction with five of his most ardent partisans, Robert Byrd, Ralph Booker, William Holcomb, James Vaughan and Richard Covington, he petitioned Governor Edward Nott for a crown grant of 8,000 acres in the great fork of the Mattapony. The Governor agreed to direct the grant provided that Byrd and his associates take up residence on this land at once. Since at the time,

the great fork of the Mattapony lay beyond the frontier it
seems that the governor in adding the residence stipulation,
sought to send Byrd to a region where anti-royalist talk did no
harm; or it may have been that Her Majesty's chief executive
in the Virginia Colony hoped that Indians were going to do
what he was afraid to do himself; kill Byrd and shut his
mouth forever.

Nothing is known of Byrd's associates in this venture except
Richard Covington, who was a chronic trouble maker for royal
authority. In his youth he sided with Nathaniel Bacon, Jr., in
Bacon's Rebellion against Sir William Berkeley and lost all his
property on account of this choice. Thirty years later after in
some manner he had managed to acquire more lands, he was
still willing to get rid of his holdings and set off into the wilderness following a new leader, who dared to oppose royal rule.

Robert Beverley, the Historian

The year before William Byrd, the Frontiersman, went to live
in the great fork of the Mattapony, another radical moved into
the upper valley of that stream. This was Robert Beverley, the
Historian, who took up residence at "The Park" or Beverley's
Park, his extensive holdings along Beverley's Run. Tradition
and the best evidence indicate that he built his manor near the
old site of Salem Baptist Church but this is not conclusive.

However this point, while interesting is actually of small
consequence, since it in no way diminishes the vast influence
Beverley exerted in setting up the pattern of civilization in
Caroline's York River basin. He owned over 5,000 acres in
what is now Madison Magisterial District, 20,000 acres in
what is now Reedy Church Magisterial District, and so much
of the area to become Bowling Green Magisterial District
that this region was practically his fief. Through granting and
refusing to grant his excess acreage, he was to control the type
of settler who took up residence in this district and because his
views on economics and politics were the most advanced in the
colony these people were a carefully selected lot.

Robert Beverley, the Historian, was born in Middlesex County, in 1673, the son of Robert Beverley, the Soldier. The older Beverley was a close friend of Sir William Berkeley and that Royal Governor's chief lieutenant during Bacon's Rebellion. For these services Berkeley added extensive grants to Beverley's already large holdings and Beverley bcame the third largest landowner in the Virginia Colony. As befitting a man of his station, he sent his son to England to school and there the youth remained until his father's death in 1687.

How long Beverley, the Historian, remained abroad on this trip is a matter of conjecture, but it is a matter of record that when he returned to Virginia, that he found the family fortune in jeopardy and that he was old enough to take action. Unstable land titles were the root of his trouble. From the days of the London Company every one with the power to make grants was notoriously generous in giving away Virginia land. British monarchs made huge grants to take care of their favorites, indifferent to the fact that often one of their predecessors on the throne, or a royal governor in the colony had already given these lands to someone else (examples; the Culpeper and Fairfax grants); and in Jamestown and Williamsburg, the same system prevailed on a smaller scale. With each new governor there was a rash of grants to take care of his followers. In the ten years between Berkeley's recall, and Beverley, the Soldier's, death, Virginia had five new governors and the demand for land to satisfy their retainers was great.

Many of these new patents included land which Berkeley had already given Beverley, and Beverley refused to surrender his claims to their title without a struggle. When direct appeals to the new governors failed, he filed suits in court, but the courts were dilatory and failed to render decisions and the litigation only served to antagonize further the sovereign's chief lieutenants in the colony. These disputes increased in bitterness until Lord Howard of Effingham (Governor of Virginia, 1684-88) disfranchised Beverley, the Soldier, for insubordination in 1686 and deprived him of the rights to sue. The next year Beverley died a broken man.

When Robert Beverley, the Historian, returned to Virginia

and attempted to save the family fortune he also renewed his father's fight against the abuse of royal authority, but these activities did not keep him from joining the social and political life of the colony. In 1697 he married Ursula Byrd, a daughter of William Byrd I, and a sister of William Byrd II, of Westover, who was in time to become the richest man in British America. The next year he won a seat in the House of Burgesses from the borough of Jamestown. Both of these events which began so auspiciously ended in tragedy.

Ursula Byrd Beverley died in 1698 after giving birth to a son, William Beverley, who in time established a family seat at Blandfield in Essex County, which to this day, (1953) his descendants still own. The wife's death was a crushing blow to the husband. Apparently, she was the only woman ever to interest him, romantically, because he never remarried, although he was only twenty-five years old at the time of her death.

In the House of Burgesses he met only frustration. When he stood for election to that body, he hoped to have it enact laws fixing land titles and controlling grants in the future. But the royal governor and his council wanted no such reforms and balked him on every term until he gave up in disgust. However, before he quit, he presented his case with such intelligence and vigor that the ruling clique in the colony became alarmed, and during that session of the colonial legislature when they voted, over his protest, to move the colonial capital from Jamestown to Williamsburg, they also voted to deprive Jamestown of a seat in the House of Burgesses and thus eliminated him as a member.

When in the course of these debates, Beverley revealed his political philosophy, he antagonized his in-laws, the Byrds of Westover, and began a feud with them which lasted the rest of his life. He regarded them as arch conservatives, who resisted further mass migration of white settlers to Virginia and all attempts to industralize the colony because they wished to set up a feudalism of a few white landowners who controlled vast acreages tilled by thousands of African slaves, while they regarded him at first as a half-baked youngster and later a dangerous man.

Failure in the House of Burgesses did not cause Beverley to give up. Instead, like his father before him, he tried to save his own lands, and at the same time clarify the land title laws by action through the courts. Again the colony's ruling clique stopped him as they stopped his sire, by directing the judges to draw out the litigation in endless proceedings. But from this point on Beverley, the Historian, proved that he was an abler man than Beverley, the Soldier, because instead of quarreling with local authorities about these dilatory tactics, he packed up his papers and sailed for England to present his case directly to the Privy Council of the Queen.

When Beverley reached England in 1702 he became more convinced than he was at home, through conversations he overheard in fashionable clubs and drawing rooms and articles which he read in the press that Virginia's ruling clique waged a vigorous campaign to discourage mass migration of white settlers to that colony because they wished to keep all the acreage for themselves and use only African slave labor for its cultivation, and he resolved to do all in his power to thwart his old enemies' aims. When an editor asked for his criticism of an article on Virginia, which his brother-in-law, William Byrd, of Westover, supplied for a new encyclopedia, he wrote, "it so misrepresents conditions to the common people of England to make them believe that the servants in Virginia are made to draw carts and plow as horses and oxen do in England."

As his reputation grew in the British metropolis as an authority on Queen Anne's oldest dominion beyond the seas, more bitter because of his attacks on that colony's local rulers. He ran a series of stories in London journals in which he accused Robert Quarry, chief collector of customs in Virginia, of outright theft of public money, and Sir Francis Nicholson, the royal governor, of raising a standing army "to overawe too much independence of spirit in the plain people."

When reports of these activities reached Williamsburg the ruling clique became enraged and pulled wires to force Beverley to return to Virginia to answer charges. Apparently the accused made no effort to resist these orders but before he left

London he made arrangements with a firm of printers to publish his notes in a volume entitled, *The History and Present State of Virginia.*

Back in Virginia there were long drawn out hearings of charges and counter charges with Beverley getting the better of the arguments until Nicholson in an attempt to shut him up by burying him in the wilderness, offered him the position as clerk of the backwoods county of King and Queen. Beverley accepted his offer because some of his largest holdings lay in that county and he wanted to live nearby and develop them. But the move failed to shut him up, for he had hardly reached his new post of duty before copies of his *The History and Present State of Virginia,* reached Williamsburg and set off the greatest uproar in colonial officialdom since Bacon's Rebellion.

Beverley divided his work into four parts: (1) First settlement of Virginia and the government thereof until 1705; (2) The natural production and convenience of the country suited to trade and settlement; (3) The Native Indians, their laws and their customs; and (4) The state of the country as to the policy of the government. It was the second and fourth sections which upset Virginia's ruling clique and they had reason to be disturbed because it was these sections which in the end proved their undoing.

The book was widely read in Europe. Its London publishers brought out a series of printings and numerous pirated editions in French appeared on the Continent. It circulated among the literate middle class, revived their waning interest in Virginia, and induced many of them to migrate to that colony; thus bringing in a new wave of white settlers to offset the ruling clique's rapid importation of Negro slaves, and in time establishing enough small landholders to outvote the great landlords at the polls.

The book also had a profound effect on the British intelligentsia in court circles. They used it as proof of misrule in Virginia and persuaded Queen Anne to send Alexander Spotswood to that colony as a reform governor.

Spotswood was Virginia's most enlightened royal governor. And among other reforms he forced the courts of the colony to grant the writ of habeas corpus for the first time, to keep the ruling clique from oppressing the poor through false imprisonment; and he set up iron furnaces at intervals throughout the entire domain to encourage industrial development to bring the colony a balanced economy to curb the agrarian regime of great landlords and slaves which the ruling clique desired.

Today (1953), although Colonial Williamsburg and the University of North Carolina Press have recently brought out a new edition of Beverley's *The History and Present State of Virginia,* only research students read this work; and most often they are primarily interested in the first and third sections. The first section although it sometimes reflects the author's prejudices, is a fairly accurate account of Virginia's first one hundred years, and it is the only history written by a historian, who lived in Virginia between John Smith and William Stith, a period of over one hundred and twenty-five years; and the third section is of incalcuable value to the anthropologist, because the first-hand observations of Indian laws and customs, which Beverley recorded, still stand uncontradicted.

Lack of general interest today, however, in no way diminishes the effect of *The History and Present State of Virginia* on the development of the pattern of American civilization. Its publication saved Virginia and perhaps the entire South, from becoming another Haiti, and permitted all the territory that was British North America to reach its present high state of culture. It had more influence on the American way of life than the words to come from the pen of any other author between the Mayflower Compact (1620) and the Declaration of Independence (1776).

Sir Francis Nicholson summarily dismissed Robert Beverley as clerk of King and Queen immediately after copies of *The History and Present State of Virginia* reached Williamsburg. But the royal governor did not summon the author to the colonial capital to answer charges and Beverley made no effort to defend himself. Instead he withdrew further into the wilderness and took up residence on his lands along Beverley's Run. Here he maintained his homestead for seventeen years and until he died in 1722.

Prudence dictated this move. Already Nicholson had granted John Baylor, a new favorite, a portion of the Beverley lands in upper Essex and King and Queen since the colonial courts seldom recognized a second grant of the same acreage, when the original grantee, or his heirs or assigns, was in residence on the property, Beverley, the Historian, sought to halt further raids on his inheritance by taking advantage of this precedent, when he set up his homestead on Beverley's Run.

Here he lived in a primitive baronial splendor and attempted to put into effect, so far as it was possible, the political and economic theories, which he had advocated in print. The use Virginia freeholders made of their land appalled him and he had bitterly attacked these practices in section 4 of *The History and Present State of Virginia*. Habitually after the planters cleared a plot of land, they cultivated it constantly in tobacco without adding fertilizer, until they exhausted its fertility, then they abandoned it for new clearings, often before the stumps of the original forest had rotted from its fields.

To show that this system was wrong and also to prove that the tilling of numerous crops made a more prosperous economy than depending solely on the staple, tobacco, Beverley instituted crop rotation and began to make permanent improvements on his fields. He cleared the slopes, giving to the east and south, which led to Beverley's Run, and set them out in grapevines, some of which he imported from Europe and others which he developed himself, and cultivated them in the manner he watched French vine culturists tend their vines, on one of his trips abroad. As soon as he was growing grapes in quantity he used French methods to make wine and the results were gratifying. Every guest who visited Beverley's Park, and left a record of his visit, and these guests included such a celebrity as Governor Alexander Spotswood, declare that the wine Robert Beverley served was the best to be found in the Virginia colony and equal to any wine in Europe. Today this vineyard has been long since abandoned but the residents of Caroline County, who live beyond Alps, still dote on the flavor of the wild grapes which grow in their section.

Beverley also established permanent pastures and turned his

attention to livestock. He improved the local breed of cattle for milk and beef, sheep for wool and mutton, and horses for both racing and farm work. His interest in horses laid the foundation for horse-racing in Caroline, which was to bring the county one of its greatest glories in the last half of the 18th century.

While Beverley resented royal governors regranting land when the title was already vested in his name, he had little patience with idle acres. He considered that he held in trust for future settlement all tracts of which he was unable personally to supervise the cultivation, and that it was his sacred duty to see that this property became the homes of the proper type of people. Shortly after he took up residence along Beverley's Run, he hired Col. James Taylor to divide his 16,000 acres along the Pamunkey-North Anna into sixteen 1,000 acres tracts. He reserved two of these subdivisions for himself and deeded the rest, one lot each, to his sisters, Mary, Margaret, Susanna, Catherine, Agatha and Judith; to his friends, William Wiley and John Wiley, Henry Gains and Bartholomew Yates and to his cousins, William, Elizabeth, Beverley and Ann Stennard. At least eight of these original grantees were women and through intermarriage and sale the bulk of this land passed to the Morris, Hunter, Wyatt and Hurt families.

North of the Mattapony, Beverley held on to his estate along Beverley's Run and a huge tract east of the site of Bowling Green to become known as "The Chase" or Beverley's Chase, as a hunting preserve, but through the years he gradually got rid of his other holdings in this region; some of the land around Milford (presumably Aspen Hill) to his relatives, the rest to outsiders. Unfortunately the early records of King and Queen County, in which this territory lay at the time, are lost, and it is impossible to trace the passing of individual tracts from Beverley to settlers. But since a record of all crown grants in Virginia is preserved in the archives of the State Library in Richmond and the Caroline Order Book in the Clerk's Office at Bowling Green go back to 1732 it seems that Robert Beverley brought, among others, the Woolfolk, Broaddus, Motley and Beazley families to the area to become Caroline County, because none of them had crown grants in the territory, but they were all intrenched on land that was originally Beverley property when the county's order books begin.

The size of the grants Robert Beverley made to new settlers varied from small plots to estates of 2,000 acres. But in no instance did they exceed 2,000 acres because he contended that a larger acreage was too much for one man to handle and only resulted in land waste. Beverley not only brought in new settlers from the outside but he enticed residents of the Rappahannock Valley to cross the watershed and build their homes in the valley of the Mattapony, (Kay, White, Gravatt, Chapman, Gouldin) and through grants he added to the holdings of substantial people who already lived in the section (Hoomes and Pitts).

In all instances before Beverley made a grant he took care that the proper person was getting the land; the type of settler he chose was a hard worker, who opposed the colony's old ruling clique and despised the feudalistic economy which they espoused. This being true Caroline's Bowling Green Magisterial District was from the beginning, and has remained through the years, a redrock of democracy, without either a fixed aristocracy or huge land estates; and while the descendants of few of the original settlers can claim that their ancestors had crown grants, the vast majority can truthfully boast that they are the only people in Virginia who sprung from selected stock.

Beverley's disgrace in colonial government circles lasted five years. Alexander Spotswood, who became royal governor in 1710 as a direct result of the publication of *The History and Present State of Virginia*, restored him to favor and until the year of his death, 1722, he remained a power in Williamsburg, although he continued his domicile at Beverley's Run.

Spotswood made Beverley numerous visits at his manor. The most celebrated was in the late summer of 1716, when the governor led his expedition from Williamsburg across the Blue Ridge into the valley of the Shenandoah, and stopped there the second night out of Williamsburg.

John Fontaine, log-keeper of the party, described this visit in

detail. He praises Beverley's lavish hospitality and dwells especially on the fine flavor of the wine made from native grapes.

The visit lasted a week, at the end of the week Spotswood
set out with Beverley as a member of his party, for the home
of William Woodford, on the Rappahannock between Moss
Neck and Snow Creek (Windsor). It is impossible to chart
the exact course the travelers followed in crossing the territory
that is now Caroline County, but evidently the major portion
of the route lay through a trackless wilderness because Spotswood left his chaise behind at Beverley's Run and proceeded
on horseback; and John Fontaine states that although the
weather was dry it took them nine hours to cover less than
twenty-five miles.

The party spent only one night at Windsor, and the next
day Woodford joined it when it moved on to Germanna. Here
it tarried for several days while Spotswood, the leader, assembled Indians, rangers and frontiersmen to act as guides, pro-
tectors and artesans when the expedition pushed into the
unmapped country which lay a few miles ahead.

Beverley found much to interest him during this stopover.
The men of Germanna were skilled German workmen, whom
Spotswood had recently persuaded to come to Virginia to
develop industry in the colony. Beverley was fascinated as he
watched them smelt iron ore in a newly set furnace and fashion
the molten metal into farming implements. Fontaine records
that Beverley took a hand himself in doing the rough work
at the forge under the Germans' guidance.

From Germanna the party moved to the crest of the Blue
Ridge, where Spotswood created his Knights of the Golden
Horseshoe, and down the west slope of the mountains into the
valley of the Shenandoah. From this point the expedition re-
traced its route, by way of Germanna and Windsor, to Beverley's Run, where the Governor parted company with Beverley
and set out in his chaise for Williamsburg.

Robert Beverley gained far more out of this trip than a
dubious knighthood, of which he never thought highly, and a
chance to explore the back country. He gained a large tract
of land. Spotswood stopped further inroads on his holdings

by the royal government as soon as he became governor, and had already added to his acreage by grants of 4,250 acres in what is now Caroline's Madison Magisterial District and 2,644 acres close by the south side of the Marocossic Swamp in 1713. But it was immediately after the expedition of the Knights of the Golden Horseshoe that Spotswood was most magnanimous. No sooner was the governor back in his capital than he patented Beverley 3,420 acres of the unclaimed land over which he passed with his party between Beverley's Run and Windsor and a huge slice of the Shenandoah Valley to become in time, the Beverley Manor Magisterial District of Augusta County.

In gratitude for these grants Beverley, at Spotswood's request, compiled *An Abridgement of the Public Laws of Virginia,* which served as the colony's first code, and dedicated the volume to the governor. Further to show appreciation, Beverley in the revision of his *A History and Public Survey of Virginia,* on which he was engaged at the time, deleted some of his most rabid attacks on the royal government and took care to explain that with an enlightened governor it was possible for Virginia to develop a sound economy with opportunities for the plain people under royal rule.

Beverley lived to regret these revisions because a short time after he sent the second edition of *The History and Present State of Virginia* to his London publisher, William Byrd II and Commissary Blair of William and Mary College succeeded in getting the doltish George I, who followed the enlightened Anne to the throne of England, to remove Alexander Spotswood as governor of Virginia on trumped up charges, and to send over in his stead the reactionary Hugh Drysdale. To Beverley this was stark tragedy, and he hastily began to revise his monumental work accordingly. But unfortunately, although he was only in his forty-ninth year, death overtook him before he got very far with this task, or succeeded in notifying his publisher to halt publication of the second edition.

Beverley died in despair. He believed that all hope for Virginia was lost and that the colony was about to sink to a feudalism of vast estates and slave labor. His fears were not entirely groundless, because although the economy he advocated, rather than which Byrd and Blair espoused, prevailed in time, Virginia did not reach this state without a long and bloody civil war whose germ reached back to the area of Beverley, Byrd and Blair.

Today according to the best evidence and tradition Beverley's remains rest somewhere along Beverley's Run, in the soil he loved so well; but after almost two hundred and thirty years the people of Caroline are still to erect a memorial to their county's greatest son. Fortunately Robert Beverley, the Historian, was too great a personage to suffer from this oversight. He created his own memorial also in the splendid Alps-Sparta-Smoots Mill agricultural community which he set up; and through the fact that Virginia has now adopted the economy which he advocated for that region in the early years of the eighteenth century.

End of the Indians

Indians plagued the settlers of the Caroline's Mattapony and North Anna-Pamunkey valleys during the greater part of the first decade of the 18th century. Raiding Iroquois, however, caused most of this bloodshed and house burning, rather than the native Algonquians and neighboring Souians.

The Pamunkeys never recovered from the defeat which Bacon inflicted upon them in 1676. For although they regained their strength sufficiently to keep their domain between the Mattapony and Pamunkey rivers relatively free of white settlers, they were unable to hold back the Souians Manohocs, who pressed against their western frontier in an effort to escape the raiding Iroquois.

In time, the English, as their settlers moved farther up the south bank of the North Anna and the north bank of the Mattapony, found themselves in the same position as their old enemies, the Pamunkeys, because the hard pressed Monohocs recognized no frontiers in their move east and butchered whites and reds alike. In 1684 the English and the Pamunkeys formed an alliance and sent an expedition to destroy their mutual foe. This campaign resulted in disaster for the allies. They suffered a rout in which the commander of the colonial troops was mortally wounded and Totopotomi, the chief of the Pamunkeys, and the flower of his braves were killed.

After this tragedy, only the quick work of a remarkable woman saved the Pamunkeys and their subtribes from extinction. This woman was the wife of the slain Totopotomi, who, upon hearing of her husband's death, seized the tribal government in the name of her young son, and ruled for the next thirty-five years as Anne, Queen of the Pamunkeys. The first act of her reign was to make her people a tributary tribe of the English. This was a bitter blow to their pride but it assured them of protection. In making this deal she drove a sharp bargain. The Royal Government agreed to let the Indians keep all the land between the Mattapony and the Pamunkey as hunting grounds.

To their credit government officials, for the most part, respected this treaty, but settlers as individuals soon began to violate it. In a few years, they moved in great numbers, across both the Mattapony and the Pamunkey and set up homesteads in the Indians' country. By the turn of the century they were so numerous in the lower part of the peninsula that they petitioned the House of Burgesses to establish a new county. The Burgesses demurred at first, but in 1701 acceded to the request and carved King William from the territory of King and Queen, which lay south of the Mattapony. This new county contained within its limits that part of Caroline which is now Reedy Church and Madison Magisterial Districts.

Anne resented this illegal taking of land in her kingdom, but she restrained her subjects, as far as possible, to prevent attacks on the unwelcome newcomers, and appealed to the royal government for relief. When the powers in the colonial capital procrastinated and her people threatened to get out of hand and go on the warpath, she brought the matter to a head herself. In 1706 she asked the royal government to revoke the treaty of 1684, and in lieu thereof patent certain tracts of land to the Indians in the same manner in which the government patented land to white settlers, except that the patents be issued to the tribes as a whole rather than to individuals. The Royal Government agreed to this arrangement and she won for her people the only lasting concession which the white man ever made the Indians in Colonial Virginia. To this day (1953) the Pamunkeys, along with their sub-tribe, the Mattaponys, and the Chickahominys, who were under their protection in 1706, still hold this land except for the part which they, of their own free will, have surrendered, and the Commonwealth of Virginia still honors all the prerogatives attached to the original granting.

This deal established permanent peace between the English and Anne's subjects, because the Indians now held titles to their property of equal dignity with the titles of white settlers. When frontiersmen moved on their land and began to build homesteads they had a remedy through the colonial courts by bringing action of ejectment and no longer had to resort to killings and house burnings to get rid of intruders.

However, peace with the English did not end Anne's troubles. For the rest of her days she was in conflict with many of her own people. They wanted to adopt the white man's way of living while she firmly believed that the only chance the Indians had to preserve their identity as a race was to retain an undiluted Indian culture. History has proven that she was right but a majority of subjects were not so farsighted. When she banned the wearing of the white man's dress and the building of houses, in her kingdom, they sought means to leave the reservations.

Colonial laws deterred this movement because they provided that an Indian must prove that he was able to earn his livelihood, so as not to become a public charge, and find a white man to go his bond to insure his good behavior before the authorities granted him permission to leave his reservation and live among the whites. Unfortunately, if an Indian were of use to the whites, it was relatively easy for him to meet these requirements. Along the frontier there was an acute shortage of craftsmen, and a sure way for an Indian to gain permission to leave his tribe was to acquire skill in a white man's trade.

In point is the case of the Indian, Robin, who stated in his petition to leave the Pamunkey Reservation in 1709, that he was a shoemaker, and that the only way for him to earn a livelihood from his trade was to live among the whites, since Anne, Queen of the Pamunkeys, forced the people of her reservations to wear moccasins.

Few Indians, however, were lucky enough to learn a white man's trade; for more of them left their reservations to become hunters. The pelts of native animals commanded a high price on the European markets and it was profitable for settlers to go an Indian bond in exchange for a monopoly on the resale of the Indian's pelts. Off the reservation the Indian were able to increase vastly the number of animals he killed, because so long as he lived among his own people the colonial laws allowed him to hunt only with the bow and arrow, but away from them, and with a white man on his bond for his good behavior, it granted him the right to use firearms.

With settlers and Indians conspiring to evade the laws, Anne sadly watched, through her declining years, many of her people leave her kingdom and adopt the white man's customs. As the number of her subjects diminished, she applied at various times to the royal government for permission to sell off a portion of their land to support those who remained, and thus set a precedent, which her successors, as rulers, followed until the lands of the Pamunkeys, Mattaponys and the Chickahominys, shrunk to the small acreages of the three present reservations.

With the decline of the Indians' power in the York River basin, the fate of the Pamunkeys' Myghtuckpassu and Catta-chiptice and the Mattaponys' Untenstack and Paussaunkack villages located in the area that was to become Caroline is shrouded in mystery. The chances are that they were drawn back into the main bodies of their parent tribes, when Anne arranged for reservations for her people. But the fate of the Dogue Indian town located between Milford Bridge and the Devils Three Jumps is a matter of record.

Since the Dogue's were a semi-independent tribe living under the protection of the Pamunkey-Mattaponys and not actually first class subjects of Queen Anne, it seems that she left them out when she made her deal with the English in 1706 because the records indicate that the Colonial Government never granted them a reservation. In fact they lived on holding the precarious title of their fathers to their hunting grounds, until 1718 when Robert Farrish patented 1,540 acres along the south side of the Mattapony "including in ye grant the saidde Dogue Indian Towne." Apparently Farrish used the Indian well because they still resided in their homes two years later when the Council granted George Braxton, John and Mary Waller, 1,000 acres located on both sides of May's Run about three miles from the Indians "living in Dogue Indian Town." This is the last reference that the author can find to the Dogues or any other Indians living as a tribe in the territory to be Caroline. It is of interest to note that this date was 1720, only seven years before Caroline became a county.

Little is known of the nature of the Dogues, but to this day there stands in the Mattapony flats and on a hill a short distance back of the flats on lands owned by Floyd Parker and Temple Coleman, within a few miles of their town site, two ancient houses, constructed with slits in their walls for guns and other devices to withstand the attacks of Indians. This may indicate that the Dogues were warlike; or it may have been that they lived peaceably alongside the whites and that the homes were built in this manner as a protection against the Iroquois, who during the first decade of the eighteenth century, raided the land that is Caroline, killing the native Indians and the white settlers alike.

The Seneca and Tuscarora tribes of the Iroquois rendered the Souians impotent a short time after Anne placed her tribes under the protection of the English; and afterwards with the Souians no longer strong enough to soften the blows, the settlers along the Virginia frontier felt the full fury of these Indians' hit-and-run attacks for over a quarter of a century.

The fort Lawrence Smith set up at Leaselands (Fredericksburg after 1727) furnished adequate protection to keep the raiders out of the Rappahannock Valley, but the settlers along other streams were not so fortunate. The House of Burgesses in each session from 1700-1712 enacted laws to set up rangers

and maintain forts for the protection of the James and York
River basins. But for all their efforts these defenses were in-
effective. As late as 1708 the Tuscaroras raided upper New
Kent, King William and King and Queen counties (now Hanover and Caroline), burned many homesteads, caused settlers
to flee in terror and killed at least one white man, Jeremiah
Pate, who lived south of the Pamunkey.

The Iroquois were the craftiest Indians who opposed the
English in Virginia. They not only kept the frontier under
constant pressure with their unheralded sporadic attacks, but
also organized disgruntled elements who lived among the
settlers to harass law-abiding people between their attacks.
About 1718, on a raid into Stafford County, they released
Black Tom, a convicted murderer awaiting the gallows, and
placed him at the head of a band which consisted of other
fugitives from justice, native Indians who dared defy their
chiefs' truces with the colonial government and attack the
whites, and recently imported Negro slaves who had run away
from their masters. This motley crew of cut-throats and
savages committed acts of murder, arson and rape, which
spread terror along the fall line from the Potomac to the
James. All the able-bodied men among the settlers who lived
in the region to be Caroline, not needed to protect homesteads,
joined a posse which pursued these brigands night and day
until they killed Black Tom and dispersed his gang.

Individual colonies never had sufficient military forces to
cope with the Iroquois and several times between 1710 and
1720 their governors met to plan concerted action but all these
efforts came to naught. It was European power politics which
finally removed them as a threat to the Virginia Colony.
Around 1720 England needed Indian allies to offset the Indian
allies of the French in her struggle with France for control of
the North American continent. As such allies, the Iroquois
were a logical choice, because they were already bitter foes of
the Indians, who had joined forces with the French. Under
pressure from London the colonial authorities made peace.
The Iroquois gained sweeping concessions in New York which
was their traditional habitat, but through a skillful maneuver

Governor Alexander Spotswood of Virginia managed to write into the treaty the provision that henceforth they were to remain north of the Potomac and west of the Blue Ridge.

The Settlement of Reedy Church and Madison

After Lawrence Smith failed to take up his patent on Reedy Swamp in 1664 the white man left the section of Caroline County lines between Mattapony and North Anne-Pamunkey alone, until William Collins set up his household on 620 acres on "Poulcatte" Creek in 1691. But the Collinses were strictly a frontier family and got on without white neighbors for almost a quarter of a century.

The next crown grants in this territory were to the colony's established landlords. In 1701 the royal governor patented 3,860 acres in what is now lower Reedy Church Magisterial District to a gentleman with the resounding name of Chickerly Corbin Thacker; and five years later Robert Beverley, always a sharp dealer when it came to land, persuaded the crown to give him 16,000 acres in the same district to compensate him for the loss of a much smaller tract along the Rappahannock-Mattapony watershed to John Baylor. The record fails to disclose what Thacker did with his land and the atuhor has already explained Beverley's subdivision.

Shortly before the Beverley grant, William Byrd, the frontiersman, and his associates moved into the great fork of the Mattapony, and these three widely separated settlements (Beverley's sub-grantees eastward from the present-day site of Morris' Bridge, Collins in the region that is now Penola, and Byrd's party between the Matta and Pony) appear to be the only instances of white people living on Caroline soil south of the Mattapony, until after Spotswood made his treaty with the Indians, which freed all Virginia east of the Blue Ridge from raids by the Iroquois.

From the records of crown grants in the archives of the Virginia State Library it seems that mass settlement of the territory included in Caroline's Reedy Church and Madison

Magisterial Districts began in 1714. That year the royal
government granted James Kimbrew 300 acres on Topping
Castle Swamp, James Terry 400 acres below the great falls
of the North Anna (Oxford), William Terrell 300 acres on
Polecat Creek, and Richard Sutton 600 acres on Reedy Swamp.
From that date onward the crown issued numerous patents
each year; and in most instances the acreage was small and to
homesteaders. This was in striking contrast to the giving away
of large tracts to the favorites of royal governors which prevailed, when the white man first claimed title to the land alongside of the Rappahannock and the north side of the Mattapony.

Settlers without drag in the colonial capital got their Crown
land in conformity with the homesteading laws of the day, 50
acres for each member of the settler's family. The authorities
in Williamsburg complied strictly with the statutes in making
grants during Spotswood's rule, but bribes, friendship and
convenience often influenced county clerks when they certified
the size of families, and county surveyors when they marked
off the land.

In 1715, Timothy Chandler, when a bridegroom, patented
100 acres on the upper branches of Polecat Creek; 50 acres
for himself and 50 acres for his wife. Three years later he
patented 100 additional acres, claiming two children in three
years which was logical for a frontier family. But after seven
more years, when he had become a big man in the new parish
of St. Margaret's, he pushed the realm of biological proba-
bility, when he demanded and secured 750 additional acres due
to natural increases in his family. It is hard to believe that
even a hardy pioneer couple produced fifteen children in seven
years. The same doubt applies in the case of William Terrell,
who like Chandler rapidly became a personage of importance
in the new country, when he claims land for 18 new sons and
daughters in a ten-year period.

From the sameness of surnames in crown grants it appears
that the first settlers south of the Mattapony were a clannish
lot. Besides Timothy, two other Chandlers patented land in the
headwaters of Polecat Creek; Robert with 150 acres in 1718
and Joseph with 400 acres in 1725. There were also three

Dickasons (Dickinson) in this same region: Thomas with one grant of 390 acres in 1717 and another of 400 acres in 1726, (eight children in nine years for Thomas); Griffin with 900 acres in 1717, and William with 400 acres in 1725. Two Samuels came to live on the "South River of the Mattapony" in 1719, Simon on 360 acres on the north fork and Anthony 400 acres on the south fork of that stream. And the homesteads of the two Terrys, James and Thomas, originally stood somewhere in the section between the North Anna and the site of Carmel Church.

Growth During the First Quarter of the 18th Century

Towards the close of the 17th century the English settlers along the south bank of the Rappahannock from Portobago Bay to the falls of the river had become so numerous that they petitioned the Colonial Council of Virginia for a church. The Council granted this request and set up St. Mary's Parish, which embraced all of Caroline's Rappahannock Valley. Shortly thereafter the settlers built in this new parish a commodious house of worship, which they located on Mount Hill about mid-distance between Portobago and Snow Creek.

This building was Caroline's first church. The exact date on which the colonists built it is not known, but documents still in existence prove that it had a flourishing congregation when its first rector of record, the Rev. Owen Jones, arrived in the parish from England in 1704.

Rev. Jones was rector of St. Mary's from 1704-24 and as was the case with most rectors in Colonial Virginia, he was a teacher as well as a preacher, and shortly after he reached the parish he set up on Mount Hill a school, which lasted for almost two centuries.

With church and school firmly established, and one trading center flourishing about Taliaferro's warehouse at the mouth of Mill Creek, and another flourishing about Buckner's tobacco warehouse further up the Rappahanock, Caroline's Rappahannock Valley had the essential elements to sustain a high order of society. On their plantations along the river, the Lomaxes, Woodfords, Conways, Catletts and other early settlers began to build comfortable homes and sometimes pretentious manors.

Across the watershed along the north bank of the Mattapony, settlers, which included the Lewises, Hoomes, Thorntons, Tompkins, and Roystons lived fairly well, but in a considerable less degree of elegance, because Indians or raiding parties from across the Mattapony still harassed this district.

In the back country wilderness between the river flats and their abutting hills lay uninhabited country except for a few disgruntled political recluses and small bands of rugged frontiersmen. To encourage the settlement of this region the royal government in Williamsburg offered bounties. In 1703 the Colonial Council granted Sam Craddock, John Core, John Echols and William Glover, 1,620 acres on Tuckahoe Swamp in "ye freshies of the river Rappahannock," for bringing thirty-three (33) persons to Virginia from England. The Council made this grant for dual purposes; to get more people into Virginia and to get them settled in the back country; because the patent specifically states that the grantees were to lose title to the whole acreage unless they planted settlers on all of it before 1706.

The grant furnishes an interesting sidelight as to the value of Caroline's real estate in the first decade of the eighteenth century. Using the current (1953) minimum Trans-Atlantic fare as yardstick, Craddock, Core, Echols and Glover paid per acre for the land about what $3.00 will buy today.

French Huguenots were among the most stabilizing settlers to reach the region that was to become Caroline during this period. The Huguenots had to leave France after 1685 when the French King, Louis XIV, revoked the Edict of Nantes, which granted immunity to Protestants in his domain. About 40,000 of them fled to England and because that country was already overcrowded the English arranged for the vast majority of these refugees to move on to Britain's colonies overseas.

This exodus brought Huguenots in great numbers to the colonies of Virginia, South Carolina and New York. The chief settlement in Virginia was at Manakin (Monocantown) on the James, thirty miles west of the site of Richmond and well beyond the white man's frontier; but a few families at least made their way into every accessible section of the colony. In the area that was to become Caroline, three Boutwell (Bouteilles) brothers secured a large tract of land near the Rappahannock in the vicinity of Jack's Hill; the LaFoes, Durretts and Fontaines moved inland and became frontiers-men, while the Picardattes (Picardees), Chennaults and others came in a group and planted a settlement in the Mattapony Valley to become known as Picadees Fork.

The Huguenots were a thrifty folk, who possessed many skills, such as glass-blowing, weaving and metal working, which were badly needed in the Virginia Colony, especially along the frontier; and their attitude towards the Indians was quite different from that of the English. Instead of fighting the red man, they made friends. The aborigines quickly recognized this difference and while they kept on shooting at the English on sight, they let the Huguenots move about unmolested. This freedom to move without fear of attack plus their skills and industry, placed them in position to make large contributions in bringing a staple culture to the frontier.

New Counties and Parishes

The rapid settlement of Caroline's York River Basin was only small parts of the western migration in Virginia during the era of Spotswood and Beverley (1710-22). The enlight-ened policies of the royal government under their guidance attracted to the colony its greatest annual volume of European settlers. Peace with the Iroquois and the Expedition of the Knights of the Golden Horseshoe led many of these new people to settle west of the fall line, where they got their land through crown grants and did not have to pay exorbitant prices for acreage to the entrenched landlords. By 1720 the

western settlements were so numerous that Governor Spotswood asked the royal government to set up a new series of
counties along the frontier.

These new counties were all anchored in Tidewater and
their western limits extended to the Blue Ridge and beyond.
Three of them, King George, Spotsylvania and Hanover,
boxed in the area to be Caroline on the north, west and south.
Because the authorities in Williamsburg fixed the eastern
boundary of a new frontier county along the present-day
Caroline-Spotsylvania line, indicates that they saw no need to
start another county by a greater reduction of the western
territories of Essex, King and Queen and King William.
Further evidence of this opinion is found in the fact that they
divided this area among parishes in existing counties.

The same year that the colonial authorities set up the new
counties, they split St. Mary's Parish, which lay along the
south side of the Rappahannock westward from Portobago
Creek, at Snow Creek. The western end became St. George's
Parish and lay wholly within the new county of Spotsylvania,
while the eastern end retained church, glebe and name, and
remained entirely within the territorial limits to be Caroline.
At the same time they divided St. John's Parish, which took
up the entire peninsula between the Mattapony and the Pamunkey-North Anna, three ways. The upper section became Berkeley Parish in Spotsylvania, the middle, St. Margaret's and the
lower remained St. John's.

St. Margaret's originally comprised all of Caroline's Madison and Reedy Church Magisterial Districts and the upper
third of King William. The Crown appointed Capt. Thomas
Terry and Macajah Chiles as its first wardens and granted
them a huge tract of land, as trustees, to set up a parish church
and glebe. These gentlemen sold a portion of the land and
built a substantial house of worship, to become known as
Chesterfield Church, on the tract of land which lies south of
the road leading from Ruther Glen to Carmel. In the third
decade of the eighteenth century this was the most central
location in all the area to become Caroline, south of the
Mattapony. It was the junction of the Indian trail which lay

along the Mattapony-Pamunkey-North Anna watershed and the trail Powhatan built along the fall line to serve as the connecting link with his Algonquin kin to the north. The early white settlers took over these roads as the only overland route to their courthouse at King William, and as soon as they came into the region this road junction became their trade center. When the royal government formed Caroline as a county, John Sutton already had a well established tavern in this vicinity to take care of transients.

The Rev. Francis Fontaine became the first rector of St. Margaret's. The first glebe was on the road leading eastward from Ruther Glen opposite Old Bagdad, but it appears that the first rector lived adjacent to the church rather than on this property because to this day (1953) the church site is known as the Fontaine tract.

The colonial authorities failed to reduce the size of St. Stephen's Parish, which lay in a narrow strip along the north side of the Mattapony from lower King and Queen to that stream's source, when they divided St. Mary's and St. John's. Spotswood and Beverley caused this oversight. To entice German immigrants, who were Lutherans, to Virginia, Spotswood shoved through the House of Burgesses and Council legislation which exempted them from paying church levies to the government. When these people took up most of the land in the upper end of the parish there was insufficient public revenue either to build or to sustain a state church in that region. While Beverley, who dominated the central section of the parish, discouraged the building of a house of worship for the official religion there because he regarded the established church of the colony as another tool which the great landlords used to hold back the advancement of the plain people.

It was 1723, after Beverley had died and Byrd and Blair had forced Spotswood out of office, before the royal government in Virginia split St. Stephen's Parish. The dividing line was somewhere in what is now upper King and Queen. The lower parish remained St. Stephen's and the upper became Drysdale, in honor of Hugh Drysdale, who at the time served as royal governor of Virginia.

Drysdale Parish did not prosper. The shape, five miles wide and fifty miles long was against it. There was no central location on which to build a church, convenient to more than a handful of the parishioners and to make matters worse neither the German immigrants nor Beverley's protégés, which formed the bulk of the population, looked with favor upon the established religion. At an early date it seems civil authorities stopped trying to enforce the compulsory church attendance law, because while there are numerous instances of fines imposed on residents of St. Mary's and St. Margaret's for not frequenting their parish church in the early order books of the Caroline Court there is not an instance when such a fine was imposed on a resident of Drysdale for a similar offense.

However, with all these handicaps, there was a house of worship in the parish. This building known as Joy Creek Church was located somewhere near the banks of Beverley's Run. In 1857 Bishop Meade wrote that in his youth elderly men told him that they had heard their grandfathers speak of such a church, but in the same paragraph he admitted that after careful exploration in the area and much inquiry he was unable to find any trace of its foundation. Other evidence which points to a short and impoverished life span for Joy Creek is the fact that the location of its site is completely lost, while the sites of Caroline Colonial churches which flourished, (Mount, Chesterfield, Bull, Reedy, Ivy and Creek) are known to even the casual research students.

Why Caroline Was Founded

After the royal government set up Drysdale Parish, it considered the political organization of the territory to be Caroline, complete. But the people who lived in this area had different ideas. As early as 1715 they had begun to demonstrate the need of a county in that section with its own local officials.

That year, when the authorities in Williamsburg placed an exorbitant tobacco tax of 85 lbs. per head on all male residents, both Negro and white, over the age of 16, the planters of St.

Mary's Parish rebelled. Instead of shipping their tobacco through a government chartered warehouse where inspectors exacted the tax, as the law required, they piled it on private wharfs along the Rappahannock, and sold it to black marketeers, who plied that stream under the cover of darkness. When notice of these tax evasions came to the attention of Leo Tarrant, the sheriff of Essex, he moved into the upper parish of his county, and through threats scared some of the more timid planters to move their crops to chartered warehouses. This, however, did not restore law and order. It only served to antagonize all but the meekest planters. On the night of April 15, 1715, the boldest of the agrieved broke into Buckner's warehouse, destroyed the scales, and burned the building in which the timid had recently stored their tobacco. Tarrant arrested no one for this crime. Instead he wrote the Governor's Council that it was impossible for him to enforce such an unpopular law, in a region so remote from his county seat.

After the settlement of St. Margaret's Parish the people of that section, too, had their difficulties because they lived in a region far removed from the center of local government. In 1726 four Negro slaves, James, Gray, Roger and Sampson, recently brought to Virginia from Africa, escaped from their master's plantation near Manakin, and fled to St. Margaret's. Here they stripped off their clothes and reverted to the life of their native jungle. These wild men darting nude about the wilderness caused a panic among the white inhabitants. But when they notified the sheriff of King William about their troubles, he refused to try to capture the escapees. Whereupon the settlers took the law in their hands and formed a posse which seized the runaways on the lands of Martin Slaughter in the vicinity of present-day (1953) Cedar Fork. After the capture the people of St. Margaret's Parish sent messages to colonial authorities in Williamsburg which bitterly assailed the sheriff of King William for being derelict in his duties and asked relief.

That same year (1726) the residents of St. Mary's found a new need for local government. When Governor Hugh Drysdale left for England, Robert (King) Carter, president of the

Council, took over as acting governor, until a new appointee of
the crown reached Virginia. Carter abused the powers that
went with his office. He closed all custom houses along the
Rappahannock except the one at Urbanna, which he turned
over to his son, Robert Jr., whom he made Collector of Customs for the whole valley. Robert Jr. exceeded his sire in
arrogance, and moved the office from the town to his manor
three miles distant from the river. This caused all ships sailing
out of Rappahannock ports to stop over at Urbanna while
their masters treaked inland for clearance. The inconvenience
vexed merchants, warehousemen and planters throughout the
section. They began to clamor for more counties with more
Burgesses to curb the governor. Among the most outspoken
were the aggrieved of St. Mary's Parish, who angrily demanded their own representatives in Williamsburg to look out
for their interest.

At the time another complaint rankled the St. Mary's people.
For many years Augustine Smith, a son of the celebrated
Lawrence Smith, who commanded the first garrison at leaseland (Fredericksburg) had been public surveyor for their
parish. They did not like him, and accused him of bringing
savage Negroes on their lands as chain bearings when they
hired him in his official capacity, and; if they objected to the
Negroes, of giving them a plat without making a survey. They
hoped that they lost him when the royal government cut off
the upper end of the parish, in which he lived, and placed it
in the new county of Spotsylvania. But these hopes proved vain
when Williamsburg authorities made him surveyor for both
Spotsylvania and upper Essex. Through the years the feud
grew more bitter until the planters were willing to try any
tactics that might result in getting rid of Augustine Smith. A
new county seemed a plausible way.

However, it was the planters of upper Drysdale and their
neighbors across the Mattapony in northwest St. Margaret's,
who made the move which resulted in the setting up of Caroline
County. Their troubles were economic rather than political.
The only way they had to send their tobacco to market was on
flat boats down the shallow, tortuous Mattapony to Aylett's

warehouse at Tidewater, where it was processed and tran-
shipped on ocean-going vessels to England. This was a great
hardship for the Thorntons, Tompkinses, Claibornes, Catletts,
Buckners, Palmers, Ginneys and other settlers, who at an early
date had established a flourishing agricultural community in
the vicinity of present-day (1953) Guinea. They soon found a
practical solution for that problem; a short overland road to
roll their tobacco in hogsheads to Conway's warehouse on the
Rappahannock. But this route lay in three counties and it was
impossible for them to get three county courts to agree on its
course and to order its clearing. After numerous attempts and
failures they decided to try another procedure. In the winter
of 1727 under the leadership of Francis Thornton, they drew
up a petition asking the royal government to form a new county
from the heads of Essex, King and Queen and King William
and thus place the whole route within one political subdivision.

The weather was rough and the time short, since the House
of Burgesses and Governor's Council were already in session.
When Thornton left for Williamsburg with the petition it only
contained the signatures of his neighbors, who were all residents of either King and Queen or King William.

The Setting Up of Caroline County

Politicians in the colonial capital ignored Thornton and his
petition until leaders of the great landlord caste took the
matter up and made it a part of their campaign to gain control
of the House of Burgesses.

The year 1727 was a crucial one for the great landlords,
who came back to power after the reactionary George I sup-
planted Alexander Spotswood with Hugh Drysdale as governor. While Drysdale and Robert (King) Carter ruled Virginia
they were safely entrenched and did not need control of the
House of Burgesses, because a friendly governor and council
blocked all legislation which the lower house proposed to their
detriment. In 1727 the situation became quite different. That
year George II followed his father, George I, to the British

throne and this new king, under the influence of his wife,
Caroline, and her advisors, all of whom the English nobility
classed as radicals, sent to Virginia another great liberal, Sir
William Gooch, as governor. When Gooch reached Willims-
burg the great landlords realized that their days of influence
on the Colonial Government were numbered unless they were
able to gain control of the House of Burgesses. They had lost
the governor and the loss of the council was only a matter of
time, since all the members of that body were appointees of
the governor and held office at his pleasure. Their only hope
was to gain a majority in the House of Burgesses and use
that body to block the governor and council, as they used
governor and council to block the Burgesses while Drysdale
and Carter ruled.

Garwin Corbin, a holdover Drysdale appointed on the Council, and George Braxton, a Burgess from King and Queen,
directed the landlords strategy in the York basin and adjacent
territory. They decided to use Francis Thornton's petition as
the basis of a gerrymander to eliminate two hostile and gain
four friendly Burgesses.

Thomas Carr who sat for King William and John Robinson
who held a King and Queen seat, were the Burgesses whom
they marked for the axe. Carr, they classed a renegade of
their caste because instead of developing the 4,260 acres
Governor Drysdale granted him in upper St. Margaret's Parish
as a great estate, he only improved a part of it and offered
the rest in small tracts to homesteaders. They were afraid of
Robinson because he was a nephew of their old enemy, Beverley, the Historian, and while yet young, he showed a strong
tendency to follow the economic and political policies of his
celebrated relative.

Carr automatically lost his seat if the royal government
cut upper St. Margaret's Parish from King William because
colonial laws provided that a Burgess must reside in the county
for which he sat. Already Robinson's seat was in controversy.
Corbin and Braxton had filed a petition in the House of
Burgesses in behalf of Richard Johnson, whom Robinson defeated the past summer, contesting the election. If the Bur-

gesses followed precedent and ordered victor and vanquished to face the voters a second time at the polls to settle the dispute, Robinson had little chance of winning with the major portion of Drysdale Parish out of the district, since in the first election he piled up his majority among the small landowners of that parish. Corbin and Braxton felt that the inclusion of St. Mary's in the new county secured two more Burgesses favorable to their cause because that populous parish, in which the great landlords predominated, could easily outvote the small landowners, who resided in upper St. Margaret's and upper Drysdale.

To execute this plan Braxton introduced a bill in the House of Burgesses on February 8, 1727, to form a new county from the heads of Essex, King and Queen and King William. This bill faced rough going from the start. Heretofore, the boundaries of all new Virginia counties extended beyond the frontier, and many Burgesses disliked the idea of setting up a new county entirely within settled territory. They feared that it might lead to the breaking up of the whole colony into tiny political subdivisions. Thomas Carr was strangely silent during the debate, but John Robinson fought back, until, midway of the discussion, the Burgesses declared his seat vacant and excluded him from the House. The Burgesses from Essex claimed that the bill ruined their county and challenged the inclusion of St. Mary's when no residents of that parish had signed the petition which asked for a new county. But Garwin Corbin had great influence along the south side of the Rappahannock. He got in touch with his friends in that region, a delegation of them showed up in Williamsburg, and forced the Burgesses from Essex to withdraw their protest.

After Braxton got around these objectors, the eastern boundary of the proposed county gave him trouble. In the original bill this line began at the mouth of Portobago Creek on the Rappahannock, and continued in a southwesterly direction parallel with the lower limits of Spotsylvania to the Pamunkey. Unlike previous arbitrary boundaries in Virginia it ran through settled country splitting plantations, and as soon as the residents of the region learned what was underway they began to clamor to be left out, or included in the new county. Braxton was willing to accommodate them, so long as their requests were not fatal to his bill. He sanctioned a series of amendments which changed the proposed eastern limits from a straight line to a deckled edge. This jockeying took up almost a month, and it was March 7th before the Burgesses engrossed the bill and put it on its second reading. Two days later they passed it, and sent it to the council for concurrence.

Garwin Corbin had his troubles in the Council. Other planters wanted their holdings shifted, but he handled them with dispatch. In three days the upper house passed the bill with more amendments altering the proposed county's eastern boundary and sent it back to the House of Burgesses. That day (March 12, 1727) the Burgesses agreed to these changes and the bill went to Governor Gooch for his signature. The governor signed promptly; Caroline became a county.

Who named the county is unknown. The name Caroline first appears in the record in an amendment a Burgess offered from the floor, when the bill to erect the county was on its second reading. The identity of the Burgess remains a mystery.

The Founding Fathers—Their Background, Duties and Problems

Governor Gooch appointed John Lomax, William Woodford, Thomas Carr, John Martin, Richard Buckner, Thomas Catlett, Francis Thornton, John Taliaferro, Francis Conway, Ambroise Maddison, John Catlett, John Battaile, John Sutton, Lundsford Lomax, Robert Woolfolk, Walter Chiles, Thomas Rucker and Richard Mauldin, as king's magistrates to set up Caroline County. The lack of records and the confusion caused by the frequent use of the same given name within a family in the new surviving documents render complete biographical sketches of these men, who were Caroline's founding fathers, impossible. But fortunately enough evidence survives to identify most of them.

In colonial Virginia the governor always ranked the magistrates in the order of importance when he listed them in appointing a panel for a county. Since this was true John Lomax was the first presiding magistrate for Caroline County. He lived in the Rappahannock Valley, east of Port Royal, on lands his wife inherited from her father, Sir Thomas Lundsford. Apparently he was an elderly man in 1727 and the chances are that Governor Gooch made him presiding magistrate largely on account of his age and the venerable position which he held in the community.

William Woodford was the most distinguished man living in the territory from which the Royal Government formed Caroline County. He was born in England and in his youth made an excellent military record. He fought with Spotswood under Marlborough at Blenheim and came to Virginia upon Spotswood's invitation after his old comrade-in-arms became governor of the colony, and took up a large tract of land he acquired through marriage in St. Mary's Parish. Here he soon set up a lavish homestead and began to cultivate the friendship of his distant neighbor, Robert Beverley, the historian, with whom he agreed on many topics pertaining to economics and agriculture. These two men were the only gentlemen in the entire region of sufficient importance to merit an invitation from Spotswood to join the expedition of the Knights of the Golden Horseshoe across the Blue Ridge. Almost as soon as Woodford reached Virginia, Spotswood made him a magistrate for Essex County. He retained this position through the years and brought a wealth of knowledge gained through experience to the first governing board for the new county of Caroline.

Thomas Carr was even better qualified through training than Woodford, to be magistrate. A long time resident of King William, he had served that county as magistrate, sheriff and burgess. In 1727 he was an elderly man with a seat at Topping Castle on the North Anna. One of his daughters was married to a Waller and another to a Minor. These alliances gave him great influence over the most substantial people in St. Margaret's Parish.

John Martin, like William Woodford, was born in England, and came to Virginia after a distinguished military career.

But unlike Woodford he came to the colony as a protégé of Drysdale rather than Spotswood. His patron gave him a small tract of land southeast of the Bowling Green, in the midst of Robert Beverley's domain. The chances are that Drysdale put him there to counteract the influences of the deceased Beverley, which still lived on, because due to his close association with the governor and the fact that he married, almost as soon as he reached the colony, Martha, the daughter of Lewis Burwell of Gloucester, the owner of some of Virginia's greatest estates, he firmly espoused the feudalistic landlord's cause.

Through the sheer ownership of property Richard Buckner easily qualified as a great landlord, but instead of blindly following this group, he wavered like his father before him, between being their partisan and a champion of the plain people. He was of the third generation of Buckners to own acreage in the area that is Caroline County. His grandfather Anthony received a joint grant with that old speculator, Lawrence Smith of 4,972 acres south of the Rappahannock in 1671. Five years later his father, John, joined Sir William Berkeley in that royal governor's attempt to crush Nathaniel Bacon, Jr. and as a reward for these services received a one-fifth interest in 10,050 acres along the Rappahannock-Matta-pony watershed, as well as 500 acres more in the Golden Vale, which Berkeley took from John Patterson, a partisan of Bacon, to hold in trust for his infant son, Richard. Control of this vast acreage, however, failed to align John Buckner with the feudalistic aristocrats. Instead of joining them, he smuggled into Virginia the colony's first printing press and in 1681 printed an abridgment of the colonial laws, which he circulated, that all who were literate might learn the law and demand their rights. Both, to own a press and to print without a license, were felonies. Lord Culpeper, the arch reactionary, who persuaded Charles II to grant him the whole Northern Neck as a personal fief, ruled Virginia at the time. He summoned Buckner to Jamestown to answer for his crimes, but the culprit after a lengthy wrangle managed to escape with no greater punishment than the loss of his press and the posting of a one hundred pound bond to print no more.

For the next twenty years John Buckner appears to have done no act to offend Virginia's late seventeenth century's ruling caste. For this loyalty Francis Nicholson granted him 3,080 additional acres in 1702 in the back country of St. Mary's Parish. But he kept in step with the times and after Spotswood came to Virginia, joined the new regime's program to expand trade and opened the second chartered tobacco warehouse on the southside of the Rappahannock, between Portobago Bay and the river's falls. His interest in commerce came to Spotswood's attention and to reward him the governor invited his son, Richard, to come to Williamsburg and serve as clerk of the House of Burgesses.

Life in Williamsburg made Richard Buckner something of a snob. He held on to this job until his father died. But when he returned to St. Mary's Parish to take over his heritage he promptly sold the warehouse to Thomas Roy, one of the tobacco inspectors who worked there, and set himself up as a country squire, untarnished by trade.

Thomas Catlett was a son of the John Catlett who gained 3,400 acres in the vicinity of Port Royal in 1677 for helping Berkeley during Bacon's Rebellion. However, he did not live on this property in 1727 but at Locust Hill (the home of Mr. and Mrs. George Cosby in 1953) across the Mattopany from Guinea. He had moved into this region because he married Martha, the daughter of Francis Thornton, who lived at Ormesby across the river. The chances are that he merited the position of magistrate on account of this connection. The only incongruity in this assumption is the fact that Gooch named him immediately ahead of Thornton on the slate of original justices.

Francis Thornton along with John Lomax and Thomas Carr composed the group of three grand old men among Caroline's founding fathers. It is interesting to note that they represented the three parishes which formed the new county. Thornton was from Drysdale, Lomax from St. Mary's and Carr from St. Margaret's. Francis Thornton sprung from one of the most prolific families in colonial Virginia. His first Thornton ancestor reached the colony shortly after the English settled at Jamestown and this man's descendants helped roll back the frontier from the Atlantic to the Pacific. Francis Thornton, the founding father, reached the area to be Caroline in his youth, when in 1675 he, with his brother, Anthony, patented 2,740 acres along the upper Mattapony. Here he demonstrated his qualities as a leader by setting up about his plantation one of the most flourishing settlements on the frontier. These fifty-two years of experience gained under local conditions made him an invaluable man among Caroline's first magistrates.

John Taliaferro has the distinction of being the scion of the first family to reach the soil that is Caroline and produce a founding father. His first Caroline Taliaferro ancestor patented 6,300 acres jointly with Lawrence Smith on the south side of the Rappahannock below Snow Creek in 1666. Seven years later Robert, the son of Robert, took up 739 acres on both sides the mouth of Peumandsend (Mill Creek), and set up on a portion of this property the region to be Caroline's first chartered tobacco warehouse. This enterprise flourished and the children of Robert, the son of Robert, multiplied until in a short time his heirs were among the most numerous and prosperous families in the region. At one session of court a few years after Caroline became a county, three of the five sitting magistrates were Taliaferros.

Francis Conway was of the second generation of Conways to own Caroline land. He lived on a tract the crown granted his father, Edwin Conway of Lancaster, in 1681 and was a successful business man, the owner of Conway's warehouse on the Rappahannock and a substantial home at Mt. Scion, in 1727. He appears to have been too much concerned with his own affairs to have much time for public life; and to have left his spectacular cousin, Edwin Conway, who represented Lancaster County in the House of Burgesses at the time, to make a name for his generation of his family in statecraft.

Ambroise Madison was a son of John Madison who had large grants in upper St. Margaret's Parish. John Catlett was a brother of Thomas, who lived on the family's original holdings near Port Royal. He had served as coroner for Essex and had some experience in public life. John Battaile came to the area to be Caroline as a tobacco inspector at Conway's warehouse. He prospered in the new county and in a short time became wealthy. He took out land, built a manor house, and established the celebrated Battaile family of Prospect Hill.

John Sutton was a St. Margaret's Parish homesteader. The chances are, that like John Taliaferro, Richard Buckner and Ambroise Madison, he was born on the soil to be Caroline. At an early date his father took up land north of the Mattapony. When the region south of the river became safe from Indians he and his brother, Richard, crossed that stream. Here they took out 400 acres, maximum each, which the law allowed settlers who were not so fortunate as to have powerful friends in Williamsburg.

Lundsford Lomax was a son of John, the presiding magistrate. Governor Gooch seems to have included him on the panel to take over in case his father became incapacitated. It worked out that way because John Lomax died shortly after the Royal Government organized Caroline, while Lundsford continued on in public life for almost forty years as one of the county's most influential men.

Robert Woolfolk, Walter Chiles and Thomas Rucker were all protégés of Robert Beverley. Woolfolk developed his grant, Shephards Hill, between Bowling Green and Milford into a thriving plantation, and became one of the new county's most useful, if sometimes eccentric, residents. Chiles lived on a portion of the land Beverley granted his father, Macajah Chiles, near Chilesburg, and contributed to the development of that section. Rucker lived on the Three Knotch Road near John Daniel's Mill (Whites in 1953), and left the region shortly after Caroline became a county.

Richard Mauldin was a St. Margaret's Parish merchant. Evidence points to the location of his business establishment at Chesterfield, and this appears correct since no stream navigable for ocean-going vessels reached that parish and its first traders set up their businesses at the junction of its two most important Indian trails.

In picking the original slate of magistrates for Caroline

County Governor Gooch chose wisely. He named representatives from all segments of the voting population; from great landlords to homesteaders; from partisans of Berkeley to protégé of Beverley; from Knight of the Golden Horseshoe to a simple trader.

King's magistrates were important officials in colonial Virginia. The scope of their duties exceeded the duties of trial justice, circuit court judge and board of supervisors combined today (1953). As individuals they each presided over a precinct which was the smallest unit of government. In this area they directed the investigation of all suspected lawless activities; and as jurist rendered judgment in minor civil and criminal cases.

As a group they formed the county court which governed the whole county. This court had broad judicial, legislative and executive powers. It tried, either with or without a jury, all civil cases above precinct level, and all criminal cases between precinct level and those which carried a maximum penalty of death for white persons. This latter category it investigated, and if it found probable grounds for guilt, certified to the General Court of the colony at Williamsburg for trial, usually before a jury drawn from the county that was the scene of the crime.

The court's jurisdiction included chancery matters as well as common law. It probated wills, appointed administrators and settled estates. It received the acknowledgment of the vendor's signature to deeds conveying real estate and ordered these instruments admitted to record. It appointed guardians for infants, sanctioned apprenticeships, and supervised the indentures of bond servants. While it was unable to grant a divorce it had the power to force a husband to put up funds for a wife's separate maintenance in case the lady proved that she suffered abuse from her spouse.

The court's quasi-judicial authority included fixing the price of alcoholic beverages, the licensing of taverns to sell these drinks, and the revocation of the licenses if the licensee ran a disorderly house. It decided the location and granted permission to build grist mills; and condemned the acreage needed to form ponds to impound water to generate power to operate these mills, in case an owner of real estate objected to the flooding of his land. It decided which new roads were to be cleared and if the routes of existing public ways might be changed.

The court acted as a local bureau of census and registry. Each year it recorded a list of all taxable persons in the county and admitted to record by age, name and name of owner, all Negro slaves and bonded whites too young to be assessed a head tax brought into the area. It registered the brand mark each planter used to identify his livestock which ranged the unfenced land.

Perhaps the court's most important function was to levy the taxes to maintain local government. This tax was in tobacco and was assessed each year against all residents, Negro and white, slave and free, above sixteen years of age, except free white women, at exactly the same number of pounds per taxpayer, regardless of the taxpayer's ability to pay. A master was liable for the tax on his slaves and servants. Today's (1953) income, inheritance, sales and property taxes indicate that the American theory of taxation has moved a long ways in two hundred and twenty-five years. The court also paid all the county's bills. These they paid in tobacco as they collected the taxes in that commodity. Little money was in circulation at the time.

In addition the court had vast appointive powers. It named a foreman to clear, build and maintain roads, and ordered people who lived along the route to help him with the work. It named census takers to count the taxpayers each year and inspectors to test measures used in trade and scales used at the chartered warehouses. It named a constable to serve as baliff for the presiding magistrate in each precinct. If an appointee failed to do his duty in the proper manner the court promptly punished him for negligence. Road supervisors were the chief offenders. This was scarcely odd considering the terrain and the equipment available to build roads. But evidently the magistrates expected these unfortunate men to accomplish the impossible because regularly as spring came they indicted a great number for failing to keep their roads in a passable condition during the winter.

Besides these direct appointments the court recommended to the governor local residents to be tobacco inspectors, three of their own number from which to pick a sheriff, and a panel from which to choose their successors in office. This panel always contained the names of the incumbents and in this manner most magistrates kept themselves in office until death, or, at least, so long as they wished to serve.

Finally the crown charged the court with maintaining a building for its sessions and a jail for its prisoners; and authorized it to spend county revenue for firewood, candles and small beer for its comfort and enjoyment while meeting. Except for buying the beer the magistrates of Caroline were derelict in performing these duties in the early years. Instead of building a courthouse and jail they met in their respective homes and charged the sheriff with keeping the prisoners at his manor. This system was not unusual at the time. The Lees built the great hall at Stratford large enough to hold the court of Westmoreland and Governor Spotswood held the court of Spotsylvania in the parlor of his residence at Germanna until his enemies contended that he exerted undue pressure on that body and forced its removal to the new town of Fredericksburg.

In Caroline the practice of holding court at the homes of magistrates continued until Benjamin Fletcher, a prisoner, whom the county's first sheriff, William Woodford, held at his home at Windsor for nonpayment of debt to Richard Sutton, escaped and the magistrates ordered the sheriff to pay Sutton Fletcher's debt in full. Woodford appealed this decision to Williamsburg, and the House of Burgesses, with the Council concurring, passed a law directing the magistrates to reimburse the sheriff and to build a courthouse and jail for their county at once to prevent a recurrence of such a mishap in the future.

The magistrates built Caroline's first courthouse in the region between Kidd's Fork, Ideal and Shumansville. They called this settlement which grew up about the new seat of government, Caroline Courthouse, and the chances are that they held their first session there in May 1732, since the order books of the courts of Caroline County now in existence begin on that date. These records are preserved in the Clerk's Office of the Circuit Court of Caroline County in Bowling Green and from this point the author uses them as the source of much of the material in this history.

Many difficulties beset Caroline's original magistrates when they went about setting up the new county. The population which numbered a scant 5,000 was scattered over almost 350,000 acres. There were no towns and only three small trading centers. Two of these were on the Rappahannock in the vicinity of Roy's and Conway's warehouses and the third was in upper St. Margaret's Parish at Chesterfield Church. A few families enjoyed the income from well established plantations with several hundreds of acres under cultivation but far more eked out a precarious existence by tilling small clearings in the wilderness still studded with stumps and belted trees, while they kept a blunderbus close at hand to kill prowling wolves. Besides these two classes of property owners fully half the people were landless. They were headrighters, white indentured servants and Negro slaves.

No north-to-south roads bounds the new county together. All cleared trails led eastward to the courthouses of Essex, King and Queen and King William; the counties of which prior to 1727 the parishes of St. Mary's, Drysdale and St. Margaret's were, respectively, parts.

All residents had one interest in common—tobacco. But the planters along the Rappahannock sold their crops through Roy's and Conway's warehouses, while those along the Mattapony floated theirs downstream to Ayletts at Tidewater and those along the North Anna-Pamunkey used that waterway to reach Crutchfield's in lower Hanover.

With neither common courthouse, market center nor church, few people in one of the three parishes which formed Caroline had even a speaking acquaintance with their neighbors in another. During the early years of the county the magistrate's greatest problem was to bind the people together and give them a community of interest.

The Crown Appointed Officers

Governor Gooch, upon the recommendation of the magistrates, made William Woodford sheriff. He appointed, with the consent of his Council, Benjamin Robinson, Clerk, and upon the nomination of the attorney general for the colony, William Robinson crown attorney. (Commonwealth Attorney in 1953.) Benjamin Robinson was a brother of John Robinson of King and Queen, who was to become the speaker of the House of Burgesses and treasurer of the colony. The family was among the most powerful and most conservative in Virginia. They were both tools and leaders of the great landlords. On the other hand William Robinson sprung from liberal stock. His ancestor had lost his land and life for supporting Nathaniel Bacon, Jr. Apparently the Robinsons were no kin and they were poles apart in political philosophy. They were only in office a short time before they became bitter enemies. This feud led to the crown removing William Robinson from office in 1735.

Rev. James Blair, rector of William and Mary College, made James Taylor, public surveyor for St. Mary's and Drysdale parishes, and Thomas Carr public surveyor for St. Margaret's and St. Martin's in Hanover. These appointments failed to give the people of Caroline one surveyor to themselves, which they desired, but the planters of St. Mary's Parish at least were rid of Augustine Smith whom most of them despised.

The Burgesses

The House of Burgesses called a special election in 1729 to permit the voters of Caroline to choose the new county's first representatives in the colony's lower legislative assembly. This election resulted in a partial victory, at least, for the feudalistic landlord caste, because the voters chose John Martin and Richard Buckner as Burgesses. Martin was definitely a member of that group; not on account of his holdings, which were large by present-day (1953) standards but modest in the Virginia of 1729, but because he was married to a Burwell and his wife's family were kingpins among the great landlords. On the other hand Buckner easily qualified for membership, due to his own vast acreage, but in spite of his position, in his votes in the House of Burgesses, he more often sided with the plain people than with the aristocrats.

Of the pair Buckner had decidedly the more distinguished career as a Burgess. He became a member of the Committee on Courts of Justice which was the most powerful committee in the House of Burgesses and yielded a vast influence on the shaping of the policies which governed the colony. On the other hand Martin's main interest in politics was local and confined to Caroline County. He and Buckner, both, continued to serve as magistrates for Caroline the whole time they represented the county in the House of Burgesses; but in this office Buckner maintained an aloof position while Martin was bitterly partisan in every dispute which arose.

While the sides Martin took in these arguments failed to increase his stature as a statesman, they often led to an increase in his wealth. His political manipulations placed the location of the first courthouse at a site much closer to his residence than the home of any other magistrate. This victory enhanced the value of his property in which no other magistrate shared.

Background was the greatest factor which caused the difference in the political careers of Buckner and Martin. Buckner was born in the colony and he knew local problems through experiences from youth, while Martin arrives in Virginia from England only a short time before he went to represent Caroline in the House of Burgesses. His knowledge of local conditions was meager and what little information he had was colored by the prejudices of his wife's people, the powerful Burwells. Buckner was a man of great wealth. His property was located in Virginia and it was essential to his own interest that the colony prosper, while Martin was an inpecunious adventurer who crossed the ocean in an effort to get rich quick. In this attempt he was successful and after he accumulated a fortune, he returned to Britain to enjoy the luxuries he was able to buy with his wealth in a highly civilized land. During his political career he was in the process of getting rich and cared more about adding to his own coffers than looking after the public welfare. Finally Martin was a professional soldier while Buckner had held a series of public offices since his youth. His experiences as clerk of the House of Burgesses in his young manhood gave him a background in parliamentary procedure and statescraft, which Martin was unable to match.

The two Burgesses hardly reached Williamsburg before they fell out. Rivalry between the factions they led dominated Caroline politics in the county's early years.

The Rule of Sir William Gooch
(1727-1749)

1. THE PLAGUES

ABOUT the time Caroline began its existence as a county a series of catastrophies befell Virginia which the colonists called "the plagues." In the spring of 1728 a multitude of caterpillars spread over the country east of the Blue Ridge and threatened to destroy all plant life. Superstitious settlers believed that the Lord sent these pests to punish them for their wickedness, and instead of trying to protect their crops, rushed to houses of worship to pray. In Caroline the churches of Mount, Joy Creek and Chesterfield were thronged.

Governor Gooch, a deeply religious Presbyterian, proclaimed May 17, 1728, "a day of fasting and humiliation to deprecate the anger of the Almighty and save ye fruits of ye earth from destruction." Fortunately the House of Burgesses adopted a more rational point of view than either the masses or the governor and passed a law which forbade the exportation of "Indian corn, wheat, peas and other grains" to conserve the food supply and prevent starvation in the ensuing winter.

Destruction of plant life by the caterpillars paved the way for the second plague. Shortage of food in the forest caused famished deer to descend on the crops which the more prudent planters strove to protect. These animals came in such great numbers that in many places it was impossible for the alarmed freeholders to drive them off. The only solution was to kill and in a short time the woods adjacent to many homesteads were littered with carcasses.

These carcasses brought on the third plague, the wolves, which concentrated about the homesteads to enjoy feasts of newly killed meat. Unfortunately the wolves did not clean up the bodies of the dead deer and move on. Instead they stayed and preyed on the settler's livestock and sometimes attacked the children and even older members of the family.

In a move to get rid of the wolves the House of Burgesses passed a law raising the bounty on wolf scalps to 100 pounds of tobacco each. This was a handsome price at a time when a laboring man only made 30 pounds of tobacco for working from sun to sun, and an indentured servant had to serve an extra month and a half for every 100 pounds of tobacco the court estimated he cost his master when he ran away. In all sections of the colony men abandoned their work and became professional wolf hunters. The two best known in Caroline were Adam Loving and Minor Winn.

The turmoil which the caterpillars, deer and wolves caused made many of the Negro slaves, recently brought into the colony from Africa, restless. On the new plantations along the upper James they began to run away in great numbers and many of these fugitives formed a settlement of their own in the Valley of Virginia near the site of Lexington. Here they built a town of boughs and grass houses in the manner of the homes in their native land, and set up a tribal government under a chief, who had been a prince among his own people before slave traders brought him across the Atlantic. The fugitives had with them many farming implements which they stole from their masters. These, they knew how to use, and since the region in which they settled was outside the area afflicted by the caterpillars their crops grew and the community prospered, but not for long. The whites located them and the next year military men mustered from all sections of the colony moved on their settlement, killed the chief and returned his followers to their masters.

This incident strained relations between the races. County courts sentenced numerous Negroes to death. In Caroline the magistrates tried and ordered the sheriff to hang Robin, a slave of Captain William Taliaferro, for breaking into the dwelling house of Thomas Royston.

Governor Gooch, however, did not wish to see the Negroes persecuted and to restore the slaves' morale, freed a Negro who concocted a medicine reputed to cure venereal disease, after paying the Negro's master his appraised value out of the public revenue.

News of this liberation spread like wildfire among the slaves. In hopes of gaining their freedom, Negroes in all sections of the colony began experiments and attempted to make medicines to cure all ailments known to man. In Caroline one of these experiments resulted in tragedy. Tom, a Negro belonging to John Garnett, made a medicine which failed to cure. Instead this concoction poisoned and killed Joe and Wick, slaves of Richard Buckner, Mingo, a slave of Francis Thornton, and Rover, a slave of John Micou. The magistrates of Caroline County, however, were lenient with Tom for causing these mass deaths. Instead of ordering him hanged, they directed that he be transported to some place outside of the Virginia colony to prevent him from causing more trouble locally.

2. THE TOBACCO TRANSPORTATION ACT

Before Virginia recovered from "the plagues" the British Parliament passed an act which threatened to ruin the colony's economy. This law, designed to help English ship owners, forbade the planters to strip, stem or cut their tobacco before shipping it abroad. The statute was so unpopular in Virginia that it led to riots which veered on open rebellion.

In 1732 the fiery Edwin Conway, who sat for Lancaster in the House of Burgesses, made a stirring speech against the act at a muster in his colony which so inflamed the planters that when night fell they burned the chartered tobacco warehouse at Corotoman. From Lancaster the trouble spread until all Virginia between the Potomac and the Rappahannock was in an uproar. Governor Gooch reported to the Crown "that bands of the meaner sort roamed the countryside, burning tobacco warehouses and comitting other crimes."

As close as the bands came to Caroline was Falmouth, where they burned Todd's warehouse. But Gooch ordered the Caroline militia mustered and placed on guard along the south bank of the Rappahannock to keep the rioters from crossing that stream and spreading trouble into other sections of the county. The Caroline militia was, at the time, under the command of Colonel Henry Armistead, crown lieutenant for the county.

The officers who served under him included Colonel William Woodford, Captain John Taliaferro, Captain William Taliaferro, Captain Benjamin Robinson, Captain Lawrence Battaile, Lieutenant Roger Quarles, Lieutenant John Taylor, Lieutenant David Sterns, Lieutenant Robert Farish, Lieutenant John Scott, Lieutenant Christopher Tompkins, and Lieutenant William Waller.

Mobilization of the militia prevented acts of violence in Caroline, but it did not keep planters from grumbling. Constables seized John Wilson for cursing King George and when he reached the court the magistrates made an example of him by ordering the sheriff to lay twenty lashes on his bare back at the public whipping post. Two justices, Thomas Rucker and Thomas Maulding, did not agree with this sentence and publicly proclaimed the fact. For this boldness and certain other remarks against the unpopular law, Governor Gooch removed them as magistrates.

While latent rebellion smouldered throughout Virginia the House of Burgesses and Governor's Council worked frantically to find a solution of the colony's economic problems. When all their petitions to the royal government in London failed to persuade Parliament to repeal the Tobacco Transportation Act they decided to attempt to reduce the poundage of tobacco on the market, and through scarcity forced up the price sufficiently to make it profitable to ship these crops uncut, unstripped and unstemmed. To put this policy into effect they passed laws which stinted the number of tobacco plants a planter might set out, based on his acreage, and laws which forbade the tending of seconds (suckers after the original crop was cut).

The laws were no better liked in Caroline than the Tobacco Transportation Act. As soon as the news of their passage reached the county a large delegation of planters headed by William Woodford descended on Williamsburg and demanded their repeal. Woodford stated that he had invented a machine to harvest tobacco and if the crop was to be curtailed the time and ingenuity he spent on his invention were in vain. But all arguments failed; neither Burgesses nor Councilors were impressed with an invention which promised to revolutionize the cultivation of the crop, that was the basis of the colony's economy. They turned the demands down, the laws remained on the statute books and Woodford quit working on his invention in disgust.

Failure of the mission to Williamsburg, however, did not cause the Caroline planters to accept the laws stinting the number of tobacco plants and banning the tending of seconds. The statutes were especially hard on the white indentured servants who were numerous in the county in its early days. Benevolent masters often permitted these unfortunate people to tend seconds after the original crop was cut and keep the money from the sale of this second growth, to accumulate the means to purchase their freedom ahead of the terms of their bonds of indenture; or to get the capital to set up a homestead of their own after they were free. But indentured servants and recently liberated indentured servants were not the only people who refused to abide by the stinting of plants and banning of tending seconds law.

The Order Books of the Caroline Court record scores of instances of their violations and many cases where the court indicted constables because they refused to enforce the law. These violators include a full cross section of the county's social strata, all the way from Kemp Taliaferro, a great landlord, who refused to cut up his plants after he harvested his crop, to Ann Barnes, a bondwoman with numerous illegitimate children, who tended seconds. The court, however, took notice of the difference in their social and financial positions, when it meted out punishments after conviction. It ordered Kemp Taliaferro to forfeit 5,000 pounds of tobacco to the Crown and the sheriff to give Ann Barnes five lashes on her bare back at the public whipping-post.

3. INTERNAL IMPROVEMENTS

While plagues threatened to destroy crops and unfavorable laws the economy, Caroline's magistrates went doggedly ahead with a road building program to unite the three parishes which formed their county and to furnish the planters with overland routes to transport their tobacco to Tidewater. Public thoroughfares at the time fell into three classes: bridle paths for riders on horseback, cart roads for horse-drawn vehicles, and rolling roads for rolling hogsheads packed with tobacco, usually propelled by oxen hitched to an axle driven through the center. Rolling roads were decidedly the most costly to build, since causeways had to be constructed across marshes and bridges over streams to keep the tobacco dry in transit.

The first major project the Caroline Court authorized was a rolling road which began at the Spotsylvania line and continued across the Mattapony at Michael Ginney's Bridge to Conway's warehouse on the Rapphannock. Robert Taliaferro laid out the route, Francis Thornton had charge of construction and the people (all free white males over sixteen), Negro slaves and white indentured servants on the plantations of Robert Taliaferro, Francis Thornton, Anthony Thornton, Thomas Catlett, Thomas Buckner, Michael Ginney, Christopher Tompkins, George Goodloe, Anthony Samuel, Rice Williams, William Lawson and Joseph Stevens did the work.

In spite of the handicap of the broad and often flooded Mattapony Valley, work progressed rapidly and in the fall of 1732 the road was opened for traffic. It was an immediate success. Planters of upper St. Margaret's and Drysdale parishes now had a way to get their tobacco to a chartered warehouse without floating it down the shallow and crooked Mattapony.

Francis Conway and John Roy, the owners of Caroline's two chartered warehouses, were quick to see the advantages of rolling roads to their establishments. The income they received from their business was based on a percentage of the tobacco they processed, and roads of this type tapping the interior promised to increase vastly the volume of tobacco they handled. In a short time they became rivals to have the termini of projected rolling roads located on their premises. In this rivalry Conway had decided advantages because he and his brother-in-laws, Thomas and John Catlett, were magistrates, while Roy was without political connections.

The next rolling road the court authorized, the celebrated

Three Knotch Road built in 1730 under the supervision of John and Charles Beazley, clearly shows this position of preferment, since it began at John Daniel's Mill (White's in 1953), cut a zigzag course across Roy's back country and funneled tobacco towards Conway's warehouse. When Roy accused the court of favoritism the magistrates replied, they authorized the road for settlers along the Rappahannock-Mattapony watershed in lower St. Mary's to have a way to reach their parish church on Mount Hill. But this was a poor excuse. A cart road was the highest type road built elsewhere in the county leading to a church.

Conway did not long enjoy this preferred position. In 1731 the traders at Chesterfield, who suffered from loss of trade due to the fact that since the organization of Caroline the planters of St. Margaret's no longer traveled the Ridge Road to reach the courthouse at King William, petitioned the magistrates to authorize the construction of a rolling road leading from Chesterfield to the Rappahannock, in hopes of bringing back traffic and reviving their businesses. When the planters of mid-Drysdale joined in this request the only practical Tidewater terminus of the route became Roy's warehouse. Francis Conway, and his relatives on the court, opposed this road but since some of the most powerful men in the county, Walter Chiles, Thomas Carr, Thomas Mauldin, and Robert Woolfolk, who were already magistrates, and Robert Farish, Robert Fleming, George Hoomes and John Baylor, who were to become magistrates, lived on, or close by the proposed route, they were unable to halt construction.

Robert Woolfolk fixed the course of this road from Chesterfield to the Mattapony at Doguetown (Milford) and John Baylor from Doguetown to Roy's warehouse. Timothy Chandler built the bridge over the Polecat at his plantation (Woodlawn) and Robert Farish and George Hoomes the causeway and bridge over the Mattapony flats and river bed at Doguetown.

Francis Conway did not sulk at this setback. Instead he mapped out an elaborate road to syphon off most of the tobacco grown in upper St. Margaret's Parish from the Chesterfield-Doguetown-Roy's warehouse road and turned it to his warehouse. This road began at Cook's ford across the North Anna back of Cedar Fork and continued roughly parallel to the Caroline-Spotsylvania line to Woodpecker (Gravatt's in 1953), where it turned to cross the Mattapony at John Downer's (Woodford) bridge and follow the north bank of that stream to Michael Ginney's, for a junction with the existing road to Conway's warehouse. The magistrates approved the project and the rolling road from Ginney's to Downer's, and the bridge across the Mattapony were built in 1733. But Francis Conway died that year and after his death there was no one left with the interest and force to push construction of the road across St. Margaret's Parish.

At the same time the magistrates authorized rolling roads to Conway's and Roy's warehouse; they also directed the building of numerous cart roads. The most important of these led from the courthouse to Burk's Ferry over the Mattapony, Henry Burk supervised the construction of a road from his ferry to Needwood Forest and Thomas Morris from Needwood to Norman's Ferry across the Pamunkey. Here the new road joined the established road from Hanover to Williamsburg.

Two years later (1734) planters in the lower part of St. Margaret's petitioned the county court to make the section of this road between Needwood and Burk's Ferry a rolling road, build a bridge over the Mattapony at Burk's, and clear a new rolling road across Drysdale Parish from Burk's to the rolling road leading from Doguetown to Roy's warehouse, in order that they might market their tobacco on the Rappahannock. The court agreed and the project was completed in 1736.

The Order Books of the Caroline Court contained many other orders establishing roads and directing their building. Some of these "from the court house, across Deep Run to the Bee Tree to the Spotsylvania line" are meaningless due to the loss of identity of landmarks. The routes for others "from Doguetown bridge by John Baylor's twigg house to the court house" can be easily traced. But taking them all together it seems that by 1736, when the court ordered road supervisors to put up markers at intersections to indicate distances and directions, that all sections of the county were well knit by a network of public thoroughfares.

The only opposition to the building of roads in Caroline, especially rolling roads, came from sources outside the county. The two chief foes were the proprietors of Aylett's and Crutch-field's warehouse. The new rolling roads in their back country shifted so much tobacco from water-borne to overland trans-portation to reach Tidewater that it threatened them with ruin. Aylett petitioned for permission to build lavish houses of enter-tainment on his premises to attract planters from a distance, especially the upper Mattapony Valley, and Crutchfield tried to deal directly with the Caroline magistrates. Both of these efforts came to naught, more and more of Caroline's tobacco rolled towards the Rappahannock.

4. New Leaders

The building of roads made a drastic change in the way of life in Caroline. The masses now had well defined routes which led to the taverns at Chesterfield in St. Margaret's, the court-house in Drysdale, Roy's and Conway's warehouse in St. Mary's and at other points scattered about the countryside. In these meeting places they discussed their problems. Here public opinion was formed and new leaders emerged. Many of these new leaders were tavern-keepers. A few were conscientious men but far more were unscrupulous and used their new posi-tions of prominence to stir people up to commit acts which increased either their wealth or their prestige.

The first instance of a case of the abuse of influence recorded in the Order Books of the Caroline Court is that of Benjamin Rennolds, a tavern-keeper at the courthouse, who incited mob violence in an attempt to gain the contract to supply the court with small beer. Robert Willis, who had the first license to run an ordinary at Caroline Courthouse, had this contract and evidently the magistrates were satisfied because he rendered bountiful service. On one occasion he passed around so much beer that some of the jury "became drunk and were not in their good senses." But the justice did not censure him for this mishap. Instead they dismissed the jury, declared the case at bar a mistrial, impaneled another jury and went on with their session. Rennolds did not care about such undecorous conduct. He wanted the contract only because it carried a fat stipend of 1,000 pounds of tobacco a year and set about to get it.

To accomplish his aims he enlisted the support of John Bruce, John Terrell, William Burdette, Charles Durrett, Moses Downer, Thomas Lantor, Mace Pickett and William Lawson who owed Willis money, since Willis was a money-lender as well as tavern-keeper, and Robert Smith, a rival loan shark. This gang descended on Willis' tavern and proceeded to reduce it to shambles. In the face of overwhelming odds, Willis, with his wife, Sarah, at his side tried to protect their property and preserve order, but their efforts were in vain. Afterwards, however, they sued Bruce, Terrell, Burdette, Durrett, Downer, Lantor, Pickett and Lawson for assault and battery and persuaded Thomas White and John Jenkins, two constables, to investigate Rennolds, the ring's leader. Upon the constable's testimony the court indicted Rennolds but a jury, composed mostly of his friends, refused to convict him. When a series of subsequent juries refused to award damages to Robert and Sarah Willis in their suits for assault and battery and often went so far as to recompense the defendants, who filed cross suits, the magistrates gave way to public opinion and revoked Willis' tavern license. With this revocation he automatically lost the beer contract.

Willis' loss was not Rennolds' gain. The court gave the coveted contract to another rival tavern-keeper, Edward Haswell, who like Willis was a protégé of that renowned politician, John Martin. After this transfer Rennolds and his gang made life so unpleasant for Haswell that in less than a year's time that betroubled tavern-keeper gave up his ordinary license and left Caroline County.

Again Rennolds failed to profit. The magistrates gave the contract to supply the court with beer to a third favorite of John Martin, Samuel Coleman, who took over Haswell's tavern, as well as the contract. But through his persistence Rennolds had made a name for himself and the magistrates, perhaps to get rid of him and over Martin's objections, made him a deputy sheriff and a collector of the county levies, which was by far a more lucrative position than supplying the court with beer. For all his chicanery Rennolds prospered. In a short time he became a merchant and money-lender as well as tavern-keeper, and along with his rival, Samuel Coleman, one of the two chief business men of the new town of Caroline Courthouse. With all these interests in commerce, however, he never gave up his interest in politics. He held on to his public office, and with the help of his friend, William Burdette, whom the court made his assistant, milked the public till for all it was worth. He made fast friends among the magistrates, and became especially close to Robert Fleming, the justice who served as sheriff, and was ex-officio his superior. But these associations never led him to respect John Martin, whom he continued to hate.

Martin was in political difficulty. His record in the House of Burgesses left him open to attack. Before he and Richard Buckner reached Williamsburg to begin their terms of office, the Burgesses passed a law which compelled St. Mary's, Drysdale and St. Margaret's parishes to pay their proportionate share for a full term, of the salaries of the Burgesses from Essex, King and Queen and King William, elected in 1727, immediately before these parishes were severed, respectively, from their parent counties. Martin's and Buckner's efforts to get this unfair law repealed were in vain. The Caroline magistrates refused to levy the additional tax needed to raise the revenue to foot the bills until the sergeant-at-arms of the House of Burgesses came into the county and forced them. By this time Buckner was dead and the levy was called "Martin's tax."

On other premises the Caroline voters had sounder grounds to censure Martin. While he opposed the Tobacco Transportation Act, he voted, under the influence of his father-in-law, Lewis Burwell, for the laws stinting the number of plants and banning the tending of seconds. Caroline had no planters in Burwell's class, which the law was designed to help primarily; and in that county the vast majority of the largest landowners

PRECINCTS
With MAGISTRATES
1735
CAROLINE COUNTY

Legend
Modern Comunities •
PRECINT LINE ————
COUNTY LINE — — —

SCALE OF MILES
0 1 2 3 4 5 6

stood shoulder to shoulder with the small homesteaders and demanded that both laws be repealed.

Rennolds quickly grasped the reasons for Martin's unpopularity. When he traveled about the county taking care of the duties of his office, and when he waited on customers at his store and bar, he brought the issue home. People thought the way he wanted them to think and when Governor Gooch dissolved the House of Burgesses in 1735 and issued writs for a new election he knew that his time of revenge was at hand.

5. THE ELECTION OF 1735

When Richard Buckner died in 1733 Governor Gooch issued a writ for a special election of a Burgess from Caroline, but this election was not held and the vacancy remained until the governor dissolved the House in 1735 and ordered new elections throughout the colony. This election turned out to be one of the nastiest incidents in the history of colonial Caroline.

John Martin offered for re-election in spite of all his mistakes and he had powerful support from Benjamin Robinson, the county clerk, Henry Armistead, the county lieutenant, and most of the king's magistrates. But these backers had very little influence with the homesteaders who, if they owned 25 acres of land with a house on it, had a vote which counted the same as the vote of a Corbin, a Baylor or a Battaile, who owned thousands of acres; and the homesteaders were by far the most numerous voters in the county. These small landowners, Benjamin Rennolds proceeded to organize. To help him with this work he enlisted the support of William Burdette, his assistant tax collector, and Thomas Roy, a tobacco inspector and part owner of Roy's chartered warehouse. Both of whom through their respective positions of tax collector and tobacco inspector were in position to exert pressure on the public through promises of favoritism or threats of reprisals in their official capacities and both were so unscrupulous as to have no qualms about exerting this pressure.

Selecting the strongest candidates posed the most delicate problems for Rennolds. To run himself was out of the question. He had come up too fast and made too many enemies along the way. The most logical places to look were among the homesteaders and the tobacco warehouse owners, for these two classes had suffered most from the laws stinting the number of tobacco plants and banning the tending of seconds which Martin supported. Among the homesteaders he found an ideal candidate, Robert Fleming, a magistrate from St. Margaret's, who had served the county as its first sheriff, who lived on the south side of the Mattapony, and who, while in that office, made him an undersheriff.

To find a candidate for the second seat proved more difficult. The Conway and Roy families, who owned Caroline's two chartered warehouses, presented poor hunting grounds. Both Francis Conway and John Roy, who had built up the business, had recently died, and Conway's sons were callow youths while Roy's were at best young men with shady reputations. The real management of both houses had fallen to the two widows, Rebecca Conway and Dorothy Roy, and woman's suffrage in Virginia was almost two centuries away. There was not an acceptable candidate in the lot.

There was another warehouse owner, however, who lived in the county, although his place of business was across the Rappahannock in King George. He was Jonathan Gibson, who already nursed political ambition and a mere approach on the subject was enough to get him to agree to run.

When the campaign began the crown or great landlord party endorsed Robert Fleming, because as a king's magistrate and ex-sheriff, he was as acceptable to them as any man in the county, who did not own thousands of acres, and centered their attack on Gibson, whom they termed an outsider and an interloper. These tactics did not work. Gibson held the upper hand throughout the campaign. But as the election drew near the Rennolds' lead group, in a drive to snow Martin under with an avalanche of adverse votes, engaged in scandalous practices which came to a climax at the polls. Gibson won handily but the conduct of his partisans gave Martin grounds to contest the election before the House of Burgesses.

A full record of this investigation can be pieced together

from the *Journal* of the House of Burgesses and Order Books of the Caroline Court. The Burgesses found: 1. The greater number of votes were cast for Gibson. 2. The manner of the election was disorderly; people drank too much liquor on election day, before and during the taking of the polls. 3. Thomas Roy, a tobacco inspector in Caroline County told scores of voters during the campaign that if they did not vote for Gibson he was going to grade their tobacco as of inferior quality, when they brought their crop in for inspection that fall and that if he heard of them electioneering for Martin that he was going to burn their tobacco stored in Roy's warehouse at once. 4. That William Burdette, a deputy sheriff and tax collector of Caroline County threatened to foreclose on all taxpayers in arrears in their payment of taxes whom he heard vote for Martin at the polls. 5. That during the election Roy and Burdette stood in the polls, issued threats and listened while each voter called the name of the candidates of their choice while casting their ballots. 6. That Gibson's partisans kept jugs of liquors at the polls and treated voters who supported their candidate both before and after they cast their ballots. 7. That Thomas Harrison and John Davis entered the polls and announced that they were going to vote for Martin but before the tally takers were able to record their votes, hoodlums snatched them outside, got them drunk and brought them back to vote for Gibson, while they were "not in their good senses." 8. That Gibson was innocent of misconduct and in no way responsible for the irregularities. Upon these findings the Burgesses ordered (1) a second election in Caroline between Martin and Gibson for that county's second seat in the House of Burgesses, (2) the sergeant-at-arms of the House of Burgesses to arrest Thomas Roy and William Burdette and bring them to Williamsburg for trial, and (3) the magistrates of Caroline to make a thorough investigation of the whole matter.

The Caroline justices had a difficult time in making investigation of the matter. Voters who knew what happened refused to testify before the local grand jury. Because of these refusals the court fined John Boutwell, Nicholas Ware, Robert Kay, Richard Buckner II, William Lawson, Joseph Rennolds, Oliver

Towles, Charles Holloway, John Holloway and Benjamin Grubbs 100 lbs. of tobacco each for contempt. But these fines failed to make them talk. When finally the court managed to get enough evidence from other sources for a few indictments, William Robinson, the crown attorney, refused to prosecute. To get around this obstacle a majority of the magistrates petitioned the governor to remove Robinson and appoint Benjamin Walker in his place.

After the governor acted favorably upon this recommendation Walker had little luck with his first cases. William Powell, John Hogg, Richard Hill, John Munday, John Robinson and John Goodwin, went on trial for misconduct at the polls before a jury composed of John Downer, William Watkins, Anthony Arnold, Joseph Martin, Michael Ginney, David Woodruff, William Herndon, George Eastham, Thomas White, William Evins, John Rogers and William Oliver, all of whom were either homesteaders, tavern-keepers or artisans. Zachery Lewis, attorney for the defense, ably defended the accused, and after a wild session of court during which the justices fined John Henderson five shillings for striking the sheriff the jury brought in a verdict of one pound of tobacco, which was equivalent to a verdict of one cent today. Johnathan Gibson and Benjamin Rennolds paid the costs of court and Lewis' fee and this ended the Caroline phase of the investigation.

In Williamsburg the House of Burgesses reduced the charges against Thomas Roy from felony to misdemeanor and fined him three pounds, seven shillings, sterling. The sergeant-at-arms failed to arrest William Burdette. He hid out while the heat was on and after the trouble blew over returned to Caroline to live to a ripe old age as a successful business man and tavern-keeper.

Gibson and Martin waged a second campaign for a seat in the House of Burgesses in the summer of 1736. William Taliaferro placed Thomas Roy under a 100 pound bond to keep the peace and John Martin, who was a money-lender as well as a politician, threatened to foreclose on all freeholders, who were in debt to him, if they voted for Gibson. In spite of these handicaps, Gibson won hands down with a larger majority than he received in 1735. In revenge Martin foreclosed on thirty-three men, who owed him money, and voted against him. All of these men lost much of their property and many of them went to jail because they were unable to pay. They were John Brown, John Williamson, John Hudson, Henry Powell, John Smith, William Watson, Henry Wood, William Powell, William Pickett, Richard Long, Thomas Fox, John Jeter, John Hogg, Richard Hill, John Carter, John Gough, Andrew Harrison, Gabriel Long, Henry Samuel, John Robinson, John Munday, Eli Griffin, William Samuels, John Lewis, William Bell, John Schooler, Edward Swanson, John Goodwin, Thomas Robinson, Thomas Royston, Daniel Brown, Richard Land, Samuel Robinson.

6. THE UPSTARTS CURBED

The elections of 1735 and 1736 focused the attention of the royal government in Williamsburg on Caroline politics. An upstart had challenged a crown-favored candidate and won. The powers, who guided the destines of the colony for their king, did not intend to let anything like this happen again.

Immediately after John Martin's first defeat Governor Gooch forced the removal of Benjamin Rennolds and William Burdette as under sheriffs and tax collectors, suspended Thomas Roy as tobacco inspector and began packing the local court with magistrates of proven loyalty of his regime. In 1735 he made the unprecedented number of eight new magistrates and in 1739-40 named six more, for the largest turnover in the personnel of the Caroline court during his twenty-two-year rule.

But these precautions were not needed. The upstarts defeated themselves. Jonathan Gibson, their titular head was not only a poor leader but also a greedy and avaricious man who neglected his public duties and tried to use the prestige which went with his office for personal gain. Custom forced Gooch to make him a magistrate after his election to the House of Burgesses, but from the Order Book of the Caroline Court it appears that during the six years he held this office he never attended a session of the Caroline Court. His record in Williamsburg was no better. Instead of representing his constituents in the House of Burgesses he engaged in a series of shenanigans to get permission to move his chartered warehouse across the Rappahannock from King George to Caroline where there was a deeper back country from which to draw tobacco. He failed to get this permission and his conduct angered the Conways and the Roys, the owners of Caroline's two long established warehouses, who were among his chief supporters in both his election campaigns.

Gibson's behavior so disillusioned many independent voters, that when Robert Fleming, Caroline's other Burgess, died in 1738 and Governor Gooch called a special election to fill the vacancy, enough of them swung behind their old enemy, John Martin, who attempted a comeback, to return him to the House of Burgesses.

Martin did not enjoy this victory of vindiction. His wife, the charming and beautiful Martha Burwell Martin, died during the campaign and was buried at her home, Clifton, in lower Caroline. After her death her husband lost interest in public affairs. He finished the term in the House of Burgesses for which he was elected but at the same time he got his property in order to turn over to his seven children, in a move to leave Caroline County and subsequently the colony of Virginia.

How Martin and Gibson got on together, after their many spats, the three years they served as Caroline's two members in the House of Burgesses the records fail to disclose. But they had this in common when Governor Gooch dissolved the House in 1741 and ordered new elections, neither was in position to run for another term. Martin quit for reasons already stated and tarried in Caroline a few years while straightening out odds and ends in his estate, but Gibson, who unfortunately had more enemies than friends during his brief political career, left the county at once.

With the official leaders of the warring factions out of public life peace came to the Caroline political front. The large planters, who lived on crown grants, which exceeded one thousand acres, got together and sponsored two of their number,

John Baylor and Lundsford Lomax, for membership in the House of Burgesses. These choices pleased the colony's ruling clique, who wanted the holding of public office confined to the great planters, because they were afraid of the homesteaders, who were often radicals and threatened to upset the status quo. Baylor and Lomax won handily and remained in office until the end of Sir William Gooch's rule.

John Baylor was one of the most distinguished residents of Colonial Caroline. He was born in 1705 at Walkerton in King and Queen, the son of another John Baylor, who was a merchant and large landowner, and a very wealthy man. The elder Baylor, as befitting a man of his station, sent his son, John Baylor II of Caroline, to England to school. Here the younger Baylor attended Putney Grammar School and Caius College at Cambridge, and at the same time picked up a great deal of knowledge about horse racing and horse flesh, a hobby he pursued for the rest of his life. When he returned to Virginia in 1726, he settled on a huge tract of land extending on both sides of the Mattapony below Doguetown (Milford) to which his family had perfected title by a grant from the crown after a long struggle with the Beverleys for much of the upper Mattapony Valley. Here Baylor set up a lavish establishment which he called "Newmarket" in honor of the celebrated racing center in England, and settled down to manage his plantation, breed and race horses, take part in public affairs and lead the life of cultured country squire. Governor Gooch first appointed him magistrate in 1739.

Lunsford Lomax was also to the manor born. He lived in lower St. Mary's Parish, on land which the crown granted his maternal grandfather, an English baronet, Sir Thomas Lundsford, in the last quarter of the 17th century. The best evidence points to the fact that he, too, was educated in England. Governor Gooch named him, along with his father, John Lomax, as an original magistrate of Caroline County. He served in this capacity throughout the Gooch regime as well as Burgess from 1741.

Lundsford, unlike Baylor, was not satisfied with his inheritance and was always trying to increase his fortune. Instead of spending his spare time in racing horses, he devoted it to business ventures. Many of these ventures ended in failures, and although, due to generosity of royal governors, he became one of the largest landlords in Virginia, he ended his days in debt.

The stern side of his nature was clearly indicated when his son, John, stole a horse to race and he agreed with the court that the boy must have fifteen lashes on his bare back at the public whipping post, as punishment for this crime.

7. HEAD LYNCH

Curbing the troublesome homesteaders and tradesmen did not end the owners of the larger crown grants troubles in Caroline. Two other elements kept them from running things entirely as they wished. One of these elements was Head Lynch, a royal favorite, who settled in the county in 1734, and the other dissenters from the Established Church.

Why Head Lynch came to Caroline is a mystery. He had powerful friends at the British royal court, and a speaking acquaintanceship, at least, with King George II. Men with his background rarely migrated to the raw American colonies; and the few who came, such as Lord Fairfax, usually crossed the ocean to take up huge crown grants and to develop their new domain. Lynch had such a grant. It was in the Valley of Virginia, at the time a part of Spotsylvania. But he did not go there to live. Instead he established his residence on lands he bought from Francis Allen, Paul Pigg and others in lower St. Margaret's and Drysdale parishes.

When Lynch reached Caroline, officials from colony to county level, treated him with deference. Gooch made him a magistrate in 1735 and in 1737, sheriff. At first he was un-assuming enough, modestly going about his official duties. In 1736 he persuaded the court to authorize a road leading along the southside of the Mattapony to Aylett's warehouse, and personally supervised the building of a bridge over Boot Swamp, connecting Caroline with King William County.

It was not until 1741 that he began to throw his weight

around and show his true colors. That year the collector of customs and chief naval officer for the York River basin died and Governor Gooch promptly appointed his son, William Gooch, Jr., to that position, which was one of the most lucrative public posts in the colony. Lynch made no effort locally to get this job when the vacancy occurred but as soon as ships had time to take a letter to England and bring back a reply he showed up in Williamsburg with a commission signed by the Duke of Newcastle, the chief privy councillor of King George, which empowered him to take over the office and to draw the accrued pay.

This threw the government of the colony into a quandary. Gooch, who was a money grabber and sought to squeeze the last shilling out of the public revenue to increase his family's wealth, refused to remove his son. Lynch laid his claim before the Governor's Council and that body split five to five. This deadlock held until Lynch contacted London and had more pressure exerted. Then the opposition crumbled. Gooch and his councillors were afraid to go against the expressed will of the King. Lynch became Collector of Customs and Chief Naval Officer of the York River basin. This was the most important position a resident of Caroline held in the colony until the Revolution.

Another post with much less pay and prominence which Head Lynch got because he was a royal favorite had a more far-reaching effect on the development of Caroline County. This was the job as the county's first postmaster. In 1737 the crown made Alexander Spotswood, who regained favor at court after George II and Caroline came to the throne, postmaster general of all England's American colonies. Spotswood was an efficient man and in time set up an overland mail route, with regular deliveries, from Boston, Mass. to Charleston, S. C. To expedite the movement of mail he established a general postoffice in each colony with a branch postoffice in each county along the way.

From New Post in Spotsylvania, the general postoffice for Virginia, the mail moved southward along the routes of Virginia Highway 2 and U. S. 301 (1953) to Needwood Forest, where it veered to the east to cross the Pamunkey at Norman's

Ferry and reach Williamsburg over the Peninsula Road. As soon as this route was established Head Lynch used his connections in court circles to secure the appointment as postmaster in Caroline County and the contract to carry the mail from New Post to Norman's Ferry. The notation that he is commissioned postmaster and an account of his qualification for office is recorded in the Order Books of Caroline Court in 1742 in the Clerk's Office of the Circuit Court in Bowling Green. The best evidence indicates that he set up the first post-office for Caroline at Needwood Tavern, which was located near his home, and in which he had an interest.

Although postage rates were high and mail went collect the revenues derived from the service were small, because the costs of transportation were high and the public wrote few letters. But in spite of this drawback the franchise to carry mail and the office of postmaster were classed political plums in the early days of the postal system. Head Lynch and his associates saw the chance to increase vastly the income derived from this source by carrying passengers for pay, along with the mail. They initiated plans which led to the setting up of the celebrated stage route which crossed Caroline County for almost one hundred years, and until the building of the Richmond, Fredericksburg and Potomac Railroad in the second quarter of the nineteenth century.

Lynch, however, did not live to develop the stage line. He died in 1734 and his wife, Prudence, administered his estate. His sons were infants and entirely too young to handle the ventures which he had begun.

8. The Dissenters

After Head Lynch died no one else with pull at court showed up in Caroline to disturb the entrenched families during the rest of Gooch's rule, but dissenters from the Established Church of the colony became increasingly troublesome.

The Quakers were the first of the local dissenters. They showed interest in the region to be included in Caroline County as early as the second decade of the eighteenth century, when

Alexander Spotswood persuaded the crown to sanction laws the Assembly passed, which exempted from parish levies the German Lutherans he settled along the Rappahannock above the fall line to work his iron forges. The Quakers insisted that the law be construed to let them come to Virginia under the same terms. But their efforts were in vain until Sir William Gooch, who was a Presbyterian and cared little for the Church of England, became governor and decided in their favor.

John Cheadle, a Pennsylvania Quaker, bought a tract of land in Caroline's, St. Margaret's Parish, from Thomas Carr in 1733, but it was five years later before Governor Gooch and his Council cleared the way for members of the sect to come to Virginia and live unmolested. In 1739 the mass migration began and the segment which came to Caroline settled on lands which John Cheadle, John Hubbard and others purchased from William Terrell on the upper branches of Polecat Creek (Stevens Mill Run in 1953) near the site of Golansville.

The *Journal* of the House of Burgesses records that Abraham Ricks, John Cheadle, William Ladd, William and John Denson, Thomas and John Pleasants, William Outland, Peter Binford, John Murdock, Robert Ellyson, John Hubbard, Samuel Sebrell, Thomas Newby and Edmound Mathew and Samuel Jerdone, Jordan or Jurdon, as leaders among the Quakers who came to Virginia at this time. But since the Caroline Order Books only mention Cheadle, Murdock, Hubbard, Outland, Newby and Jerdone as appearing before the Caroline Court in any capacity it may be assumed that the others settled elsewhere.

Caroline's Quaker settlement lasted one hundred and fourteen years. Worship was held regularly at the Golansville meeting-house and members of the congregation lived in all sections of upper St. Margaret's Parish. The sect included not only the original migrants and their descendants but also Quaker families which came later, such as the Ricks, Johnsons, Stanleys and Nesses; and converts gained mostly through intermarriage among families already in the section. These families included the Terrells, Cobbs, Swans, Wrights, Coates, Olivers and Hacketts.

The Quakers officially moved this congregation to North Carolina in 1853, because the sect had come to oppose Negro slavery and was not in accord with the prevailing public opinion in the section. But stray Quakers remained, and within the last sixty years, a Mr. Moore, the last of the Caroline Quakers, was a regular attendant of County Line Baptist Church. Today (1953) all that remains in the county as tangible evidence of the colony's existence are two Quaker graveyards with unmarked tombstones. One of these is located at Golansville and the other on the Ness place in the triangle formed by the roads leading from Chilesburg to Partlow and from Chilesburg to Blantons.

The Quakers, however, did not oppose Negro slavery when they came to Caroline. The leader of their sect in America, William Penn, owned slaves, and the Caroline Quakers used slaves to till their land. As late as 1745 the county's head Quaker, John Cheadle, registered two young Negroes, Sam and Gilbert, ages 10 and 11, he purchased from a slave trader, who had imported them directly from Africa, in the County Court. But from the beginning of their settlement the Quakers' attitude towards slavery differed from that of their non-Quaker white neighbors in Caroline. They refused to stand watch at night to keep slaves from prowling around; and after John Woolman, a Philadelphia Quaker, brought out a pamphlet dealing with the treatment of slaves in 1746 they quit buying and selling slaves, but for some time after this they continued to work the slaves and the descendants of the slaves they already owned.

The Quakers' attitude towards slavery alarmed Caroline's large planters and homesteaders alike; and this attitude instead of toning down, as time went on, became more radical. But in spite of these differences, the Quakers were good subjects of the king. They faithfully performed all duties, which the law imposed. In the Order Books of the court their names often appear as jurors, appraisers of estates and road workers. For many years John Cheadle was charged with keeping in repair the road from the Quaker meeting-house (Golansville) to Chesterfield; and at no time was he indicted for failing to perform his duties, which was rare for a Caroline road supervisor, who held office over a period of years.

Governor Gooch was tolerant of other dissenting sects besides the Quakers, and he was especially lenient towards members of his own faith, the Presbyterians. In 1743 a Hanover carpenter, Samuel Morris, who had been holding religious services at his home, reading the scriptures and rendering his own interpretation of the Bible, which was not at all in keeping with the tenets of the Established Church, got hold of a "Confession of Faith" and decided that he was a Presbyterian. When notice of his conduct came to the attention of the Governor, Gooch granted him permission to hold assemblies, rather than censor him as the authorities in Williamsburg expected. With the boost, Presbyterians spread in Hanover. In a short time there were several congregations with a regular ordained minister, the celebrated Samuel Davies.

Samuel Morris had a cousin, Thomas Morris, who lived in lower St. Margaret's Parish, and Thomas probably through family associations became a Presbyterian. He made converts among his neighbors and in 1748, this group sponsored by Samuel Davies, petitioned Governor Gooch for authority to form a congregation (Burk's *History of Virginia,* pages 111-112). Gooch granted this request over the vigorous protest of Edmund Pendleton, who was at the time already a leading member of the Caroline bar, and the congregation built a meeting-house near "the Reeds," somewhere west of the site of Point Eastern.

The Baptists, who were in time to become Caroline's largest denomination, were known in the county as early as 1744. That year, according to the Order Books, Daniel Stover of Orange County came into the Caroline Court to reclaim a horse stolen from him by Daniel Garity and refused to take an oath because he was a Baptist (the Order Books record the word with a small b). Whereupon the court after examining him, decided that he had the same rights as a Quaker, with which they were familiar, and permitted to forego the making of the oath and give his affirmation.

Virginia's ruling caste did not share Governor Gooch's tolerance of dissenters. In 1742 they presented the Governor with a petition protesting "the countenance of Quakers by men in high station." Later the Burgesses with the Council concurring, passed laws to strengthen the position of the Established Church and to increase the penalties for stirring up dissension. But these statutes had little effect so long as Gooch was Governor, because he presided over the General Court of the colony and refused to cite them when he gave the charge to grand juries.

9. THE ESTABLISHED CHURCH TROUBLES IN ST. MARGARET'S PARISH

Between 1744 and 1748 the ecclesiastical authorities of the colony made numerous changes in the personnel of the church wardens of St. Margaret's Parish in a frantic effort to halt the spread of religious dissent in that parish. In 1744 they removed John Sutton and James Elliott, who had succeeded Thomas Terry and Micajah Chiles, the original wardens, some time prior to May 11, 1732, the date of the first entry in the Order Books of the Caroline Court, and appointed Rice Curtis and Thomas Wild. Curtis and Wild were followed in rapid order by John Anderson and John Wyatt (1746), William Connor and Hugh Noden (1747), and Timothy Chandler and Thomas Marshall (1748).

All of these men, with the exception of William Connor, were substantial settlers. Curtis, Wild, Wyatt and Noden served the county with distinction as king's magistrates. They failed as church wardens because of the temperaments of the people of the parish, a female busybody, Margaret Connor, and an inapt rector, the Rev. John Burnskill.

The residents of St. Margaret's were predominately homesteaders, only a generation removed from frontiersmen. In accordance with their backwoods background, they resented any restraint of their liberties. Over three-quarters of the standard fines of five shillings, or fifty pounds of tobacco, the Caroline Court imposed for missing church for two months' stretch between 1732 and 1744, were imposed on residents of St. Margaret's. Elliott and Sutton, who were the church wardens at the time were responsible for few of these arrests because they realized the parish's peculiar problems and decided that leniency was the best policy.

Mistress Margaret Connor, who lived in the great fork of the Mattapony in the upper end of the parish, stirred up most of the trouble. In 1735 she reported the record number of seventeen persons for missing church and her testimony before the court led to fines of five shillings or fifty pounds of tobacco for the lot. Heavy spring rains and the resulting high water were the defenses of most of these accused. But Mrs. Connor argued that if she was able to get to church, so were they, and her arguments convinced a majority of the magistrates.

In 1747 the authorities made William Connor, the husband of Margaret, church warden, perhaps in an effort to shut this woman up, whose sex barred her from holding the office herself. William Connor was unfit for this post. He had lost the position of under-sheriff in 1733, for misconduct in office; he had spread malicious lies about John Martin in the campaign in 1735, and he had been censured by the court for the disorderly way in which he ran his tavern at Downer's Bridge. During the brief period he served as warden he was fined for shooting crap and gambling with cards at James Martin's tavern, and for failing to report to the court for grand jury service. However, during his tenure of office, perhaps due to the watchful eye of his wife, no one was accused in St. Margaret's Parish of missing church. Many, however, attended unwillingly. William Isbell and John Martin (not the magistrate) were fined five shillings each for coming to church drunk.

While the ecclesiastical authorities of the colony removed church wardens at the drop of a hat, they refused to touch the Rev. John Brunskill, rector of St. Margaret's Parish, who was probably the poorest excuse of a man to attempt to preach in the county's 225-year history. The Rev. Brunskill was too engrossed in trying to make a fortune to take care of his pastoral duties. But he lacked business acumen and all his attempts ended in failure. His first try was a grist mill on Reedy Creek in 1735. This venture brought him in debt to Samuel Garlick, Charles Dick and other local merchants. Undismayed that his credit was no longer good at home he ran up bills with Mathew Bogle, of Glasglow, and Humphrey Bell of London, merchants abroad, who did an extensive business in the county. When they pressed him for their money he borrowed small amounts from James Southworth, William Terrell, John George, Josiah Wood and other prosperous parishioners to make token payments and forestall foreclosures. After he gouged these men for all the traffic would bear, he got additional funds from William Hunter, a professional money-lender of his parish. When Hunter cut him off, scores of his creditors demanded payment. Beginning in 1740 the pages of the Caroline Order Books are crowded with suits for debt against the Rev. John Brunskill. But some way, maybe because he was rector, he managed to stave off bankruptcy.

While preoccupied with his financial troubles Brunskill neglected his duties as rector. To take care of his parishioners north of South River, who claimed that they were unable to reach the parish church on account of high water in 1745, the court ordered him to hold regular services at a "chapel of ease" (brush arbor) set up in the great fork of the Mattapony. But Brunskill defied this order and a year later the court inconsistantly indicted the minister for refusing to preach and parishioners for failing to go to church at the same session. In 1739 Benjamin Walker, crown attorney for Caroline, cited Brunskill to church authorities in Williamsburg for not holding religious services on regular schedules anywhere in his parish. In 1744 James Elliott and John Sutton, among their last acts as church wardens, charged him with abusing the glebe property entrusted to his care. For this offense the court fined him fifteen shillings and ordered him to repair the property at once.

For relief from some of his official duties and to have more time for his private ventures, Brunskill farmed out his obligations to teach the youth of the parish's gentry first to his son-in-law, John Scott, and later to Joseph DeJarnette. Scott was drunk so much he had to quit, but Brunskill had a competent substitute in DeJarnette, a well-educated young man who came to Caroline from Gloucester and in time founded one of Caroline's most celebrated families. The rector failed to pay DeJarnette for his services, and in a short time all teaching stopped and a new series of law suits began.

Other defects in Brunskill's character included rowdyism, vanity and outright graft. He was constantly in tavern brawls which resulted in suits for assault and battery, and he engaged in a feud with Mace Pickett, the parish bully, which lasted over twenty years.

The most celebrated instance which reflected his vanity, and also showed his willingness to engage in graft, began in 1734, when he engaged William Johnston, a neighbor about to set out on a business trip to London, to buy him a mirror, of sufficient length to reflect the human image from "crown of the hat to sole of the boot." Johnston made and delivered the purchase, and Brunskill, while he did not open the package in Johnston's presence, received it, and subsequently announced that he was satisfied. But try as he may, Johnston was never able to force payment for the mirror, and after he died a few years later, his administratrix, Frances Jourdane, and Thomas Hamilton, the London merchant, who supplied the merchandise, brought suit for the purchase price. At the trial of the case Brunskill contended that the mirror was broken before delivery, and there is a great deal of testimony in the record as to whether the parcel "jingled." But after the trial had been underway several days it became apparent that Brunskill was going to lose the suit, and in a frantic attempt to avoid the loss he tried to bribe each individual juryman. These acts of infamy came to the court's attention and the magistrates imposed fines of fifteen shillings for each attempt.

10. NEW CHURCHES

Only the efforts of conscientious laymen kept the Established Church of the colony from falling into complete disrepute in St. Margaret's Parish. These men sought to get rid of the rector, sheer off the King William portion of the parish to facilitate administration, and set up more churches for the convenience of the worshipers. But they worked against great odds. Ecclesiastical authorities blocked every reform until the

Quakers threatened to take over the upper end of the parish and the Presbyterians the lower section in Caroline.

In 1741 John Sutton, one of the church wardens of the parish, Richard George whom the court had fined for non-attendance of church upon the information of Margaret Connor, John Wiley, Moses Hurt and John Dyer, gained permission to build a church on the lands of Richard George near Reedy Mill. This building became known as Reedy Church. Traces of its foundation still remain (1953) on a site near Edmund Pendleton School. Two years later James Elliott, the second warden of the parish at the time, Daniel Tompkins, who also had been fined for non-attendance of church upon the information of Margaret Connor, Richard Hewlett, Henry Harris, Josiah Wood and others secured permission to build a house of worship on the lands of Charles Yarbrough, a short distance south of the south fork of the South River (Campbell's Creek) in the upper end of the parish. This building became known as Bull Church. The ruins of its foundations are located on the north side of the road leading eastward from Ladysmith (1953).

Bull Church had the distinction of housing a congregation of the Church of England, or Episcopal Church, longer than any other building in the history of Caroline County. Due to this fact the assumption arose that it was the mother church of St. Margaret's Parish. This assumption is incorrect. Frequent references to Chesterfield Church on Fontaine's grant are found in the Order Books of the Caroline Court from the date of the first entry in 1732. Entries about the church on the lands of Richard George near Reedy Mill begin in 1741, while the first entries about Bull Church do not begin until 1743 and Charles Yarbrough did not come into court and acknowledge his deed for the church lot to vestry of the parish until 1747.

In addition to the myth about priority in building a great many legends have developed about the odd name "Bull Church." One legend holds that the workmen who constructed the building ate only bull meat while on the job; and another, that after the structure was completed, but before its dedication, a fierce bull took possession of the new building and refused to be ousted until parishioners slaughtered the brute and dragged his carcass outside. To celebrate this victory the parishioners cut off the animal's horns and nailed them to a sapling in the churchyard, where they remained until only their tips were exposed after the sapling grew into a tree. Rationalists try to explain the myths away by contending that the church got its name from the fact that its building was authorized by a "bull" (church legal document) from the Bishop of London, who had supervision over the church in Virginia. But this research student has been unable to uncover any evidence to substantiate this theory.

After the building of Reedy Church and Bull Church many new roads were cut to their locations; from Anderson's plantation on the Reeds to Reedy Church in 1743; from Richard Hewlett's to the new church now "abuilding" in the upper end of the parish in 1744. But with the new churches and the new roads the Rev. Brunskill held on as rector, and the status of the Church in the parish improved only slightly. In 1744 ecclesiastical authorities reluctantly consented to another change, and set up the new parish of St. David's in upper King William from the lower end of St. Margaret's and the upper end of St. John's. This move put all of St. Margaret's in Caroline, and gave that county's court jurisdiction over the whole parish. But the reform failed to bring the improvements that its sponsors hoped.

While St. Margaret's seethed with turmoil over religion, St. Mary's was placid. The staid planters on large crown grants in that parish had no patience with "new faith." Benjamin Robinson and William Woodford, two of the most illustrious men in the county, held office as church wardens the entire twenty-two years Sir William Gooch ruled Virginia. The Reverends Jones and Dawson served as rectors. Legends hold there were several houses of worship in the parish, but the Order Books of the Caroline Court record only one; venerable Mount Church on Mount Hill.

The people of Drysdale were neither interested in "new faiths" as were the people of St. Margaret's nor steadfast in their loyalty to the Established Church as were the people of

St. Mary's. For the most part they were not interested in organized religion; perhaps due to the influence of Robert Beverley, the historian, who sponsored the entry of many of their families into the region, since Beverley held that a strong church was an agency of the rich to oppress the poor. Their attitude evidently distrusted the ecclesiastical authorities in Williamsburg because while Gooch ruled Virginia they had as many church wardens as St. Margaret's; John Taylor and Mordicai Throckmorton, William Byrd Richards and Christopher Beverley, James Wood and James Taylor, Thomas Buckner and Mungo Roy, Henry Lynde and Edmund Pendleton. But these frequent changes until Pendleton took over failed to accomplish the desired results.

The parish's shape, extending along the north bank of the Mattapony from upper King and Queen to Caroline-Spotsylvania line in a narrow strip never more than six or seven miles wide, was almost as great a handicap as the indifference of the residents. From its earliest days the parish had a church known as Joy Creek in its lower end. This site was inconvenient for a vast majority of the parishioners, especially those who lived in the thriving settlement around the north end of Guinney's Bridge. Evidence substantiates that the wardens took the geography of the parish and the nature of the inhabitants into consideration because the Order Books do not record a single instance of a resident of Drysdale being fined for non-attendance of church from 1732-1749 while during the same period the court fined scores from St. Margaret's and tens from St. Mary's for this offense.

The growth of the trading center about Caroline Courthouse magnified the need of a more substantial house of worship in Drysdale Parish. In 1743 Humphrey Bell, a Caroline boy reared in the parish, who had gone to London and made good as a merchant, decided to give the vestry two acres for a new church and perhaps some money to construct the building. This site was near Marocossic Creek (lands of Frank Beazley and Maxie Broaddus in 1953). The building was constructed under the supervision of William Pendleton and Moses Penn, and became known from the time of its completion as the Ivy

Church. Bell's deed to the vestry for the property was not recorded until 1748. This delay may have been caused by the fact that the vestrymen had to wait until the busy merchant had time to visit Virginia and acknowledge his signature in open court; or it may have been that Bell refused to part with the title to the property until he was sure that it was going to be used for religious purposes.

11. FOREIGN WARS

The British crown called upon its American colonies to furnish troops to fight in foreign wars for the first time in 1740. Virginia's quota was 400 men. Alexander Spotswood was in command of this force until he died and Sir William Gooch succeeded him. These colonial soldiers fought on many fronts and with indifferent results. The Spaniards repulsed them when they attacked Cartagena in the West Indies; the French drove them back when they invaded Canada. Their only success came when they prevented a combined French and Spanish expedition from landing on the coast of Georgia.

Lawrence Washington, the eldest half brother of George Washington, served with distinction in these campaigns. He named his plantation, which was in time to become an American national shrine as the home of the first president of the United States, Mt. Vernon, for the commanding officer of the participating British fleet.

Caroline produced no Lawrence Washington during these wars. Its only soldier of record was John Brooks, a deserter. Brooks left his mother, Phoebe, a widow, when he went off to fight at Cartagena and Canada. But when he returned on furlough after the second campaign he found her remarried to Richard Long, who had moved into his home and was enjoying fully the inheritance left him by his father. Brooks resented this. To keep peace, his mother joined him in selling the family lands to John Sanderson. When the young soldier got his share of the estate, he did not return to the army but stayed in Caroline and went on a wild spree. In time military authorities notified the sheriff of Caroline to arrest him, if he were in his native county, and bring him to Williamsburg to stand trial for desertion. The sheriff found Brooks with ease and after his arrest turned him over to William Herndon, a constable, for transportation to the colonial capital. On this journey Brooks escaped. He was never heard of in Caroline again. But the military officials court-martialed Herndon, and sentenced him to serve the prison term usually imposed on deserters.

While Brooks' conduct may be attributed to the irresponsibilities of youth there were at the same time many mature men in Caroline who felt little loyalty to the British crown. The families with the larger crown grants held their acreage due to the generosity of the Stuart kings, Charles II and James II, or those monarchs' deputies in Virginia, and it rankled many of this class that the British throne had passed from the heirs of their patrons to the House of Hanover. In addition to this group there were scores of homesteaders in the county, who came to Virginia at a later date to escape punishment for participating in various plots against the reigning family; and indentured servants bound only upon conviction of political crimes against the king. The larger planters, who disliked the Hanoverians, were afraid to grumble because they had too much to lose from royal disfavor, but both homesteaders and indentured servants spoke their opinions freely.

When Charles Edward Stuart, Bonney Prince Charley, landed on the Isle of Skye off the coast of Scotland in 1745 to make his greatest attempt to gain the English and Scottish thrones, the sympathies of the vast majority of the people in Caroline were with the young prince. They were disappointed when King George II's younger son, the Duke of Cumberland, defeated Charles Edward and his supporting Scottish Highland clans at Culloden, with the aid of the Campbells of Argyle treachery, and saved the crown for the House of Hanover, and they were resentful when their members of the House of Burgesses, John Baylor and Lundsford Lomax, signed a resolution congratulating George II on this victory.

However, neither the Stuart Pretender's defeat nor Baylor's and Lomax's congratulations stemmed the rising anti-Hanoverian tide in Caroline. After Culloden the crown took punitive action on the supporters of Charles Edward. To escape punishment these men, mostly Scots, came to Virginia in droves. They took over the new town of Port Royal and scattered Scottish customs all over the county, which survive in modified forms to this day (1953).

Baylor and Lomax regained much of their lost prestige with their constituents by the stand they took on another issue which confronted the House of Burgesses later in 1747. The capitol of the colony had burned and there was a widespread demand throughout Virginia to move the capital from Williamsburg to a site "more centrally located and advantageous to trade" when the structure was rebuilt. The people of Caroline who were finding at the time that their own county seat was in the wrong place, were, with the exception of the powerful Corbin family, solidly for the change. Their magistrates unanimously passed a resolution asking that the shift be made. Baylor and Lomax voted in accord with the wishes of the magistrates and lay settlers of their county. The Burgesses passed a bill authorizing the removal but the Governor's Council killed this legislation because several councillors were heavily invested in Williamsburg real estate and potential decreases in land values in that town if the capital was removed, threatened them with financial ruin. The Capitol was rebuilt on the same spot and the capital remained in Williamsburg until British rule ended in Virginia.

12. EXPANDING TRADE

Caroline shared with the rest of the colony in the expanding economy which called for new trade routes and new trading centers in the decade prior to the burning of the capitol. After Alexander Spotswood pushed back the frontier to include most of the area of Spotsylvania County in settled territory two mariners sailing out of the southwest England port of Bristol, Captain Henry Sweet with the sailing vessel *Priscilla* and Captain William Dunlop with the sailing vessel *Elizabeth and Ann,* began making regular calls along the Rappahannock to the river's falls at Leaseland (Fredericksburg). Many references to these two ships and their masters are found in the earliest Order Books of the Caroline Court. The chief merchant in Caroline with whom they did business was George Tilley, who prior to the first entry in the oldest Order Book, had set up a wharf and warehouse on the south side of the Rappahannock at a site near Conway's warehouse, marked on old maps as Heard's or Hoard's landing. Tilley not only supplied the larger planters but also retail stores scattered through the county; Thomas Mauldin and Samuel Garlick at Chesterfield, Benjamin Rennolds and Samuel Coleman at the Court House, Charles Dick in upper St. Margaret's Parish, Josiah Baker near Conway's warehouse and Humphrey Bell's outlet in lower Drysdale.

This system functioned in a fairly satisfactory manner, in spite of the rapid growth of the county, until George Tilley died in 1742 and his chief clerk, Thomas Heard or Hoard, took over the business. Hoard was a hard man. As soon as he was in control he began to curtail credit and demand payment of past due accounts. His actions caused unrest all over the county until James Bowie, an immigrant who had recently reached Caroline from Scotland, took advantage of the dissatisfaction and opened a rival trading house at Roy's warehouse.

Bowie chose Roy's as a site for his new business on account of established harbor facilities, a ferry across the Rappahannock, a network of roads leading inland, and the chartered tobacco warehouse and the adjacent tavern of Mistress Dorothy Roy. (James Bowie remained a bachelor. Caroline's celebrated Bowie family descended from James' brother, John, who came to Caroline with him, married Judith Catlett, the daughter of John Catlett, and took care of the family plantation while James took care of trade.)

Ships began to dock regularly at the point to become known as Roy's early in the eighteenth century after John Buckner chose this site to set up a chartered tobacco warehouse. Through the years as the tobacco business prospered under the direction of John Buckner, John Roy and Dorothy Roy, in turn, more and more ships used the harbor and the port facilities improved until they far surpassed any other installations along the Caroline sector of the Rappahannock.

Ferries were important to any commercial development on the Caroline side of the river to bring trade from King George. The first ferry of record was established in 1732 and ran between Moss Neck and James Hackley's plantation. This route lasted only six years. Garwin Corbin, who owned the land along the south side of the river blocked the road leading to its Caroline terminus because he, like many of the great landlords of the colony, was opposed to the expansion of the commerce and trade. The next ferry set up in 1734 linked Roy's warehouse with Gibson's landing, and the third, two years later, Conway's warehouse with Berry's plantation in King George.

After 1736 ferry facilities at Roy's and Conway's warehouses, which had become keen rivals for trade, were about the same. But a wide discrepancy was developing in the roads which led to the back country where most of the trade originated, and this discrepancy favored Roy's. The rolling road from Chesterfield across Doguetown Bridge (Milford) to Roy's warehouse split Caroline in almost equal halves. A feeder rolling road leading from Needwood Forest across Burk's Bridge joined it at New Hope (Bowling Green) and it syphoned off much of the traffic originally intended for Conway's which passed westward along the Three Knotch Road, at Rollins Fork. This trunk route with its tributaries gave Roy's undisputed control of the commerce in the lower half of the county and permitted it to challenge Conway's on even terms for trade with the upper half. Much of the tobacco sold through Conway's originally came from Spotsylvania but with the growth of Fredericksburg this business steadily declined.

After the death of Francis Conway I, the founder of Conway's warehouse in 1733, roads as a rule leading to Roy's warehouse were in better shape than those leading to Conway's. Terrain, supervision and know-how accounted for this difference. Caroline people had trouble maintaining the county's roads from the time that they were built. Each spring the court appointed local residents to look after roads in all sections of the county and the next spring indicted at least a fourth of them for failing to perform their duty. Until 1736 these men got off with a rebuke from the magistrates but after that date a regular fine of fifteen shillings (150 pounds of tobacco) was imposed for neglect. These fines fell upon the rich and the poor alike; from bankrupt Thomas Lantor to magistrates and great landowners, George Hoomes and Thomas Buckner.

Due to the nature of the soil roads leading to Conway's were harder to keep in repair than roads leading to Roy's, but Francis Conway I personally supervised the maintenance of the trunk rolling road leading from Guinney's Bridge to his warehouse until his death, and kept it, at all times, in passable shape. After he died, while his widow, Rebecca Catlett Conway, struggled to keep the family business together, until her sons were old enough to take over, the care of this road passed to John and Joseph Stevens, and the Stevenses were poor roadmen. One or the other of this pair was fined for failure to keep this road in condition each year from 1736 until 1745. The fines they paid tripled the fines assessed against the supervisors of any other road in the county. Why the court kept reappointing such incompetents remains a mystery but the fact stands out that their negligence hamstrung development about Conway's warehouse and turned trade and traffic towards Roy's.

In striking contrast to the Stevenses, the Beasleys, John and Charles, kept the feeder roads leading to Roy's warehouse from lower Drysdale Parish in excellent condition. They enjoyed the distinction, along with John Cheadle, of being the only road supervisors in colonial Caroline who were never fined. On account of their records the court sent them to rebuild roads, which gave trouble, in sections of the county remote from their homes in the vicinity of John Daniel's Mill (White's in 1953). But oddly enough they were never authorized to put in shape a road leading to Conway's warehouse.

When Francis Conway II gained full control over Conway's warehouse after the deaths of his brothers, Catlett in 1744 and Reuben in 1745, he took immediate steps to improve the roads leading to his place of business in an effort to revive trade. He persuaded the court to get rid of the incompetent Stevens and to authorize rolling roads connecting the warehouse with all sections of upper Caroline. These improvements increased the volume of tobacco which passed through the warehouse, but came too late to bring other trade, because already the major business houses in the county were centered in the new town of Port Royal at Roy's.

Bridges for a time threatened the emergence of Roy's as Caroline's chief center of trade. Since settlers first came into the region to be the county, the rambunctious Mattapony had frequently flooded and severed all routes for transportation which lay across its course. In 1738 after the bridges at Guinney's, Downer's, Doguetown and Burk's had all washed away, the planters of St. Margaret's began to clamor for a bridge across the Pamunkey at Littlepage's to connect them with warehouses at Crutchfield's in lower Hanover and in the new town of Richmond. The court gave in to their demands and hired John Harris to build the bridge over the Pamunkey for 4,912 pounds of tobacco.

Harris was an inapt bridge builder. His first attempt fell into the stream, and the magistrates refused to accept the second because it was unsound. While he tried to strengthen this structure under the supervision of William Carr, a magistrate, to meet the specifications, the court indicted Harris, declared his bond forfeited, sued his sureties and appointed three of its own members, Thomas Wild, Thomas Johnston and Hugh Noden, to build the bridge.

These activities consumed time. It was 1745 before the court fined Harris and took over the construction of the bridge. In the meanwhile other magistrates, Arch Macphearson, Thomas Buckner, George Goodloe, Robert Farish and George Hoomes, had rebuilt all the bridges across the Mattapony, commerce had resumed its normal channels and the planters of St. Margaret's were placated. James Bowie had been joined at Roy's by Robert Gilchrist, Oliver Towles, John Harvey of Essex, and other merchants. Port Royal had become a town.

13. DOROTHY ROY

Mistress Dorothy Roy reigned like a queen over the growing commercial settlement about Roy's warehouse. From the day James Bowie chose the site as a likely spot for a trading house, merchants, speculators, cheats and planters met at her tavern to discuss business deals and make plans for the expansion of commerce. She was a central figure in these talks and schemes. Men from all walks of life came to her for advice.

Dorothy Roy gained the background for her reputation through the school of hard knocks. She came to live in the territory to be Caroline County while Alexander Spotswood ruled Virginia, when her husband, John Roy, got the job as tobacco inspector for the chartered warehouses, and stayed in the background rearing her children, Thomas, John Jr., Reuben, Mungo, Richard, Betty and two more girls whose names are lost, while her husband took over Buckner's warehouse upon the death of John Buckner, and the ferry across the Rappahannock at this warehouse, and grew rich.

But around 1730, John Roy began to slip financially and two years later Benjamin Rowe, a Caroline planter, put him in jail for the non-payment of debt. With this catastrophe, Dorothy became interested in the family's finances, an interest which she retained until her death. To get her husband out of prison she borrowed from friends, and paid Rowe off which automatically brought his release.

Before John Roy recovered from this blow to his standing in the county's business circles he was in trouble again. The next year Lionel Lyde, a London merchant, accused him of passing a hogshead of tobacco, which rotted in transit, because it was prized in too high order, and sought to have the royal government of Virginia revoke his charter for a public warehouse and remove him as a tobacco inspector. These accusations led to a lengthy investigation, conducted by Thomas Lee, of Westmoreland, president of the Governor's Council, Nicholas Smith and George Grymes, of King George, and John Taylor, of Caroline. Their findings exonerated Roy but the strain of the hearings exhausted him and he died shortly thereafter, a broken man.

Upon his death, his eldest son, Thomas, and his wife, Dorothy, administered his estate, and Thomas took over as tobacco inspector and owner of the chartered warehouse and ferry.

To bolster the family's finances strained through adversity, Dorothy secured a license to run a tavern in the vicinity of the warehouse. This was the first ordinary license issued to a woman in the history of Caroline County.

Thomas' career as inspector and proprietor was short. He was too much interested in politics to be a good business man. His conviction by the House of Burgesses in 1736 for the disgraceful part he played in the campaign which defeated John Martin, carried with it prohibitions to hold positions of public trust, which automatically revoked his franchises for public warehouse and ferry and forced him to vacate his position as tobacco inspector. To save the business for the family, Dorothy Roy asked the authorities in Williamsburg to put title to the warehouse and ferry in her name because her second and third sons, John Jr., and Reuben were heavily in debt and her younger sons were minors. In a superb tribute to her personal magnetism the authorities granted her unheard of request, and she became the first and only woman to own a chartered to-bacco warehouse in colonial Virginia. Specific evidence of this ownership is found in the Order Books of the Caroline Court, Vol. II, page 282.

Dorothy Roy was not content with being merely the nominal owner of the warehouse after she got its title registered in her name. She assumed active management at once. Her career as a business woman did not always run smoothly. In 1737 she persuaded the Burgesses to remove the disabilities they placed on her son, Thomas, and allow him to resume his position as tobacco inspector. Thomas Roy did not justify his mother's faith in him. No sooner was he back in office than he joined with Richard Booker, the second inspector at the warehouse, and forced planters to grant them kickbacks of 20 per cent before issuing certificates for tobacco in storage. Irate planters reported this graft to Benjamin Walker, crown attorney of Caroline, and Walker directed three of the county's magistrates, John Micou, John Taliaferro and Richard Taliaferro, to investigate the complaints. Their findings resulted in the removal of Roy and Booker as inspectors, and the appointment of James Boutwell and Francis Stern. This correction was not enough to satisfy the rabid planters. Shortly thereafter they burned a storehouse at Roy's warehouse in revenge.

Dorothy Roy refused to let Thomas drift after this most recent evidence of his crookedness. Instead she promptly engineered his marriage to a woman much older than he, Judith Beverley Kenner, the widow of the Rev. Rodham Kenner, late rector of Drysdale Parish, who, through her inheritance from the Beverleys, was one of the richest women in the county. This time Thomas justified his mother's faith because he not only succeeded in gaing control of all of Judith's property, but also embezzled trust funds belonging to her young son by the Reverend Kenner without getting caught. With these fortunes behind him Thomas Roy became one of the most influential business men in Caroline County. Beginning in 1748 his name no longer appears in the Order Books as plain "Thomas Roy," it had become "Thomas Roy, gent."

Dorothy Roy's scruples when it came to money were hardly better than her son's. In 1742, after the traders had begun moving their businesses to the neighborhood of her establishments, she joined with Col. William Woodford in a move to discredit Conway's warehouse and keep the community in which it was located from sharing the boom. Woodford accused William Allcocke, an inspector at Conway's, of passing cut tobacco for Lawrence Battaile. The court ordered an investigation and the hearings to be held, of all places, in the parlor of Mistress Dorothy Roy. But even this hostile atmosphere failed to prejudice the findings. The investigators found no basis for complaint. History, however, has proven that it was needless for Dorothy Roy to engage in such underhanded tactics because the die was already cast, and her warehouse, not Conway's was to be the site of Caroline's town on the Rappahannock.

In dealing with servants Dorothy Roy was as hard-boiled as when she dealt with her business rivals. When her indentured servant, Ann Sanders, stole an Irish poplin shirt from her storehouse, valued at 20 shillings, she was disappointed when the magistrates let the girl off with 20 lashes at the whipping post, rather than sending her to Williamsburg to stand trial for her life before the General Court of the colony.

Edmund Pendleton was the most celebrated resident of Caroline to stand in awe of Dorothy Roy. He married her daughter, Betty, in 1741 "against my friend's consent, also my master's." (Pendleton's Autobiography in Richmond *Enquirer* for April 11, 1828.) Betty was an infant at the time and her mother, as her guardian, had custody of her share of her father's, John Roy's estate. When she gave birth to a child, and both she and the child died, shortly over a year after the marriage, title to her property passed to Pendleton. He qualified on her estate and demanded it at once. But try as he may he was unable to get it so long as Dorothy Roy lived. (Caroline Order Books, Vol. IV, page 412.)

Although Pendleton and the landed aristocrats to whom he catered looked down on Dorothy Roy and her family, the men who controlled Caroline's commerce did not. They continued to flock to her tavern and named the trading center about it "Port Royal" in her honor.

Unfortunately the lady did not live long to enjoy this honor. Shortly after the founding of the town she became ill, and when she failed to respond to treatment from her physician, Dr. John Symmer, left her family and took up residence in a small house in Port Royal belonging to Colonel Waller with three Negro slaves and a white bondsboy to look after her creature needs. While she lingered she made over most of her property to her children, keeping only title to the chartered warehouse and her four attending servants in her name. These assignments led to bitter disputes between her creditors and her heirs after her death in 1746, which came to a head with 15 pages of testimony in the Order Books of the Caroline Court in 1758 (Vol. IV, pages 397-412) (the longest case of record). The court forced the heirs to settle with the creditors, but even the payment of her debts in full took only a small part of her alleged estate. Her executor, Richard Roy, denied he knew what happened to her silver tankards and plate, which one creditor, Oliver Towles, swore was "the most valuable in Virginia."

14. THE BOOM AT ROY'S

Sites near chartered warehouses appealed to traders as likely business stands because the settlers drew the pay for their tobacco either in script or in sterling through the warehouses. Most of the settlers were so hard up for goods manufactured abroad to keep their homesteads and plantations running that they made purchases of such merchandise as soon as they were able to reach a market where it was offered for sale after their money came into their hands. If stores were located in the vicinity of the warehouse they stocked up before beginning the journey home after disposing of their crops.

Since Roy's was Caroline's larger and more centrally located warehouse it was the natural focal point for trade. After James Bowie went into business there he was joined in short order by Robert Gilchrist, or Gilcrease, another Scottish immigrant, John Bell, the agent of Humphrey Bell of London, the Caroline native who had done so well as a merchant in lower Drysdale Parish that he moved his headquarters to the British metropolis and John Gartsboro, factor for a new firm made up of William Dunlop, the mariner, who had transported cargoes between wharves on Caroline's sector of the Rappahannock and Great Britain since the earliest days of the county, and Robert Boyd, a Glasgow merchant. In the spring of 1744 Oliver Towles, an impecunious speculator, managed to gain control of the venerable trading house founded by George Tilley, from its current owner, the tight-fisted Thomas Hoard, for a small down payment, and move it from its old site at Hoard's Landing to a new site at Roy's. This shift made Roy's the undisputed economic capital of Caroline County.

The greatest handicap confronting the new trading center was the title to the land on which it stood. Richard Taliaferro set out to remedy this situation (Vol. V., Hening's *Statutes-at-Large,* pages 287-292). He was the executor for Robert Smith in whom fee simple title to 500 acres adjacent to Roy's warehouse vested at the time of his death. But this title had many clouds. In 1707 Charles Smith, Robert Smith's father and predecessor in title, had leased the land to three London merchants, Thomas Lane and Macajah and Richard Perry, for 1,000 years for a flat fee of 690 pounds and an annual rental of an ear of Indian corn, with the proviso that Smith, or his heirs, might take up the lease, at the end of a year for 731 pounds, eight shillings, or at a time after that date upon the payment of the redemption price with interest. The mortgage was not redeemed and in 1719 Macajah and Richard Perry, the surviving London merchants, sold their interest in the property to Rowland Thornton and John Catlett.

The status of the title became even more confused with the deaths of Thornton and Catlett, and Charles Smith and his son and heir, Robert Smith. Fortunately Robert Smith left a will in which he directed Richard Taliaferro to sell the 60 acres of the land adjacent to Roy's warehouse in lots for a town to pay his creditors and to divide what was left of his estate between his wife and his four infant children. To accomplish this Taliaferro filed a suit of chancery in the General Court of the Colony against the heirs of Thornton and Catlett, and petitioned the General Assembly to set up a town on the property. Both Court and Assembly acted favorably. The former entered a decree allowing Smith's heirs to redeem the land and the latter, in September 1744, passed a law to establish a town at Roy's warehouse "to be called Port Royal." This act authorized Richard Taliaferro to have the town site surveyed and divided into lots and named Charles Carter, William Beverley, Lundsford Lomax, Richard Taliaferro, Thomas Turner, John Baylor and Oliver Towles as trustees to convey the lots to purchasers.

Immediately thereafter the first land boom in the history of Caroline County got under way. The lots sold quickly and all manner of people took up residence in the new town. They ranged from Robert Gilchrist and James Bowie, the merchants, to Thomas Sanders, who opened a race-track near by, Joseph and Elizabeth King, who were bootleggers, and Mary Crawley and Catherine Straughn, who set up houses of prostitution.

The boom was genuine and the town continued to prosper in spite of its many unsavory characters. Mathew Bogle, James Berries, John Murdock and John Graham, merchants of Glasgow, and William Black, Johnathan Forward and William Hamilton, merchants of London, sent factors to compete with the factors of Dunlop and Boyd of Glasgow and Humphrey Bell of London, already set up in the new town, for business. John Harvie of Essex, a merchant who drew much of his trade from lower Caroline, moved his headquarters to Port Royal, and Patrick Mitchell bought and expanded the trading post begun by Dorothy Roy.

For all the rivalry for business the traders worked together for the common good. They set up a guild to promote commerce at Port Royal in 1745 under the direction of Robert Gilchrist. This was Caroline's first chamber of commerce and one of the earliest organizations of this type in Virginia. In 1746 it directed memorials to the Royal Governor, his Council and the House of Burgesses, asking public improvements and legislation regulating commerce for their town. Unfortunately the text of these petitions have been lost.

With the boom the number of taverns increased in Port Royal fourfold, when John Miller, Oliver Towles and George Todd took out ordinary licenses in 1745 as well as Dorothy Roy. But this phenomenal rise in the number of licenses failed to take care of the thirst of the traders, planters, speculators, cheats and hangers-on, who congregated in the new town because at the same time Joseph and Elizabeth King did a lively business bootlegging.

George Todd was a physician as well as a tavern-keeper. In addition to Todd, John Symmer and Daniel Fergusson practiced medicine in Port Royal from the town's earliest days. Symmer was the physician of Dorothy Roy and attended her in her last illness. (Order Book IV, page 414.) Fergusson like Todd engaged in business while he practiced his profession. He was a tailor and ran a tailor shop under the direction of Thomas Smith, his chief apprentice.

John Miller had a grist mill on Peumandsend a short distance out of town, and Lundsford Lomax was engaged in the manufacture of runletts from native wood which he shipped to the Madeira Islands for the storage of Madeira wine, which the Virginia traders imported in great volume. These two enterprises completed the list of industries in the vicinity of the new town.

15. The Great Crime Wave

Caroline's first crime wave followed in the wake of the founding of Port Royal. Prior to that time the county was remarkably free of serious crime. With the exception of one case of forgery (Robert Baber in 1737) the early Order Books record only convictions of failure to work roads, non-attendance of church, violation of the tobacco laws, sale of alcoholic beverages without a license, disrespect for the court, the King and the militia, adultery, bastardcy, swearing, drunkenness and youthful pranks among the free white inhabitants. On the surface this looks like a formidable list but actually the trial justice of a Virginia county today (1953) has jurisdiction over practically all cases in these categories, if they remain crimes.

In this period the magistrates investigated only one homicide. This was in 1733 when John Partlow shot Thomas Downer. In this trial the court held Downer's death accidental and exonerated Partlow after hearing the testimony of eye-witnesses, William Oliver, William Smith, Henry Barlett and Moses Downer. The magistrates failed to certify a single free white person to Williamsburg for trial before the colony's General Court. Thomas Roy and William Burdette by the House of Burgesses for the part they took in the defeat of John Martin, and Edward Herndon by court martial for permitting his prisoner, John Brooks, the deserter, to escape, were the only Caroline residents, with the exception of a handful of indentured servants, tried in the colonial capital.

Booming Port Royal changed this situation. Crooks and speculators, as well as hardheaded business men, crowded that thriving trading center and roamed the adjacent countryside looking for ways to get rich quickly. In 1745 Alexander Sweeney showed up on the streets of the town and offered gold bricks for sale at a modest price. In a prevailing atmosphere of reckless speculation he made numerous sales before a purchaser discovered the bricks were made of base metal. This disclosure led to his arrest but the magistrates were lenient with him at his trial. After branding him as a "common cheat" they offered him his freedom if he were able to post bond of 50 pounds sterling for his good behavior. Jacob and Charles Burruss of St. Margaret's Parish supplied this bond and the court released Sweeney, with the admonition "go your way and sin no more."

Patrick Welsh was the arch criminal of this lawless era. His arrest in 1747 led to the uncovering of a crime ring with its headquarters in Port Royal which extended its activities to all sections of Virginia. The fact that Welsh was a crook came as a surprise to his neighbors, because for twenty years after he reached Virginia and sold his headrights to Richard Taliaferro he clearly concealed his criminal activities from the people of his home community. The disclosure of his true nature came with his arrest for the relatively minor crime of breaking into the storehouse of Thomas Johnson in Drysdale's Parish and carrying away 18 yards of German serge and other goods. Johnson was a magistrate and through diligent inquiry learned the identity of the thief. A search of Welsh's home not only uncovered the serge but also revealed stacks of silver communion plate and equipment to counterfeit coinage in shillings from this metal. A portion of the plate was identified, and confronted with this evidence, Welsh confessed. He admitted that he and his confederates, Manus Fegan, Edward Danerley, George Fox, Ann Dugan and Patrick and Catherine Roan, all residents of Caroline, had stolen communion service sets from churches in Upper and Lower Brandon parishes in Prince George, St. David's Parish in King William, Yorkhampton Parish in York, Southwork Parish in Surry, and other parishes in Southampton, Lunenburg, Stafford, Northumberland and Richmond counties and brought their loot to Port Royal, where they broke it up and used it for material to counterfeit coinage, which they passed into circulation. The Caroline Court after an inquest certified Welsh and Fegan to the General Court of the colony to stand trial for grand larceny, breaking and entering and counterfeiting; and Patrick and Catherine Roan for receiving and breaking up stolen property and issuing counterfeit coins. It held that the charges against Danerley, Fox and

Ann Dugan were not proven and only bound them to keep the peace.

The magistrates regarded Welsh as such a dangerous prisoner that they hired John Robinson, John Smith, George Bullard, Thomas Jeter, George Brassfield, James Potter and Francis Stell, at the cost of 1,470 pounds of tobacco, to act as his guards on the journey to Williamsburg.

After the trial in the colonial capital Welsh was duly hung. But upon the completion of a short term of imprisonment Fegan, who came to Virginia as an indentured servant, returned to Caroline County. The records fail to disclose the fates of Patrick and Catherine Roan.

An attempt to get rich quick also led Francis Bearding to crime. To secure capital with which to speculate he broke into the storehouses of Benjamin Hubbard of lower Drysdale Parish and carried away 350 pounds of tobacco. The Caroline magistrates had jurisdiction to try Bearding since neither the value of the goods he stole, nor the breaking and entry of an outhouse during daylight were sufficient to constitute a felony. But they preferred not to exercise this right and sent him to Williamsburg to stand trial for his life in the General Court, because in colonial Virginia the theft of tobacco, which was the basis of the economy, was treated very much like horse-stealing, at a later date, in the American West. Hanging was none too good for the thief.

Two oddly dissimilar Caroline residents, George Hoomes and Thomas Roy, tried to help Bearding. Hoomes got the doomed man's property, and Roy his debts, for their trouble.

The biggest unsolved crime of the period was the burning of John Bowie's dwelling, quarters, dairy, stables, storehouse, meat house, and hen houses on the hill overlooking Port Royal, during the nighttime. Bowie accused John and Catherine Noden, who were engaged in a bitter controversy with his brother, James, the merchant, over debts, of setting the fires. While the Nodens were out of jail on bail awaiting trial, parties unknown under the cover of darkness cut up every tobacco plant on Bowie's plantation, and Bowie filed additional charges against the pair to cover this crime. But at the trials he was unable to bring enough evidence before the court to secure convictions. In both cases the magistrates returned Scottish verdicts of "not proven," and instead of either clearing or punishing the accused, ordered them set free after they had posted bonds of 20 pounds sterling, each, to keep the peace for one year. The fact that Hugh Noden, father of the accused John, was among the magistrates, who presided over the trials, may have influenced these inconclusive verdicts.

John Hoomes did not fare so well when he faced the court, although his father, George Hoomes, was a magistrate. The court sentenced him to twenty lashes on his bare back at the public whipping post for the theft of a bell belonging to Thomas Buckner, another magistrate, although he was a mere youth, perhaps not more than fifteen years of age.

16. The Panic

Over-expansion and speclation strained credit to the breaking point during the Port Royal boom. The crash began with the failure of John Harvie of Essex in 1747. Harvie was in bad shape financially when he moved the site of his business to the new town. Settlers in all sections of upper Essex and lower Caroline owed him money and he in turn was in debt to local planters for produce and to merchants overseas for merchandise. Influx of new traders caused many of his paying customers to take their business elsewhere, his customers who were in debt to him shunned him because there were new sources of credit, and the planters to whom he owed money pushed him for payment to get funds to join in the wild spending spree.

To revive his ebbing trade, Harvie was in dire need of some of the new goods which his new rivals stocked to draw buyers to his store. But he was without either money or credit to make these purchases. To get around this difficulty he robbed Robert Gilchrist and brazenly offered for sale the silk stockings, shoe buckles and bells which he stole. When Gilchrist missed his goods, and found out where they were, he summoned Harvie to court. But for some unknown reason, perhaps because Gilchrist was a kindly man, the magistrates were lenient with

Harvie. Instead of certifying him for trial before the General Court of the colony, they dismissed all the charges after he returned the property he stole to its rightful owner.

This leniency, however, failed to save John Harvie. It only served to stir up his creditors. Immediately after the trial John Beazley, to whom he owed a considerable sum, attached a chest of silver which was his most liquid asset. As the news of this seizure spread other creditors acted and soon gobbled up his entire estate. When there was nothing left to take care of the mounting claims, the unfortunate man went to jail for debt. The trading house of John Harvie, of Essex, was at an end.

Harvie's failure made only a ripple but the failure of Oliver Towles a year later rocked Caroline County from stem to stern. The trading house he headed was the oldest in the county. It had prospered in turn under the proprietorship of George Tilley, its founder, and Tilley's successor in title, Thomas Hoard. Through the years under these managements it built up a large volume of trade and unlike many of the new businesses mushrooming in Port Royal had a firm foundation on which to stand.

In addition Oliver Towles was well liked. In his early years in the county he paid a fine rather than testify before the grand jury investigating John Martin's complaints against the supporters of Johnathan Gibson in the election contest of 1735. This stand won him friends among the plain people without alienating the upper crust. He was favorably known to the officials of the royal government in Williamsburg. Governor Gooch esteemed him sufficiently to make him one of the original trustees of Port Royal. He had enough influence with the Caroline magistrates to get them to hold some sessions of the county court in a room he rented them in his home at Port Royal for the convenience of the people of the new town of which he was a trustee. With this background people expected him to succeed, but Towles was too soft-hearted to operate successfully on his limited capital in the prevailing economy of dog-eat-dog. When Josiah Baker, who ran a retail store in the vicinity of Conway's warehouse, was unable to meet his obligations and all other importers cut him off, Towles took in partial payment an assignment of 21 small accounts of his large outstanding debt and extended more credit. A study of the Caroline Order Books over two centuries later reveals that most of the 21 accounts Baker put up as security were worthless. Patrick Boswell, James Burden and Henry Cooper had taken the poor debtor's oath. John Buckner, Walter Chiles and Thomas Brown were dead; their estates had been settled and all their assets dispursed by the court. Thomas Hoard, who was a keen business man, knew these facts and chafed while he watched Towles exercise such poor judgment.

Josiah Baker did not appreciate Towles' consideration. He continued to part with his stock of goods for mere promises to pay, and began bootlegging to supplement his income. When the court convicted him for selling hard liquors without a license, he went to jail because he did not have the means with which to pay his fine. While he was incarcerated his business went to pot and the huge account he owed Towles became worthless. With this loss Hoard, who was becoming more and more impatient with the lax manner in which Towles conducted business, decided to act. He demanded that Towles pay the full price he contracted to pay for the trading house at once. Hoard had the right to make this demand because his contract with Towles provided that the full purchase price was payable on demand if the buyer fell behind in making partial payments when they became due.

James Bowie and Robert Gilchrist, two of the leading merchants on Port Royal's "Wall Street" tried to save Towles. They wanted no major failure to hamper the development of the new trading center where they staked their earnings and careers. To halt this failure they took deeds of trust on Towles' real estate and chattel, mortgages on his merchandise and offered to back him until he worked himself out of his financial difficulties. But Hoard refused to sanction this arrangement. Instead he hired Edmund Pendleton, who was making a reputation for himself as a lawyer at the local bar at the time, to set the deeds and mortgages aside and foreclose on Towles.

Pendleton moved and was upheld in court. Towles was

unable to pay up and went to jail. Hoard repossessed the trading house and ran it in conjunction with a partner, James Mills. While this was unfortunate for Towles it did not materially effect business conditions in Caroline until Pendleton, at Hoard's instigation, entered suits against all the firm's debtors, which numbered into the hundreds and included many of the most prominent people in the county. Few of these debtors had either a defense or the means to pay. Forty-two went to jail for debt after one session of the court.

Panic swept the county. The prisons at Port Royal, the courthouse and Johnston's Tavern in lower St. Margaret's were full to overflowing, and the magistrates rented "the late residence of John Martin" in lower Drysdale for a temporary lockup. No one but Pendleton, Hoard and Mills knew who might go to jail next.

Towles sought to testify before the court in an effort to save some of the debtors, but Pendleton persuaded the magistrates to deny this request and to order Towles testimony taken in depositions while he remained in jail. When these documents finally reached the court, Pendleton argued that they were not in the proper form and succeeded in blocking their admission as evidence. The snowballing of debtors to prison went on.

The break came when Hoard moved to lock up Jane Tompkins, one of the most prominent women in the county, because she was unable to pay her debts to his firm. This outrage caused James Bowie and Robert Gilchrist, who already felt the pinch of declining trade, to decide that they must take drastic steps to keep fear and panic from giving the local economy a knockout blow from which it might never recover. Joining together they hired Zachery Lewis, the crown attorney and Pendleton's chief rival at the bar, to defend all persons in debt to Hoard. Lewis soon proved that he was a better lawyer than Pendleton and invoked the statute of limitations, which heretofore Pendleton had refused to allow the debtors to plead. After a bitter legal fight the court sustained Lewis and its ruling automatically released fully three-fourths of the debtors from jail. Pendleton appealed the decision to the General Court of the colony, but the high court refused to reverse the Caroline magistrates, and the recently released prisoners remained free.

The court's ruling did not help Towles. His debts to Hoard were in date and he stayed in jail. During the remainder of Governor Gooch's rule in Virginia, he was shunted back and forth, between the prisons at the courthouse and in Port Royal. His long incarceration, however, failed to break his spirit, and he was to live to regain his prestige in Caroline County while Robert Dinwiddie and Francis Fauquier ruled Virginia.

17. THE COURTHOUSE

On June 10, 1748, the Caroline Court instructed the sheriff to ask permission of the royal government to move the county seat. The location of the original courthouse in the Ideal-Kidds Fork-Shumansville triangle (1953 names) was no longer convenient for a vast majority of the residents of the county due to the growth of trading centers and the establishment of new trade routes. Already some sessions of the court were being held on two other sites; in a room the justices rented from Oliver Towles in Port Royal for 500 pounds of tobacco a year, and at the "late residence of John Martin"; and there were four jails, at the courthouse, in a cellar rented for 200 pounds of tobacco a year from Johnston in lower St. Margaret's Parish, and an outhouse at the "late residence of John Martin."

Caroline magistrates had shown a great interest in the county's first courthouse since it was built around 1732. Who supervised the construction is not known because the building was completed before the first entry in the existing order books of the court. But entries in these documents do reveal in detail many incidents concerning improvements and repairs.

The first extensive alterations of county buildings came in 1736 after the brawls attending the Martin-Gibson election dispute demonstrated the need for a more substantial courthouse and a better equipped jail. At this time the court authorized Henry Armistead, the county lieutenant, to build a chimney for the jail; Samuel Coleman, a local tavern-keeper, who served as jailor, to put iron bars in this chimney and across the courthouse windows; and William Taliaferro and George

Hoomes, two of the justices, to supply the bricks and to purchase the iron bars.

In 1739 the magistrates engaged Charles Bridges, a celebrated English artist visiting in Virginia, to paint a mural of the kings arms on the courthouse walls. This work cost 1,600 pounds of tobacco, which was considerably more than either county clerk or crown attorney drew in annual salaries. But evidently the money was well spent because critics acclaimed the painting the finest of its kind in British America. Unfortunately it has been lost. Not even a facsimile of it remains.

It may have been destroyed in the fire of 1742 which burned the jail and damaged the courthouse. After this disaster the court rented Samuel Coleman's cellar as a temporary jail, and authorized Coleman to build another permanent structure to hold prisoners. But Coleman in order to keep renting his cellar to the county dallied with this job until the court became disgusted with him and turned the completion of the building over to Joseph Stevens, with Thomas Buckner, a magistrate, to supervise his work. John Baylor, another magistrate, took charge of repairing the courthouse. The court instructed him to lay the floor with smooth stone and find glass to mend the windows.

But with all this expenditure for building, repair and art work, it was not until November 2, 1745 that the magistrates got around to purchasing the land on which the county buildings stood. On that day they bargained to buy two acres surrounding the court and jail from Samuel Coleman for 20 pistoles (Spanish gold coins), and directed Robert Farish, a magistrate, to lay out the lot by metes and bounds. But the completion of the deal lagged because the court was unable to get together so much gold, until eventually Coleman agreed to deed the land to the county for 2,000 pounds of tobacco, which was about 7½ per cent less, at the current rate of exchange, than the original asking price. Justices Thomas Buckner, Robert Farish, George Hoomes and John Baylor supervised the improvement of buildings and green as soon as the title passed to the county.

A flourishing community grew up at the county seat. There

were at least three taverns and general stores from the earliest days. One of these establishments was run in turn by Robert Willis, Edward Haswell, Samuel Coleman and Betty Wyatt Coleman, Samuel's widow, who took over after his death; a second by Benjamin Rennolds at first and later by his chief henchman, William Burdette, and the third by John Brown. When court was in session a public market flourished on the green where peddlers, craftsmen and planters offered all manner of merchandise for sale, and where during the court's recesses auction sales were held. Richard Straughn, for many years, was public crier for the county. The most celebrated sale dealt with a race-horse offered by Ephriam Buckner, which both John Micou and John Baylor claimed as the highest bidder. This transaction is reported in detail in the section of this history dealing with sports. The record of the litigation over the ensuing dispute recorded in the Order Books reveals that huge crowds attended sessions of the courts, and that scores which included court officials and jurymen, as well as spectators, were so drunk as "not to be in their good senses"; and that fights which ranged from personal feuds to public brawls were commonplace.

In addition to the jail which was used primarily to hold debtors, accused charged with a capital offense awaiting transportation to Williamsburg for trial before the General Court of the colony and runaway Negro slaves and indentured servants from other counties captured in Caroline, other instruments to punish law-breakers located on the court green included pillory, stocks, whipping-post and scaffold. After Edmund Pendleton became a church warden for Drysdale Parish in 1746 he persuaded the court to set up a ducking pool in nearby Lantor's Pond (Collins in 1953) to afford a more humane way to punish female criminals. But the Order Books contain no record of a woman being sentenced to be ducked.

Pillory and stocks were used sparingly. Only Robert Baber convicted of forgery in 1742 was punished in the pillory; and the Order Books disclose but three instances when the magistrates made use of the stocks. In all these cases this punishment was imposed for disrespect for the court. Thomas Blassingame was the culprit in 1742, and Thomas Lantor in 1742 and 1745. While Blassingame was confined he broke the stocks and ran away. Immediately thereafter the court paid John Brown, the tavern-keeper, five shillings, "to make strong the lock on the stocks on the court green."

The scaffold was only used for Negroes. Whites executed for capital crimes were hung in Williamsburg. Few Negroes were put to death in Caroline while Sir William Gooch ruled Virginia. (See chapter on Negro slavery.)

The whipping-post was the court's favorite instrument for inflicting punishment. Hardly a month passed without numerous public whippings. The culprits punished in this manner included people from all stratas of society; from John Lomax and John Hoomes, who were sons of a Burgess and a sheriff, to white indentured servants and Negro slaves. The number of lashes, always "well laid on the bare back" varied from five for a white woman for having a bastard to thirty-nine for a Negro slave for stealing a hog.

Over the colorful court green while the court was in session waved the county standard, attached to a flagstaff atop the courthouse. Mrs. Betty Wyatt Coleman kept this standard in repair and reputedly designed it. Unfortunately all traces of its pattern are lost.

Governor Gooch failed to act on the magistrates' petition to move the courthouse before he left Virginia. Some of the sessions of the court were held at the old site until the end of his regime. The magistrates did not neglect the care of the public building while they waited for the royal government of the colony to act upon their request. On September 9, 1748, three months after they filed their petition, they directed William Boulware, under-sheriff of the county, to improve the premises by taking out the old windows and installing new sashes with small panes of glass.

18. WESTWARD MIGRATION

In 1748 all Virginia hummed with excitement over the settlement of the West. That year the royal government chartered six companies to develop huge tracts of land on and beyond the frontier. Caroline people played important parts in at least five of these enterprises.

The oldest, and today the best known, of the organizations was the Ohio Company charter to develop a huge tract of land in the vicinity of the site of Pittsburg. John Handbury, a fabulously wealthy Quaker merchant of London, put up the money to finance this undertaking, and the thirteen Virginians who held title to the land, share and share alike, included Lawrence and Augustine Washington, the half brothers of George Washington, Thomas Lee of Stratford, Thomas Nelson of Yorktown, George Fairfax, the heir of Lord Fairfax, and Francis Thornton of Ormesby in Caroline.

The second company, headed by Bernard Moore of Chelsea in King William, a son-in-law of Alexander Spotswood, was chartered to develop 100,000 acres on the New River. Benjamin Hubbard and Duncan Graham, two of the richest merchants in Caroline, were among the ten owners. They put up much of the money to carry out the project. Although neither of these men moved to the raw frontier, several of their sons did, and to this day (1953) their descendants are among the most prominent and affluent people in Southwest Virginia.

Peter Jefferson, the father of Thomas Jefferson, headed a third company which had a grant of 800,000 acres along the North Carolina border (Tennessee in 1953). John Baylor, Francis Thornton, Francis Thornton, Jr., John Thornton, John Dixon, William Hudson and Charles Dix of Caroline were among the forty proprietors.

The fourth company was relatively small. It held only 4,000 acres, which like the lands of the company in which Hubbard and Graham were interested, lay along the New River. Edmund Pendleton and John Madison of Caroline were among the owners, and Madison, who was a magistrate and important personage in his native county, moved to the Southwest.

Samuel Redd of Cedar Vale in Caroline, who had taken over the mercantile business of Samuel Garlick at Chesterfield, was one of the five owners of a company formed to develop 50,000 acres west of the Ohio River. This was the first attempt to make mass settlements beyond that stream, and because of Redd's interest in the enterprise many of the original pioneers who moved into the Midwest were from Caroline County. These settlers included Redds, Temples, Tompkinses, Broadduses and Minors, the children, grandchildren and in-laws of Samuel Redd, the proprietor.

The only company organized to settle western land, which effected Caroline prior to 1748, was one organized in the 1730's by Edward Barradell of James City, who was the most celebrated lawyer of his time and the dean of the Virginia bar. Barradell often practiced in the Caroline Court and married Sarah Fitzhugh of the county. When he secured a grant to 30,000 acres along the Cow Pasture and Calf Pasture rivers in the upper James River Basin, and formed a company to settle this region, he recruited many of the settlers in Caroline while on visits to his wife's relatives.

The granting of large acreages to individuals, however, was an established custom. The Thorntons, Taliaferros, Carrs, Taylors, Baylors and many other pioneer families came into the area to be the county to settle on crown grants, and so long as they and their offspring remained loyal to the crown, the royal governors kept adding to their acreage with additional grants of western land. In the earliest days of the county, Thomas Carr profited most from this generosity. He already owned a large slice of St. Margaret's Parish and a sizable acreage across the North Anna in Hanover when the county was organized, and shortly thereafter he patented jointly with his son-in-laws, John Minor and William Waller, 6,000 acres on the south side of the James in Piedmont Virginia, and 100,000 acres in his own name alone in Goochland, Hanover and Spotsylvania. His descendants which included Dabneys, Minors, Sizors and Wallers, as well as Carrs, took up residence in this territory.

Another prime favorite throughout the Gooch regime was William Woodford of Windsor. Among the lands, the royal governor granted him were huge tracts in Lunenburg County, which in several places extended across the border into the adjacent province of North Carolina. Many of the first white people to settle on this land were from Caroline. Shortly before the Revolution they were joined by John Penn, a lawyer from their native county, who was to achieve eternal fame by signing the Declaration of Independence.

Towards the close of Gooch's rule, Lundsford Lomax of Caroline was the chief recipient in the whole colony of the governor's bounty. He received large grants of crown land along the Pedlar River in Albemarle and Nelson counties. About the time of the formation of the six companies to settle the West, Gooch added to Lomax's holdings 100,000 on "the Dutch Path beyond the mountains." This pushed him into top place for all landlords who resided in Caroline County.

Most grants, however, while substantial were more modest. Francis Conway I, for example, received a grant for 1,000 acres "on the Rapidan, near the mountains" in 1730 on which his son, Robert, went to live; and Walter Chiles received successive grants of 2,000 acres "above the mountains" and 1,800 acres in "Western Goochland," which took many of the Chiles from Caroline.

From the beginning Caroline bred explorers and pioneers as well as land-grabbers. Nathaniel Terry of Caroline was one of the most celebrated Indian fighters along the frontier, and Christopher Gist of Maryland, who accompanied Washington westward in 1753, spent a portion of his youth in the county. Surplus sons of local homesteaders migrated to the West, and the younger sons of the gentry moved on to build new manors in the wilderness. Orange, which contained the closest unsettled land, became a virtual colony of Caroline. John Baylor of New Market, who, among the largest landowners in both counties, spent his summers there to escape the mosquitos and malaria of the Mattapony Valley. At one time during this dual residence he was County Lieutenant for Orange, and magistrate and Burgess for Caroline.

In addition to the Baylors, the Taylors, Madisons, Conways, Stevenses, Buckners, Clarks and Joneses were among the families which did much to develop both Caroline and Orange. In fact people moved so frequently between the two counties that research students have had difficulty in establishing the lineage of many illustrious Americans. Early historians frequently made John Taylor of Caroline a native of Orange, became completely baffled over the birthplace of William Clark and claimed James Madison for Caroline at the expense of King George.

This historian is convinced that John Taylor and William Clark were born in Caroline and that James Madison was born in King George. But after making this statement he wishes to observe that Madison was actually a son of Orange and a grandson of Caroline. His parents were Col. James Madison and Elinor Rose (Nelly) Conway Madison, both of whom were born and grew up in Caroline County. They were married from Mt. Scion, the ancient Conway seat, where Nelly lived with her mother, Rebecca Catlett Conway, who at the time, was the widow of Francis Conway I, and went as a bride and groom to live on lands which Col. James Madison's father, Ambroise Madison, an original magistrate of Caroline, had patented in Orange. Here they remained domiciled for the rest of their lives. After Nelly left home, Rebecca Catlett Conway, the widow, married John Moore, who had taken over Johnathan Gibson's chartered warehouse across the Rappahannock from Port Royal at Gibson's Landing (Port Conway in 1953) in King George, and went to live with her new husband. Nelly Conway Madison was visiting her mother when her fourth child, James, who was to become the fourth president of the United States, was born. She remained with her mother only a few months after his birth, when she returned to Orange, where James Madison became domiciled, and remained domiciled, during his long eventual life.

Tradition holds that the residence of John and Rebecca Catlett Conway Moore was a small house located on the banks of the Rappahannock at Port Conway, which fell into the river about forty years ago, due to erosion, and most modern historians have accepted this as fact. But many early authorities, including Charles Campbell, whom numerous critics consider the most authentic historian of Virginia prior to the Civil War, give Caroline County as the place of Madison's birth. (Charles Campbell: *History of the Colony and Ancient Dominion of Virginia,* page 704.)

The Rule of Dinwiddie

I. THE INTERLUDE

THIRTY months elapsed between the departure of Sir William Gooch and the arrival of Robert Dinwiddie, his successor as Deputy Governor. During this interim, John Robinson, Sr., Thomas Lee and Lewis Burwell served successively as Chief of State by virtue of their positions as presidents of the Governor's Council. These three did little to interfere with the administration of local government. Robinson was remembered in Caroline for his friendship for Oliver Towles, Lee for attempting to enforce the tobacco laws and Burwell the statutes compelling attendance at services of the established religion.

No sooner was Robinson in office than he sent his personal attorney, Obediah Merriott of King and Queen, to Caroline to help Oliver Towles, who had languished in jails for over a year either because he refused to surrender all his assets, which consisted mostly of uncollected accounts, to a trustee for distribution to his creditors and take the poor debtor's oath, or because his chief creditor, the vindictive Thomas Hoard, persuaded the court to refuse to accept his oath. The record is not clear on this issue.

Merriott was a crafty lawyer. He was to achieve fame or infamy a few years later for his advice to his original patron's son, John Robinson, Jr., which lead the younger Robinson, who was treasurer of the colony at the time, to lend to friends, rather than to burn, redeemed treasurer's notes. This resulted in the greatest scandal in the history of the colony.

But Merriott did not have to resort to tricks to secure the release of Towles. Hoard's death simplified matters. James Mills, the surviving partner, and Luke Burford, who took over Hoard's interest in the firm, were more lenient men. They agreed to sanction Towles' freedom, when Robert Gilchrist and James Bowie, renewed their offer to go security for his debts. After Towles' release Robinson Sr. ordered Charles Carter, the Secretary of the Colony, to pay him a fee and to reimburse him for expenses for his part in setting up the town of Port Royal, to supply the capital on which to get a new start in life. The acting governor, also arranged an apprenticeship for Towles' son, Oliver Jr., with Obediah Merriott, and gained for that youth the opportunity to study law under one of the most skillful lawyers in the colony.

Thomas Lee, the builder of Stratford and father of the Lees of Revolutionary fame, was a large planter and trader. He believed that prosperity depended on strict enforcement of the laws to limit the tobacco produced for export, and in keeping with his belief ordered county courts to force all constables to make oath that they had visited every plantation in their precincts and determined if the laws stinting the number of plants under cultivation and banning the tending of seconds were being obeyed before paying them for their services. In Caroline, constables, George Hoomes, Jr., Robert Dudley, and William Herndon, refused to make this oath and forfeited their fees. Afterwards Hoomes and Dudley lost their positions but Herndon changed his mind and in order to keep his post made a careful inspection of his precinct and arrested John Smith, Thomas Pittman, Mordecai Abraham, William DeShazo, James Mastin and Titus Stevens for tending seconds. Other constables arrested Simon Poe, William Watson, John Blanton, William Bullard, Barnabas Arthur, Richard Powell and Drury Smith for the same offense. While these charges were pending, John Wiley sponsored a petition asking the royal government to change the law in favor of the small planters and homesteaders. But the Burgesses were not in session and Lee refused to take action. All the accused were fined. The next spring constables rearrested Bullard and Pittman, along with John Daniel and Ann Sanders for violating the statute stinting the number of tobacco plants which might be set out for each tithable, but a jury made up of Caroline small planters and homesteaders, angered by Lee's attempts at strict enforcement, refused to convict them.

Lewis Burwell, scion of a great English family transplanted to Virginia, had watched with disgust Gooch's lax attitude towards the enforcement of the laws compelling all free persons to attend services of the established religion, which he along with his fellow members of the great landlord caste regarded as a bulwark of the existing order. Immediately after he became governor he took steps to correct this situation. His actions led to the fining of ten persons in Caroline "for failing to frequent their parish church for a period of two months." This was the largest number fined for this offense at a single session of the local court since Margaret Connor used the law to indulge in personal spites. Those punished were in no sense from the riffraff. They included Mary Catlett, a member of one of the county's most cultured families, John Bowie, a thrifty planter and brother of the celebrated James Bowie, John Miller, a constable and leading business man of Port Royal, William Parker, who in a few years was to become a king's magistrate, and Thomas Hackett, a Quaker, whom the court had no right to fine.

Burwell had close relatives in Caroline. Some of his grandchildren, the children of his daughter, Martha, and Col. John Martin, lived in the county. But he showed them no favors while he was acting governor, although one of them, John Martin, Jr., who practiced law at the local bar, was in position to benefit from appointment to public office.

In the interim between deputy governors, King George II bestowed upon a part time resident of Caroline County the greatest honor he was able to grant a Virginia subject. On May 7, 1750 he made Richard Corbin a member of the Governor's Council. This body was the colonial House of Lords. It acted both as the upper chamber of the legislative assembly and as the supreme court of the colony. The king appointed all members and they held office at his pleasure. They never numbered more than a dozen and by virtue of their positions, were the most powerful men in Virginia, since they were able to override the will of the people by refusing to join the Burgesses in passing legislation. In addition to the other perogatives which went with the office, the pay was excellent, 600 pounds sterling a year, which was one-fifth as much as the salary of the deputy governor in residence.

Richard Corbin was born in King and Queen but spent much of his time at "The Reeds," his plantation in Caroline's lower St. Margaret's Parish. His career as a councillor was marked by a slavish devotion to the crown. Stirring speeches in praise of the king and the king's deputies in Virginia, form the bulk of the record of his activities, in office. But this conduct, while distressing to small planters, homesteaders and merchants, made him in time the leader of the royalist faction in the colony.

2. ROBERT DINWIDDIE, HIS BACKGROUND AND PROGRAM

Robert Dinwiddie was a new type of deputy governor for Virginia. He was the only trained civil servant to hold this office in the history of the colony. A well-educated Scotchman of the minor gentry, he began his career as a clerk in a West Indian customs house, and through successive promotions became Surveyor General of Customs for all His Majesty's colonies before coming to Virginia as commissioned representative of the crown in residence. For the first three years of his rule he acted as deputy for William Anne Keppel, Earl of Albemarle, and later for John Campbell, the Earl of Loudoun, neither of whom left Great Britain while "Captain General and Governor of Virginia." But for all of Dinwiddie's faithful service to his king, and acting for nobility, George II failed to reward him, not even with a knighthood. He died plain "mister."

The colonist from great landlord to homesteader did not know what to expect from this new type of governor. But Dinwiddie's first speech after he reached Williamsburg did much to reassure all classes. He announced that the primary objective of his regime was to improve the personnel of the courts and to speed up litigation, and to encourage a more rapid settlement of the frontier.

No new magistrates had been appointed since Gooch left Virginia thirty months before and in most counties there were many vacancies due to deaths and removals. Caroline's normal panel of twenty-four had dropped to sixteen. To bring this back to its maximum Dinwiddie made Edmund Pendleton,

Edward Dixon, Robert Gilchrist, Waller Chiles, John Sutton, William Buckner, Peter Copeland and Joseph Hoomes, magistrates.

Pendleton, Dixon, Gilchrist and Copeland were the first magistrates to sit on the Caroline court, since Francis Conway and Richard Mauldin, who derived the major portion of their income from sources other than agriculture. Their appointments brought to the local judicial-legislative body, men equipped by training and experience to deal with a variety of matters concerning which the old type of magistrate was ignorant. Pendleton, an excellent lawyer, was able to advise on the technical application of the law, and Dixon, Gilchrist and Copeland, all successful merchants, the customs and usages of trade, which in recent years had become of such vital importance to the county's economy.

Waller Chiles was the first Quaker to serve on the Caroline court, and John Sutton represented the ever increasing number of small freeholders, who had become great planters. The new appointments, however, did not revolutionize the court. It remained safely in hands of the county's larger landlords and established families, among the new justices, Waller Chiles, William Buckner and Joseph Hoomes, who were all descendants of patentees with large grants in the area, years before Caroline became a county, and all of them and one or more close relatives, who were, or had been magistrates. The Taliaferros, Buckners, Thorntons, Taylors, Hoomeses, Baylors, Lomaxes and Woodfords, with thirteen of the twenty-four seats, still controlled the court.

Dinwiddie handled the advancement of settlement along the western frontier with equal political finesse. He granted 500,-000 additional acres to the Ohio Company and became a full partner in that enterprise. He proposed that public funds be expended to encourage friendly relations with the Indians of the interior to reduce the hazards of pioneering for homesteaders along the frontier.

To get funds for government aid to carry out this project Dinwiddie had to call the Burgesses together. The legislative assembly of the colony had not met since Sir William Gooch left Virginia, and that royal governor had dissolved the lower chamber immediately before his departure. Elections were mandatory before a new session.

Lundsford Lomax, who had been a Burgess from Caroline for a decade, managed to survive this contest, but the freeholders of the county replaced John Baylor with Edmund Pendleton as their second representative. Conservatives still regarded Pendleton an upstart, and hooted at the affrontery of this skilled but rustic lawyer, with no better education than the training Benjamin Robinson was able to give him as an apprentice in the local clerk's office, and without means except his slender savings and the small inheritance he gained from his first wife, Betty Roy, challenging the urbane, Cambridge-educated master of New Market plantation, who owned thousands of acres scattered throughout the colony and, who was known both in Virginia and abroad for his fine stable of thoroughbred race-horses. But Pendleton turned Baylor's attributes in the eyes of the rich to handicaps in the eyes of the poor, and after a stirring campaign convinced homesteaders, small planters and traders that Baylor was too rich, too well-educated and too aristocratic, and spent much of his time away from New Market at his plantation in Orange, to be familiar enough with their problems to represent them properly as a Burgess.

The first session of the legislative assembly of Dinwiddie's regime, which met on February 27, 1752, was one of the most constructive in the history of the colony. Because of the good will which existed between Governor and Burgesses many laws were passed which brought long needed reforms. To finance Dinwiddie's program to strengthen the militia and improve relations with the Indians, to help the settlers along the western frontier and to raise additional revenue to pay off the debt which remained for rebuilding the capitol after the fire of 1747, the legislative assembly renewed the 5 per cent tax on the purchase price of Negro slaves brought into the colony. Homesteaders and artesians, who resented the competition of slave labor and the intelligentsia, who looked with disfavor on a feudalistic society, welcomed this law as a check on the ever increasing stream of Negro slaves being brought into the colony each year. Because times were prosperous no other tax measure was needed.

Immediately before the session adjourned on April 20, 1752, the Burgesses with the Council concurring voted the governor a gratuity of 500 pounds sterling out of the public funds, as a token of their esteem.

3. LOMAX AND PENDLETON AS BURGESSES

Lomax and Pendleton promptly established themselves as leaders of the House of Burgesses of 1752. Of the 104 men which composed that body, two each from the 50 counties, and one from the city of Jamestown, the borough of Norfolk, the town of Williamsburg and the college of William and Mary, respectively, they held more committee assignments than any other two members. They both had seats on the eleven-member committees on Privileges and Elections and the thirty-one member committee on Grievances. Pendleton gained for a Caroline Burgess a place on the powerful eleven-member committee on Courts of Justice for the first time since the death of Richard Buckner in 1734, and Lomax became chairman of the eleven-member Committee on Trade. All told Caroline had a representative on every standing committee except one.

As chairman of the committee on trade, Lomax introduced and secured the passage of bills to build a lighthouse at Cape Henry, to prohibit the importation of Madeira wine in pipes in sizes less than standard gauge, to fix standards and to provide for the inspection of hogsheads, staves and shingles manufactured in the colony for export, to prevent ships from dumping ballast into naviable streams, to force counties to keep standard units of measure at their clerk's offices to check the accuracy of units in use commercially, and to provide for the inspection of beef, pork, turpentine, tar and pitch. When these bills became laws, the Caroline Court appointed John Miller and Daniel Triplett to bring ashore the ballast from ships, which docked at Caroline wharves along the Rappahannock, John Boutwell and Adam Lindsay to be inspectors of beef, pork, turpentine, tar and pitch, and Edward Dixon to send for one bushel, one-half bushel, one peck standard measures and brass ell and yardsticks to be kept at the courthouse by William Johnston, the jailor.

As a member of the committee on Courts of Justice, Pendleton successfully sponsored legislation to force the owners of indentured servants accused of crime to pay the cost of prosecution, to make mandatory the release of poor debtors from prison within twenty days after they took the pauper's oath, to improve the condition of the jails, and to inspect and audit the clerk's offices. After these statutes went into effect the Caroline magistrates ordered William Boulware, undersheriff of the county, to recondition the courthouse jail, and after he finished this work directed William Johnston, the jailor, to equip it with chamber pots, purchased with county funds. This is the first effort at public sanitation in the history of the county. The magistrates named three of their number, William Taliaferro, Edward Dixon and Robert Gilchrist to examine the records in the Clerk's Office, the first audit of public accounts in Caroline. Lomax and Pendleton, jointly and with other members of the Committee on Privileges and Election, secured passage of legislation to prohibit the sale of alcoholic beverages on election day. Some form of this law has remained on the statute books of Virginia until this time (1953).

As members of the committee on Grievances the Caroline Burgesses were not so fortunate. They succeeded in getting out of committee and through the House a bill incorporating the recommendations in Wiley's petition for revising the tobacco stint laws to favor families who tilled their own soil. But this bill never became a law. It was defeated in the Governor's Council.

Lomax and Pendleton also sponsored considerable local legislation. Perhaps their most important bill provided for the improvement of navigation on the Mattapony from Aylett's Warehouse to Burke's Bridge. When the bill became a law the governor named Lomax, Pendleton, Richard Corbin, John Baylor, Thomas Turner, John Robinson, Henry Robinson and Thomas Johnston, directors in charge of the operations. Another joint local bill established a ferry across the Rappa-

hannock from Nicholas Battaile's in Caroline, to Anderson
Donivan's in King George. A third prohibited sheep and swine
from running at large in the town of Port Royal. But the
Burgesses cut out the section banning sheep, and the Governor's
Council, who had more sympathy for a man trying to raise
domestic animals than a man trying to build a town, killed
the whole bill.

On some issues Lomax and Pendleton did not see eye to eye.
Lomax was heavily in debt although he was among the largest
landowners in Virginia. A rising market was his only hope to
stay solvent and throughout his legislative career he sponsored
and supported measures which lead to inflation. Pendleton, a
conservative lawyer, believed in a sound currency. But Pendleton was not adverse to voting against the public interest to
conserve John Roy's estate, in which, through inheritances
from his wife, Betty Roy, he had an undivided interest. He
managed to defeat a bill sponsored by Lomax to permit Edward Dixon, Duncan Graham, Robert Gilchrist, James Bowie
and other merchants in Port Royal to operate a free ferry
from that town across the Rappahannock to the lands of Col.
Thomas Turner, in King George, because the free ferry threatened to destroy his source of revenue from the toll ferry
owned by Roy's estate. He also successfully opposed bills to
set up a tobacco warehouse on the land of his old patron,
Benjamin Robinson, on the Rappahannock between Port Royal
and Portobago, and a ferry between the estates of John Micou
in Caroline and Leedstown, in Westmoreland.

Roy's Warehouse had more business than it was able to
handle. The Caroline court had forced Thomas Roy, who was
in charge, to construct additional buildings. James Jameson
and John Evins, the tobacco inspectors, sometimes permitted
tobacco to stay in storage for two years before they had time
to grade and process it for shipment overseas. Jameson and
Evins had petitioned the governor for extra help and been
turned down. To remedy the situation the planters who lived
to the south and the east of Port Royal asked Lundsford
Lomax, who was their neighbor, to secure passage of a law to
set up another warehouse on Robinson's land. Pendleton op-

posed this bill because the new proposed warehouse threatened to take business away from Roy's. After he succeeded in defeating the bill, he managed to secure the passage of laws providing for a third inspector at Roy's and forcing the inspectors at that warehouse to grade and process all tobacco within eighteen months of the time that it was brought for storage, as sops to placate his aroused constituents in the lower end of the county. When these laws went into effect Jameson and Evins promptly asked pay increases although they now had James Boutwell to help them with their work. The royal governor turned down their request.

Before Caroline became a county a ferry ran for a time from the region immediately above Portobago Bay across the Rappahannock, and was abandoned because of lack of travel. But with the growth of Leedstown as a commercial center in the mid-eighteenth century there was a demand for its restoration and Lomax obligingly introduced a bill in the House of Burgesses to accomplish this purpose. Pendleton, however, blocked its passage, because he wanted no new routes of transportation to draw trade away from Roy's Warehouse and traffic from the Port Royal ferry.

Pendleton also used his skill as a lawyer to draw bills to dock the sales of entailed land, which he pushed through the House of Burgesses. Many of the people for whom he did this work were not his constituents, and while there are no records to prove that he charged them a fee, it follows logically that this was another of his extra-curricula activities to earn money while a Burgess.

4. THE FRENCH AND INDIAN WAR

The colonists' admiration for Robert Dinwiddie was shortlived. It ended immediately after the first session of the legislative assembly of his regime adjourned, when he announced a pistole (Spanish gold coin worth about $3.50 in U. S. currency before the Federal Government cut the gold content of the dollar) for affixing his signature and seal to all land patents. Almost a thousand applications for crown grants had accumulated in the office of the Secretary of the Colony because there had been no commissioned representative, of the crown, in Virginia, to sign and pass valid title, since Sir William Gooch left the colony. Technically Dinwiddie was within his rights to make this charge but the colonists did not see it that way. They classed the fees, which promised to bring the governor a sizeable fortune, as outright graft. As soon as the policy was announced Lundsford Lomax, Burgess from Caroline, and one of the most frequent patentees of the crown land in Virginia, wrote to Dinwiddie and asked "is the payment of the fee demanded by your direction, and if it is please acquaint us with the authority that empowers you to make same?"

While the storm over the pistole fee swept the colony, Dinwiddie found himself in desperate need of money. The French threatened to take over the Ohio Valley and the public treasury was without funds to equip an army to meet this threat. The 5% tax on the purchase price of slaves failed to yield the anticipated revenue. Before the passage of the act, an average of sixty Negro youths under the age of sixteen, recently imported from Africa, had been registered in the Caroline Court alone each year, but the year after passage not a single young Negro was registered. Alexander Rose (Ross), a Port Royal lawyer and tavern-keeper, who speculated in slaves as a sideline, went to jail because he sold Negroes short to Robert Garrett, a tavern-keeper and merchant at Conway's warehouse, and James Mills, a Port Royal merchant, and was unable to make deliveries.

As a last resort before calling the Burgesses back into session and asking them to levy additional taxes for defense, the governor decided to send a message with a letter to the commander of the French forces marching southward from the Great Lakes and warn him that region was part of Virginia. Dinwiddie selected the youthful George Washington for this mission.

Dr. Douglas S. Freeman surmises that Washington crossed Caroline County in the early stages of this trip. Entering the county from King William and proceeding by way of Burke's Bridge to the Spotsylvania line in the vicinity of Corbin, Washington's companion and guide was Christopher Gist, who was a native of Maryland, but who, from records in the Caroline Order Books, spent much of his early life in Caroline County with a relative, Samuel Gist. Because of this Pendleton asked the House of Burgesses to pay Christopher Gist a gratuity for his work in connection with the mission.

After a journey fraught with peril, Washington and Gist, made their way through the wilderness beyond Alexandria, and reached the headquarters of the French commander, located about 40 miles south of Lake Erie. The French commander received them politely, but his reply to Dinwiddie's letter was a firm denial that the French were encroaching on Virginia's territory.

With this information before him, the Virginia governor had no alternative but to call the Burgesses together and ask for money, or surrender the whole Ohio Valley to the French. The second session of the legislative assembly of Dinwiddie's regime accomplished little. The Burgesses refused to raise taxes and spent their time assailing the governor for imposing the pistole fee. This attack was led, in a large measure, by Edmund Pendleton. When Dinwiddie refused to give ground, the Burgesses took matters in their own hands and arranged to send Peyton Randolph to London to plead their cause before the Board of Trade, which had final control of the colony's affairs. The governor indignantly vetoed an appropriation to bear the expense of this mission and adjourned the legislative assembly. But before the Burgesses left Williamsburg they met in rump session and voted to underwrite the expense of Randolph's trip from the public treasury.

Settlers from Virginia continued to move into the Ohio Valley although the Burgesses failed to finance the strengthening of military forces for their protection. Tales of their massacre by Indians instigated by the French drifting back to the settled sections of the colony so aroused the people that public sentiment forced the Burgesses and governor to iron out enough of their disagreements to act. When the Burgesses met for their third session of Dinwiddie's rule they agreed to appropriate 10,000 pounds sterling for the defense of the western frontier. This money was to be made available at once through issuing bonds for five years, bearing interest at six per cent. The bonds were to be redeemed by taxes on ordinaries, slaves, wheeled vehicles and legal documents. This appropriation was far short of the amount that Dinwiddie asked and not enough to equip an adequate force. Finally, the Burgesses hamstrung its effectiveness by writing into the appropriation act the provision that none of the money was to be spent except with the consent of a committee from the House of Burgesses. Edmund Pendleton was a member of this committee.

Dinwiddie gained the Committee of Burgesses' approval to use this limited appropriation to equip a small body of militia which he placed under the command of George Washington and sent to defend the western frontier. Washington built a small fort at Great Meadows about forty miles to the east of the main French fortification in the fork of the Ohio which he called Ft. Necessity. He was unable to hold this position. The French seized his fort but let him withdraw his troops to the settled region of Virginia.

At least three residents of Caroline County accompanied Washington on this expedition; William Woodford, Henry Wyatt and John Ogelby (Ogeltrie). Woodford, son of William Woodford, the first sheriff, and long time magistrate of Caroline, was a young officer in the militia. His valorous conduct on this campaign was the beginning of one of the most distinguished military careers in the annals of Virginia. His ability attracted Washington, who was two years his senior, and led to a close association which lasted until his death in the closing years of the Revolution. He became one of Washington's most trusted lieutenants and a distant connection through marriage.

Henry Wyatt was a soldier in the ranks. His name is recorded because he lost his life in battle, and his will was subsequently proven in the Order Books of the Caroline County. So far as this author has been able to determine, Wyatt was the first resident of Caroline to be killed by an enemy while in uniform on the field of battle. John Ogelby (Ogeltrie) was another soldier in the ranks. A record of his services exists because he complained to the Caroline Court that he was discharged from the militia, after he lost his health from "constant duty" under Washington at Great Meadows; and asked that the court authorize the payment of his back pay and grant him relief for physical disabilities. The court granted these requests and he became the first resident of Caroline to receive a pension for military service.

The loss of Ft. Necessity caused only a ripple of excitement in Caroline. The people were too engrossed with domestic economic problems to be upset by the adverse fortunes of war on the distant frontier. The new struggle between England and France had closed the markets of Europe to their tobacco and the worst drought "within the memory of the living" gripped the land. They had exhausted their tobacco certificates and were without prospects for more. All classes from great planters to head righters were having a hard time finding the means to survive. Regular taxes were in arrears and new levies ignored.

Sussannah White, John Carneal and John Dyer let their tavern licenses lapse because of the tax on ordinaries, and Thomas Roy sold the public house which he inherited from his mother, Dorothy, in Port Royal to Benjamin Long. The next year Long failed on account of the added tax and the decline of business due to the drought and lack of shipping brought on by the war in that port town. Bootleggers moved in to fill the demand for alcoholic beverages which arose from the closing of taverns. The Caroline Court convicted John Penn (not the Signer of the Declaration of Independence) for selling rum contrary to laws and John Kitcham for retailing cider without a license.

The Caroline sheriff made no attempt to collect the new tax on wheels, and few owners of luxury vehicles volunteered to pay these levies. They remained in arrears until 1762 when Francis Fauquier, who succeeded Dinwiddie as governor, forced their collection by ordering the local courts to indite all delinquent taxpayers. The list of the indited reads like "who is who" in Caroline for the decade 1752-62. It included almost everyone of social prominence or wealth; John Baylor, Burgess, magistrate, colonel in the militia and apparently the only owner of a chariot in the county, and the following owners of chaises; Benjamin Robinson, the county clerk, George Muse, the county lieutenant, Lundsford Lomax, Burgess and magistrate, Robert Taliaferro, magistrate, Richard Buckner, magistrate and sheriff, William Buckner, magistrate, Thomas Buckner, magistrate and sheriff, Edward Dixon, Port Royal merchant, magistrate and sheriff, James Miller, Port Royal merchant and magistrate, Robert Gilchrist, Port Royal merchant, magistrate and sheriff, James Jameson, magistrate and tobacco inspector, John Thornton, magistrate, Francis Taylor, magistrate and merchant, John Sutton, magistrate and sheriff, John Baynham, physician and magistrate, Harry Beverley, magistrate, George Guy, magistrate, Waller Chiles, magistrate and Quaker leader, Thomas Roy, proprietor of Roy's chartered warehouse, Sarah Conway, widow of Francis Conway II, proprietor of Conway's chartered warehouse, John Miller, tobacco inspector, tavern-keeper and under-sheriff, John Boutwell, tobacco inspector, John Evans, tobacco inspector, William Allcocke, tobacco inspector, Ambrose Hoard, planter, William Micou, planter, Lawrence Taliaferro, planter, Thomas Royston, planter, George Catlett, planter, Thomas Collins, planter, Benjamin Catlett, planter, Thomas Samuel, planter, William Taylor, planter, John Clark, planter, Joseph Woolfolk, planter, Francis Fleming, planter, George Holloway, planter, Thomas Scott, planter, Seth Thornton, planter, Thomas Landrum, lawyer, Rev. Musgrave Dawson, rector of St. Mary's Parish, Thomas Terry, officer in the militia and explorer, John Scott, officer in the militia, William Stevens, officer in the militia, William Johnston, tavern-keeper and jailor, John Thilman, tavern-keeper, John Allmond, tavern-keeper, Duncan Graham, Port Royal merchant and developer of the West, John Elliott Payne, merchant of lower Drysdale Parish, six other widows in addition to Sarah Conway; Mary Buckner, Ann Taliaferro, Mary Gillison, Mary Taliaferro, Elizabeth Riddle, Sarah Slaughter, and Elizabeth Marshall, and Benjamin Milwerd(?) and William Larkem(?), whom this author has been unable to identify.

The unpopular tax laws made numerous magistrates reluctant to serve on their county courts. Robert Farish, who had served longer than any justice in Caroline with the exceptions of William Woodford and Lundsford Lomax, quit; John Baylor, the best educated magistrate, stayed away from sessions and Waller Chiles resigned because he was a Quaker and the Quakers opposed war. This coupled with the deaths of Arch MacPhearson, George Hoomes, John Taliaferro, John Taylor and Thomas Wild, the removal from the county of Rice Curtis, the frequent absences of Edmund Pendleton and Lundsford Lomax to attend sessions of the House of Burgesses, and the sad plight of William Woodford, who after one of the most distinguished careers in the history of the county had grown senile in his old age and was in constant trouble with his white indentured servant girls, made it difficult to get enough magistrates together to hold a session of the court. In an attempt to remedy this situation Caroline's conscientious magistrates, Richard Buckner, Thomas Johnston, Edward Dixon, William Taliaferro, Robert Gilchrist, Francis Taylor, Peter Copeland and Joseph Hoomes, met in a special session to make recommendations to the governor for additional appointments to their court. This proved a stormy meeting. The justices fell out over the qualifications of Edmund Taylor, a tavern-keeper, to be magistrate. In the end they left his name off the proposed slate and nominated Anthony Thornton, William Taliaferro, Jr., and James Jameson, whom the governor immediately approved.

Conditions which prevailed in Caroline were general throughout the colony. Dinwiddie was unable to make the people realize the seriousness of the threat from the French and the Indians along the frontier. When he called the Burgesses into session he only got additional abuses for imposing the pistole fee. The lawmakers refused to add extra taxes for defense. Finally as a last resort he laid his problems before the crown and the government of George II answered with a positive program.

The Board of Trade settled the pistole dispute. It held that Dinwiddie was within his rights in charging a fee, but at the same time it abrogated all fees on patents applied for before the governor announced the charge and prohibited the charging of fees for issuing patents on all land west of the Blue Ridge, and all grants of less than 100 acres east of the mountains, in the future. This ruling while saving Dinwiddie's face, effectively nullified the practice. In addition the crown sent 10,000 pounds in specie to bolster the colony's finances and promised an expeditionary force to drive the French out of the Ohio Valley.

In return for these considerations Dinwiddie asked the Burgesses to levy 20,000 pounds in additional taxes for defense, and to draft every tenth man into the militia. The lawmakers were grateful for the concessions and inclined to coöperate but they were not grateful enough to grant the governor his full program. They halved the appropriation requested, changed the draft law to read "every man without visible means of support," and retained the committee of their own members to control the expenditures for defense, which Dinwiddie found so distasteful.

Pendleton, who kept his seat on this committee, was soon at loggerheads with the governor again. Dinwiddie wanted to send Virginia troops and military stores for the defense of Ft. Cumberland, which after the fall of Ft. Necessity was the only barrier between the French and Virginia's Potomac and Shenandoah Valleys. Pendleton blocked this move. He argued that since Ft. Cumberland was in Maryland that colony was solely responsible for its garrison and supplies.

On another matter Pendleton was not so shortsighted. He drew and pushed to passage a bill to reorganize, train and equip the Virginia militia. This act set up a hard core of native troops to defend the colony in the darkest days of the French and Indian War, and who, at a later date, formed the nucleus of Virginia's contribution to the Continental Army during the Revolution.

The announcement that Gen. Edward Braddock was about to sail for Virginia with a force of British regulars to drive the French out of the Ohio Valley brought the first burst of enthusiasm for the French and Indian War in that colony. The

Virginians hoped that this expedition was going to bring a quick end to the war and reopen the seas for safe shipment of their tobacco to the trans-Atlantic markets. The Burgesses quickly appropriated 10,000 pounds to equip the colonial militia to fight with Braddock, and to make these funds available at once, ordered the Secretary of the Colony to issue legal tender notes, to be funded prior to June 30, 1756 through annual taxes of one pound of tobacco on tithable Negroes and 15 pence on 100 acres of land and additional duty on rum.

Lomax as chairman of the Committee on Trade guided the tax bills to passage in the House of Burgesses, and Pendleton as an anti-inflationary measure attached a rider to make the new government notes good for payment of all debts of the colony and its political subdivisions, including the salaries of Burgesses and other officers. This rider lead directly to the Parson's Case nine years later. In addition Pendleton also secured the passage of a law to garrison Ft. Duquesne militiamen after it was captured by the British regulars to forestall the Pennsylvanians, who also claimed the territory in which the fort was located, from moving in.

Pendleton was too optimistic in securing the passage of the last mentioned act. The stories of Braddock's defeat in the wilderness and Washington's ensuing heroism are among the best known incidents in American history. Of the 1,000 colonial troops who went with the British general on this ill-fated expedition this author has been able to identify only one who was from Caroline. He was Edward Goodwin "late soldier of the Virginia regiment whom the House of Burgesses voted a gift of five pounds and awarded an annuity of the same amount for life because he behaved himself well in the campaign with Gen. Braddock against Ft. Duquesne and because he is unfit for further military service due to a wound which he received in battle."

After Braddock's defeat Dinwiddie rushed the militia to the frontier to hold back the French and to check the rampaging Indians. The Caroline unit under the command of William Woodford, son of the county's first sheriff, William Woodford, drew an assignment in Frederick County, which at the time extended to a boundless western frontier. Here they built and garrisoned a stronghold called Ft. Mindenhall (Order Books of the Caroline Court). Anthony Thornton, James Taylor, Jr., James Taylor, the younger, Eusabious Stone and Benjamin Robinson, Jr., were junior officers and Woodford's lieutenants in this command.

A chastened House of Burgesses voted an additional issue of 40,000 pounds in legal tender notes for defense. They scheduled this new issue to be redeemed in four years by continuing the fifteen pence per 100 per annum tax on land, the pound of tobacco tax on Negro tithables and extending the head tax to include tithable whites. They also passed laws to pay bounties for enlistments, and the procuring of enlistments in the armed forces, for the punishment of deserters and a ten-pound award for a hostile Indian's scalp.

Unfortunately the governor and Burgesses had a drought and an economic depression as well as a war with which to contend. The great drought of 1754 became even more severe in 1755, Edmund Pendleton and Benjamin Waller introduced a bill in the House of Burgesses "to limit the price and regulate the supply of Indian corn." Later that year the General Court granted Samuel Hargrave and Roger Quarles permission to build milldams across the main channel of the North Anna for the first time, because the water heads of the ponds in Caroline and Hanover counties were too low to furnish power to grind flour and meal. These measures failed to bring relief. When Benjamin Long and John Powell, both of whom had been men of property in Caroline County, were brought to trial in the fall of 1755 for breaking into the house of a widow, Jane Cooper, their defense before the court was that they were hungry and merely looking for food.

Many colonists moved to the frontier where there was adequate rainfall, preferring the hazards of life among the Indians to the drought. In Caroline the chief participants in this mass migration were the Quakers. Scores of families of that sect left their homes in upper St. Margaret's Parish to pioneer in Bedford (now Campbell) County. Much of the correspondence between the daughter meeting house on South

River in Bedford, and the parent meeting house at Golansville, in Caroline, is preserved in *Our Quaker Friends of Ye Olden Times* published by Bell Bros. of Lynchburg. The letters from Caroline are all dated Golansville and signed by Samuel Hargrave, the Secretary of the Meeting. This data indicates that Golansville has the fourth oldest name held by any postoffice in Caroline County today (1953). Being anteceded only by Guinea, Port Royal and Bowling Green, and at that time Bowling Green was only a plantation and not a community.

Other colonists moved west without their families and earned their livelihood from bounties on hostile Indian's scalps rather than from the crops they grew in the new country. Nathaniel Terry was the best known of these adventurers from Caroline County. The House of Burgesses awarded him special gratuities "for taking several persons disguised as Indians, who robbed and plundered the inhabitants along the frontier," in addition to the bounties he gained for scalping redskins.

Less hardy colonists did not bother to go to the frontier to attempt to take advantage of the new laws awarding bounties. Alexander Sweeney "the common cheat," who only a few years before had been convicted for selling "gold bricks" on the streets of Port Royal, procured a commission from the governor to recruit soldiers. After a few months' "work" he presented the Secretary of the Colony a bill for twenty-seven pounds sterling "for expenses and bounties for recruits." A committee from the House of Burgesses investigated this claim and was unable to find a single soldier whom he induced to enlist. But again "the common cheat" on account of his glib tongue managed to escape punishment although he lost his bounties.

The most celebrated case of recruiting for bounty in Caroline centered around the enlistment of twelve and one-half year old Samuel Duval, the apprentice of Gabriel Mitchell, a carpenter. Duval became dissatisfied with his apprentiseship and ran away from his master. While he was in hiding he made contact with Richard Johnston, who was authorized to make enlistments, through Abraham Mitchell, a tavern-keeper, his master's brother, and joined the army. After his induction he was shipped immediately to a battalion on the western frontier, where he distinguished himself for bravery under fire in spite of his tender years. But he did not stay at the front very long because Gabriel Mitchell found out where he was and had him brought back to Caroline as a fugitive apprentice. A lengthy trial ensued in the local court. Johnson swore that he was ignorant of the youth's age and apprenticeship and enlisted him because "he looked like an able bodied man fit to be a soldier." Young Duval testified that he considered his apprenticeship forfeited because his master forced him to spend all his time "tending tobacco and corn" and made no attempt to teach him carpentry. The magistrates believed both witnesses. They let Johnson keep his bounty and ordered Duval to return to his battalion. Only the Mitchells suffered; Gabriel lost an apprentice and the court fined Abraham twenty shillings because he knew all the facts and acted as go-between.

Few Caroline residents shared young Duval's enthusiasm for a military career. One man, at least, attempted to escape service through violence. He was Benjamin Tankersley, who threatened the life of George Muse, the county lieutenant, when Muse ordered his induction into the armed forces. The Caroline Court convicted Tankersley of "notorious breach of the peace" because of this crime and placed him in the custody of the sheriff until he posted two bonds for the huge amount of 25,000 pounds sterling each. Tankersley made no effort to find bondsmen. He preferred incarceration in the county jail to fighting on the frontier.

Desertions by men in uniform were frequent. The most notorious which involved a resident of Caroline County was that of Benjamin Catlett, who quit his battalion at Ft. Mindenhall and returned to his home. William Woodford, who was in command of Ft. Mindenhall, sent two of his lieutenants, Anthony Thornton and James Taylor, Jr., to Caroline with orders to arrest Catlett and bring him back to his duty station for trial by court martial. But the fugitive after his arrest managed to get his case before the local civil court, and at the ensuing trial the magistrates exonerated him of desertion and ordered his release from the militia on the grounds that further service imposed an undue hardship upon him and his family.

The magistrates were sympathetic with Catlett because a majority of them were in a position similar to his: men of property going broke. They wanted to give him a chance to straighten out his finances before it was too late. British merchants were about to take over Virginia. The planters ran their operations on credit and paid their bills with the certificate they received when they brought their tobacco to the chartered warehouses for processing. The droughts of 1755 and 1756 had ruined all crops. There was no tobacco for processing and no warehouse certificates with which to pay bills. The creditor merchants refused to admit that the lack of rainfall was an act of God and grant moratoriums. Instead they insisted upon the payment of all accounts in full when they fell due. Thomas Buckner, Zachery Taliaferro, James Taliaferro, Lundsford Lomax, Joseph Redd and John Plant, who, like Benjamin Catlett, were among the wealthiest planters in the county before the crop failures, were on the brink of bankruptcy. Relatives saved Buckner, the Taliaferros and Catlett, temporarily at least, and Lomax managed to salvage a portion of his estate because he was among the largest landowners in Virginia, but Redd and Plant were forced to surrender all their property to their creditors and take the pauper's oath.

In attempts to lessen their obligations, settlers from all classes tried tax evasions. In 1755 the Caroline Court fined John Hart 2,000 pounds of tobacco because he failed to report four tithables for assessment. But the next year with the amount of tobacco available for the payment of taxes growing constantly shorter due to the continuing dry weather, the magistrates let Benjamin Hubbard, Peter Lantor, John Kay and Elizabeth Zachery off with warnings when they failed to report twenty-seven, five, three and two tithables, respectively, for assessments. Unfortunately the sheriff was responsible for all taxes whether he collected them or not. These evasions and other circumstances which arose from the drought and the war caused Thomas Johnston, sheriff of Caroline County, to default on his accounts.

Johnston was an honest man. Leniency and bad judgment

led to his disgrace. Early in his administration (1755-1756) he dismissed William Boulware, his under-sheriff, and William Burdette, a deputy, because they relentlessly pushed the collection of accounts for British merchants in order to get their commissions, and appointed in their steads James Taylor and John Burk, whom he instructed to ease up on the local people at the expense of the traders overseas. Boulware and Burdette resented their dismissal and demanded settlements of their accounts with the sheriff's office at once. When Johnston was unable to meet this demand on short notice, the pair of dismissed underlings immediately filed suits for 3,000 pounds of sterling and thirty thousand pounds of tobacco and attached all his property to satisfy anticipated judgments while these actions were pending in court.

Taylor and Burk proved more lenient than even Johnston expected. They not only refused to levy on the property of distressed planters but also let poor debtors in their custody escape. For this negligence the sheriff dismissed the pair from office and named John Miller, Jr., under-sheriff, and John Penn, deputy, to fill the vacancies. But already his personal finances had suffered serious blows since he had to make up out of his own funds the claims of creditors against the fugitive debtors.

With the plight of the people about him going from bad to worse Johnston refused to attempt to collect any of the new levies the royal government imposed for defense. In 1756 Thomas Nelson, Secretary of the Colony, sent his personal attorney, Obediah Merriott, to Caroline with instructions to collect the one pound of tobacco for each tithable (3,725 pounds of tobacco), from the sheriff's estate. Johnston pled ignorance of the law and went through the form of having the local magistrates send to Williamsburg for a new copy of the statutes. But Merriott refused to accept this plea as a defense, and before the case came to trial filed an additional suit against the sheriff to collect 398 pounds, eleven shillings and nine pence sterling because two of his deputies, John and Edmond Taylor, were short in their accounts for the collection of quit rents. This suit was the final blow. Johnston had to pay out a large sum and poundage of tobacco at once, or go to jail, and he was without either liquid assets or the means to raise the needed funds and poundage. All he had left was his real estate, a huge tract of 2,956 acres on the north side of the Mattapony below Burke's Bridge, and this land was entailed. Edmund Pendleton saved him from prison by shoving through the General Assembly a bill which permitted him to sell this property in fee simple to Lewis Turner, and get the means to square his accounts with the Secretary of the Colony.

After this incident Johnston was a ruined man. But the Caroline magistrates did not prosecute him for his shortages. Instead they let him leave the county and take up residence on land which his wife had inherited in Louisa. However, the local court had learned a lesson; when Governor Dinwiddie appointed Edward Dixon, the Port Royal merchant, to succeed Johnston, the justices forced the new sheriff to post adequate bond to cover all taxes the law required him to collect in the county before accepting his oath which qualified him for office.

While the Caroline taxpayers enjoyed a limited relief because the unfortunate Johnston failed to collect the defense levies, Lundsford Lomax, one of their representatives in the House of Burgesses, sponsored legislation to make cheap money available to pay off their mounting debts. He advocated that the royal government of the colony issue 200,000 pounds in paper notes, when Dinwiddie asked for more funds to press the war against France in 1756.

Lomax's motives were not altogether altruistic in sponsoring this legislation. He was making a frantic effort to save himself from bankruptcy as well as other hard pressed planters throughout Virginia. According to the Order Books of Caroline Court he was in debt to four creditors alone (Johnathan Lyndenham and the partnership of Robert Tucker and Henry Witherburn, London merchants, John Younger of Whitehaven, and his Caroline factor, William Boulware, and Mitchell and Gray of Port Royal for 686 pounds, eleven shillings and tuppence. At the existing rate of exchange it would take all the tobacco grown on 1,715 acres under normal weather conditions to clear up this debt.

Dinwiddie bitterly opposed Lomax's proposal. As a trained civil servant he knew that all the paper money issued in New England and the Middle Colonies led to inflations which burst when the money of a particular issue became worthless. He wanted nothing like this to happen in Virginia while he was governor, and insisted upon the continuance of pay-as-you-go for defense. Lomax countered that system had not worked since already all the short term bonds issued to finance the war were in default. The greatest debate between Bacon's Rebellion and the Parson's Case stirred Virginia. Lomax was a talented leader, and as Chairman of the Committee on Trade, which handled all tax matters in the House of Burgesses, exerted great influence. In a short time he had enough Burgesses lined up to assure the passage of a bill authorizing the colonial government to issue paper money. But before he was able to push this legislation through the General Assembly, Dinwiddie dissolved the House of Burgesses and ordered new elections throughout the colony to give the freeholders of the colony a chance to vote on the issue.

Dinwiddie's campaign to purge the House of Burgesses of its inflationary block was only partially successful. The freeholders of the colony returned 61 per cent of the membership in the election of 1756, but the casualties included far more advocates of cheap money than the supporters of a firm currency. The Caroline electorate defeated Lundsford Lomax, the arch champion of inflation, and returned John Baylor of New Market to represent the county along with Edmund Pendleton.

Both Baylor and Pendleton were sound money men. Baylor held mortgages on the property of scores of planters and merchants and did not want to get back pounds with less purchasing power than the pounds he loaned, in payment for these debts. He expressed his views on this subject in strong language, in letters to John Backhouse, his London banker. Pendleton, although in time willing to take a leading part in the Revolution, actually was an ultra-conservative throughout his long and distinguished career. Born into a plain family and limited in education to what he was able to pick up in the county clerk's office under the tutorage of Benjamin Robinson, he wormed his way into the propertied class through a fortunate marriage, ability as a lawyer and penny pinching thrift. He fought inflation because it threatened to undermine his position of prominence in the county, which was based primarily on a goodly supply of ready cash. In 1752 he had been flattered when Lundsford Lomax, who at the time appeared well on the way to amassing one of the largest fortunes in the colony, backed him to defeat John Baylor for a seat in the House of Burgesses. But four years later, after circumstances brought on by drought and war, revealed that, Lomax instead of being rich was on the verge of bankruptcy, he did an abrupt about face and shifted his allegiance from Lomax to Baylor in the campaign of 1756.

Lomax, however, did not quit the fight for inflation after his defeat. The stakes were too great; their essence were his own solvency. Instead of giving up he became a lobbyist to advance the cause which cost him the election. He worked at home, in Williamsburg, and elsewhere throughout the colony, and became so engrossed in this task, that he had no time to perform his duties as magistrate in Caroline. The new House of Burgesses felt the pressure he exerted a few days after it went into its first session of the new term when it received "a petition by the freeholders and merchants of the county of Caroline, setting forth that by reason of the great scarcity of cash, occasioned by the shortness of the two preceding crops, a proper medium is wanting to support the necessary occasion of trade, whereby they are rendered unable to support their families and pay those taxes which the incursions and depredations of a bloody and faithless enemy make so necessary at this time, and praying that this House would apply a proper remedy, where by the great inconvenience of the want of specie, either by erecting a bank and loan office or such methods as the House shall think fit." (*Journal* of the House of Burgesses.)

The Burgesses referred this petition to a committee composed of Baylor and Pendleton, where it lay buried until similar petitions inspired by Lomax from the freeholders of Goochland, Hanover, Chesterfield, Charles City and Halifax, forced

the lawmakers to act. The bill, which they passed, was sub-
stantially the same legislation that Lomax proposed during the
last session. It authorized the Secretary of the Colony to issue
about 180,000 pounds in paper money, backed by annual taxes
of a shilling per tithable and a shilling on each 100 acres of
land. This new currency was good for the payment of all
private debts but taxes had to be paid in tobacco. A section of
the law known as the "Two Penny Act" shifted the rate of
exchange between tobacco and currency from one and one-half
to two pennies a pound.

This new law offered some immediate relief to the hard
pressed planters, since with the new rate of exchange an acre
of tobacco paid off six pounds, fourteen shillings and four
pence of their debts rather than the even four pounds of the
old. But long range prospects were not good. Prices automatically arose 66⅔ per cent and taxes increased sixfold.

As hedges against inflation Pendleton introduced bills to fix
the wages of artificers (skilled workmen), and to pay the
salaries of Burgesses and other public officials in paper money.
He also secured the passage of an act to create the office of
treasurer at the colony to direct the issuance of the new currency, and to supervise the withdrawal of redeemed notes from
circulation. The first of these laws led to the "Parson's Case,"
and the second to the defalcation of the treasurer and the
biggest scandal in the history of the colony.

As an interesting sidelight in the issuance of the new currency, the House of Burgesses appointed Pendleton to sign all
shilling and shilling thruppence notes. Bills of these denomi-
nations were by far the largest of the issue, and the assignment
meant that he must sign his name 66,000 times. How long this
took him is not of record.

The 180,000 pound issue of paper money worked no miracles in Caroline. Times were still hard and the war with France
unpopular. The morale of the people was low and a crime
wave swept the country. Shadrack and William Watts stole
tobacco from Conway's warehouse and resold it at Royston's,
in Fredericksburg. They were apprehended and sent to Williamsburg to stand trial before the General Court of the colony

for this crime. John Harvie, who ten years before robbed Robert Gilchrist, in a futile attempt to get goods for resale and avert failure as a merchant in Port Royal, raised a number of the new currency notes, from one to ten pounds; but again the Caroline Magistrates dealt lightly with him and let him off with another warning. Joseph Head, John Mitchell, William Blanton, Henry Tarrent, Andrew Fletcher and John Long were in court for swearing and drunkenness; Henry Tarrent, Daniel Roberts and John Lewis for neglecting the care of their children, Mace Pickett and Samuel Jeter for disturbing the peace, and Ann Green for having a bastard.

The unrest also extended to the servant classes. Among the indentured servants, John and Reuben Daner sued their master, Edward Powers, for their freedom, John Stanley ran away from William Taliaferro, Robert Kay had Mary Cox bound to keep the peace, and Catherine Bohannon and Mary Martin, servants of Oliver Charles and Abraham Estis, respectively, had bastards. Among the slaves William Baker, a mulatto belonging to John Billups, ran away and spread terror through the countryside, Jack Hickory, another mulatto, broke into the dwelling of William Dudley and was hung, and Sley, a Negro, was burned in the hand and given 39 lashes at the whipping-post for stealing hogs.

Civil cases as well as criminal, clogged the docket of the local court. Lundsford Lomax, in spite of his frantic efforts to preserve his solvency, was in serious financial difficulties. Over two score suits for debt pended against him. Benjamin Chapman, William Grimsley and John Howworth gave up their fight to preserve their property and took the pauper's oath; and John Chandler, Samuel Johnson, Benjamin Johnson and William Clutterbuck pled age and infirmity and asked to be made levy free. In quest of additional income to liquidate their debts Timothy Smith, Joseph Stevens and Jeremiah Canady tended tobacco seconds and were caught.

The people were quarrelsome because of the strain under which they lived, and filed a multitude of suits, based on slander and assault and battery, which further strained the functioning of the judiciary. The most noteworthy of these suits was an action for slander by Samuel Gist, Washington's friend and business associate, against Samuel and Caroline Riddick, alleging that they ridiculed his efforts in the French and Indian War.

Witnesses, preoccupied with their personal problems and not wishing to become engaged in these controversies, ignored summons to court at will. To break up this lawless arrogance, the Caroline magistrates fined four absentee witnesses, William Isbell, William Buckner, Dr. John Southerland and Philip Johnston, the huge sum of 2,000 pounds of tobacco each, at one term of court for contempt.

But the greatest handicap to the enforcement of law and order in Caroline County during the last years of Dinwiddie's rule was the lackadaisical attitude of the magistrates themselves. Only Edmund Pendleton, Robert Gilchrist, Edward Dixon and William Tyler took their duties seriously. Lundsford Lomax, John Baylor, Harry Beverley and Francis Taylor, failed to swear to their commissions and qualify to continue service after the Governor reappointed them in 1756; William Taliaferro died that year, Thomas Johnston left the county on account of his disgrace, Waller Chiles quit the court because he was a Quaker and the Quakers had decided all wars, including the current war with France, were sinful, and the remaining magistrates only showed up when it suited their convenience. Often not enough were present at a regular term, to form a quorum.

In an attempt to remedy this situation, the serious magistrates, Pendleton, Dixon, Gilchrist and Tyler, petitioned Governor Dinwiddie to add James Taylor, John Boutwell, Benjamin Robinson, Jr., Phillip Taylor, Robert Taliaferro, Jr., Christopher Tompkins and William Parker to the Caroline Court. The Governor granted this request, but Boutwell and Tompkins refused to accept commissions, and the Caroline petitioners offered the names of William Boulware and Lundsford Lomax, Jr., as substitutes. Dinwiddie resigned as governor and left Virginia before he acted on this second petition.

Caroline's non-Quaker population dismissed Waller Chiles' resignation from the county court "because all wars were sinful" as the act of a religious crank. But these same people, became first alarmed, and later angry, when Samuel Hargrave, the Secretary of the Golansville Quaker Meeting, announced that all Quakers were leaving the military service for the same cause. The Quakers, who lived in Caroline, were now the largest group of Quakers south of the Mason and Dixon Line and members of the sect formed an appreciable percentage of the county's population. Samuel Hargrave, their new leader, was a forceful man. He took over as Secretary of the Golansville Meeting in 1754, when John Cheadle, who brought the first Quakers from Pennsylvania to Caroline, died. He was a native of Caroline County and the son of William Hargrave, overseer for Benjamin Hubbard, a large planter and prosperous trader in lower Drysdale Parish. Benjamin Hubbard was the son of John Hubbard, a Quaker, who came to Caroline from Pennsylvania with John Cheadle. In time, after he became rich, he left the faith of his father and became a communicant of the Established Church. But not before he trained the precocious son of his overseer. He instructed young Samuel in business methods, as well as religion, and also gave him an excellent general education. (His letters as Secretary of the Golansville Meeting to the Meeting on South River in Bedford (Campbell in 1953) County, preserved in *Our Quaker Friends of Ye Olden Times,* are faultlessly written in a lucid style.)

After Samuel Hargrave grew up he acquired several tracts of land in upper St. Margaret's Parish and became a prosperous planter. Modeling his career on his mentor, Benjamin Hubbard, he went into trade and prospered. At the time of the Revolution he was among the largest importing merchants in Caroline County, although his place of business was located in St. Margaret's Parish and a great distance from navigable water. But financial success did not cause him to abandon his religion and turn to the Established Church in an attempt to get into local "society" as it had Hubbard before him. Instead he remained true to his faith, and when John Cheadle died in 1754, the Quakers of the Golansville Meeting House made him their leader, or the secretary of the congregation. The Quakers never had reason to regret this choice. One of his first acts as Secretary of the Golansville Meeting, was to secure permission from the General Court to build a milldam across the main channel of the North Anna, to generate water power to grind grain, that his people and other people of the county, the Quakers were always unselfish, might have flour and meal for bread during the great drought.

Hargrave, like most proselytes, was more zealous in enforcing a strict observance of the tenets of his faith than his predecessor, Cheadle, a life-long Quaker. While Cheadle was Secretary of the Golansville Meeting he paid scant attention to the rulings of the sect's hierarchy in Philadelphia. The chances are that he would have ignored the ruling of Quaker leaders in England and Pennsylvania "that all wars were sinful" and that no Quaker was to bear arms as a soldier, sailor or militia-man in the future. But the newly elected Hargrave decided to enforce it and gave orders that all members of the Golansville Meeting, serving with the Virginia regiment and the Caroline militia, must lay down their arms and return to their homes immediately, or face expulsion from Meeting. The ensuing exodus of Caroline Quakers from the armed forces at a time when the French and Indians threatened to overrun the Virginia colony caused anger and bitterness among their non-Quaker neighbors. But they were not moved by public opinion, and threats and appeals, which included an appeal to Robert Dinwiddie, the royal governor, failed to stop them.

The Quakers soon proved, however, that quitting the armed forces, was not based on cowardice. Because while they refused to fight in organized military units, they kept on moving to the western frontier with their families, and setting up homesteads, in spite of the dangers from hostile Indians. Few other pioneers dared risk such perils, and the Quaker settlements became the most effective check which kept the redskins from raiding the older sections of the colony. Members of the Golansville Meeting left Caroline en masse to make homes in Bedford County (all of Southwest Virginia in 1953).

Shortly after Braddock's humiliating defeat in the drive on Ft. Duquesne the French fleet made it unsafe for a ship flying the British flag to sail the seas. This interference with navigation had far more effect in Caroline County than the military reverses in the West, because the frontier was far away and navigable water close at hand. Caroline merchants lost vessels and cargoes, and trade in the town of Port Royal diminished to the vanishing point.

In 1757 a French man-of-war captured the *St. Mungo*, a freighter belonging to John Gray, a merchant of Port Royal, and mastered by John Lindsey, also of that town, in the West Indies, and towed it into a port on the French island of Guadeloupe, where the French governor condemned it as a prize of war. Lindsey twice protested this seizure without avail, and when the news of the loss reached Port Royal, Gray took the matter up, first with the Caroline Court, and afterwards with the royal government of the colony in Williamsburg. But all his efforts to force the French to release the ship and its crew failed. Losses of goods on the high seas because of the French ruined another Port Royal trader. The "minutes of the Kilwinning Cross Lodge" of Masons for March 3, 1758, record "William Miller, a indigent brother, who met with many misfortunes and suffered much by our implacable enemy, the French, having applied to the Right Worshipful, the Master, he with the advice of several members of this lodge, thought proper to give him forty shillings out of the treasury."

Perils at sea made many seamen loath to sail with their ships. In 1758 John Archer, a seaman on the *Virginia* jumped ship while that vessel was docked at Port Royal. But John Bowcock, the *Virginia's* master got an order from the Caroline Court and made Archer return to his duty station before the vessel sailed. (Order Book of the Caroline Court.)

Peter Corne, another seaman who lived in Port Royal, was made of sterner stuff. He was willing to sail in the face of adversity, but knowing the dangers prepared for the worst. An entry in the minute book of the above mentioned Masonic Lodge records "Peter Corne on his humble petition to the Lodge, is initiated an Entered Apprentice according to the usual form and solemnity, on paying the accustomed dues, and the Lodge taking into consideration the disadvantages of the sd. Peter Corne layd under not having the time or opportunity of learning the mysteries of the Art requisite to make himself known among Masons and considering that a Certificate from his worshipful Lodge of his being regularly admitted and initiated as an Entered Apprentice therein might in some measure supply that defect and be of singular service to him in case of misfortune by war he should fall into the hands of the enemy, ordered that a Secretary prepare, and draw such a Certificate to be signed by the Master Wardens and Secretary and the seal of the Lodge apprehended thereon."

With few ships risking a voyage overseas, tobacco from the first good crops after the great drought piled up in the chartered warehouses. The mounting volume made extra storage space necessary, and both Thomas Roy and Francis Conway II, the owners of Caroline's two chartered warehouses, claimed that they did not have the means to build these additional facilities, since the incomes they received from this business were based on a percentage of the tobacco they processed and during the dry years this income dropped to a pittance. The local court accepted their excuses and ordered Richard Buckner and Peter Copeland to build additional storage space at Conway's, and Edward Dixon and Robert Gilchrist to construct the needed buildings at Roy's and the owners to give them liens on the transfer tobacco in storage as security for the funds they advanced for the work.

Years of heavy rainfall followed the years of drought and the tobacco held over in the warehouse on account of the blockade began to rot. In a desperate attempt to prevent further deterioration someone conceived the idea of installing furnaces in the warehouses where the tobacco was stored to keep the crop dry. Again Francis Conway II, and Thomas Roy reported to the court that they lacked the means to make improvements and the magistrates ordered Richard Buckner and Thomas Allcocke to install a furnace at Conway's and Edward Dixon and James Jameson to install a furnace at Roy's and impounded more of the owners transfer tobacco to take care of the costs.

The furnace at Crutchfield's warehouse, on the Pamunkey, in lower Hanover caused a catastrophe. It exploded and the warehouse with the bulk of the tobacco in storage burned. This was stark tragedy for planters in Hanover, Charles City, King William and Caroline's lower St. Margaret's Parish, who sold their crops through this warehouse because they lost the major portion of the tobacco which they had raised since the great drought. The House of Burgesses, however, took official notice of their plight and passed legislation which authorized the Secretary of the Colony to issue them warehouse certificates for tax tobacco to cover a percentage of their losses.

The blockade proved Dinwiddie's undoings as governor of Virginia. Since the honeymoon period with the Burgesses early in his regime he had become increasingly more disillusioned with his job. He was willing to admit that he was wrong on changing the pistole fee for land patents but on the other major issues which confronted him during his rule he insisted that he was right. He only signed the bill authorizing the colonial government to issue paper money, when ordered by John Campbell, the Earl of London who was his superior and actual governor of Virginia. After this, relations between Campbell and his deputy were strained. They reached the breaking point when Dinwiddie, who, in spite of the rebuffs he received from the Burgesses, retained a firm interest in the welfare of Virginia, insisted that Campbell use his influence at the court of George II, to have the British fleet break the French blockade before the economy of that colony disintegrated to total chaos. When Campbell refused to intercede Dinwiddie resigned his position and set sail for England, unmourned by either the people whom he ruled or the masters whom he served.

The Rule of Francis Fauquier
(1758-1768)

1. END OF THE FRENCH AND INDIAN WAR

THE British crown gave its tacit approval to inflation in Virginia when it sent Sir Francis Fauquier to succeed Robert Dinwiddie as deputy governor. Fauquier, the son of a refugee French Huguenot physician, was reared in poverty in London, and through sheer drive became a director in the South Seas Company, where through experience he became an expert at issuing paper used in financial transactions with face value far beyond its actual worth. This background made him sympathetic, at least, with Virginia's inflationary block.

The first wave of the new deputy governor's popularity, however was based on luck. The French and Indian War, so far as Virginia was concerned, ended a short time after he reached Williamsburg, and the colonists acclaimed him a conquering hero, when actually he had little or nothing to do with the victory. It was the capture of Ft. Duquesne by General Forbes and a British Expeditionary Force assisted by Washington and a body of colonial troops on November 25, 1758, which relieved the western frontier from danger of invasion by the French.

Two soldiers of record from Caroline took part in the campaign against Ft. Duquesne. They were Thomas Riddle who lost all the fingers on his right hand and William Blanton who was shot through the thigh. Their names are preserved because the House of Burgesses voted them pensions on account of their wounds.

After the defeat of the French, other residents of Caroline with claims less meritorious than Riddle's and Blanton's, rushed to Williamsburg and demanded compensation at the public's expense, for losses sustained or for services rendered during the war. The Burgesses appropriated funds to pay Dr. John Southerland for treating soldiers wounded in battle after they returned to their homes; William Johnson, the Caroline jailor, for the food he fed deserters while they were locked up in the local jail, between the time they were picked up in the county and military personnel arrived to take them back to their command; and Elizabeth Burk for three beeves a company of troops confiscated and barbecued when camped before her son's tavern at Burke's Bridge, while they waited for a raging flood of the Mattapony, which blocked their way to the front, to subside. At the same time the Burgesses denied the claim of Harry Beverley for an indentured servant inducted into the Virginia regiment (Thomas Slaughter had already collected for this man's services), and the claim of John Miller for the meals he supplied stray soldiers at his tavern in Port Royal, without authorization from the military high command.

Unfortunately the defeat of the French and their Indian allies did not bring peace to Virginia. Indians, who had been friendly up to this time, began to give trouble. During the darkest days of the French and Indian War, Governor Dinwiddie invited the Cherokees, a tribe of the friendly Iroquois, to make their homes in the area that is now (1953) Southwest Virginia, south West Virginia and east Kentucky, and act as a buffer between the settled regions of the colony and the hostile Indian tribes to the west. From the date of issue, this invitation was unpopular. Hardy pioneers, including a large body of Caroline Quakers (*supra*), continued to push into the section and build homesteads. The Cherokees resented this invasion of their new hunting grounds and accused the royal government of the colony of bad faith, and when authorities in Williamsburg failed to give redress, they took matters in their own hands. Scalpings and the burning of homesteads became commonplace.

Many people in Caroline in addition to the Quakers had a vital stake in this disputed land. In 1748, the crown had granted much of the acreage to companies in which Duncan Graham, Benjamin Hubbard, Francis Thornton, Francis Thornton, Jr., John Thornton, Edward Dixon, William Hudson, Charles Dick, Edmund Pendleton and John Madison were directors; and since that time, these directors had sent members

of their families and their neighbors to develop their prop-
erties. When the Cherokees began their outrages, the hue and
cry throughout the county was great. The local court arranged
to send a company of soldiers under the command of Captain
John Quarles, to serve with the forces of Col. Andrew Lewis,
in a campaign to crush the redskins as soon as the militiamen
returned to their homes after the defeat of the French.

But in making this decision, the court failed to reckon with
the dispositions of the militiamen. Few of them wanted to
fight. Having just finished one war they had no desire to take
part in another. Their families and private finances needed
attention. The magistrates were powerless to make them join
in the campaign against their will since the trouble lay beyond
the limits of the county. In an attempt to bring Captain Quarles'
company up to normal strength before it set out for the frontier,
the court engaged recruiting agents to enlist men for bounties.

Richard Johnston, Thomas Booth and Richard Doggett
were the most active participants in this work. Among them
they managed to sign up thirty-one men. But these thirty-one
were perhaps the sorriest lot of soldiers ever to represent
Caroline. When, after many delays, Quarles' troops finally
reached the frontier, Col. Lewis immediately discharged three
of Booth's recruits as "too small and unfit for military duty,"
and three of Doggett's deserted in the heat of the first battle.

The Caroline Court obligingly certified its recruiting agents
bills for bounties advanced, commissions and expenses, to Secretary of the Colony for payment. But the secretary refused
point blank to reimburse Booth for the men who were unfit,
and Doggett, for the men who deserted. Between them, they
were thirty-seven pounds and fifteen shillings hard cash out of
pocket for the enlistment bounties they had paid.

Other soldiers, who served under Lewis in the campaign
against the Cherokees, appear to have been of no higher calibre
than the troops from Caroline. The war dragged on until 1762
when Governor Fauquier sent William Woodford into the area
to see if he might bring it to a conclusion. Woodford was
highly successful on this mission. He accomplished through
negotiation, what Lewis failed to gain on the field of battle.

Working with pioneer scouts, he managed to reach the Chero-
kee headquarters, where, after considerable argument, he persuaded a party of braves to accompany him to Williamsburg
and deal face to face with the governor. The ensuing confer-
ence in the colonial capital, brought a division of the disputed
lands which was mutually satisfactory to the Indians and the
whites, and established a peace in Virginia which lasted over a
decade. A grateful House of Burgesses voted Woodford a
gratuity of thirty pounds before he returned to his home in
Caroline.

2. INTERNAL IMPROVEMENTS

After the fall of Ft. Duquesne the Caroline Court resumed
a program of internal improvements for the county which the
war and the dry weather had interrupted. The magistrates
ended a ten-year argument, and decided to rebuild the courthouse on site, "nigh unto the old," (Ideal-Shumansville-Kidds
Fork triangle). They upped the county levy from nine to
seventeen pounds of tobacco, per tithable in 1759, to finance
the project and named three of their own number, Edmund
Pendleton, John Baylor and Robert Gilchrist, to select a design
and to supervise construction. This committee chose "the style
and the dimensions" of the courthouse at King and Queen for
a model, and hired John Wiley to put up the building. (Caroline Order Book V., page 93.)

Wiley was a grafter. He dallied over the job while trying to
squeeze extra compensation from the court. This went on until
1765 when the court, exasperated by his conduct, ordered him
to name either Richard Brooks, a surveyor, or David Stern, a
builder, as his representative to meet with George Rogers,
another builder, who represented the county, and magistrates,
Edmund Pendleton, John Baylor, Robert Gilchrist, and Anthony Thornton, to view the courthouse and place a value on
his work. Meetings of this committee resulted in the firing of
Wiley. The courthouse was never completed, although the
court used the unfinished building to hold some of its sessions
for many years.

The selection of the site "nigh unto the old," to rebuild the courthouse was unpopular with the rank and file of the people in Caroline. It was chosen irrespective of their wishes, because it lay mid-distance between the homes of Edmund Pendleton and John Baylor, who, at the time, were the county's Burgesses and most influential magistrates. In attempts to placate public sentiment, the court ordered the repair and clearing of roads leading from the thriving commercial center of Port Royal and populous St. Margaret's Parish; and William Johnson, the jailor, under the supervision of James Taylor and William Parker, magistrates, to build a large stable on the county lot for the public's convenience.

While the relocation of the courthouse at the old site displeased many people in Caroline, it pleased many of the residents of upper King and Queen. It was close to their homes, and their own courthouse was far away. In 1762 a group of these people petitioned the House of Burgesses to cut off the upper end of King and Queen and add the area to Caroline. The Burgesses acquiesed to the request and the Caroline Court named Edmund Pendleton and Francis Taylor to meet with commissioners from King and Queen and run a new line between the counties. When this was done, the Caroline magistrates added this new section of their county to the precinct of Benjamine Snead, who was already constable for the district about Daniel's (White's in 1953) Mill. This addition brought the area of Caroline up to its present size (1953).

When Fauquier began his rule of Virginia there was a greater need for reform of the ecclesiastical boundaries in Caroline than the civil. The shape of Drysdale Parish, which extended in a narrow strip along the north side of the Mattapony from the Spotsylvania-Caroline line well into King and Queen, continued to give trouble. With Ivy, the upper house of worship of the parish located in the vicinity of Sparta, the people of the Guinea community were practically unchurched, and with the glebe located below the lower church in King and Queen, over forty miles from the upper end of the parish, the parishioners in Caroline found it difficult to summon their minister to conduct funerals, perform marriages and render other services for their families.

After the close of hostilities with the French, the ecclesiastical authorities of the colony in Williamsburg took steps to correct these inequities. In 1760, they authorized the building of a new church for the upper end of the parish. This church was located on a hill, overlooking the Marrocossic Creek, north of the site of Bowling Green, on lands owned in 1953 by C. A. Broaddus. It was called "the Creek Church" because at this period, the Marrocossic had assumed such importance in the county, that it was referred to constantly in the records as "the Creek," rather than by its full name. The new church retained its original name until 1780 when St. Asaph's Parish was carved from the upper end of Drysdale, and it became the chief church of the new parish.

Shortly after the building of Creek Church, the devout of upper Drysdale petitioned the House of Burgesses, to arrange for the sale of the glebe of their parish and use of the funds derived from the sale, to purchase another more centrally located. The Burgesses secured this permission, and Governor Fauquier appointed Anthony Thornton, Thomas Buckner, William Buckner and William Parker to make the sale and the purchase. This transaction may have been tainted with fraud because Thornton, the two Buckners and Parker used the funds derived from the sale to purchase a new house to be used as a glebe from one of their own number, William Parker and his wife Elizabeth.

This author has been unable to determine where the new glebe was located. The best evidence indicates that it was on the road leading from Milford towards Sparta, because an order in the Caroline Order Book for 1765 directs the repair of the road from Doguetown (Milford) bridge to the new glebe of Drysdale Parish. Since the same order authorizes the repair of a second road, leading from Doguetown bridge, by way of "the Bolling Green" to the Creek Church, the new glebe falls into the area to the southeast of Milford by the process of elimination. Incidentally this order is the first time the name Bowling Green, appears in the official records of Caroline County. The fact that it was prefixed by the definite article "the" indicates that it was a place of some type of activity, probably horse-racing. The chances are that the spelling Bolling, instead of Bowling Green, was due to the ignorance of the recording magistrate, and without historical significance.

Concurrent with the rearrangement of Drysdale, there was agitation on the south side of the Mattapony, for rearrangements in St. Margaret's. One group of residents filed a petition to divide the parish and another to cut off its lower end, and add it to St. David's in King William. Both of these petitions came to naught. The fact that the notorious Rev. John Brunskill died in 1762, after serving the parish as rector for almost forty years, may have influenced the agitators to drop their grievances.

While rebuilding the courthouse and encouraging the establishment of a new church and a more centrally located glebe for Drysdale Parish, the Caroline magistrates pushed the repair of bridges and causeways in the county, neglected during the war and damaged in the wet years which followed the great drought. They joined with the magistrates of Hanover, to hire John Wiley to rebuild Littlepage's across the Pamunkey, and at the same time gave him an additional contract to repair the bridge and causeway across the Mattapony at Downer's (Woodford). Wiley managed to finish the job at Littlepage's in a satisfactory manner, but he stalled on Downer's as he did on the courthouse, trying to get more money for his work, until the court declared his contract forfeited and named William Tyler, Robert Taliaferro and Aquilla Johnson to finish the job. At the same time, Benjamin Hubbard and George Kenner rebuilt the bridge at Burke's, and Anthony Thornton, Thomas Buckner and William Buckner repaired the bridge and causeway at Guinney's. The bridge over the Mattapony at Doguetown appears to have been the only major bridge in the county which did not need attention.

3. THE REVIVAL OF TRADE

Trade boomed between Virginia and Great Britain after the British fleet regained control of the seas in 1759. Several vessels in the trans-Atlantic trade made Port Royal their home port. They included the *Virginia* owned by Mitchell and Gray and mastered by John Lindsay, who had returned to Caroline after his escape from Guadeloupe, the *Molly* sailed by William Lyne for Dunlop and Crosse, and the *Beverley* of Robert Montgomery and the *Christian* of Captain Stanley, who apparently operated on their own.

Port Royal needed better wharfage facilities to take care of these ships and others not of record. When Thomas Roy who owned the existing docks pled poverty and failed to make the needed repairs, the Caroline Court ordered him to build a new pier according to plans submitted by Edward Dixon, Robert Gilchrist and James Jameson, who were Port Royal business men as well as magistrates. Roy got one sop in this transaction, the House of Burgesses awarded him a gratuity of twenty-five pounds sterling to speed up construction.

With a new wharf for Port Royal on the way, the Caroline magistrates next turned their attention to Conway's and Roy's, the county's two chartered tobacco warehouses, and found the storage houses at both falling to pieces. When the court ordered these buildings repaired at once, Thomas Roy, the owner of Roy's, replied that this work should be done at the public's expense, since the sad plight of the storage houses was brought on by loss of revenue, during the drought and the war which were perils beyond his control. He had grabbed one subsidy from the government to improve his property and did not intend to miss a chance to grab another. But the magistrates brushed aside his argument and when he refused to obey their order, directed a committee composed of Richard Buckner, Edward Dixon, Robert Gilchrist and Benjamin Robinson, Jr., to put the storehouses in first class condition and levy on the transfer tobacco Roy held for his commissions, to pay for the repairs.

The situation at Conway's was different. Francis Conway II, the proprietor, had recently died, and the warehouse was being operated temporarily by the executors of his estate. When the executor contended that they were without authority to make the repairs, the court appointed Benjamin Robinson, Jr., Richard Buckner and James Taylor to supervise the work and granted them a lien against the estate's income from the warehouse to cover the costs.

With a new pier and Roy's warehouse reconditioned, Port Royal entered one of its greatest periods of prosperity. Edward Dixon, Robert Gilchrist, James Bowie, Duncan Graham, Patrick Coutts, John Crosse, Patrick Mitchell, William Fox, James Jameson, James and John Miller, Edward Powers, William and Collin Dunlop, Thomas and Richard Roy, Richard and William Bullock, John and William Gray and John Bowcock were among the chief business men of the town. Mathew Boogle, James Murdock, Hugh Lennox, Archibald MacCall and Andrew Cockran of Glasgow and Peter Horn and John Younger of Whitehaven, at least, had factors in residence. Alexander Loggie, Archibald Ritchie of Tappahannock, John Glassell of Fredericksburg, Robert Tucker of Norfolk and Thomas Nelson of York (town), were among the traders with headquarters elsewhere in the colony who made frequent visits to town. There was much coming and going of factors and realignment of partners in business ventures. (See chapter on Traders and Trade.) The inhabitants for the most part were a penny pinching hard drinking lot, who cared little or nothing for culture and were primarily interested in amassing wealth. The Rev. Johnathan Boucher, who lived in Port Royal throughout Fauquier's regime as governor of Virginia, first as tutor for the sons of Edward Dixon and later as rector of St. Mary's Parish, wrote in his autobiography, "In all the years I lived in Port Royal I did not form a single friendship on which I can now look back with approbation, though I had numerous acquaintances and many intimacies." (*Notes and Queries,* London, 1885-86.)

The Port Royal traders were so afraid that they might drive away trade, if they punished visitors for misconduct, that the port became the most popular in Virginia for sailors on liberty. In 1762 when James Campbell and John Scott, two seamen on Captain Robert Montgomery's *Beverley,* ran amuck on a drunken spree and brutally assaulted Edward Dixon, Robert Gilchrist, Robert Allen and John Snead, the injured refused to press charges, and Campbell and Scott sailed with their ship, unpunished.

Thomas Roy, backed by Edmund Pendleton, who for a short time was his brother-in-law, represented the conservative element in Port Royal. Roy started out a radical but became a conservative after he became a man of established wealth. From his mother, Dorothy Roy, he inherited the town's chartered tobacco warehouse, wharf and ferry across the Rappahannock, and he feared if the place grew too rapidly that it might attract the attention of men with enough influence in Williamsburg, to secure permission to set up a rival warehouse, wharf or ferry.

Pendleton backed Roy because he retained an interest in the Roy estate through inheritance from his first wife, Betty Roy Pendleton. Together they made an effective team. Pendleton's influence in Williamsburg, where he served as one of Caroline's two members of the House of Burgesses, and Roy's efforts locally, blocked all attempts to break the Roy family's stranglehold on public services and utilities in the vicinity of Port Royal prior to Thomas Roy's death in 1772. In 1764 they defeated a second attempt of Harry Beverley, John Gray and John Lindsay to set up a free ferry and move by the planters of upper Essex and lower Caroline to secure a charter for a new tobacco warehouse at Port Micou on Portobago Bay, after the chartered warehouse at Occupacia had fallen into disuse.

Traders elsewhere in Caroline, beyond the limits of Port Royal, for the most part prospered, while Francis Fauquier ruled Virginia. They included Henry Mills and Robert Garrett in upper St. Mary's Parish, Peter Copeland and Charles Dick, who also had a business establishment in Fredericksburg, in upper St. Margaret's, William and later James Hunter of lower St. Margaret's, Samuel Redd and Samuel Garlick of Chesterfield and Francis Coleman and William Johnson of the Courthouse.

The most extensively organized trader in the county was Benjamin Hubbard. He and his associates and underlings dominated the commerce of the Mattapony Valley from the Bowling Green to Ayletts. Hubbard had come to Caroline as a small child with John Cheadle and the Quakers from Pennsylvania. But he strayed from the Quaker fold and first operated a plantation and later a tavern he purchased from Stephen Haynes in the section that is now (1953) Sparta. This tavern grew into a trading center. It became an outlet for goods brought into Virginia through Ayletts which was the head of navigation for ocean-going vessels on the Mattapony. In time Hubbard wormed his way into a minor partnership in Aylett's chartered warehouse, and took over the whole business when Phillip Aylett, the chief owner, died and his heirs, the Ayletts and the Buckners, engaged in a dog fight over his estate. (See Chapter on Traders and Trade.)

Hubbard's energy attracted the attention of Richard Corbin and John Baylor, and they let him handle the local business of The Reeds and New Market, two of the largest and most prosperous plantations on the Mattapony. With this backing he branched out and engaged in joint ventures with the Hunters of lower St. Margaret's and the principal merchants of Port Royal. His chief lieutenant in the early days of his career was John Elliott Payne, who in time became his full partner. Among his later associates was Robert Broaddus, who was in charge of a tavern near present-day Sparta (probably the home of Miss Ivy Carter) and manager of Hubbard's Caroline outlet. His other associates included James Taylor, the Elder, who may have at one time been his father-in-law and William Cowne.

The political philosophy of Hubbard was more liberal than any other merchant of his time with the probable exception of Samuel Hargrave, whom he trained. Robert Dinwiddie made him a magistrate for Caroline in 1754 but he was never happy as a member of the court. He quarreled with the other magistrates and when he refused to sit with them they fined him 5 pounds, sterling, for "grossly insulting the court." He quit the court altogether in 1761 because he refused to swear allegiance to George III.

4. THE GREAT PLANTERS' EXTRAVAGANCE

While most Caroline merchants prospered during the early years of Fauquier's regime, the financial positions of a vast majority of great planters grew steadily worse. The Rev. Johnathan Boucher in his autobiography describes the planters about Port Royal as being in "middling circumstances" when he took up residence in that locality in 1759. But five years later John Baylor of New Market in a letter to John Backhouse, his London banker, asking for an advance of 140 pounds to meet obligations in Great Britain because he was unable to collect 3,000 pounds owed him by planters in Caroline, paints a far darker picture. In conclusion, he observed, "Poor Virginia, what art thou coming to. She is held in derision by merchants and factors. Surely this will open the eyes of my countrymen and make them more frugal."

Baylor's observations were correct. The great planters were becoming economic vassals of the merchants, because of their extravagance. This was utter folly because they had the acreage and slaves to prosper if they were thrifty. The soil of Caroline was not yet worn thin through over cultivation and insufficient refertilization as it was the case in counties closer to the Chesapeake Bay. It still produced tobacco of quality in quantity. Edmund Pendleton, in his argument before the House of Burgesses in 1766 to break the will of John Corbin and let his son and heir, Gawin Corbin, sell the lands of the estate in Lancaster which were entailed, and keep the lands of the estate in Caroline which were in fee, contended that this was necessary because the Lancaster lands were exhausted and the Caroline lands "in shape to grow fine tobacco for at least another generation." The Burgesses agreed with Pendleton and docked the tails of the Corbin's Lancaster lands, which permitted their sale and allowed young Gawin to take up residence in Caroline. (*Journal* of the House of Burgesses for 1766.)

Extravagance was the great planters' curse. They were more interested in luxuries than in preserving their estates. They considered clothing of imported fabrics and furniture manu-

factured abroad essential to maintaining a position in their
caste. Clothes of homespun and homemade furniture were
the badges of inferior social standing.

The accounts of Lundsford Lomax, Sr., Burgess and king's
magistrate, with Patrick Mitchell and John Gray and Edward
Dixon of Port Royal, and John Younger of Whitehaven,
England, are preserved in the Caroline Order Books (Vol. V,
pages 171-182). To clothe himself and his family, Lomax
owed for bales of scarlet cambric, plaid, flannel, drab, black
and yellow challis, German serge, white and checked linen
and cotton cloth, hanks of silk, yards of lace, metal buttons,
felt hats, Holland hose, London shoes, indigo to dye the cloth
and skeins of hair from which to fashion the great wigs in
vogue at the time. His debts for luxury food and drink included casks of Port and Madeira wine, rundlets of rum, chests
of tea and large quantities of coffee, ginger, nutmeg, spices and
brown, loaf and fine sugar. House furnishings and building
materials for which he owed included china, candle sticks, table
knives and forks (in spite of the popular impression that table
forks were not in use at this early date), locks, hinges and bed
sheets. Among the miscellaneous articles were bearskins, buck-
ram, paper, saddles, bridles, camphor, and most peculiar of all,
snuff, brought from abroad into a country where tobacco was
the staple crop. Finally there were articles needed on the
plantations; broad and narrow axes, chisels, hand saws, grind-
stones, lanterns, nails, twine and rope.

The merchants demanded payment for these goods in tobacco certificates, or some other medium of exchange acceptable in
Great Britain. They refused to accept the paper money issued
in Virginia because it was worthless outside the territorial
limits of the colony. Lomax had Virginia money in quantity
but he lacked the tobacco certificates to meet his obligations,
and his creditors reduced his debts to judgments and placed
liens against his real estate. After this misfortune he was strap-
ped to meet the accruing interest to prevent foreclosure. He
had become an economic vassal of the merchants, since the
larger share of his income went to keep them appeased.

Many other large planters were in positions similar to

Lomax. But in spite of the fact that their credit was extended to the breaking point they continued their extravagant way of life until the break actually came. They evaded taxes and resorted to crime in frantic attempts to put off the day of reckoning, and got drunk in efforts to forget their troubles. Thomas Boothe rode around in a luxurious chaise on which he was unable to pay the tax, and Robert Tompkins, Benjamin Hurt and William Ellis failed to list either their land or their tithables with the assessors. Robert Burdette counterfeited sterling coinage and forged the names of Robert Gilchrist, Edward Dixon, John Broaddus, John Baylor and Benjamin Hubbard on bills of exchange. James Farish, the most pathetic of the lot, got drunk each time he went to court to answer the summons of his creditors and paid a five shilling fine for the use of the poor of Drysdale Parish until he assigned all his property to Thomas Coleman, who paid off his debts and kept him out of jail.

Dry weather in 1760 ended the fight to survive for many of the debt ridden planters. With the short crop due to the drought, they did not have the tobacco certificates to meet the interest on their debts, and their creditors foreclosed. The sale of land, to satisfy debts through chancery suits, was a long and tedious way to collect money, and Phillip Taylor, a local merchant, inaugurated a more efficient means to accomplish the same purpose when he attached the slaves of William Isbell in the spring of 1761. No sooner was this method begun, however, than crafty planters tried to evade it. When Lundsford Lomax learned that Patrick Mitchell, the Port Royal merchant, was about to attach his Negroes, he deeded them in parcels to James Hunter, James Mills and John Garnett, but retained possession of the lot to have hands to work his fields. When this fraud came to Mitchell's attention that merchant promptly filed suit to set the conveyances aside. He was successful in this litigation and only the intervention of Lundsford Lomax, Jr., with enough cash to pay off Lomax Sr.'s debt to Mitchell, saved Lomax Sr. from jail.

Success in the attachment of slaves led creditors to attach the personal property of their debtors, as well. In 1762 the sheriff levied on, and sold at public auction, the farming equipment and household furniture of Lazarus Yarbough to satisfy the judgments of William Spiller, a local merchant. A few months later John Younger of Whitehaven used the same means to ruin Robert Taliaferro, a magistrate.

By 1763 not even crops growing in fields were safe from creditors' claims. During the summer of that year, Robert Gilchrist and James Miller, Port Royal merchants, levied on Benjamin Catlett's growing tobacco. After the levy, Catlett promptly abandoned the crop, and Gilchrist and Miller sought an injunction to force him to cultivate and harvest it to prevent waste. The ensuing litigation brought Peyton Randolph and George Wythe, two of the most eminent lawyers in Virginia, to Caroline as counsel. The local court's decision to grant the injunction was sustained by the General Court of the Colony and became ruling case law in Virginia.

In 1764 an epidemic of smallpox, the worst in the county's history, added to Caroline's economic woes. Negro slaves, as well as whites, died by the hundreds. Tobacco, badly needed for export, went to ruin in the field from the lack of hands for its cultivation. In the face of this adversity numerous planters gave up the fight to survive and went to jail for their debts. Conditions in the local prisons, already overcrowded with debtors and criminals, became intolerable. Because of the congestion the disease spread rapidly and the inmates died like flies. In an attempt to relieve this situation the court named three of its members, Anthony Thornton, John Baylor and William Parker, to supervise the building of a separate prison for debtors. Thornton, Baylor and Parker engaged Daniel Barksdale to put up the building. He finished the job in a few months and the court paid him 112 pounds, Virginia currency, for his work. This was Caroline's first debtors' prison and the last public building erected at the site of the first courthouse in the Ideal-Kidds Fork-Shumansville triangle.

William Parker one of the three magistrates who supervised construction was among the first inmates of the new debtors' prison. He was locked up upon the complaint of Alexander Rose (Ross), a Port Royal lawyer, because he was unable to meet his obligations to Glasgow merchants. But he did not stay in prison long. John Baylor, who backed most Caroline men in public life from the Mattapony Valley section of the county while Fauquier ruled Virginia, advanced funds to pay off his pressing obligations and secured his release. Out of jail, Parker immediately resumed his position on the bench and handed down decisions which put other debtors behind the bars.

Another Caroline official was not so fortunate. When Edmund Pendleton sold all the lands of Francis Taylor, sheriff of the county, in 1765, to satisfy the judgments of Peter Horn of Whitehaven, Fauquier removed Taylor as sheriff because he had become ineligible to hold that office without real estate in his name, and appointed John Sutton II to finish his incompleted term. After Taylor's ruin, the court bound his son, James, to Nathaniel Anderson, a house joiner, as apprentice, and began a cleavage in the Taylor family, which has lasted until this time (1953).

5. Germ of the Revolution

While Caroline's great planters struggled to maintain their solvency they were beset on one hand by oppressive measures of the British government, overseas, and on the other by the demands of their neighbors, the small freeholders, for a greater voice in a management of local affairs. For over a decade they fought on two fronts, trying to preserve their supremacy from the onslaughts of both forces, at times making temporary alliances with one to stem the advance of the other. It was not until 1774 that they split into two factions, the patriots and the tories, with the far larger faction, the patriots, making common cause with the smaller freeholders in opposition to the crown. The king, Hillsborough Proclamation, Parson's Case, fight for religious freedom, Stamp Act and other tax laws enacted by Parliament were all issues in this odd three-sided contest.

Only two kings ruled Caroline. The first, George II, was popular with all classes throughout his long reign (1727-60). But many people in the county mistrusted the second, George

III, from the day they learned that he was on the throne. They knew that he was reared away from the court of his grandparents, tolerant King George II and enlightened Queen Caroline, under the direction of his father, Frederick, Prince of Wales, whom his great grandsire, the narrow-minded bigot, George I, trained, and they were afraid of an abandonment of the moderate policies of George II and a return to the despotism of George I with the new reign.

The merchants in particular were alarmed. They feared a program to enrich the merchants of Britain at the expense of merchants in Virginia. Because of this fear the five Caroline merchants, who held commissions as magistrates in the local court, refused to take the oath of allegiance to the new king. After two years' consideration Robert Gilchrist changed his mind and swore allegiance but he was the only one of the five to relent. Peter Copeland died and Phillip Taylor moved away a few years after the new king ascended the throne, but Benjamin Hubbard and Edward Dixon remained in business in Caroline, without taking the oath, until after Virginia refused to acknowledge George III as king. Hubbard had not qualified on his last commission, and his refusal may have been based as much on pique against the other magistrates as dislike for the new king. But Dixon was a magistrate in good standing with a long record of service in the court. He was one of Caroline's original rebels.

To make matters worse Dixon was the magistrate, who served as sheriff at the time. To meet this emergency the court permitted his deputies, William Harrison and John Miller, Jr., who had no scruples against taking the oath of allegiance to the new king, to act until Governor Fauquier named John Sutton II to finish out Dixon's incompleted term.

A short time later (1763) all Caroline was aroused when George III, through his ministry, issued the Hillsborough Proclamation, which denied all the residents of Britain's coastal colonies in America, the right to patent additional land west of the Alleghenies. The people of the county thought they had won the right to develop the Ohio Valley because of the aid they rendered the crown during the French and Indian War.

They looked upon this vast region as their land of opportunity. It offered the great landlords chances to grow rich through speculation, homesteads for the younger sons of the small freeholders, and land for indentured servants after they completed their terms of indenture. Lundsford Lomax and John Baylor, who already were among the largest holders of western land in Virginia, refused to perform their duties, as magistrates on the Caroline Court, in protest.

This protest made no impression on Governor Fauquier. He promptly declared their seats vacant, along with the seats of Benjamin Hubbard and Edward Dixon, and named John Baynham, John Taylor, Lawrence Taliaferro and Grabriel Throckmorton to fill the vacancies.

The ink on the Hillsborough Proclamation was hardly dry before the Parson's Case rocked Virginia. While this celebrated case was actually tried in Hanover, events leading up to the trial began across the Pamunkey in Caroline. In 1757, immediately after the General Assembly of the colony enacted a law to pay civil servants in Virginia currency rather than in tobacco, the Rev. John Brunskill, Sr., who had served for thirty-six years as rector of Caroline's St. Margaret's Parish, got up a petition addressed to the king, asking the sovereign to annul the statute. (*Journal* of the House of Burgesses for 1757.)

George II ignored the petition when it reached his court. As a constitutional monarch he decided that he had no more right to set aside an Act of the Virginia Assembly than he had to set aside an Act of Parliament. But the new king, George III, had different ideas on the subject. After he reached the throne and the petition finally came to his attention in 1762, he annulled the law and decreed that vestries in Virginia must pay their rectors in tobacco.

The ruling came too late to help John Brunskill, Sr. He was on his deathbed when he got the news and did not have time to file a suit against the vestry of St. Margaret's. After his death (1762) the burden of forcing the colonial authorities to act in accordance with the king's dictates fell to the Rev. James Maury of Hanover, the second signer of the petition. Thus by a quirk of fate the Parson's Case was tried in Hanover rather than Caroline, and Patrick Henry got the chance to set in motion the series of acts which won him immortal fame.

No other Caroline clergyman took part in events leading up to the Parson's Case. The Rev. Musgrave Dawson of St. Mary's and the Rev. Robert Innis of Drysdale were both ill at the time. (Dawson died in 1763 and Innis in 1764.) Neither of them were among the signers of Brunskill's petition. After their sad experience with Brunskill the people of St. Margaret's took extreme measures to keep their new rector, the Rev. Robert Barrett, from getting involved. They trumped up charges against him, the nature of which the Caroline Order Books (Order Book V, page 350) unfortunately fail to reveal, of sufficient strength, to convince the magistrates that there was probable cause to believe that he had committed a felony. After an investigation the Caroline Court certified him for trial before the General Court of the Colony and directed the sheriff of the county to pay John Emerson 400 pounds of tobacco to guard him on the journey to Williamsburg. What happened to Barrett after he reached the colonial capital this author has been unable to determine. But it is a matter of record that he never returned to Caroline and that St. Margaret's Parish was without a rector during the trial of the Parson's Case. After the trouble subsided the vestry engaged the services of the Rev. Archibald Dick, the son of Charles Dick, a prominent local merchant. He was reared at Twickenham, the home of Robert Bullock in 1953, and was the first native of Caroline to become rector of a parish in the county.

Although the trial of the Parson's Case caused no upheaval in Caroline, Governor Fauquier considered the county a potential trouble spot and took steps to be prepared to meet an emergency if one arose. He sent British troops into the county and appointed Lawrence Taliaferro quartermaster, to find billets for these soldiers in private homes and collect supplies from the people for their support. In a move to strengthen the local militia, he commissioned small planters and tavern-keepers as officers for the first time. Heretofore, all officers were from the ranks of the descendants and relatives of the patentees of the large crown grants. The governor made this change in an attempt to curry favor for the crown with the rising middle class. He tried to pick this new type of officer from among men known for their loyalty to the Established Church. Ironically one of his appointees was John Broaddus, the father of Andrew Broaddus I, the founder of one of the most celebrated lines of Baptist ministers in America.

6. THE STAMP ACT AND ITS CONSEQUENCES

The crown angered the Caroline freeholders for a third time within two years when Parliament passed the Stamp Act in 1765. This statute forced the colonists to put revenue stamps on legal documents, pamphlets, newspapers and almanacs. The tax was small and only effected a few people but Patrick Henry and Richard Henry Lee argued that it was unjust because it was levied by a legislative body, in which the people taxed were without representation. All Virginia became inflamed over the issue. Two young idealists John Penn and Francis Coleman led the fight on "taxation without representation" in Caroline.

The fight in Caroline went far beyond the Stamp Act. Penn and Coleman enlarged its scope to include county and parish taxes, as well, which they contended were also "taxation without representation" since the magistrates and vestrymen, who levied these taxes were appointed by the royal governor, and no more representatives of the people than the members of Parliament, who enacted the Stamp Act. On levy day in 1765 small planters, traders and artesians descended on the Caroline Court in such numbers that the magistrates postponed the laying of the levy for the next year. Nothing like this had happened before. Traditionally after given notice, as the law required, the magistrates authorized the sheriff to pay the county's current bills and fixed the tax rate for the coming year, in a few hours of one session of their December term.

After this December postpostment there were additional delays in January and February and it was not until March 1766 that the magistrates were able to set the levy for that year. This levy was only two pounds of tobacco per tithable, a decrease of over 400% from the previous year, and the approximate yield far less than the country's anticipated cost of operation. The magistrates knew that they were creating a deficit but they were afraid to act otherwise on account of the pressure from the aroused people.

When news of the magistrates surrender to the people reached Williamsburg Governor Fauquier became alarmed over the situation in Caroline, and upon the advice of John Baylor of New Market, his chief advisor on Caroline affairs, sent William Goode, an outsider, to the county as sheriff. This move was without parallel in the annals of Colonial Caroline, before Goode's appointment and afterwards, the sheriffs were all local residents and the presiding magistrate of the court. The move was the sharpest censure that the governor was able to impose on the magistrates, short of removing them from office.

The magistrates, however, refused to accept this rebuke placidly. Prodded by the people they cut the powers of the sheriff as far as they dared. Heretofore that official not only enforced the laws, but also collected taxes and kept in his custody public funds until the court authorized him to use them to pay the county's bills. The magistrates were afraid to interfere with the sheriff's law enforcement and tax collecting powers, but they deprived him of the right to hold tax funds after they were collected. To effect this change they created the office of treasurer of the court and named one of their own number, James Taylor, an uncle of John Penn, the plain people's champion, to fill the position.

While the freeholders who held small acreages were throwing their newly-found weight around in Caroline, they did not fare so well in Williamsburg where their duly elected representatives to the House of Burgesses, Edmund Pendleton and John Baylor, failed to act in accord with their wishes. Pendleton was too preoccupied amassing a personal fortune to have time for general legislation. He had established the reputation as one of the most competent estate lawyers in the colony. Between 1758 and 1765 in addition to the estate of John Corbin, he was attorney for the heirs of Alexander Spotswood, Ralph Wormley, Henry Scarbrough, William Colston, Richard

Todd and many other patentees of large crown grants. Much of the land in these estates was entailed and by virtue of his membership of the House of Burgesses, he was able to introduce bills to dock or reassign tails to suit the pleasure of his clients. His seat was too much of an economic asset to be jeopardized by taking a lead on controversial issues. He had already left Williamsburg when Patrick Henry introduced his famous "resolves," in opposition to the Stamp Act, in the closing days of the session of 1765 and did not return to the colonial capital to take part in the ensuing debate.

John Baylor was present and argued and voted against the "resolves" because he regarded them as treasonable. This course of action cost him his seat as Burgess. When Fauquier dissolved the lower house of the General Assembly after it passed a portion of Henry's "treasonable" measure and ordered new elections for Burgesses, throughout the colony, the Caroline freeholders defeated Baylor at the polls and sent Walker Taliaferro to represent them in Williamsburg, along with Edmund Pendleton, whom they retained in office because he had not declared himself publicly on "the resolves" and during the campaign did a first class job on straddling the issue.

Baylor's defeat embittered him and he spent a great part of what remained of his life in getting even with the Caroline politicians who opposed him. He not only persuaded Governor Fauquier to rebuke the Caroline magistrates en masse, by sending William Goode to the county as sheriff, but he also used his influence with the governor to injure the powerful Robinson family, which formed the backbone of his opposition.

Benjamin Robinson, the greatly beloved first clerk of the county, died in 1762, after thirty-five years of public service, and his son, Joseph Robinson took over the office. But the position of clerk was too great a political plum for a son to inherit from his father, uncontested. Local politicians intervened and persuaded Governor Fauquier to use the office to provide sustenance for undistinguished sons of distinguished sires. The governor revoked Joseph Robinson's temporary appointment and named Robert Armistead, a son of Henry Armistead, Caroline's first county lieutenant, as clerk, with

Catesby Woodford, a son of Major William Woodford of Windsor, the county's first sheriff, as chief deputy, and John Timberlake of plain stock as second deputy to do the actual work attached to the office.

This arrangement continued for three years until Armistead died, Woodford moved out of the county and Joseph Robinson slipped back into office. But Robinson's second tenure as clerk was no longer than the first, because he, and his brothers, Benjamin Jr. and Charles, dared oppose the powerful Baylor in his campaign for re-election to the house of Burgesses in 1765. After Baylor's defeat he joined Thomas Nelson, Secretary of the Colony, in a move which resulted in the removal of Joseph Robinson from office and the naming of Thomas Nelson, Jr., a son of Thomas Nelson, to be clerk of Caroline, with John Nelson, another son of the secretary of the colony, as deputy. This indicates the extremes to which Baylor was willing to go to get his revenge, because at the time of their appointments neither Nelson was a resident of Caroline and it was customary for the governor to name only local residents to fill county offices. His actions enraged his neighbors, but he was unruffled by their reactions and promptly posted bond for the Nelsons, to guarantee that they properly fulfilled their duties in the clerk's office. (Vol. V, page 212, Order Books of the Caroline Court.) He remained their surety until his death in 1772.

Charles Robinson was the next Robinson to suffer from Baylor's wrath. In 1766 when Zachery Lewis, crown attorney for Caroline, moved his residence from the county the local court declared the position vacant, and petitioned the governor to name Charles Robinson, who was a competent attorney, trained by his father along with Edmund Pendleton and numerous other lawyers in the Caroline clerk's office, to fill the vacancy. But Baylor blocked this move. He went to Williamsburg and persuaded Fauquier to retain Lewis, who had supported him in the campaign of 1765, as crown attorney for Caroline, although Lewis was now living in another county and unable to perform any of the duties of the office, and ordered the Caroline Court to pay him the full salary as provided by law. After this decision the Caroline magistrates in desperation hired Charles Robinson to do the work of crown attorney, as deputy in residence. Fauquier ratified this agreement but at the same time decreed that Robinson was to receive only a deputy's salary for his services.

Opposition to the Stamp Act which generated opposition to all "taxation without representation" and John Baylor's moves for revenge, because of his defeat in the election of 1765 after he took the unpopular side of the issue, placed Caroline in an awkward position. The three most important offices in the county, sheriff, clerk and crown attorney, were all held by non-residents. After a careful search of the records this author has been unable to find an instance when a royal governor punished another county so severely. But this search also reveals that no other county went so far in its opposition to "taxation without representation" after the passage of the Stamp Act. Elsewhere opposition was confined to that law, but in Caroline, the people carried the issue to its grass roots, and declared that local taxes levied by crown appointed vestrymen and magistrates, were as much "taxation without representation" as a tax enacted by a lawmaking body overseas. Apparently their contention so alarmed Fauquier that he "meted out punishment to fit the crime."

7. PENDLETON AND THE ROBINSON SCANDAL

Edmund Pendleton was lucky in his campaign for re-election to the House of Burgesses in 1765. He not only straddled the issue of "taxation without representation" to the satisfaction of both his great landlords and small freeholder constituents, but he also managed to keep under cover the biggest scandal in the history of the Virginia colony until after the voters expressed their preference for representatives in the lower house of the General Assembly at the polls. This scandal was the shortage of John Robinson, Speaker of the House of Burgesses and first treasurer of the colony, in his public accounts. Pendleton was personal attorney to Robinson while he lived and co-executor of his estate after his death.

The treasurer of the colony was more controller of the currency than treasurer. His chief duties consisted of issuing new notes of Virginia paper money and destroying the older after they were redeemed. Robinson was derelict in performing the latter duty. Instead of destroying all of the redeemed notes he loaned a great many of them to his debt ridden great planter friends. When he died early in 1765 over one hundred thousand pounds in this worthless paper was in circulation.

Rumors of this shortage were widespread in Williamsburg before Governor Fauquier dissolved the House of Burgesses for passing the "treasonable" resolves protesting the Stamp Act. Richard Henry Lee and other radicals tried to bring the matter into the open and make it an issue in the impending campaign. But Pendleton, Wythe, Bland and their fellow conservatives blocked the move.

Subsequently, after the truth became known to the public, Henry and Lee charged Pendleton with partial responsibility for the crime, citing his close personal and professional association with Robinson during the speaker-treasurer's lifetime, and the fact that as co-executor of the estate he knew of the shortage months before he acknowledged its existence to the lawmakers of the colony, who were vitally concerned because it involved public funds. Unfortunately these charges are well founded, for while there is no proof that Robinson acted upon Pendleton's advice in making the illegal loans, there are adequate grounds to believe that Pendleton at least knew what was going on. In 1763 within two years of the speaker-treasurer's death, Robinson as speaker of the House of Burgesses appointed Pendleton to examine the books of the treasurer in behalf of the House. Pendleton made this examination and reported that the books were in "Perfect Order." (*Journal* of the House of Burgesses for 1763.) The shortages began long before this date. Pendleton either was negligent in making this examination or discovered the shortage and concealed his findings. The chances are that the latter was true because he was one of the most meticulous of men, and there is no other record of negligence through oversight in his long career.

There is no doubt that Pendleton was under great obligations to Robinson. He was a gawky, uncouth countryman, when he arrived in Williamsburg in 1752 to sit as Burgess from Caroline in the place of the suave and polished John Baylor, of New Market, and the speaker, who was already a great man in the colony took him in tow. The reason for this may be attributed to the fact that Speaker Robinson was a brother of Pendleton's old mentor, Benjamin Robinson, Clerk of the Caroline Court and that Pendleton in spite of his appearance and lack of general education, had a fine mind and excellent legal training, which he received under Benjamin Robinson in the Caroline clerk's office. Speaker Robinson, with all his transactions, many of dubious legality, needed a skillful lawyer, whose personal devotion he did not doubt, at his beck and call.

This association grew more intimate through the years. Robinson, as speaker, pushed Pendleton, as Burgess, until the latter became one of the most powerful men in the House. In gratitude for this consideration Pendleton decided with his sponsor on all important issues and used his growing influence as Burgess to strengthen the position of speaker. After the House, against his wishes, passed the law which authorized the colony of Virginia, to issue paper currency, backed only by anticipated tax collection, to finance the French and Indian War, he insisted that the office of treasurer be created, to control these funds and that Robinson be appointed to fill this position. Later he resisted all moves to force Robinson out of this job when young radicals in the House, such as Henry, Lee and Carr, insisted that the office of speaker and treasurer ought not be filled by the same man.

Pendleton was well paid for his devotion to Robinson in addition to the prominence it gained for him in the House of Burgesses. His close association with the speaker put him in contact socially with many of the most aristocratic people in Virginia. Back in Caroline during his youth, the homes of most of the minor gentry were closed to him because he was a poor apprentice without prospects of wealth, and an unsuitable prospective husband for marriageable daughters. His two wives, both of whom he married in his young manhood, were from families of means but with modest social ranking at the time. These slights made him sensitive and one of his chief aims became full acceptance by the great landlord caste.

In Williamsburg under Robinson's tutelage these aims were fulfilled. He became an intimate of the Byrds, Pages, Burwells, Carys, Braxtons, Blairs, Tayloes, and other great families of the colony to whom the aristocrats of Caroline with the exception of the Corbins, Beverleys and Baylors, were small fry. Pendleton served his new friends well. In 1765 he reversed his position on sound money and was co-sponsor of a plan, for the colony to borrow 240,000 pounds sterling, from British merchants and issue 140,000 pounds of additional paper money, to float the currency further in an attempt to keep the debt-ridden aristocrats solvent. Fortunately this scheme was defeated. Had it been enacted into law, the chances are that Virginia would not have been able to finance her share of the Revolution.

Pendleton also profited financially from his association with Robinson. When Obediah Merriott died in the 1750's, the speaker made him his personal attorney. After he was engaged by this celebrated personality he gained many other important clients. In a short time he had one of the most lucrative law practices in the colony and was well on the way to amass a fortune, in keeping with his new found social station. To his credit, he was one of the most competent lawyers in Virginia, and able to dispatch to the satisfaction of his clients, the huge volume of business which came his way.

The way Pendleton handled the deceased speaker-treasurer's estate, as attorney and co-executor, did much to restore his prestige, badly damaged by the Robinson scandal, throughout the colony. When John Robinson died, he was one of the largest landlords in the highly developed section of Virginia, between the James and the Rappahannock. He owned 4,000 acres in King and Queen, 6,500 acres in Spotsylvania, 4,250 acres in Hanover, 1,200 acres in King William, 3,200 acres in Caroline along Marrocossic Creek, 400 acres in James City and a house and lot in Williamsburg. His appraisers valued the slaves, alone, on this property at 3,000 pounds. In addition to these tangibles there were intangibles which included a mortgage by Bernard Moore of Chelsea, in King William, the son-in-law of Governor Spotswood, on 6,039 acres of land in Caroline's St. Margaret's Parish. Pendleton disposed of this estate to such an advantage that he was able to keep the heirs independently wealthy and take up all but 12,000 pounds, which he was unable to find, of the redeemed treasury notes, illegally in circulation. This feat curtailed inflation, and preserved the solvency of the Virginia colony.

The plantation along Marrocossic Creek was among the lands sold. Pendleton and Lyons, as executors of the estate, transferred it to Richard Todd. Moore tried to preëmpt on the foreclosure of the mortgage on the St. Margaret's Parish property by conveying it to Samuel Redd. But Pendleton had the Caroline Court set this conveyance aside, and sold it in subdivided tracts to William Fulcher, John Sizer, James Conner, Benjamin Mason, Timothy Parish, William Chewning, George Tribble and Anthony Arnold.

To protect the interest of the estate Pendleton sued the individuals to whom Robinson originally turned over the redeemed treasury notes, after he paid the current holder and gained possession of the paper. Only one of these suits was against a resident of Caroline. This was against Gawin Corbin, to recover the face value of redeemed currency, which Robinson turned over to Corbin's father, who was at the time of the transaction a resident of Lancaster.

8. The Increasing Importance of the Jury

Unpleasantness caused by the Stamp Act and the Robinson scandal soon blew over for Caroline's ruling caste. Parliament repealed the unpopular law in 1766 and Pendleton's management of Robinson's estate revived overseas sources of credit. But these reliefs failed to end their troubles. Freeholders, who were not so fortunate to inherit a position of leadership in the county, continued to demand a larger voice in the direction of the government.

Members of this rising class ranged from artisans, crossroad traders and tavern-keepers through small planters to great planters, who accumulated their vast acreages through their own perseverance and ingenuity, and who were often in far better financial circumstances than the descendants of the patentees of large crown grants. These people formed a lopsided majority of Caroline's electorate, but they were unable to gain control of the county's government, because a self-perpetuating group of great landlords, who inherited their estates, monopolized the positions as magistrates on the court.

There were ways, however, by which they made their influence increasingly felt. The most important of these was through the jury. In accordance with the best British traditions, all freeholders were eligible to serve in this capacity. Because the privilege was commonplace, planters of the ruling caste shunned it, as beneath their dignity, and the panels were made up almost entirely of men without inherited wealth. After the plain people began to demand more consideration, they soon learned that it was to their advantage to have their cases decided by a jury rather than the justices who formed the court. In 1764, when the magistrates fined Zachery and Errom Coghill, two small planters, ten shillings, each, for aggravating assault on Jacob King, bootlegger, the Coghills appealed for a jury trial and won their acquittals. A year later, a jury granted William Campbell, another small planter, a large judgment against the celebrated John Hoomes of Bowling Green, and when Hoomes refused to honor their verdict, ordered him to jail. Hoomes paid the judgment to get out of prison, but this did not end the matter. His friends hired a roughneck, John Spaulding, to give Campbell a thrashing, because he dared push a suit against a "gentleman" to such extremes. Ironically Campbell won the ensuing fight and Spaulding filed a suit for compensation for the injuries he sustained. When the case came to trial, Campbell demanded a jury, and again his faith in the common man was justified, because the jurors dismissed the charges and assessed the costs against the plaintiff.

Unfortunately, verdicts rendered by juries were as often as biased in favor of the plain people as the verdicts by the magistrates were biased in favor of the great landlords. While one jury sent John Hoomes, the great landlord, to jail for debt,

another refused to convict George Wiley, a small planter, and
Henry Mills, a crossroads trader, for breaking out of debtors'
prison. The court took judicial notice of this arbitrary miscarriage of justice, and angrily dismissed the jury, which was
composed of Samuel Reed, a rich man, who made his own
fortune as merchant at Chesterfield and planter on the North
Anna, and William Kidd, Thomas Taylor, Thomas Jones,
John Pemberton, James Gatewood, Thomas Pittman, Thomas
Coghill, John Garnett, Abraham Wilson, Anthony Sale and
Daniel Isbell, who were all thrifty small planters, for failing to
perform its duty.

After this fiasco debtors escaped from prison in increasing
numbers and went unpunished because of lenient juries until the
court fired William Johnston, the jailor, for getting drunk on
the job, and letting inmates walk away almost at will. This
move worsened rather than improved the situation because
Johnston's successor, Francis Coleman, was a young radical
and staunch desciple of Patrick Henry, who indoctrinated the
prisoners with the new liberalism sweeping across British
America, before allowing them to escape. When the court
found out what he was doing, they fired him, employed workmen "to make strong the locks" of the debtors' prison and
hired Bernard King, William Hobart, John Ferguson and
Harvey Harkless, landless headrighters without the right to
vote, to stand a twenty-four hours a day watch.

Juries did so well for the plain people at home that in 1767,
a group of Caroline small planters petitioned the General
Assembly to repeal the law which required that all white
persons accused of a capital crime be transported to Williamsburg for trial before the General Court of the Colony. The
reason that the petitioners gave for this request was convenience, which was indeed a part of the motive, but there were
other reasons as well. The small freeholders believed that
while juries in all cases were usually drawn from the county
that was the scene of the alleged crime, that the jury had a
better chance of dominating the trial and rendering a verdict
of their own making in the familiar surroundings of their home
courthouse, than in the strange environment of Williamsburg

with the governor's councilors, the most powerful men in the colony, presiding as trial magistrates.

A few years before (1763) a case tried in Williamsburg, which arose in Caroline, shocked the county. James Kay was tried for the murder of his wife, Mary Kay. This was the most heinous crime committed in Caroline until this date. It was the first time in the history of the county that a free white person had been accused of murder, and to make matters worse, the accusation was of a husband killing his wife.

The Kays were prominent people, not of magistrate rank but descendants of the original patentees of Caroline land. Facts in the case were garbled and opinion as to guilt was sharply divided. There was a preliminary hearing in the local court but the crown only presented enough evidence to establish probable guilt. Caroline people did not get a chance to hear the testimony of William Johnston, Nathaniel Carpenter, William Pemberton, Elizabeth Pemberton, Thomas Griffin, Mildren Griffin, Simon Kay, John Eastborough and Hannah MacDonald, who appeared in Williamsburg as witnesses. In due time Kay was convicted and hung. James Taliaferro administered his estate and found apprenticeships for his sons. But the rank and file in Caroline were never satisfied with the outcome because they were unable to learn all the facts in the case. There was a lingering doubt as to Kay's guilt, and many people were convinced that he might have a fairer trial before the court of his home county.

Pendleton promptly endorsed the Caroline freeholders' petition and introduced a bill to enact it into law. But his motives were quite different from those of his constituents. He wanted to get the cases away from Williamsburg because the people who came to the colonial capital from all sections of Virginia at the government's expense as jurymen and witnesses, were becoming increasingly troublesome. Instead of sticking to the business which brought them to Williamsburg they meddled in any problem which happened to be before the General Assembly. The influence they wielded on members forced the House of Burgesses to adopt four of Patrick Henry's "resolves" in opposition to the Stamp Act. But Pendleton was unable to get the measure enacted into law. It passed the House, but was defeated in the Council, where great landlord councillors lacked the foresight of great landlord Burgesses.

While the small freeholders sought to extend their powers through jury service the great landlords, who served as magistrates on the court, sought to curb them. Prior to 1767 the Clerk of the Caroline Court drew the names of freeholders out of a box for jury duty, indiscriminately. But beginning that year the justices began to pick the names put in the box from which the drawings were to be made. This new system was only partially successful, because seemingly it mattered not how hard the magistrates tried a preponderance of the jurors on the panels remained from the ranks of the artisans, crossroads traders and small planters.

9. THE SMEAR CAMPAIGN

After the court tried to fix juries by excluding the more troublesome freeholders from jury service, the landowners without social position or political influence struck back with a smear campaign designed to embarrass individual magistrates sufficiently to force them to resign from office. This skulduggery worked only in one case. John Sutton was the victim.

He was a native of Caroline County, the son of a former magistrate, and a leader among the small freeholders, although he was a great landlord before Governor Dinwiddie elevated him to the bench. But once a member of the court his position rapidly shifted and he soon became one of the royal government's staunchest partisans in Caroline. The crown rewarded him for this change. Dinwiddie named him to finish the incompleted term of Thomas Johnston as sheriff when Johnston resigned from office because of a shortage in the public accounts, and Fauquier appointed him to take over for Francis Taylor when Taylor gave up the office of sheriff under similar reasons, and for Edward Dixon, when Dixon refused to swear allegiance to the new king, George III.

These demonstrations of the confidence of royal governors in Sutton's integrity only added to the Caroline masses' desire to tear him down. But they were without grounds to attack him publicly and their resentment smouldered until 1767, when a suit was filed against him which exposed grievous defects in his character. The masses now had ammunition for their attacks and these attacks brought his political ruin.

Sutton, long since a widower, had made Sarah Mann, a servant woman, his mistress. Her term of service had expired and she demanded her freedom, but Sutton claimed he needed her services to minister to him in his old age and refused to let her go. His fellow magistrates on the court agreed with him, and Sarah remained in bondage and the story of his relations with the woman under cover until William Boulware, one of the ablest and most radical lawyers in the county, agreed to take her case without a fee, and enter suit against Sutton for her freedom.

Under Boulware's skillful handling Sutton's sordid relations with the woman were exposed. She was no ordinary indentured servant, transported from Great Britain to Virginia to serve a term of from three to seven years. She was instead the daughter of a white mother and a Negro, or mulatto, father bound to serve a master until she reached the age of thirty-one years, after which she must be set free and allowed to join society as a white person, in accordance with the law governing the children of white mothers and non-white fathers in force at the time. Boulware proved these facts, and the fact that Sarah Mann was thirty-one years old. But faced with this evidence, Sutton tried to intimidate the woman instead of setting her free. If she left him he threatened to send all their children to the "far west" to live among the Indians and grow up as "savages." He boasted that she would neither know where they were nor see them again.

This threat proved Sutton's undoing. Its barbaric nature shocked the great landlord magistrates, as well as the smaller freeholder public. A man's willingness to sacrifice his own children, even though they were illegitimate, was too drastic for either class to ignore. The court transferred Sarah Mann to Anthony Thornton for safekeeping while her case was pending and petitioned the governor to remove Sutton from office at once.

Governor Fauquier granted this request, and Sarah Mann

won her freedom. But this did not end the matter because a fierce controversy arose over the status of the children. There were at least five boys, Frank, Romulous, Remus, Caesar and Pompey (Sutton appears to have gone in for Roman names) and one girl Charlotte. All six of these people using the surname, Mann, rather than Sutton, brought suit for their freedom. While the law governing the children of white mothers and non-white fathers, which applied to Sarah, was clear, the law governing the status of a child born of a mother, who was the daughter of a white woman and a non-white man, while she was still in bondage, and a white father, had not been settled. Sutton contended that they were the slaves of the master to whom the mother was in bondage at the time of their birth. While the children acted through William Boulware, their attorney, contended that they automatically gained their freedom when their mother was set free. The cases dragged on until finally the General Court of the Colony rendered a compromise verdict, and ruled that the children were in the same position as their mother, and might be held in bondage until they were thirty-one, when they must be set free.

As an interesting sidelight, although Sutton was in disgrace and forced from the court, he remained a church warden for St. Margaret's Parish. His holding on to this position did not help the cause of the Established Church in the fight with the Baptist and other dissenters which was about to break out in that parish.

While public attention in Caroline was focused on the fitness of John Sutton for office, and the suits brought against him by the Manns, the British Parliament reasserted its right to tax the colonists by enacting duties on glass, paper, painters' colors and tea, brought into the colonies. These new taxes, unlike the Stamp Act, brought no great uproar in Caroline, where the people made a distinction between internal and external levies by the crown. Instead of protesting, the public, from small freeholder to great landlord, quit using the articles taxed.

With the question of Parliament's latest attempt to tax the colonist unsettled and the suits of the Mann children against John Sutton pending in the courts, Francis Fauquier died in Williamsburg and his rule of Virginia came to an end.

The Rule of
Botetourt and Its Aftermath
(1768-1771)

1. THE DISSENTERS ARE OPPRESSED

JOHN BLAIR, president of the Council, became acting governor of Virginia after Fauquier's death. He was a religious bigot and used his position to oppress the dissenters in the colony. The great landlords readily subscribed to this program because they believed that it was a means to keep the troublesome rising middle class in place.

In spite of the fact that by statute the Established Church of England was the Established Church of Virginia a large degree of religious tolerance was firmly embedded in the colony. Alexander Spotswood had opened the way for non-conformists to settle, when he persuaded the General Assembly to exempt the German Protestants, he brought to the upper Rappahannock Valley, from parish levies and compulsory attendance of services at the Government Church. William Gooch followed this precedent when he allowed the Pennsylvania Quakers to migrate to Virginia in 1732, and enlarged it a few years later, when he licensed Presbyterian ministers to preach and to hold divine services.

Other sects took advantage of this tolerance and established themselves in Virginia without official sanction. The Baptists became especially strong along the frontier where the royal government was more interested in a settler's stamina than his faith. From the beginning these settlers were able to visit the older regions of the colony without fear of persecution for their faith. When Daniel Stover of Orange, the first Baptist of record to enter the territorial limits of Caroline County, appeared before the Caroline Court in 1744, to reclaim a horse stolen from him, by Daniel Garity and removed to that county, the local magistrates did everything in their power to help him, rather than attempt to prosecute him after they learned that he was a dissenter. Although apparently no member of the court had ever heard of a Baptist before, the justices accorded him the privileges of the Quakers with which they were familiar and accepted his evidence upon affirmation, rather than under oath.

The only instances of religious persecution in Caroline, prior to 1768 were sporadic attempts to enforce the law which required all free persons, except those especially exempt by statute, to attend divine services at the Established Church. The punishment the court meted out for this offense was seldom more than a five shilling or fifty pounds of tobacco fine. The wholesale arrest for unorthodoxy and neglect of worship, which came in the wake of John Blair's assumption of office, as acting governor, caused one of the greatest upheavals in the county's history.

At the March term of the Caroline Court for 1768, which was the first term of the court under Blair's rule, a grand jury brought in presentments against John Burruss for "illegally preaching" at the home of Jacob Burruss in St. Margaret's Parish and at the home of Phillip Tinsley in Drysdale, Jacob Burruss for permitting the holding of "unauthorized" divine services in his home in St. Margaret's and Phillip Tinsley for permitting the holding of "unauthorized" divine services in his home in Drysdale, and John Thompson, James Gatewood, Thomas Terrell, Robert Chandler, George McNails, William Blades, Christopher Terrell, Robert Woolfolk, the son of Joseph Woolfolk, Thomas Burk, Martha Noden, Rachael Terrell, and Henry Terrell for attending "unauthorized" religious services at the home of Jacob Burruss and William Tinsley for attending "unauthorized" religious services at the home of Phillip Tinsley and Francis Fleming, William Earlington, John Pruitt, Thadeus Pruitt, Benjamin Pruitt, John Carden and Griffin Moody, of Drysdale, Lodowick George, John Southworth, Joseph Redd, Henry Tarrent, John Wyatt and John Burruss of St. Margaret's and Thomas Roy, James Bowie, Jr., William Parker, Jr. and John Bowie of St. Mary's for failure "to frequent their parish church for a period of two months." At the same session the grand jury returned presentments against Charles Carter of King George, a grandson of "King" Carter, for not keeping the road in repair across a milldam he owned in St. Mary's Parish, and William Sutton, Richard Edmundson, Robert Foster, Cornelius Reynolds and John Penn for letting their hound dogs run at large.

The court, which was composed of Edmund Pendleton, Robert Gilchrist, James Taylor, Robert Taliaferro, William Parker, James Miller, Thomas Lowry, John Armstead, promptly dismissed the charges against Carter, Sutton, Edmundson, Foster, Reynolds and Penn. For "reasons sufficient unto themselves" and deferred the presentments for crimes against the men and women accused of violating the laws governing religion, for action at a future session.

This postponement was fortunate for the accused. Their relatives and public opinion worked in their favor. Joseph Woolfolk got the charges against his son, Robert, dismissed at the April term of court, on the grounds that the accused was a callow youth, without the discretion to realize what he was doing when he listened to John Burruss preach. With this precedent established, the magistrates in time, dismissed the charges against all members of Burruss' congregations, and extended the ruling to include Jacob Burruss and Phillip Tinsley, for allowing their homes to be used for unauthorized religious services.

The Caroline Order Books are obscure about John Burruss' fate for preaching because several pages are missing. But the best evidence indicates that he escaped punishment temporarily by having two suritors post bonds of 25 pounds each for his good behavior. On the second charge against him he was not so fortunate because he, like all the rest accused of "not frequenting their parish church for two months," paid the customary fine of five shillings or fifty pounds of tobacco.

"Failure to frequent the parish church" was an old crime in Caroline and the court had set rules of precedent in regards to handling it. But "illegal preaching" and "attendance of unauthorized divine services" were something new. There were no established rules to guide the magistrates. They moved slowly, afraid of arousing public sentiment to the point of causing trouble. By the time they had disposed of all the cases arising out of John Burruss' preaching at Jacob Burruss' and Phillip Tinsley's, Lord Botetourt had replaced John Blair as governor of Virginia and religious persecutions for the time were over.

There is no record of the denominational faith of any of the accused, charged with violating the statutes, governing religion, in 1768 in the Order Books of the Caroline Court. But other sources clearly establish that John and Jacob Burruss, at least, were Baptists. Dr. L. M. Ritter in *A Memorial to Imprisoned Baptist Preachers* states that John Burruss was a native of Spotsylvania, and "was known as a 'helper' of John Waller" a celebrated dissenting minister of that county. This may be true but he was a resident of Caroline at the time of his arrest in 1768 because he was charged with failure "to frequent his parish church" as well as "illegal preaching" and only the court of the county in which the accused was a resident, had jurisdiction over the former offense. This charge also indicates that he was nominally, at least a communicant of the Established Church, for had he been reared a Quaker or a Presbyterian he would have been exempt from attending services of the state religion by the Toleration Act.

Our Quaker Friends of Ye Olden Times records that Jacob Burruss was originally a Quaker. The fact that he was not accused of "failure to frequent his parish church" gives supporting evidence to this fact. When he was converted to the Baptist faith is not known, but evidently it was some time before he allowed John Burruss to preach at his home in 1768. From records in the Caroline Order Books he was a man of considerable means and influence at the time of this arrest. His home was located in the area between Golansville and Carmel Church. There is no way to gauge how long Baptist services were held there, before they were made a matter of record by the religious persecutions of 1768, because public officials made little, or no, attempt to stamp out dissenting religious groups prior to that date. But afterwards they were held with a fair degree of regularity in spite of persecutions, and the men and women who met at Jacob Burruss' home to worship became the nucleus of Carmel, Caroline's oldest Baptist church.

The Terrells, who formed a substantial portion of John Burruss' first congregation of record, were Quakers, and there is no evidence to support the theory that they abandoned their old faith in favor of the new. In fact, several of their names are recorded as members of the Golansville Meeting in *Our Quaker Friends of Ye Olden Times* after they attended the services at Jacob Burruss'.

James Gatewood, Robert Chandler and Thomas Burk were leaders of the rising middle class and the chances are that their attendance was motivated more by politics than religion. They considered the Established Church as a tool of the great landlords and were interested in any movement which threatened to weaken it. But they did not feel this keenly enough to drop their membership in the State Church and join the new faith. They were never charged by the court with "failure to frequent their parish church." The Caroline Order Books fail to divulge any pertinent information about John Thompson, George Mc-Nails and William Blades, except that they were small planters and in debt. Robert Woolfolk was a mere youth, who went to hear John Burruss preach without his parents' consent, and Martha Noden was the daughter of Hugh Noden, a king's magistrate and great landlord. She was plagued by two notoriously dissipated brothers and apparently sought a more virulent faith than the one offered by the Established Church for solace.

John Burruss' attempt of 1768, to evangelize in Drysdale Parish, caused little interest. He attracted only two worshipers, Phillip and William Tinsley. Little is known of either of these men.

There is no evidence that any of the men, charged with failure to frequent their parish church, at the March term of the Caroline Court, in 1768, with the notable exception of John Burruss, had any interest in the Baptist faith. On the other hand there is proof that several of them did not. The Bowies, who appear to have been Presbyterians, had been in trouble periodically ever since the family settled in Caroline, because they refused to subscribe to the tenets of the Established Church. Thomas Roy and William Parker, Jr. were nominal communicants of the State Church beyond a shadow of a doubt. Neglect of church attendance, based on indifference, led to their arrest.

2. BOTETOURT IN WILLIAMSBURG

After Fauquier's death, George III and his advisors decided that the next commissioned representative of the crown, in Williamsburg, be the actual governor of Virginia, rather than his deputy because of the tension which existed, between that colony and the mother country. Deputies had ruled Virginia for sixty-three years and the king's clique attributed the growing disrespect of the colonists, for the crown, in a large measure, to the lack of a royal governor in residence. But no one with enough prestige to merit the job wanted the appointment with this requirement attached. Lord Jeffry Amherst, who held the position, promptly resigned, and eight months elapsed before the king persuaded Norborne Berkley, Baron deBotetourt, to give up the luxuries of London and go to Williamsburg.

Lord Botetourt was an affable, bumbling peer, a lord of the bedchamber and an accomplished courtier. But at the time of his appointment some members of Parliament questioned his ability to read and write. This lack of schooling, however, did not upset the Virginia aristocrats, because in many instances their education was no better.

Flattered because George III chose a peer to govern them, the colonists gave Botetourt a royal reception when he reached Williamsburg. The new governor reciprocated by launching a series of levees and balls at his palace. Social life for the aristocrats reached its greatest brilliance of the colonial era, and great landlords and their families from all sections of Virginia flocked to Williamsburg to attend the "Governor's Court." Lundsford Lomax spent so much time in the capital that he neglected his duties as magistrate in Caroline. He failed to attend a session of the county court while Botetourt was governor.

Contacts at "Court" with the governor, strengthened the aristocratic great landlord's position in the colony. Almost without an exception Botetourt filled appointive offices from their ranks. He made Henry Armistead, John Minor, William Buckner, Jr. and James Upshaw magistrates in Caroline, to take the place of Gabriel Throckmorton, who had moved out of the county, William Jones and Thomas Slaughter, who had refused to qualify on their last commissions, because they disapproved of punishing dissenters for violating laws governing worship, and Robert Gilchrist, a merchant extensively engaged in the import trade, who strenuously objected to the duties parliament levied on tea and other commodities coming into the colony.

Botetourt's failure to reappoint Gilchrist, caused widespread disapproval throughout Caroline. He was the second ranking magistrate on the court and had served the county well in that capacity, for over a decade. No governor since Gooch had failed to reappoint a Caroline magistrate, who wished to continue to serve. But Gilchrist was not of the landed aristocracy and that alone was enough to justify Botetourt's action among his chief advisors.

Frequent meetings at the "Governor's Court" caused more coöperation among the ruling aristocrats in developing the colony. George Washington formed a company to drain the Dismal Swamp, in which Samuel Gist, of Caroline, was a director. The magistrates of Caroline and Hanover agreed to build a series of bridges across the Pamunkey-North Anna connecting their counties. This was quite an accomplishment because after forty years of bickering they had only succeeded in getting one bridge (Littlepage, for the stage and mail) built. The first of these new structures was completed at Cook's ford in the fall of 1769. Several more were built the next year.

Discussions at the "Governor's Court" led to many plans to rid Virginia of dissension over religion. Botetourt persuaded the General Assembly to appoint a committee to study the question and directed county courts to quit punishing dissenters until after this committee filed its report. In Caroline only five persons, Firth(?) Gilkin, Francis Fleming, James Southworth,

Griffin Moody and John Brown, were punished for violating the laws governing worship, while Botetourt was in residence as governor, and their convictions were all for non-atteance of religious services, rather than participating in the services of a dissenting sect.

Edmund Pendleton was a chairman of the joint committee of Burgesses and Governor's Councillors, which studied the problems of dissent over religion, rampant in the colony. This committee under Pendleton's dominance sought means to strengthen the Established Church rather than to promote tolerance. It became interested in a movement, which originated in the north and was being promoted in the south by the Rev. Johnathan Boucher, of Caroline's St. Mary's Parish, to have the king create a bishop for his American colonies. Virginia churches were under the jurisdiction of the Bishop of London, and Boucher and his associates thought that the Bishop was too remote to exercise the proper discipline, and because of this lack of discipline the dissenters had gotten out of hand.

The Virginia Burgesses, led by Henry, refused to sanction this plan, contending that to place a bishop in charge of the enforcement of laws, governing worship and chancery matters dealing with estates and guardians and wards, as Boucher advocated, with courts and officials subject to the bishop, rather than the governor, was to "create a government within a government." Boucher rebutted this argument with a sermon at St. Mary's, on Mount Hill, in which he stated that Virginia's refusal to consent to the appointment of a bishop was "to unchurch the church."

Henry and other leading Burgesses construed Boucher's position as an attempt to win the office of bishop for himself. There is no evidence that this is true but he was eminently qualified for the post. He was one of the best educated clergymen in America and rector of one of the richest and most aristocratic parishes. His rectorship at St. Mary's had proven that he was a capable administrator, who knew how to deal with dissenters. New light sects such as the Baptists, failed to gain followers in St. Mary's while he was rector. Because of his success there he was called upon by the ministers of neighboring parishes, to help them with their people. Boucher in his autobiography attributes his success to the fact of "avoiding all disputation with their (the dissenters') ministers, whom I spoke of as beneath such condescension, on the score of their ignorance and impudence. And when one of them publicly challenged me to a public debate, I declined it but at the same time set up one, Daniel Barksdale, a carpenter of my parish, who had a good front and a voluble tongue, and whom therefore I easily qualified to defeat his opponent, as he effectually did. And I am still persuaded that this method of treating sectarian preachers with well judged ridicule and contempt, and their followers with gentleness, persuasion and attention, is a good one."

Boucher's plan, while successful locally, did not stop the spread of sectarianism in Virginia, and Pendleton's committee of Burgesses and Councillors offered no solution for the mounting controversy between dissenters and the Established Church. The fight for religious freedom continued.

3. BOTETOURT'S FAILURE AND DEATH

Botetourt was no more successful in reconciling the colonists to the payment of taxes levied by the British Parliament than he was in ironing out their differences over religion. He angered the Burgesses with the argument that since all the current levies were duties on imports, which in no sense fell directly on the person, property or income of an individual, they were not "taxation without representation."

This anger smouldered until the governor endorsed the action of the crown, in sending agents to Massachusetts, to make investigations for treason and bring suspects of this crime, to England for trial by a special tribunal, and the Burgesses in reprisal passed the celebrated resolves of 1769. These resolves reaffirmed the right of only the Burgesses to tax the colonists, denied the right of the sovereign to remove an accused from a colony to Britain for trial, and called for concerted action by all the colonies to defend themselves from further encroachments by Parliament and the king. When Botetourt heard of the Burgesses' actions he promptly dissolved that body and ordered new elections throughout the colony.

Caroline's Burgesses, Edmund Pendleton and Walker Taliaferro, both voted for the resolves of 1769. But evidently the freeholders of the county were dissatisfied with the part they played in securing passage, because in the ensuing election they defeated the placid and cautious Taliaferro and sent fiery Francis Coleman, to represent them in Williamsburg, in his stead.

Francis Coleman was the Patrick Henry of Caroline. He was born at the Courthouse, about 1740, where his parents, Samuel Coleman and Betty Wyatt Coleman, ran a tavern and trading post. He received the bulk of his education by attending court and formed his opinions after listening to arguments on the courthouse green and in his parents' tavern. His father died when he was a mere youth and he got his business training from his mother, who took over and operated both tavern and store. Through his father, he descended from homesteaders, and through his mother, from the patentees of large crown grants. But the large holdings of his maternal ancestors did not place him among the hereditary aristocrats, who controlled the county, because the Wyatts seldomly sought public offices or alliances with the great families through marriage.

While his immediate family cared little for high society, it was well-to-do. His father, Samuel Coleman, opened a tavern and store at the courthouse shortly after the first county seat was located in the Ideal-Kidds Fork-Shumansville triangle, and prospered. He secured contracts to supply the court with beer, to furnish fuel and light for the public buildings, and to feed the prisoners. For many years he was undersheriff of the county. But these public duties, while lucrative, did not keep him from pushing his private enterprises. He developed a large trade with people attending court. As his capital increased, he went more and more into the money lending business, until he was among the largest bankers in the county. He was doing so well that when the court considered moving the courthouse to a more central location, he sold the county the courthouse lot, which he happened to own at a modest price, to prevent the move. After his death his wife, Betty Wyatt Coleman, proved as astute in business as her spouse. She managed to keep all his enterprises going although her children were infants. At her death young Francis, was co-heir to a tidy fortune.

Francis Coleman, unlike his idol Henry, was successful in business from his youth. But this success did not cause him to cast his lot with the landed aristocrats. He was always on the side of the poor and the oppressed. He knew their problems through conversations he overheard on the courthouse green from childhood, and because he sympathized, was ready to fight their battles. When he took over as jailor, after the court dismissed William Johnston for getting drunk on the job, he became keenly interested in the plight of poor debtors.

Patrick Henry found an ardent disciple in young Coleman after he won a reputation in the Parson's Case and begun to spend the night at Coleman's tavern while looking after his expanding practice in the Caroline Court. Under his guidance the youth developed into a local leader in the fights for religious freedom and against taxation without representation; his greatest ambition became to win a seat in the House of Burgesses and join his mentor in the crusade for liberty. To make himself a more formidable candidate he qualified as a lawyer in 1768, and like Henry, literally moved from bar (tavern) to bar (court).

When Botetourt dissolved the Burgesses in 1769 because of the "resolves" and ordered new elections throughout the colony, Coleman got his chance to be a candidate. Edmund Pendleton and Walker Taliaferro, the Caroline incumbent Burgesses, were shocked at his audacity, and the great landlords, who controlled the local court, were alarmed. They knew that he was a radical from the arguments he advanced in discussions on the court green. All conservative forces joined hands to bring about his defeat. But these elements worked in vain. The small freeholders, whose cause he espoused, rallied to his support. When the election came he topped Pendleton in the vote and eliminated Taliaferro from the House of Burgesses.

The results, while flattering, were only partially satisfactory to Coleman and his partisans, because it was Pendleton rather than Taliaferro whom they and their advisor, Henry, wanted to defeat.

Coleman's reputation preceeded him to Williamsburg, and because he was a radical, Botetourt refused to name him to the Caroline Court, an appointment which traditionally came automatically with the election as Burgess. This slight gave him the distinction of being the only Caroline Burgess, who was not a magistrate. But Botetourt's slight appears not to have upset him. Instead of sulking he joined the fight against taxes levied by Parliament and oppressive laws governing worship. Unfortunately he died within a few months after he took his seat as Burgess. His death cut short the career of one of the most promising leaders of the Revolution; a career which promised to emblaze his name in eternal fame along with the names of Henry, Mason and Lee. After his death the Caroline voters returned the cautious Walker Taliaferro to Williamsburg in a by-election.

4. THE NELSON INTERIM

Governor Botetourt died in Williamsburg on November 15, 1770. His death took the government of George III by surprise and almost a year elapsed before the king's ministers were able to find a suitable man to send to Virginia as commissioned representative of the crown in residence. During this interim William Nelson, who had succeeded John Blair as president of the Council, was acting governor.

Nelson like Blair and other Councillors was a leader among the aristocrats with hereditary wealth, who were more afraid of the demands of the lower orders of society than oppression by the crown. He agreed with his fellow Councillors that Virginia needed a strong State church to help keep "troublesome" elements in their place and to put this program in force ordered a renewal of persecution of dissenters, begun by Blair but held in abeyance by Botetourt.

The reinauguration of this program made itself felt in

Caroline in May 1771, when John Young was brought before the local court and charged with "preaching the gospel at Thomas Pittman's contrary to law." A grand jury of which George Muse, a great landlord, was foreman, indicted Young for this offense and at the same time returned true bills against John Goodrich, Thomas Collins, Charles Chewning, Micajah Stevens and Edmund and Elizabeth Beazley for attending the service. When arraigned Young offered no defense and "acknowledged that he preached the gospel at Thomas Pittman's to a number of people, not having Episcopal ordination or being licensed as a dissenting preacher, contrary to the Acts of Toleration. 'Tis therefore considered by this court that he be committed to the gaol of this county and their (sic) remain, 'til he give security for himself in the penalty of 50 pounds and two surities each, for his good behavior for one year and one day." (Caroline Order Book for 1771.)

Edmund Pendleton, John Taylor, Thomas Lowry, Walker Taliaferro, Anthony Thornton and John Minor were the magistrates, who formed the court which imposed this sentence. The same court quashed the indictments against members of Young's congregation.

This conviction, however, did not stop Young, who was a small planter and a constable, until he got into difficulties with the law, in lower St. Margaret's Parish. He appealed his case to the General Court of the Colony and continued to preach while it pended. His efforts with the assistance of the Presbyterians led to the establishment of a church to be known, in time, as Mt. Horeb, Caroline's second oldest Baptist congregation.

Young appears to have made a more lasting impression on his hearers than John Burruss, the first dissenter of record to preach in Caroline in violation of the law, in their early sermons, because of Young's congregation the families of Thomas Pittman, John Goodrich and Charles Chewning became prominent in the spread of the Baptist faith while of John Burruss' hearers of record only Jacob Burruss took part in the movement. Within two months after the Caroline Court convicted John Young for preaching at Thomas Pittman's, it convicted

James Goodrich, Bartholemew Chewning and Edward Herndon for "preaching and teaching the gospel without Episcopal ordination or a license from the court" and sentenced them to prison until they furnished bond of twenty pounds each, to keep the peace for a year and a day. These men were small planters of St. Margaret's Parish. Goodrich and Chewning were the descendants of homesteaders and while Herndon's original Caroline ancestor was the patentee of a large crown grant, by his generation the family's holdings were reduced to relatively small tracts. The Order Books of Caroline Court reveal that the trio were interested in the civic and commercial life of their community as well as the religious. They served as constables, road supervisors, jurors and appraisors of estates. There is no evidence to indicate that they were either bigots or cranks about religion. The chances are that they regarded themselves as teachers rather than preachers, because of the long list of accused brought before the Caroline Court charged with violating the law governing worship, they alone were charged with "teaching the gospel" contrary to law.

In mid-summer 1771, the struggle for religious freedom in Caroline County entered a new phase. Prior to that time only local residents had taken part in the movement and it had been confined primarily to St. Margaret's Parish. John Burruss' missionary journey of 1768 into Drysdale, met with indifference. He gained no converts at his only service of record at Tinsley's. The erratic but brilliant Johnathan Boucher had little trouble in keeping new light preachers out of his aristocratic parish of St. Mary's. This situation changed when Lewis Craig, an outsider, came into the county and chose Drysdale Parish as the field of his missionary activities.

Craig, who held a license to preach without Episcopal ordination under the Toleration Act, was a native of Spotsylvania and one of the earliest leaders of Baptist evangelism in the territory between the Rappahannock and the James. He helped organize the first Separate Baptist Church in that region (Upper Spotsylvania or Craig's in 1767) and had been imprisoned at least twice for abusing his license to preach under the Toleration Act, in Spotsylvania jail, before he came to Caroline.

The appearance of an outsider in Drysdale preaching a dissenting faith caused Caroline's great landlords to act. Heretofore they found no cause for alarm lest sectarians take over the county, because a handful of residents in St. Margaret's chose to become Baptist. Traditionally that parish was the home of non-conformist in worship. It had harbored a large colony of Quakers since 1732 and a Presbyterian congregation since the 1740's. Neither of these sects had gotten out of control. There was no reason to assume that native Baptists in that region, could not be held in line by the normal functioning of the court. But the appearance of an outsider in Drysdale preaching the Baptist faith was quite another matter. The magistrates directed Anthony Thornton, member of the court, ex-sheriff and county lieutenant, to take the necessary steps to curtail the propagation of the Baptist faith in Caroline County.

Thornton arrested Craig at once and kept him in jail until the next session of the Caroline Court. Brought before the magistrates for trial the accused "acknowledged that he had preached the gospel without Episcopal ordination and contrary to the license granted him by the General Court." (Order Books of the Caroline Court.) Upon hearing this confession the magistrates ordered Craig to post bond of twenty pounds to keep the peace for a year and a day. When he refused to obey this order they sent him back to jail.

Although Craig's first ministry in Caroline was short lived, he planted seed which in time germinated and flourished. This work led to the formation of Tuckahoe Church, later to be known as Upper Zion, which was Caroline's third oldest Baptist congregation.

As the fight for religious freedom grew more intense non-conformist faiths specifically protected under the Toleration Act felt the heavy hand of persecution as well as the Baptists. When Benjamin Faulkner, John and Walter Mackie appeared before the Caroline Court in 1771 and asked permission for the Presbyterians, who had been holding regular services in lower St. Margaret's Parish for over two decades, to build a house of worship on the lands of Melchezedeck Braime near Needwood, Edmund Pendleton, Walker Taliaferro, Thomas

Lowry and William Buckner, the magistrates who heard the petition, turned the request down "for lack of jurisdiction."

Not all the great landlords of the hereditary aristocracy, however, were intolerant. James Taylor, sheriff of Caroline in 1771, was opposed to persecution of dissenters. Because of this attitude a majority of the magistrates on the court regarded him a traitor to his caste and sought to embarrass him by naming Anthony Thornton as their special agent to deal with Lewis Craig and other sectarian leaders. After this move failed to force Taylor to change his position the court trumped up charges that he was short in his accounts in an attempt to force him out of office. Upon its recommendation Thomas Nelson, Secretary of the Colony, presented him a bill for 6,446 pounds of tobacco. Taylor realized his unfortunate position, made up the alleged shortage out of his private fortune, and completed his term of office.

The Rule of Dunmore

(1771-1776)

1. THE BEGINNING OF HIS RULE

WHEN John Murray, Earl of Dunmore, whom the ministers of George III finally chose to succeed Botetourt in Williamsburg, reached Virginia early in 1772, he found the colony suffering from the freshets of 1771. These rainfalls raised streams to unprecedented heights. Floods washed away crops and homesteads and drowned numerous people. Milldams broke and bridges collapsed. When the waters subsided in many places thick deposits of sand covered once fertile fields and newly accumulated bars diverted the channels of rivers and blocked navigation.

The new governor immediately launched a program of internal improvements to repair, so far as possible, the ravages caused by the catastrophe, and to restore the morale of the people. This program included a project to improve navigation and control floods along the Caroline section of the Mattapony. The House of Burgesses refused to appropriate any funds for this purpose but the crown granted a charter to a company to clear the channel and collect tolls from navigation for reimbursement. This company was organized under Pendleton's guidance but it got little work done before the Revolution began.

Taking its cue from the example set by the governor the Caroline court authorized the rebuilding, or the repair, of all bridges across the Mattapony, and engaged workmen to build the first new bridge across that stream in twenty-five years. This structure was at Samuel Hawes' plantation and connected St. Margaret's Parish with the new trading center growing up near the Bowling Green.

The Hanover and Caroline magistrates had trouble over agreements to restore bridges across the North Anna until Samuel Hargrove offered to take over the job, rebuild all the bridges at once, and allow the counties to pay him in seven equal instalments, extending over seven years, for his work.

The Caroline court granted seven permits to build gristmills, the permit for the restoration of another, and rejected the applications for two, in 1772 as a result of the freshets, in the greatest gristmill building boom in the county's history. Heretofore the magistrates moved slowly in granting permits for new mills. They first made the applicant prove a definite need. But after the floods broke practically every dam in the county they decided that there could not be too many mills if the county were to be prepared when another such emergency arose.

Four of these new mills were in upper St. Margaret's Parish. Henry Terrell secured leave to dam the north fork of the upper Polecat, James Dismukes a branch of that stream, Benjamin Winn, the headwaters of South River (the Rattle-trap or Temple's or Davis' Mill in 1953), and James Harris a stream which this author is unable to locate, over the protest of William Chiles, because the new pond threatened to flood his bottom lands. Two of the mills were in St. Mary's; one with a pond entirely on the lands of Garwin Corbin at "the Neck," and the other to be operated by Nicholas Ware with a pond extending over the land of numerous property owners in the upper end of the parish. The seventh was in upper Drysdale. Seth Thornton secured permission to build a mill after he promised to furnish free grinding for all freeholders whose lands were flooded by the proposed pond. The restored mill also was in Drysdale. James Garnett received permission to rebuild a mill formerly operated by Col. Cole Digges in the lower end of the parish.

One rejection was on account of a peach orchard and the other resulted in a bitter lawsuit. When John Sutton asked permission to rebuild a mill he once operated near Burk's Bridge, the court denied the request because Thomas Burk had brought into production a fine peach orchard on Burk's portion of the old pond bed. Peaches were a luxury in the county and the basis of the most expensive locally distilled brandy. The Caroline Order Books fail to make clear the details of the lawsuit which brought about the second rejection, but they emphasize its bitterness. James Reynolds asked permission to build a mill on Woodson's branch and it was turned down after a jury composed of Abraham Wilson, John Durrett, William Wright, Henry Goodloe, Benjamin Harrison, Thomas Coghill, James Coleman, Thomas Hawes, Nicholas Oliver, Thomas Goodrich, George Madison and Thomas Laughlin spent days tramping over the proposed site.

Two deaths occurred in Caroline the first year of Dunmore's rule, which profoundly effected the social, political and economic life of the county. The two who died were John Baylor and Thomas Roy. Baylor was perhaps Caroline's richest resident. He certainly had established the county's highest standard of living. His residence at New Market was a show-place, and his imported thoroughbreds were known on race-tracks throughout the colony. He was a close friend of royal governors and a top leader in the great landlord caste. His death was a blow to the royalists because his sons who took over his vast holdings were liberals, and they used the family fortune to advance the patriots' cause during the Revolution. Roy was the owner of the county's larger chartered warehouse and one of its most influential business men. After his death his son and heir, John Beverley Roy, broke up his estate. Young Roy sold the chartered warehouse to James Miller, a Port Royal merchant and magistrate. Miller continued to operate the warehouse as "Roy's" but he made changes which the public did not like. One of the most objectionable was the removal of the main entrance from the street side of the building to the river side which was only reached by a long and narrow gangplank extending high over the Rappahannock. After several planters, who imbibed too freely in alcoholic beverages in Port Royal taverns while waiting for inspectors to process their crops, fell into the water when they attempted to return to the warehouse and pick up their tobacco certificates, a delegation complained of the change to the court. The magistrates were sympathetic and although the proprietor was a fellow justice they ordered him to restore the entrance to its original position. This change was trivial but there were more far-reaching consequences resulting from the transfer about which the public did not complain. The Roys were patriots and James Miller was a Tory, and the sale caused the assets of the warehouse to be used in behalf of the king rather than the rebelling colonists during the Revolution.

Although John Beverley Roy sold the chartered warehouse he retained the major portion of Thomas Roy's other business enterprises. The tavern, which for a long time Thomas Roy had leased out, he turned over to William Buckner, who was married to his daughter, Dorothy Roy II. Buckner took over the active management of the tavern. His ordinary license was among the first the Caroline Court granted to the descendant of the patentee of a large crown grant. The granting of this license indicates that a change was taking place in Caroline County. The next year Robert Woolfolk took out a license in his own name to operate a tavern at Needwood, and the year thereafter John Hoomes applied for a license "to run an ordinary in his new buildings at Bowling Green." A new day was dawning with the approaching Revolution and many old line aristocrats were no longer too proud to engage in trade.

2. RENEWAL OF THE FIGHT FOR RELIGIOUS FREEDOM

The Baptists of Caroline took advantage of the courtesy session of the General Assembly that Governor Dunmore called in 1772, to file with the House of Burgesses a petition which asked for their sect the right of freedom of worship under the Toleration Act.

This petition read in part, "The Society of Christians called Baptists are not indulged with the Free Exercise of their Religion, and they are deprived of the benefits of the Toleration Act, though they are willing to conform to the Spirit of it, and are quiet and loyal subjects; that their teachers are persecuted, while liberty of Conscience is permitted to Protestants of other Persuasions, and therefore praying that the Petitioners meet the same kind of Indulgence in Religious matters as the Quakers, Presbyterians and other different Protestants do enjoy." (*Journal* of the House of Burgesses for 1772.)

This was the first instance of record when the Baptists of

Virginia officially asked the royal government of the colony for their rights under the Toleration Act. The fact that the request came from Caroline indicates the strength and the quality of the leadership of the faith in that county. The text of the petition summed up the position of the Baptists at the time. They were in no mood to rebel but only wanted equal rights with other dissenters. They did not protest against the law, but the interpretation of the law by the great landlord magistrates who formed their local court.

Leaders of the Established Church in Caroline, also acknowledged the rising strength of the Baptists in that county, at the same session of the General Assembly, by petitioning the Burgesses to consolidate the upper ends of St. Margaret's and Drysdale parishes in a new parish centering on Guiney's Bridge. These leaders realized that unless something was done at once to make minister and church more convenient to the residents of this district, that the bulk of the small planters, and their families, were going over to the Baptists, because the Bull Church below South River and the Creek Church near the Bowling Green, were too far away for regular attendance without undue hardships. But tight-fisted great planters in the region filed a counter petition opposing the plan on account of the expense of building a new house of worship if it were adopted.

Governor Dunmore prorogued the Assembly before the Burgesses acted on any of these petitions and the persecution of Baptists in Caroline was revived with renewed vigor. In short order Nathaniel Holloway and James Ware were arrested for preaching without a license and John Waller, a licensed minister, was locked up for conducting an unauthorized revival.

Holloway was a veteran of the French and Indian War, whom the Caroline Court had rewarded with the position of constable before he became a Baptist. He was arrested for preaching at the home of John Partlow, another ex-constable, in upper St. Margaret's Parish. Local law enforcement officers arrested both Holloway and Partlow. When their case came to trial they refused the magistrates' offer to post bonds of twenty pounds, each, to keep the peace for a year and a day, and went to jail.

Ware's arrest for preaching at James Pittman's tavern in Drysdale Parish marked another turning point in the propogation of the Baptist faith in Caroline County. Heretofore services were held only in private homes or out of the way places, this was the first instance of record when unauthorized worship was conducted openly in a tavern. In addition Ware was a member of the county's minor gentry, he held a commission in the militia, while heretofore the leaders of new light faiths had come from plainer stock.

Powerful friends came to Ware's rescue after he "got into trouble." William Taliaferro and Christopher Singleton, rich planters of the great landlord caste, offered to post bond for his good behavior. This was the first instance of record that great landlords befriended a Baptist in Caroline since Daniel Stover faced the local court, over two decades before. But Ware was not willing to accept this bond on the usual conditions, supported by Taliaferro and Singleton he contended that "keeping the peace" he construed literally and not as a bar to preaching. The magistrates refused to accept this construction and Ware remained in jail for sixteen days while they wrangled. At the end of this period the magistrates gave in and ordered his release, without a provisor against preaching in the bond to keep the peace. John Waller's arrest for conducting an unauthorized revival at Henry Goodloe's residence in upper St. Margaret's Parish shortly after James Ware's release from jail, brought members of the landed aristocracy openly into the fight for religious freedom in Caroline, because while Ware was minor gentry, Waller and Goodloe were major, and they acted to make converts rather than to help a friend, as was the case with Taliaferro and Singleton.

Waller was a member of one of the great families of Virginia, and while he was a native of Spotsylvania his ancestors had large crown grants in Caroline and he had numerous cousins in the county. He was reared in the traditions of the scions of the landed gentry, and in his youth because of his dissipations was known as "Swearing Jack Waller" and "the

Devil's Adjutant" until his conversion to the Baptist faith in 1767.

Henry Goodloe at whose home Waller preached, was a son of George Goodloe, an early magistrate, who served as sheriff of Caroline County, and who had a crown grant in upper St. Margaret's Parish. Through wealth and inheritance Henry Goodloe easily qualified as a member of the ruling caste.

The combination of Waller preaching at Goodloe's so alarmed the aristocracy that the court sent Anthony Thornton, the county lieutenant, whom it had delegated to deal with dissenters, because of the lax attitude of James Taylor, the sheriff, to lead a raid on one of these services, at the head of a band of constables. The raid resulted in the arrest of Waller and Goodloe but not before Thornton had trouble with lay members of the congregation. When he ordered the assembled worshippers to disperse, they defied him until he ordered his accompanying constables to take three of their leaders, Andrew Ross, Thomas Kelley and Mathew Gale, into custody for "failure to obey a legal command, and disrespect to the person of Anthony Thornton, a magistrate."

At the ensuing trial Samuel Daniel and Betty Chewning, two other members of Waller's congregation, defied the court and refused to obey its sumons and appear as witnesses for the crown. The magistrates fined them each, three hundred and fifty pounds of tobacco for this offense in absentia, and proceeded with the trial of the case with only the evidence of the arresting officers. The verdict was five pounds, sterling, fines for Ross, Kelley and Gale for their impudence, and bonds of ten pounds for Goodloe and forty pounds for Waller to keep the peace for a year and a day. Ross, Kelley and Gale paid the fines, although they were excessive, but Goodloe and Waller refused to post the bonds and went to jail.

History has proven that Goodloe and Waller did not make their sacrifices in vain because from the services they held at Goodloe's plantation, located on the north side of Campbell's Creek between U. S. Route One and Blanton's Post Office (1953 names) developed Bethany and County Line Baptist churches, which through the years have been the rural churches with the largest memberships in Spotsylvania and Caroline counties.

Despite persecutions, the Caroline Baptists were strong enough by 1763 to hold regular services of their faith in organized congregations. The first of these congregations met on Jacob Burruss' plantation in upper St. Margaret's Parish with John Burruss as minister. In colonial times it had three names; "Polecat" from Polecat Creek which flowed nearby, "Burruss" from the names of the plantation owner and minister, and "Roundabout" because the members used roundabout ways to reach the place of worship to avoid detection and arrest by law enforcement officers. After many years of distinguished service this congregation adopted its current name "Carmel" in 1838.

Shortly after the organization of the meeting at Jacob Burruss', John Young, who was out of jail on bail while an appeal on his conviction for preaching without a license in the Caroline Court pended in the General Court of the Colony, began holding Baptist services each Sabbath Day, in "an outhouse" on his plantation in lower St. Margaret's. The word "outhouse" to describe the building in which Young conducted the services appears in the record of his trial for holding unauthorized worship in the Order Books of the Caroline Court. Since the magistrates who wrote these records were communicants of the Established Church to whom only a building dedicated exclusively to worship in accordance with the rites of the State religion was a church, the chances are that they used the term in its derogatory sense and the building Young used for worship was actuallly a building dedicated to the worship of God. If this assumption be true Young's "outhouse" was actually the first Baptist church building in Caroline County.

John Young's second conviction was the last record in the Order Books of the conviction of a Baptist in Caroline County for violating the laws governing worship. Semple, the great historian of the early Baptist Church in Virginia, states that Hipkins Pittman, a resident member of Reed's (John Young's) Church, "was taken up and threatened to be whipped but was discharged without further injury" in 1775, and that same

year "in the bounds of Tuckahoe (later Upper Zion) Church
—Younger Pitts, a preacher, and a man by the name of
Pickett were taken up and carried by force some distance, as if
with a view to bring to a magistrate, but after some abuse etc.
they set them at liberty." (Beale's *Semple,* page 156.)

In addition to the two instances cited above, unofficial sources
reveal many other acts of violence against Baptists in pre-
Revolutionary Caroline, which in some cases may be exaggera-
tions, since the records were written by Baptists either during
or shortly after the fight for religious freedom in the county.
Lewis Peyton Little in his *Imprisoned Preachers and Religious
Liberty in Virginia,* pages 229-231, gives two versions of the
abuse of John Waller. The first, from Morgan Edwards'
Volumes, page 34, reads, "In the spring of 1771 as he was
holding divine worship in Caroline County the minister of the
parish (Morton) and his clerk (Thomas Buckner) with the
sheriff (William Harris) came to the place. Mr. Morton
strode up to the stage on which he stood and with his whip
tumbled over the leaves of the book as Mr. Waller was giving
out the psalm; but Waller held his thumb on the place until
the whole was sung; then Mr. Waller began to pray; and his
reverence Morton ran the butt end of his whip into Waller's
mouth and silenced him. After that the clerk, Buckner, pulled
him down and dragged him and whipped him in so violent a
manner (without the ceremony of a trial) that poor Waller
was presently in a gore of blood and will carry the scars to his
grave. However, Waller, sore and bloody as he was, remounted
the stage and preached a most extraordinary sermon.

The second version was from Elder John Williams' *Journal,*
reputedly written within two weeks after the incident happened,
from information Waller gave Williams as they rode together
to the Baptist association. This version reads "Brother Waller
informed us about two weeks ago on the Sabbath Day down in
Caroline County he introduced the worship of God by singing.
While he was singing the Parson of the Parish would keep
running the end of his horsewhip in his mouth, laying the whip
across the hymn book etc. When done singing he proceeded to
prayer. In it he was violently jerked off the stage; they caught

him by the back part of his neck, beat his head against the ground, sometimes up, sometimes down, they carried him through a gate that stood some considerable distance, where a gentleman gave him something not less than twenty lashes with his horsewhip. After that they carried him through a long lane. At the end thereof they stopped in order for him to dispute with the parson. The parson came up and gave him abominable ill language, and away he went with his clerk and one more. Then Brother Waller was released, went back singing praise to God, mounted the stage and preached with a great deal of liberty."

Careful reading reveals considerable difference in the two versions of this incident. The older version given by Elder Williams makes no mention of the sheriff taking part in the disgraceful affair, and identifies neither the parson nor his clerk by name. The latter version by Edwards has the sheriff, William Harris, whipping Waller and identifies the minister of the Established Church as Mr. Morton and his clerk as Thomas Buckner. His identifications are in part, at least, inaccurate, because pre-Revolutionary Caroline never had a sheriff named William Harris. James Taylor, a kindly man, who opposed persecution of dissenters, was sheriff of Caroline at the time the incident occurred, the chances are that while Waller was abused, the extent of his abuse has been grossly exaggerated by Baptist partisans.

The only occasion of record of physical violence inflicted on dissenters being countenanced by the court in Caroline concerns Presbyterians rather than Baptists. In 1773 when Samuel Mackie, Sr. and Samuel Mackie, Jr. charged Thomas Reynolds with entering their home near Needwood while drunk and breaking up the Presbyterian services in progress, the court instead of punishing Reynolds for this crime, exonerated him, and ordered the Mackies to post bond for ten pounds each to keep the peace for a year and a day because of the injuries they inflicted on Reynolds while ejecting him from their home. The Mackies refused to post this bond and went to jail.

While from the records of the Order Books, the Caroline Court rarely went further than to order violators of the laws

governing worship to post bond to keep the peace after conviction, and to incarcerate them until they posted such bonds,
the magistrates at an early date used other statutes, both civil
and criminal to harass dissenters. When law enforcement
agencies were unable to break up the holding of Baptist services
at Jacob Burruss' plantation the court ordered Burruss to open
an unused road to his gristmill, and when he was unable to
comply with this order in a limited time, fined him ten pounds,
sterling. Next the magistrates charged him with failing to keep
his milldam in repair, and fined him an additional ten pounds
although he produced evidence in court that it was in excellent
condition. After these two attempts failed to break Burruss'
will his enemies stirred up his creditors against him and the
court forced him to settle all his accounts at once at a time
when extended credit was the accepted practice.

In 1773 when Archibald Dick, the rector of St. Margaret's
parish, Samuel Hargrave, Secretary of the Golansville Quaker
Meeting, and Thomas Pittman, who let Lewis Craig hold
Baptist services in his home, all failed to list their chaises for
taxation, the court excused Dick but fined Hargrave and Pittman 500 pounds of tobacco each.

The crudest discrimination took place when Robert Month
was brought to trial for breaking into Nathaniel Holloway's
home while Holloway was in jail because he refused to post
bond to keep the peace after his conviction of preaching at
John Partlow's. In this trial the magistrates refused to accept
the testimony of Mary Holloway, the wife of Nathaniel, because she was a Baptist, and William Taliaferro because he
posted bonds for James Ware and James Pittman, and Month
went free because of the lack of evidence to sustain a conviction. Devout adherents to the Established Church also used
harsh means to control members of their families who went
over to the New Lights. The Goodloes had the court declare
Henry Goodloe insane after he let John Waller preach at
his home.

Discrimination and persecution, however, failed to halt the
establishment of religious freedom in Caroline. As time went
on more and more prominent people joined the crusade for

tolerance. In 1773 Joseph DeJarnette, the teacher, and William Boulware, the lawyer, were among the accused who paid fines of five shillings for failing to frequent their parish church.

3. AUTOCRATIC RULE

Lord Dunmore soon demonstrated that he had little patience with democratic processes. His program of internal improvements turned out to be largely a ruse to divert the attention of troublesome Burgesses from more controversial issues during the session of the General Assembly, custom forced him, as a new governor, to call shortly after he arrived in Williamsburg. When he complied with this formality he prorogued the lawmakers and set up personal rule. In his choice of magistrates for the county courts he was no more democratic, and tried to fill all vacancies with Tories.

Seven vacancies existed on the Caroline Court. Lundsford Lomax, Jr., Benjamin Robinson, Jr., and John Baynham were dead. John Taylor had left the colony, William Tyler had resigned on account of old age, and George Taylor and Jeremiah Rawlings refused to serve because they disapproved of the royal government's tax program and the persecution of dissenters. To fill these vacancies Dunmore named Henry Armistead, Garwin Corbin, Roger Quarles, William Harrison, Anthony New, George Guy and Robert Gilchrist. Armistead, Corbin, Quarles and Harrison were descendants of the patentees of large crown grants and members of families with reputations of loyalty to the king. New was the stepson of John Baynham and took Baynham's place on the court. George Guy was a lawyer, already favorably known in royal circles in Williamsburg before he decided to settle in Caroline. Robert Gilchrist had served for many years on the court before Botetourt refused to reappoint him because he was a trader rather than a landed aristocrat. His reappointment was popular with all classes in the county, and the new appointees the governor named were satisfactory. Dunmore, however, was only partially successful in his attempt to pack the court with Tories. When the colonists declared their independence of Great Britain,

Harrison alone of the new appointees remained steadfast in his loyalty to the crown throughout the Revolution, although it took Gilchrist several months and Corbin almost half a year to make up their minds to foreswear their allegiance to the king and become active participants in the patriots' cause.

The court as now constituted, Edmund Pendleton, James Taylor II, Anthony Thornton, Sr., Walker Taliaferro, John Buckner, William Buckner, Jr., James Miller, William Parker, Thomas Lowry, James Upshaw, John Armistead, Samuel Hawes and the seven new members, was the last court to govern Caroline for the crown. The court began its regime by trying to look out for the interest of the great landlords and the king, but before the Declaration of Independence ended its rule most of the magistrates, who formed its membership had abandoned the king and were only concerned about the position of the great landlords in the new era which was at hand.

One of the first acts for the new court in behalf of the crown was to bring John Penn to trial for treasonable speech. Penn was one of the most brilliant lawyers at the local bar and a leader of the county's radical element. The grand jury indited him upon information furnished by Chillion White, a constable, and William Dew, for making remarks critical of the royal government and the king, the exact wording of which the Caroline Order Books, unfortunately, fail to disclose, in the interim between Botetourt and Dunmore while William Nelson, as president of the Council, ruled Virginia. After the indictment Penn's trial lagged, perhaps, because three of his relatives, James, John and George Taylor were magistrates. But with the naming of the new court only one of these relatives retained a seat and he was brought before the bar of justice.

In the trial the Caroline magistrates instructed the jury to bring a verdict for the crown as the Hanover magistrate had done nine years before in the trial of the Parson's Case. But the Caroline jury, with Richard Roy as foreman, also followed precedent set in Hanover, and brought in a verdict for one penny.

As a result of this verdict the monetary costs to Penn for his injudicious statements was slight. In addition to the penny fine,

he only had to pay 12 pounds of tobacco to White and Dew
for appearing in court against him. But the disgrace was great.
After his conviction he lost interest in Caroline and began
setting his affairs in order in preparation to move his residence
from the county. This took over two years because he was
engaged in a variety of undertakings with numerous people.
When it was finally done he departed to establish a new home
in Granville County, North Carolina, where close kinsmen
had already settled. Abuse, however, strengthened rather than
weakened Penn's faith in liberty. Two years after he left Caroline, he attended the Continental Congress in Philadelphia, as
a delegate from his adopted province, North Carolina, and
achieved immortal fame as a Signer of the Declaration of
Independence.

The conviction of Penn brought a rash of accusations by
royalists against radical patriots for seditious speech in the
Caroline Court. In rapid order the grand jury indicted Amy
Taylor, who appears to have been Penn's aunt, Thomas Ditmar, John Montague, Mitchael Crenshaw, one of the Robert
Woolfolks, (there were at least three men of this name in
Caroline at the time) and Thomas Collins. But sympathetic
juries, in spite of the pressure from the magistrates, refused to
convict Amy Taylor, Montague, Crenshaw and Woolfolk.
Collins did not fare so well. He was tried by a jury with John
Broaddus, who up until this time remained one of the staunchest royalists in the county as foreman and fined five pounds,
sterling, "for making remarks about the crown which led to a
breach of the king's peace."

After Collins' conviction the Caroline Court continued to try
cases of sedition almost to the eve of the Declaration of Independence. William Boulware, the attorney, successfully defended Thomas Tennant in the most celebrated of these cases
in 1775. But in March 1776, within four months of the Fourth
of July, which was to change the course of world history,
William Harrison, one of the Caroline magistrates, who was
to remain a Tory throughout the Revolution, succeeded in per-
suading his fellow megistrates on the court to bind John Melear
for twenty pounds, and James Munday and Thomas Pickett

for ten pounds each, to maintain a respectful attitude towards the king and his government for a year and a day.

The magistrates were even more zealous in forcing lay residents to show respect to their persons than in forcing the respect of the king. In addition to the notorious case of the court fining Andrew Ross, Thomas Kelley and Matthew Gale for disrespect to Anthony Thornton at George Goodloe's (*supra*), the court fined Robert Woolfolk of Needwood five pounds for cursing John Baynham, although Baynham was dead, and summoned William Sutton to face charges of insulting Anthony New, Baynham's successor on the court. Sutton was more fortunate than Woolfolk and escaped punishment for his crime.

Favoritism in the enforcement of the tax laws remained a favorite device for the magistrates to reward their friends and punish their enemies. In 1772 when John Armistead, William Micou, Thomas Royston and John Roy failed to report their wheeled vehicles for taxation the court excused Armistead, who was a magistrate, and Micou, who was the son of a magistrate, but fined Royston and Roy 500 pounds of tobacco each. The Order Books fail to divulge what the magistrates had against Royston, but it is obvious that they were angry with Roy, because he was foreman of the jury, which brought in a verdict of only one penny fine against John Penn, after being directed to bring in a verdict of guilty by the court.

The next year Armistead took advantage of the indulgence offered him by the court and as tithetaker for his home district failed to report any of his own tithables for taxation. His neighbors reported this attempt to defraud the government of its taxes, and the magistrates forced him to add his tithables to the tax list. But they imposed no penalty for the crime, which at the same time they fined John Broughill, Joseph Willis, Andrew Ross, John Nunn, Francis Fleming, Elizabeth Fortune, William Smithers, Sr., and John Smith 500 pounds of tobacco each for each tithe, which they concealed. John Smith was the only taxpayer discriminated against, who dared complain, and it took a liberal dosage of alcohol to make him bold enough to air his grievances before the court. His efforts got him nothing. The magistrates ignored his charges and fined him for being drunk.

4. THE REVOLUTION BEGINS

High-handed tactics of the government of George III in efforts to enforce the collection of the taxes the British Parliament had imposed on the American colonists finally caused the vast majority of Virginia's ruling aristocrats to abandon the crown and join the plain people in the fight to preserve their liberties. In 1773 all elements in the colony were shocked when Parliament passed an ex post facto act to transport Rhode Island patriots to England for trial after they were accused of burning a vessel in Narragansett Harbor, which the British government had sent across the Atlantic to enforce the collection of the tax on tea.

When this news reached Virginia, the Burgesses called back in session by Dunmore, much against his will, because of the widespread counterfeiting of the local currency, decided to act at once. But there was great disagreement over the nature of this action until Dabney Carr, the grandson of Thomas Carr, an original magistrate of Caroline, who represented Louisa in the House of Burgesses at the time, moved for a committee of correspondence to keep the legislatures of each colony informed as to what was going on in the other colonies and set up interlocked plans of defense.

The Burgesses unanimously adopted Carr's motion and created a committee, which included men of every shade of political opinion in the body from Patrick Henry to Edmund Pendleton. In accepting his appointment Pendleton wrote "My object is to raise the spirit of the timid to a general united opposition, and to oppose the violent, who wish to adopt rash measures."

Governor Dunmore promptly dissolved the Burgesses for their impudence and nonchalantly set off for a tour of inspection along the frontier. But he was unable to halt so easily, a chain of events which had begun. Even a bloody Indian War, which engulfed the western regions of the colony, failed to divert the Virginians' attention from the oppressive measures imposed by the crown. They applauded the Bostonians for destroying tea on shipboard in Boston Harbor on the night of

December 16, 1773, and were angered when George III's ministers ordered the port of Boston closed in reprisal.

The latter deed brought the Burgesses back to Williamsburg. But they returned as an independent convention acting on·their own, rather than in their official capacity, as the lower house of the General Assembly, because Dunmore refused to call them together, or even to sanction their meeting. Edmund Pendleton and James Taylor, duly elected by the freeholders as Burgesses, but not as delegates, represented Caroline in this convention.

The convention passed resolutions protesting the latest outrages perpetrated by the crown, and named six delegates to represent Virginia in a congress, with representatives from all the colonies, to meet in Philadelphia. George Washington, Edmund Pendleton and Patrick Henry formed half of the Virginia delegation. This trio met at Mt. Vernon and traveled northward together. Tyranical acts inspired by George III and his ministers had gone a long ways towards solidifying public opinion in Virginia to cause Pendleton and Henry, the leaders of the conservative and radical elements of the colony, to set off on a mission with a common purpose.

This Philadelphia convention to become known in history as the First Continental Congress, ratified agreements to boycott all trade with Great Britain until the crown and parliament revoked or repealed all edicts and laws which encroached on the rights and the liberties of the colonists, to formulate a plan of common defense during the emergency and to set up a committee of safety in each county or town, elected by the freeholders, to prevent profiteering because of the sacrcity of goods during the boycott, to train men and to accumulate arms for the common defense, to preserve order locally, and to carry out other programs, which the Congress might in time direct.

The records of the proceedings of the committees of safety for only four Virginia counties now exist. The records of Caroline are in this short list. The original minutes are in the Huntington Library and Art Gallery in San Marino, California, where they finally turned up after being stolen from the Clerk's Office in Caroline County during the Civil War. The

Virginia State Library printed a limited number of copies of this remarkable document in 1929. The next section of this volume is a digest of this record.

The first Caroline election for public safety committeeman was held on November 10, 1774. All freeholders entitled to vote for Burgesses had a vote. This was the first election for local officials in the history of the county. The voters chose two committeemen for each precinct, just as the crown appointed two magistrates from each of these political subdivision. Eleven magistrates became committeemen. They were Edmund Pendleton, James Taylor, Anthony Thornton, Walker Taliaferro, Thomas Lowry, William Woodford, John Minor, James Upshaw, John Armistead, Samuel Hawes and George Guy. These eleven included the ablest and most influential magistrates on the court; Edmund Pendleton, Burgess and acknowledged leader throughout the colony, James Taylor, Burgess and leader of the local liberal faction, Anthony Thornton, the county lieutenant and head of the local militia, Walker Taliaferro, ex-Burgess and current sheriff, and William Woodford, one of the most seasoned military men in Virginia.

Why the remaining nine magistrates did not serve on the original committee is a matter of conjecture. The record fails to reveal if they ran for office and were defeated or refused to be candidates. Correlating known facts the positions of some are easy to surmise. Garwin Corbin was from a family of tories, and he was serving as a Governor's Councillor. James Miller, William Buckner, Jr. and Robert Gilchrist were Port Royal merchants extensively engaged in the import trade and the boycott threatened to ruin them. William Harrison was such a dyed in the wool royalist that he remained, along with Justice James Miller, a Tory throughout the Revolution. John Buckner wanted to be sheriff and actually became the last sheriff of Caroline appointed by a royal governor. He was afraid of antagonizing Dunmore and ruining his chances to gain this highly lucrative post, if he took part in any movement protesting the actions of the crown.

The positions of Anthony New, Roger Quarles and Robert Taliaferro are more difficult to surmise. New and Quarles, who were soldiers, may have been out of the county on a military mission at the time, and Robert Taliaferro may have decided not to become a committeeman and offend the crown, to keep the Taliaferro family on top, it mattered not which side won, since his relative Walker Taliaferro was a member of the committee. It is interesting to note that of the three families who furnished the most magistrates for the Caroline County, that the Taylors were all patriots from the beginning of the Revolution, that the Taliaferros were divided in their allegiance in the early stages of the struggle, and that the Buckners remained royalist until only a few months before the actual proclaiming of independence, when they deserted the king en masse and espoused the patriots' cause.

The Caroline freeholders elected George Taylor, Benjamin Hubbard, Thomas Lomax, George Baylor, John Tennant, William Nelson, John Jones, Edmund Pendleton, Jr. and Richard Johnston, who were not magistrates, to the first committee of safety. Taylor and Hubbard had served as magistrates and given up their seats because they differed with the policies of the royal government, although Hubbard's were more personal than over issues. He accepted a seat on the committee, however, when other large merchants of the county, Robert Gilchrist, James Miller and William Buckner, Jr., refused to serve. Lomax and Baylor were the scions of families, who traditionally held seats on the county court, and who had been deprived of this prerogative because royal governors feared their trend towards liberalism. Their elections indicated that many of the richest and most powerful hereditary aristocrats were siding with the patriots, and that the smaller freeholders, who held the bulk of the votes believed them to be trustworthy.

Tennant also was of Lomax's and Baylor's caste. He was a physician, born in Caroline, educated in part at least at William and Mary College, and married to a daughter of Harry Beverley. At first he lived on an estate his wife inherited from her father near Port Royal, and later on another portion of her inheritance near the Bowling Green. He was a liberal, already recognized for his brilliance and his charity when the Revolution began.

Pendleton, Jr., a nephew of the great Edmund Pendleton, was acting crown attorney, and Nelson was the clerk of the court. Their elections to committee of safety tied the chief administrative officers in the county to the patriots' cause, and strengthened the committee's control over the local government.

Jones, a young officer in the militia, was the son of William Jones, who quit the court rather than enforce oppressive laws. His selection appears to have been in recognition of his father's services rather than anything that he had done himself because up to this time he had done nothing to attract the public's attention.

Richard Johnston was a tavern-keeper, and while a man of wide influence, he was not of the caste from which governors traditionally chose magistrates. All told, the personnel, were considerably more liberal than the personnel who customarily made up the court.

5. RULE OF THE FIRST COMMITTEE OF SAFETY

The Caroline Committee of Safety held its first meeting on November 10, 1774, and elected Edmund Pendleton, moderator, and Samuel Hawes, Jr., clerk. The only other order of business was to set in motion the machinery to prove that it had the power to enforce its orders and directives and the orders and directives of the Virginia Convention and the Continental Congress. All through the campaign to elect committeemen, the unruly element of the county, as well as the royalist, had scoffed at the idea of a committee of safety, challenged the authority under which it was being set up, and boasted that they intended to defy it, if and when it came into being. Now that the committee was an accomplished fact it first moved to prove that it had the power to act.

To gain this objective the committeemen decided to make an example of John Morris who was among the most loudmouthed in his boast. Before they adjourned they ordered Morris to appear before them at their next meeting on December 16th and explain his remarks. They also summoned Richard Stevens, Speill Davis, Peter Tribble, Robert Durrett, Benjamin Tompkins and Killis Durrett to appear as witnesses.

Morris' bark proved fiercer than his bite. When December 16th rolled around he appeared before the committee and after listening to the testimony of several witnesses confessed that he "made use of certain expressions foreign to the good of this country," begged forgiveness and promised that his conduct would give no cause for complaint in the future.

With this victory achieved the committee turned its attention to the more difficult task of forcing the importing merchants of the county to open their books for inspection to determine if they continued to bring in goods from Great Britain, or had raised the prices on their merchandise since the embargo went into effect in defiance of the Continental Congress' directives. The committee named William Woodford, John Tennant, James Upshaw, Thomas Lomax, Thomas Lowry, George Taylor and Benjamin Hubbard to examine the books of the merchants of Port Royal, Walker Taliaferro, Anthony Thornton, John Jones, John Armistead and Samuel Hawes the books of Patrick Kennan, factor for Dunlop and Cross, at the Bowling Green in upper Drysdale, and Richard Johnston, John Minor, George Guy, George Baylor and William Nelson the books of Samuel Hargrave, the Quaker merchant of St. Margaret's. The committee exempted Benjamin Hubbard, of lower Drysdale from this order, and it subsequently developed that Robert Gilchrist and Robert Johnston were not included among the merchants of Port Royal. Since they were among the largest importers of the county the only reasons that the author can attribute for the omissions are Hubbard's membership on the committee, the widespread respect for Gilchrist throughout the county, and Johnston's kinship to Richard Johnston, a committeeman.

Edmund Dixon and James Bowie, Jr. of Port Royal and Samuel Hargrave of St. Margaret's "delivered up their books without hesitation" when the inspecting committeemen called and after examining these records the committeemen announced that these merchants were "doing business agreeable to the directives of the Association." But James Miller, James Dunlop of Dunlop and Cross, John Wallace, Andrew Leckie and William Dixon, merchants of Port Royal, and Patrick Kennan were not so coöperative. They refused to produce their books for inspection. After this rebuff the Committee of Safety at its next meeting adjudged the non-coöperative merchants "enemies of their Country until they gave Satisfaction," advised the people not to deal with them, and directed that notice of their refusal to coöperate be published in the Williamsburg *Gazettes*.

This action angered rather than intimidated the merchants. Instead of knuckling to the committee they joined together and printed a pamphlet, in which they denounced the committeemen as busybodies without authority to act, declared that they were not importing goods from Great Britain and had not raised their prices since the embargo went into effect, and begged the public to continue to trade with them. They circulated this paper throughout Caroline County. Its publication stymed the committee. But not for long because the pamphlet had exactly the opposite effect than that for which the merchants hoped. Rather than placating the freeholders it angered them and caused the more hot-headed to make plans to lynch the merchants, pillage their stocks and burn their places of business. Edmund Pendleton, always the conciliator, wanted no such lawlessness. In an effort to prevent violence, he wrote the offending merchants a letter, in which he stated that if they were neither importing goods from Great Britain, nor had raised the prices of their merchandise since the embargo went into effect as they claimed in their pamphlet, that they had nothing to fear from the committee. He advised them that the committee was meeting the next day to consider further action against them, but promised that if they attended this meeting, the committeemen would consider their cases without prejudice, in spite of the fact that they had slandered the committeemen in their publication. In conclusion he promised safe conduct to and from the meeting for any merchant who wished to appear.

All the offending merchants accepted Pendleton's offer and showed up before the committee the next day. They "gave in a paper certifying that the Gentlemen of the committee might examine their books and acknowledged themselves sorry for the misunderstanding that had happened and their having published a paper to the people of the county." The committee, pleased at having established its power to act without greater difficulties, was magnanimous, it accepted the merchants' apology and offered to hold its next meeting in Port Royal to examine their books at their convenience.

At this Port Royal meeting held six days later (January 19, 1775) Edward Dixon and James Bowie, Jr. showed up with the rest of the merchants of the town. Evidently they suffered pangs of conscience when they saw all their competitors trying to do the right thing, because they both confessed that although they opened their books for inspection when first requested by the committee and escaped detection, that they did not stop trading with Great Britain when the embargo went into effect. Dixon confessed that he still had in stock "two Cart Bushes" brought in since that date, and Bowie confessed he had two pair of shoes. The committee after hearing their confessions decided that deception was worse than open opposition and refused to forgive them as it had forgiven the other merchants. Instead it ordered "William Woodford, Thomas Lomax and John Tennant, or any two of them, to sell the aforesaid Bushes and Shoes and apply the money agreeable to the Association."

Even though the merchants were willing to coöperate the committee still had to take drastic steps to stop the flow of goods from Britain to Caroline County. A few days after Dixon and Bowie turned in the cart bushes and shoes, the ship *Favorite* arrived at Port Royal from England with a cargo of coal consigned to Payne (John Elliott Payne) & Co., a subsidiary of the trading firm of Benjamin Hubbard. The committee ordered the coal seized and sold and the proceeds used for the purchase of arms and ammunition to defend the county. Although Hubbard was a member of the committee he did not protest this action. The chances are, however, that the British sellers rather than the Caroline purchasers lost the price of the coal by the seizure, because while the committee confiscated the cargo it made no effort to take over the vessel, which was owned and captained by William Fletcher of Port Royal.

Continued strict enforcement of the embargo made itself increasingly felt on Caroline's economy. By the Spring of 1775 only Robert Johnston, whose books the committee had exempted from inspection, had a variety of goods manufactured outside of Virginia in his stock for sale. This caused considerable resentment among his competitors and they aroused the consumers to complain that he was charging more for his goods than the price prior to the time that the embargo went into effect. The committee investigated these complaints, found that they were true and "Ordered the case be published and that he be allowed to trade on the same terms that other merchants do in this county that do break the Association."

Johnston refused to accept this rebuke without making a defense. A month later (May 1775) he appeared before the committee with memoranda which proved that all goods he was accused of selling at an advanced price, had been purchased in Philadelphia and not in Great Britain. The committee admitted this evidence and amended its order to absolve him from guilt of trading with the enemy, but refused to exonerate him of profiteering until he reduced the asking price of his goods to their pre-1775 level. Rather than abide by this ruling Johnston withdrew his Philadelphia goods from the market. He did not, however, go out of business. Instead he began replenishing his stock with merchandise imported from the non-British West Indies. These goods he sold at an advanced price and the committee again took action against him for "breaking the rules of the Association." But this time because of mounting shortages, the committee was not so harsh. It named John Tennant, Thomas Lowry, James Upshaw and Thomas Lomax, all of whom were committeemen and Robert Gilchrist, who was not a member of the committee, to fix the prices of his non-West Indies goods at the prevailing prices for such goods in Port Royal for the year preceding "the Continental Association," but in the same order allowed him to retain his current prices on all West Indies goods. Johnston agreed to this arrangement and his controversy with the committee ended.

While the committee wrangled with Johnston it was engaged in even a more acute controversy with James Dunlop. When in the summer of 1775 the Continental Association agreed to the clearance of a number of ships from Virginia ports bound for Europe to transport the tobacco crop to the overseas market, Dunlop did not ask for the clearance of one of his own ships, and he was among the largest shipowners in Virginia, but sought and gained permission from the local Committee of Safety to send a sloop loaded with forty-six hogsheads of tobacco from Port Royal down the Rappahannock and Chesapeake for transhipment aboard the *Prospect* lying at anchor in the mouth of the York River. When the sloop reached the *Prospect* York and Gloucester County planters had already taken up all the available space on the vessel and the sloop returned to Port Royal with its cargo on board. To get out of this unfortunate position Dunlop applied to the Caroline committee for relief and the committee granted him permission to send the tobacco to Europe on any ship that was available. With this permission in hand he decided to use the sloop *Olive* which he owned jointly with Henry Lyburn.

The *Olive* left Port Royal early in October 1775. Before it sailed Dunlop instructed the captain to ignore the agreement he had with the Caroline Committee of Safety when the ship reached Europe, and instead of unloading the tobacco and immediately beginning the return voyage to Virginia to put in at a British port and take on a cargo of goods, which were greatly in demand in Caroline on account of the embargo. News of Dunlop's breach of faith preceding the ship's return to its home port, and while it sailed up the Rappahannock in the direction of Port Royal the Caroline Committee of Safety met to decide on a course of action. After much discussion the committee decided to turn the matter over to a "Select Committee" consisting of John Tennant, Thomas Lowry, James Upshaw "with regard to stopping aforesaid vessel." The "Select Committee" ordered Captain Richard Taylor, who was in charge of the patriot navy patrolling waters adjacent to Caroline at the time, to seize the ship.

Taylor complied with this order. The ship was seized and

its cargo confiscated and sold, in spite of Dunlop's protest. But after this setback Dunlop did not give up, he continued to wrangle, seeking to regain control of the vessel. This dispute went on for almost six months and until the Caroline Committee of Safety at its last meeting of record (May 21, 1776) reluctantly agreed to hand the *Olive* back to Messrs. Dunlop and Lyburn.

6. RULE OF THE FIRST COMMITTEE OF SAFETY

a. *Caroline is Armed*

While the Caroline Committee of Safety squabbled with the importing merchants over trade regulations it moved steadily ahead in its attempt to solicit contributions "of every person in their respective precincts for the purchase of arms and ammunition for the use of this county." Evidently this move was successful because a month later (March 8, 1775) the committee had funds available to purchase five barrels of gunpowder "made by Col. James Taylor and Capt. William Woodford."

But the committee did not denude the county of gunpowder for local defense when it authorized the powder manufactured by Taylor and Woodford transported to Fredericksburg for Washington's use, because at the same session, at which it issued this authorization, it also directed the seizure of all the powder in the stocks of merchandise of Edward Dixon, James Bowie, Jr. and John Wallace in Port Royal, and the division of this powder into seven pound lots, one lot going to each member of the committee, to be taken home by him, and kept for use in his precinct in case of trouble. This order provided ammunition for defense at the grass roots.

The "Proceedings of the Caroline Committee of Safety fail to disclose how Dixon, Bowie and Wallace reacted to this seizure, and if the committee paid for the powder, or if its taking was outright confiscation." The chances are the merchants were paid because they registered no complaint of record.

Additional evidence, that the committee paid, is found in the fact that shortly after the seizure its treasury was devoid of funds. At a meeting a little over a month later it decided that it was unable to depend any longer solely on voluntary contributions to purchase arms and ammunition for the defense of the county and levied a tax of two shillings on every tithable person for this purpose. This was the first attempt of the committee to levy a tax on the freeholders, and from the "Order Books" and the "Proceedings of the Committee of Safety," which are the only official records of happenings in Caroline at this time, neither the court nor the people objected, although the committee was purely a de facto body and totally without authority to act under the law. The fact that a majority of the magistrates on the court also formed a majority of the committeemen on the committee explains the court's failure to protest, and the manner in which the committee handled the merchants and other residents who dared try to defy its directives, had convinced freeholders of all political complexions, including the staunchest Tories, that opposition was futile.

The committee delegated the committeemen to collect the special tax in their respective precincts. The collection was more rapid than even the most hopeful member of the committee anticipated, and within two months of the time that the tax was levied, enough funds were on hand for the committee to instruct William Woodford and John Tennant "to engage 1,000 pounds of powder and hire persons for that purpose and pay them out of the money collected for ammunition etc." (June 8, 1775.) This was far more, than all the powder which the committee had previously obtained. Unfortunately for the patriots' cause it was so much that Woodford and Tennant, in spite of their best efforts, were able to secure only a small portion from local sources, and the committee was compelled to send George Thornton on an ammunition buying expedition to Baltimore in the late Summer of 1775 and pay him six pounds out of the committee's treasury for his "trouble and expense."

Caroline needed men as well as arms for defense and the local Committee of Safety was afraid to trust the county militia with the former function. Because, while Col. James Taylor, the County Lieutenant, and many other officers of the militia were ardent patriots, this military organization remained an arm of the royal government subject to Dunmore's orders, and some of its officers were still loyal to the king. Due to this distrust the Virginia Convention of 1774 directed the formation of "independent" companies of troops in each county under the control of the local Committee of Safety. These soldiers were organized on precinct level with a company for each precinct. They drilled and learned military tactics in small units in their home communities rather than at county-wide musters as was the case with the militia. Some of the troops in the "independent" companies were also enlisted in the militia while others were not, but practically all the officers of the "independent" companies were commissioned in the militia.

Robert Mickleberry, John Broaddus, John Jones, Richard Buckner, Phillip Johnston, William Marshall, Edmund Pendleton, Jr., Samuel Redd, James Upshaw, Edward Dixon and Anthony Thornton originally drilled the "independent" companies in Caroline's eleven precincts. The local Committee of Safety contributed arms to each of these units from the date of their organization, and in August 1775, ordered all able-bodied white males over the age of sixteen to take part in their precinct drills.

Compulsory military service in the "independent" companies with another military organization, the militia, in existence in the county apparently did not work because the Caroline Committee of Safety ordered the merger of the two outfits within thirty days of the time it ordered compulsory military service. The royal government was now too weak to oppose this move successfully, but it led to other difficulties. The precinct leaders who trained the "independent" companies were with three exceptions relegated to the position of captain and all officers of headquarters' rank were chosen from the old commanding officers of the militia. The officers, who had trained the "independent" companies felt slighted and aired their grievances openly. But only two of them, Edward Dixon and Samuel Redd, quit. The committee named Peyton Stern and John Minor to take their places, and at the same time appointed

William Stresherly and Robert Ware to fill the two other vacancies, which existed among the captains, because James Upshaw had been promoted to major on the general staff and Anthony Thornton had resigned to accept a commission in the Continental Army.

After the reorganization the troops continued to drill regularly in their respective precincts, and were known as "Minute Men" because of their ability to muster upon short notice, rather than by their old name of "independent" companies, when they existed as military units without official recognition. In their new status they only faced one serious difficulty, Tories and patriots drilled side by side in the same ranks. None of the officers knew how their Tory troops were going to act in case of an emergency. Many feared that they might betray the mission in which they were engaged or fire on the patriot soldiers marching at their sides. This distrust became so great that the Caroline committee, in conformity with a Resolution of the Virginia Convention, on November 6, 1775, excluded all residents of the county, who were natives of Great Britain from bearing arms, unless they wished to join the patriots, and were able to satisfy the committee that sincerity rather than deception motivated their willingness to drill. Thus purged, the Caroline "Minute Men" were ready to play their part in the Revolution.

7. RULE OF THE FIRST COMMITTEE OF SAFETY
b. *Morale*

Caroline, along with many other counties in Virginia, attempted to contribute food for the relief of the Bostonians, who suffered because the government of George III had closed their port in reprisal, after they dumped the tea from British ships into their harbor. Early in 1775 the committee placed William Woodford, John Tennant, James Taylor and Thomas Lomax in charge of soliciting pledges of corn and wheat from the freeholders to be shipped north after that year's harvest. Woodford, Tennant, Taylor and Lomax were signally successful in this work and secured pledges for great quantities of grain from all landowning classes in the patriot element. But their job was hardly complete before it developed that 1775 was going to be a poor crop year, and the planters became alarmed at the prospect of having to make their pledges good when they did not expect to produce enough food stuff for their own use. To relieve the pledges of this obligation if it worked an undue hardship, the committee at its May 18th session passed a resolution permitting the payment of pledges in currency at the rate of four shillings and six pence per bushel of wheat and two shillings per bushel of corn.

A great many pledges took advantage of this offer, while others preferred to fulfill their obligations in kind. The mixed contributions resulted in confusion. There was not enough grain to fill a vessel for shipment and no available supply from which to purchase more. The committee named James Upshaw, John Tennant and William Woodford "to dispose of the grain received for the relief of the Bostonians as they or either of them shall think best." After a considerable delay Upshaw, Tennant and Woodford sold the grain to Robert Johnston, the Port Royal merchant. But Johnston refused to make payment until the committee ordered him to turn the funds over to George Taylor, who acted as its treasurer at the time. When Taylor finally got the money apparently he had not the faintest idea what to do with it, because it remained in his custody until February 8, 1776, when the second committee, which by that time had taken over from the first "Resolved that James Taylor, George Taylor, Abner Waugh be incorporated with the former Gen't. app'd to dispose of the donations collected from this county for the use of our Bostonian brethren." The "Gents" disposition of the collection is not of record. The chances are that none of it reached Boston and that Caroline's first attempt at countywide charity ended in a farce.

Another act the Caroline committee attempted to show the county's sympathy for the Bostonians was more successful, but it is highly doubtful if the Bostonians ever heard of it. As soon as the committee established its power to enforce its directives, it ordered every resident of the county to surrender all the tea in their possession to a member of the committee, who was to seal it, store it and give the owner a receipt as to quantity. The residents complied with this order without protest but there is no record of the tea being returned.

While the people of Caroline were not particularly concerned about being deprived of their tea they were concerned about the shortage of material for clothing brought on by the embargo on British goods. In December 1774, the local Committee of Safety fixed the price of cotton in the seed at four pence a pound, and seeded at fifteen pence, and the price of wool at ten pence a pound, unwashed, and fifteen pence a pound washed. To keep planters who produced a surplus of these commodities from profiteering at the expense of other residents of the county, who were not so fortunate, and who had to make purchases of the raw material for cloth to keep themselves properly clad and warm. The next Spring the Caroline committee named Anthony Thornton, William Woodford, George Taylor, James Taylor, and John Tennant to inquire into a scheme to manufacture linen in the county. Nothing came of this scheme and by Fall the planters, who had raised a surplus of cotton and wool, were complaining about the fixed prices on those staples. Their complaint was based on the fact that the inhabitants from the back counties who had no such price regulations, were buying up their surplus at a cheap price, transporting it to the hill country and reselling at huge profits. After the committee was convinced this was true, it annulled the regulations fixing the price on cotton but let them stand on wool because while the upland counties were unable to produce cotton, they produced wool in abundance.

Besides cloth, salt was the most keenly felt shortage in Caroline during the rule of the first Committee of Safety. People living in the inland sections of the county accused those who lived along the Rappahannock, especially about the port of Port Royal, of hoarding large amounts of salt brought in on ships. The argument became so acute that it threatened to split the county into two dissenting geographical areas. In an attempt to avert this crisis the committee named a "Select Committee" composed of John Tennant, James Upshaw, Thomas Lowry, Thomas Lomax and John Armistead "to inquire in the district about Port Royal of salt, and if any person is found there with more in his possession than they (the Select Committee) shall think proper for his own use, that they the aforesaid Committee shall seize same and distribute it among the people at the price they think proper." This arrangement satisfied the inlanders for a short time.

Faced with the threat of open warfare the Caroline committee adopted a stern attitude towards all types of frivolity. In April 1775, it decided to make an example of Rodham Kenner, grandson of Judith Beverley Kenner Roy and one of the richest men in the county, for allowing gambling in his home. Alexander Parker, John Long, Joseph Cooper and loud-mouthed Daniel Barksdale, who had been the scourge of dissenters, gave evidence against Kenner and the committee found him guilty as charged. But the only punishment it meted out was publication in the *Virginia Gazettes* that he "had violated the Association in gambling at his home." This curious punishment appears to have been enough because the committee tried no one else for frivolity for the next nine months. The first offender, Rodham Kenner, was also in the second group of accused, and the charges were the same crime, gambling. Only the scene of the crime was different, a Port Royal tavern rather than in Kenner's home, and this time other gamblers, William Murray, Turner Dixon, Richard Buckner, Francis Buckner, Joseph Cooper, John Cooper and William Poe, were charged with him. The first committee ended its tenure of office before these men were brought to trial.

The first committee in its dying days also decided to ban horse-racing, Caroline's most popular sport, during the emergency. Many residents of the county refused to take this ban seriously and the committee delegated John Jones, John Minor and Michael Yates to investigate a race reputedly to have been sponsored by David Woodruff, Fielding Woodruff and Nicholas Lewis. This sub-committee's report is not of record but evidently the accused were exonerated because they were never punished for the offense.

8. THE CALL TO ARMS

While the first Committee of Safety ruled Caroline the tension between Britain and her American colonies continued to mount. Early in 1775 patriot leaders called for a second congress in Philadelphia to consider the next moves for the common defense.

Edmund Pendleton and James Taylor represented Caroline in a convention held in St. John's Church, in Richmond, to elect delegates to represent Virginia in the congress. No sooner was this convention seated than it split into conservative and radical factions with Pendleton leading the former and Henry the latter. The radicals wanted an open break with Great Britain while the conservatives argued that such a drastic step was utter folly due to the colonists' lack of arms, ammunition and manpower and must ultimately lead to their destruction. Pendleton and his associates' persistence in advancing this argument caused Henry to explode with his immortal "Give me liberty or give me death" speech. Neither the conservatives nor the radicals won a clearcut victory in the Richmond convention. Both Pendleton and Henry were among the six delegates that it chose to represent Virginia in Philadelphia. But the truce which existed between the pair was ended. They were openly enemies again.

Much happened, however, before they resumed their argument on the floors of the congress. Governor Dunmore forbade the Virginia delegates to go to Philadelphia and when they prepared to set out in open defiance of his orders, he commanded British sailors and marines to remove the gunpowder from the magazine in Williamsburg in an attempt to intimidate them and the people whom they claimed to represent. This move backfired and brought about exactly the opposite results for which the governor hoped. Henry put off his trip to Philadelphia, called together the Hanover independent companies and marched on Williamsburg.

When news of Henry's action spread across the Pamunkey-North Anna the Caroline Minute Men mustered at the Bowling Green and prepared to set out to reinforce the troops from

Hanover. The local Committee of Safety in session at New Hope Tavern approved the plan and authorized the soldiers to carry along the powder stored in their respective precincts for use in an emergency. But Pendleton was violently opposed to the move and rushed to the Bowling Green and attempted to stop it. The Minute Men refused to obey his orders to disperse but he finally persuaded them to await the advice of Peyton Randolph, speaker of the House of Burgesses, moderator of the Virginia Convention, president of the Continental Congress and one of the most prominent men in America, who was expected momentarily to pass through Caroline on his way to Philadelphia.

From conferences at the Richmond convention, Pendleton knew that he and Randolph were in accord on their opinions of Henry and the Williamsburg expedition. They both publicly proclaimed that they opposed the maneuver because it was an independent campaign which jeopardized the common defense since it was not controlled and directed by the Congress. Actually they were jealous and afraid of Henry. Their following was chiefly among the aristocrats while he was the idol of the masses. They feared that he might use his influence with the plain men who made up the independent companies to set up a government more radical than either the convention or the congress sanctioned. Such a calamity, to Pendleton especially, was unthinkable.

When Randolph arrived, he addressed the troops but his eloquence made no more impression on the Caroline Minute Men than Pendleton's. The soldiers marched in spite of the opposition of the statesmen, and Randolph and Pendleton sadly set out on the journey northward together. At Fredericksburg their spirits rose because the troops assembled there dispersed at their command and refused to march on Williamsburg, much to the disgust of Hugh Mercer, the local Minute Men's commander. By the time they reached Philadelphia they again hoped that open warfare with Great Britain might be averted. Pendleton actively opposed a unified command before the congress although he had espoused such a command in his attempt to block Henry. He was dead set against Washington assuming charge of all military operations and was the last member of the Congress to withdraw his objections.

While Randolph and Pendleton spoke in vain to the Caroline Minute Men the arguments they advanced in their speeches to the troops had considerable effect on the more conservative members of the Caroline Committee of Safety. These gentlemen began to wonder if they acted wisely in sanctioning the Williamsburg expedition. They became particularly concerned because they let the soldiers carry away the powder stored in their precincts, and decided that when the troops returned that they must adopt stern measures to keep the independent companies under control.

Unfortunately no accurate record exists of the part Caroline troops played as a unit in Henry's campaign to recover the gunpowder the British removed from the magazine in Williamsburg. But from the "Proceedings of the Caroline Committee of Safety" it seems that the tall tales the soldiers told upon their return to their home county gave conservative members of the committee additional reason to believe that they must be disciplined. In a meeting at New Hope Tavern on August 29, 1775, the committee ordered troops enrolled in the independent companies to turn over to the committeemen from their precincts all the arms they took from the Governor's House and magazine in Williamsburg and brought back to Caroline. This order was based on misinformation, evidently the boasts of braggarts among the Minute Men, trying to impress the gullible with their deeds of daring during their first military mission, because well-authenticated accounts of the Williamsburg campaign definitely establish that the colonial troops did not break into the Governor's House and spring guns set by the British kept them from removing arms from the magazine.

When the Minute Men failed to turn in any arms under this order because they had no weapons of the category in their possession the conservative committeemen became even more alarmed and personally conducted searches of the premises and living quarters of each soldier who took part in the expedition. When these searches failed to uncover a single concealed weapon the suspicious committeemen ordered "independent troops to turn in all arms in their possession purchased by the public." The soldiers complied with this order without protest and were now totally disarmed except for the guns which they owned personally. But the conservatives of the committee were still afraid of them while less suspicious committeemen became alarmed about the deterioration of the county's defenses. To remedy this situation in less than a month's time, the committeemen acting in accordance with directives from the Virginia Convention placed all troops in the county under the command of Col. James Taylor, the county lieutenant. (Sec. 7—Rule of Dunmore, *supra*.)

9. CAROLINE IN THE SADDLE

During the twelve months immediately preceding the Declaration of Independence Caroline made her greatest contribution to leadership. Few American counties have produced so many leaders in such a short time. Edmund Pendleton was acting governor for the patriots, William Woodford commanded the colonial troops in the field, Richard Corbin, who may not have been domiciled in the county but who had a residence there where he spent much of his time, was the acting royal governor, John Tayloe Corbin, a bona fide resident of Caroline, was chief espionage agent for the British and liason officer between the acting and actual royal governors, and Richard Taylor, a native of Caroline who may have been domiciled in Orange at the time, was head of naval operations for the colonists with Port Royal as his headquarters.

When Dunmore learned that the Continental Congress planned a general defense of the colonies and had made George Washington commander-in-Chief of all military forces, he abandoned the Governor's Palace in Williamsburg and took refuge first on a British man-of-war anchored in York River, and later in the peninsula made up of Princess Anne and the major portion of Norfolk counties. Before he left Williamsburg he designated Richard Corbin, president of the Council, to act for him in his absence. John Tayloe Corbin took over the position of maintaining contact between the actual and acting governors. To avoid detection he sent messengers or went himself on the more important missions on the long circuitous route overland from Williamsburg to the Rappahannock (Fredericksburg, Port Royal or Urbanna) thence down that stream and the Chesapeake by vessel to Norfolk County. Sometimes numerous messengers were used to cover different legs of this journey. But in spite of all John Tayloe Corbin's precautions, he was caught by the patriots in October 1775 and thrown into the guardhouse at Williamsburg, where he languished without the benefit of a trial until the Spring of 1776, when he was brought before the Committee of Safety for the colony at the specific direction of Edmund Pendleton, and offered his release from prison if he agreed to remain in that section of Caroline County between the Pamunkey-North Anna and the Mattapony Rivers (St. Margaret's Parish) upon the penalty of a ten thousand pound bond until hostilities ceased between Britain and her American colonies. John Tayloe Corbin accepted this offer and sat out the war in Caroline. Richard Corbin received a more pleasant reward for his services to the crown. He managed to follow Dunmore to London after the royal government completely collapsed in Virginia, where he was lavishly entertained by the leaders of the anti-American party.

After Dunmore's flight from Williamsburg the House of Burgesses constituted itself into a convention and named a Committee of Safety to govern the colony during the emergency. Edmund Pendleton and James Taylor, Caroline's Burgesses, represented the county in this convention. Pendleton was named to the Committee of Safety, and upon its organization became its chairman. This position made him chief of state for the de facto government, or the first governor of Virginia of a regime which Britain refused to recognize.

Immediately after organization the central Committee of Safety authorized the raising of two regiments of troops to defend the colony from attacks by Dunmore and his British regulars, and named Patrick Henry to command the first and William Woodford to command the second. Pendleton bitterly opposed the selection of Henry, and when he was unable to block it, as chief of state completely ignored the first regiment and assigned all field operations to the second. While this choice was based on spite it was actually sound, because Henry was without military experience while Woodford was a seasoned commanding officer from distinguished service rendered during the French and Indian War.

Woodford's first military mission was to drive Dunmore and his troops from the Princess Anne-Norfolk peninsula. The royal governor had chosen wisely when he picked this location to make a stand because water almost severed it from the rest of Virginia and it contained the well-developed port of Norfolk. His strategy was to hold the colonial forces at bay until reinforcements reached him by sea. On the other hand it was essential to the success of the patriots' cause to defeat Dunmore before these reinforcements arrived.

Dunmore's exact position was unknown. But Woodford at the head of the second regiment and an auxiliary force of 200 Minute Men crossed the James River at Sandy Point in November 1775 and found it rapidly enough. The British occupied a fort at Great Bridge, guarding the only overland approach to Norfolk. This fort was surrounded by a branch of the Dismal Swamp with only a plank gangway connecting it to dry land. It was armed with cannon and since the Virginians were without artillery for support Woodford was afraid to attempt a frontal assault and settled his forces behind breastworks for a siege.

During the siege Woodford had trouble discipling his troops, who were all raw recruits. They were more interested in shooting the wild boar which roamed the Dismal Swamp than the British. Fortunately for the Virginians the siege did not last long. A servant boy, who deserted the patriots and went over to the royalists convinced Dunmore that there were not more than 300 men in the attacking force. Assuming that this was true the governor decided to send troops out under the cover of darkness and overwhelm the Virginians. On the morning of December 9, 1775, about an hour before daybreak, the attack began. Sixty British grenadiers, marching six abreast, started across the gangway towards Woodford's position. Although it was yet dark the Virginians detected their approach, and Woodford ordered his men to open fire, directing their aim in the direction of the gangway. The result was an instant success. British soldiers by the score toppled into the morass of the Dismal Swamp. Dunmore hastily set out a second wave of troops and they suffered a similar fate. After this loss he quit, but Woodford, because of the cannon, did not dare attempt to storm the fort. The British, however, were so depleted that Dunmore realized the futility of trying to hold out, and that night, after sunset, evacuated his forces by sea leaving the overland route to Norfolk open to Woodford. The royalists lost over 100 men while the patriots did not suffer a single casualty, in this first battle of the Revolution to be fought on Virginia soil.

Although victory at Great Bridge gave the Virginians Norfolk, the British shortly thereafter burned the city from the sea. This dastardly act aroused patriots throughout the colony. As soon as the news reached Caroline the local Committee of Safety sent a newly trained company of regulars from the county under the command of Samuel Hawes, Jr. to reinforce Woodford.

Further raids by the British from their ships lurking off shore so jeopardized the safety of the inhabitants of Princess Anne and Norfolk counties that the Virginia Convention made plans to move them inland. When James Taylor, one of Caroline's representatives in the convention, wrote to the Committee of Safety of his home county and asked how many of these refugees Caroline would receive, the Caroline committee promptly replied "1,000 souls at least." (Proceedings of the Caroline Committee of Safety for May 21, 1776.) For all this generous offer there is no evidence that a refugee from either Princess Anne or Norfolk ever came to Caroline. The reason that they were able to remain at home in safety was due in a large measure to the efforts of another native of Caroline, Capt. Richard Taylor.

Dunmore only had a small garrison of British troops in Virginia. The central Committee of Safety realized that the

greatest threat to the success of the patriots' cause lay in rein-
forcement from overseas rather than in the forces already
present. Shortly after it authorized the raising of two regiments for defense it inaugurated a ship-building program.
These ships, in a large measure, were built on the Chickahominy, at Fredericksburg under the supervision of Washington's brother-in-law, Fielding Lewis, and at Frazier's shipyard
on the Mattapony (east of Caroline), which were all sheltered
spots easily protected from marauding British men-of-war. The
ships these yards turned out, while small, were swift and
sturdy and accomplished amazing fetes when handled by seamen familiar with local waters. Captain Richard Taylor with
a flotilla of these vessels based at Port Royal cleared the
Rappahannock of British shipping in 1775 and forced ships of
Virginia registry to abide by the Continental Congress' directives governing shipping. (See case of the *Olive, supra.*) The
patriots armed one of the ships, the *Speedwell*, which Taylor
seized, and sent it to the French West Indies for arms and
ammunition.

In the Spring of 1776 Edmund Pendleton, as head of the
central Committee of Safety, turned the command of the
colony's naval forces in operation over to a native of his home
county, as he had already done the land forces in the field,
when he placed William Woodford in charge of the expedition
against Dunmore, and ordered Richard Taylor to protect the
residents of Princess Anne and Norfolk from royalist water-
borne raids. Taylor got together what Charles Campbell calls
"a squadron of Virginia built ships" for this work, and he was
so successful that he was on the job only a short time before
Dunmore not only stopped sending raiding parties ashore but
also withdrew all his forces from the Hampton Roads area to
Gwynn's Island off the coast of Gloucester (now Matthews
County) in the mid reaches of Chesapeake Bay.

Taylor followed Dunmore to Gwynn's Island. He did not
dare engage the Governor's fleet in an all out battle due to a
great difference in the size and fire power of the opposing
vessels, but he continued his harassing tactics, the most effective
of which was the seizure of practically all foodstuff Tories on

the mainland tried to send the beleaguered royalist forces. When troops under the command of General Andrew Lewis, who took over control of field operations from William Woodford after Patrick Henry as governor of the Commonwealth succeeded Edmund Pendleton as chief of state, reached a point on the mainland opposite Gwynn's Island, Dunmore's forces were so nearly starved out, that the royal governor decided that it was no longer prudent to attempt to hold out for reinforcements in the face of an impending attack. When Lewis set up a battery and began to fire on the island, Dunmore loaded his men on his ships and set sail down Chesapeake Bay. Before the colonials were able to cross the narrow strait separating the island from the mainland all the British had fled. In this ignoble manner ended almost 170 years of royal government in Virginia.

10. THE SECOND COMMITTEE OF SAFETY

In the Fall of 1775 the Committee of Safety for the colony ordered elections of new Committees of Safety in each county in Virginia as a part of its program to prove to the people that their new rulers held office subject to public approval. In accordance with this directive the Caroline committee on October 12th, ordered its clerk to advertise through the churches of the county that an election was to be held at the courthouse on November 9th, and that all freeholders qualified to cast a ballot for Burgess were eligible to vote for committeemen.

Of the old committee Edmund Pendleton, William Woodford and George Baylor did not offer for reelection. Pendleton was busy in Williamsburg as chairman of the Committee of Safety for the colony, William Woodford commanded the Virginia troops pursuing Dunmore and George Baylor was in Massachusetts serving as an officer on Washington's staff. George Guy was defeated and to fill these four vacancies and a new seat the committee created the electorate chose William Boulware, John Pickett, Robert Mickleberry, Michael Yates and Benjamin Tompkins. But for some reason which the Proceedings of the Caroline Committee of Safety fails to divulge, the central Committee of Safety declared that this election was held improperly and ordered a second election in Caroline. The second election took place on February 7, 1776. Its returns resulted in two more changes in the personnel which composed the committee. William Nelson, a holdover, and Benjamin Tompkins, a new member, lost their seats to John Catlett and the Rev. Abner Waugh.

The second election was a victory for the political faction headed by Patrick Henry in the colony and a sharp rebuke to Edmund Pendleton and his partisans. Two of the new members, John Pickett and Robert Mickleberry, were captains in the old independent companies of troops, and their election indicated that the rank and file voters of the colony disapproved of the conservatives' moves in disarming the independents and merging them with the militia. William Boulware was a radical lawyer and so opposed to royalty that Francis Fauquier had refused to make him a magistrate after he had been endorsed for this position by the county court. Michael Yates was a self-made man. Although the court had bound him to his uncle, Michael Guinney, the tavern-keeper, in his youth when his father, William Yates, failed to "instruct him in the doctrines of Christianity," he had by some means succeeded in getting an excellent education and become one of the leading physicians of the county. John Catlett was the first member of his family to gain a seat on the governing board of Caroline since the ruling great landlord clique became angry with the Catletts for supporting Johnathan Gibson rather than John Martin in the bitterly contested election for Burgess in 1735. The Rev. Abner Waugh was rector of St. Mary's Parish. But his election was no victory for the conservatives. It proved, instead, that many strict adherents of the Established Church were breaking away from their traditional moorings and joining the patriots.

Changes in the relative number of votes that the successful candidates received at the polls reveals even more forcibly that public sentiment in Caroline was shifting to the left. Richard Johnston, the tavern-keeper, jumped from ninth place in the first poll, to first in the second, and liberal Dr. John Tennant

moved from twelfth to second. While conservative great landlord, Walker Taliaferro, fell from third to thirteenth place
and conservative William Nelson from fourth place to defeat.
Only the positions of moderates like James Taylor, who was
second in the first and third in the irregular and the second
polls, remained relatively the same.

After the second election there was only one change in the
Caroline Committee of Safety's personnel. When the Virginia
Convention instructed its delegates in the Continental Congress
at Philadelphia to move for independence, pressure from high
churchmen forced the Rev. Abner Waugh to resign. Waugh
apparently quit the committee much against his will, in an
attempt to avoid dissention in his church brought on by discipling him for taking part in political activities, if he kept his
seat, because, although shorn of official position, he remained a
staunch patriot throughout the Revolution.

John Buckner succeeded Waugh on the committee. He was
the first member of the powerful Buckner family, other than
half-baked youngsters in the militia, to espouse openly the
rebels' cause. In addition he was sheriff, the last sheriff a
royal governor appointed for Caroline. His willingness to
accept a seat on the committee indicated that the crown's rule
had crumbled into impotency in the county by this time, mid-
Spring of 1776, and within three months of the actual Declaration of Independence.

While the second committee lost only one member, it also
lost its secretary. Samuel Hawes, Jr. had served in this capacity
since the first committee was organized. He had even purchased the book from Purdie of Williamsburg in which a
record of the proceedings of the committee were kept. But
Hawes was a soldier as well as a statesman and while he
served the committee as secretary he was busily engaged in
training troops. When the second committee met for its first
meeting on February 1, 1776, his troops were ready for action
and William Woodford attempting to protect the inhabitants
of Princess Anne and Norfolk counties from raiding parties
from British ships anchored in Hampton Roads was sadly in
need of reinforcements. To supply this need the committee

ordered Hawes and his company to join Woodford. Before leaving the county on this mission he resigned as secretary of the committee. The committeemen accepted his resignation, voted him a purse of ten pounds in recognition of his services and named Samuel Temple to fill the vacancy.

The second committee was considerably bolder than the first. Instead of holding its meetings in the public rooms of New Hope Tavern at the Bowling Green, Dr. George Todd's Tavern at Villeboro and the taverns of Port Royal, it sat in the courthouse and in a building often used as a courthouse near the Bowling Green. But its problems were the same. The county had to be armed, men trained to engage in the colonies' common defense, shortages in foodstuffs and other supplies overcome, Tories curbed and the public morale sustained.

Full mobilization of the county for war proved one of the second Committee of Safety's easiest tasks. It left Col. James Taylor, the county lieutenant, in command of all military forces but restored the young officers, who had trained the independent companies, to the command of precinct units. This move proved so popular that men in all sections of the county flocked to the colors. In a short time precinct units, which had shrunk to a mere skeleton, were so swollen that the committee had to organize six new companies and increase the number of companies in the county from eleven to seventeen. One of these new companies was in upper St. Margaret's Parish under the command of Roger Quarles, another in lower St. Margaret's under the command of James Johnson, while James Fletcher commanded a third in Drysdale and John Armistead, John Pickett and Charles Vivion commanded the remaining three in sections of the county which the Proceedings of the Caroline Committee of Safety fails to specify.

In addition to the seventeen militia companies there was at least one company of regular troops in the Continental Army at this early date. This company was under the command of Samuel Hawes, Jr., as captain, with Thomas Jones, as first lieutenant, James Upshaw, as second lieutenant, and Thomas Catlett as ensign.

The second committee at its first meeting on February 2,

1776, split the county along the Mattapony into two regions for a better defense. It placed Abner Waugh, John Tennant, Thomas Lomax, John Catlett and Thomas Lowry in charge of fortifying the district north of the river, and Richard Johnston, William Boulware, Samuel Hawes, Sr., Robert Mickleberry and John Jones, the district south of the stream.

In only one instance of record did the second committee have trouble maintaining discipline among the soldiers and this instance proved a false alarm. When Capt. Charles Vivion accused Capt. William Marshall of purposely retarding "the minute service" the committee investigated the charges and exonerated Marshall after it was satisfied that Vivion made them without cause.

The control of trade proved more difficult. Merchants' stocks became depleted of imported goods because of the embargo on trade with Britain, and after they sold out they closed their shops instead of looking for sources to replenish their merchandise. In a short time many essential commodities were on the critical list. In an attempt to alleviate this situation the second committee reversed the precedent set by the first and sought to stimulate trade with the neighboring colonies. At its meeting on February 8, 1776 it was "resolved that any person hath leave to export Grain and Tobacco to Our Sister Colonies under the restrictions made by Congress upon giving bond and security to the Committee, and taking the oath prescribed by them, and pointing out the place of its destination."

The British merchants in residence in Caroline ignored this offer and continued to sulk in their closed shops. But Robert Johnston, a native trader, decided to take advantage of it, although he had fared badly when he brought goods into the county from Philadelphia the previous year. He posted bond and imported a quantity of goods from the North. But Johnstan's imports fell far short of supplying the local market and Caroline people needed goods produced in the South as well as in the North. In another move to overcome shortages the committee sent George Hampton and Robert Bridges on a trade mission to South Carolina in the Spring of 1776. Hampton and Bridges both had relatives in that colony. But how they came out on their mission is not of record.

The scarcity of salt continued to be the most acute shortage in the county. This shortage was felt not only in Caroline but all through Virginia. It developed to such extremes that the central Committee of Safety sent abroad for a supply and rationed it among the counties of the colony. When Caroline's ration of 130 bushels arrived the local Committee of Safety promptly split it in even portions for distribution among the people who lived on the south side and the north side of the Mattapony to prevent a recurrence of the threat of civil war between the two sections over salt which upset the county during the rule of the first committee.

In spite of shortages the second committee was fair to the British merchants in residence and their Tory followers although they shirked their duty in attempting to maintain trade. In February, 1776, it granted Archabald Ritchie, a Scottish merchant of Tappahannock, permission to remove grain he had purchased from Richard Corbin, the acting royal governor, grown on Corbin's Caroline plantation, to Essex upon giving bond. Two months later it granted James Dunlop, the Port Royal merchant, who had tried to evade the embargo, similar privileges upon the same terms.

For all this indulgence one Tory dared criticize the committee. He was Robert Graham, a Scot, who had inherited an interest in the trading house founded by his father, Duncan Graham, in Port Royal. Reuben Royston overheard the remarks and reported Graham to the committee, which charged him with "abuse uttered against this committee." These charges were still pending when the committee gave way to the court set up by the new Commonwealth of Virginia.

Oddly enough patriots gave the second committee a great deal more trouble because of misconduct than the Tories. This was due, perhaps, to the fact that the former became restless while awaiting the outbreak of mass hostilities while the latter were surly. Rodham Kenner, who was to distinguish himself a few years later as a naval officer, continued constantly in trouble for gambling. Joseph Cooper and John Long also defied directives making gaming a crime. But the most interesting case of misconduct involved Robert Mickleberry, a committeeman. At the last session of the committee of record (May 21, 1776), he filed charges against himself, Robert Woolfolk, John Thilman, George Guy and Nathaniel Norment for drunkenness and gambling. In his charges he alleged that he had attended the May term of the Hanover Court and gotten drunk, and that on his way home he stopped at Needwood Tavern, where he drank and gambled far into the night with Robert Woolfolk, the tavern-keeper, John Thilman, George Guy and Nathaniel Norment. After hearing the charges the committee summoned all the accused to appear before its next session and stand trial. This session was never held. The Virginia Convention had already framed a Constitution for the Commonwealth. The Declaration of Independence was only six weeks away.

The Commonwealth

(1776-1781)

1. The Declaration of Independence

CAROLINE was the first county in Virginia to cut her ties with the royal government after the Continental Congress proclaimed the Declaration of Independence. Edmund Pendleton called the local court together to consider the emergency after a messenger on horseback passed through the county carrying the tidings from Philadelphia to Williamsburg. This session was held in the courthouse on July 11th, 1776. It is reported in detail in the Caroline Order Book for 1776 beginning on page 103.

Only six magistrates attended this session. They were Edmund Pendleton, James Taylor, Thomas Lowry, William Buckner, Samuel Hawes and George Guy.

There were three vacancies caused by death on the court and William Woodford was away leading the Continental troops in the field. But the remaining twelve magistrates either did not get the summons in time to attend the session or received it and stayed away because they were not ready to foreswear their allegiance to the king. The record of the other officers was even worse. John Buckner, the magistrate, who served as sheriff, Edmund Pendleton, Jr., the acting crown attorney, and William Nelson, the county clerk, were all absent.

Undismayed by this lack of support the six sitting magistrates "severally took the oath required by the late ordinance of the General Convention, entitled 'An ordinance to enable the present magistrates and officers to continue the administration of justice and for setting the general mood of proceeding in criminal cases 'til the same can be more adequately provided for." This abbreviated court also swore in John Buckner's deputies, Joseph Richerson, Thomas Ship and Phillip Johnston, to perform the duties of sheriff, William Harrison, Jr., deputy clerk, to act as clerk, and William Boulware to take over as prosecuting attorney, and before they adjourned directed the deputy sheriffs "to wait on all gentlemen named in the commission of peace, and other county officers appointed by the crown, and to desire that they will attend the next session of the court to take the oath appointed by the General Convention for a justice and other public officers to take."

Four of the absentees showed up at the next term (August). They were Roger Quarles, Walker Taliaferro and John Armistead, magistrates from upper St. Margaret's Parish, and John Buckner, of upper Drysdale, the sheriff. The chances are after considering the prominent parts that Quarles, Taliaferro and Armistead played in furthering the patriots' cause under the Committee of Safety, that they did not hear of the Declaration of Independence in time to attend the July session of the court because they all lived in remote sections of the county. But Buckner's case was different. It appears he had purposely stayed away from the first session, and his attendance at the second not only aligned the powerful office of sheriff with the Commonwealth but also indicated the way sentiment was shifting.

This trend continued and in September, James Upshaw, John Minor, Anthony New and Robert Taliaferro resumed their seats on the court. But the shift was not fast enough to suit the more radical magistrates, and at the September term they persuaded the court to issue an order for all holdout crown appointed officials to attend the October session and swear allegiance to the Commonwealth or resign. Magistrates Anthony Thornton, James Miller and William Harrison and Clerk William Nelson came to this session. Thornton, who had served the most conservative Tory element in the colony when he acted as special agent to arrest religious dissenters, stated that he had "a change of heart," and that he was in full accord with the revolutionary movement. But he contended that he was now too old to take an active part in government and resigned as magistrate after urging the court to recommend the appointment of his son, Anthony Thornton, Jr., (who was a member of the Committee of Safety) to fill the vacancy.

James Miller and William Harrison made no excuses. They

boldly announced that they were Tories and had no intention of abandoning the king and espousing the Commonwealth. They declared that they intended to hold on to their seats so long as "it pleased the royal governor" and that the only way the other magistrates could get rid of them was to kick them off the court. The sitting magistrates rose to this challenge and declared their seats vacant.

James Miller's position is easy to explain. He was one of the richest of the Port Royal merchants and believed that war with Britain and the stoppage of trade spelled his ruin. William Harrison's position is more difficult to understand. He was a large planter and the vast majority of his large planter neighbors were patriots. In addition his son, William Harrison, Jr., had already renounced his allegiance to the king and resumed his position as deputy clerk of the county. The only light which his stand sheds is the division in the great families of the county between the Tory and Patriot camps.

William Nelson complied with the directives of the court and again began to perform the duties of clerk without offering any explanation of record. The chances are that his holding out was based on pique. The voters of the county had denied him a seat on the second Committee of Safety after he had served on the first. He had taken this defeat as an insult and the odds are that he was reluctant to join forces with a group which failed to appreciate his services.

Neither magistrate Garwin Corbin, nor acting attorney Edmund Pendleton, Jr. attended the October session of the court, despite the magistrates' orders. Corbin was a member of one of the most prominent Tory families in Virginia. One relative, Richard Corbin, had been acting royal governor of the colony after the flight of Dunmore from Williamsburg. Another, John Tayloe Corbin, was confined to St. Margaret's Parish for the duration of the hostilities for acting as chief go-between, between Richard Corbin and Dunmore. Numerous kinsmen were already refugees in England. To espouse the patriot's cause meant ostracism by his blood kin. To side with Tories meant the loss of his vast estates for the time being at least.

He had a momentous decision to make and did not intend to be stampeded into making it hurriedly.

Pendleton, Jr.'s absence was not based on the lack of patriotism. He stayed away for personal reasons. Zachery Lewis, in spite of the fact that he had long since moved his residence from Caroline, still held office as crown attorney and drew the salary, while Pendleton, Jr., as his deputy, did all the work and drew only a deputy's pay. Pendleton, Jr. wanted to make sure that this situation was not going to continue after he foreswore his allegiance to the king and resumed his duties. Patrick Henry, who was governor and had the power to make the change, refused to offer this assurance because of his dislike for the Pendletons, and Edmund Pendleton, Jr. continued to hold out.

The court recognized Corbin's and Pendleton, Jr.'s peculiar position and refused to declare their offices vacant and send recommendations to the governor for replacements, although it asked Governor Henry to name Anthony Thornton, Jr., Samuel Temple, John Page, Jr., Dr. John Tennant, Thomas Lomax and Richard Johnston to fill the six vacancies on the court, and John Hoomes of the Bowling Green to take the place of Edmund Pendleton, who resigned because of the press of his duties as Speaker of the House of Delegates, at the end of the October term. Henry acted favorably on all the recommendations and the full slate of new magistrates joined the court. At the same time abiding by the magistrates' precedent he wisely refrained from forcing the issue over Corbin and Pendleton, Jr. Corbin's post remained vacant until February 1777 when he finally decided to cast his lot with the patriots and reoccupied his seat on the court. He was the only Corbin of prominence to foreswear allegiance to the king. The Pendleton case was longer drawn out. It remained stalemated with William Boulware acting as Commonwealth's attorney without a commission, until Edmund Pendleton, Sr. became President of the Court of Chancery in the Fall of 1777 and gave the post to his nephew, Edmund Pendleton, Jr., in name as well as in fact.

2. CURB OF POTENTIAL TROUBLEMAKERS

Before the Caroline Court completed the purge of its own ranks of Tories it moved to curb other elements in the county which might, either wittingly or unwittingly, aid the British. These elements included the Negro slaves, the Quakers, leaders in the Established Church and the importing merchants.

Lord Dunmore after his flight from Williamsburg had issued a proclamation offering freedom to all Negro slaves who deserted their masters and joined his forces. Few Negroes took advantage of this offer but it created consternation throughout Virginia. The Caroline Committee of Safety set up a patrol headed by Michael Brown Roberts, a constable, to keep Negroes from roaming around at night. The first court under the Commonwealth made this de facto arrangement de jure for the duration of hostilities and shifted command of the night patrol from Michael Brown Roberts to Robert Broaddus.

This precaution proved unnecessary. Caroline Negroes gave less trouble the year immediately after the Declaration of Independence than any preceding year in the county's history. There was only one arrest among the servants for crime. This was the arrest of a Negro named Jack accused of the attempted rape of Mary Vaughan. The Court found Jack guilty, but instead of imposing the customary sentence of death by hanging let him off with thirty-nine lashes at the whipping post. The reason for this relatively mild sentence was due, perhaps, to the fear of inflaming the Negroes with a public hanging.

While the night patrol was not needed to control the Negroes it irritated the Quakers. This sect, which formed one of the most numerous blocks of population in St. Margaret's Parish, had become pacifist during the French and Indian War. After incorporating this doctrine into its creed, its leaders turned their attention to slavery and by the time of the outbreak of the Revolution had decided that slavery was wrong. They had not gone so far, however, as to prohibit Quakers from owning slaves. But they had decreed that Quakers must neither buy nor sell Negroes nor interfere with a slave's freedom of movement. Serving on the night patrol was in violation of this latest tenet of their faith and they refused to serve. Ardent patriots classed this refusal as traitorous and threatened acts of violence in reprisal until Samuel Hargrave, Secretary of the Golansville Meeting and leader of the sect in Caroline, convinced the public that Quakers opposed all forms of tyranny and that they classed the night patrol as much tyranny for Negroes as the rule of the royal government was for the freeholders.

The attitude of the leaders in the Established Church posed a more difficult problem. Many high churchmen throughout the colony held that to repudiate the king was to repudiate the Church since he was its titular head, and remained royalist. Edmund Pendleton, who was striving to keep the Established Church of the colony as the Established Church of the Commonwealth, wanted none of this deflection in his home county of Caroline. The political philosophies of the incumbent rectors of the three Caroline parishes aided him in bringing the local church to the side of the patriots. Had he attempted this move at an earlier date when the rapscallion Brunskill was rector of St. Margaret's, the intolerant Morton, rector of Drysdale, and the brilliant but archly Tory Boucher, rector of St. Mary's, his plan would have been foredoomed to failure before its inauguration. But Brunskill was dead, Morton out of the county and Boucher a refugee in England, and temperate Archabald Dick, mild Samuel Shields and Abner Waugh, who was one of the few ministers in Virginia to be elected to a colony Committee of Safety, occupied the pulpits of St. Margaret's, Drysdale and St. Mary's parishes, respectively. These three men, unlike their predecessors, welcomed rather than opposed a break with Britain.

But the vestrymen proved more difficult to line up than the ministers. Some of them were out and out royalist, some were indifferent to the Revolution, and others sought to use the crisis to create a permanent break between church and state. In all three parishes the vestries dallied until their failure to take a stand wore Pendleton's patience thin. Early in 1777 he persuaded the Caroline Court to order all vestrymen in the county to swear allegiance to the Commonwealth, or resign. Edmund

Pendleton, Benjamin Hubbard, Thomas Lowry, James Upshaw, Edmund Pendleton, Jr., William Harrison, Jr. and Anthony Thornton, Jr., of Drysdale, took the oath at once to place over fifty per cent of the vestry of that parish on the side of the patriots. But only William Woodford, James Taylor, Thomas Lomax and John Catlett of St. Mary's and Walker Taliaferro, John Armistead and William Boulware of St. Margaret's took the oath.

Pendleton exerted more pressure and the next month John Buckner, John Thornton, Robert Gilchrist, Edward Dixon and Garwin Corbin of St. Mary's, and Samuel Hawes, Samuel Redd and Robert Mickleberry of St. Margaret's fell in line. The patriots now held twenty-two of the thirty-six seats on the vestries of the county, and the other seats the court declared vacant. Some of these were filled, in time, by members of the younger generation, John Sutton, Jr., of St. Margaret's, and John Page, Jr. and John Hoomes, of Drysdale. But the vestries of Caroline never again operated with full membership so long as there was a state church in Virginia.

The importing merchants soon proved to be the most dangerous partisans of Great Britain in Caroline. Their activities in aiding and abetting the enemy were so pronounced that the magistrates in January 1777 ordered all foreign born residents engaged in trade to appear before the court and take the oath of allegiance to the Commonwealth, or be expelled from the colony and forfeit their property to the State. Patrick Kennon appeared and took the oath, but his assistant, John Monroe Morris, and James Gordon, fled. While James Craigie and James Stark, assistants to Dunlop and Cross, John Gray, his assistant, James Coates, and factor, Andrew Leckie, John Wallace and his assistant, Archabald MacLean, John Thompson, a clerk for James Miller and James Markey ignored the summons. The court judgment on this group, ordered them expelled and their holdings forfeited. Port Royal lost many of its most prominent residents. Andrew Leckie, however, in some manner managed to evade expulsion and remained in Caroline, an avowed Tory throughout the Revolution.

John Pendleton was the only individual to gain financially

from this mass expulsion. His celebrated uncle, Edmund, who was never adverse to nepotism to help a relative, secured him the job of escheator and he grew rich from his commissions on the sale of the expelled merchants' forfeited estates.

3. THE WAR AT SEA—THE *Liberty* AND THE *Mosquito*

After the soldiers who served under Gen. Woodford at Great Bridge the next Caroline men to see action against the enemy were sailors and marines. To keep the sea lanes open and to prevent the stoppage of imports from abroad was essential to the success of the patriots' cause. Besides, armed ships on the high seas brought in British merchantmen as prizes of war, whose cargoes increased the colonist stocks of critical materials they needed to wage war.

Scores of Caroline men worked overtime at Frazier's shipyard on the lower Mattapony and at Fielding Lewis' shipyard in Fredericksburg to build these ships. Henry Lyburn of Port Royal, captain and joint owner with James Dunlop of the ill-fated *Olive,* which was seized, while attempting to enter the port of Port Royal with a cargo of British goods, by Captain Richard Taylor upon orders of the Committee of Safety, turned patriot after the Declaration of Independence and piloted the newly-built ships through the treacherous waters of the Mattapony and the upper Rappahannock to the open sea.

Caroline furnished many men to man and command these vessels. George Catlett got his first taste of war as a lieutenant in the marines aboard the *Pocahontas,* Thomas Chandler, Sr. served as a lieutenant first on the *Northampton* and later on the *Patriot,* Robert Conway as captain of the *Adventure,* Rodham Kenner, as an officer on the *Proctor* and the *Dragon,* Thomas Landrum II, a Port Royal physician, as surgeon's mate on the *Tartar* and the *Tempest,* Christopher Tompkins as a lieutenant on the *Henry,* and Richard Taylor, who had already won renown as a sea captain under the Committee of Safety, commanded a squadron from his flagship, the *Hornet.*

But the two ships of which the records reveal the most information on which Caroline men served were the *Liberty* and the *Mosquito*. The log for the *Liberty* was as ignoble as the log of the other, the *Mosquito* was glorious.

The government of the new Commonwealth of Virginia sent the *Liberty*, which was a large man-of-war with eighteen guns, to Baltimore in August 1776, to be outfitted for the protection of the York River. Thomas Lilly of Gloucester, was captain of the vessel and John Royston, steward, Thomas Coleman, pilot, and John Chick, gunner, all of Caroline, among the crew. Royston kept a diary and the information set forth in this paragraph is from his record. Lilly was unfit to be a commanding officer, and among other things he forced the officers and the enlisted men to dine together and sleep in the same quarters. In a short time the enlisted men lost all respect for their superiors and the officers were unable to keep them from disgraceful conduct ashore. This revel continued until all the money gave out and when Lilly failed to get funds from Virginia to meet the ship's payroll over half the crew deserted. With only half crew and without funds conditions aboard the ship went from bad to worse. In the end Royston reports that he was forced to sell his clothes to pay his washwoman. The *Liberty* was never outfitted to serve as a man-of-war.

The *Mosquito* was outfitted in Portsmouth in the Summer of 1776 for a cruise into the West Indies to prey on British commerce. Governor Henry ordered Maj. Alexander Dick, of Fredericksburg, a son of Charles Dick, the Fredericksburg and Caroline merchant, and brother of the Rev. Archibald Dick, rector of St. Margaret's Parish to recruit marines to form the military force on this voyage. Dick picked the company of twenty-five commanded by Capt. George Catlett of Port Royal, for the mission. All of Catlett's company were Caroline men. They included Thomas Chandler, Jr. and Roger Quarles, lieutenants, William Coleman, chief petty officer, and Anthony and Nicholas Dixon, Reuben and William Chandler, James Quarles, Larkin Farish, Jesse Hipkins, Francis Pickett, Reuben Brooks, George Doggett, Benjamin Tankersley and three Dishman brothers, two of whose names were James and William. This outfit left Port Royal on December 4, 1776, and went aboard the *Mosquito* at Urbanna a few days later.

In addition to the numerous marines, several sailors on the ship were from Caroline. They included Henry Rains, Moses Stanley, William Mitchell and William Thorp. Stanley kept a diary which was published in the *New England Historical and Genealogical Register* and the Dishmans wrote a series of letters to their sister, Mrs. Sarah Beazley, of Caroline, which have been preserved. The author drew the information about the voyage of the *Mosquito* and what happened to her crew from these sources along with the applications for land bounties from servicemen in the Revolution.

The cruise of the *Mosquito* began auspiciously enough. She reached the West Indies without mishap and captured the British merchantman, *Snow John,* laden with clothes, beef, bacon, candles and flour, worth 80,000 livres, off Antigua. The men aboard were elated. They figured that their shares of the spoils were worth sixty louis each. But Capt. Collier, the commander of the ship, refused to let them enjoy their good fortune. He put in at Guadeloupe, but instead of selling the booty there engaged a Frenchman, M. Souliez, to transport it to Martinique where the market was better, while the crew got the *Mosquito* ready to continue the voyage. A Dominican privateer seized M. Souliez's sloop with the booty aboard while it was on the seas between Guadeloupe and Martinique, and although Collier protested he was unable to get redress. The *Mosquito* sailed from Guadeloupe with a saddened crew.

Back at sea misfortune struck again and smallpox broke out on board. Captain Collier turned the ship about and returned to Guadeloupe to inoculate every man in his crew. William Dishman wrote his sister, Mrs. Beazley in Caroline, that the inoculation did no great harm, as was often the case, but much time was lost while the men convalesced.

This delay proved the *Mosquito's* undoing. The British found out where she was and sent the *Ariadne*, a twenty-gun man-of-war to blockade Guadeloupe. But when his men were again in shape the American commander decided to try to run this blockade. Moses Stanley reports that it was a futile gesture. The *Mosquito* was soon overhauled by the larger and heavier armed British ship. The surrender took place on June 4, 1777.

The British promptly divided their American officer and enlisted men prisoners. The enlisted men were incarcerated in Bridgetown, Barbados jail, and the officers sent on to Fortune prison, at Gosport, near Plymouth on the south coast of England.

Officers and men, alike, suffered from many indignities. The British forced Francis Pickett, Reuben Brooks and William Chandler, although they were marines and not seamen, to serve as sailors on British ships, where at least two of them were seized with fever and died from lack of necessities.

The Dishman brothers were more fortunate. The Frenchmen, M. Souliez, came to their rescue. He managed to smuggle clothes to them in the Bridgetown jail which they used as a disguise to escape to Jamaica. After a long wait on that island a Dutch merchant let them work their way to Philadelphia on one of his vessels. They reached their destination the night the whole city was illuminated to celebrate the signing of the treaty of military alliance between France and the American colonies.

After seven months at Bridgetown, according to Moses Stanley, all the remaining American marines and seamen were transported to Gosport. In Fortune jail with the officers, William Thorp furnished the wherewithall for him and George Catlett to bribe a jailor and escape. Once outside the prison they stole a small boat and crossed the English channel to France. Thorp's fate after this escapade is not of record. But Catlett did not get back to Virginia until the Spring of 1781. After he got home he declared "that his feelings against the British were so violent from the treatment he received while in jail that he would never leave the service so long as there was a chance of fighting" and immediately left for the front. He was true to his word because he was one of the Caroline men at the surrender of Cornwallis to Washington at Yorktown.

Catlett and Thorp's flight caused other Americans locked up in Fortune prison to try to escape. Led by William Mitchell, a group succeeded in undermining the prison walls, seizing a vessel and crossing the channel to France, where they joined John Paul Jones, and finished the war as members of his crew.

With the second successful flight the British became wary of the Americans and offered all who remained, pardons if they agreed to take the oath of allegiance to the king. Upon hearing of this offer the Americans replied "Damn King George, and his pardon, too."

The remaining Americans apparently remained locked up for the rest of the war. During this period Moses Stanley completed his *A Yankee Privateersman in Prison in England* referred to above.

4. THE MILITIA, THE ARMY AND SMALLPOX

Activities at sea, while vital, were merely a side thrust. Caroline made her main contribution towards winning the Revolutionary War through her soldiers, who fought on land.

After the magistrates purged their own ranks and curbed the Tories they next turned their attention to total mobilization of the county. Walker Taliaferro succeeded James Taylor, as county lieutenant, and Governor Henry, upon recommendation of the court, gave him a staff consisting of Thomas Lowry, colonel, James Upshaw and Anthony Thornton, lieutenant colonels, and Richard Buckner and John Minor, majors, to supervise the training of troops. Phillip Buckner, Samuel Temple and William Buckner succeeded Richard Buckner, John Minor and Anthony Thornton, respectively, as company commanders, when the latter were promoted to staff rank.

The staff immediately organized a new company in the county and placed it under the command of Robert Graham, who had changed from rank Tory to rank patriot, to raise the total number of companies in the local militia to seventeen. This placed, at least, eight hundred and fifty men in the militia alone. In addition there were over three hundred and fifty in the regular Continental Army (figures from the Archives of Virginia State Library) and numerous others in the Navy and the Marines, to make a total of well over twelve hundred and fifty men from Caroline in the armed forces. This was a remarkable feat for a county with a population of less than nine thousand white inhabitants.

Unfortunately, no record exists of where Caroline men

fought as a unit during the Revolution. But it may be assumed that they were fighting in the main theaters of the war under the command of the ranking officers from the county, since at that time men from a county fought together under the command of local officers.

Gen. William Woodford and Col. George Baylor were the ranking officers from Caroline who served in the Revolution. Woodford joined Washington's main body of troops in the middle colonies after he successfully completed the Norfolk campaign against Dunmore. He commanded the First Virginia Brigade, composed of the Third, Seventh, Eleventh and Fifteenth Virginia Regiments. The Seventh Regiment was literally cut to pieces in the battle of Brandywine (September 1777) and General Woodford, its commanding officer, was so severely wounded that he had to retire from the battlefield. The chances are that many of the men in this regiment were from Caroline because of the great number of soldiers' estates admitted to probate in the Caroline Court in the Fall of 1777, and the fact that subsequently a postoffice in the county was named Brandywine to commemorate the valor of the men who died in that battle.

Col. George Baylor was a cavalry leader and an aid to Washington. The Continental Congress voted him a charger in appreciation of his services in the battle of Trenton. Later he was shot through the lung and captured by the British while fighting with Washington's army at Tappan, N. Y. It is logical to believe that there were Caroline men in his command both at Trenton and Tappan.

Many other Caroline men were wounded in battle as well as Woodford and Baylor, and a great number were killed. But disease soon proved a greater scourge to the county, brought on by war, than casualties on the battlefield. As early as February 1777, smallpox broke out in Port Royal. From records in the Order Books it is hard to determine if the disease entered the county through soldiers home on furlough or if it was brought in by sailors on the ships calling at Port Royal. But in either case the epidemic developed from circumstances arising out of the war.

A Negro wench belonging to Dr. William Johnston, of Port Royal, was the first patient of record. The court ordered her moved to an outhouse in an attempt to prevent the spreading of the disease. This precaution did little good because a few days later another Negro woman, the property of Edward Dixon, the Port Royal merchant and neighbor of Dr. Johnston, became ill. The court took more drastic steps in this case and ordered Dr. John Tennent to inoculate all the Negroes in Dixon's slave quarters.

Shortly after the second case was reported to the court, the outbreak reached epidemic proportions when most of the Negroes at Dr. Johnston's contracted the disease. Terrified, the doctor asked permission of the court to move his family, who up to this point had escaped contagion, to the home of Phillip Buckner, a relative, who lived in the high country beyond the river flats. The magistrates consented to this move, provided that every one on Buckner's plantation was inoculated against smallpox before the Johnstons joined them.

While the magistrates pondered over how to stop the spreading of the disease about Port Royal, Henry Pemberton, a planter from St. Margaret's appeared before the court and presented a claim of six pounds for nursing Thomas Dudley, a soldier on furlough, who was ill with smallpox, and who had died of the disease in his home. The court paid the claim and while it was a substantial sum of money, it was small remuneration to the Pembertons for taking the stricken Dudley into their home, because at least four of them had contracted the disease from the soldier, and the illness brought on their deaths.

When Thomas Pitts, a planter of Drysdale Parish, learned that the court had paid Pemberton for nursing Dudley, he presented a bill for nursing his son, David, another soldier on furlough, who was ill with smallpox. The court paid the elder Pitts four pounds. But he became alarmed when he heard that four of the Pembertons had contracted smallpox from Dudley and died, and quickly removed his son from his home, in an attempt to save other members of his family, and entrusted the youth's nursing to one, Rennolds McKenney. Why McKenney agreed to take over this dangerous job, the Order

Books fail to reveal. The best explanation is his love of money. What financial arrangement Pitts made with him is not of record, but subsequently the court paid him three pounds. As a happy postscript to this incident, young Pitts, in spite of the shunting about, recovered from the disease and was able to return to his post of duty in the army.

Few people who contracted smallpox were as fortunate as David Pitts. Most of them died. The epidemic mounted to such proportions that the court in March 1777, instructed Dr. John Tennent "to provide a convenient house for the purpose of inoculation," and passed an ordinance which forced people who had been exposed to contagion to go there for treatment. Dr. Tennent set up the house, which was, in effect, the first hospital in the history of Caroline County. But many of the people who had been exposed to smallpox did not take kindly to the idea of forced inoculation, which in some instances was almost as bad as the disease itself, since it consisted of infecting the patient with smallpox in a mild form to build up his resistance to a more virulent attack, and stayed away from the house of treatment in open defiance of the ordinance. The disease continued to spread until the court refused to countenance this disobedience and in mid-Spring 1777 named a committee composed of Robert Gilchrist, Walker Taliaferro, John Armistead, William Buckner, Thomas Lomax and Anthony Thornton to investigate all cases of smallpox reported in the county, determine everyone, who might contract the disease through contagion, and force them to go to the inoculation center. This committee did its work well and compelled scores of people, who stood a chance to contact smallpox, to take preventive treatment.

While the court worked in this manner Dr. John Tennent, who was one of the most brilliant physicians in Virginia, ran countless experiments to cure the disease, or at least to cut down its rate of fatalities. He was partially successful, and between his new system of treatment and forced inoculations by the committee the epidemic was at length brought under control.

5. SHORTAGES, INFLATION AND MORALE

Shortages in many lines of merchandise and the mounting costs of living were the greatest domestic plagues to scourge Caroline, in addition to smallpox, during the years immediately after the Declaration of Independence. The gallant patriots in the navy and the marines were unable to keep the sea lanes open, and it became increasingly difficult to bring in goods from abroad. In January 1777 the local court created the position of port master for Port Royal and gave the post to Edward Dixon. His duties included the improvement of wharfage facilities in an attempt to attract ships, which managed to elude the British blockade, to Port Royal and give the people of Caroline a chance to purchase their cargoes.

Caroline had another advantage over other Virginia counties: James Dunlop, one of the largest ship owners in the colony, made Port Royal his headquarters, and he kept his ships constantly on the seas. Dunlop's motives, however, were based on hopes of personal gain rather than patriotism. He had attempted to defy the Continental Congress' regulations governing trade by sending the *Olive* to England for a cargo of goods before the Declaration of Independence, and now he risked the loss of vessels and merchandise by ordering his ships to run the blockade. His motto appears to have been that trade must go on regardless of the hazards, and the attitude of the government in power.

But Dunlop and the other shipowners, who attempted to elude the British on the high seas, tempered daring with reason. Instead of sending their vessels to northern Europe for badly needed manufactured goods, they sent them to Africa for slaves and to the West Indies for tropical products where the risk of falling prey to an enemy man-of-war was much less than nosing along the coast of Great Britain. As a result, Caroline taverns were stocked with the finest wines, while the merchants lacked manufactured metal articles for sale. Two French merchants in Martinique, Antoine Gautieu and Jean Collineau, tried to cash in on this situation and imported large quantities of merchandise of north European manufacture in Dutch,

French and Spanish bottoms for transhipment to the revolting colonies on American ships. The part of this venture which concerned Caroline met with scant success. The Port Royal merchants, who received the goods, had little of value with which to pay Gautieu and Collineau, and the transactions ceased after the institution of numerous suits for payment, which clutter up the Caroline Order Books for the decade beginning with 1778.

The lack of manpower to till the fields because of the ravages of smallpox and the number of men away in the armed forces caused a shortage of native grown staples to develop alongside the shortage of goods manufactured abroad. People became hungry and profiteers began roaming the countryside offering diluted foodstuffs for sale. In an attempt to break up this racket, the court, in August 1777, made John Catlett and Vivion Minor inspectors of flour.

A crime wave was another result of the shortage of food. In 1778, the court, in an unprecedented move, certified John Hackett to the General Court of the Commonwealth for trial for the theft of three lambs from James Miller. No one had been sent to the General Court for such a minor theft before and to make the case even more unusual Hackett was a patriot, and Miller an ardent Tory. When quick-tongued Daniel Barksdale heard this verdict, he cursed magistrates and Miller alike in open court. The magistrates fined him ten pounds for this crime.

Barksdale was not the only patriot to curse the court. The magistrates were becoming more and more unpopular because of their attempts to cure economic distress with ordinances. When they ruled that tavern-keepers must take in travelers and furnish them "cold diet and lodging for nine pence a night" (slightly over 10 cents at the present rate of exchange) and furnish stableage and a minimum of six bunches of fodder for horses at one shilling, thruppence (slightly over 16 cents at the present rate of exchange) Robert Woolfolk, proprietor of Needwood Tavern, became so enraged that the Order Books report that he "insulted, abused and degraded the court at sundry times and declared that the whole of this court were a set of damned rascals." The magistrates ordered Woolfolk to appear at the next court and show cause why he delivered these tirades and summoned George Turner, John Fitzhugh, John Thilman and Daniel Turner to testify against him. But the Woolfolks were old hands at cursing the court, and Robert of Needwood, like other members of his family before him, managed to make his remarks and escape punishment.

Rising prices and the shortage of foodstuffs had their most disastrous effects on the families of men out of the county in the armed forces. If no able-bodied person remained in the household to till the land and raise grain these families were frequently in acute need. In August 1777 William Johnston, who had served the county as jailor, appeared in court and declared that he was "infirm and unable to support his family in the absence of two sons in the service of the United States." The magistrates considered his case and appropriated ten pounds sterling for the maintenance of the family, to be spent as directed by James Taylor, John Hoomes, James Upshaw and John Minor.

When news of this award spread numerous other persons, (James Anderson, the wife of William Carneal, Leah Hampton and Caty Bryan, the next day) appeared before the court and made similar claims. Having set a precedent the magistrates began to make appropriations for them all. (The complete list is set out in the supplement to this history.) These awards mounted so rapidly that it soon appeared, unless drastic steps were taken, they were going to break the county, although they were all to be spent under the personal supervision of a subcommittee of magistrates named by the court. In an attempt to set the fiscal affairs of the county straight, James Upshaw, an elderly man, resigned as treasurer of the court, and the magistrates named John Hoomes of the Bowling Green, one of the most astute young businessmen in the county, to fill the vacancy. But Hoomes was unable to work miracles, and it was soon apparent that the only chance to keep the county solvent was a substantial increase in taxes, because the awards were recurring obligations, demanding supplemental appropriations each time they were exhausted, so long as the war lasted. Besides the chances were that a large number of new awards must be made each year.

The tax levy for Caroline for 1777 was only three pounds of tobacco per tithable, one of the lowest rates in the county's history. The magistrates had purposely lowered it, the first year they functioned under the Commonwealth, as a morale booster, and in further consideration to the spirits of the people had ruled, that for the first time, the taxpayers might pay the levy, either in tobacco or in currency, at the rate of six pence a tithable head. The freeholders appreciated this concession. The county was flooded with continental currency, issued to pay the expenses of the war, which was valueless to make purchases of goods imported from abroad, while tobacco, which might be used for this purpose, was scarce. But Hoomes' wizardry as a financier was able to save neither the low tax rate nor the privilege of paying taxes in specie. Instead he boldly recommended that the right to pay taxes in specie be revoked, and the tax levy be raised from three to sixteen pounds of tobacco per tithable. The magistrates adopted this report and time proved that Hoomes figured accurately. Awards for the year totaled 52,732 pounds of tobacco, or almost eleven and one-half pounds for every tithable head, and consumed all but about one and one-half pounds per tithable head of the raise. It is interesting to note that in a day (1953) when it is a common complaint that such a large percentage of the public revenues must go to maintain the armed forces and for the national defense, that in 1778 Caroline County spent over 70 per cent of her total tax intake for the support of the families of service men from the county.

6. UNREST

Allotments failed to keep the men in the armed forces and their families satisfied, although the awards were wrecking the county's finances. The war went badly for the colonist in 1778-79 and wounded men and deserters returned to their homes in droves. John Powell Edmundson, who had lost a leg in battle, appeared before the Caroline Court and asked for a pension.

The magistrates listened to his request sympathetically but turned it down because they had no funds for pensions. This refusal caused an uproar through the county, and when a few days later the widow of Mason (Mace) Carneal, who had been killed in combat, appealed for help the magistrates were afraid to deny her; and instead of tempering her request with reason they went all out and authorized the huge award of 1,000 pounds, sterling, evidently in hopes of regaining the favor of the masses. This award amounted to the tobacco from 250 acres. If it were all paid in a year it meant an additional assessment of over forty pounds of tobacco on every tithable in the county.

John Hoomes of the Bowling Green, realizing the futility of his attempts to balance the county budget in the face of such extravagance by the magistrates, resigned as treasurer of the court in disgust. After some delay the magistrates persuaded John Baylor, of New Market, to fill the vacancy. Baylor made some drastic changes. He took the county off the "tobacco" standard and decreed that taxes might be paid in Continental dollars, and that the families of the service men must accept their allotments in this currency. This move sanctioned mounting inflation which Hoomes had sought to curb when he ordered a return to the "tobacco" standard, but it eased for the time being the financial pressure. But it angered the families of the service men when they realized the purchasing power of their allotments had been cut. They became even angrier when Baylor persuaded the court to announce that it was going to award no more pensions for wounds and deaths and leave this function to the government of the Commonwealth and the Continental Congress.

In an attempt to placate the aroused service personnel and their kin the court pointed out that soldiers might claim land bounties. This announcement brought loud guffaws in the taverns throughout the county, because veterans recalled that the royal government had offered land bounties for service in the Virginia Regiment during the French and Indian War, and after the conflict was over, practically nullified the promise with the Hillsborough Proclamation, which prohibited residents of the colonies from taking up land beyond the Alleghanies where most of the crown land, fit for settlement, was located. The masses had no more faith in the promises of the government of the Commonwealth than they had in the government of the colony, and having been stung once they did not intend being stung again.

To restore the doubters' faith the magistrates offered to make good at once the crown's promise of free land for service in the French and Indian War, and opened the court for proof of claims of all local veterans who fought in that conflict, or their heirs if they were dead, to certify to the governor of the Commonwealth for immediate action. Forty French and Indian War veterans in Caroline took advantage of this offer. They were George Muse, Reuben Ross, Thomas Ayers, Thomas Moss, Thomas Smith, John MacDonald, Benjamin Rennolds, William Smithers, James Arnold, Richard Riddle, James Satterwhite, William Sepot (?), Thomas Hitchcock, John Harvey, Benjamin Oliver, Francis Self, William Field, James Russell, John Sampson, Edward Brown, James Samuel Lewis, William Mutchell, Thomas Dickinson, Achiles Whitlock, George White, James Taylor, George Hicks, William Robinson, John Carter, Samuel Taylor, Thomas Thorpe, James Ryan, John Johnstone, Nathaniel Holloway, John Powell, William Rennolds, John Munday, James Sessell (Cecil), Reuben Munday and Henry Sessell (Cecil).

Not all of the disgruntled element was so mercenary. Many patriotic men were losing faith in the Revolution, because it had not brought the reforms its leaders promised. For a short time before the Declaration of Independence, Caroline enjoyed local representative government, while the freeholders elected the Committee of Safety, which ran the county. But, now after independence had been declared, this reform was lost, and the governor of the Commonwealth named the magistrates, who sat on the court, in the same autocratic manner as the royal governor. Many leaders, including Pendleton, felt that the people were not ready to govern themselves. Governor Henry felt otherwise. But he was powerless to act without a change in the Constitution. He did, however, make all the amends possible, and named Mungo Roy, John Garlick, James Jameson and Richard Johnston to the Caroline Court, who were popular leaders and without any great claim to aristocracy.

Keeping the Established Church of the colony as the Established Church of the Commonwealth was even a greater cause of disillusionment, because more people were interested in religious freedom than civil rights. Pendleton, again, was the chief leader who opposed change. He was determined to keep the state church at all costs. In an attempt to appease his neighbors he maneuvered through the General Assembly a bill to divide Drysdale Parish, whose ill-shape had been a great inconvenience to its freeholders since it was formed in 1723. The new parish, to be called St. Asaph, was formed from Drysdale's upper end and included most of Caroline west of the Marocossic and north of Phillip's Run to the Mattapony and the St. Mary's Parish line. It was officially sanctioned in February 1780, and was the last parish set up by law in Virginia. The Creek Church, between the Bowling Green and the temporary courthouse became its chief church, and Anthony Thornton, Jr., John Hoomes, Mungo Roy, Edmund Pendleton, Edmund Pendleton, Jr., David Jameson, Phillip Johnston, Charles Todd, Charles Woolfolk and Thomas Buckner became its vestry.

The setting up of St. Asaph did not save the Established Church. Before its vestry held its first meeting the General Assembly passed a law to allow ministers of other faiths to perform the marriage ceremony. Nathaniel Holloway, veteran of the French and Indian War, ordained Baptist minister and victim of persecution (he had served a jail sentence for his faith) during the attempt to oppress dissenters, was the first non-conformist minister to qualify to perform marriage ceremonies in the Caroline Court. This was only a beginning. The Established Church of the colony as the state church of the Commonwealth was doomed. The people were going to win their liberties in spite of their conservative leaders.

7. LAST YEARS OF THE REVOLUTION

In an effort to boost morale Caroline patriots began calling Port Royal, Port Roy. (Order Book for 1778, page 80.) This was in accord with a vogue prevalent throughout the rebelling colonies. From New Hampshire to Georgia places and institutions shed their names associated with royalty. Kings College (now Washington and Lee University) in the Valley of Virginia became Liberty Academy, Kings College in New York became and remained Columbia, but fortunately Port Royal reverted to its original name after the Revolution because the first name is more euphonious and has greater historical significance. But the temporary shift gave rise to a legend that Port Royal was first called Port Roy. This legend is untrue. The General Assembly named the town Port Royal in the same act it authorized its founding. The only time it was ever called Port Roy was by a few ardent patriots during the last three years of the Revolution.

Unfortunately name changing did not revive trade. The British blockade effectively stopped all sea-borne commerce. Port Royal became a dead town. The plight of its merchants was desperate. In 1778 Andrew Leckie, a Tory factor, who attempted to last the war out in Caroline, opened a tavern in an effort to make ends meet.

The shutting off of foreign trade was not the only cause of Port Royal's business doldrums. Production of local crops was at the lowest level since the great drought of 1755-56 and the French and Indian War. There were plenty of slaves to cultivate the fields but most of the men to make them work were away in the armed forces, weeds choked crops on large acreages and scores of Negroes enjoyed a shiftless holiday. Able-bodied free white men to work were so scarce that Sarah Bowie personally took over the supervision of the operation of the ferry across the Rappahannock between Port Royal and King George after her husband, James Bowie II, died, and farther upstream Mary Taliaferro supervised the operation of another ferry after the death of her husband, Francis Taliaferro.

An unusual number of deaths further reduced the number of men too old for the armed forces, who were capable of managing businesses. In addition to both James Bowies, William Johnston, merchant and tavern-keeper at the make-shift second courthouse (near the main gate of the A. P. Hill Military Reservation 1953), Benjamin Hubbard and John Elliott Payne died. The deaths of this trio paralized trade in central and lower Drysdale Parish, which they had dominated.

In this economic turmoil the people soon lost faith in the dollar, which was the new currency issued under the authorization of the Continental Congress, because it steadily depreciated in value. In 1788 when Robert Baker, a free mulatto, and David, a Negro slave of James Bowie's estate, broke into the Port Royal home of Patrick Rouke and took away goods which they sold on the black market for $800.00 Rouke refused to accept this money in restitution for his merchandise and persuaded the court to bind Baker to servitude for a term of seven years and direct his master to pay his earnings as reimbursement as hedge against the inflation. David, who was already bound, received thirty-nine lashes at the whipping-post in punishment.

The greatest new burdens placed on the freeholders already hard-pressed by the warn-torn economy, were the ever increasing demands of the Commonwealth for more food and clothing for the Continental Army, and more food for the French allies. In 1777 the General Assembly passed laws which authorized the confiscation of grain, flour and men's clothing held in storage by profiteers, and a tax in kind on all grain produced by planters. The Caroline Court placed Robert Gilchrist of St. Mary's, Edmund Pendleton, Jr. of Drysdale and Walker Taliaferro of St. Margaret's in charge of confiscations and collections in their respective parishes. Gilchrist and Pendleton Jr. did not long remain on this job. The work made them unpopular and they resigned. The court named William Buckner and John Hoomes to take their places. The public resentment against "Grain Collectors" contined to mount and Buckner, Hoomes and Taliaferro all quit. After they refused to serve the magistrates had difficulty in finding replacements.

The freeholders were so thoroughly aroused that to hold the position had become dangerous. The more rabid threatened to mob any man who came to take away a portion of their grain. At length the court persuaded John Brand to take the job for St. Mary's, John Bayley for Drysdale and John Sutton for St. Margaret's on purely a mercenary basis. Brand and Bayley were either obscure personages of little consequence in Caroline, or men especially brought in to do the work, only Sutton was a man of prominence in the county. But this trio managed to hold on through the Revolution. They did their work well and were well paid. In one of the last orders in the Order Books before the battle of Yorktown the court directed that John Brand be paid $5,000 for the storage of grain at Port Royal, that John Bayley be paid $5,000 for the storage of grain at the Bowling Green, and that John Sutton be paid $4,000 for the storage of grain at Chesterfield. This pay was in inflated Continental dollars.

The grain tax and the confiscation of grain, flour and clothing owned by speculators soon proved inadequate to feed and clothe the Continental Army and feed the French allies, and the Governor of the Commonwealth directed the county courts to employ agents to purchase additional supplies on the free market in an attempt to fill Virginia's enlarged quota without increasing the tax. The Caroline Court employed Thomas Jones to do this work in St. Mary's, John Broaddus to do it in Drysdale and Daniel Coleman in St. Margaret's, and made John Broaddus supervisor of the whole project. The work did not go well. The freeholders refused to sell their surplus food and material for clothing for Continental dollars. Their obstinacy provoked the court and the magistrates ordered them to sell at fixed prices until the county's quota was filled. Jones, Broaddus and Coleman became the most unpopular men in the county in carrying this program out, more unpopular even than the Grain Collectors. But they stuck to their jobs, more perhaps for financial gain than patriotism, because the work paid well. John Broaddus collected 25 shillings a day for each beef he stabled after purchase. It is interesting to note that he insisted in being paid in pounds, sterling, rather than dollars because of lack of faith in the patriots' cause.

The terrible winter of 1779-80 proved that the current system of getting food and supplies for the army was not enough. The Continental Congress revised the quotas of each of the States upward, and the States sub-divided their new quotas among their counties. To buy the needed supplies at fixed prices or to acquire them by outright confiscation had become out of the question in Virginia because the freeholders hid all the foodstuffs and clothing material that the army might use when they heard that a government collector was in the vicinity of their homestead. To overcome this handicap the General Assembly enacted a law which divided each county into a multitude of small units and required each unit to furnish a completed soldier's uniform, consisting of a pair of overalls, two linen or cotton shirts, two pair of stockings, a pair of shoes and a wool, fur or leather hat, and one beef weighing at least 300 pounds. If a unit failed to fill its quota in sixty days constables were to seize and sell enough of the personal property of its inhabitants to purchase the uniform and beef; if enough personal property was not available for this purpose a lien was to be placed against the real estate. (Hening's *Statutes-at-Large,* Vol. 10, page 398.)

The new law assigned 93 units to Caroline. This was more units than were assigned to any other county with the exception of Amelia with 112 and Northampton with 93, and indicates that Caroline was tied for second place as the most populous and affluent county in Virginia at the end of the Revolution since the numbers of assigned units was based on the number of tithables and the value of assessed wealth. Among Caroline's neighbors Hanover was divided into 87 units, Spotsylvania into 60, King George into 38, Essex into 34, King and Queen into 38, and King William into 56.

The Order Books fail to reveal the boundaries of Caroline's 93 units but state that the committee charged with the purchase of food and supplies for the army, Thomas Jones for St. Mary's, John Broaddus for Drysdale and Daniel Coleman for St. Margaret's, was assigned to supervise the collections from the units in their parishes. There is no record that any of Caroline's 93 units failed to meet their obligations.

But before the collections were in it became apparent that they were not going to be enough to fill Virginia's quota of food and clothing for the army. In desperation Governor Jefferson directed the collectors in all counties to make additional purchases on the free market. When this directive reached Caroline John Broaddus wrote Jefferson in a letter dated Jan. 24, 1881, "I have been informed by Col. Thornton that Mr. James Warren of Fredericksburg desired all pork and stalled beef be gotten and sent to him for which a reasonable price will be paid. No additional supplies can be purchased in Caroline. The planters are holding out for $8.00 a pound for stalled beef and $300 for a hundred weight of pork. This is heresay and I cannot vow for the truth. But it is desirous that fixed prices be established for the whole Commonwealth."

8. THE END OF THE REVOLUTION

The shooting phase of the Revolution returned to Virginia in the Winter of 1781 when Benedict Arnold set out from Portsmouth to ravage the valley of the James and Lord Cornwallis crossed over into the Commonwealth from North Carolina. This was the first major attempt of the British to regain their oldest colony since Lord Dunmore fled from Gwynn's Island in 1776. Caroline, like the rest of the counties in the fledgling state was unprepared for this new threat. It lacked men and arms. Most of the able-bodied men had been inducted into the armed forces of the Continental Congress, and were either fighting with armies to the north and south, or had been killed or captured, or incapacitated by battle wounds and returned to their homes. When Governor Jefferson wrote Edmund Pendleton, Jr. to send 260 Caroline militia men at once to Williamsburg to oppose Arnold's march up the valley of the James, in due time Pendleton Jr. replied "after the greatest exertion I have succeeded in collecting only 190." But in the same letter he implied there were other men in Caroline who were able to fight but refused when he added "the unfavorable

season of the year may be the cause why so many have dis-
obeyed orders." It was mid-Winter.

The Caroline militia men did not remain in Williamsburg
long. Their commanding officer, Col. Anthony Thornton,
marched them home again, and wrote the governor that he
acted on the orders of Gen. Thomas Nelson, who ordered him
to march the troops back to Caroline and hold them in readi-
ness for further orders. The trouble was that the Caroline
soldiers were without weapons. Thornton ends this letter with
a plea for 250 muskets, stating "we can do nothing without
arms."

The troops that the Virginians attempted to put in the field,
who were certainly the last scrapings of the man-power reserves,
were not only without weapons, but their leaders were without
maps. This deficiency extended from the governor, and technical commander-in-chief, to field officers. On February 12, 1781,
John Baylor, fearful lest the British invade Caroline and the
local militia be unable to determine their position wrote Jefferson, "Hoping that you have supplied yourself with an American atlas in the space of six or eight months, you will please
deliver, General Weedon's care, my atlas to New Market."

When it became apparent that the local militia was help-
less to stop either Arnold or Cornwallis, Washington sent
LaFayette to Virginia. Among LaFayette's troops was a regiment commanded by Col. George Baylor, and in this regiment
served many men from Caroline. Col. Baylor had either
escaped from, or been exchanged by, the British after his
capture in the battle of Tappan, N. Y. The chances are that
he had been exchanged since he suffered a lung wound at
Tappan, which rendered him "unfit" for action. This "unfit-
ness," however, did not keep him from resuming command.
He fought gallantly through the rest of the Revolution. But
it did lead to his death. He died in Barbados, British West
Indies, in 1784, where he went after the battle of Yorktown
in an attempt to regain his health, impaired because of the
injury to his lung, and was buried in the churchyard of St.
Michael's Cathedral, Bridgetown.

Gen. William Woodford, Caroline's ranking military officer,

was even more unfortunate than Col. George Baylor, the county's second ranking officer. The British captured Woodford during the siege of Charleston, S. C. and transported him by sea to New York, where he died a prisoner of war on November 13, 1780. A persistent rumor holds that he was buried in Trinity churchyard. But he has no marked grave in the well known graveyard of Trinity Church at the head of Wall Street, and the custodian of this famous cemetery contends that there is no record of him being buried there.

LaFayette was able to stop Arnold but he lacked the manpower to cope with both Arnold and Cornwallis. The latter moved into Hanover and sent his chief lieutenant Tarleton to destroy the ordnance plant and ammunition stored at Falmouth. This expedition meant the invasion of Caroline. All the people of the county were alarmed. The local court ordered each of the 95 districts into which the county was divided to furnish supplies for the army to provide a covered wagon and four horses with a driver to haul food and ammunition to the soldiers at the front and to remove the military supplies from Falmouth. The freeholders complied with this order, but there was grumbling. As late as 1797 Charles Vivian of Caroline petitioned the General Assembly for compensation "for wagon and team, impressed and taken into public use in 1781."

These preparations failed to stop Tarleton. He crossed into the extreme southwestern corner of Caroline at Anderson's Bridge on June 4, 1781. Apparently he chose this circuitous route to Falmouth because of the information furnished by Sancho, a Negro slave belonging to William Evans, who also acted as his pilot in his advance across the county. But in spite of Sancho's help, Tarleton's expedition into Caroline was not a success. Washington dispatched Gen. Anthony Wayne from Pennsylvania to aid LaFayette in Virginia, and since Wayne's forces were nearing Falmouth, Tarleton turned west in Caroline, entered Spotsylvania, recrossed the North Anna at Devenport's Bridge and moved on Charlottesville in an attempt to capture the governor and General Assembly, who had set up a temporary capital of the Commonwealth there, rather than risk battle with Wayne over Falmouth. This change of plans rendered the unfortunate Sancho valueless and the British abandoned him. Shortly thereafter he was captured by the Americans, court-martialed and hung. Four years later the General Assembly compensated his master, William Evans, eighty pounds for his loss.

With Wayne's arrival the Americans' position in Virginia steadily improved. In time Cornwallis was forced to withdraw all the British forces in the Commonwealth to the peninsula between the York and the James. When Washington heard of this move he set out for Virginia in an attempt to capture the enemy before it escaped by sea. Two legends have arisen about this Washington trip concerning Caroline. They hold that Washington camped at the Old Mansion (the Bowling Green) on his way to Yorktown and gave a gala dinner in honor of LaFayette at the same estate on his return. Unfortunately neither are true. On the way south Washington became so concerned over a rumor that the French fleet had suffered defeat at sea he heard after he reached Fredericksburg, that he rode straight through to Williamsburg without even breaking the journey for a night's rest. There was no major stop in Caroline. On his return journey, after the victory at Yorktown, the whole Washington family was grieved because of a personal tragedy. Jack Custis, Washington's stepson and his wife's last surviving child, contracted camp fever during the Yorktown campaign and died a few days after the victory at Eltham, the home of a relative in King William. Washington, personally, arranged the funeral, and after it was over on November 11, 1781, set out with his wife by coach for Mt. Vernon. They were in no mood to celebrate. There was no gala dinner for LaFayette at this time.

In fact there is no record of any kind of celebration in Caroline because of the victory at Yorktown, and the chances are that there was none. The county was too depleted by the long war for festivities. It had to rebuild to play its rôle in the new nation of which it was now a part.

The People

CAROLINE'S non-Indian pre-Revolutionary settlers fall into five classes, the patentees of crown grants, freeholders who acquired their real estate through marriage or purchase, headrighters, indentured servants and Negro slaves.

1. Patentees of Crown Grants

Patentees of crown grants consisted of favorites, homesteaders and speculators, but no clearly cut lines of demarcation divided the three classes. Favorites were often speculators and homesteaders striving to become favorites. To get title to as much as possible, by hook or crook, was a characteristic common to all classes. The chief distinction among them lay in the fact that favorites were able to gain title to acreage by working on the vanities of royal governors while less fortunate men and women had to conform to the statutes governing patents.

a. *The Favorites*

Grantees, who received larger tracts of Caroline real estate than the acreage allotted to settlers under the homestead laws, were for the most part minor gentry, who had been lucky enough to worm their way into the favor of the ruling royal governor or his lieutenant in residence. None of them had any drag with the reigning monarch. English kings and queens gave away whole colonies, or at least several counties to their friends, *i.e.* Maryland, Pennsylvania, the Northern Neck of Virginia, rather than a paltry few thousand acres. Only two proprietors of crown grants of land in the area which became Caroline were noblemen, and they, Sir Ralph Wormley and Sir Thomas Lundsford, were of minor rank, baronets at best. Neither of them established a residence within the territorial limits of the county. Wormley lived in Middlesex and Lundsford sent his son-in-law, John Lomax, to settle his land, to which this author has been unable to find a record of the patent although he has come across numerous references to its existence.

Although favorites got title to their land without complying with the provisions of the homestead laws the vast majority had to follow strictly the statutes governing seating to retain possession. Careless favorites often lost their property. This was especially true if they delayed seating until after there was a change of royal governors and they were no longer favorites. This laxness caused numerous tracts in Caroline to be patented several times before a patentee finally perfected title through possession.

The author made up the following tables after a study of land grants in New Kent, old Rappahannock, Essex, King and Queen, King William and Caroline counties, and listed tracts that he was able to identify as located in the area now contained in Caroline.

Grants in excess of 1,000 acres made by Sir William Berkeley to his favorites:

Date	Grantee	Acreage	Description
1655	William Lewis	2000	North side of the Mattapony below the main fork of the river. (Millwood)
1664	Lawrence Smith	4600	South side of the Mattapony at the mouth of Reedy Creek. Smith never seated this tract.
1666	Lawrence Smith & Robert Taliaferro	6300	On the Rappahannock eastward from the mouth of Snow Creek.
1667	Thomas Hoomes	3000	On a swamp leading into north bank of the Mattapony, below the Lewis grant.
1667	John Meadors & Henry Peters	4200	Three miles from the Rappahannock up Peumandsend Creek.
1667	Alexander Fleming	2750	Two miles from the Rappahannock up Peumandsend Creek.
1667	Robert Smith	1900	On the Rappahannock beginning two miles above Portobago Bay.
1667	Henry Corbin	5776	On the Rappahannock eastward from the mouth of Ware Creek.
1668	Thomas Gouldman	1200	Inland from Robert Smith's grant.
1670	Augustine Warner	1400	On the main swamp of the Mattapony, nigh opposite the Smith-Taliaferro grant on the Rappahannock and

Date	Grantee	Acreage	Description
			12 miles through the woods from the great falls of the Rappahannock.
1671	Thomas Bowler (Boulware)	1460	Two miles above Portobago Bay, and three miles in the woods from the Rappahannock.
1671	John Buckner Robert Smith & Thomas Royster	3553½	In the valley of Goldenvale Creek.
1672	Augustine Warner	10100	On the north side of the Mattapony, immediately east of the 1,400-acre Warner grant.
1672	Col. Thomas Goodrich	2200	Upper reaches of Tuckahoe Swamp, lost through escheat after Bacon's Rebellion.
1672	Anthony Buckner & Lawrence Smith	4972	On Rappahannock above Portobago Bay.
1672	Thomas Mott	2000	On Tuckahoe Swamp, lost to George Morris after Bacon's Rebellion.
1673	John Prosser & Thomas Pannell	5200	On the Mattapony-Rappahannock watershed and along a creek between Snow and Ware creeks flowing into the Rappahanock, known as Prosser's Creek.
1673	Thomas Hall & John Pigg	3831	Northside of Mattapony westward from the mouth of Marocossic Creek.
1673	John Bagby & William Herndon	2600	Northside of the Mattapony west of Hall-Pigg grant.
1673	_____ Robinson	3400	In the forest between Peumandsend and the Goldenvale inland from the Rappahannock, this land passed to John Catlett by escheat after Bacon's Rebellion.
1673	William Herndon & Robert Bagby	1000	Inland from John Bagby-William Herndon grant.
1674	Robert Beverley	15000	Part in present-day Essex, King and Queen and Caroline, around and to the east and north of Beverley's Run, part subsequently lost to other grantees, after the Beverleys lost royal favor.

Date	Grantee	Acreage	Description
1674	Lawrence Smith & Robert Beverley	6500	North side of the Mattapony opposite the mouth of Reedy Creek.
1674	George Morris	3000	On Tuckahoe Swamp between Mott grant and the Mattapony.
1674	Joshua Storey, Thomas Wyatt & William Morris	3200	North side of the Mattapony between the Bagby-Herndon and Smith-Beverley grants
1674	John Smith, John Buckner, Phillip Lightfoot, Thomas Royston & John Lewis	10050	Beginning at the upper corner of the 3,831-acre grant to Hall and Pigg.
1675	Francis & Anthony Thornton	2740	North side of the main run of the Mattapony above the main fork of the stream.
1675	Ralph Wormely	2200	On the Rappahannock, including Portobago Indian town.
1675	John Catlett	3400	The Robinson tract gained through escheat.
1675	Thomas Hawkins	2611	On the Rappahannock 2 miles above Portobago Indian town
1675	James Taylor	1050	In the freshies of the Mattapony above the Smith-Beverley grant.

Grants of less than 1,000 acres to favorites by Sir William Berkeley:

Date	Grantee	Acreage	Description
1673	William Herndon	430	Inland from Bagby-Herndon grant.
1673	Anthony Buckner & Lawrence Smith	716	On Rappahannock between the first Buckner-Smith grant and the lands of Hawkins.
1673	Robert Taliaferro, the son of Robert Taliaferro	739	On the Rappahannock, including both sides of the mouth of Peumandsend.
1674	Robert Beverley	600	Part of the Pigg-Hall grant, taken by Berkeley from Pigg and Hall and given to Beverley.
1674	Thomas Hoomes	523	Immediately south of first Hoomes grant.

Grants in excess of 1,000 acres to favorites by governors from Berkeley to Spotswood (1676-1710):

Date	Grantee	Acreage	Description
1681	Edwin Conway	1200	On the Rappahannock below Snow Creek and beginning on the northwest side of a small creek known as Prosser's Run.
1683	Joshua Storey & William Morris	5000	On the north side of the Mattapony west of the mouth of Reedy Creek.
1683	George Morris	5000	In the valley of Tuckahoe Swamp, a reaffirmation of a previous grant of 3,000 acres with the addition of 2,000 lost by Mott for supporting Bacon during the rebellion.
1683	William and Augustine Smith	6500	Same land granted Lawrence Smith and Robert Beverley in 1674.
1686	Thomas Terry	1000	North side of the Mattapony beginning by "two white oaks" corner of Hall-Pigg grant.
1686	Martin Palmer	1500	North side Mattapony, south of Thornton grant.
1686	Stephan Binbridge & Richard Tunstall	8500	In the freshies of the Mattapony, back in the woods and adjacent to Robert Bagby, William Herndon, Joshua Storey and William Morris. This land overlapped numerous other grants and the record indicates that it was never seated.
1687	Edwin Thacker	1563	Upper reaches of Tuckahoe Swamp.
1687	Benjamin Arnold	1754	Freshies of the Mattapony, including 1,050 acres granted James Taylor in 1675 and sold by Taylor to Anthony Arnold.
1688	Thomas Todd	2828	Inland from the north bank of the Mattapony, well below the Palmer grant (Villborro).
1691	Joshua Storey	19060	Two grants north side of the Mattapony some distance from stream and on the west side of the Marocossic beginning at a large branch of that creek.

Date	Grantee	Acreage	Description
1693	Joshua Storey, James Taylor & Johnathan Fisher	9150	"beginning by ye head of a small branch of the Marocossic above 19060 Storey grants."
1693	Arthur Spicer	2750	About two miles up Peumandsend.
1694	Robert Beverley	6500	First granted Lawrence Smith and Robert Beverley, later to William and Augustine Smith, lost by Beverley a second time in 1698 to Bartholomew Fowler.
1695	Ralph Wormely	19420	Portobago Bay and inland, part in present-day Essex, title always disputed with Hawkins, the Beverleys and others.
1695	Peter Beverley	4500	North side Mattapony opposite Dogue Indian town.
1695	Edwin Thacker	2634	On the path leading from Portobago to Tuckahoe Creek.
1695	Edward Thomas	2750	Two miles up Peumandsend, same land granted Arthur Spicer who failed to seat.
1696	Robert Beverley	2359	On the Mattapony - Rappahannock watershed, bound on the east by the path from Portobago to Chickahominy Indian towns.
1698	Richard Covington	1091	Upper valley of Ware Creek, lost to Thomas Merriweather in 1704.
1698	Benjamin Harrison & William Leigh	3474	On the Mattapony - Rappahannock watershed above the head of Marocossic Creek.
1698	Bartholomew Fowler	6500	First granted to Lawrence Smith and Robert Beverley, later to William and Augustine Smith and in 1694 to Robert Beverley again.
1701	Chickerley Corbin Thacker	4060	Between the North Wales path and the Pamunkey (two grants).
1703	Henry Nelson	2340	On the North Wales path.
1703	Harry Beverley	3050	Two grants, St. Mary's Parish adjacent the lands of Sir Thomas Lunsford.

Date	Grantee	Acreage	Description
1704	Thomas Tinsley	2400	Two grants on Portobago-Tuckahoe Creek path, adjacent the lands of Edwin Thacker.
1704	Thomas Merriweather	1091	Ware Creek, the same land granted Richard Covington in 1698 and by him deserted.
1704	James Taylor	4500	Head of Beverley's Run extending between the two main branches.
1705	Robert Thomas	1650	Two grants in the forest between Ware Creek and the Long Branch of the Massaponax.
1705	John Hay	3288	Two miles from the Rappahannock back of Moon's Mount.
1706	Robert Beverley	16000	From the head of North Wales path along the Pamunkey-North Anna.
1706	James Taylor	2763	Between the branches of Beverley's Run to the corner of Beverley's Park.
1706	William and Robert Byrd, Ralph Booker, William Holcomb, James Vaughan & Richard Covington	8000	In the great fork of the Mattapony. These men were not favorites. The governor granted them this vast expanse of land beyond the frontier to get rid of them.
1706	Richard Wharton, Henry Lightfoot & Robert Ambroise	6500	This was the fifth grant of this tract. It was first granted to Lawrence Smith and Robert Beverley in 1674.

Grants to favorites of less than 1,000 acres by governors between Berkeley and Spotswood:

Date	Grantee	Acreage	Description
1684	William Leigh	920	Inland from the Hall-Pigg and Bagby-Herndon grants.
1686	Jacob Tompkins	565	North side of the Mattapony, near Thornton grant.
1693	Joshua Storey	300	"beginning on a great run issuing into the Marocossic Creek."
1694	Francis Taliaferro & Henry Price	806	On the Rappahannock above the mouth of Peumandsend.
1704	Clara Robinson	860	Ware Creek, escheat land of Elizabeth Hazelwood.

Date	Grantee	Acreage	Description
1704	Ann Hay	685	Ware Creek, escheat land of Elizabeth Hazelwood.
1704	Benjamin Robinson	655	Ware Creek, escheat land of Elizabeth Hazelwood.
1705	John Taliaferro	220	Upper end of Peumandsend.
1705	Richard Covington	646	Upper end of Peumandsend.
1705	Charles Taliaferro	966	Between Ware and Mount Creeks on a path called Solomon's Garden.

Grants in excess of 1,000 acres made by Alexander Spotswood to his favorites:

Date	Grantee	Acreage	Description
1710	Richard Johnston	2765	On north side of Mattapony River (below Burke's Bridge).
1711	Gawin Corbin	1234	Adjacent to land of Prosser and Creighton, part of the 5,776 acres granted Henry Corbin in 1667.
1712	Larkin Chew	2143	On the south side of a run issuing into the Mattapony from its north bank, about a mile above the lowest stones of the falls of said river.
1713	Robert Beverley	2644	Coming to the upper corner of Lawrence Smith's land close by the south side of Marocossic Creek.
1713	Edmound Jennings	3330	On the southwest side of the Mattapony and the lower side of Reedy Swamp.
1713	Robert Beverley	4250	Between the Polecat and the South River, well into the forest.
1714	John Madison & Samuel Coleman	2000	Adjacent to Larkin Chew.
1715	John Baylor	1330	North side the Mattapony, adjacent James Taylor, and the lands John Watkins bought from Johnathan Fisher and Joshua Storey.
1716	Robert Beverley	1420	On the head branches of Marocossic Creek (The Chase).
1717	John Madison, John & Peter Rogers	1860	North side of the Mattapony, two miles above the stones or falls of said river.

Date	Grantee	Acreage	Description
1717	Robert Beverley	15000	Reaffirmation of title, land east of Beverley Run mostly in present-day Essex and King and Queen.
1718	Robert Farish	1540	South side of the Mattapony, including Dogue Indian town.
1718	Harry Beverley	1980	On the south side of the northern-most branch of the Mattapony.
1718	John Robinson	2200	South side of first great branch of the Mattapony. (South River)
1718	Edward Jennings	1150	Between the east side of Reedy Swamp and the Mattapony.
1719	William Hall	1080	The center section of Tuckahoe Valley.
1720	Lawrence Smith	2025	Beginning two miles back in the forest at the inland limits of the 4,600-acre tract granted Lawrence Smith and Robert Taliaferro on the Rappahannock below Snow Creek in 1664, and extending to the Long Branch of the Massaponax.
1720	Francis & Anthony Thornton	2740	Reaffirmation of title to Thornton grant of 1675.
1720	John Robinson	2000	Across the South River from first Robinson grant and extending to the middle branch of the Mattapony.
1720	George Braxton, & William Waller	1000	Both sides of May's Run about two miles from Dogue Indian town.
1721	Catesby Cocke, Chickerly Corbin Thacker, Francis Thornton & William Strothers	6000	From the long branch of the Massaponax to the north bank of the Mattapony.
1721	Harry Beverley	1830	North bank of the Mattapony below Dogue Town.
1722	Richard Buckner	4500	In the forest south of the Mattapony-Rappahannock watershed, adjacent to the lands of Prosser and Pannel.
1722	William Robinson	1500	East of the Buckner grant, described above.

Grants by Spotswood of less than 1,000 acres to favorites:

Date	Grantee	Acreage	Description
1711	Lawrence Taliaferro	220	Upper valley of Peumandsend.
1712	Larkin Chew	220	Above the falls of the Mattapony on the north side of the stream.
1715	Richard Buckner	180	Adj. to his estate.
1715	Francis Thornton	100	Adj. to his estate.
1718	Thomas Carr	800	About three miles above the falls of the North Anna at the mouth of Topping Castle Creek, called Turkey Neck.
1719	Harry Beverley	831	On Peumandsend, beginning at the flood gate of Taliaferro's Mill, at the east end of mill-pond.
1719	John Baylor	800	South side of the Polecat between the lands of William Terrell and Timothy Chandler.
1720	Thomas Carr	400	South side of the Polecat, adj. Douglas.
1722	Robert Farish	775	North side of the Mattapony nigh unto the great fork.

Grants by Drysdale of 1,000 acres and over to favorites:

Date	Grantee	Acreage	Description
1723	James Taylor	4260	South side Polecat beginning at Rook's Branch.
1723	Augustine Moore	1088	North side the North Anna on both sides of Hawkins Creek.
1724	Thomas Carr	4500	On the North Anna above the falls at Topping Castle Creek.
1725	John Madison	2150	Between the South River and the main run of the Mattapony.
1726	Hon. John Carter	4740	On North Anna above the Carr grant.
1726	John Baylor	3360	North side the Mattapony beginning about three miles below Dogue Indian town. (New Market)
1726	John Baylor	8400	South side of Mattapony and north side Polecat in the angle between the streams.
1726	Robert Baylor	2650	Both sides South River, part in Caroline and part in Spotsylvania.

Date	Grantee	Acreage	Description
1726	Nathaniel Sanders	1200	Both sides of South River at the great fork.
1727	Richard Buckner	1100	Adjacent to his plantation on the Rappahannock.

Grants in excess of 1,000 acres by Sir William Gooch:

Date	Grantee	Acreage	Description
1728	Augustine Moore	6950	Middle branch of the Mattapony, part in Spotsylvania and part in Caroline.
1728	Thomas Terry	1500	On Woodyard Swamp in St. Margaret's Parish.
1730	William Beverley	4252	A reaffirmation of title, along Beverley Run, in King and Queen, Essex and Caroline.
1732	Thomas Carr	2530	Inland from Topping Castle.
1733	Thomas Catlett	1376	St. Mary's Parish, adj. Royston and Taliaferro's land and Gabriel Long's mill-dam.
1734	Richard Long	1165	Tract known as Solomon's Garden, adj. Nicholas Battaile in St. Mary's Parish.

Grants by Sir William Gooch of 900 to 1,000 acres:

Date	Grantee	Acreage	Description
1728	William Brunskill	900	St. Margaret's, between Ridge Road and the North Anna.
1728	John May	980	St. Margaret's, between the Mattapony and the South River.
1732	Robert Beverley	928	St. Margaret's, no further description.

Grants by Dinwiddie in excess of 1,000 acres:

Date	Grantee	Acreage	Description
1754	William Daniel, Jr.	1000	Drysdale, adj. Daniel's mill-pond and on the south side of Beverley's Run.

b. *The Homesteaders*

Settlers not so fortunate as to bask in the favor of royal governors had to conform to the law to get land. The statutes permitted all free white persons to claim 50 acres of crown land for a homestead and to purchase 100 acres more for each tithable person among their retainers (Indentured servants and Negro slaves) at the rate of 10 acres for a shilling until their holdings reached 400 acres and 200 acres at the same rate for all their retainers above five until their holdings reached 4,000 acres. Since few settlers without influence in Williamsburg, who wished to establish homesteads along the frontier, had many retainers their crown grants seldomly exceeded 400 acres. But as the size of their establishments grew due to the birth of children and the purchase of indentured servants and slaves, they were able to add to their acreages until in some instances they became great landlords.

Royal governors granted the major portion of the acreage in Caroline's St. Mary's and Drysdale parishes to their favorites while that region lay beyond the frontier. But homesteaders succeeded in getting original title to much of the land in St. Margaret's from the crown. The following tables show grants to homesteaders by parishes.

St. Mary's Parish

Date	Grantee	Acreage	Description
1671	Francis Farmer	150	Inland from Robert Smith's 1,900-acre grant.
1671	John Godfrey	300	Adj. to Farmer, lost by escheat.
1673	Simon Miller	817	Head of Peumandsend.
1673	_____ Rollins	650	Immediately south of Simon Miller grant.
1673	John Patterson	500	Goldenvale, lost to Buckner by escheat.
1682	Thomas Blanton	200	In the forest, beyond Peumandsend.
1683	William Sayer	550	On Ware Creek.
1683	Cornelius Vaughan	300	Same land granted to Godfrey, who lost it by escheat for supporting Bacon.
1684	John Prosser	408	Head of Goldenvale.
1687	Thomas Blanton	266	Adjacent to first Blanton grant.
1688	Thomas Pitts	376	Area beyond the head of Peumandsend.
1693	Anthony Seal	200	Upper side of Peumandsend.
1693	John Battaile	560	On the Rappahannock about two miles below Snow Creek.

Date	Grantee	Acreage	Description
1698	John Battaile	570	Adj. to first grant.
1698	Robert Kay	132	Tuckahoe-Portobago path.
1704	William Scott	96	Above Sir Thomas Lundsford's.
1704	John May	191	Two miles from Rappahannock on Tuckahoe path.
1704	Michael Guinney	210	Upper branches of Goldenvale.
1705	Francis Shackleford	395	On Tuckahoe path.
1713	Catherine, Eleanor & Walter Proverb	517	Peumandsend, adj. Peters, Meadors and Fleming.
1713	John Long	104	Upper branch of Peumandsend.
1715	John Sanders	621	St. Mary's (inland from Port Royal).
1715	John Wriding (?)	263	Between Long Branch of the Massaponax and Francis Thornton's land.
1715	James Carne	400	Adj. to Wriding tract.
1718	Edward Scrimshaw	91	St. Mary's above Portobago.
1719	Robert Slaughter	470	Upper St. Mary's.
1720	Elias Downs	400	Adj. lands of William and John Holloway.
1724	Daniel Hornbe	550	East side of Mt. Swamp.
1759	William Lindsay	290	On a run of Portobago Creek.

DRYSDALE PARISH

Date	Grantee	Acreage	Description
1682	Robert Terrell	170	On Mattapony above the William Lewis grant.
1683	John Joy	317	Inland from the Pigg grant (two grants).
1684	Cornelius Vaughan	300	Deep Valley.
1689	Alexander McKenny	790	Adj. to Thomas Todd's grant.
1691	William Fenney & William Cardwell	200	Mattapony—opposite mouth of Polecat Creek.
1692	John Clarke & Cornelius Vaughan	288	Beginning near the head of Great Meadows.
1694	Thomas Jones & Cornelius Vaughan	420	Adj. to grant above.
1702	James Taylor & Thomas Pitts	576	In valley of Beverley's Run.
1704	John Wyatt	700	Mattapony above the Herndon grants.
1720	Robert Pollard	290	West side of Tuckahoe Creek.

ST. MARGARET'S PARISH

Date	Grantee	Acreage	Description
1720	John Martin	120	West side of Beverley's Run.
1724	John Martin	190	Adj. to first Martin grant.
1724	William Daniels	100	Upper end of Beverley's Run.
1729	Henry Rains	686	Mattapony-Rappahannock watershed near Spotsylvania line.
1732	William Fell	162	Near Frances and Anthony Thornton.
1738	Samuel Coleman	100	On Marocossic Creek "just below a dam where Col. Baylor's line crossed the water."
1740	Joseph Beverley	286	Between Beverley and Baylor.
1691	William Collins	620	On lower Polecat Creek.
1701	Thomas Carr	546	North Anna near Topping Castle.
1701	John Oliver	446	Oliver's Spring branch.
1701	James Terry	418	Adj. to Thomas Carr.
1702	Martin Slaughter	137	On Topping Castle path.
1713	John Waller	200	Upper South River.
1713	Nicholas Guillintine	200	About a mile back in the woods from Powell's ford.
1714	William Henry	400	Below the falls of the North Anna.
1714	James Terry	400	Between William Henry and falls of the North Anna.
1714	William Fleming	400	At the falls of the North Anna.
1714	John Kimbrow	320	On Long Branch.
1714	John Kimbrow, Jr.	300	On Long Branch.
1714	Thomas Thompson	200	On Long Branch Creek.
1714	William Terrell	300	South side the upper fork of the North fork of the Polecat.
1714	John Sutton	500	South side of the Mattapony below Dogue Town.
1714	Thomas Terry	500	In the fork of Woodyard Swamp.
1714	John Buckner & Robert Bullard	400	South side of fork of South River issuing into Mattapony.
1714	Thomas Thompson	200	Above the falls of the North Anna back of William Flemings.
1714	Timothy Chandler	100	On the Polecat, mid-distance.
1715	William Terrell	100	Adj. to first Terrell grant on Polecat.
1715	Michael Mixer (?)	500	On West side of Boot Swamp.

Date	Grantee	Acreage	Description
1715	William Terrel	400	Both sides of the Polecat adj. to first Terrell grant.
1715	Thomas Cartwright	400	North side of Reedy Swamp.
1717	William Terrell & Robert Chandler	300	South side south fork of the Polecat adj. their own land.
1717	Christopher Smith & William Cockran	200	North side of Reedy Swamp.
1717	Richard Mauldin	400	On Mattapony about ¾ mile above Powell's Ford.
1717	John Hurt	450	On upper side of Reedy Swamp.
1717	John Watkins	400	On both sides of Polecat, adj. John Baylor.
1717	Thomas Dickinson	390	On North Anna at mouth of Hawkins Creek.
1717	Griffin Dickinson	400	On North Anna above Thomas Dickinson grant.
1717	John Sutton	370	On the Polecat.
1717	William Terrell and his son, William Terrell	400	On the north side of the Polecat.
1718	Arthur Smith	390	On south side of South River above the mouth of May's Run.
1718	Henry Goodloe	400	Both sides of Stoney Lick Run.
1718	Henry Goodloe	350	Both sides of Stoney Lick Run.
1718	Thomas Walker	400	South side South River, adj. Benjamin Woods.
1718	William Terrell, Jr.	174	On main fork and north side the north fork of the Polecat.
1718	Timothy Chandler	100	Adj. his plantation of the Polecat.
1718	Robert Chandler	150	On the south side of the Polecat.
1718	Thomas Carr, Jr.	600	About 3 miles above the great falls of the North Anna.
1718	John and David Crenshaw	300	Below William Terrell's on the Polecat and two miles below the main fork of said stream.
1718	Robert Fleming	400	Two miles above falls of the North Anna.
1718	William Anderson	400	North side North Anna above Topping Castle.
1718	Robert Baber	500	Upper end of Reedy Swamp.

Date	Grantee	Acreage	Description
1718	Walter Evins	420	North fork of Reedy Swamp.
1718	Nicholas Dillard	200	On the head of Gum Branch between Reedy Swamp and the Polecat.
1718	William Terrell	400	Both sides the north fork of the south fork of the Polecat.
1718	William Terrell, Jr.	220	Adj. to William Terrell, Sr. grant above.
1719	Joseph Hayle	400	South branch of south fork of Polecat.
1719	George Eastham	400	On branch of Middle River adj. Rogers.
1719	John May	400	North side White Run adj. Coleman.
1719	Thomas Madison	330	Adj. May grant above.
1719	Thomas Carr, Jr.	400	Both sides of South fork of north fork of Polecat.
1719	Philemon Hawkins	400	Polecat Valley, back line of Thomas Terry's.
1719	Philemon Hawkins	200	Adj. above grant.
1719	George Mussick	250	Between May's Run and the South River.
1719	Thomas Carr, Jr.	400	South side of Polecat adj. Douglass.
1719	Anthony Samuel	400	Both sides the north fork of South River adj. George Eastham.
1719	John Rogers	400	South side of middle fork of Mattapony, adj. his own land.
1719	John Rogers	400	Adj. above mentioned grant.
1719	John Ellis	400	North side South River and upon the back of John Madison's line.
1719	John Ellis	400	Both sides the North fork of the north fork of the South River.
1719	John Ellis	400	On both sides the north fork of the South River and between Madison and Ellis upper grant.
1719	Adolphus Kendrick	400	Above Turkey Neck on the North Anna.
1719	John Madison, Jr.	400	Both sides the north fork of South River beginning above Hubbards.
1719	Benjamin Wood	400	South side South River adj. Jones.
1719	John Fisher	400	Gum Swamp between Reedy Swamp and Polecat.

Date	Grantee	Acreage	Description
1719	John Hubbard	250	North side South River adj. Daniel Coleman.
1719	Edward Green	125	Both sides of Long Creek.
1719	John Brownfield	100	North branch of Boot Swamp.
1719	Paul Pigg	200	North fork of Reedy Swamp.
1719	Charles Durrett	400	Adj. John Baylor.
1719	John Quarles	400	In the forks of the north fork of the Polecat adj. William Terrell.
1719	John Sutton	165	Adj. his land on the Mattapony.
1720	Phillip Todd	400	Between Polecat and Reedy Swamp.
1720	John Waller	400	On south side the Mattapony adj. Mary Waller and Phillip Todd.
1720	Mary Waller	400	South side Mattapony adj. John Waller, Phillip Todd and Taylor.
1720	John Hawkins	410	Beginning at Dolphus Kendricks corner.
1720	Richard Turner	300	Between Reedy Swamp and Jack Pond Branch.
1721	Samuel Norment	430	Between Jackpond & Reedy branches.
1721	Richard Turner	400	Across Reedy Swamp from first Turner grant.
1721	Samuel Norment	325	Above the mouth of Reedy Swamp, beginning about ¾ mile above Powell's Ford across Mattapony.
1721	Henry Armistead	400	On the south side of the south fork of the South River.
1721	Robert Charlesworth	425	In the forest between the Polecat and Reedy Swamp.
1721	William Fenney	400	On both sides Topping Castle Road and the north side of Long Creek.
1721	Robert Hinds	270	On the south side of the Middle River, adj. Rice Williams and John Downer, Jr.
1722	James Carey	400	On the south side of the north fork of Reedy Swamp.
1722	Thomas Jones	765	On upper Woodyard Swamp in St. Margaret's Parish.
1723	Richard Davis	150	Beginning at Davis line.

Date	Grantee	Acreage	Description
1723	Edward Arnold	400	On the south side of the north fork of Reedy Swamp.
1723	Charles Durrett, Jr.	400	On a branch of the Mattapony adj. his own land.
1723	John Watkins	400	Adj. Richard Walker and Thomas Carr.
1723	William Higgins	400	On south side the south fork of South River, adj. Robert Bullard.
1723	Thomas Evins	200	Upon branches of Reedy Swamp and branches of North Anna.
1723	John Hurt	400	Between Polecat and Reedy Swamp.
1723	William Yarbrough	400	On the west side of Long Branch adj. Robert Baber and William Cockran.
1723	Mathew Creed	200	On both sides of Beaverdam Swamp, back on James Terry's land on North Anna.
1723	William Smithey	400	In the forks of the south fork of the north fork of South River, adj. Henry Roodloe.
1723	Thomas Hamm	400	On the north side of the north fork of the Polecat, adj. Robert Axton.
1723	Thomas Walker	400	South side of South River adj. Benjamin Wood.
1723	John Holladay	400	On north side of North Anna about 10 miles above North Wales.
1724	Zachery Martin	400	South fork of South River-Stoney Lick Run, beginning Robert Powell's line.
1724	Richard Fowler	420	Both sides of Stoney Lick Run, back of Zachery Martin's.
1724	Edward Shepard	485	Adj. Richard Mauldin and Robert Powell.
1724	Christopher Beverley	400	Between Polecat and Reedy Swamp, adj. Timothy Chandler and George Douglass.
1724	Timothy Johnson	283	North side of Long Branch on both sides of Topping Castle Road, adj. John Hollaway.
1724	Francis Durrett	400	Both sides south fork of South River adj. John Rogers & Johnathan Clerk.

Date	Grantee	Acreage	Description
1724	John Rogers	400	In fork of north fork of South River, adj. Anthony Samuel.
1724	Samuel Norment	450	On the branches of Chandler's branch on the south side of the Polecat, adj. the lands of Chandler, Baylor and Walker.
1724	David Murray	400	South fork of Polecat adj. Robert Holmes.
1724	James Harrison	400	In the fork of the north fork of Reedy Swamp adj. Hurt.
1724	Peter Rogers	400	North side the middle fork of the Mattapony adj. Harry Beverley and Ambroise Madison.
1724	Robert Baber, Jr.	300	North side the south fork of Reedy Swamp adj. Cockran.
1724	James Jones	350	South side of the Mattapony, southwest of Douguetown Branch, adj. land of John Baylor.
1724	John Watkins	350	Both sides of Saddle Swamp, adj. Nicholas Gillintine.
1724	Daniel Coleman	400	South side of South River, adj. Thomas Walker.
1724	Daniel Coleman	344	Adj. above, adj. to John Rogers and Thomas Walker.
1724	James Powell	458	Forest between South River and Polecat, adj. William Richardson.
1724	James Powell	256	Adj. above and William Terrell.
1724	Thomas Ware	150	Branches of Beaverdam Creek in St. Margaret's Parish.
1724	John Holladay	400	On Beaverdam Creek.
1724	John Holladay	400	Adj. above to Topping Castle Creek.
1724	Nicholas Dillard	200	Both sides Reedy Creek, adj. Paul Pigg.
1724	William Yarbrough	400	Forest between Reedy Creek and North Anna.
1724	Joel Terrell	400	St. Margaret's adj. William Terrell.
1724	Paul Pigg	243	South side of north fork of South River, adj. Henry Goodloe and Thomas Allen.
1724	William Hurt	400	Between Polecat and Reedy Swamp.

Date	Grantee	Acreage	Description
1724	Robert Axton	400	Up a branch of Beaverdam Swamp.
1724	John Dawson	200	Back of James Taylor and John Baylor, north side of Polecat.
1724	Thomas Carr	850	Two tracts, both sides the south fork of the Polecat.
1724	William Terrell	237	On south side the north fork of the Polecat.
1724	Robert Powell	400	On South River, beginning at the mouth of a creek.
1724	James Powell	436	Above John Dawson on a branch of the Polecat.
1725	Henry Goodloe	472	Adj. Ellis in St. Margaret's Parish.
1725	George Braxton	400	Between May's Run and South River.
1725	Col. James Taylor	835	Two tracts between James Powell's and Richardson's grants.*
1725	Whithead Ryon	325	Both sides the north fork of the south fork of South River above Stoney Lick Run.
1725	John Stone	175	Forest between Reedy Swamp and Polecat.
1725	Thomas Cain, Jr.	400	North side of Long Creek below Thomas Thomas' line.
1725	William Bigger	400	On North Anna adj. Dolphus Kendrick.
1725	Thomas Allen Goodloe	243	South side of the north fork of South River adj. Henry Goodloe.
1725	William Dunn	600	Two tracts, south side the south fork of South River, adj. James Taylor, Roger Tandy and John Buckner.
1725	John Ellis	400	Both sides Stoney Lick Run on south fork of north fork of South River.
1725	Robert Axton	300	Both sides north fork of the Polecat.
1725	Charles Yarbrough	400	South side of South River beginning at Richard Mauldin's.
1725	James Hurt	368	Forest between Reedy Swamp and Polecat adj. Hurt.
1725	John Yarbrough	400	North side Reedy Swamp adj. John Sutton.
1725	Samuel Norment	140	Between Reedy Swamp and Mattapony adj. Norment and Paul Pigg.

Date	Grantee	Acreage	Description
1725	Thomas Hackett	400	Both sides the south fork of Polecat and extending across watershed into North Anna Valley.
1725	Joseph Crenshaw	300	Below William Terrell's on Polecat Swamp and about two miles below a fork of said swamp.
1725	Samuel Davis	400	Both sides Stoney Lick Run and adj. Zachery Martin's lower tract.
1725	Thomas White	400	On North side of Reedy Swamp.
1725	Robert Williamson	200	Adj. to White grant on Reedy Swamp.
1725	William Cockran	350	Both sides of south fork of Reedy Swamp adj. to his earlier grant.
1725	Robert Baber, Jr.	150	Back of his grant on Reedy Swamp.
1725	Hanse Kendrick, Jr.	100	On north fork of Boot Swamp.
1725	Hanse Kendrick, Sr.	200	Between Reedy and Boot Swamps and adj. to Col. Jennings.
1725	Philemon Hawkins	800	Two grants, bound by Polecat and the Ridge Road and the lands of Thomas Carr and Augustine Moore.
1725	Thomas Hampton	100	Both sides the main branch of Boot Swamp.
1725	Jacob Burruss	400	Adj. the lands of John Hawkins.
1726	Robert Baber	400	Middle fork of Reedy Swamp adj. William Cockran.
1726	Timothy Chandler	390	Forest between the South River and Polecat, adj. Chandler and Charles Yarbrough.
1726	Timothy Chandler	400	On east side the main road to Mauldin's trading house in St. Margaret's Parish.
1727	Joseph Chandler	400	Between the South River and north fork of the Polecat adj. Hamm and William Terrell.
1727	Robert Baber	514	Two tracts, both sides the main fork of Reedy Swamp.
1727	Charles Goodall	578	Two tracts, 215 acres on south side of Long Creek, and 363 between Long Creek and Ridge or Topping Castle Road.
1727	William Yarbrough	250	North side south fork of South River adj. Francis Durrett.

Date	Grantee	Acreage	Description
1727	Samuel Davis	400	North fork of north branch of Mat River, adj. Ellis and Rogers.
1727	Capt. James Terry	400	Adj. his land on the North Anna.
1727	John Hubbard	234	South side of White's Swamp.
1727	John May	980	Between Mattapony and South Rivers, adj. John Baylor, below Mattapony and South River fork.
1727	Robert Powell	580	South fork of South River, adj. earlier grant.
1727	Joseph Buckley (?)	400	Both sides Ridge Road, adj. Robert Chandler's.
1727	John Golding (?)	400	Adj. James Taylor, Francis Durrett and John Rogers.
1727	Henry Wood	258	Adj. above and also next to Francis Durrett.
1727	Thomas Hamm	400	Both sides Reedy Swamp, adj. Arnold, Axton and others.
1727	John Martin	400	On the branches of middle fork of Mattapony.
1727	William Dickinson	400	On the North Anna.
1727	John Martin	400	On White's Run, adj. to Martin grant above.
1728	Richard Yarbrough	400	Between branches of Reedy Swamp and North Anna.
1728	Jury (?) Smith	400	Between branches South River and Polecat, adj. James Taylor, Timothy Chandler and John Wright.
1728	Griffin Dickinson	400	Adj. previous grant, on North Anna.
1728	William Higgins	250	Maple Swamp, adj. John Quarles.
1728	John Wright	400	Between branches of South River and Polecat, adj. land of Francis Durrett, James Taylor and John Golding.
1728	Phillip Todd	400	Between branches of Polecat and South River adj. Timothy Chandler.
1728	George Douglass	400	South side the Pilecat adj. Timothy Chandler.
1728	Joel Terrell	698	Two tracts adj. William Terrell and Roger Quarles.
1728	John See	150	Branches of Beaverdam Creek, adj. Thomas Thomas.

Date	Grantee	Acreage	Description
1728	John Quarles	400	In the forks of Polecat adj. William Terrell.
1728	Mary Oglevie	550	North side of Reedy Swamp.
1728	Roger Quarles	400	Adj. Henry Wood and John Rogers.
1729	John Cheadle Thomas Hackett	400	South branch of Polecat, Quaker land.
1729	Robert Hoomes	317	North side Topping Castle Road.
1729	John Sutton	175	Adj. to his estate on the Mattapony.
1729	Edward Yarbrough	200	South fork of middle fork of Reedy Swamp.
1729	Daniel & Henry White	500	North of South River.
1729	Isaac Allen	50	On Reedy Swamp.
1730	John Partlow	200	On South River.
1730	Thomas Hamm	380	Adj. to his estate.
1730	Micajah Chiles	379	On Topping Castle Road.
1730	John Clark	207	Adj. Clark Grant.
1730	Thomas Carr	570	Adj. Carr grants at Topping Castle.*
1730	John Harris	162	North side of north fork of Reedy Swamp.
1730	Richard & Francis Fowler	137½	Adj. to their estate.
1730	Robert Chandler	357	Adj. to his estate.
1730	John Ellis	530	Adj. to his estate.
1730	William Marshall	150	Adj. to John Ellis.
1731	John Ellis	538	Adj. to his estate.
1731	Zachary Martin	306	Adj. to his estate.
1731	John Scandland	400	On Long Creek.
1732	Richard Mauldin	387	Adj. to his estate.
1732	John Sutton	400	Between the South River and the Polecat on the east side of the main road to Mauldin's.
1732	Lewis Burwell	400	On branches of the middle fork of the Mattapony and White Run.
1732	Charles Goodall	915	Adj. to his estate on Long Creek.
1735	Benjamin Walker	200	On White Run.

*Made to favorites rather than homesteaders.

Date	Grantee	Acreage	Description
1735	George Wilson & John Clark	277	On Ridge or Topping Castle Road, at the Spotsylvania line.
1735	George Woodruff	400	South side of the south fork of South River.
1737	Hugh Rea	118	Adj. Richard Mauldin.
1740	Thomas Collins	90	North side of Doguetown Run.
1741	William Crutchfield	596	Herring Creek.
1743	William Trigg	157	Reedy Swamp and Spring Branch.
1752	Richard Devenport	396	On the road from Chesterfield to Mangohick.
1761	John Sutton	400	North side and head of Beaverdam Creek.
1767	John Chiles	255	Adj. to Micajah Chiles estate.

c. *The Speculators*

Statutes permitted enterprising colonists to claim 50 acres of crown land for every settler they brought to Virginia. The chances above are that numerous small grants to two patentees jointly were to the immigrant and his sponsor who paid his way across the Atlantic; *i.e.* the John Buckner and Robert Bullard grant and the Christopher Smith and William Cockran grant. Buckner and Smith were established residents of the area at the time while Bullard and Cockran were newcomers.

In addition to the above mentioned arrangement there were men who made a business of bringing settlers to Virginia for the reward. They worked alone or in groups. The table below lists known men of this class and their acreage.

Date	Grantee	Acreage	Description
1703	Samuel Craddock John Care John Eckols William Glover	1620	In the branches of Tuckahoe Creek. The details of this grant are outlined in the Journal of the House of Burgesses. The patentees brought in 33 immigrants to get the land.
1703	John Care John Eckols	600	In the branches of Tuckahoe Creek.
1704	Edward Merrick William Wakeley	1014	Along little Tuckahoe Creek.

Date	Grantee	Acreage	Description
1704	Andrew Harrison Richard Long Samuel Elliott	813	In the Goldenvale adj. to the west the land of John Buckner.
1715	Richard Mauldin John Sutton Thomas Terry	600	Between the Mattapony and Reedy Creek, adj. Turner and Yarbrough's land.
1721	William Glover	200	On Tuckahoe Creek west of Eckols grant.
1724	Samuel Craddock	1300	On Tuckahoe Creek west of Glover grant.
1724	Richard Mauldin	350	On Maple Creek.
1724	Richard Mauldin	385	South side the south fork of South River, adj. his home estate.
1724	Richard Mauldin	400	North side the south fork of the Polecat.
1724	Richard Mauldin	400	Both sides the south fork of the South River, at the lower end of his home tract.

In addition to the tracts listed above the crown granted favorites and homesteaders alike, small tracts of unclaimed land adjacent to their estates to round out their boundaries. The claiming of this type of land continued under the Commonwealth until almost the close of the nineteenth century.

Two islands in the streams which bound Caroline claimed the settlers' special attention. After numerous attempts Richard Buckner succeeded in perfecting title to Featherstone, or Goat Island consisting of 37 acres in the Rappahannock between Hazelwood and Cleves in 1719, and Roger Quarles succeeded in patenting Fleming's Island consisting of 15 acres in the North Anna a short distance below the river's falls in 1739.

Two tracts of Caroline land were granted to the church rather than to individuals. They were both to the vestry of the parish of St. Margaret's in 1722. One, known as the Fontaine tract from the name of the first rector, was located near Chesterfield and was the site of the parish's earliest church. It consisted of 300 acres. The second was located on the south side of the Ridge Road opposite what is now (1953) known as Bagdad. It consisted of 1,830 acres and was many years the parish glebe.

The crown leased for a term of 500 years a tract of 2,660 acres in the section which became Drysdale Parish across the Rappahannock-Mattapony watershed from the headwaters of Peumandsend to John Holloway in 1710. Holloway sold this lease to Robert (King) Carter of Lancaster for seven pounds sterling and six Negroes. Carter never lived on this property, but he and his heirs maintained a plantation there for many years with an overseer in charge.

2. MARRIAGE AND PURCHASE

Patentees of crown grants began dividing their estates with their children and selling off their surplus acres as soon as they perfected their titles. Because of these transactions many of Caroline's oldest families gained their first holdings in the area to be the county through the marriage of their first male Caroline ancestor to the daughter of the patentee of a crown grant or through purchase. Unfortunately, the records of most of these transactions have been lost. It seems certain, however, that John Lomax gained his property through marriage to a daughter of Sir Thomas Lundsford, and the chances are that Dorothy Roy was the daughter of John Buckner.

Descriptions of crown grants in the land books reveal the names of a few purchasers of adjacent land. They are listed below:

Date	Freeholder	Description
1683	Jacob Flippo	Land adj. to Joshua Storey-George Morris 5,000-acre grant on the north side of the Mattapony.
1688	John Gatewood	Land adj. to Thomas Pitts (grant beyond the head of Peumandsend.
1720	Elias Blackburn	Land adj. to John Martin's grant on Beverley's Run.
1720	William & John Holloway	Land adj. to Elias Downs' grant in St. Mary's Parish.
1721	Rice Williams	Land adj. to Robert Hinds' grant in St. Margaret's.
1721	John Downer	Land adj. to Robert Hinds' grant in St. Margaret's.

Other references reveal the identity of a few more Caroline freeholders before the first entry in the Order Books in 1732. They are:

Date	Freeholder	Source of Information
1716	William Woodford	John Fontaine's *Journal of the Expedition of the Knights of the Golden Horseshoe.*
1727	Robert Woolfolk	*Journal of the Governor's Council.* Named magistrate and the law required a magistrate to be a freeholder.
1727	Thomas Rucker	Same as Robert Woolfolk.

3. THE HEADRIGHTERS

Some immigrants preferred to remain in the settled regions of the colony rather than to push on to the frontier and claim the 50 acres of free land the crown allowed. These immigrants included professional men, traders, artesans, crooks and criminals, all of whom needed a developed community in which to exercise their vocations for the greatest profits. But many of them did not wish to lose completely the crown bounty for coming to Virginia and sold their headrights for what the traffic would bear. These transactions were recorded in the courts of the counties in which the vendor or vendee were residents. A few men made a racket of buying up headrights. Their aim was to secure the right to enough 50-acre tracts to make up a sizeable estate which they might dispose of at a profit.

The table below list the sales recorded in Caroline with the date of the immigrant's entry into the colony after his name in parenthesis, when it is disclosed in the Order Books. It is noteworthy that the immigrant was often in Virginia many years before he sold his headrights.

Headrights purchased in 1735 by John Vaughter; Andrew Phillips, Johnathan and Ann Webster (Ann and her daughter, Mary, became prostitutes after Johnathan's death), John Wilson, Robert Linday (seaman), James Vaughan, John Fox (seaman).

Headrights purchased in 1736 by Richard Taliaferro; William Barnes, David Dixon, Henry and Mary Nichols, John Wallis Summers, Thomas Price, Sarah Tibbs, Edward and Elizabeth Savage, James Atkins, George Brassfield (horsetrader), John Green, Emanuel Penn, Benjamin Hawes, Patrick Welsh (arch-criminal, hung), Thomas Elliott.

Headrights purchased in 1737 by John Holloway; John Pickett, Thomas Durningham.

Headrights purchased in 1737 by George Maunch; Joseph and Sarah Bales.

Headrights purchased in 1738 by Benjamin Rennolds; Joshua and Elizabeth King (sold their headrights a second time in 1754—bootleggers and Elizabeth was also a prostitute), Thomas Portwood, Sarah and Mary Crawley (prostitutes), Catherine Staughn (immoral, married and sued her husband for separate maintenance).

Headrights purchased in 1739 by John Pickett, Jr., John Stuart and Patrick Murphy.

Headrights purchased in 1742 by Richard Taliaferro; John Johns (1742—tailor who became a bankrupt), John Miller (1742—trader, impoverished by the French and Indian War), Robert Gilchrist (1739—merchant and magistrate), Archibald Richie (1740—merchant), Thomas Wild (1740—tavern-keeper and magistrate).

Headrights purchased in 1750 by John Madison; Thomas Turner, Thomas Landrum (lawyer), Dr. John Shores (physician), George Frazier, Edward Dixon (merchant and magistrate), Patrick Coutts (merchant), James Donald, John and William Gray (merchants), Robert Scott.

Headrights purchased in 1754 by James Taylor; Thomas Berry (1715), Fox Stirling (1740—merchant), Robert Robinson (1727), Joshua and Elizabeth King (1711—sold headrights for the second time, caught and punished), William Holmes (1754), Peter Copeland (1743—merchant and magistrate), William Cowne (1733—merchant and slave dealer, a henchman of James Taylor, who purchased his headright), Thomas Rogers (1752), Benjamin Whitehead (1725—tavern-keeper), John Spaulding (1741), Daniel LaFoe (1734—weaver), Herbert Price (1732), John Mitchell (1744).

Headrights purchased in 1755 by Francis Taylor; Richard (1715) and Mary Ann Corey (1734), Timothy Smith (1742).

Headrights purchased in 1755 by James Taylor; John Semple (1752—merchant), John Whaling (1734—entered colony as an indentured servant).

Headright purchased 1755 by Adam Lindsay; James Summers (1725).

4. THE INDENTURED SERVANTS

A large number of settlers came to Virginia as indentured servants. A few of these people had been transported from Britain after their convictions for common law crimes such as robbery and housebreaking. But many more were sent overseas in servitude because they supported the House of Stuart instead of the House of Hanover in dynastic wars. Others voluntarily bound themselves to serve a term of years to pay their transportation to the new world. The most tragic were youths of tender years, kidnapped in British port cities by sea captains and sold in Virginia. These youths, if literate, were in demand by merchants to keep their accounts because local youths often had little schooling and even less inclination for office work. Finally a few residents of Virginia were sold into bondage for a term of years by the local court because they were in debt.

Terms of servitude varied from two to seven years, or until the servant reached age of twenty-one, if he were a juvenile. At the end of an indenture all servants were entitled to freedom dues. The freedom dues for which William Brown sued his master Benjamin Grubbs in 1737 were typical. They consisted of a young mare, a suit of Kersey clothes, two shirts, two pair of hose, a pair of shoes and a hat.

There is no way to determine the number of indentured servants in colonial Caroline. The only ones of record are those who had cause to appear in court. The table below, compiled from the Order Books, list these servants, their masters and why they were in court.

Year	Servant	Master	Why in Court
1732	John Dererieux	Henry Rains—Escaped 4 days; 4 months and 16 days added to service.	
1734	Sussannah Baker	John Ralls—Escaped 6 days; 4 months and 16 days added to service.	
1734	Charity Burns	George Douglass—Had mulatto bastard; 5 lashes at whipping-post.	
1734	Mary Close	George Douglass—Had mulatto bastard; 5 lashes at whipping-post.	
1735	John Johnson	Zachery Martin—A witness.	
1736	Elizabeth Williams	John Herndon—Adultery with Negro slave; 9 weeks added service and 200 lbs. of tobacco fine.	
1736	Joseph Williams	John Herndon—The husband of Elizabeth Williams.	
1736	John Jenkins	John Ralls—Escaped for 20 days; serve according to law.	

Year	Servant	Master	Why in Court
1736	Christine Smith	Edward Vaughter — Had b a s t a r d; Emanuel Penn paid fine.	
1736	Elizabeth Sanders	Samuel Coleman—Had mulatto bastard; Peter Lantor paid fine.	
1737	Edward Martin	John Jeter — Escaped for 6 days; 6 months extra service and 300 lbs. of tobacco fine.	
1737	John Johnson	William Burdette—Escaped 5 days; 15 months extra service. 2nd offense: Johnson had been sold by Zack Martin to Burdette between his escapes.	
1737	Edward Powers	James Miller — Escaped 24 days; 12 months added service and 800 lbs. of tobacco fine.	
1737	Robert Stuart	James Hubbard — Age registered — 14 years old.	
1737	William Brown	Benjamin Grubbs — Sued for freedom dues.	
1738	Ann Gold	Robert Baber—Complained her master beat her. Baber placed under bond not to beat servant.	
1738	William Rigsby	Thomas Catlett—Released by master's will, as reward for educating master's children.	
1739	Sarah Matts	William Woodford—Broke into master's storehouse; sent to General Court —prior conviction in Britian.	
1739	Constatine Mathews	William Woodford — Same crime; to General Court.	
1739	James Moore	William Woodford — Receiving stolen goods; to General Court—prior conviction in Ireland.	
1739	James Harris	William Woodford—Criticized sending Sarah Matts to General Court; 15 lashes at the whipping-post.	
1739	Ann Gold	Robert Baber—Disrespect to master; 15 lashes at whipping-post.	
1740	John Cook	John Embrey—Complains of hard usage by his master—asked to be sold— request denied.	

Year	Servant	Master	Why in Court
1740	Isaac Eccles	John Ralls—Escaped 5 days; 7 months, 11 days extra service.	
1740	Mary Rawlings	Dr. George Todd—Released upon cancellation of freedom dues.	
1740	Jeannett Coleman	Dr. George Todd—Bound to Charles Stuart in Glasglow—Stuart left Caroline before servant arrived—transferred to Dr. Todd when he paid her transportation.	
1740	Nicholas Mullins	John Glantor—Escaped; bound to serve according to law.*	
1740	Dorcas Barnett	John Glantor—Escaped with Mullins, a romance; bound to serve according to law.	
1740	Morris Paris	Nicholas Jeter—Escaped for 20 days; serve 9 months 6 days extra, fined 200 lbs. of tobacco.	
1740	Robert Butler	Lodowick Murray—Age registered—14 years old.	
1740	Harry Montgomery	Robert Gilchrist — Age registered — 10 years old.	
1740	Lewis Morgan	Robert Gilchrist — Age registered — 9 years old.	
1740	Joseph Hunt	William Burdette — Sued for freedom dues.	
1740	Isaac Edes	John Ralls — Escaped for 10 days—5 months service and 475 lbs. tobacco.	
1740	Ann Sanders	Dorothy Roy—Stole from mistress—20 lashes at whipping-post.	
1741	Daniel Potter	John Micou — Released for educating master's children.	
1741	James Young	Bartholomew West—Escaped, serve according to law.	
1741	Ann Danton	Lawrence Battaile—Sold for a year for misconduct in her master's home.	
1741	Timothy Mathews	Richard Straughn—Escaped for 24 days—7 months, 18 days extra service.	
1744	Joseph Neplett	Bennett Beazley — Age registered — 12 years old.	
1744	John Whaling	John Dyer—Sued for freedom dues.	

Year	*Servant*	*Master*	*Why in Court*
1744	Daniel Garrity	of Orange—Horse thief.	
1744	Thomas Lloyd	Oliver Charles—Sued for freedom dues.	
1745	James Young	Thomas Riddle—Escaped for 8 days—18 months extra service and 100 lbs. of tobacco fine. 2nd offense —Young sold by West to Riddle after first escape.	
1745	Mary Hunt	John Wallis—Freed upon cancellation of freedom dues.	
1745	Nick Mallin	Thomas Roy—Escaped for 3 days—6 months extra service and 523 lbs. of tobacco fine.	
1745	Dorcas Sebastian	Thomas Roy—Escaped with Nick Mallin—same punishment.*	
1745	Nicholas MacClain	John Glantor — Escaped 8 days — 16 months extra service.	
1745	John Stuart	James Bowie—Escaped for 36 days—6 months, 16 days extra† service and 523 lbs. of tobacco fine.	
1745	Mary Cockran	James Bowie—Escaped for 36 days with John Stuart—same punishment.	
1745	Thomas Hailey	Richard Powell—Escaped for 36 days with John Stuart—same punishment.	
1745	Morris Paris	Nicholas Jeter — Escaped with John Stuart, absent 35 days, same punishment.	
1745	Robert Lyons	John Lomax—Freed upon cancellation of freedom dues.	
1745	John Dovel	Lawrence Battaile — Escaped, returned to master on own free will, forgiven.	
1745	James Nolting	Henry Cooper—Complained against his master—complaint denied.	
1745	James Tool	Richard Taliaferro—Purchased his freedom for 17 pounds, 18 shillings and 6 pence.	
1745	Andrew MacKenzie	—Age registered—12 years old.	
1745	John Farley	Rice Curtis—Age registered—11 years old.	

Year	Servant	Master	Why in Court
1746	Charles Sprunt	Thomas Roy—Freed upon cancellation of freedom dues.	
1746	Charles Bone	William Wallis—Freed upon cancellation of freedom dues.	
1746	Bartlett Hart	Peter Copeland — Age registered — 12 years old.	
1746	Isabella Gibbins	John Wiley—Freed upon cancellation of freedom dues.	
1747	Francis Barnham	John Pickett—Escaped, serve master according to law.	
1747	John Thompson	Thomas Roy—Age registered—10 years old.	
1747	Elizabeth Massey	Joseph Lewis — Bastard by William Cockran—5 lashes at whipping-post.	
1747	Daniel Clark	Robert Robinson — Age registered — 14 years old.	
1747	William Cockran	Joseph Lewis—Complained against his master—complaint dismissed.	
1748	Eleanor Dogood	Joseph Spicer — Escaped — serve master according to law.	
1748	Arch Chambers	William Robinson—Sued for freedom after master's death—lost case.	
1748	Jane MacKenzie	William Woodford—Complained against her master—dismissed.	
1749	Jane MacKenzie	William Woodford—Complained against her master. Master ordered to treat her better.	
1749	Fatty Moon	William Rogers—Age registered in court 18 years old.‡	
1749	Michael MacCurd	Peter Holland — Age registered — 10 years old.	
1749	Honor Mundowney	Adam Lindsay — Bastard — 5 lashes at whipping-post.	
1749	John Cardin (Carter?)	Henry Rains — Escaped 11 days — 11 months extra service and 200 lbs. of tobacco fine.	
1750	Patience Moss	James Mason—Sued for freedom dues.	
1750	James Moss	John Jeter—Sued for freedom dues.	

Year	Servant	Master	Why in Court
1750	Morris Paris	Nicholas Jeter—Freed upon cancellation of freedom dues.	
1751	Charles May	Richard Taliaferro—Sued for freedom when master refused to release him as the end of indenture.	
1751	Elizabeth Witchfield	Thomas Berry—Bastard, 5 lashes and extra year service.	
1752	Samuel Young	Edward Powers—Escaped for 19 days—serve master according to law.	
1752	Henry Thomas	Mordicai Abraham — Indenture cancelled because master was a Jew.	
1752	Alexander Southerland	Jeremiah Pierce—Escaped for 15 days—serve master according to law.	
1752	Elizabeth Whitlock	Elizabeth Campbell—Bastard—5 lashes at whipping-post and serve mistress an extra year.	
1753	Alexander Isaacs	James Kay—Escaped for 8 days—serve according to law.	
1753	Alexander Southerland	Jeremiah Pierce — Escaped — never recaptured.	
1754	John Mayfield (poor debtor)	Mordicai Abraham—Escaped for 11 days —serve master according to law.	
1754	Mary Clark	George Muse—Freed upon cancellation of service dues.	
1755	Patrick Fisher	John Sutton—Escaped for 4 days—serve according to law.	
1755	Solomon Higgins	William Boulware—Released upon cancellation of freedom dues.	
1756	John Mayfield	Mordicai Abraham—Sued for release because masters were Jews—suit denied because servant was a poor debtor and not a true indentured servant.	
		& Jacob Isaacs	
1756	Thomas Perrin	Timothy Smith—Escaped for 5 days—serve according to law and 200 lbs. of tobacco fine.	
1756	Catherine Bohannon	Oliver Charles—Complained against her master—dismissed.	
1756	John Penny	Thomas Johnston—Released upon cancellation of freedom dues.	

Year	Servant	Master	Why in Court
1756	Dennis MacCarty	Oliver Charles—Released upon cancellation of freedom dues.	
1757	Mary Martin	Abraham Estis—Bastard, 5 lashes and a year extra service.	
1757	James Stanley	James Taliaferro—Released upon cancellation of freedom dues.	
1757	Sussannah Cockran	Peter Copeland—Released upon cancellation of freedom dues.	
1757	Catherine Bohannon	Oliver Charles—Bastard, 5 lashes and extra year service.	
1757	Catherine Bohannon	Oliver Charles—Freed upon cancellation of freedom dues.	
1758	Henretta Andrews	William Allison—Freed upon cancellation of freedom dues.	
1758	Mary Cox	Robert Kay—Misconduct—master gave bond for her good behavior.	
1758	John Danner	Edward Powers—Sued for his freedom dues.	
1758	Reuben Danner	Edward Powers—Sued for his freedom dues.	
1760	Thomas Craig	Mary Lyons—Released upon cancellation of freedom dues.	
1760	James Munday (poor debtor)	William Davis—Sued for freedom.	
1760	George Whitlock	George Wiley—Freed upon cancellation of freedom dues.	
1760	Richard Carter	John Watkins—Complained against his master—complaint dismissed.	
1765	Francis Lodge	Robert Garrett—Sued for freedom at end of indenture—won.	
1765	Dorothy Bourton	James Clayton—Bastard—5 lashes, year added service.	
1766	Merryman Fox	Johnathan Douglass — Complained against master—ordered sold.	
1769	Mary Johnson alias Tunney	George Spicer—Sued for her freedom.	
1770	Martha Murrah	Henry Pemberton—Sued for her freedom.	
1771	James Gordon	James Miller—Sued for his freedom.	

Year	Servant	Master	Why in Court
1772	John Young	James Martin—Escaped for 70 days—serve according to law.	
1772	William Christopher	William Emerson — Escaped 10 days, serve according to law.	
1773	Annie Whittaker	Nellie Mitchell—Bastard, 5 lashes and extra year service.	
1773	Mary Budd	James Baber—Complained against her master—master ordered to treat her better.	

*Nicholas Mullins and Dorcas Barnett may have been the same persons as Nick Mallin and Dorcas Sebastian. If this is true they made two escapes for romantic purposes.

†The mass escape led by John Stuart was the only mass escape of indentured servants in the history of Caroline County. The number of Stuarts in the county leads to the conjecture that they were fugitives from Britain's dynastic wars.

‡The law required that all white servants be registered with the court if they were under 18 years of age, when they were brought into the county. The Caroline court held that Fatty Moon was over 18.

Additional Comment: Major William Woodford of Windsor appears to have been the only freeholder to have trouble with his indentured servants because they were criminals.

Edward Powers was the most successful indentured servant, who remained in Caroline after he gained his freedom. He was trained by James Miller, the merchant, his master, and became a prominent business man. He operated a tavern, and Humphrey Bell of London deeded him land and made him his factor. Powers in time owned indentured servants himself. From the records of the Order Books he had trouble with three of them.

5. THE NEGROES

Negroes have formed a substantial percentage of the population of Caroline County since the Indians lost control of the territory. The first white settlers brought Negro slaves with them to help till the soil and the number of Negroes constantly increased. 405 young Negroes, under the age of sixteen, were registered by their masters in the Caroline Court as soon as they were imported from abroad, as the law required, between the first entry in the Order Books in 1732 and the outbreak of the French and Indian War in 1734. During the same period the number of tithables in the county, free white males and indentured servants over the age of eighteen and Negro slaves over the age of sixteen, only increased by 505.

Few freeholders were large slaveholders in colonial days. Instead most of the men and women who owned land owned a few slaves. Evidence of this is found in the large number of freeholders who registered young slaves with the court, and the fact that registrations by the same freeholder were usually one or two at the time and continuing sporadically through the years. The names of the Caroline freeholders who registered young slaves with the court follows with the number of registrations after their names:

William Allcock 1, Thomas Ayers 1, John Apperson 2.

Thomas Berry 1, Henry Bell, Roger Bell 1, Easter Bell 1, George Braxton 2, Thomas Buckner 3, Morgan Bridges 1, John Brown 4, William Brown 2, Abraham Brown 1, Sarah Brown 1, Benjamin Brown 1, Thomas Bankes 3, Elias Blackburn 1, Richard Booker 4, William Broughill 1, Jacob Burruss 1, John Burk 2, James Bowie 1, Ambroise Bullard 2, Moses Benson 1, Daniel Barksdale 1, Richard Bradford 1, Harry Beverley 1, Thomas Brassfield 1, William Blanton 1, Charles Blanton 1, Richard Blanton 1, John Beazley 2, Charles Beazley 5.

John Clark 1, Thomas Collins 2, Thomas Croutcher 3, William Croutcher 2, Timothy Chandler 1, Richard Chandler 1, William Carr 1, Daniel Coleman 1, John Coleman 1, Samuel Coleman 1, Robert Coleman 1, James Coleman 1, William Coleman 1, Patrick Cowan 1, William Campbell 1, Thomas Cook 1, John Cheadle 2, William Coates 1, James Chapman 3, Nathan Chapman 1, Peter Copeland 2, William Conner 6, William Curd 1, Moses Carneal 2.

Adam Dick 1, John Dyer 3, William Dyer 1, Elizabeth Dickinson 1, Thomas Dickinson 1, William Daniels 3, David Daniels 1, John Daniels 1, Richard Davenport 1, Francis Durrett 1, Joseph DeJarnette 1, George Dillard 1, William Dudley 1, Ambroise Dudley 1, Rev. Musgrave Dawson 1, John Dixon 2.

Thomas Estis 1, Abraham Estis 1, John Estis 2, John Eubank 1, Elizabeth Evins 1.

John Fox 1, James Fletcher 1, Benjamin Faulkner 3, William Faulkner 2, Robert Farrish 5, Thomas Floreson 1, Elizabeth Franklin 1.

Michael Guinney 1, Reuben George 1, John Griffin 2, Robert Goodloe 1, William Gray 1, John Guy 1, John Graves 1, John George 1, Samuel Garlick 4.

George Hoomes 2, John Hoomes 1, Joseph Hoomes 5, Samuel Hawes 2, James Hoarde 1, John Hudson 1, Jasper Haynes 1, Margaret Hewlett 1, Richard Hale 1, Thomas Hackett 1, Thomas Holland 2, Robert Huntley 1, William Holden 1, David Herndon 2, George Herndon 1, John Herndon 1, Francis Haile 1, John Hudgins 1.

Jacob Johns 1, William Jeter 1, Thomas Jeter 1, Sherwood James 2, James Jameson 1, Equitter Johnston 1, James Johnston 3, Thomas Johnston 1.

Ambroise Kemp 1, James Kay 1, Zachery Kendricks 1, William Killum 1.

Head Lynch 2, Robert Lowery 2, Andrew Lyon 1, John Long 1, Augustine Leftwitch 2, Ann Lahone 1, William Loving 2, Robert Lyon 1, William Lee 2, Joshua Lindsay 1, James Lindsay 1, Caleb Lindsay 1, John Lindsay 2.

John Micou 5, William Marshall 3, Edward Mastin 1, Arch. Macphearson 4, Francis Murray 1, Joseph Minter 1, James Miller 1, James Martin 4, George Martin 1, John Martin 1, William MacGehee 2, John Major 1, John Meadors 1, John Mitchell 1.

John Nichols 1, Joseph Norment 2, Henry Newton 1, Hugh Noden 2.

Nicholas Oliver 1, John Oliver 1.

John Penn 2, George Penn 1, Honorous Powell 2, Edmound Pendleton 4, John Price 1, Thomas Pickett 1, John Pickett 7.

John Quarles 2.

Ralph Richards 1, John Rogers 2, Thomas Richerson 1, John Ralls 2, William Riddle 1, James Riddle 2, Sarah Rennolds 1, James Rennolds 2, Thomas Roy 7, Charles Rorey 1.

Peter Sanders 2, John Sanders 1, James Ship 1, Thomas Ship 1, Joseph Ship 1, Thomas Ship 1, Stephen Stone 1, John Sneed 2, Thomas Scott 1, James Satterwhite 1, John Satterwhite 1, William Stevens 2, Joseph Stevens 5, Dr. John Shores 1, John Southworth 1, William Southworth 1, John Scandland 1.

James Taliaferro 1, Walker Taliaferro 1, William Taliaferro 2, Richard Taliaferro 2, Francis Thornton 1, Reuben Thornton 1, George Todd 1, Daniel Triplett 1, James Taylor 9, John Taylor 2, Edmound Taylor 2, John Thilman 1, Henry Terrell 7, John Turner 1, William Turner 2, James Turner 1, Thomas Turner 1, William Thomas 2, David Tinsley 5, Phillip Tinsley 1.

Ambroise Vaughan 1, John Vaughan 1, Cornelius Vaughan 1.

William Woodford 4, Benjamin Wood 1, John Wyatt 2, William Watkins 2, Mary Watkins 1, Joseph Woolfolk 6, Richard Woolfolk 2,

Henry White 1, Benjamin Walker 5, Robert Wright 1, Mathew Willis 1, Richard Walden 1, John Walden 2, Abraham Wilson 1, Benjamin Winn 1, Thomas Wellard 1, Nicholas Ware 1, Edward Ware 2.

Charles Yarbrough 2, Michael Yates 2, James Young 3.

Registrations of young Negroes imported from abroad by years were:

1732, 10; 1733, 21; 1734, 28; 1735, 7; 1736, 19; 1737, 13; 1738, 6; 1739, 8; 1740, 29; 1741, 1; 1742, 18; 1743, 16; 1744, 4; 1745, 13; 1746, 1; 1747, 0 (Port Royal panic); 1748, 10; 1749, 59; 1750, 25; 1751, 63; 1752, 31; 1753, 22.

The tax placed on Negroes entering the colony, by the General Assembly to help finance the French and Indian War, and the control of the seas by the French, caused an abrupt end to the registration of young Negroes in the Caroline Court. If any were brought into the county during the next eight years they were not registered. With the return of peace 14 were registered in 1763; by William Allcock 2, Robert Standfield 1, John Minor 3, Micajah Terrell 1, Francis Taliaferro 2, Robert Hall 2, Moses Carneal 1, James Bowie 1, and Edmound Pendleton 1. But the renewal of the importation of Negroes did not continue, British tax laws and the upheaval in the wake of the Revolution interrupted the traffic again. After 1763 only two more young Negroes were registered prior to the battle of Yorktown by John Burruss in 1770 and John Partlow in 1771.

The foregoing tables indicate that the great landlords imported few Negroes after 1732. Not a single young slave was registered by a Baylor or a Corbin, and only one by a Beverley, Caroline's three families with the most extensive estates. Of families of only slightly lesser importance not a slave was registered by a Lomax, a Catlett, a Armistead, a Sutton, a Battaile, or a Conway. The Carrs registered only one, and the Thorntons and the Buckners only two. The chances are that these families had enough slaves to till their plantations from the natural increase of their Negroes acquired before 1732 and were not interested in additional importations from abroad. Of the gentry only the Taylors, Taliaferros, Hoomes and

Woolfolks who were more prolific than their Negroes, had to purchase slaves to staff the homesteads of younger sons.

The chief registrants of young imported Negroes, however, were tavern-keepers, members of their families and the men who loafed in taverns, such as sailors when ashore, small-time speculators and minor office holders. Roy's Tavern at Port Royal, Brown's at the Courthouse, Dyer's at Douguetown (Milford) Bridge, James Martin's at Guinney Bridge, Sneed's at Daniels' (White's) Mill and Thomas Bankes at Chesterfield were early centers of slave trade. In addition to the tavern-keepers and members of their families other traders included the seafaring Lindsays, the horse-trading Picketts and Saunders, and the Beazleys, who frequently served as road supervisors and constables.

Unfortunately there is no record of the adult Negroes brought into Caroline. But it is known that the number was considerable and that a great many of them came from the West Indies rather than from Africa. This is borne out by slaves' names in the Order Books in business transactions and in crime, which were often typically Spanish; Pancho, Sancho, Diego, Pedro, Mungo, Mingo, Lucia, Juanita and Maria. The adult Negro imported from the West Indies was of considerable greater value than the adult Negro imported from Africa. The former was civilized while the latter was still a savage.

While planters usually let their West Indian Negroes keep their original names they gave a wide variety of names to their other slaves. Of the young Negroes registered in the Caroline Court, forty-eight received the names of Greek and Roman gods and heroes with eight Cupids and seven Cæsars heading the list. Twenty-seven were named for cities with Bristol (6) being the most popular. Twenty-five received the names of Biblical characters, which included four Hams. The most popular name for a woman was Daphne. There were sixteen. Some names were pure fantasy. Henry Terrell named six of his slaves Pansar, Paisar, Potah, Sonah, Pakah and Tulah. Samuel Hawes named a Negro, Money, John Apperson a Negro, Breakup, and Sarah Brown, apparently afraid that hers was going to run away, Don't-forget-me.

a. *Crime*

Caroline Negroes were well behaved for the most part. The only major crimes in which Negroes were the accused recorded in the Order Books are listed below:

1734—Robin, slave of William Taliaferro, burned dwelling of Thomas Royston—*hung.*

1734—Dirk, slave of Francis Thornton, tried to poison Robert Dudley and others—master gave bond for his good behavior.

1736—Andrew, slave of Richard Bradford, convicted of the rape of Elizabeth Williams—*hung.*

1739—Phil, slave of Henry Lawless, burned Thomas Emerson's dwelling—hung and head cut off and set up in a public place.

1744—Tom, slave of John Garnett, poisoned Joe and Wick, slaves of Richard Buckner, Mungo, slave of Francis Thornton, and Rover, slave of John Micoy—ordered transported from the colony of Virginia.

1747—Robin, slave of Francis Thornton, struck Simon Morgan, with a knife—39 lashes at the whipping-post.

1751—Cuffey, slave of Robert Coleman's estate, poisoned Betty, a slave of Robert Coleman's estate—*hung.*

1751—Harry, slave of Henry Armistead's estate, stole gun from Joseph Whitehead—*hung.* This was a second offense; previously Harry had broken into the house of Hugh Davis and stolen a gun. (He had been burned in the left hand in open court and given 39 lashes at the whipping-post upon conviction of this crime.)

1761—Daniel, slave of John Pickett, killed Pronton, slave of Sam Major—*hung.*

1762—Bob, slave of Archibald Dick, broke into the storehouse of Theodore Morrison—sentenced to hang. Broke out of jail the day before the day set for the hanging, never heard from again.

1762—Roger, slave of George Arnold, participated in the crime above—*hung.*

1762—Tom, slave of Thomas Coleman, participated in crime above—39 lashes at the whipping-post.

1762—Peter, slave of John Wiley, poisoned Nicodemous and Jeffry, slaves of Francis Taylor, *hung.*

1762—Cupid, slave of John Allmond, killed Frank, slave of John Cheadle—*hung.*

1762—Abel, slave of Nicholas Oliver, participated in crime above—*hung.*

1762—Sam, slave of John Burk, participated in crime above—39 lashes at the whipping-post.

1763—Peter, slave of Martin Phillips, poisoned other slaves—*hung*.

1763—Nan, slave of John Sutton, crime obliterated—*hung*.

1764—Tom, slave of Henry Gilbert of Hanover, broke into numerous Caroline homes—*hung*.

1764—Hannah, slave of Samuel Sutton, convicted of burning her master's home, sentenced to hang—pardoned by the king.

1765—Aaron, slave of Robert Armistead, broke into master's home—*hung*.

1765—Dick, slave of John Wright, accused of poisoning Guy, slave of Samuel Stevens—Court held poison administered as medicine without intent to kill—ordered burned in left hand in open court and 39 lashes at whipping-post—allowed the benefit of clergy.

1772—Abraham, runaway Negro from Goochland, broke into John Baylor's stable, stole horse and clothing—*hung*.

1775—Gloucester, slave of Dr. William Johnston, broke into store of James Bowie—*hung*.

1776—Jack, slave of ———, attempted rape of Mary Vaughan—39 lashes on bare back.

1779—Patt, slave of William Dandridge—accused of killing her child— not guilty.

Minor Crimes: Negroes were frequently in court for minor crimes. The most prevalent were theft and escape from servitude. Food was the article most often stolen. On numerous occasions a group of slaves seized a hog and carried it into the woods far out of the reach of a white man's habitation for a barbecue. The punishment for this was the most drastic the court imposed short of the death sentence, 39 lashes at the whipping-post and burning of the left hand in open court for the leaders, and a lesser number of lashes for the followers. The theft of articles other than food was not very profitable for Negroes after 1752, when the General Assembly passed a law which made it a felony for a free man to have a business transaction with a slave. But in spite of this law, Gilbert, a slave of Thomas Roy, stole eleven rugs from the schooner *Molly* anchored in Port Royal harbor in 1762. He was burned in the left hand and given 39 lashes at the whipping-post for this crime.

Escape was the commonest of all crimes. It was committed by bound children, apprentices and indentured servants as well as Negro slaves. The escapees roamed the countryside committing crimes to live. The General Assembly passed drastic laws to punish the offenders because they were the source of so much trouble while on the loose. Escapees after capture were publicly whipped in each county they passed through while on the way back to their masters in custody, and their captors received liberal rewards. The reward was paid by the secretary of the colony out of public funds, but it had to be made up by the owner of the escaped servant. In cases of servants bound for a term of years the servant had to serve additional time after the termination of his indenture to reimburse his master. But in the case of Negro slaves there was nothing that the master was able to do but take his loss. The reward was so liberal that numerous men made a living capturing runaways. The most celebrated in Caroline was Thomas Lantor, who had failed at everything else he tried in life.

After Dinwiddie became governor two sessions of the Caroline Court each year were set aside to certify claims to the secretary of the colony for the capture of runaways in the county. The claims certified for the Fall term of 1752 follows:

Captor, Who Claimed Bounty	Runaway	Name and Address of Master
Henry Burk	George—Negro slave	William Naiper of Goochland.
Joseph DeJarnette	Gabriel—Negro slave	Benjamin Milward of Caroline.
James Gatewood	Negro "who either refused or was unable to give his name."	William Arnold of Gloucester.
John Carson	Cate—Negro slave	John Corbin of Essex
Richard Corey	Cato—Negro slave	John Spotswood of Spotsylvania.
Abraham Willson	Alexander Southerland, indentured servant.	Jeremiah Pierce of Caroline
Nathan Chapman	Alice—Negro slave	Richard Corbin of King and Queen.

Captor, Who Claimed Bounty	Runaway	Name and Address of Master
Patrick Cockran	Michael MacMath & Samuel Stanley, indentured servants.	John Cook of Norfolk borough.
Joseph Lankford	Manger—Negro slave	John Corbin of Essex.

The above list was typical. An average of over twenty-five escapees were captured in Caroline each year between 1745 and 1775. Some fugitives managed to travel a great distance before they were captured. One indentured servant from Northampton County was captured in Caroline.

Negro Progress. The Negro's position improved rapidly in Caroline. From uncouth barbarian he became, in many instances, a skilled worker able to read and write. With his enhanced value to his master as an artisan his living standards improved. In time the freeholders accorded him many of the common law rights which were a British heritage. By the time of the Revolution hundreds of Caroline Negroes were Christians and a few were no longer slaves.

There is only one instance of record of the miscarriage of justice in regards to a Negro in the Caroline Courts prior to 1782. This was the hanging of Andrew, for the alleged rape of Elizabeth Williams, a white indentured servant, when the evidence indicates that she acquiesced to the sex act. In this case both the man and the woman were first convicted of adultry. But when a certain element in the county was not satisfied with the verdict, the court set it aside and condemned Andrew to death for rape. When the Negro was hung his paramour took to the woods and remained a fugitive for nine days. She was sentenced to serve nine additional weeks at the end of her term of indenture and pay a fine of 200 lbs. of tobacco after her capture. After this unfortunate episode the Caroline Court made no attempt to punish the Negro father when white women gave birth to mulattoes. Charity Burns, Mary Close, Sussanah Baker and Elizabeth Sanders were all whipped for this crime, but there is no record of any punishment being imposed on the child's father.

The only act of barbarism by whites towards a Negro was early in the county's history. Three years after the hanging of Andrew, or in 1739, the court ordered the head of Phil cut off and set up in a public place after he was hung for the burning of the manor house of Thomas Emerson. Arson is an awful crime, and the court's attitude is understandable. The magistrates wanted to make an example of Phil and deter others from committing a similar offense. But even this reasoning does not excuse the atrocity.

In other instances of attacks of Negroes on whites the court was more lenient. It merely ordered Dirk placed under bond for his good behavior after he attempted to poison Robert Dudley, and Dirk's master, Francis Thornton, put up this bond. It only sentenced Robin, another slave of Francis Thornton, to thirty-nine lashes at the whipping-post after he wounded Simon Morgan with a knife. In this case all the defense witnesses were Negroes while many of the prosecuting witnesses were whites.

In 1770 Harding Chewning, a white man, was charged with the murder of Jack, the Negro slave of John Smith. The court acquitted Chewning and there is no evidence of his guilt. But it is interesting to note that whites were being tried in Caroline at this time if they killed a Negro.

Negroes had certain civil responsibilities along with their rights. In 1762 Isabelle and Daphne, the slaves of John Beazley, were sentenced to 15 lashes at the whipping-post for perjury after they were convicted of lying on the witness stand in the trial of Daniel, slave of John Pickett, for the murder of Pronton, slave of Samuel Major.

As early as 1760 there is evidence that Negro slaves in Caroline were beginning to win their freedom through acts of benevolence of their masters. An unusual statement in Order Book V (1759) reads: "It is ordered that Lavendar, a Negro servant belonging to Benj. Hubbard, gent., serve her master, three months after her term of service expires."

The first positive evidence that there were free Negroes in Caroline appears in the same Order Book on page 203, when the magistrates order John Gillison to appear in court and explain "why Daniel, a free Negro, should not be bound." Gillison answered the summons and stated that he intended for Daniel to be free, "whereupon the court let the Negro go his way."

But life for Daniel, as a free man, was not easy. Irresponsible whites picked on him until in desperation he sued Jacob Tinsley for assault and battery (Order Book V, page 449). In this epoch-making case the jury, which of course was all white, found for the Negro although they only allowed him a penny in damages. Tinsley, however, had to pay the costs, which were considerable.

The next step towards civil rights for Negroes came in 1764 when Hannah, the slave of Samuel Sutton, received a king's pardon after the Caroline Court convicted her of burning her master's home and sentenced her to hang. Hannah was the only person, Negro or white, pardoned by the king in Caroline during colonial times. Significant as this act was she could not have secured the sovereign's forgiveness without powerful friends to plead her cause in Williamsburg before the royal governor. The chief of her friends was William Boulware, her attorney. It was a common practice for the court to appoint lawyers to defend Negroes accused of crime. The leading members of the Caroline bar served in this capacity at some times during their careers.

Around 1765 the court began to take cognizance of the fact if Negroes were Christians when they appeared as witnesses or as the accused. If Christian Negroes were caste in the later rôle and convicted the magistrates either allowed or disallowed the benefit of clergy when enduring punishment, depending on the degree of the crime, as they did with the whites.

While undoubtedly there were Christians among the Caroline Negroes prior to 1765 the mass Christianization of colored slaves appears to have taken place about that date. The Rev. Johnathan Boucher in his autobiography writes, "On the 24th day of November, 1765, I baptized in St. Mary's Church one hundred and fifteen Negro adults, and on the 31st of March 1766, being Easter Monday, I baptized three hundred and thirteen Negro adults, and lectured extempore to upwards of a thousand. I question whether so extraordinary an accession to the Church of Christ, by one man and in one day, can be paralleled in the journals of the Popish missionaries."

Rev. Boucher, however, appears to have been interested primarily in baptizing Negroes and saving their souls, rather than in making them communicants of his church. He held that they were not ready for church membership until they were better educated. He writes "in my humble judgement it is injudicious to attempt to instruct them (the Negroes)*** in its mysterious doctrines. I may add, moreover, with strict truth, that I had under my care many Negroes as well informed, as orderly and regularly pious, as country people usually are, even in England. Corresponding with the society called the Associates of Dr. Bray, I had set up two or three serious and sensible blackmen as school masters to teach the children around them merely to read at their leisure hours, and chiefly on Sunday afternoons,***. I had in consequence almost every Sunday, twenty or thirty, who could use their prayer books and make the responses, and I had towards the last of my ministry there (St. Mary's) thirteen black communicants."

But in the long run economic reasons, rather than an interest in saving souls, caused the education of more Negroes. Masters taught their brighter slaves to read and write that they might more perfectly practice skilled trades. As time went on more and more Negroes became artesans until skilled slaves made indentured servants unprofitable and doomed the apprentice system. John Baylor in his will probated in the Caroline Court in 1772 lists his skilled Negroes by name.

Race Relations. Strong bonds of affection sprung up between the Negroes and the whites. Elizabeth Goodwin renounced her husband's will to keep her Negro maid. But it was again the loquacious Parson Boucher who left the most comprehensive account of race relations. Upon leaving Caroline for Maryland he wrote in his autobiography, "To my slaves I gave the option either to go with me or to choose themselves masters in Virginia. All the unmarried ones chose the former; and the others I sold by their own desire, chiefly to gentlemen, who having been my pupils, had lived with me. It affords me more comfort that I can express to recollect that I had nothing bad to charge myself with on the score of severity towards my slaves. No compliment ever paid me went so near to my heart, as when a gentleman was one day coming to my home, and having overtaken a slave, asked him to whom he belonged, to which the slave replied "To Parson Boucher, thank God."

Mulattoes. Half breeds caused the greatest race problems in colonial Caroline. The children of white fathers and Negro mothers were classed as Negroes and gave no trouble, because they remained slaves. But the children of white mothers and Negro fathers were quite a different matter. They formed a class of their own since the law allowed them to be held as slaves only until they reached the age of thirty-one when it required them to be set free as white persons. This led to many lawsuits because masters were often reluctant to part with able-bodied servants in the prime of life.

The most celebrated cases of this type in Caroline involved Cloe, Dinah, Swaney, Doll, Sarah and Scilla Burdette. These mulattoes were the servants of Hugh Noden, the magistrate, and when he died while they were still children, his son and heir, Charles Noden, attempted to remove them from the colony of Virginia in an effort to keep them slaves all of their lives. When his intentions came to the attention of the court the magistrates issued a writ to stop him, and when he prepared to defy the writ they remanded him to jail. To get out of jail he promised to remain in Virginia and treat his servants as the law required. The first part of his promise he honored but the last part he did not. The Burdettes were forced to sue individually to gain their freedom when they reached the age of thirty-one. These six suits took days of the court's time.

In some instances mulatto slaves claimed that their mothers were white and their fathers were Negroes, in efforts to gain their freedom when they reached the age of thirty-one, when actually their mothers were Negroes and their fathers were white, and they were not entitled to be set free under the law. How many mulattoes got by with this is not known, but one, at least, was exposed and lost his suit. He was Harry Ralls, who sued his mistress, the widow of John Stevens, in 1770. He lost because of the testimony of Sarah Mullins which is recorded in detail in the Order Book of the Caroline Court for 1770 at page 244. This testimony reads, "the Deposition of Mariah Mullins, aged fifty-seven, deponeth and saith, that sometimes in the spring of the year thirty-nine, the granney that attended the delivery of a woman in the neighborhood came to my house. I asked where she came from. She answered that she came from Mr. John Stevens where she had delivered Beck of a son and that it was the whitest child that she had ever seen to have so dark a mother, and that she was sure that it was a white man's child. Sometimes after that being heavy with child I was desirous of drinking some new cider, and being told by my husband, John Mullins, that they were beating cider at Mr. Stevens, I went there to get some and saw Beck with this man Harry, which was then a small child, I well remember them to be the same."

A more complicated case was the status of a child born out of wedlock to a mulatto woman, the daughter of a white mother and Negro father, while she was still in bondage and before she reached the age of thirty-one. The Caroline Court settled this question when the father of the child was white in the cases of Ceasar, Romulus, Frank, Charlotte and Hannah Mann. The Manns were the children of John Sutton, and his mistress, Sarah Mann, a mulatto, whom he held as a bond-servant until she reached the age of thirty-one. As Sarah's term of service neared the end she claimed that her master must also liberate her children, when he set her free. But Sutton, who did not wish to give his mistress up, insisted that the law allowed him to keep the children as slaves, in hopes that if he kept them, that she would also remain. But instead of agreeing Sarah appealed to the court, and the magistrates ruled in her favor. This, however, did not end her troubles. Sutton threatened to ship the children to the Indians and transport her from the colony immediately before her term of service expired. In the end each of the Manns, the mother as well as the children, had to sue for their freedom. They all won. The Caroline Court never passed on a case when the father of the children of mulatto woman in service until she was thirty-one, was a Negro.

The unusual status of mulattoes born of white mothers made some of them restless. William Baker, the son of Sussannah Baker, escaped from his master, John Billops, so many times, and behaved so badly, that Billops set him free before he reached the age of thirty-one to get rid of him. Robert Baker, another mulatto son of Sussannah, tried the same tactics but did not fare so well. His master, Charles Sterns, set him free in 1769, ahead of time, because he was incorrigible. But this consideration failed to cure him of his restlessness and law-breaking. He continued a career of minor crime and suffered numerous whippings for punishment until 1778 when he joined David, a Negro slave of James Bowie, Jr., and broke into the merchantile establishment of Patrick Rourke in Port Royal and carried away goods to the value of $800. The pair was captured and while thirty-nine lashes at the whipping-post was the most severe sentence the court was able to impose on the slave, David, the magistrates ordered Baker whipped and sold into bondage for seven years and his earnings paid to Rourke as restitution for the loss.

Fortunately all of the mulattoes were not like the Bakers. Many were well behaved during their period of servitude and settled down to become trustworthy residents after their liberation. The best known of these was John Chambers of St. Mary's Parish. Already a free man in 1775, he assisted in the capture of Will, slave of Francis Thornton's estate, after this slave broke into the slave quarters of John Thornton.

OTHER RACES

In 1750 an East Indian jumped ship in Port Royal and fled into the interior. He sired several children before he was captured the next year by William Mathews, and deported from the colony. As a result of this episode there is a trace of East Indian blood in the veins of numerous descendants of old time Caroline residents.

THE OFFICE HOLDERS

Caroline office holders during the colonial period fell into these classes; officers elected by the freeholders, officers appointed by the crown and officers appointed by the court.

a. *Elected Officers*

The crown sanctioned the election of only one class of officers; Burgesses to represent the freeholders in the lower house of the General Assembly of the county. There were two Burgesses from each county, regardless of the county's area and population. Caroline's Burgesses are listed below. The main issues of the principal campaigns are recorded in the main text of this history.

1729-33	Richard Buckner and John Martin.
1733-35	John Martin. One seat vacant.
1735-38	Robert Fleming and Johnathan Gibson.
1738-41	Johnathan Gibson and John Martin.
1741-52	John Baylor and Lundsford Lomax, Sr.
1752-56	Lundsford Lomax, Sr. and Edmund Pendleton.
1756-66	Edmund Pendleton and John Baylor.
1766-69	Edmund Pendleton and Walker Taliaferro.
1769-70	Edmund Pendleton and Francis Coleman.
1770-73	Edmund Pendleton and Walker Taliaferro.
1773-76	Edmund Pendleton and James Taylor.

After the Declaration of Independence both houses of the General Assembly were elective. Caroline continued to elect two members to the lower house (the House of Delegates), and jointly with Hanover elected one member to the upper house (the Senate).

Members of the House of Delegates:

1776-77	Edmund Pendleton and James Taylor.
1777-78	Edmund Pendleton and Thomas Lowry.
1778-79	Thomas Lowry and Thomas Lomax.
1779-80	Thomas Lomax and John Taylor.
1780-81	John Taylor and Thomas Lowry.

Senator of the district composed of Caroline and **Hanover**:

1776-77	Thomas Lomax of Caroline.
1777-81	James Taylor of Caroline.

During the period immediately preceding the Revolution there were numerous conventions with representatives from all counties in the colony. These representatives were always the counties' duly elected representatives in the House of Burgesses unless there were extenuating circumstances. Extenuating services only applied to Caroline once. That was when Burgess Edmund Pendleton was absent in attendance of the Continental Congress in Philadelphia. On this occasion the Caroline Committee of Public Safety, not the freeholders, chose William Woodford to sit in Pendleton's place in the Virginia Convention (1775).

The only local officers elected in Caroline County prior to the end of the Revolution were the members of the Committee of Safety, and these men were members of a de facto and not a de jure government. There were three elctions of committeemen by the freeholders. One of these, the second, was declared illegal by the Virginia Convention and the third election took its place. The table below shows the three committees and the number of votes each successful candidate received.

The first election held Nov. 10, 1774. Number of votes not given, only the ranking of the members in the voting.

Edmund Pendleton	1	George Baylor	11
James Taylor	2	John Tennant	12
Walker Taliaferro	3	John Minor	13
William Nelson	4	Thomas Lowry	14
James Upshaw	5	Benjamin Hubbard	15
Anthony Thornton	6	John Jones	16
George Taylor	7	George Guy	17
William Woodford	8	Samuel Hawes	18
Richard Johnston	9	John Armistead	19
Thomas Lomax	10	Edmund Pendleton, Jr.	20

The second election. Held Nov. 9, 1775 (illegal). Number of votes shown.

Samuel Hawes	185
John Tennant	176
James Taylor	166
Richard Johnston	163
Anthony Thornton	161

The third election. Held Feb. 1, 1776. Number of votes shown.

Richard Johnston	233
John Tennant	227
James Taylor	225
Thomas Lowry	224
Samuel Hawes	220

(The second election—cont.)			*(The third election—cont.)*		
William Boulware	. . .	159	James Upshaw	. . . .	208
Thomas Lowry	. . . .	156	Thomas Lomax	. . . .	196
James Upshaw	. . . .	150	William Boulware	. . .	186
John Jones	. . . . .	146	Anthony Thornton	. . .	177
Thomas Lomax	. . . .	122	John Jones	. . . . .	165
William Nelson	. . . .	115	John Armistead	. . . .	134
Walker Taliaferro	. . .	115	Edmund Pendleton, Jr.	.	131
Edmund Pendleton, Jr.	. .	108	Walker Taliaferro	. . .	121
Benjamin Hubbard	. . .	104	John Pickett	. . . . .	118
John Minor	. . . . .	104	John Minor	. . . . .	115
Benjamin Tompkins	. . .	101	John Catlett	. . . . .	114
George Taylor	. . . .	94	George Taylor	. . . .	104
John Pickett	. . . .	90	Abner Waugh	. . . .	102
Robert Mickleberry	. . .	88	Michael Yates	. . . .	100
John Armistead	. . . .	81	Robert Mickleberry	. . .	100
Michael Yates	. . . .	80	Benjamin Hubbard	. . .	89

Under the Committee of Safety the Virginia Convention divided the colony into defense regions. James Taylor, George Taylor and Anthony Thornton represented Caroline on the first regional committee, and James Taylor, George Taylor and Walker Taliaferro on the second.

b. *Officers Appointed by the Crown*

Officers appointed by the crown included magistrates, sheriff, clerk of court, crown attorney, surveyor and coroners. After the Declaration of Independence the Commonwealth retained these appointive powers through the Revolution although they were far from democratic.

1. MAGISTRATES

The magistrates were the most influential men in the county. Their powers and duties are set forth elsewhere in this history (see Index). The table below lists the men who served Caroline County as magistrates from 1728-81, with the dates of their appointment. For the end of their terms consult table of administrations of estates and main body of this history through Index. They all served until they died unless it is specifically stated that they quit, resigned, left the county or were removed from office.

The founding fathers:

William Woodford I (1728)—great planter.
John Lomax (1728)—great planter.
Thomas Carr (1728)—great planter.
Richard Buckner I (1728)—planter and Burgess.
John Martin (1728)—Burgess, adventurer—left county.
Thomas Catlett I (1728)—great planter.
Francis Thornton (1728)—great planter—resigned.
John Battaile (1728)—great planter—tobacco inspector.
Ambroise Madison (1728)—great planter.
Francis Conway (1728)—proprietor of chartered tobacco warehouse.
John Catlett (1728)—great planter.
John Taliaferro I (1728)—great planter.
John Sutton (1728)—homesteader and tavern-keeper.
Robert Woolfolk (1728)—great planter—quit court in a huff.
Lundsford Lomax, Sr. (1728)—great planter—resigned because of debts.
Walter Chiles (1728)—small planter.
Thomas Rucker (1728)—homesteader—removed because of opposition
    to tobacco laws.
Richard Mauldin (1728)—trader—removed because of opposition to
    tobacco laws.

Other magistrates appointed by Sir William Gooch:

John Micou (1732)—great planter.
William Taliaferro (1732)—great planter—died in office.
Robert Fleming (1732)—small planter—Burgess—died in office.
John Taylor I (1732)—great planter—died in office.
John Scott (1734)—schoolmaster—recommended but never appointed.
Robert Farish (1734)—great planter—carpenter—died in office.
Thomas Buckner I (1734)—great planter—miller—died in office.
George Goodloe (1734)—homesteader—died in office.
John Wyatt (1734)—great planter—died in office.
Lawrence Battaile (1734)—great planter—died in office.
Nicholas Battaile (1734)—great planter—died in office.
Head Lynch (1734)—adventurer—king's favorite—died in office.
John Scott (1734)—appointed but never qualified.
Richard Taliaferro (1734)—great planter—promoter—died in office.
George Hoomes (1735)—great planter—died in office.
James Taylor I (1735)—great planter—died in office.
Johnathan Gibson (1735)—tobacco warehouse—Burgess—quit when
    defeated for Burgess.
John Thornton (1736) great planter—resigned.
John Baylor (1740)—great planter—Burgess—frequent resignations—
    but served a part of the time, at least until his death.

Richard Buckner II (1740)—great planter—died in office.
Arch Macphearson (1740-54)—great planter—died in office—a Thornton in law, and held Thornton seat from upper Drysdale.
John Madison (1740)—great planter—migrated from Caroline.
William Carr (1740)—great planter—refused to continue to serve.
Hugh Noden (1740)—physician and planter—died in office.
John Taliaferro II (1740)—great planter—died in office.
Thomas Johnston (1743)—planter and tavern-keeper—resigned when short in accounts as sheriff.
Thomas Wild (1743)—tavern-keeper—merchant—died in office.

Magistrates appointed by Robert Dinwiddie:

Edmund Pendleton (1751)—lawyer—resigned because of other public duties.
Edward Dixon (1751)—merchant—refused to take oath of allegiance to George III.
Robert Gilchrist (1751*)—merchant—left off the court by Botetourt but returned by Dunmore.
Peter Copeland (1751)—merchant—migrated from Caroline.
Waller Chiles (1751)—Quaker—planter—quit court during French and Indian War because Quakers opposed war.
Joseph Hoomes (1751)—great planter—died in office.
Rice Curtis (1743)—great planter—moved to Spotsylvania—became Burgess from that county.
Francis Taylor (1753)—great planter—left Caroline.
James Jameson (1753)—planter—tobacco inspector—died in office.
Harry Beverley (1753)—great planter—promoter—died in office.
Edmound Taylor (1754)—planter and trader—left Caroline.
Anthony Thornton I (1754)—resigned after Declaration of Independence—great planter.
Benjamin Hubbard (1754)—trader—resigned after he insulted other magistrates—refused to swear allegiance to George III.
William Tyler (1757)—great planter—resigned because of age.

Magistrates appointed by Sir Francis Fauquier:

Benjamin Robinson, Jr. (1758)—great planter—lawyer—died in office.
Phillip Taylor (1758)—great planter—trader—left county.
William Parker (1758)—small planter—tavern-keeper—died in office.
James Taylor, Jr. (1758*)—great planter—Burgess—surveyor.
John Sutton II (1758)—great planter—forced from court because of conduct with mulattoes.
Christopher Tompkins (1758)—small planter—recommended but not appointed.
William Boulware (1758—lawyer—recommended but not appointed.

Robert Taliaferro (1758)—great planter—died in office.
John Boutwell (1758)—planter and tobacco inspector—died in office.
Joseph Robinson (1761)—lawyer—died in office.
John Taylor II (1761)—planter—trader—left Caroline.
John Baynham (1761)—physician—died in office.
Gabriel Throckmorton (1761)—small planter—left Caroline.
Lawrence Taliaferro (1761)—great planter—resigned.
Jeremiah Rawlings (1761)—small planter—resigned in protest of the persecution of dissenters.
Lundsford Lomax, Jr. (1761)—great planter—died in office.
Walker Taliaferro (1764*)—great planter—Burgess.
James Miller (1764)—merchant—Tory—refused to take oath of allegiance to the Commonwealth.
William Woodford II (1764)—soldier—resigned because of active duty in Revolution.
John Buckner (1764*)—great planter.
William Buckner, Jr. (1764*)—tavern-keeper and merchant.
Thomas Lowry (1764*)—small planter.
George Taylor (1765)—trader—planter—resigned in protest of persecution of dissenters and tax laws.
John Armistead (1765*)—great planter.
Samuel Hawes (1765*)—great planter.
Thomas Slaughter (1765)—small planter—resigned in protest of tax laws.
William Jones (1765)—small planter—resigned in protest of tax laws.

Magistrates appointed by Lord Botetourt:

James Upshaw (1768*)—great planter.
John Minor (1769)—great planter—resigned.
Henry Armistead (1770)—great planter—left Caroline.
William Harrison (1772)—great planter—refused to take the oath of allegiance to the Commonwealth.
Roger Quarles (1772*)—great planter and soldier.
George Guy (1772*)—lawyer.
Anthony New (1772*)—soldier—great planter—chair-maker.
Gawin Corbin (1772*)—great planter.

Magistrates appointed by Patrick Henry:

John Tennant (1776*)—physician.
Anthony Thornton II (1776*)—soldier—great planter.
John Hoomes (1776*)—great planter.
John Page, Jr. (1776)—resigned.
Richard Johnston (1776)—died.
Thomas Lomax (1776*)—lawyer and great planter.
Samuel Temple (1776*)—planter.

Magistrates appointed by Thomas Jefferson:

Mungo Roy (1780*)—planter.
Vivian Minor (1780*)—great planter.
Richard Buckner III (1781)—great planter.
John Washington (1780*)—great planter.
John Garlick (1780*)—trader and planter.
David Jameson (1780*)—planter.

*Served through the Revolution and after.

Comment. The patentees of crown grants in excess of 1,000 acres and their descendants controlled the Caroline Court through the colonial period and Governors Henry and Jefferson made no attempt to break their hold during the Revolution. The county was divided into from nine to twelve precincts with two magistrates from each precinct, and some of these precincts practically became fiefs of certain families. The Lomaxes supplied one and sometimes both of the magistrates in the precinct of St. Mary's adjacent to the Essex line. The Thorntons and the Buckners and their in-laws furnished all the magistrates from upper Drysdale. The Carrs and their in-laws the Minors kept one seat almost continuously from a precinct in western St. Margaret's. This control was accomplished with ease since the surviving magistrates made recommendations to the governor to fill vacancies on the court and the governor seldomly ignored their recommendations.

In time three families dominated the Caroline Court. They were the Taylors, Taliaferros and Buckners, who furnished eight, seven and six magistrates, respectively, or over twenty per cent of the total membership and a much larger percentage of the terms of service. They accomplished this by the elimination of certain families from the court when their representative among the magistrates died, and alliances with certain other families, who were not so prolific, and the traders and strong men of the county. The allies were the powerful Baylors, Beverleys, and Corbins, who were too rich to be concerned over local politics, so long as politicians did not interfere with their personal fortunes and habits, and only accepted a seat on the court occasionally, as a civic duty. The Thorntons, Woodfords, Hoomes, Robinsons, Lomaxes, and Carr-Minors, who were all concerned primarily with a small area of the county, the merchants of Port Royal and the strong men, who arose sparodically in St. Margaret's Parish, but who were not strong enough to found a dynasty. The families who were eliminated from the court consisted of the Catletts, the Battailes, the Chiles, the Madisons and the Conways. The Catletts lost their seats because they engaged in a two-decade feud with the Thorntons over the estate of Thomas Catlett, who married Martha Thornton. Thomas Catlett tried to deed all his interest in the Catlett grants in the Goldenvale to his brothers and sisters because he had spent all his time and energy in developing his residence, Locust Hill, in St. Margaret's Parish, which was originally his wife's property, and which he believed was enough for her and his heirs after his death. Martha Thornton Catlett knew his intentions and refused to join in any of the conveyances. After his death she sued for her dower in each tract her husband had sold. Tempers became so aroused during the extended litigation that the Thorntons and their allies succeeded in eliminating the Catletts from the court. The Battailes incurred the ire of William Woodford of Windsor over tobacco inspections and he succeeded in blocking the appointments of other members of the family to the court after their incumbent representatives died. The Chiles turned Quaker, and refused to serve after the Quakers decided to disapprove of the French and Indian War. The Madisons and Conways lost their seats because of the lack of suitable candidates in their families.

These were unpleasantries among the ruling families. The Taliaferros were particularly quarrelsome. In the 1740's they engaged in a family spat that rocked the county. John Taliaferro I, John Taliaferro II, and William Taliaferro sued Richard Taliaferro. They were all magistrates and their disputes became so unpleasant that other magistrates stayed away from the court. At last the suit was decided by a minimum quorum of five. John, John Jr. and William voted together and won the case.

Only twice were the ruling families upset. Johnathan Gibson

won a seat in the House of Burgesses over their opposition in 1735 and 1736, and Francis Coleman won in spite of them in 1769. But these victories in no sense changed local rule because the freeholders were unable to vote for magistrates.

The Juries. Juries formed the most effective curb on the magistrates for the freeholders without political influence. All free persons in accord with the tenets of English common law had a right to demand to be tried by a jury of their peers. The Caroline Court tried to control the juries through control of the selection of freeholders for jury service. But it was only partially successful in this attempt. Caroline juries at times refused to convict tax evaders, turned poor debtors out of prison and assessed fines of only a penny, or a pound of tobacco when directed to bring in a verdict against the accused by the court.

Caroline juries are recorded in the Order Books from 1732 to 1745. They reveal the freeholders in whom the magistrates had confidence, and the degree of this confidence by the number of times each juror served. The names of these jurors are listed below.

Caroline Jurors, 1732-45, with number of panels on which they served are opposite their names are listed below.

Anthony Arnold	10	William Burdette	6
Lawrence Anderson	3	Thomas Blassingame	11
William Allcock	1	Henry Blassingame	5
		Thomas Bullard	4
John Buckner	1*	Jacob Burruss	2
Thomas Buckner	1*	Mark Boulware	3
John Baylor	1*	Richard Booker	3
John Bell	6	Mathew Brooks	1
Henry Bell	4	John Bradley	8
Thomas Bankes	10	Henry Burk	9
Thomas Burch	5	William Blanton	3
William Brown	14	Elias Blackburn	2
Robert Baber	12	Thomas Burk	1
Edward Baber	1	Charles Beazley	4
Spencer Baber	2	John Beazley	10
Duncan Bohannon	7	Bennett Beazley	1
Richard Bradford	2	William Buckley	1

(Caroline Jurors, 1732-45—Cont.)

Richard Billops	3
Francis Bearding	2
William Broughill . . .	4
Timothy Chandler . . .	7
James Collins	12
Thomas Collins	4
Thomas Coleman	1
Richard Coleman	7
James Coleman	2
Daniel Coleman	4
Thomas Carey	1
William Carr	3*
Robert Charlesworth . . .	2
William Chewning . . .	1
Samuel Chapman	4
George Chapman	1
John Carter	4
Matthew Crank	1
William Chase	1
John Clark	1
Peter Claybrook	1
Thomas Croucher	2
William Cammack . . .	1
William Conner	16
George Chapman	1
John Downer	12
Benjamin Downer . . .	2
William Daniels	18
Robert Dudley	3
John Dudley	6
Thomas Dudley	3
William Durrett	11
Richard Durrett	1
Thomas Durrum	3
Richard Devenport . . .	1
James Dismukes	10
John Dyer	10
William Dyer	3
John Davis	1
George Dillard	2
Joseph DeJarnette . . .	1

John Ellis	9
Timothy Ellis	6
Thomas Estis	2
Abraham Estis	6
Phillip Estis	4
Bryon Edmoundson . . .	1
Thomas Emerson	1
George Eastham	5
William Evins	2
Richard Eubank	5
Austin Ellis	3
Thomas Fortune	6
Robert Farish	1†
Thomas Foster	1
Robert Foster	1
James Fortson	1
Thomas Fortson	1
Robert Fortson	1
John Fox	1
Nathaniel Fogg	1
George Goodloe	2†
John Gooch	2
Benjamin Grubbs	5
John Griffin	7
John Garrett	5
John George	8
Richard George	3
Robert George	2
Thomas Guy	1
Charles Goodall	2
John Goodby	2
John Garnett	2
John Glanton	1
Michael Guinney	14
Phillip Herndon	4
James Herndon	10
William Herndon	13
Joseph Herndon	4
Edward Herndon	6
John Herndon	1

(Caroline Jurors, 1732-45—Cont.)

George Holloway	6	John Jeter	1
Charles Holloway	8	Sheerwood James	4
John Holloway	7	Nicholas Jeter	1
Samuel Hawes	4†		
George Hoomes	2*	Robert Kay	3
Benjamin Hoomes	4*		
Joseph Hoomes	2*	Richard Long	7
John Hurt	6	John Long	6
Titius Hurt	1	Gabriel Long	5
Richard Hampton	1	Henry Long	6
William Hampton	1	Reuben Long	2
Henry Hampton	2	Adam Lindsay	1
Robert Hall	1	James Lindsay	11
Thomas Hackett	1	David Lindsay	2
John Hubbard	2	Robert Lyon	5
William Hudson	5	John Latham	6
John Hutchinson	1	William Lawson	7
Henry Honey	1	Thomas Lowry	3
John Honey	3	James Lewis	1
Thadeus Harson	1		
John Hart	1	Joseph Meacham	1
Joseph Harvey	1	William Marshall	20
William Holland	1	James Martin	11
John Holland	1	Zack Martin	1
Anthony Howorth	2	Arch Macphearson	1*
Henry Harris	11	James Micou	1*
Robert Hudleston	1	John May	1
Paul Harrolson	3	James Mason	1
Thomas Hamm	4	William Mason	2
Henry Haynes	2	Samuel Major	4
Hans Hendrick	2	Catlett Mann	1
		Thomas Morris	2
Henry Isbell	2	Robert Mickleberry	5
		William Mickleberry	1
Jacob Johns	11	George Marsh	4
John Johns	5	Thomas Madison	8*
Stephan Johnston	3	Rogert Madison	7*
Johnathan Johnston	4	John Miller	7
William Johnston	1	James Miller	1
John Jones	2	John Morgin	2
James Jones	1	Charles Morgin	3
Robert Jones	7	James Munday	1
James Jameson	2†	William MacGehee	4

(Caroline Jurors, 1732-45—Cont.)

John Madison	1*	Samuel Robinson	1
		Thomas Rucker	2‡
John Norment	1	Thomas Royston	1
Samuel Norment	4	Joseph Rennolds	3
Joseph Norment	1	John Rogers	3
John Nichols	3	George Rogers	1
Thomas Normon	1	James Riddle	5
James Neville	1	Benjamin Rowe	1
John Newton	3	William Rowe	9
		Jeremiah Rawlings	1†
Nicholas Oliver	3	John Ralls	3
William Oliver	2	Thomas Roy	5
Peter Oliver	1	Richard Roy	1
John Owins	1	Mungo Roy	1
William Ogelbie	2	Henry Rains	3
		Edward Rouse	6
John Plant	10	Ralph Richards	1
James Powell	5		
Henry Powell	2	John Sutton II	25*
Honorous Powell	4	William Sutton	3
William Powell	1	Richards Straughn	15
Robert Powell	2	John Samuel	1
William Pemberton	2	James Samuel	3
John Penn	3	Thomas Samuel	1
James Pendleton	4	John Sneed	4
Benjamin Poe	1	Joseph Stevens	2
John Partloe	1	James Stevens	13
William Poe	1	John Stevens	2
Thomas Pickett	1	William Stone	4
William Pickett	3	Nicholas Stone	1
John Pickett	7	Eusabious Stone	1
Michael Parrott	1	Thomas Schooler	1
Mathew Peatross	1	William Stapleton	1
Thomas Peatross	2	John Scott	3
John Pierson	1	Robert Stuart	4
Thomas Pittman	2	John Stuart	1
Moses Pittman	1	William Southworth	7
Jeremiah Pierce	2	Thomas Shipp	8
		David Stern	3
Roger Quarles	7†	Francis Stern	3
		Phillip Sanders	2
Thomas Richerson	1	John Sanders	8
John Robinson	5	Joseph Sanders	1

(Caroline Jurors, 1732-45—Cont.)

Robert Smith	6	Thomas Vaughan	1
James Sullinger	4		
Thomas Streasherley . . .	1	William Willer	1
Joseph Sanderson	2	David Woodruff	1
Robert Stanfield	2	Henry Woodcock	6
		John Wright	1
William Terrell	10	William Watkins	5
Henry Terrell	2	Edward Watkins	1
John Terrell	2	Thomas White	12
James Terrell	9	Robert Williamson . . .	4
John Thomas	5	Rice Williams	8
Edward Tinsley	1	Nicholas Ware	12
William Tinsley	1	Joseph Woolfolk	3†
David Tinsley	2	John Woolfolk	3†
Richard Tankersley . . .	5	Robert Woolfolk	1†
William Taylor	1*	William Wafford	3
Benjamin Tompkins . . .	1	Benjamin Wood	12
Daniel Tompkins	2	Josiah Wood	1
Robert Tompkins	12	Henry Wood	1
Daniel Triggs	3	Charles Walden	3
James Trice	5	William Wyatt	2†
John Tennant	1†	Benjamin Watts	1
George Todd	1	Thomas Walker	6
John Taliaferro	1*	George Wilson	1
Kemp Taliaferro	3*	George Wiley	1
Richard Taliaferro . . .	1*	John Wiley	2
Robert Taliaferro	7*	Joseph Woodson	1
George Tribble	5	Richard West	1
Oliver Towles	6		
James Turner	1		
John Turner	1	Charles Yarbrough . . .	6
Richard Turner	1	William Yarbrough . . .	6
George Tilley	3	Griggs Yarbrough . . .	2
Francis Thornton	1*	Charles Yarbrough . . .	3
Owin Thomas	3	James Young	1

---

*Jurors from families of the magistrate caste. Members of the ruling families believed it beneath their dignity to serve on juries and only served under extenuating circumstances. No Battaile, Woodford, Corbin, Conway, Beverley or Catlett served on a Caroline jury during colonial times. A Baylor, a Thornton and a Taylor served only once, and a Buckner only twice. The Taliaferros were the only exception. Members of this family served on twelve panels. The chances are that they were willing to sacrifice their dignity to influence cases in which they were interested.

†Advanced to magistrate rank at a latter date; or members of a family which furnished only one magistrate.

‡Served after being removed as magistrate, or resigned from the court.

Grand Jurors, 1746-47. The grand juries for 1746 and
1747 are recorded in the Order Books. They are listed here
because they indicate that new families were finding favor with
the court.

GRAND JURORS FOR 1746: Robert George, James Jameson, William
Conner, Jacob Johns, Joseph Meacham, James Terrell (2), Richard
Murray,* William Daniels (2), James Martin (2), James Dismukes,
Thomas Madison, Peter Holland, John Bowie,* John Godby, Elias
Blackburn, Nicholas Ware, Samuel Norment, John George (2), John
Downer, William Lawson, John Miller, John Pickett, Richard George,
James Lindsay, Timothy Chandler, David Tinsley, Robert Lowry,
Joseph Woolfolk, Thomas Samuel, Thomas Dudley, Robert Mickle-
berry, Charles Holloway, Thomas Bankes, Peyton Smith, Thomas
Coghill.*

FIRST GRAND JURY FOR 1747: John Griffin, Nicholas Ware, Charles
Holloway, John Satterwhite,* John Sneed, Peyton Smith, Edward
Ware, William Hampton, Robert Stuart, Richard Long, Jr., Robert
Coleman, John Bradley. (Grand juries consisted of one juror from
each precinct.)

---

*First representative of a family to serve on a Caroline jury.

NOTE: The juries which rendered verdicts in crucial cases are recorded in
the chronological section of this history—see Index.

2. THE SHERIFF

The sheriff was the chief executive of a county. He presided
over the court, enforced the laws and collected the taxes. He
was appointed by the governor from a panel of three magistrates recommended by the court for a term of a year. He was
ineligible for immediate reappointment but his term often ran
over due to the indifference of governors. Thomas Buckner
served as sheriff of Caroline for three years (1747-50), and
William Taliaferro threatened to quit and leave the county
without a sheriff unless the governor named his successor at
once (1740). The sheriff's pay was the best a public official
received in the county. It was based on a percentage of the
tobacco collected as taxes, varying with the distance of the
county from tidewater since the sheriff had the expense of
transporting the tax tobacco to a wharf and loading it on a
ship bound for Britain. The percentage for Caroline was ten
per cent.

Deputies did most of the work while the sheriff drew most of the pay. These assistants were trained public officials and usually held on serving under many sheriffs. The sheriffs of Caroline and their chief deputies follow:

Year	Sheriff	Deputies
1729	William Woodford	Benjamin Rennolds & William Conner.
1731	John Taliaferro	Benjamin Rennolds & William Burdette.
1732	Robert Fleming	Benjamin Rennolds & William Burdette.
1734	Walter Chiles	Benjamin Rennolds & William Burdette.
1735	Robert Farish	Benjamin Rennolds & William Burdette.
1737	George Goodloe	William Boulware, George Todd & Robert Dudley.
1738	Head Lynch	William Boulware, George Todd & Robert Dudley.
1740	William Taliaferro	William Boulware, George Todd & Robert Dudley.
1741	Lawrence Battaile	William Boulware & George Todd.
1742	John Micou	William Boulware & George Todd.
1743	John Taylor I	William Boulware & George Todd.
1744	George Hoomes	William Boulware & George Todd.
1745	Robert Taliaferro	William Boulware & George Todd.
1747	Thomas Buckner	William Boulware, George Todd, Richard Blanton & Robert Dudley.
1750	James Taylor	William Boulware, Edmound Taylor & Phillip Taylor.
1751	George Hoomes	William Boulware & William Harrison.
1753	Richard Buckner	William Boulware & William Harrison.
1755	Thomas Johnston	James Taylor, the younger, & John Burke.
1757	Edward Dixon	William Harrison & John Miller, Jr.
1758	Phillip Taylor	John Burke & Andrew Harrison.
1759	Robert Gilchrist	William Harrison & John Miller, Jr.
1760	John Sutton	William Harrison, John Miller, Jr., William Sutton, the son of John Sutton.
1762	Francis Taylor, Jr.	William Harrison & John Miller, Jr.
1763	John Sutton	William Harrison & John Miller, Jr.
1764	Anthony Thornton	William Harrison & John Miller, Jr., James Harrison, Andrew Harrison & Thomas Pollard.
1765	William Goode	John Miller, Jr. & Andrew Harrison.
1767	William Tyler	John Miller, Jr. & Andrew Harrison.
1769	James Taylor, Jr.	Andrew Harrison, Henry Lyne, William Harrison, Thomas Ship & Joseph Dickinson.

Year	Sheriff	Deputies
1773	Walker Taliaferro	George Richerson, Henry Lyne, Thomas Ship.
1775	John Buckner	George Richerson, Henry Lyne, Thomas Ship.
1778	Thomas Lowry	George Richerson & Thomas Ship.
1780	John Armistead	George Richerson & Thomas Ship.

3. THE COUNTY CLERK

Benjamin Robinson served as clerk of the Caroline Court from the date of the setting up of the county until his death in 1762 (34 years). He was followed by his son, Joseph Robinson. Governor Fauquier ousted Joseph Robinson in 1763 and gave the position to Robert Armistead, a crown favorite, with Catesby Woodford, another crown favorite, as first deputy, and John Timberlake, who was not a crown favorite, as second deputy to do the work. Robert Armistead died in 1764 and Joseph Robinson took over the clerkship again on a temporary appointment. But he did not last long, because he opposed John Baylor in the election for Burgess in 1765, and when Baylor lost he persuaded the governor to remove Robinson and make Thomas Nelson, Jr., the son of the president of the Council, and an outsider, clerk of Caroline, with his brother, William Nelson, another outsider, as deputy. The Nelsons held the position through the Revolution, although they were unpopular in the county.

4. THE CROWN ATTORNEY

William Robinson was the first crown (prosecuting) attorney for Caroline. He held this office from the organization of the county until Governor Gooch removed him for refusing to prosecute the supporters of Johnathan Gibson accused of misconduct in the campaign for Burgess between Gibson and John Martin in 1735. Benjamin Walker followed Robinson as crown attorney. His tenure lasted until he died in 1740, when Zachery Lewis took over and held on until the Declaration of Independence. Lewis moved his residence from Caroline County in the early 1760's but continued as crown attorney. Charles

Robinson served as deputy in residence, until he grew tired of doing all the work and getting only deputy's pay. When he quit Edmund Pendleton, Jr. took the position under the same arrangement. After the Declaration of Independence Pendleton Jr. refused to serve unless he was made prosecuting, now Commonwealth, attorney in name as well as in fact. William Boulware acted in this emergency, and until Governor Jefferson forced Lewis to resign and gave the job to Pendleton Jr.

5. THE CORONER

Robert Farish was the first Caroline coroner of record. He was acting in 1741. After Farish, Thomas Buckner 1743, William Taliaferro and George Hoomes 1749, Peter Copeland 1754, and Robert Gilchrist and Francis Taylor 1757, held this position. Around 1760 the Caroline Court apparently decided that a physician, rather than a layman, was the proper person to view a corpse and determine the cause of death, because that year it paid Dr. George Todd 442 pounds of tobacco for viewing the body of a dead Negro. After this date Caroline had other coroners but the doctors did the work.

6. THE SURVEYOR

James Taylor, Sr. was the first surveyor for Caroline's St. Mary's and Drysdale parishes, and Thomas Carr, the first surveyor for St. Margaret's, a position he held along with the position of surveyor for St. Martin's Parish in Hanover. Carr, however, soon resigned because of old age and Taylor took over as surveyor for the whole county. Taylor lasted until 1744 when William Woodford, John Taliaferro and John Battaile accused him of making surveys favorable to himself and persuaded the masters of William and Mary College to remove him from office. After this removal Robert Brooke, of Essex, became surveyor of Essex and Caroline. Brooke managed to keep this troublesome post until another great dispute over surveys broke out in 1763 and the Caroline Court ordered him to turn his books in and petitioned William and Mary for a new surveyor. The College granted this request and named James Taylor, Jr.

James Taylor, Jr. held the position through the Revolution, and it is amazing that he had time to take care of its duties along with all of his other obligations, since he was at the same time a magistrate, and sometimes sheriff, Burgess, chairman of the Committee of Safety, and delegate to numerous colony and Commonwealth conventions. He did have a deputy, Edward Vaughter, and there were several members of his own family, as well as the Brooks and their apprentices, on whom he was able to call for assistance.

In recent years the first survey book of Caroline County was found in the clerk's office of Campbell County, Kentucky, where presumably it was taken by members of the Taylor family, who migrated from Caroline to Kentucky. A photostatic copy of this book is in the clerk's office of the Circuit Court of Caroline County.

c. Officers Appointed by the Court

Road supervisors, constables and tithetakers were the chief officers appointed by the county court.

1. ROAD WORKERS

All tithable persons, free and slave, were subject to call for work on public roads, and all freeholders had to take turns supervising the construction and maintenance of the public roads adjacent to their property. The latter was a thankless task. Fully a fourth of the road supervisors were fined by the court for failing to do their duty. This failure was seldomly the supervisor's fault. It was often impossible to build and keep up roads on Caroline's muddy and marshy terrain with the materials and tools available.

To list the road supervisors is to list the freeholders of the county. The author does not attempt to name them here. He merely lists the supervisors for 1733, the first complete year of record, as an example.

ROAD SUPERVISORS FOR 1733: John Beazley, Edward Tinsley, Richard Straughn, Francis Stern, Charles Goodall, Silvanus Sanders, James Trice, Rise Williams, Michael Guinney, John Stevens, James Pendleton, William Wafford, John Taylor, Robert Tompkins, John Dudley, Robert

Williamson, James Meadors, George Tribble, Jacob Burruss, Robert Taliaferro, David Terrell, John Anderson, Robert Smith, James Turner, John Catlett, David Murray, Henry Burke, Charles Beazley, Kemp Taliaferro, Richard Buckner, William Marshall, John Hubbard, John Hay, George Goodloe and Henry Isbell.

Shipley Broaddus' gang to maintain a road in lower Drysdale Parish for 1765 was typical. Besides the supervisor it consisted of John Chennault, Ralph Farmer, Thomas Samuels, Richard Beazley, David Landrum, William, Thomas and Abel Cook and "their people."

2. THE CONSTABLES

The court named a constable for each precinct to serve the magistrates in residence as baliff, to enforce the law and to maintain order. This office was without a fixed term. Constables served until they resigned, moved away, died or were removed by the court. It was a position of high fatalities. Most Caroline constables either resigned or were removed from office.

Caroline Constables (1732-76):

	Date Appointed		Date Appointed
William Carr	1732*	Daniel Triplett	1737
Henry Rains	1732†	William Harrison	1737
Joseph Rennolds	1732‡	Richard Billops	1737‡ & 1745
Sheerwood James	1732*	Henry Isbell	1737
Robert Baber	1732† & 1738	John Sanders	1737
John Dudley	1732 & 1741	Peter Claybrook	1737
John Hurt	1732 & 1751	John Wiley	1737
William Wafford	1732	Robert Jones	1737‡
Zach Martin	1734†	William Herndon	1737 & 1745
Charles Walden	1735†	Robert George	1739‡
Benjamin Powell	1735	Timothy Ellis	1739‡
Charles Goodall	1737‡	Timothy Ellis	1739‡
Thomas Blassingame	1737‡	William Evins	1739‡
Henry Haynes	1737†	John Dyer	1740‡
William Oliver	1737†	Charles Beazley	1740‡ & 1742
Robert Dudley	1737 & 1751	John Kerchevall	1740‡
John Smith	1737	Richard Long	1740‡
Francis Bearding	1737	Charles Binion	1740‡

Date Appointed   *Date Appointed*

Reuben Long .	1740‡ & 1746	James Turner 1752
John Penn, Jr. . . . . 1740‡		James Young 1753
Thomas Buckner . . . 1741*		James Pemberton . . . 1755
Samuel Buckner . . . 1741*		Richard Young . . . 1756
Thomas Jones 1741		Edward Brassfield . . . 1756
John Brown 1741		Francis Long 1757
Joseph Stevens . . . 1741		Daniel Barksdale . . 1757
Nicholas Ware 1741		Thomas Pittman . . . 1757
James Allen 1741		Stephen Lowe 1757
John Dillard 1741		John Penn II 1758
Phillip Estis 1741		Richard Fortune . . . 1758
John Mitchell 1741		Samuel Norment . . . 1758
John Newton 1742		Jeremiah Pierce . . . 1759
Elias Blackburn . . . 1742		Thomas Watkins . . . 1759
William Daniels . . . 1744		James George . . . 1759
George Tribble 1745		William Hewlett . . . 1759
William Durrett . . . 1745		John Scandland . . . 1759
James Lewis 1745		Richard Fortune . . . 1759
Richard Slaughter . . 1745		James Richerson . . . 1760
William Dyer 1745		Charles Byron 1760
Stephen Terry 1747		William Schooler . . . 1760
Joseph Meacham . . . 1747		William Duval 1760
John Townsend . . . 1747		John Harrison 1760
Thomas Burch 1747		Edward Goode 1761
Robert Dawson 1747		William Samuel . . . 1763
Charles Blanton . . . 1749		Benjamin Sneed . . . 1763
Thomas Bankes 1749		Thomas Harris 1765
George Hoomes . . . 1749*		Humphrey Hargrave . . 1765
John Conner 1749		Thomas Samuel . . . 1765
Benjamin Duval . . . 1749		William Motley . . . 1765
Richard Hill 1749		Samuel Sutton 1765
William Goodall . . . 1750		Shipley Broaddus . 1765 & 1769
Ambroise Blackburn . . 1750		Benjamin Vaughan . . 1765
Nicholas Jeter 1750		Joseph Richerson . . . 1767
John Burk 1747		William Mitchell . . 1767
John Miller, Jr. . . . 1751		Thomas Sorrell 1767
Richard Tankersley . . 1751		Peter Bullard 1767
Richard Straughn . . . 1751		Peter Estis 1769
James Samuel 1751		Chillion White 1769
William Foster 1751		Samuel Sale 1770
Robert Mickleberry . . 1751		John Eubank 1770
Moza Hurt 1752		John Harris 1770
Phillip May 1752		Michael Brown Roberts . 1770

	Date Appointed		*Date Appointed*
Phillip Estis	1771	William Hoarde . . .	1775
Samuel Partlow . . .	1772	James Loving	1775
Robert Broaddus . . .	1774	Thomas Samuel . . .	1775
Harvey Stuart	1775	Israel Sneed	1773
Reuben Young	1775	George Major	1773
Elliott Emerson . . .	1775		

*Only five members of the great landlord families were constables, and they held the position in times of stress. The job was not for the aristocrats, and many substantial smaller freeholders did not like it. The enforcement of harsh laws made constables unpopular. There were many resignations and removals after the Gibson-Martin election scandals,† during attempts to enforce the tobacco laws,‡ the persecution of dissenters and after the passage of tax acts. Few constables served for more than three years.

The order books record no new appointment of constables after 1775. Therefore, the author presumes that the incumbents after that date held on through the Revolution if there were any constables at all.

3. THE TITHETAKERS

Each spring the court named several of its own number to count the number of persons and wheels on each plantation to be taxed. This tax was a levy on Negro slaves over the age of fifteen, indentured servants and free white males over the age of seventeen, and each set of wheels under a passenger vehicle, in pounds of tobacco. The owner of the plantation on which the person was domiciled or the vehicle was carriaged was responsible for the tax. Since the magistrates rotated the position of tithetaker among themselves to name the men who held this office is merely to repeat the magistrates. But the rate of annual tax and the number of tithables is interesting and that is set out below:

Year	Tax rate in lbs. of tobacco per tithables	No. of tithables	Year	Tax rate in lbs. of tobacco per tithables	No. of tithables
1732	14½	2039	1738	6½	2497
1733	10	2132	1739	9	2540
1734	11¼	2188	1740	6	2649
1735	10½ plus 3⅔	2328	1741	6	2780
1736	11¼	2383	1742	4	2876
1737	6	2486	1743	10	3137

Year	Tax rate in lbs. of tobacco per tithables	No. of tithables	Year	Tax rate in lbs. of tobacco per tithables	No. of tithables
1744	7	3239	1763	9	4244
1745	9	3340	1764	6	4628
1746	Omitted in record		1765	10	4696
1747	8	3351	1766	17	4374
1748	6 plus 9	3632	1767	3	4355
1749	2	3752	1768	9	4455
1750	4	3850	1769	3	4604
1751	8	3832	1770	5	4609
1752	Omitted in record		1771	Omitted in record	
1753	8	3845	1772	8	4597
1754	6	3934	1773	5	4716
1755	6	3723	1774	Omitted in record	
1756	Omitted in record		1775	2	4719
1757	5	3701	1776	5 lbs. tob. or	
1758	5	3937		7½ pence	4697
1759	17	4196	1777	3 lbs. tob. or	
1760	11	4174		6 pence	4706
1761	Tax day changed		1778	16	4622
	from Dec. to Jan.		1779	3 plus 4	4720
1762	9	4274	1780	5	4703

Comment. The number of tithables in Caroline increased each year from 1732, the first year of record, until 1755 when the county was beset by the great drought and the French and Indian War. It got over this setback by 1758 and the number continued to increase through the Revolution, although some years there were intermittent falling offs, caused more by the concealing of tithables than the loss of population.

The counting of the tithes was the only census in colonial times. Between 1732 and 1781 the number for Caroline increased 132%. Assuming that half of the inhabitants were below the tithable age and a fifth were free white women the total population rose from 6,796 to 15,667. This is probably a fair assumption.

Tax evasion was commonplace. The table below list Caroline evaders of record and the penalty imposed by the court.

1742—James White, Moses Pittman and James Hamm—refusing to list tithables—punishment unknown.

1754—John Hart—failed to account for four tithables—2,000 lbs. of tobacco fine.

1762—John Baylor—failed to list chariot for taxation; John Baylor, Mary Buckner, Richard Taliaferro, Richard Buckner, William Buckner, Thomas Buckner, Edward Dixon, Robert Gilchrist, James Miller, James Landrum, John Miller, John Boutwell, Ambroise Hoarde, Ann Taliaferro, Lundsford Lomax, William Micou, Thomas Roy, James Jameson, Lawrence Taliaferro, John Evins, Mary Gillison, Thomas Royston, George Muse, William Allcock, Nicholas Battaile, Sarah Conway, John Thornton, George Catlett, Mary Taliaferro, Rev. Musgrave Dawson, William Parker, William Johnston, Elizabeth Riddle, Thomas Collins, Paul Thilman, Benjamin Catlett, Francis Taylor, John Sutton, John Baynham, Thomas Samuel, Sarah Slaughter, John Elliott Payne, Harry Beverly, Thomas Terry, Duncan Graham, George Guy, Waller Chiles, John Thilman, John Allmond, John Scott, William Taylor, John Clark, Gabriel Throckmorton, Elizabeth Marshall, Benjamin Milward, Joseph Woolfolk, Francis Fleming, William Stevens, George Holloway, Thomas Scott, Seth Thornton, Benjamin Robinson—failed to list chaise for taxation—excused by the court upon the payment of the tax.

1764—Thomas Boothe—failed to list chaise—fined 500 lbs. of tobacco. Robert Mickleberry—concealed two tithes—fined 1,000 lbs. of tobacco.

1765—Mary Taliaferro, John Evins, Thomas Samuel—failed to list chaise for taxation—fined 500 lbs. of tobacco each.
William Parker—failed to list chaise for taxation—excused.
Edward Powers, Gabriel Toombs, John Sullinger—failed to list land for taxation—verdict unknown.

1766—John Harvie—failed to list tithables—already in prison.
William Ellis—failed to list tithables—jury refused to convict.
Sarah Harney, Benjamin Hurt—failed to list land for taxes—excused by court upon listing land and paying penalty.
Robert Tompkins—failed to list one Negro—500 lbs. of tobacco fine.

1768—Rev. Johnathan Boucher, David Stern, Peyton Stern, Thomas Boothe, Benjamin Pruitt, James Chick, Justinian Wells—failed to list chaises for taxation—excused by court upon the payment of taxes and penalties.

1768—John Clark, John Sutton, Harry Beverley, Sarah Battaile, Robert Taliaferro—failed to list chaises for taxation—excused by court after paying taxes and penalties.
Thomas Dudley—concealed one tithe—fined 500 lbs. of tobacco.

1769—Charles Yarbrough, James Yarbrough, James Gatewood, Michael Yates, Richard George—concealed tithes—fined 500 lbs. of tobacco per tithe.

1770—John Penn, James Chick, Gilpin Moody, John Elliott Payne, William Buckner, James Payne, Benjamin Hubbard, Elizabeth Fortune, Benjamin Spicer, James Lankford—concealed tithes—fined 500 lbs. of tobacco per tithe.

1771—Nathaniel Holloway, Long Wharton—failed to list tithables—punishment unknown.

Thomas Scott, Sarah Young, Thomas Pittman, John Sutton, John Montague, John Baynham, Estate of Ann Taylor, Augustine Ellis, Richard Lewis, Thomas Rennolds, William Rennolds —failed to list chaise for taxation—500 lbs. of tobacco fine each.

1772—Richard Woolfolk, John Young, John Smith, John Lucas, Benjamin Hubbard, William Goodall, Elizabeth Fortune, Chitwood Parr—concealed one or more tithes—fined 500 lbs. of tobacco per tithe.

Richard Micou failed to list two chaises—excused by court.

John Armistead—failed to list chaise—excused by court.

Richard Roy, Thomas Royston—failed to list chaise—fined 1,000 lbs. of tobacco.

1773—John Smith—concealed one tithe—fined 500 lbs. of tobacco. Robert Cobb—failed to report six tithes—excused by the court when he put them on the proper list.

Thomas Pittman, James Johnston, Samuel Hargrave—failed to report chaise for taxation—fined 500 lbs. of tobacco.

Benjamin Milward—failed to report chaise for taxation—died before case came to trial.

Rachael Lipscombe, Ruth Dismukes, Elizabeth Woolfolk, Rev. Archabald Dick—failed to list chaise for taxation—excused by the court.

John Armistead—failed to list any tithes—excused by the court.

John Broughill, Joseph Willis, John Nun, Francis Fleming, Elizabeth Fortune, William Smithers, Sr., Andrew Ross—concealed one or more tithes—fined 500 lbs. of tobacco per tithe.

1774—William Smithers, Elizabeth George, Thomas Torrence—concealed one or more tithes—fined 500 lbs. of tobacco.

1778—Capt. James Fletcher, Dolly Alsop, John Scandland—concealed one or more tithes—fined 500 lbs. of tobacco for each tithe.

Levy Free. The court exampted a few persons from the payment of tithes and working on the roads because they were either old or infirm. They are listed below:

1732—Jacob Minter, John Zachery.

1733—John Sizer.

1736—Richard Long, Thomas Hawes.

1738—Laurence Anderson.

1739—Mathew Hamm.

1740—Daniel Tompkins, for road work only.

1744—Bartholomew Ramsey, William Partlow.

1749—Jane Annaway,* the wife of Henry Annaway, William Watson, William Chewning, Thomas Griffin, Richard Proctor.

1752—Samuel Walden.

1753—John Draper.

1755—Lodowick Murray, James Burton, William Burdette, Griffin Jones, Isaac Pierce, Robert Westley.

1756—Robert Dudley.

1758—John Chandler, Benjamin Johnston, Samuel Johnston, William Clatterbuck.

1759—William Davis.

1760—William Pemberton, Francis Huggins, Thomas Bullard, John Hurt, Sr., Benjamin Allen, John Berry, Francis Chandler, John Robinson, Phillip Estis.

1761—Christopher Acuss, John Clatterbuck, John Lucas.

1762—James Boulware, Joshua King, James Ford.

1763—William Coburn.

1764—John MacGehee, the son of Joseph MacGehee, until 21, Thomas Hailey, Johnathan Smith, John Tiller.

1765—William Thornton, Cornelius Chapman, Thomas Brown, Rennolds MacKenny, Francis Hale.

1767—John Curent (?), Henry Mills, William Crawley, Thomas Clayton, Ambroise Jeter, John Davis.

1769—Joseph MacGehee.

1770—Walter Ross.

1771—Nicholas Mullins, John Wallis Summers, John Winterton.

1778—Covington Surles.

1780—Robert Young, William Page.

1781—John Brooks, James Sacrey (Sacra).

---

*Unexplained—a woman should not have been taxed.

THE ARMED FORCES

1. The Militia

Although the crown appointed all local officers it took no chances with a purely civil government. There was an unit of the militia in each county. It was commanded by a county lieutenant, named by the royal governor, and all free white males above the age of eighteen were subject to call for military training and drill. The crown commissioned a group of the county's most prominent residents to assist the county lieutenant in the command of the troops.

a. *The County Lieutenant*

Caroline's County lieutenants with the exact terms of their service are hard to determine from the records. The *Journal* of the Governor's Council, however, conclusively proves that Henry Armistead was the first man to hold this position and the chances are that he held it until his death in 1738.

After Armistead's death there is confusion. Records in the archives of State Library shed little light and the Caroline Order Books indicated that William Woodford of Windsor and John Baylor of New Market served intermittently in this capacity until Rice Curtis took over in 1756. Curtis only held the position a short time before he moved to Spotsylvania and George Muse became county lieutenant of Caroline upon his return from the French and Indian War. He died in 1765 and the post passed to Anthony Thornton, who held it until he retired on account of old age in 1774. Upon Thornton's retirement the crown vested command of the Caroline military unit in James Taylor, Jr. The press of other duties forced Taylor to resign in 1775, and Walker Taliaferro succeeded him. Taliaferro was the last Caroline County lieutenant under the royal government and the first under the Commonwealth. He kept the post until after the end of the Revolution.

b. *Officers of the Militia*

The qualifications of all officers in the militia on their commissions are recorded in the Order Books of the Caroline court. Commissions prior to May 11, 1732 are missing. But after that date they are complete. They are given below:

1733—John Scott, Capt.; William Waller, Lt.; Robert Tompkins, Ensign.

1738—William Woodford, Col.; John Taliaferro, Capt.; William Taliaferro, Capt.

1740—John Taylor, Capt.; Robert Farish, Capt.; Head Lynch, Capt.; William Carr, Capt.

1743—Roger Quarles, Capt.; David Sterns, Lt.; Robert Kay, Lt.; Joseph Stevens, Lt.

1745—Oliver Towles, Capt. of the Foot Company; Stephen Terry, Coronet.

1750—John Miller, Capt.; John Stevens, Capt.; Joseph Robinson, Capt.; James Tennison, Capt.; Ambroise Hoard, Lt.; James Dismukes, Lt.; William Boulware, Lt.; John Evins, Lt.

1752—Thomas Buckner, Capt.; Thomas Johnston, Capt.; Francis Taylor, Lt.; Joseph Hoomes, Lt.; William Marshall, Lt.; Robert Mickleberry, Lt.; Edmound Taylor, Lt.

1753—Charles Noden, Capt.

1754—Benjamin Robinson, Jr., Capt.; William Woodford II, Capt.; Eusabious Stone, Lt.; James Taylor, Jr., Lt.; James Taylor, the Younger, Lt.

1756—Rice Curtis, Col.

1762—James Taylor, Jr., Capt.; Francis Taylor, Capt.; William Buckner, Capt.; John Miller, Capt.; Edmound Pendleton, Capt.; Anthony Thornton, Capt.; William Parker, Capt.; John Thilman, Lt.; John Hawes, Lt.; Michael Yates, Lt.; James Jameson, Lt.; Thomas Pollard, Lt.; Thomas Buckner, Jr., Lt.; Henry Ware, Lt.; Nicholas Ware, Lt.; Robert Garrett, Ensign; Roy Griffin, Ensign; Thomas Griffin, Ensign; Gabriel Throckmorton, Ensign; Samuel Redd, Ensign.

1763—Samuel Redd, Capt.; Thomas Lowry, Capt.; Ambroise Hoard, Capt.; William Hoarde, Lt.; John Thompson, Ensign; Henry Stuart, Ensign.

1764—John Broaddus, Lt.; John Clark, Lt.; Richard Allcock, Lt.

1765—Samuel Hawes, Capt.; John Jones, Lt.; John Graham, Lt.; George Madison, Ensign.

1766—Anthony Thornton, Col.; Edmund Pendleton, Jr., Lt.

1768—Duncan Graham, Lt.

1769—John Broaddus, Capt.; William Kidd, Lt.; Vincent Vass, Lt.

1770—George Holloway, Capt.; William Dismukes, Lt.; William Buckner, Jr., Lt.; Peter Thornton, Ensign; Francis Coleman, Ensign.

1771—William Woodford II, Lt. Col.; Henry Ware, Capt.; Aquilla Johnston, Capt.; John Jones, Capt.; Leroy Hipkins, Capt.; Henry Taliaferro, Capt.; James Dunlop, Capt.; Anthony New, Capt.; Henry Ware, Jr., Lt.; Phillip Buckner, Lt.; Robert Ware, Lt.; Henry Harrison, Lt.

1772—Edmund Pendleton, Co.; Anthony Thornton, Col.; James Taylor, Col.; Thomas Lowry, Maj.; James Upshaw, Capt.; Anthony Thornton, Jr., Capt.

1773—Turner Dixon, Capt.; Richard Buckner, Capt.; Phillip Johnston, Capt.; Phillip Sterns, Lt.; Christopher Blackburn, Lt.; William Stresherley, Lt.; John Hipkins, Ensign; Henry Micou, Ensign.

1777—Organization of the Caroline Militia for the Revolution:

STAFF OFFICERS

Lt. Col. Anthony Thornton, Jr., James Upshaw

Col. Walker Taliaferro, Thomas Lowry

Maj. Richard Buckner, John Minor

COMPANY OFFICERS

1st Co.—Phillip Buckner, Capt.; George Turner, 1st Lt.; Thomas Allcocke, 2nd Lt.; James Kay, Ensign.

2nd Co.—Samuel Temple, Capt.; John Fitzhugh, 1st Lt.; John Thompson, 2nd Lt.; George Terrell, Ens.

3rd Co.—William Buckner, Capt.; John Downer, 1st Lt.; George Thornton, 2nd Lt.; Francis Conner, Ens.

4th Co.—John Jones, Capt.; George Madison, 2nd Lt.; Daniel Coleman, Ens.

5th Co.—William Marshall, Capt.; Richard Durrett, Lt.

6th Co.—Edmund Pendleton, Jr., Capt.; Richard Pemberton, 2nd Lt.; David Jameson, Ens.

7th Co.—William Stresherley, Capt.; William Reynolds, 2nd Lt.; James Reynolds, Ens.

8th Co.—Roger Quarles, Capt.; John Tyler, 1st Lt.; George Tyler, Ensign.

9th Co.—Edmound Jones, Capt.; James Norment, 1st Lt.; Chillion White, 2nd Lt.; Thomas Jones, Ens.

10th Co.—John Thilman, Capt.; Anthony New, 1st Lt.; James Faulker, 2nd Lt.; Daniel Turner, Ens.

11th Co.—James Johnston, Capt.; William Sutton, 2nd Lt.; Samuel Norment, Ens.

12th Co.—(?) Fletcher, Capt.; Thomas Broaddus, 2nd Lt.; Samuel Sale, Ens.

13th Co.—George Guy, Capt.; Joseph Richerson, 1st Lt.; James Sutton, 2nd Lt.; Joseph DeJarnette, Ens.

14th Co.—Robert Graham, Capt.; William Graham, 1st Lt.; Gregory Baynham, 2nd Lt.; William Collins, Ens.

John Marshall for John Jones, who resigned as Captain of the 4th Company before the end of 1777.

1777—New Companies formed.

15th Co.—John Long, Capt.; Charles Woolfolk, 1st Lt.; John Woolfolk, 2nd Lt.; Mungo Roy, Ens.

16th Co.—Phillip Johnston, Capt.; Samuel Coleman, 1st Lt.; Lewis Timberlake, 2nd Lt.; William Long, Ens.

1778—Reorganization of the 5th Company: William Durrett for William Marshall as Capt. Richard Durrett remains 1st Lt. Benjamin Winn becomes 2nd Lt. and William Conner, Ens.

9th Co.—James Boutwell made 1st Lt.

Ens. James Rennolds, Ambroise Jeter, Companies not stated.

Promotion: William Collins, Ens. to 2nd Lt.; Thomas Jones, Ens. to 2nd Lt.

1779.

Promotion: Phillip Johnston, Capt. to Maj.; Samuel Coleman, 1st Lt. to Capt.; William Long, Ens. to 1st Lt.; John Gravatt made Ens. (reorganization of 16th Co., when Phillip Johnston promoted to staff rank).

17th Co.—John Hall, Capt.; John Woolfolk, 1st Lt.; Duncan Graham, 2nd Lt.; Samuel Woolfolk, Ens.

Promotions: 13th Co.—George Guy, staff officer; Joseph Richerson, Capt.; James Sutton, 1st Lt.; Joseph DeJarnette, 2nd Lt.; Thomas Terry Guy, Ens.

Promotions: 4th Co.—John Marshall, staff officer; George Madison, Capt.; Daniel Coleman, 1st Lt.; Julius Coleman, 2nd Lt.; Thomas Hawes, Ens.

1780.

Promotions: 12th Co.—Thomas Broaddus, 1st Lt.; Samuel Sale, 2nd Lt.; James Daniel, Ens.; Jeremiah Upshaw, 1st Lt. Co. not stated.

1781.

18th Co.—John Downer, Capt. (from 3rd Co.) ; John Hoarde, 1st Lt.; Watts Parker, 2nd Lt.; Richard Shipp, Ens.

19th Co.—James Sutton, Capt. (transferred from 13th Co.) ; William F. Gray, 1st Lt.; Thomas Beazley, Ensign.

While commissions in the militia were reserved for the gentry and upper middle class, the officers corps was not an exclusive organization like the court. It contained some exceedingly rough customers, although socially they stood well enough. One of the roughest was Capt. John Scott. He was frequently in court for fighting, cursing, getting drunk and failing to go to church. From his record he was the biggest reprobate in the county. When at length he decided to go to church to avoid the payment of more fines he went there drunk. He was married to Elizabeth Brunskill, daughter of the notorious Rev. John Brunskill, and having to listen to the sermons of his father-in-law was his excuse for his condition.

2. The Regular Army

a. *The French and Indian War*

Troops from Caroline fought with the Virginia regiment in the French and Indian War. The names below appear in the Order Books of the county court in claims for land bounties for services rendered.

George Muse, Lt. Col., Reuben Ross, Christopher Blackburn, Thomas Ayers, Thomas Moss (drummer), Thomas Smith, John Mac-Donald, Benjamin Rennolds, William Smithers, James Arnold, John Munday, Richard Riddle, James Satterwhite, William Sepott (?), Reuben Munday, Thomas Hitchcock, John Harvey, Benjamin Oliver, Francis Self, William Field, James Russell, John Sampson, Edward Brown, James Samuel Lewis, William Mitchell, Thomas Dickinson, Henry Sessell (Cecil), James Sessell (Cecil), Achiles Whitlock, George White, James Taylor, George Hicks, William Robinson, John Carter, Samuel Taylor, Thomas Thorpe, James Ryan, John Johnson, Nathaniel Holloway, John Powell, William Rennolds, James Chick, James Callyhand, Thomas Hutchinson, Newman Boulware, James Ingram, Biddy Bankes, Joseph Stevens, Richard Johnston, Reuben Voss, Samuel Daniels, Michael Brown Roberts, Samuel Duval, Henry Wyatt,* William Blanton,† John MacDonald,† Richard Riddle.†

*Killed in battle. †Wounded.

b. *Caroline Soldiers and Sailors of the Revolution*

(From the archives of the Virginia State Library)

Nathaniel Pendleton
William Allen
John Allen
Charles Anderson
John Anderson
Richard Anderson
William Anderson
William Armistead
John Athey
Thomas B. Atkins

Gray Barber
Joshua Barlow
Ephriam Barlow
Joseph Barlow
Henry Bartlett
Thomas Baylor
John Baylor
James Baylor
William Baylor
Walker Baylor
George Baylor
John Baynham
Edmound Beadles
Cornelius Beazley
Edmund Beazley
Ephriam Beazley
Reuben Beazley
William Bernard
Thomas Bernard
John Bernard
Miller Bledsoe
John Blanton
Samuel Boulware
Mark Boulware
Obediah Boulware
Samuel Boutwell
Muscoe Boulware
Samuel Boulware*
Thomas Boutwell
Thomas Bowers
John Bowers

Edward Broaddus
James Broaddus
Richard Broaddus
William Broaddus
Robert Broaddus
James Bradley
William Brown
William Brown*
John Bruce
Thomas Buckner
Samuel Buckner
Phillip Buckner
Samuel Buckner*
Thomas Buckner*
William Buckner
Mathew Burk
Cornelius Burk
John Burk
James Burk
Obediah Bullock
John Burruss
James Butler
Samuel Butler
Daniel Barksdale

Hugh Campbell
James Campbell
John Campbell
Richard Campbell
Samuel Campbell
William Carr
Thomas Carson
John Carson
Daniel Carson
Joseph Carter
William Carter
Samuel Carter
Thomas Carter
Thomas Catlett
Thomas Chandler
Robert Chandler
Jesse Chandler

Richard Chandler
William Chandler
William Chapman
Benjamin Chapman
Reuben Chapman
John Chapman
Thomas Chapman
Robert Chewning
Charles Chewning
Thomas Chiles
William Coates
James Coates
William Clark
John Clark
Robert Clark
Frederick Coghill
James Coghill
Robert Coghill
Wyatt Coleman
James Coleman
Nathaniel Coleman
Richard Coleman
George Collins
Joseph Collins
William Conway
Joseph Conway
William Cook
Isiah Corbin
Hicks Cosby
Thomas Cosby
John Cox
Jeremiah Cox
Thomas Cox
William Cross

Joseph Daniels
E. B. Dickinson
Edmound Dickinson
Martin Dickinson
William Dickinson
James Dixon
Thomas Dixon

Claiborne Durrett
James Durrett

Martin Elliott
Samuel Elliott
Wyatt Elliott
Ambroise Eubank
Royal Eubank
William Eubank

James Farmer
Richard Farish
Joseph Flippo
William Fitzhugh

Richard Garrett
William Garrett
Richard Gatewood
Edmound Gatewood
William Gatewood
William George
Jesse George
Reuben George
John George
Innis Goodwin
Toler Godwin
James Gordon
George Gilchrist
Jesse Gouldin
William T. Gouldin
John Graves
John Gravatt
George Gray
Francis Gray
William Gray
James Green
Samuel Green
William Green
Gabriel Green
Moses Green
Richard Green
Samuel Guy
Joseph Guy
William Guy

James Harris
John Harris
William Harris
William Harris*
John Hay
Mourning Hay
John Hewlett
Baylor Hill
George Hill
Gideon Hill
Martin Hill
Benjamin Hoomes
David Hoomes
Isaac Hoomes
James Hoomes
Thomas C. Hoomes
John Hoomes
Thomas Horde
James Hoard
Benjamin Hurt

Hugh Innis
John Innis
Robert Innis

Turner Jesse
Jessie Jones
John Jones
John Jordan
Mark Jordan

James Kay
John Kay
James Kemp
William Kemp
Benjamin Kidd

Benjamin Long
James Long
Christopher Loving
James Luck

George Marshall
Robert Martin
Reuben Martin

Farish Martin
Moses Martin
James Martin
Gideon Martin
John Martin
William Madison
Thomas May
Thomas Miller
John Minor
Peter Minor
Vivian Minor
William Minor
John Morgan
David Motley
Joseph Motley
William Motley
Thomas Munday

William P. Napier
Jacobs New
Andrew Nixon
John Norment

John Oliver
Thomas Overton

James Parker
Thomas Parker
John Parker
William H. Parker
Richard Parker
James Pendleton
Nathaniel Pendleton
John Pendleton
Abraham Penn
William Penn
David Pitts
William Pitts
Simon Perry
Reuben Plunkett
Robert Powers
John Pratt
William Pratt

James Quarles

John Quarles
William P. Quarles

James Rains
William Rennolds
Robert Reynolds
George Richerson
Bernard Rogers
Joseph Rowe
John Rogers
Beverly Roy
Jacob Roy

Leonard Sale
Henry Samuel
James Samuel
William Samuel
George Sanders
Richard Sanders
John Sanders
Joseph Sanders
William Sanders
Daniel Sanders
Presley Sanders†
Robert Satterwhite
Gray Samuel
Robert Scott
Joseph Scott
John Shackleford
John Singleton
Elisha Sorrell
John Sorrell
Richard Sorrell
William Sorrell
William Southworth
Sanders Smith
Reuben Smith
James Smith
William Shepherd
Charles Swan

John Swan
Martin Sutton
Benjamin Sutton
Moses Stanley
John Sutton
George Shackleford

Francis Taliaferro
Richard Taliaferro
Walker Taliaferro
Bartholomew Taylor
John Taylor
Reuben Taylor
James Taylor
James Taylor
Thornton Taylor
Samuel Temple
Richard Tennant
James Tennant
Samuel Terrell
John Thomas
Reuben Thomas
Catlett Thomas
Elijah Thomas
James Thomas
Buckner Thomas
Anthony Thornton
James Thornton
John Thornton
Reuben Thornton
Patrick Thornton
Joseph Thornton
Mathew Todd
William Todd
John Todd
Bernard Todd
Robert Todd
Christopher Tompkins
Henry Tompkins
William Tompkins

Robert Tompkins
Richard Torrent
Joseph Tribble
William Toombs
Francis Turner
Joseph Turner
Charles Tyler
John Tyler
Joseph Tyler
William Tyler
Edward Travis

Charles Walden
George Walden
Edmound Waller
William Waller
John Washington
William Washington
Abner Waugh
Benjamin A. Welsh
James Whittaker
John Whittaker
Joseph White
John White
Robert Wood
William Woodford
Elisha Wyatt
Pittman Wyatt
Edmund Wyatt
Robert Wright
William Wright

James Yarbrough
Joel Yarbrough
John Young
Lewis Young
Robert Young
Benjamin Taliaferro
John Taliaferro

---

*May be a duplicate.
†Sometimes spelled Saunders.

This list is incomplete.

3. ALLOTMENTS

Because families were destitute while their men were away in the armed forces the Caroline court granted numerious allotments to alleviate suffering. Those which appear in the Order Books are listed below:

Year	Name of the Petitioner	Relative in Armed Forces	Award
1777	William Johnson	2 sons	15 pounds
1777	James Anderson	1 son	15 "
1777	Wife of William Carneal	William Carneal	15 "
1777	Wife of Elliott Emerson	Elliott Emerson	10 "
1777	Mary Nutt (?)	husband	10 "
1777	Leah Hampton	1 son	4 "
1777	Caty Bryan	husband	4 "
1777	Pattie Rose	"	7 pounds, 10 shillings
1777	Mrs. Eubank	2 sons	5 pounds
1777	John Crutchfield	2 sons	5 "
1777	Ann Lusgley (?)	husband	10 "
1777	Mary Daniels	"	10 "
1777	Robert Chewning	1 son	8 "
1777	Wife of William Lyod	William Lyod	8 "
1778	Frances Ashburn	William Graves Ashburn (husband)	15 "
1778	Family of Robert Fletcher	Robert Fletcher	6 "
1778	James Boulware	1 son	10 "
1778	Mary Dodd	husband	10 "
1778	John Pitts	2 sons	10 "
1778	Thomas Chandler	son	10 "
1778	Mary Martin	husband	15 "
1778	James Barden	3 sons	15 "
1778	Dicie Dollins	William Dollins (husband)	10 "
1778	James Satterwhite	1 son	10 "
1779	Nicholas Mullins	1 son	10 "
1779	James Allen	1 son	15 "
1779	John Mullins	John Cook (grandson)	10 "
1779	Mary White	husband	15 "
1779	Elizabeth Thorpe	"	10 "
1779	John Brooks	1 son	10 "
1779	Rowland McKenny	1 son	10 "
1779	Betty Carr	husband	6 "
1779	Mary Long	2 sons	10 "
1779	Sarah Burns	1 son	10 "

Year	Name of the Petitioner	Relative in Armed Forces	Award	
1779	John Ferguson	2 sons	10	"
1779	Ann Marshall	husband	10	"
1779	Johnathan Smith	1 son	10	"
1779	Ann Griddy (?)	2 sons	10	"
1779	Frances Fortune	1 son	6	"
1779	Ann Davis	1 son	6	"
1779	Esther Hooper	husband	10	"
1779	Leah Hampton*	1 son	10	"
1779	Francis Morgan	1 son	10	"
1779	Frances Ashburn*	William Graves Ashburn (husband)	15	"
1780	Elizabeth Roberts	husband	10	"
1780	John Mullins*	John Cook (grandson)	10	"
1780	Nicholas Mullins*	1 son	10	"
1780	Elizabeth Vaughter	husband	6	"
1780	Alice Wright	"	10	"
1780	John Pitts*	3 sons	15	"
1780	Elizabeth True	husband	6	"
1780	Esther Hooper*	"	10	"
1780	Family of Robert Fletcher*	Robert Fletcher	10	"
1780	Mary Morgan	husband	6	"
1780	Thomas Chandler*	1 son	10	"
1780	Isabelle Marshall	1 son	10	"
1780	Ann Roberts	son	6	"
1780	Jane Green	husband	10	"
1780	Mary Anderson	"	6	"
1780	Sarah Burden*	3 sons	15	"
1780	Rowland MacKenney*	1 son	10	"
1780	Ann Davis*	1 son	6	"
1780	Mary Malone	husband	10	"
1780	John Brooks*	1 son	20	"
1780	Mary Cox	husband	10	"
1780	William Booth	son	15	"
1780	Mary Daniels*	husband	10	"
1780	Martha Emerson*	Elliott Emerson (husband)	12	"
1780	Leah Hampton†	1 son	12	"
1780	Pattie Rose*	husband	15	"
1780	Mary Morgan*	1 son	12	"
1780	William Schooler	1 son	12	"
1780	Elizabeth Trainham	husband	12	"
1780	Elizabeth Carr*	"	12	"
1780	Robert Chewning*	1 son	12	"
1780	Sarah Chandler	husband	12	"

Year	Name of the Petitioner	Relative in Armed Forces	Award	
1780	John Mullins†	John Cook (grandson)	12	"
1781	Sarah Chandler	husband	12	"
1781	Sarah Shelton	"	12	"
1781	Rowland MacKenney	1 son	15	"
1781	Elizabeth Carr†	husband	15	"
1781	Mary Puller	"	12	"
1781	Family of Robert Fletcher	Robert Fletcher	15	"

*Second Award.   †Third award.

In addition to the allotments to the families of men in the service the Caroline court made several special awards to residents of the county for their care to sick soldiers on leave. These awards follow:

1777—Henry Pemberton—6 pounds for nursing Thomas Dudley, ill with smallpox.

1777—John Pitts—4 pounds for nursing his son David Pitts, ill with smallpox.

1777—Rennolds (Rowland) MacKenney—3 pounds for nursing David Pitts—smallpox.

1777—William Arnold—10 pounds for nursing Henry Rains, ill with smallpox.

1777—Dr. Michael Yates—10 pounds for attending Henry Rains.

1777—Henry Pemberton—3 pounds more for taking care of Thomas Dudley.

1777—John Turner—5 pounds for services to John Bullard, a sick soldier.

1778—Benjamin Poe—6 pounds for nursing his son, a soldier, sick on furlough.

1778—George Yates—10 pounds for services to Henry Rains, ill with smallpox.

1779—Dr. Michael Yates—10 pounds for attending John Ross, a sick soldier.

THE ECONOMY

1. INTRODUCTION

Colonial Caroline was a middle class county. There were no massive houses in the manner of the great mansions of lower Tidewater and along the James. Homesteads of the era, which survive in 1953, were modest at best. They include Bowling Green (the Old Mansion) and Oakridge, seats of the Hoomes; Locust Hill, the seat of Thomas Catlett; Ormesby, the seat of Francis Thornton; Mill Hill, the seat of Thomas Buckner; Gaymont, the seat of James Miller; Shepherds Hill, the seat of Robert Woolfolk; Mt. Scion, the seat of Francis Conway; Stanhope, the home of Mr. Wesley Southworth (1953); White Plains, a seat of the Pendleton family; and a few residences in Port Royal. Most, if not all, of these houses have been enlarged since the close of the Revolution. The Newton home on the west side of Route One between Ladysmith and Golansville (1953) is perhaps the best example of undefiled colonial architecture in the county.

Household furniture was plain and utilitarian although much of it was brought in from abroad. The household effects of Robert Dudley are listed in detail in the Order Book for 1740, and Dudley was a rich man. The reason they were listed was because the heirs of George Goodloe accused him of getting rich too fast by stealing a portion of the commissions when he served as deputy while Goodloe was sheriff. Dudley was exonerated of this charge, but a complete inventory of his household goods remains. They were: one desk, two looking-glasses, one large Bible, one box of knives and forks, one box of spoons, one heater with triplett, two brass candlesticks, two candle boxes, one warming pan, three stone jugs, two beds and furniture in inward room, two beds and furniture in outward room, one carbine gun, one tea-kettle, one set of saucers, one spinning-wheel, one grindstone, one hand saw, one pair of andirons, one flesh fork, one frying-pan, two pots and hooks, one tin kettle, one copper sauce pan, two pairs of wool cards, two chests, three butter pots, two spits, three powdering tubs, a three-gallon runlett, an old man's saddle and a bright bay horse with a blaze in its forehead.

While estates in St. Mary's and Drysdale parishes were sometimes large the land actually under cultivation was usually small. Most planters had servants but the number of slaves and indentured servants owned by the vast majority of freeholders was limited. Unfortunately the early tax rolls of Caroline

County no longer exist, but the Order Books do reveal the tithables on whom various individuals paid taxes. A few examples follow. The tithables include all Negro slaves over the age of sixteen, all indentured servants over the age of eighteen, and all free white males over the age of eighteen in residence on the lands of the taxpayer.

Year	Taxpayer	Number of Tithables	
1748	Henry Cooper	3	
1758	Benjamin Hubbard	27	
1758	Peter Lantor	5	
1758	John Kay	5	
1761	Elizabeth Riddle	9	
1761	John Terrell	4	
1763	Sussannah Hoomes	8	(her dower)
1773	Robert Cobb	6	
1774	William Woodford	20	
1774	Hannah Battaile	9	
1774	James Taylor	28	
1774	Jacob Daniels	5	
1774	Haye Battaile	17	
1778	William Nelson	16	
1778	Richard Johnston	11	
1778	Cheadle Burch	6	
1778	Johnathan Douglass	1	
1778	William Southworth	10	
1778	Thomas Buckner	8	
1778	Richard Taylor	2	
1778	Charles Collins	4	
1778	William Flippo	2	
1778	William Buckner	33	
1778	Francis Buckner	7	

Most planters supervised their farming. There were few overseers in the county. Listed below are the only overseers of record.

Year	Planter	Overseer
1735	Henry Armistead	John Mastin
1735	James Taylor I	John Hubbard
1736	Col. Cole Digges	James Coleman
1736	"King" Carter's heirs	John Adams
1737	Henry Armistead	William Dillion

Year	Planter	Overseer
1739	James Taylor I	John Adams
1743	"King" Carter's heirs	Henry Bell
1744	Benjamin Hubbard	William Hargrave
1766	Col. Richard Corbin	Christopher Daniels

Dates indicate one citation in Order Books. In some planter-overseer relationships there were other.

Col. Cole Digges, "King" Carter's heirs and Col. Richard Corbin were the only absentee landlords of record in colonial Caroline. They had to employ overseers to keep their plantations going.

The heirs of James Coleman, John Hubbard, Henry Bell and William Hargrave profited handsomely because their sires were overseers. Col. Cole Digges set James Coleman's son, Samuel, up as a tavern-keeper and merchant at the county's first courthouse. John Hubbard married Col. James Taylor I's daughter and their son, Benjamin, became one of the leading business men of Virginia and a partner of the Taylors in many of their ventures, the Carter family backed Henry Bell's son, Humphrey, in a merchantile business in lower Caroline which prospered to such an extent that he moved his headquarters to London, and William Hargrave's son, Samuel, because of Benjamin Hubbard's training became the celebrated Quaker merchant and leader. In a pioneer economy planters were forced to offer inducements to keep overseers because land was cheap and plentiful along the frontier. It was easy enough for the overseer to move on if he became dissatisfied. Henry Armistead's inducements backfired. He promised Mastin and Dillion, each, six Negroes at his death, if they worked for him a term of years. Both overseers complied with their side of the agreement, but when Armistead died his heirs refused to deliver the Negroes. The overseers sued and the Caroline court cut the awards to 12 pounds, 7 shillings and 10 pence, sterling, which was not enough to buy one able-bodied Negro. With Zachery Lewis as their attorney Mastin and Dillion appealed to the General Court of the colony. The outcome of their appeals is not of record.

With all the inducements an overseer's life was not an easy one. William Hargrave was overseer for Benjamin Hubbard when Francis Bearding robbed the plantation of tobacco and was hung in Williamsburg for the crime. A segment of the public insisted that Bearding had inside help, and Hargrave was investigated, although no evidence was turned up that he was an accessory in the crime. John Adams was not so fortunate. He lost his position at Carter plantation on Peumandsend because while he was overseer five Negroes escaped and spread terror through the countryside.

The number of overseers appears to have declined rather than increased during the colonial period. In 1766 the freeholders who lived in the vicinity of Reedy Mill were incensed because Col. Richard Corbin sent his overseer, Christopher Daniel to supervise the maintenance of a section of the public road rather than taking charge of the work personally although he was in residence in King and Queen and the overseer was managing his "Reed's" plantation.

2. CURRENCY

Five types of currency were in circulation in colonial Caroline; British money, Virginia specie, Spanish gold coins, bills of exchange and tobacco certificates. The amount of British pounds sterling, was limited. Most planters spent the purchase price of their tobacco, which was their only product with value abroad, before payments reached Virginia. Virginia specie was issued by the government of the colony to finance the French and Indian War. It constantly decreased in value and creditors shunned it as payment for debt. On the other hand, Spanish gold coins, the pistoles, were greatly desired. They were the only gold in circulation. Contracts frequently specified that payment was to be made in this medium. But the clause often had to be changed if payment was to be made at all since the number of pistoles in circulation was so limited that the creditor was unable to get enough to pay his bill. Bills of exchange were no stronger than the credit of the maker and his endorsers. They were used generally in local trade but were valueless for purchases abroad. The most effective monetary unit was the tobacco certificate and all through Caroline's colonial history it was the standard medium of exchange. Prices were fixed generally in pounds of tobacco rather than pounds sterling, and to get tobacco to pay their bills and to make purchases planters dropped the cultivation of other products and concentrated on this crop.

3. OTHER CROPS

From the earliest days of the Virginia colony there were attempts by the more enlightened colonist to diversify agriculture. But all these attempts ended in failure. The freeholders wanted tobacco which was equivalent to money. Special effort was made on the production of material for fabrics since all fine cloth was brought in from abroad. The planters, even in latitudes as far north as Caroline, raised sufficient cotton for plain garments, and enough wool to keep them warm. But while garments of cotton and wool were good enough for their servants, they wanted clothing of silk and linen for themselves. The cultivation of flax for linen and mulberry trees and caterpillars for silk became pet projects, but they all went wrong and the importation of silk and linen continued.

Foodstuffs were raised in abundance but shipping rates made it unprofitable to sell them abroad. In an effort to encourage the greater production of livestock the Caroline magistrates in 1740 passed an ordinance to permit planters to register their stock marks with the court and let their cattle range the county's unfenced land. Only two planters took advantage of this ordinance and registered their stock marks with the court. They were James Taylor I and Benjamin Rowe. Their marks were a swallow fork on each ear and two crops and two slits on the right ear and one slit under the heel of the left ear, respectively. The planters' attitude may be explained by the relative prices of livestock and tobacco. In 1764 in Caroline one acre of tobacco was worth 6½ cows, 30 sheep or 40 hogs.

4. THE TOBACCO LAWS

The London Board of Trade and the Virginia General Assembly promulgated decrees and passed laws designed to boost the prices of tobacco. They limited the number of plants per acre and prohibited the tending of seconds in attempts to reduce the poundage on the market and keep the price up through scarcity. These decrees and laws were unpopular in middle class Caroline County. Constables refused to make arrest unless prodded, and juries frequently refused to convict after arrests were made. But the court, in spite of these handicaps, attempted to enforce them. The residents of Caroline tried for evading tobacco laws are listed below, with the penalties imposed, if revealed in the Order Books:

1736—John Miller—failed to cut up tobacco suckers—500 pounds of tobacco fine.

1737—Richard George, Bryan Edmoundson, George Hamm, Ann Brown, Harry and Elizabeth Thomas—tending seconds—1,000 pounds of tobacco fine each, for George, Edmoundson, and Hamm, and 500 pounds of tobacco fine, each, for Ann Brown and the two Thomases.

1738—John Pierce—tending tobacco seconds—4,000 lbs. of tobacco fine.

1738—John Coeburn, Henry Catlett, John Herndon—accused of tending seconds—tried by jury—found not guilty.

1741—Mary Burton, Richard Walker—tending seconds—fined 500 lbs. of tobacco, each.

1742—George Brunley, Benjamin Spicer, Kemp Taliaferro—tending seconds—Brunley and Spicer fined 1,000 lbs. of tobacco each; Taliaferro fined 4,000 lbs. of tobacco.

1744—John Griffin—tending seconds—fined 1,000 lbs. of tobacco.

1745—Kemp Taliaferro—tending seconds—fined 5,000 lbs. of tobacco.

1749—Simon Poe—tending seconds—fined 1,000 lbs. of tobacco.

1752—John Blanton, William Bullard, Barnabas Arthur, John Smith, Thomas Pittman, Mordicai Abrahams, William Deshazo, James Mastin, Titus Stevens, Richard Powell, Drury Smith—tending tobacco seconds—fined 1,000 lbs. of tobacco each.

1753—Ann Sanders, John Daniel, Thomas Pittman, William Bullard— tending seconds—jury refused to convict.

1753—James Mastin, William DeShazo, Titius Stevens—tending

seconds—Mastin and DeShazo fined 500 lbs. of tobacco each, Stevens fined 1,000 lbs. of tobacco.

1754—Mourning Cooper—tending seconds—fined 500 lbs. of tobacco, or 50 shillings.

1756—Timothy Smith—tending seconds—jury refused to convict.

1758—Joseph Stevens, Jeremiah Canady (Kennady)—tending seconds— jury refused to convict.

1760—John Mason, Reuben George—tending seconds—jury refused to convict.

1762—Benjamin Whitehead, John MacDonald—tending seconds— 1,000 lbs. of tobacco fine.

TOBACCO PRICES

The legal rate of exchange between pounds of tobacco and pounds sterling was a pound of tobacco for a penny until 1755 when the General Assembly passed the so-called "Two Penny" Act because of the Great Drought and the French and Indian War and a pound of tobacco became officially, at least, worth two pennies. But laws which fixed the exchange rate had little practical effect. Prices fluctuated on a free market. The best example of this is the prices speculators paid for transfer tobacco at Roy's and Conway's chartered warehouses. A few examples are given below:

Year	Price at Roy's in pence per lb.	Purchaser at Roy's	Price at Conway's in pence per lb.	Purchaser at Conway's
1761	1.64	John Taylor	1.89	Robert Gilchrist
1762	1.88	James Jameson	2.02	William Spiller
1763	1.98	Robert Gilchrist	1.98	Robert Gilchrist
1766	2.00	James Robb	1.87	John Glassell

CHARTERED WAREHOUSES

Laws forced planters to market their tobacco through chartered warehouses where it was graded and the tax extracted before it was shipped abroad. These warehouses issued certificates for the planters to hold until their crops were sold, and the certificates which planters, who were not able to wait so long, used for money.

Before Caroline became a county the tobacco grown along the North Anna-Pamunkey passed through Page's and Crutchfield's warehouses in lower Hanover, the tobacco from the Mattapony Valley through Aylett's warehouse in King William and the tobacco from the Rappahannock area through Conway's and Roy's. But after Caroline was organized the bulk of the tobacco from the whole county passed through Conway's and Roy's with the building of well placed rolling roads leading to the Rappahannock.

John Buckner secured a charter for the warehouse that was to become known as Roy's early in the eighteenth century. When he died a tobacco inspector, John Roy, purchased the business from his heirs. John Roy died in 1734 and for over a decade his widow, Dorothy Roy, operated the business. She had the distinction of being the only woman in British America to have a warehouse chartered in her name. At her death the business passed to her son, Thomas Roy, and he ran it until he died in 1772, when his son and heir, John Beverley Roy, who was one of the richest men in Caroline County, sold it to James Miller, a celebrated Port Royal merchant. Although Miller was a Tory he operated the warehouse through the Revolution, but he prudently continued to call it Roy's.

Francis Conway I was the manager-owner of Conway's warehouse on the south bank of the Rappahannock eastward from the mouth of Snow Creek when Caroline became a county. He died in 1733 and his widow, Rebecca Catlett Conway, another resourceful woman, supervised the business in behalf of his estate during the infancy of his sons, Reuben, Robert, Catlett and Francis II. Robert settled on family land grants in the new county of Orange, Reuben and Catlett died while young men, but Francis II took over the warehouse and brought it to its greatest era of prosperity. When he died in 1756 he left a flourishing business. But unfortunately his widow, Sarah Taliaferro Conway, lacked the business acumen of his mother, Rebecca Catlett Conway, and management of the warehouse passed to the Taylor family. When his sons grew up they had little knack for trade and the Taylors continued in the managerial rôle. The court, according to the

Order Books, divided the profits between the two families, one-third for the Taylors and two-thirds for the Conways.

THE TOBACCO INSPECTORS

Tobacco inspectors were among the most important officials of the county. They graded the crop, supervised its prizing and shipped it abroad. In the early years of Caroline's history tobacco inspectors were as unpopular as land surveyors. William Woodford of Windsor accused Richard Booker of showing favoritism towards Lawrence Battaile, Dorothy Roy attempted to discredit the inspectors at Conway's and cause planters to ship their crops to her warehouse at Roy's, and Thomas Roy used his position as inspector to intimidate the voters in the Gibson-Martin campaign. But after 1738 Caroline inspectors had little more trouble, they stayed out of politics and kept their noses clean.

Until 1732 Roy's and Conway's on the south side of the Rappahannock and Gibson's on the north side of the stream opposite Roy's were grouped in one inspectorship with John Champe, Francis Conway and John Roy as inspectors. After 1732 the district was split up and each warehouse had two inspectors of its own, with additional inspectors for Roy's in time of stress. The governor appointed the inspectors annually from a slate of men "who knew tobacco" furnished him by the local court. Caroline inspectors beginning with 1732 follow:

TOBACCO INSPECTORS AT ROY'S AND CONWAY'S WAREHOUSES

Year	Roy's	Conway's
1732	John Roy, Richard Booker	John Taylor, Rice Curtis
1733	Thomas Bryan, Richard Booker	John Taylor, Rice Curtis
1734	John Sutton, Peyton Smith	John Taylor, John Griffin
1735	Thomas Roy, Richard Booker	Phillip Clayton, Thomas Slaughter
1736	Thomas Roy, Richard Booker	Phillip Clayton, Thomas Slaughter
1737	John Miller, John Sutton	Phillip Clayton, Thomas Slaughter
1738	Thomas Roy, Richard Booker	Phillip Clayton, Thomas Slaughter
1739	Thomas Roy, Francis Stern	Phillip Clayton, Thomas Slaughter
1740	Francis Stern, John Boutwell	William Allcock, Thomas Slaughter
1741	Francis Stern, John Boutwell	William Allcock, Robert Garrett
1742	Francis Stern, John Boutwell	William Allcock, Robert Garrett
1743	Francis Stern, John Boutwell	William Allcock, Robert Garrett

Year	Roy's	Conway's
1744	Francis Stern, John Boutwell	William Allcock, Nicholas Ware
1745	Francis Stern, John Boutwell	William Allcock, William Conner
1746	Francis Stern, John Boutwell	William Allcock, William Conner
1747	Francis Stern, John Boutwell and Daniel Triplett	William Allcock, John Garrett
1748	Francis Stern, John Boutwell and Daniel Triplett	William Allcock, John Stevens
1749	Francis Stern, Daniel Triplett	John Stevens, Robert Farish
1750	Francis Stern, Daniel Triplett	William Allcock, John Stevens
1751	Daniel Triplett, John Evins and James Jameson	William Allcock, John Stevens
1752	Francis Stern, John Evins	William Allcock, John Stevens
1753	Francis Stern, John Evins	William Allcock, Nicholas Ware
1754	James Jameson, John Evins	William Allcock, Nicholas Ware
1755	James Jameson, John Evins	William Allcock, Nicholas Ware
1756	James Jameson, John Evins	William Allcock, Nicholas Ware
1757	James Jameson, John Evins	William Allcock, Nicholas Ware
1758	James Jameson, John Evins	William Allcock, Nicholas Ware
1759	James Jameson, John Evins	William Allcock, Nicholas Ware
1760	James Jameson, John Evins	William Allcock, Nicholas Ware
1761	James Jameson, John Evins	William Allcock, Nicholas Ware
1762	James Jameson, Richard Roy	William Allcock, Nicholas Ware
1763	James Jameson, Richard Roy and John Miller, Jr.	William Allcock, Nicholas Ware
1764	Richard Roy, Simon Miller and John Miller, Jr.	William Allcock, Nicholas Ware
1765	Richard Roy, Simon Miller and John Miller, Jr.	William Allcock, Nicholas Ware
1766	Richard Roy, Simon Miller	William Allcock, Nicholas Ware
1767	John Miller, Simon Miller	William Plunkett, Robert Garrett
1768	John Miller, Simon Miller	William Plunkett, Robert Garrett
1769	Richard Roy, John Miller	Thomas Allcock, Robert Ware
1770	Richard Roy, John Miller	Thomas Allcock, Robert Ware
1771	Richard Roy, John Catlett	Thomas Allcock, Robert Ware
1772	Richard Roy, John Catlett	Thomas Allcock, Robert Ware
1773	Richard Roy, John Catlett	Charles Todd, Robert Ware
1774	Richard Roy, John Catlett	Charles Todd, Robert Ware
1775	Richard Roy, John Catlett	Charles Todd, Robert Ware
1776	Richard Roy, John Catlett	Thomas Allcock, Robert Ware

There were no more changes until after the Revolution. The incumbents were reappointed each year.

MERCHANTS AND TRADERS

a. *Port Royal (St. Mary's Parish)*

TILLEY-HOARDE-TOWLES MILLS. George Tilley was the first merchant of record to do business within the territorial limits of Caroline County. His place of business was originally on the Rappahannock in the neighborhood of Conway's warehouse. It passed to Thomas Hoarde, his clerk and junior partner, when he died in 1742. Hoarde sold the business to Oliver Towles on credit in 1744 and Towles moved it to the new town of Port Royal, and repossessed it when Towles failed in 1748. Again in possession he operated it in conjunction with James Mills until he died in 1756. After his death the business declined in volume until it was of little consequence in the economic life of the county.

DUNLOP-BOYD-CROSS. The house of Dunlop was the second business house established in the area to be Caroline. The family were primarily mariners and did their trading at first from a boat which plied the Rappahannock. But after Port Royal became a town they set up store ashore in conjunction with Robert Boyd of Glasgow and placed John Gartsborro as factor in residence. About 1750 Boyd withdrew from the business and the Cross family took his place. Both Dunlops and Crosses came to live in Port Royal and remained among the town's most prominent residents through the Revolution. Through the years the Dunlops continued in charge of shipping while trading was largely in the Crosses hands.

BOWIE. James Bowie opened a merchantile establishment at Roy's warehouse in 1732 and operated it successfully until his death forty years later (1772). After he died his nephew, James Bowie II, took over. But the younger Bowie only survived his uncle a few years, and his widow, Sarah Bowie, managed the business through the Revolution.

GILCHRIST. Robert Gilchrist was James Bowie's competitor and friend. He opened a Port Royal business in 1744 and for over thirty-five years was an important figure in the town's

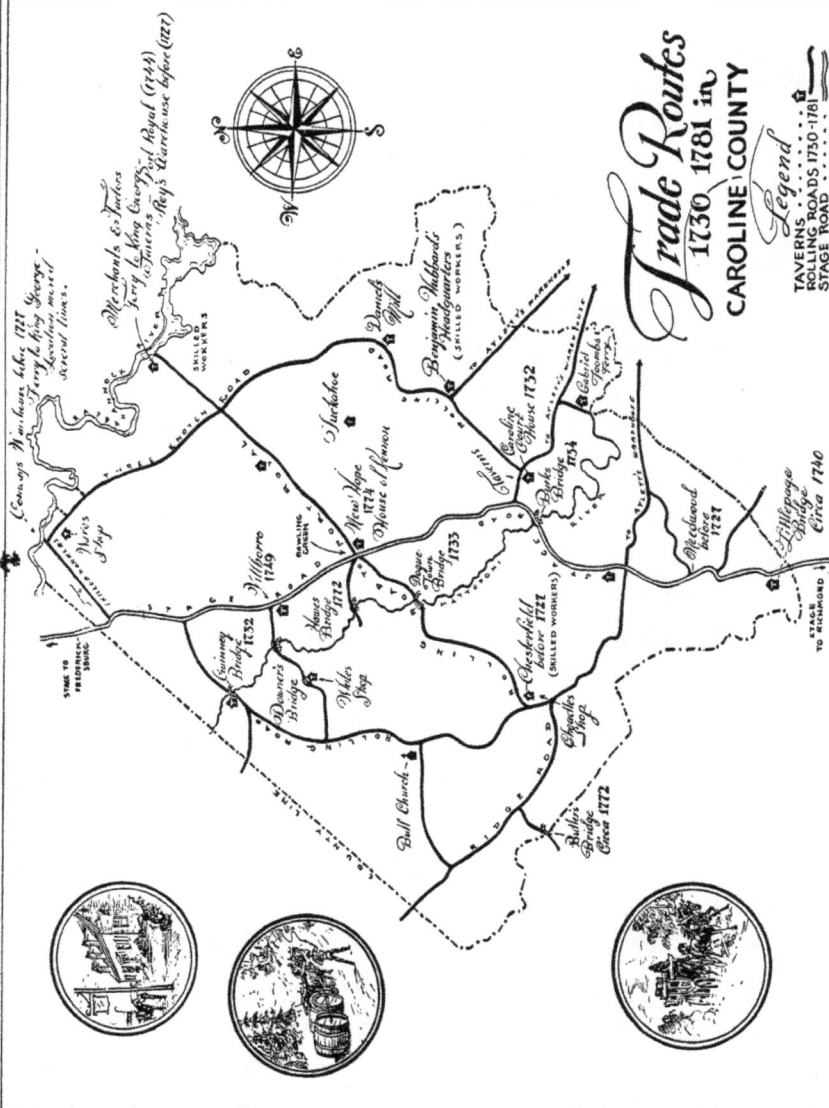

Trade Routes
1730 · 1781 in
CAROLINE COUNTY

Legend

TAVERNS
ROLLING ROADS 1730-1781
STAGE ROAD
BRIDGES

trade. The royal governor made him a magistrate and after he grew rich he gradually withdrew from active management of business and became an investor and financier.

MITCHELL. Patrick Mitchell purchased Dorothy Roy's store after her death. He and his son, John Mitchell, ran this business until after the Revolution.

BOOGLE. Mathew Boogle set up a business in Port Royal shortly after the founding of the town although he worked through factors and continued to live in Glasgow. Around 1760 he sent his son, Robert, to be his representative in residence.

GRAHAM. Duncan Graham came to represent his brother John Graham, a Glasgow merchant, in Port Royal in the 1740's, and remained to go in business on his own. He became interested in the development of western land and most of his family became pioneers in Southwest Virginia, although some of them remained in business in Caroline through the Revolution.

DIXON. Edward Dixon came to Port Royal and set up as a merchant about 1750. The firm he founded lasted through the Revolution, and he and his sons became well known figures in Caroline commercial circles. Like Robert Gilchrist, Edward Dixon was a magistrate.

GRAY. John Gray arrived in Port Royal about the same time as Edward Dixon, and like the Dunlops was a shipowner as well as merchant. His business prospered until the Revolution, when he and most of his sons fled because they were Tories, leaving their affairs in charge of Andrew Leckie, as factor.

COUTTS. Patrick Coutts, also, reached Port Royal about the same time as Gray and Dixon, and he and his relatives owned another important trading house through the rest of the colonial period.

MILLER. The house of Miller was engaged in many Port Royal businesses throughout the colonial era. James Miller, a merchant, purchased Roy's warehouse in 1772, and operated it throughout the Revolution although he was a Tory.

ROY. After the Roys got their start, they were more financiers than business people. John and Dorothy Roy actively engaged in trade, their son, Thomas Roy, supervised a chartered warehouse, and their grandson, John Beverley Roy, only watched over his investments. It takes three generations to make a gentleman and in three generations the Roy's were made.

FAILURES. In addition to Oliver Towles these Port Royal merchants failed. John Harvey of Essex failed during the panic of 1748, the Great Drought (1755-56) ruined Richard and William Bullock, Aaron Quisinberry was a victim of the inflation caused by the French and Indian War, and James Craigie fled and left his business on the outbreak of the Revolution.

b. *Drysdale Parish*

TAYLOR. James Taylor I was one of the few patentees of great crown grants to engage actively in trade. His family remained in business after his death both in lower Drysdale and upper St. Mary's Parish.

HUBBARD. Benjamin Hubbard became the head of the Taylor's business enterprizes in lower Drysdale Parish upon the death of Col. James Taylor (*circa.* 1750) and remained in active command until he died during the last year of the Revoluction. He was assisted at first by John Elliott Payne and Eusabious Stone and later by Payne and Robert Broaddus. Hubbard was unscrupulous in his business transactions. As a young man he broke Stephen Haynes, seized Haynes' tavern and bound Haynes sons out as paupers. Later he wormed his way into Aylett's warehouse as a minor partner and when the Ayletts and Buckners engaged in a bitter family quarrel over Phillip Aylett's estate seized control of the business. Although he owned Ayletts he moved neither his residence nor his headquarters to King William. They remained in a tavern he took over from Stephen Haynes, which appears to have been located in the vicinity of present-day (1953) Sparta. Oddly enough, although an astute business man, Hubbard was a radical in politics. He quit the Caroline court rather than swear allegiance to George III and was a prominent member of the Caroline Committee of Safety prior to the Revolution. Contrariwise in religion he was conservative, reared a Quaker, he became a staunch supporter of the Established Church of the colony.

BRADFORD. Richard Bradford was Hubbard's only competitor after he disposed of Haynes for almost two decades. Bradford did not last long, Hubbard broke him and forced him to flee to North Carolina to escape imprisonment for his debts.

KENNON. Patrick Kennon became factor for the Port Royal trading house of Dunlop and Cross at the Bowling Green, or New Hope as it was then called, in the early 1770's. This was Bowling Green's first store of record. The location was ideally suited for trade because the rolling road from Chesterfield to Port Royal was the Stage Road from the northern colonies to Williamsburg crossed at this point. Nearby the county court had begun to hold many of its sessions in a building the magistrates rented from the Johnstons, and the building of Hawes Bridge across the Mattapony brought shoppers from populous upper St. Margaret's Parish. Kennon prospered immediately after he opened his place of business, but his prosperity did not last long. At the outbreak of the Revolution he refused to renounce King George III and swear allegiance to the Commonwealth of Virginia. The Caroline court expelled him for his obstinacy and his thriving business came to an end.

c. *St. Margaret's Parish*

MAULDIN. Richard Mauldin was the first trader of St. Margaret's of record. He operated a trading post at Chesterfield when Caroline County was organized. Governor Gooch made him a magistrate but removed him from the court for criticizing the tobacco laws. After his removal from the court Mauldin sold his business at Chesterfield to his partner, Thomas Mallory, and opened a new establishment further north in St. Margaret's. He remained in business here until about 1750 when he sold out to Peter Copeland, and left the county.

MALLORY-GARLICK-REDD. Thomas Mallory took Samuel Garlick as a partner at Chesterfield after he split with Mauldin. Garlick bought the whole business from Mallory and in time sold half of it to Samuel Redd. The new partnership continued until around 1760 when Redd forced Garlick out. Redd continued in business in Chesterfield through the Revolution.

SUTTON. John Sutton III became Samuel Redd's competitor during the Revolution. At the end of that war he appears to have had the larger business.

DICK. Charles Dick was an early importing merchant of St. Margaret's Parish. In time he moved his headquarters to Fredericksburg but continued to do much of his business in Caroline. His brother, Archibald, remained in Caroline, as rector of St. Margaret's Parish.

GOODALL. The Goodalls were Quakers. The family came to Caroline from Pennsylvania with John Cheadle and almost immediately thereafter went into trade. They were importers and exporters and their place of business was located either at Chesterfield or near Golansville. Of all Caroline traders they appear to have made the most frequent trips overseas. Leaders in the house were John, Charles and William Goodall. The house went out of business about the mid 1750's when Samuel Hargrave forged ahead as the leading Quaker merchant of Caroline.

HUNTER. The Hunters like Charles Dick operated both in Fredericksburg and Caroline. Their Caroline headquarters were in lower St. Margaret's Parish. After William Hunter's death in 1759 the family retired from active trade and became money-lenders and financiers.

HARGRAVE. Samuel Hargrave was the most celebrated merchant of St. Margaret's Parish. He was the head of the Quakers and religious leader as well as business man. Of all the Caroline merchants he was the most coöperative with the Committee of Safety prior to the Revolution. Although his business career began prior to the French and Indian War he lived until after the end of the eighteenth century and was trying to found a town, the town of Oxford at the falls of the North Anna, when he died.

COPELAND. Peter Copeland came to Caroline as factor for his brother William Copeland, a Glasgow merchant, and remained to take over Thomas Mauldin's second business in St. Margaret's Parish. He operated this business successfully for over twenty years, and until he left the county. He was another business man who served as magistrate.

BRITISH FIRMS AND THEIR FACTORS

Prior to the founding of Port Royal most of Caroline's overseas trade was with Bristol. But after the founding of that town it shifted to London and Glasgow, especially Glasgow, and in time Port Royal became almost an outpost of that thriving port.

THE BRISTOL MERCHANTS. John Younger, Lionel Lyde, Mathias, William Gayle and Peter Horn were the principal Bristol merchants doing business in Caroline. They all had factors in Port Royal, and Younger had additional representatives in Drysdale and St. Margaret's. William Boulware was his factor for a short time in St. Margaret's and after that William Temple. George Pitts represented him for a much longer period in Drysdale. Pitts respected him to such an extent that he named one of his sons Younger, a not uncommon practice in colonial Virginia, to name a child for a merchant.

LONDON MERCHANTS. William Black, Johnathan Forward and William Hamilton were the first London merchants to send factors to Port Royal. Representatives of William Dunningham, Samuel Bosworth and William Spiller took up residence in the town shortly thereafter. But Humphrey Bell was the most interesting London merchant with factors in Caroline. A native of the county he was backed by the money of "King" Carter's family for whom his father was overseer. He got his start in lower Drysdale Parish before Benjamin Hubbard dominated that region. He prospered to such an extent that he moved his headquarters to London and left his brothers, John and Henry Bell, behind in Caroline, as his factors. After this move he always signed his name as "Humphrey Bell of London, Merchant." But in spite of this pretentious signature he remained loyal to his native county. He deeded a lot for a new church in Drysdale Parish (the Ivy Church) and when he died he still owned a great deal of property in Caroline. His will was brought across the Atlantic for probate.

SCOTTISH MERCHANTS. Most of the foreign merchants doing business in Caroline were Scots. They included Lennox, Scott and Co., Alexander Aberdeen, William Copeland, Murdock, Donald & Co., Campbell & Craig, Allen Dreghorn, Andrew Cockran, Archibald Govan, William Mackie, Nianan Glenn, Thomas MacCreeder, Robert Berries & Co., Archibald Mac-Call, Anthony MacKiltrick, William Montgomery & Sons and Alexander Loggie. The names of these firms changed frequently and partners varied. Lennox, Scott & Co. was sometimes Hugh Lennox, Daniel Campbell traded sometimes alone, and sometimes as a partner of Andrew Craig, and Donald Murdock did business with both Duncan Donald and Allen Dreghorn. All the Scottish merchants were from Glasgow or Aberdeen. There were none of record from any other city.

IRISH MERCHANTS. John Martin, the magistrate and Burgess, after he left Virginia, set up in Dublin as a merchant with one or more of his sons as a partner. This firm had a factor in Caroline.

FRENCH MERCHANTS. After the Declaration of Independence Antoine Gautier and Jean Collineau of Martinique in the French West Indies had representatives in Port Royal.

VIRGINIA MERCHANTS. Richard Ambler and Thomas Nelson of Yorke(towne), John Glassell of Fredericksburg, and Archibald Ritchie, Semple and Baylor, and Muscoe Garnett of Essex did business in Caroline and were frequent business visitors in the county.

MARYLAND MERCHANTS. Maxmillian Calvert of Baltimore began developing a Caroline market in the mid 1760's. From this beginning Baltimore dominated the economic life of Caroline's Rappahannock Valley for over 100 years.

THE FACTORS

Relatives of the owners, hired clerks and local men served foreign firms as factors in colonial Caroline. James Berries represented his father, Robert Berries, Robert Boogle, his father, Mathew Boogle, John Cockran, his brother, Andrew Cockran, Peter Copeland, his brother, William Copeland, and Duncan Graham, his brother, John Graham. Copeland and Graham elected to remain in Virginia. Among the hired clerks Archabald Buchannon represented Murdock and Dreghorn; Andrew Anderson, William Mackie; and Andrew Leckie, John Gray & Co. Among the local residents who served as factors the employees of John Younger; William Boulware, George Pitts and William Temple, are the best known.

Some factors represented a number of firms. The most celebrated of these were John Wallace, John Thompson and James Gordon. Thompson and Gordon had been kidnapped in Scotland in their youths and forced to serve terms as indentured servants in Port Royal business houses. They were well versed in local conditions and did well as factors, but both were Tories and fled rather than be expelled after the Declaration of Independence.

CLERKS

Factors in many cases had with them numerous assistants and clerks, making a whole retinue of foreign-born living in Caroline, and not considering the county their permanent domicile. The names of people of this class are only revealed once in the Order Books. That was in 1776 when the court ordered the expulsion of foreign-born who refused to take oath of allegiance to the Commonwealth. They included James Monroe Morris, assistant to Patrick Kennon, James Craige and James Stark, assistants to Dunlop & Cross, James Coates, assistant to Andrew Leckie and Archibald MacClean, assistant to John Wallace.

The Rev. Johnathan Boucher was not favorably impressed with the Caroline merchants, factors and assistants. Upon his arrival in Port Royal in 1759, he wrote in his autobiography, "on the 12th of July I landed at Urbanna and soon after got up to my place of destination which was Captain Dixon's at Port Royal in Caroline County. Here I met a cordial reception. Being hospitable as well as wealthy, Captain Dixon's house was much resorted to, but chiefly by the toddy drinking company. Port Royal was inhabited by factors from Scotland and their dependents. * * * literary attainments beyond mere reading and writing, (were not) at all in vogue or repute."

SHIPS AND MERCHANTS

The Caroline Order Books and Proceedings of the Committee of Safety reveal that the following vessels were engaged in trade between Port Royal and overseas ports during colonial times.

Ship	Owner	Master	Trade Route	Period Circa
Priscilla	——	Henry Sweet	Trans-Atlantic	1730-45
Christian	Wm. Montgomery	—— Stanley	Trans-Atlantic	1730-45
Elizabeth and Ann	Wm. Dunlop	Wm. Dunlop	Trans-Atlantic	1730-50
St. Mungo*	John Gray & Co.	John Lindsay	West Indian	1752-57
Virginia†	John Bowcock	John Bowcock	Trans-Atlantic	1750-65
Port Royal	Wm. Fox	Wm. Fox	Trans-Atlantic	1755-71
Beverley‡	Montgomery & Co.	Robt. Montgomery	Trans-Atlantic	1760-75
Molly	Dunlop & Lyne	William Lyne	Trans-Atlantic	1765-76
Favorite	John Elliott Payne	Wm. Fletcher	Trans-Atlantic	1765-76
Olive	Dunlop & Lyburn	Henry Lyburn	Trans-Atlantic	1765-76

*Captured by the French during the French and Indian War.
†John Archer a seaman aboard.
‡James Campbell and John Scott seamen.

William Fox, also had a Port Royal tavern license. His wife, Ann, ran the tavern while he was at sea. Other members of the Montgomery, Bowcock, Lindsay and Dunlop families were seafaring men as well as those listed above.

RETAIL STORES

Retail stores sprung up in all sections of Caroline County, but few survived. Importers sold to consumers as well as retailers and they were unable to stand the competition. Their only advantages lay in the fact that they were able to buy a little cheaper than the smaller planters and artesans since they purchased in volume, the costs of transportation inland in bulk was less, and they had a more intimate knowledge of credit in their home communities than the importers who lived at a distance. This last asset often became a liability because the retailers in attempts to build up trade under handicaps often overextended credit. This led to their undoing and they failed.

The most successful retail stores in Caroline were those at the first courthouse and those run by the remarkable Johnston family. The courthouse was a natural site for trade. Many people congregated in the vicinity at regular intervals and there were no importing houses nearby. Samuel Coleman and Benjamin Rennolds operated the leading retail stores at the courthouse in the early years. Coleman's business passed to his wife, Betty Wyatt Coleman, after his death in 1748, and from her to William Johnston, their clerk, who also served as jailor. When Samuel Coleman's son, Francis, grew up he wanted the business and had a quarrel with Johnston over ownership. Coleman won and Johnston moved to a new site northeast of the Bowling Green, where shortly before the outbreak of the Revolution his son, James, who took over the business at his death, persuaded the magistrates to hold some sessions of the county court in a building on the premises. All of the sessions of the court were held here, in time, and this rented building became the courthouse of Caroline County until the county seat was set up at the Bowling Green in the period from 1793-1803. Benjamin Rennolds sold his courthouse store to his clerk and political henchman, William Burdette, in 1735. Burdette ran it until around 1750 when the shifting of trade from the courthouse to more advantageous sites forced him to close it because of lack of business.

In addition to William and James Johnston with stores at the first and second courthouses, numerous other members of the Johnston family, at one time or another, ran retail stores in widely divergent sections of Caroline County. The most successful of these was Robert Johnston, the only member of the family to go into the import trade. He brought goods into Caroline during the Revolution from the northern colonies.

Among the retailers who failed were Josiah Baker, Thomas Boothe and Francis Thorpe. All three failures were due to overextend credit. The debtors of Josiah Baker, who ran a store near Conway's warehouse, are set down in the Caroline Order Book for 1747. They were with the amount of their debts in pounds, shillings and pence, as follows:

John Buckner 0/3/4½; James Burden 1/0/½; Patrick Boswell 0/3/6; William Bullard 0/1/6; William Buckner 0/3/10; Thomas Blassingame 0/4/3; Thomas Brown 0/1/1½; William Barksdale 0/3/7½; Thomas Bullard 0/0/2½; Brevard Cowley 0/14/8; Catlett Conway 0/1/3; Wyatt Coleman 0/0/6; William Campbell 0/0/9; Henry Cooper 0/7/10; Waller Chiles 0/8/9; Streman Chilton 0/10/½; James Downer 1/9/1½; Ambroise Dudley 0/10/½; John Dillard 0/8/3½; Thomas Drummond 0/6/4; Thomas Emerson 0/11/7.

The total amount was only five pounds, fourteen shillings and one and one and a half pence, sterling, or less than the price of the crop from two acres of tobacco at the prevailing rate of exchange. But it was enough to force Baker into bankruptcy.

Another entry in the Order Books reveals the stock of goods, in part, carried by retailers. This was the stock of Joseph Coleman, a merchant of St. Margaret's Parish, set down as articles stolen when two Negroes broke into his storehouse in 1746. The list of stolen goods follows:

> 8 worsted caps, 6 yds. of colored cotton cloth, 3 lbs. of brown thread, 5 cutting knives, 5,000 pins, 8 horn combs, 2 parcels of ribbon, 5 pair of shoe buckles, 1,500 other pins, 2¼ yds. other ribbon, 3 papers of thread, 2 other horn combs and a piece of handkerchief.

THE PEDDLERS

Several peddlers moved about the countryside in Caroline during colonial times selling goods from packs. All of these men of record were Jews. The Sterns were the most celebrated

Caroline family of Jewish extraction but they had passed beyond the peddler stage, if ever they were peddlers at all, before the county was organized and had become tobacco inspectors, planters and successful business men.

Peter Marks was doing an extensive business as peddler at the time the county came into being. He made his headquarters at William Dennis tavern at Chesterfield, and was Dennis' executor when the tavern-keeper died in 1735.

The most troublesome peddler in Caroline's history was Mordicai Abraham. In his many scrapes with the law the magistrates described him as a "peevish, fretful man." He arrived in Caroline sometime prior to 1751 and began traveling the county as a peddler with Henry Thomas, an indentured servant, carrying his pack. His troubles began when the local court ordered him to set Thomas free because the law forbade Jews, Mohamedians and Negroes to own indentured servants.

After the loss of Thomas, Abraham purchased John Mayfield, a poor debtor, to carry his pack, and, when Mayfield complained, succeeded in convincing the court that the law barring Jews from owning white servants only applied to servants brought in from abroad and did not apply to persons bound in Virginia. After this verdict Mayfield set to work raising tobacco seconds to get the means to purchase his freedom. He was caught, but at his trial the magistrates, evidently overcome by a wave of sympathy, after fining him for raising seconds, reversed their opinion as to the ownership of poor debtors by Jews and ordered Abraham to set him free.

With this second loss Abraham decided to buy a Negro. The law did not forbid a Jew to own a Negro slave. But he made a mistake in the type of Negro he purchased. Instead of buying a domesticated servant, he purchased a slave recently imported from Africa because the latter was cheaper. He made this purchase from a batch of Negroes recently brought into Virginia by James Taylor, the Younger, and kept in the cellar of a tobacco warehouse at Ayletts, their port of debarkation, under the supervision of William Cowne. Abraham carefully looked over the lot and picked the fattest Negro, against the expressed disapproval of no lesser personage than

Nathaniel Burwell of King William, who warned him that skinny Negroes lived longer and made better servants. After the transaction Abraham took his servant and set out for his home in Caroline selling goods along the way. When he reached his destination the Negro was ill. Abraham immediately put the black fellow in a feather bed, had his wife nurse him and sent for a doctor. But for all this tender care the Negro died. Afterwards one of the most unusual suits in the history of Caroline County arose. Abraham accused Taylor and Cowne of selling him a Negro whom they had made ill by keeping him in a damp tobacco cellar and demanded that they return the purchase price. Taylor and Cowne countered that the Negro was in good shape when they sold him, but that Abraham had impaired his health by forcing him to sleep on the wet ground on the selling trip from Ayletts into Caroline, giving him little to eat because he was fat and forcing him to drink much water. Dr. Campbell of King William testified that the Negro was all right when he left Ayletts, and Dr. George Todd and Dr. John Sutherland of Caroline testified that he died of plurisy, but they both refused to state where they believed he contracted the disease.

When it appeared that Abraham was about to lose his case he made an impassioned speech to the court. He stated that he had been discriminated against all his life because he was a Jew and was "much dejected" when he came to Virginia, where he expected to find conditions much better in a "new world." But that he had been badly mistaken in this conjecture and that every one had conspired against him since he reached Caroline. Evidently the magistrates were much impressed with this oration because they rendered a compromise verdict. After branding Abraham as "vexatious, setigeous and complacent" and holding that his suit was "supported with money by some evil disposed person," they ruled that he might recover the profits that Taylor and Cowne made on the sale of the Negro, which amounted to twelve pounds.

Abraham failed to appreciate this partial victory. He became more troublesome than ever. He sued every one that spoke to him harshly, or made a motion towards him for slander or assault. The docket of the Caroline court was cluttered with his suits. Only one of these did he win. A suit against James Powell for assault and the jury only awarded him damages of a penny. He was no respector of persons. His most lengthy litigation was with Anthony Thornton, magistrate, sheriff and county lieutenant. These suits were pending at his death.

Failure to pay for the goods that he sold from his pack led to Abraham's downfall. In 1765 Lennox and Scott became tired of waiting for their money and sued him for debt. Abraham purchased a bill of exchange from Duncan Graham and paid off this obligation, but when his paper fell due he made no effort to take it up. Graham sued and while this suit was pending William Dunlop seized Abraham for other debts and had him put in jail. Joseph DeJarnette, a professional bondsman, put up the collateral and he got out of the lockup. But his health was seriously impaired and died before any of the cases pending against him came to trial. When his son, Joseph, threatened to follow in his footsteps as a troublemaker, the Caroline magistrates took no chances and indicted the Younger Abraham in blank in 1769. Young Abraham did not wait to see what the charges might be. He hastily fled the county.

Isaac Jacobs, another Jewish peddler, was quite different. He was easy to get on with, people liked him, and he prospered.

INDUSTRY

There was little industry in colonial Caroline besides grist mills and artisans' shops. Charles Dick tried to manufacture potash and pearlash from native woods during the Great Drought (1755-56) to make crops grow in the parched land. Lundsford Lomax manufactured barrels and runlets and shipped them to the Canary Islands and the West Indies in exchange for wine, molasses and sugar in an effort to stave off bankruptcy after the French and Indian War. Neither of these attempts were successful.

a. *The Grist Mills*

The number of Caroline grist mills were legion. From the Order Books it seems that half of the deep bottoms in the county have been under water at some time. Because they were so numerous and the descriptions so confusing this author has been able to identify only a few of them. These are listed below:

Year Built or First Mentioned	*Owner*	*Stream* (a) *or Parish*	*Name Today*
Before 1732	William Daniel	Beverley's Run	White's
Before 1732	Francis Durrett	May's Run	Gray's (Henderson's)
Before 1732	Thomas Catlett	Drysdale	Cosby's
Before 1732	Peter Lantor	Drysdale	Collins or Ideal
Before 1732	Corbin family	Reedy Creek	Reedy Mill
Before 1732	Col. Cole Digges	Drysdale	
Before 1732	William Taliaferro	Peumandsend	Delos (1)
Before 1732	Edward Scrimshaw	St. Mary's	
Before 1732	Henry Ware (2)	St. Mary's	
Before 1732	John Miller	Peumandsend (Mill Creek)	Harris
Before 1732	John Sutton I.	Polecat	
1735	Rev. John Brunskill	Reedy Creek	
1739	John Baber	Long Branch of the North Anna	
1742	William Terrell (3)	Polecat	Stevens—gone
1742	John Rogers	St. Margaret's	
1743	Benjamin Robinson	St. Mary's	
1744	Richard Murray	Drysdale	Jones or Rolphs
1745	Thomas Royston	Peumandsend	
1745	Henry Burk (4)	Jackpond Creek	
1746	James & John Taylor	Marocossic	
1754	Thomas Cheadle	Polecat	
1754	Mathew Peatross	Reedy Creek	
1756	Robert Gilchrist	Peumandsend	Delos (1)
1756	Samuel Hargrave	North Anna	Oxford (5)
1756	William Quarles	North Anna	
1757	John Baylor	Drysdale	
1758	Harry Berry	Prosser's Run	
1759	James Lindsay	Drysdale	
1759	Edmound Pendleton	Marocossic	
1765	Thomas Roane	Marocossic	
1768	Charles Carter	Peumandsend (6)	
1771	Henry Terrell (3)	Polecat	Stevens (gone)

Year Built or First Mentioned	Owner	Stream (a) or Parish	Name Today
1771	Nicholas Ware (2)	St. Mary's	
1771	Seth Thornton (7)		
1771	James Garnett	Rebuilt Col. Cole Digges' old Mill—Drysdale Parish	
1771	James Dismukes	St. Margaret's	
1771	James Rennolds	Woodson's Branch	
1772	Samuel Burruss	Polecat (8)	
1773	James Harris		
1773	Benjamin Winn	Upper South River	Temples or Rattletrap
1773	Thomas Jones	Jones Spring Branch	
1773	Peyton Stern	Peumandsend (9)	
1774	Robert Mickleberry	Polecat—near Cheadles	
1774	Timothy Chandler	Polecat (10)	
1774	Thomas Trevillian	St. Margaret's	
1774	John Minor	North Anna	
1778	Reuben George	St. Margaret's	
1778	Richard Buckner	Same mill as Seth Thornton's	
1780	Rodham Kenner	Bottle Swamp	
1780	James Sutton	St. Margaret's	

(a) Stream may mean the main or the branch of a stream.

(1) May be the same mill. (2) May be the same mill. (3) May be the same mill.

(4) Sutton's milldam had broken and Henry Burk won the right to build this mill after a lawsuit with the Sutton family. After he built it he set out a peach orchard on his part of the floor of Sutton's pond and forestalled an effort of John Wiley to rebuild Sutton's Mill.

(5) Samuel Hargrave secured permission to build the first milldam across the North Anna during the Great Drought. When normal conditions returned the Caroline court ordered him to remove it because it considered the North Anna a navigable stream. Hargrave appealed this order to the General Court of the Colony and won.

(6) An old mill, mentioned because the dam broke.

(7) Seth Thornton gained permission to build this mill after a controversy with all the owners of the land, which he proposed to flood. To secure permission he agreed that the owner of the mill would grind the grain of the owners of the land adjacent to the millpond without pay, forever.

(8) An old mill. Samuel Burruss was ordered to fix his milldam to punish him for allowing Baptist worship at his home.

(9) Peyton Stern and James Miller engaged in a lawsuit over the ownership of the mill near the mouth of Peumandsend (Mill Creek), which was one of the most desirable mills in the county due to its location near Port Royal. James Miller won the suit but at the same time the court granted Stern the right to build a mill further upstream on Peumandsend.

(10) An old mill, mentioned in a guardianship account.

ARTISANS

In the early years of Caroline's history the artisans were among the most favored groups of the county's people. There was a shortage of skilled workers and they were paid well for their services. In 1742 the freeholders had to send all the way to Westmoreland to hire James Senior, a wheelwright. But as the number of Negro slaves in the county increased the position of the free skilled workers became more precarious. Planters taught their more intelligent slaves trades. Many free artisans became bankrupt.

Skilled workers lived in all sections of the county. But many of them had their homes around White's shop in upper St. Margaret's, Cheadle's shop near Chesterfield, Ware's shop near Conway's warehouse and in Port Royal.

Listed below are the skilled workers whose names appear in the Order Books. The date given is the first time a name appears. Most artisans continued to live in the county many years after this date.

Joiners and Carpenters: 1732—Benjamin Duval, Robert Farish*, Daniel Duval; 1736—Edmound Graves, Robert Rains; 1741—Adam Lindsay‡; 1744—William Lindsay†, John Montague, John Wiley*; 1746—Daniel Barksdale; 1748—Joseph Rogers; 1749—a Mourning Richards; 1750—John Holloway; 1751—Thomas Montague, Moses Sheets; 1753—James Pattie‡; 1754—Jacob Lindsay†; 1755—Gabriel Mitchell; 1757—John Mitchell, William Davis; 1760—George Wiley*; 1761—David Sterns*; 1764—John Small; 1765—Nathaniel Anderson; 1769—John Wiley, Jr.*; 1774—Thomas Merriweather.*

Coopers: 1739—Mathew Brooks; 1740—John Embrey; 1746—Sheerwood James.

Bricklayers: 1736—William Weller, John Mann; 1740—Thomas Sanders; 1749—Jacob Kendricks, John Johns.

Shoemakers: 1734—William Woodcock; 1740—Henry Woodcock; 1744—Thomas Jones; 1746—Francis James; 1755—Peter Bullard; 1771—John Griffin.

Tanner: 1762—Michael Brown Roberts.

Blacksmiths: 1754—Thomas White, Thomas Cheadle, Henry Ware, Nicholas Ware, Benjamin Arthur; 1756—Thomas Arthur; 1766—William Richerson.

Weavers: 1734—Daniel LaFoe; 1753—James Pattie.

Tailors: 1744—Dr. Daniel Fargusson; 1750—Jacob Johns; 1751—Thomas Smith.

Millwrights: 1734—Thomas Loving; 1741—Adam Lindsay‡; 1744—Lindsay‡; 1754—Jacob Lindsay.‡

Chairmaker: 1773—Anthony New.

---

*More nearly a contractor than a mere carpenter. Thomas Buckner I, may be added to this class.

†James Pattie had an odd combination of skills—weaver and carpenter.

‡The Lindsays were both carpenters and millwrights.

CREDIT

a. *Bankers and Money Lenders*

Only four Caroline families employed London bankers to look out for their interest abroad. They were the Baylors and the Beverleys who employed John Backhouse, the Corbins who employed John Handbury, the great Quaker banker, and the Lomaxes, who employed Nicholas Bosworth. After the French and Indian War the Lomaxes were more liability than assets as clients. They were in debt far beyond their means and in constant lawsuits with their banker.

Lesser Caroline families used the British mercantile firms with factors in residence in the county to look out for their affairs overseas as the occasion arose.

While the larger landowners borrowed from either their bankers or the British merchants to operate their plantations the smaller planters were hard put to find the capital to get on. They borrowed from the local merchants and tavern-keepers and after they exhausted this source of credit went to the professional money lenders, who flourished in Caroline from the county's earliest days. The more prominent included John Champe, and afterwards his son, William, and James Robb, of St. Mary's Parish, William and later James Gatewood and John Sutton of St. Margaret's and James Taylor, the elder, James Taylor, the younger, John Martin and John Broaddus of Drysdale.

In one term of the Caroline Court (1766) Broaddus sold out James Loving, Ralph Farmer, Henry Pemberton, John Gaunt and Thomas Brooks. Broaddus' attitude may be accounted for, in part, by the fact that his father, William Broaddus, died heavily in debt to William Shackleford and James Gaines, and he had to pay this debt before coming into his share of the estate.

Unfortunately, the reckoning day came for the vast majority of Caroline freeholders in debt. Hundreds went to jail and scores surrendered their holdings and took the pauper's oath. In a frantic attempt to save a portion of their property some debtors arranged for special bail to get out of jail and hold their creditors off while they worked. The men who furnished this bail charged up to fifty per cent, and if the debtor defaulted he went back to prison where he remained until he surrendered all his property to meet his obligations and bound himself out to earn enough to pay off the rest. Bail bondsmen did not begin operating in Caroline until after the French and Indian War. They included Joseph DeJarnette I, John Woolfolk and his son, Joseph, Paul Thilman, John Beverley Roy, Roger Quarles, and numerous members of the Taylor family. Joseph DeJarnette even went so far as to post bail for Mordicai Abraham, when the Jewish peddler was in jail for debt.

POOR DEBTORS WHO SURRENDERED THEIR PROPERTY AND TOOK THE PAUPER'S OATH IN CAROLINE COUNT

1732—William Shelton.
1733—Thomas Lantor.
1735—Edward Crawley.
1736—Richard Evins, John English, William Ochletree, Nicholas Lankford.
1737—John Hawkins, Richard Morris.
1738—John Mayfield.
1739—Patrick Boswell.
1741—John Hudson, Elizabeth Martin, Jeremiah Swan.
1743—John Partlow, James Stepp.
1744—John Hart.
1745—Thomas Pickett, William Knighton, Benjamin Lankford.
1747—John Harvie.

1748—Henry Wood, John Grimsley, John Dayson.

1749—Jacob Kendrick, George Stone, Henry Cooper.

1751—Ambroise Blackburn, Cornelius Vaughan.

1754—William Smith.

1755—John Graves, Benjamin Long.

1756—Joseph Redd.

1757—John Plant.

1758—William Grimsley, Benjamin Chapman, John Howworth, Richard Chapman.

1759—Jacob Johns.

1762—John Hackett, John Price.

1764—Robert Chapman, Joshua King, Peter Bullard, John Ashburn, John Small.

1765—Henry Mills, Elizabeth Meacham, Richard Vaughan.

1766—James Burton.

1767—John Gurent, William Crawley, Thomas Clayton, Ambroise Jeter, John Davis, William Ballard.

1773—William Mitchell.

The estates the poor debtors forfeited varied greatly in size. A few are listed below in detail.

Estate of Benjamin Long (1755): Negro girl, large black horse, 2 beds and furniture, 1 chest of drawers, 2 spinning-wheels, 1 case and bottles, 1 large chest, 1 large trunk, 3 chairs, 1 box iron and heater, 1 small glass, 2 large pails, 1 piggin, 2 pt. pots, 1 frying-pan, 1 small trunk, 1 flowered sugar box, 4 pewter dishes, 1 dz. plates, 3 cannisters, 1 pr. fire tongs, 2 iron pots, 1 gun, parcel old china and earthenware, 5 table knives, 8 forks, 2 iron candlesticks, large money scales.

Long was a tavern-keeper who operated Roy's tavern in Port Royal under a lease. Robert Gilchrist was his chief creditor.

Estate of Joseph Redd (1756): 6 Negroes, 13 head of cattle, 10 head of sheep, 7 hogs, 2 horses, 3 feather beds and furniture.

Redd was the most prominent Caroline planter to give up his property and take the poor debtor's oath. Edmound Taylor was his chief creditor.

Estate of Thomas Pickett (1745): parcel of corn, 14 hogs, 1 meal tub, 1 washing tub, spinning-wheel, 3 chairs, 1 cow hide, 1 bed, one sheet, 2 bedsteads and one side saddle.

Estate of John Grimsley (1748): one horse and saddle.

Estate of Henry Wood (1748): 1 chest, 1 pot, 1 runlett, 1 iron pistol, parcel of pewter, 1 pr. Holland and 4 pr. old hoes, 1 fiddle and a hominy grinder.

Estate of John Mayfield (1738): 1 old bed and furniture, 1 pig, 2 small dishes, 1 old mare running at large, and 1 small crop left in the field when he went to prison.

Estate of Joshua King (1764): 1 boolster and blanket.

SOCIAL LIFE

1. THE TAVERNS

Much of the social life in colonial Virginia centered about the taverns. Here planters, traders, professional men and artisans met to discuss business and politics. Here cheats and speculators plied their crafts and wastrel hung out so long as they had, or were able to borrow, the means for dissipation. Here traveling troups gave shows and games of chance flourished. Cards and dice were the favorite devices for gambling on the inside of the building, while on the outside bets were placed on wrestling matches, cock-fights, gander head-pulling contests and horse-races.

The Caroline court granted licenses to ninety applicants to operate taverns between 1727 and 1781. These licensees are listed below with the locations of their taverns if the sites are disclosed in the Order Books.

Date	Licensee	Location and Remarks
?-1733	John Sutton	South side of the Mattapony at Burk's ferry (bridge).
?-1734	George Senior	Location unknown—license revoked by court.
?-1735	William Dennis	Chesterfield.
1731-32	Robert Willis	First courthouse—the court tavern.
1732-33	Edward Haswell	First courthouse—court tavern—Willis stand.
1733-34	John Brown	First courthouse—Willis stand.
1733-39	Benjamin Rennolds	First courthouse.
1733-48	Samuel Coleman	First courthouse—court tavern.
1734-50	Thomas Burk I	Sutton's stand; south side Mattapony at Burk's bridge.

Date	Licensee	Location and Remarks
1734-80	John Sutton II	Chesterfield.
1735-45	Michael Guinney	South side Mattapony at Guinney bridge.
1735-56	Thomas Bankes	Chesterfield.
1735-45	Dorothy Roy	Roy's warehouse, or Port Royal.
1736-45	William Conner	(Woodford) bridge.
1737-55	John Dyer	South side Mattapony at Doguetown (Milford) bridge.
1738-41	William Mason	St. Margaret's Parish—Needwood.
1738-41	John Littlepage	Littlepage ferry (bridge), moved across the Pamunkey.
1739-49	William Burdette	First courthouse—Benjamin Rennolds stand.
1740-44	Edward Ware	Near Conway's warehouse.
1741-44	William Boulware	Location unknown.
1741-43	John Wiley	Needwood—Mason's stand.
1741-43	John Neiville	"at his home"—location unknown.
1741-49	James Dismukes	First courthouse—John Brown's stand.
1741-74	John Sneed	Daniel's (White's) Mill.
1742-47	Phillip Johnston	Dolly Wrights fork (1953 name).
1744-48	Josiah Baker	Near Conway's warehouse — Edward Ware's stand.
1744-46	Sarah Parrott	Bull Church.
1744-52	Gabriel Long	Upper Drysdale, near B u c k n e r 's (Morse) Mill.
1745-50	Thomas White	White's (Burk's) Shop.
1745-59	James Martin	Guiney bridge — Michael Guiney's stand.
1745-81	Gabriel Toombs	Toombs ferry across Mattapony — east edge of county.
1745-48	Oliver Towles	Port Royal.
1745-65	John Miller	Port Royal.
1745-49	Thomas Wild	Needwood.
1745-52	Richard Murray	Drysdale Parish—near Sparta.
1745-51	Thomas Roy	Port Royal.
1746-49	Dr. George Todd	Port Royal—moved to Villborro.
1747-56	Thomas Johnston	Dolly Wright's fork—Phillip Johnston's stand.
1748-57	Richard Whithead	St. Margaret's Parish, maybe White Chimney's.
1748-58	Robert Garrett	Near Conway's warehouse, Ware-Baker stand.

Date	Licensee	Location and Remarks
1748-49	Betty Coleman	First courthouse — Samuel Coleman's stand.
1748-55	Luke Burfoot	Port Royal—Oliver Towles stand.
1749- ?	John Pendleton	"late home of John Martin"—Clifton, Drysdale Parish.
1749-53	Edmound Taylor	St. Margaret's Parish—Needwood.
1750-52	Alexander Ross	Port Royal.
1750-62	Henry Burk	Thomas Burk I's stand; Burk's bridge.
1750-57	Sussannah White	Thomas White's stand — White's (Burk's) shop.
1750-81	Dr. George Todd	Villborro.
1750-59	William Johnston	First courthouse — Samuel Coleman's stand.
1751-52	George Keeling	St. Mary's Parish—site unknown.
1752-56	Stephen Haynes	Lower Drysdale — Richard Murray's stand.
1752-73	Thomas Pittman	Tuckahoe valley.
1752-55	Benjamin Long	Thomas Roy's stand—Port Royal.
1753-57	Phillip Taylor	Needwood—Edmound Taylor's stand.
1754-56	John Carneal	Upper St. Margaret's, exact site unknown.
1755-75	William Fox	Port Royal.
1756-80	Benjamin Hubbard	Lower Drysdale — Stephen Haynes stand.
1756-62	John Allmond	Doguetown bridge—John Dyer's stand.
1756-69	William Meacham	St. Margaret's Parish—Chesterfield?
1757-65	John Dudley	St. Margaret's, perhaps White Chimneys.
1758-72	Paul Thilman	Needwood.
1758-62	Abraham Mitchell	Near Conway's warehouse—Garrett's stand.
1759-71	Francis Coleman	First courthouse — Samuel Coleman's stand.
1759-74	Aquilla Johnston	Guinney bridge, north side of Mattapony.
1760-70	William Johnston	Second courthouse, moved to new location after Francis Coleman became of age and demanded Coleman's tavern; his son, James, persuaded court to hold some sessions in building nearby.
1761-63	Zachery Benson	Location unknown.
1762-65	James Gouge	Port Royal "in a room of his home."

Date	Licensee	Location and Remarks
1762-73	George Taylor	Near Conway's warehouse.
1762-72	Thomas Burk II	Burk's bridge; the Burk family's stand.
1763-65	John Bowcock	Port Royal.
1763-64	William Graves	Location unknown.
1763-66	William Parker	"at his home"—lower Drysdale Parish.
1766-81	Edward Powers	Port Royal.
1767-76	James Yarbrough	Bull Church.
1769-76	Humphrey Edmounds	Chesterfield.
1770-78	Richard Johnston	Second courthouse — William Johnston's stand.
1772-81	John Alexander Still	Port Royal.
1772-76	Nathaniel Norment	Reedy Mill.
1772-81	Hannah Coleman	First courthouse — Samuel Coleman's stand.
1773-81	John Burk	Burk's bridge—Burk family's stand.
1773-81	Robert Woolfolk	Needwood.
1773-81	Ambroise Dudley	Near Conway's warehouse—Garrett's stand.
1774-81	William Buckner	Port Royal.
1774-81	John Hoomes	his "new buildings at the Bowling Green."
1774-81	Benjamin Sneed	Daniel's Mill—Sneed family stand.
1774-81	James Head Lynch	St. Margaret's, probably White Chimneys..
1775-81	Mildred Palmer	Guinney bridge.
1775-81	Ann Fox	Port Royal—William Fox stand.
1776-81	Robert Broaddus	Lower Drysdale—Hubbard's stand.
1777-81	Peyton Stern	St. Mary's, perhaps "The Trap."
1777-81	John Sutton III	Chesterfield.
1777-81	George Madison	St. Margaret's (Clyde Coleman Store, a Welch—1953).*
1779-81	Nancy Johnston	Second courthouse — William Johnston's stand.

*Present-day Madison Magisterial District, and Madison Precinct took its name from this tavern, and not from the fourth President of the United States.

Most taverns showing the last license granted in 1781 continued after that date.

The Order Books give complete descriptions about the Port Royal taverns. Humphrey Edmoundson and John Sutton III at Chesterfield, Dr. George Todd at Villborro, Paul Thilman and Robert Woolfolk at Needwood, the Johnstons at Wright's

Fork, the Burks at Burk's Bridge, Michael Guiney and James Martin at Guiney Bridge, the Sneeds at Daniel's Mill, John Hoomes at the Bowling Green, the Murray-Haynes-Hubbard-Broaddus in lower Drysdale, the taverns at the first and second courthouses, and many others. But the author had to establish the location of some taverns by indirect evidence, or not try to place them at all. Especially difficult were the early taverns along the Rappahannock and at Chesterfield, which were the first houses of public entertainment in the area which became the county.

Of Caroline's colonial taverns only four remain standing in whole or in part in 1953. They are George Todd's Tavern at Villborro, Thomas Johnston's at Wright's Fork, the Murray-Haynes-Hubbard-Broaddus' Tavern which is now the home of Miss Ivy Carter at Sparta, and Robert Farish's printing shop in Port Royal, which houses several taverns of that town. A building, the Bowling Green Hotel, stands on the site of John Hoomes' Tavern at the Bowling Green but the best evidence indicates that this is not the building which housed the colonial tavern.

The Caroline Court at first was quite strict with licensees but in time it grew more liberal. The magistrates revoked the licenses of Robert Willis (1732) and George Senior (1734) and refused to grant licenses to Henry Berry (1737) and Henry Long (1739). They also turned down Gabriel Long when he first applied (1742) because he was a convicted boot-legger. But relented and granted him a license (1744) when Edmound Pendleton posted bond as his surety.

The Bootleggers: Leniency did not eliminate bootleggers. The first of whom was the above mentioned Gabriel Long. The court convicted him for selling punch without a license to Thomas Buckner and John Catlett, two of the king's magistrates in 1736, and fined him 2,000 lbs. of tobacco, although Buckner and Catlett refused to testify against him in court and were fined 350 lbs. of tobacco each for contempt.

Joseph and Martha King did a flourishing bootleg business in the early days of Port Royal (1743-47) and were fined several times for this crime. Josiah Baker sold liquor without a license after he got out of jail for debt in an attempt to make a comeback until he was caught in 1749. John Penn (not the patriot) was convicted for selling rum and John Ketcham for selling cider without licenses in 1755, when it was a great temptation to bootleg because of the high tax on ardent spirits to help finance the French and Indian War. Ann Dudley, the last bootlegger of record during Caroline's colonial period, was convicted of selling liquor to soldiers without a license in 1779.

The Drinks: Caroline bars offered a wide variety of drinks for the tiplers and the prices were fixed by the court. These drinks included French brandy and Canary, Teneriff, Madeira, port and claret wines for the wealthy, rum distilled in the northern colonies, Virginia peach and apple brandy and English beer for the well-to-do, and Virginia beer, cider and hot meal, the colonial equivalent of "old hen" of the Volstead era, for the poor. There were many fancy drinks for the fastideous. They included lemonado, or Sangaree, orchard punch and citron water. Prices were relatively high. In 1750 a working man was able to buy a half gallon of rum, or two gallons of ale, for a day's wages.

2. GAMBLING

Virginia laws forbade wagering on cards and dice in taverns, but since magistrates, in precinct courts, had jurisdiction to punish violators the only cases of record in the Order Books are appeals to the county court. There are only one set of these appeals in the Order Books of Caroline. They arose in 1746 because of gambling at James Martin's tavern at the north end of Guinney Bridge. Thomas Buckner, the waggish magistrate of upper Drysdale precinct fined Martin 5 pounds sterling, for each offense of allowing gambling at his tavern on June 21, August 2 and August 7, and Thomas Garnett, John Dyer, Thomas Pickett, Francis Pickett, William Hewlett, William Conner, Joseph Stevens, Samuel Pryor, George Yates and Joseph Read 5 pounds each for shooting crap in the tavern on June 21, Equitter Johnston, Phillip May, Micajah Pickett,

Thomas Garnett, Samuel Pryor and Francis Pickett, 5 pounds each for shooting crap at the tavern on August 2, and Thomas Garnett, John Dyer, William Hewlett, Francis Pickett, Phillip May and Samuel Pryor for betting on cards at the tavern on August 7. Together these fines amounted to a large sum. They equaled the sales price of the tobacco crop from over thirty-eight acres. On appeal the county court made drastic reductions. It exonerated James Martin completely, which was a boon for him, since a conviction for permitting gambling in his tavern meant the loss of his license. It also dismissed all other fines except the 5 pounds assessments against Thomas Garnett, John Dyer, Francis Pickett, Phillip May and Samuel Pryor for their second convictions of crap-shooting. The amount paid in fines fell from 125 to 25 pounds, sterling.

The only other case of gambling in taverns, of record in colonial Caroline, took place at Needwood in 1776. Robert Mickleberry, according to the "Precedings of the Caroline Committee of Safety" reported to the committee that he got drunk at Needwood with Robert Woolfolk, the tavern-keeper, John Thilman, George Guy and Nathaniel Norment, and gambled all night while on the way home from attending Hanover Court. Because of the end of the rule of the Committee of Safety shortly thereafter, there is no record of what happened to this report.

The only statutes controlling betting away from the taverns until the rule of the Committee of Safety were laws which prohibited "excessive" gambling. Only three Caroline residents tried to escape the payment of their debts by pleading these laws. They were John Miller, the Younger, John Beverley Roy and Rodham Kenner II. In each instance they failed, juries held that their wagers were not excessive and that they must pay in full.

Thomas Morris was perhaps the most unfortunate gambler in the history of colonial Caroline. In 1737 he gambled all night and until ten o'clock the next day in the home of Robert Farguson, with Farguson, Robert Williamson and James Smith, and in the course of the game lost all he possessed including the horse he rode to the party. But in spite of the loss he mounted the horse to ride away when he departed. Farguson, who was the winner, tried to stop him by seizing the horse's bridle. A fight ensued and Morris won the fight, but afterwards Farguson sued him for assault and battery. A jury awarded Farguson punative damages and in a side issue, which was not germane to the case, confirmed his title to horse and harness. Mary Chiles was present during the card game, and testified in court, but the Order Books fail to reveal if she were a party to the gambling.

With the rule of the Committee of Safety public officials tried to break up gambling in homes. They twice summoned Rodham Kenner II to appear and answer charges, and summoned William Murray, Joseph Cooper, John Cooper and William Poe to appear against him. How Kenner came out is not a matter of record.

3. HORSE-RACING

Traditions hold that the Hoomes family raced horses at the Bowling Green prior to 1700. This may be true because Caroline was the cradle of horse-racing in colonial Virginia. But the first record of a horse-race in the county was in 1739 when John Latham sued Joseph Hoomes alleging that his horse,

Yellow Jacket, had defeated Hoomes' horse, *Blue Bonnet,* in a race. The court awarded Latham the wager and the first Hoomes race-horse of record has a defeat marked opposite his name.

The next year (1740) another horse-race of record took place. William Waller bet John Miller, the Younger, sixteen pistoles (Spanish gold coins), that his bay horse could outrun a gray horse belonging to John Green, twenty yards in half a mile, and the parties gave Arch MacPhearson, a magistrate the stakes to hold. In the course of the race the Waller horse was at least 35 yards of the pole, when "a stranger did suffer a dog to run at the Waller horse and cause him to fly the path," and run at his disadvantage some 30 yards before his rider was able to get him back on the track. But in spite of this mishap the Waller horse managed to cross the finish line some 10 yards ahead of the horse owned by Green. Because of the confusion the judges refused to render a decision and both Waller and Miller claimed the stakes. MacPhearson held on to all the money in the face of their demands and Miller sued. The court ruled against him and awarded the wager to Waller. An interesting sidelight to this case was the amount of money bet. The wager totaled enough to buy an able-bodied slave at the prevailing market price.

Seven years later (1747) another case was tried in the Caroline court which revealed the large amounts that the gentry of the county were willing to spend on race-horses, and horse-racing. The year before Ephriam Buckner of Orange had shown up at a session of the Caroline court with a horse he directed Richard Straughn, the auctioneer, to put up for sale to the highest bidder, on the court green. Edward Brassfield and John Emerson offered competing bids until the bidding reached 6 pounds, 15 shillings, by Brassfield, and Elias Blackburn, an onlooker, advised the auctioneer to disregard Brassfield because he was drunk. Upon hearing this Straughn demanded that Brassfield show his money, and Brassfield replied by opening his purse. There were only five or six shillings inside and Straughn proceeded to knock the horse out to Emerson for his last bid of 6 pounds, 12 shillings, in spite of Brassfield's protest. While this argument was going on John Baylor of New Market, paid 6 pounds, 13 shillings, directly to Buckner, mounted the horse and rode off. The crowd was aghast at this conduct, but Emerson was too awed to attempt to do anything because Baylor was such an important personage, until John Micou, another gentleman with great prestige, championed his cause. Micou announced that Emerson was merely acting as his agent and sent word to Baylor demanding the horse. Baylor refused to surrender the animal and Micou sued for possession. In the trial of the case Baylor testified that Brassfield was acting for him as much as Emerson was acting for Micou. Witnesses testified that while Brassfield was "tipsy" he was "not out of his senses" and asked the age of the horse and other pertinent questions before he began to bid. The trial lasted for twenty days and in the end a jury ruled that Baylor might keep the horse but that each of the litigants must pay his own witnesses. Witness fees were sizeable because many witnesses had been summoned several times from Orange and other distant counties. The total bill ran to over 12,000 lbs. of tobacco, which was over eight times the sales price of the horse.

But what the Buckner horse cost John Baylor was mere pocket change to the amount he paid for *Fearnaught* seventeen years later. In 1764 he brought this celebrated stud to New Market from England at the costs of over 1,000 guineas. This sum was more than the sales price of the crop from 125 acres of tobacco at the time. A decade later John Hoomes of the Bowling Green imported *Stirling*. These two horses were the progenitors of the most famous race-horses in America.

Horse theft in colonial Caroline was a serious crime. The magistrates sent Richard Munford to stand trial in the General Court of the Colony in Williamsburg in 1739 for breaking into the stable of William MacKie and carrying away a large bay gelding, saddle and bridle, and ordered 25 lashes at the whipping-post for his partner in crime, John Lomax, a youth of sixteen. Twenty-five years later another set of magistrates sent David Gordon to the colonial capital for trial after he stole a horse belonging to Francis Fleming, and shortly thereafter sentenced a runaway Negro to hang for the theft of a horse and saddle from John Baylor. While the punishments imposed on Munford and Gordon is not known, the chances are they suffered the same fate as the Negro because accused were only transported to Williamsburg to stand trial for crimes punishable by death, and neither of them returned to Caroline.

Race-tracks: While doubtlessly there were race-tracks at New Market and the Bowling Green during colonial times, the only race-track recorded in the Order Books is Sanders Race-track near Port Royal. This track is first mentioned in the Order Book for 1744, and there are frequent other references to it in the Order Books covering the period extending from that date through the Revolution. This track was for the masses. Here the gentry, small freeholders, traders, artisans and roustabouts rubbed shoulders and placed their bets.

4. HUNTING

Caroline people have always been huntsmen and interested in hunting laws. The last wolf of record was killed in the county by David Terrell in 1747. As early as 1738 laws were enacted for the protection of deer, to force owners to keep hounds and beagles tied except when on the chase, and to make unlawful the use of fire, or the burning over of land, in hunting game.

5. OTHER AMUSEMENTS

The records contain little information about other forms of amusement in colonial Caroline. Henry Wood was a fiddler and played for the public's entertainment, until he fiddled himself into bankruptcy and lost his fiddle when he surrendered all his property and took the poor debtor's oath in 1748.

Bishop Meade in his *Old Churches and Families of Virginia* relates that a group of traveling players came to White Chimneys' in 1772 and arranged to give a play, and that when one of the actors became sick and was unable to play his rôle, a substitute was found in a bookseller guest at the tavern. This bookseller was named Weems. Afterwards he became a minister and achieved fame as rector for George Washington. In time he wrote the celebrated *Parson Weems' Life of Washington.*

DOMESTIC RELATIONS

1. MARRIAGE

Romance may have blossomed in colonial Caroline but the marriages of record in the Order Books were mercenary affairs. A few of them are reported in detail below.

Roy-Kenner: The Rev. Rodham Kenner of Drysdale Parish was hardly cold in his grave in 1733 when Dorothy Roy engineered the marriage of his widow, Judith Beverley Kenner, to her son Thomas Roy, although Judith was at least ten years older than Thomas. Judith had inherited a large slice of the vast Beverley fortune and Dorothy coveted this property for the Roys. There is no evidence to indicate that Thomas and

Judith were unhappy together, but they were in constant difficulty with the court because of their attempts to rob George
Kenner, Judith's son by her first husband, of his share of the
estate. Their misconduct was so flagrant that the clergy became aroused since young George was a minister's son, and
upon a parsons' petition the court transferred custody of
George's property from his mother to his uncle, Hausen
Kenner.

Dugard-Kenner: George Kenner died a rich man in 1772, and
his widow, Margaret, promptly remarried. Her new spouse
was John Dugard, an adventurer, who only recently had moved
to Caroline from Baltimore. This marriage displeased her son,
Rodham Kenner II, a sporting youth much given to betting
and drink, and when the newly wed pair cut down on his
allowance for dissipation, he took a trip to Baltimore to see
what dirt he might dig up on his step-father. He dug up plenty.
Dugard already had a wife in Maryland when he married
Margaret Kenner in Caroline. Young Rodham got affidavits
to prove this from the Rev. Thomas Chase, rector of St. Paul's
Parish, Baltimore, and the Governor of Maryland and returned
home with these documents. The Caroline court speedily convicted Dugard for bigamy. But Dugard refused to accept this
conviction and employed Patrick Henry to appeal his case to
the General Court of the Colony in Williamsburg. Henry was
successful in the appeal, and Dugard returned to Caroline a
free man. But he refused to pay Henry his fee, and Henry,
who was a close collector, turned on him in his wrath and saved
the Kenner fortune for Rodham II.

Fleming-Hoomes: When Joseph Hoomes of the Bowling
Green died in 1753, his widow, Sussannah Waller Hoomes,
married dashing Francis Fleming, who was many years her
junior, before she took time to go to court and probate the will
of her first husband. After reading the document Fleming
persuaded her to renounce her legacy and claim her dower.
When this was done he moved the court to assign her title to a
widow's share of the Negroes and other personal property of
the estate in fee, and after the court granted this motion he

prevailed on his wife to make a will leaving him every thing she owned. With this document drawn Fleming lived at the Bowling Green in great style, carrying on the great Hoomes tradition of horse-racing. His extravagance threatened to undermine the whole Hoomes fortune until Joseph Hoomes' relatives became alarmed and hired Edmound Pendleton to preserve what was left of the property for Joseph Hoomes' children. Pendleton did a thorough job and Fleming's entertaining was curtailed. But his dissipation continued, and Sussannah's affection for him cooled as she grew older. Before she died in 1772 she was made another will leaving all her property to her children. Fleming ignored this will and tried to probate the first. When the magistrates found out what he was up to they ordered him to produce the second will at once, and when he refused fined him for contempt. After this show of force Fleming produced the will and paid the fine but brazenly retired to the Bowling Green and challenged the Hoomes family to force him to leave. He did not enjoy this refuge long. Pendleton brought a suit of ejection and the court ordered the sheriff to put him out. He passed the rest of his life in poverty, a broken down sport.

Although Joseph Hoomes' children regained the property, the trouble with Fleming sharply curtailed the size of the estate. In an effort to rebuild the family fortune young John Waller Hoomes opened a tavern at the Bowling Green in 1774. This move led to the building of the town that is now (1953) Caroline's county seat.

Long-Griffin: In 1746 John Griffin told Gabriel Long several times while he was drunk, that he would give his grist mill and fifty pounds, sterling, to one of Long's sons, if the young man married his daughter, Betty. Long repeated this offer after he got home and his son, Gabriel, Jr., immediately began to court Betty. In time he won her hand, but when he went to her father to make the financial arrangements, on which the match depended, John Griffin welshed. He claimed that he was unable to part with his mill property and countered with an offer a Negro woman and fifty pounds. Young Long accepted this compromise and the marriage took place. At the wedding feast Griffin was again very drunk, and while in his cups waxed so enthusiastic over the match that he doubled Betty's dower to two Negro women and a hundred pounds. But the next morning he was sober and unwilling to part with any of his property when the young couple got ready to set out for their new home. He protested that he had neither Negroes nor money to give away. After an ugly scene Betty prevailed upon her father to offer a chest, a cow and a calf, and her husband to accept the offer.

After this settlement Long made no further demands on his father-in-law until ten months later when his wife died giving birth to a child. After her death he demanded the payment of her dower in full. Griffin refused to pay and Long sued. The suit lasted eleven days and at its end the court ruled that Griffin was not responsible for the doubled offer of dowery he made at the wedding feast while drunk, but that he must pay Long the value of the originally proffered dowery when sober of a Negro woman and fifty pounds, less the value of the chest, cow and calf, Long took away when he carried his bride from her father's home.

Hoyle-Holloway: In 1747 Charles Holloway offered two Negroes and 100 pounds sterling to any eligible young man, who married his daughter, Ann. What was wrong with Ann the records do not disclose, but it must have been quite bad because no young man in Caroline took advantage of the offer. It remained open for over a year, and until Edward Hoyle of King George heard of it and came courting. Holloway was a shrewd man and after he had Hoyle hooked he managed to cut the dowery down to one Negress. Matters moved smoothly after this compromise for a time. The marriage was celebrated in Caroline and afterwards Ann took the Negress, who was her personal maid, Lucy, to live with her in King George. But when Ann died Holloway demanded Lucy's return. Hoyle refused to part with the woman and Holloway sued for her possession in King George. The King George court denied his claim and he returned to Caroline and sulked. But he did not sulk long, because one night under the cover of darkness he crossed the Rappahannock, went to the Hoyle plantation and spirited Lucy away, along with her children born since she went to live in King George. Back in Caroline, Holloway dared Hoyle to try to regain the Negress and her offsprings. Hoyle ignored this challenge for lawlessness and accused Holloway of kidnapping in the Caroline court and demanded that the Caroline magistrates order his property returned. But the Caroline magistrates dismissed all the charges and ruled that Holloway had only reclaimed what was rightfully his own.

An interesting side light in the testimony recorded in Order Books covering this case reveals that Holloway's daughters called him "Daddy." But the magistrates, who took down the testimony, carefully points out that "Daddy means Father."

2. ADULTRY

Not all Caroline people were faithful to their marriage vows. The cases of adultry which came to the attention of the court follow:

1732—William Terrell and Rachael Jourdanne—excused when Terrell promised to support the child. Thirteen years later he deeded a plot of land to Joannah Jourdanne.

1733—William Hallett and Ann, the wife of George Downer—20 pounds bond not to meet for a year and a day.

1734-38—John Terrell and Elizabeth Harrison—this couple was before the court in 1734, 1735 and 1737 for adultry. Terrell had taken the woman into his home although he had a wife, Sarah Terrell. Three children were born to the couple out of wedlock. Each time they were tried, they were placed under a larger bond not to meet. But this did not stop them. They fled the colony of Virginia in 1738 to escape punishment.

1736—Thomas Pierce and Sarah Shelton—20 pound bond not to meet for a year and a day.

1739—Richard Coleman and Margaret Clark—40 pound bond not to meet for a year and a day.

1741—Edward Crawley and Martha King—40 pound bond not to meet for a year and a day.

1748—Jacob Johns and Ann Welsh—punishment not of record.

1763—Isaac Baker and Mary Cox—20 pound bond not to meet for a year and a day.

1771—John Mason and Ann Blanton—indited and placed under a 50 pound bond for a year and a day.

3. SEPARATE MAINTENANCES

Divorces were not allowed except by acts of Parliament but county courts granted women separate maintenance from their husbands, if facts warranted such grants. Separate maintenances granted by the Caroline court follow:

1733—Sussannah May from John May.

1740—Sarah Terrell from John Terrell. The court granted Sarah Terrell permission to take over the estate of her husband, John Terrell, because he had fled the colony with Elizabeth Harrison.

1744—Margaret Clark from John Clark. The court granted this woman separate maintenance from her husband although it had convicted her five years before for adultry with Richard Coleman. She was a sister of Richard Straughn, the auctioneer, and he had great influence with men in authority.

1747—Ann White against James White. This woman was another sister of Richard Straughn. When James White failed to put up the funds for her separate support as ordered by the court, Straughn sued as her next friend, and the magistrates granted him the right to seize a Negro slave named Ben, who was the property of White, hire the Negro out for 500 lbs. of tobacco a year, and pay the funds he collected for the hire, to his sister for her support.

1748—Ann Gough Oakley against Thomas Oakley. Ann Gough was bound to Thomas Oakley as a child. He married her after she grew up. Later she sued him for separate support.

1754—Mary Payne from David Payne.

1760—Elizabeth Cannady from Jeremiah Cannady (Kennedy)—Jeremiah Cannady did not have to pay an annual stipend to his wife, as was true in all other cases. When they parted the court ordered James Kay and Giles Samuel to split his estate and assigned her half. Afterwards the magistrates placed him under a 20 pound bond to keep the peace. Elizabeth Cannady's flirtations with James Kay subsequently caused Kay to murder his wife.

1781—Ann Blanton Renolds from Thomas Reynolds. Ann Blanton was lucky to have a husband. Ten years before she had been convicted of adultry with John Mason, and subsequently borne several bastards. One of whom she claimed that John Beverley Roy was the father. But Roy managed to escape when she sued him for the child's support. In spite of this unsavory background the court ruled that Thomas Reynolds must pay for her separate maintenance.

4. SUITS FOR DOWER

Caroline women were capable of looking out for their interest after their husband's deaths. If the legacy the husband left them in his will was less than their dower they renounced the will and claimed the dower. The following widows renounced wills and claimed dowers.

1739—Martha Thornton Catlett renounced the will of Thomas Catlett.

1740—Rachael Binion renounced the will of Samuel Binion.

1744—Sarah Dickinson renounced the will of Thomas Dickinson.

1745—Frances Hoomes renounced the will of George Hoomes.

1747—Judith Long renounced the will of Jeremiah Long.

1748—Elizabeth Goodwin renounced the will of George Goodwin to keep her Negro slave Lucy.

1748—Ann Bell renounced the will of John Bell.

1753—Mary Mills renounced the will of Mathew Mills.

1753—Sussannah Hoomes renounced the will of Joseph Hoomes.

1757—Ann Taylor renounced the will of James Taylor.

1760—Mary Buller renounced the will of John Buller.

1759—Sarah Herndon renounced the will of William Herndon.

1771—Mary Brown renounced the will of John Brown.

1772—Jane Taylor renounced the will of Francis Taylor.

1776—Elizabeth Thornton renounced the will of Peter Thornton.

5. UNWANTED SUITORS

A few men were too persistent in their courtships and the women asked the court for protection. These cases in Caroline follow:

1744—Mace Pickett placed under a 50 pound bond upon the complaint of Thomas and Dorcas Wilshire. Pickett was trying to seduce a married woman.

1745—Mace Pickett placed under a 50 pound bond to stay away from Peggy Dunn upon the complaint of Thomas Pickett. Pickett was trying to take his brother's girl.

1745—Sussannah Allen complains against Hugh Croucher. Complaint dismissed.

6. RAPE

There were no convictions of a white man for rape in colonial Caroline and only twice was the crime charged.

1745—Ann Campbell accused Samuel Pryor of rape. But Francis Thornton and Richard Buckner swore that Pryor was out of the county on the day of the alleged crime and the court dismissed the charge.

1774—Mourning Phillips, the wife of Jeremiah Phillips, accused Chillion White, a constable, of rape. He was indited but a jury refused to convict.

7. BASTARDS

Bastards were commonplace in colonial Caroline, although the punishment for a white woman, free or indentured, who bore an illegitimate child was 5 lashes at the whipping-post, or a 50 shilling or 500 lb. of tobacco fine. Few women had the money or tobacco to pay the fine and most of them were whipped. A list of the white women who had bastards follows. All were whipped unless specifically stated otherwise.

1733—Elizabeth Sanders, fine paid by Thomas Lantor, Charity Burns, child a mulatto, Mary Close, child a mulatto, Jane Ross, child a mulatto.

1734—Margaret Pence, Mary Scott.

1735—Mary Bell.

1736—Elizabeth Sanders, Christine Smith, Emmanuel Penn the father but fine paid by James Vaughter.

1737—Eleanor Douglass, Margaret Pence, Mary Billops, Elizabeth Sanders, child a mulatto but Thomas Lantor paid the fine, Margaret Crew.

1738—Elizabeth Rains.

1739—Mary Scott, child a mulatto.

1740—Lucy Fortune.

1741—Sussannah Brooks.

1742—Mary Rankin, Agatha Marshall, William Clatterbuck paid the fine.

1743—Mary Scott, child a mulatto.

1744—Mary Prosser, Mary Anderson, Grace Vaughan, Mary Blassingame.

1745—Rachael White, Elizabeth Barnes, Mary Wilshire, Jeanette Grant, Elizabeth Gregory,* Lettis Powell.

1746—Sarah Gibson, Isabella Griffin.

1747—Elizabeth Massey, William Cockran the father paid the fine.

1748—Sussannah Baker, a mulatto child, Mary Scott, a mulatto child, Mary Wilshire, Ann Welch, George Black paid the fine, Mary Blassingame.

1749—Honor Mundowney.

1750—Sussannah Baker, a mulatto child.

1751—Elizabeth Whitchfield, Ann Bankes, Sarah Parnell, Angelina Searles.

1752—Elizabeth Whittaker.

1753—Elizabeth Peatross, Elizabeth Murray.

1757—Mary Martin, Catherine Bohannon, Ann Green.

1758—Frances Robinson.

1760—Sarah Jones, Elizabeth Major, Martha Hamm.

1761—Sussannah Griffin, Mary King, Elizabeth Quarles.

1764—Sussannah Jones, Ann Haynes.

1765—Dorothy Bourton.

1769—Mary Bell, Ann Meacham, Elizabeth Crawley, Ann Holland, Mary Smith, Ann Blanton.

1770—Priscilla Edmoundson.

1771—Ann Blanton, Mary James, Ann Brown.

1772—Pattie Riddle.

1773—Ann Whittaker, Nellie Mitchell, Elizabeth Lankford, Eleanor Allen.

1774—Dicey King.

1778—Elizabeth Gray.

---

*Elizabeth Gregory was a resident of King William County. After her child was born she fled to Caroline. Phillip Buckner and William Russell, wardens of St. David's Parish, came to Caroline and forced her to return and take her punishment.

Contrary to popular belief men were frequently punished for fathering bastards, or at least they were charged with the

child's support. The following men appeared in the Caroline
County court to answer charges of this type.

1745—Robert Berry bound to Gabriel Long because he failed to support
his bastard child born to Jeanette Grant, or pay Jeanette's fine.

1748—William Faulkner jailed until he gave bond to support the child
"Mary Blasingame is now big with." John Jones and Thomas
White gave bond for 20 pounds each and Faulkner got out of jail.

1754—Thomas Snodgrass—"It is ordered that Richard Straughn deliver
a bastard to Thomas Snodgrass," the only notation in the Order
Books.

1763—Ambroise Fletcher—bound for fathering a bastard child—name
of child's mother omitted.

1771—John Beverley Roy—denied that he was the father of Ann Blanton's child—charges dismissed.

1771—William Chiles—ordered by the court to keep off the parish the
"child he begot on the body of Ann Brown."

1772—John Dickinson—Pattie Riddle made oath that he was the father
of her child. The court ordered him to support the child.

CHURCHES
of
COLONIAL PERIOD
CAROLINE COUNTY

Legend

PRESENT COUNTY LINE ----------
COLONIAL BOUNDARIES - - - - -
EPISCOPAL CHURCH ......
BAPTIST CHURCH ......
PRESBYTERIAN CHURCH ......
QUAKER MEETING HOUSE

ST. MARY

Mount Church 1700

Port Royal

DRYSDALE

Creek Church with St. Asaph 1781 Roaring Creek

Trinitahoe 1744 (later Upper Zion)

Ivy Church 1745

Salem 1953

Ivy Creek Chapel 1722

Chapel Ease 1749

The Reeds (now North) 1773

Rock Church 1744

Presbyterian Church 1740

ST. MARGARET

Bull Church 1745

St. John's 1736

Burbess or Roundabout 1772 (New Carmel)

Chesterfield Church 1726

MATTAPONI RIVER

SCALE OF MILES

THE CHURCH

1. PARISHES

When Caroline was organized as a county the area placed in its boundaries was already incorporated into three parishes of the Established Church. The area between the Mattapony-Rappahannock watershed and the Rappahannock River formed St. Mary's Parish, which had been set up before 1700. The area between the Mattapony-Rappahannock watershed and the north bank of the Mattapony was in Drysdale Parish, which had been set up in 1722, and the area between the Mattapony and the North Anna-Pamunkey formed St. Margaret's Parish, which had been set up in 1720. St. Mary's Parish was always wholly within Caroline County. Drysdale extended from the Caroline-Spotsylvania line to deep in King and Queen. In 1780 the General Assembly cut off the upper end of this parish and formed St. Asaph which was wholly in Caroline, while what was left of Drysdale remained divided between Caroline and King and Queen. St. Margaret's at first extended from upper King William to the Caroline-Spotsylvania line. But in 1742 the General Assembly added its King William portion to upper St. John's Parish to form the new parish of St. David's, and from this date all of St. Margaret's was in Caroline.

2. THE CHURCHES

There was only one church in St. Mary's Parish during colonial times. This was venerable Mount Church on Mount Hill overlooking the Rappahannock, built prior to 1700. Drysdale had three churches: Joy, or Joy Creek, located to the east of Beverley's Run and built at some time before Caroline became a county; Ivy, located on the Marrocossic near Sparta (1953 name) and built in the late 1740's; and Creek, located near the homestead of Charles Broaddus (1953), northeast of the Bowling Green and built in the early 1760's. Creek Church became the main church of St. Asaph's Parish after it was formed. Chesterfield was the first church of St. Margaret's Parish. It was built on the Fontaine tract between Carmel and

Ruther Glen (1953 names) about 1720 and used as a house of worship until the Bull Church was built in the upper end of the parish and the Reedy Church was built in the lower end of the parish in the first half of the 1740 decade. Bull Church was located on the north side of the road leading from Ladysmith eastward, and the Reedy Church was located near Edmound Pendleton School (1953 names). In addition there was a chapel of ease located between the great forks of the Mattapony near Woodpecker. (For more specific information about parishes and churches see the index and main body of this history.)

3. MINISTERS

The following men served as rectors of Caroline parishes during colonial days:

St. Mary's Parish	Drysdale Parish
———— Jones (?-1733)	Rodham Kenner (?-1733)
Musgrave Dawson (1733-64)	Robert Innis (1733-65)
Johnathan Boucher (1764-72)	Thomas Morton (1765-74)
Abner Waugh (1772-?)	Samuel Shields (1774-?)*

St. Margaret's Parish
Francis Fontaine (1720-39)
John Brunskill (1729-62)
Robert Barrett (1763-65)†
Archibald Dick (1766-?)

*Became rector of the new parish of St. Asaph in 1781.
†Rector of St. Martin's in Hanover and probably no more than supply rector in Caroline.

4. WARDENS AND VESTRY

Vestries governed the parish. They consisted of twelve men appointed by the royal governor, or agencies to whom he delegated this power. Two wardens, senior and junior, were the executive officers of the vestry. They disbursed alms to the poor and had custody of the unfortunates in the parish. The early vestrymen are not recorded in the Order Books of the Caroline court, but the names of the senior and junior wardens are there. They are as follows:

St. Mary's Parish

> Benjamin Robinson and William Woodford of Windsor (1727-52)
> Thomas Roy and William Allcock (1752-63)
> James Miller and Gen. William Woodford (1763-?)

Drysdale Parish

> John Taylor and Mordicai Throckmorton (1727-38)
> William Byrd Richards and Christopher Beverley (1738-44)
> Edmound Pendleton and Henry Lynde (1744-45)
> Thomas Buckner and Mungo Roy (1745-47)
> James Wood and James Taylor, the younger (1747-52)
> John Baylor and Henry Lynde (1752-61)
> William Parker and Thomas Lowry (1761-66)
> John Baylor and Henry Lynde (1766-72)

St. Margaret's Parish

> Thomas Terry and Micajah Chiles (1720-27)
> Phillip Aylett and John Anderson (1727-35)
> John Anderson and John Wyatt (1735-41)
> John Sutton II and James Elliott (1741-45)
> Hugh Noden and William Conner (1745-46)
> Thomas Wild and Rice Curtis (1746-48)
> William Marshall and Timothy Chandler (1748-51)
> Roger Quarles and John George (1751-52)
> Peter Copeland and William Conner (1752-53)
> Samuel Wortham and Christopher Tompkins (1753-59)
> Robert Taliaferro and Phillip Taylor (1759-62)
> Gabriel Throckmorton and Samuel Hawes (1761-62)
> John Sutton II and Samuel Redd (1763-65)
> Walker Taliaferro and John Baynham (1765-?)

The above dates are approximate but the wardens served at least through a major portion of the designated periods. Phillip Aylett lived in King William. He served when a part of St. Margaret's lay in that county.

Most of the men listed above were vestrymen before and after they served as senior and junior wardens. In addition to them the Order Books disclose that the following men served on vestries in Caroline. The date after each name is the date that person first appears as a vestryman. Most of them served many years after that date.

St. Mary's Parish: John Boutwell (1752), James Lindsay (1762), Seth Thornton (1764), Gawin Corbin, John Evins and John Buckner (1772), Richard Taylor (1774), James Taylor, Thomas Lomax, John Thornton, Edward Dixon, John Catlett and Richard Buckner (1777)* and Charles Lindsay (1778), Thomas Allcocke (1778).

Drysdale Parish: Robert Woolfolk (1739), Benjamin Hubbard (1762), John Rogers, Anthony Thornton I, William Buckner, Gregory Baylor, John Richards, James Jameson and Richard Todd (1766), John Penn (1767), William Harrison and William Nelson (1774), Edmound Pendleton, Jr., John Hoomes, Anthony Thornton, Jr., Charles Todd and John Buckner (1777).*

St. Margaret's Parish: Head Lynch (1738), Samuel Hawes, Gabriel Throckmorton (1762), William Tyler (1770), Thomas Dickinson (1772), William Boulware, James Sutton, Robert Mickleberry, Robert Robinson, John Thilman (1777), John Fitzhugh, Anthony New (1778), George Baylor (1780).

---

*Vestrymen listed for 1777 were incumbents at the time of the Declaration of Independence, who renounced the king and swore allegiance to the Commonwealth. Most of them were in office as vestrymen long before that date.

Vestrymen of St. Asaph's Parish (original vestry—1781): Edmound Pendleton, Edmound Pendleton, Jr., Anthony Thornton, Jr., John Hoomes, Mungo Roy, David Jameson, Phillip Johnston, Charles Todd, Charles Woolfolk and Thomas Buckner.

5. THE DISSENTERS

The Quakers settled in Caroline in the 1730's, the Presbyterians built a meetinghouse near Needwood in the 1740's and the Baptist evangelized the county in the late 1760's and early 1770's. The progress of these three faiths and their problems are covered in detail in the main body of this history. See Index for specific references.

6. PERSECUTIONS

Laws governing worship were strict and evasions were frequent. Listed below are the people who appeared in the Caroline court charged with violations of the laws governing worship:

1734—William Hutchinson and Timothy Terrell—failing to frequent their parish church for two months—5 shillings or 50 lbs. of tobacco fine.

1735—Rev. John Brunskill—failed to preach at chapel of ease—case dismissed.

1735—Zach Martin—failed to frequent his parish church for two months—5 shillings or 50 lbs. of tobacco fine.

1736—George and Ann Long—failed to frequent their parish church for two months—5 shillings or 50 lbs. of tobacco fine.

1738—John Ellis, William Durrett, Henry Haynes, Benjamin Wood, James Coleman, Richard George, George Eastham, Timothy Chandler, William Southworth, William Terrell, Thomas Hamm, Christopher Acres (Acuss—Acors), James Collins, John Smith, John Stepp—failed to frequent their parish church for two months—5 shillings or 50 lbs. of tobacco fine.

1740—John Fry, William Harris and John Newton—failed to frequent their parish church for two months—5 shillings or 50 lbs. of tobacco fine. Newton ran away rather than pay fine.

1741—Rev. John Brunskill—destroyed church property—fined 15 shillings, ordered to repair property.

1742—Joseph Buller, Jason Meadows, Jonas Meadows, Richard Binnion, John Hamilton—failed to frequent their parish church for two months—5 shillings or 50 lbs. of tobacco fine.

1744—William Isbell, Charles Goodall, Richard Billops—failed to frequent their parish church for two months—5 shillings or 50 lbs. of tobacco fine.

1745—William Isbell—going to church drunk—5 shillings.

1749—William Isbell—drunk in church—5 shillings.

1751—Thomas Hackett, William Whitlock, Robert Williamson—failed to frequent their parish church for two months—5 shillings or 50 lbs. tobacco.

1751—Mary Catlett, John Bowie, John Miller, William Parker—failed to frequent their parish church for two months—5 shillings or 50 lbs. of tobacco fine.

1756—Elias Blackburn—failed to frequent his parish church for two months—5 shillings or 50 lbs. of tobacco.

1758—William Whitlock, John Hackett, William Goodall—failed to frequent their parish church for two months—5 shillings or 50 lbs. of tobacco.

1763—Samuel Long, Richard Straughn, John Pruitt and John Pruitt, Jr.—failed to frequent their parish church for two months—5 shillings or 50 lbs. of tobacco.

1765—William Johnston, Richard Fortune, John Elliott Payne, Thadeus Pruitt, John Pruitt and Robert Jordan, failed to frequent their parish church for two months—5 shillings or 50 lbs. of tobacco fine.

1765—John Pruitt (2nd offense that year), Richard Fortune—failed to frequent their parish church for two months—5 shillings or 50 lbs. of tobacco fine.

1768—Francis Fleming, William Earlington, John Pruitt, Thadeus Pruitt, Benjamin Pruitt, John Carden, Griffin Moody, Ledowick George, Joseph Redd, Henry Tarrent, John Wyatt, John Burruss—failing to frequent their parish church for two months—5 shillings or 50 lbs. of tobacco fine.

1768—Jacob Burruss, Phillip Tinsley—allowing home to be used for unauthorized worship—charges dismissed.

1768—John Burruss—preaching without a license—bound not to preach again.

1768—John Thompson, James Gatewood, Thomas Terrell, Robert Chandler, George McNeils, William Blades, Christopher Terrell, Robert Woolfolk, the son of Joseph Woolfolk, Thomas Burk, Martha Noden, Rachael Terrell and Henry Terrell, William Tinsley—attending unauthorized worship—charges dismissed.

1768—Thomas Roy, James Bowie, Sr., John Bowie, William Parker, Jr.—failed to frequent their parish church for two months—5 shillings or 50 lbs. of tobacco. Frederick Fleming, Gilpin Moody, James Loving, Justinian Wills, James Chick—failed to frequent their parish church for two months—5 shillings or 50 lbs. of tobacco.

1771—John Young—preaching the gospel contrary to law—50 pound bond to keep the peace for a year and a day. Appealed case to general court.

1771—Thomas Pittman—allowing unauthorized religious services in his home—charges dismissed.

1771—John Goodrich, Thomas Collins, Jr., Charles Chewning, Micajah Stevens, Edmound Beazley, Elizabeth Beazley—attending unauthorized worship—charges dismissed.

1771—Bartholomew Chewning, James Goodrich, Edward Hearndon—preaching and teaching the gospel without a license—ordered to post twenty pound bond to keep the peace for year and a day—went to jail.

1771—Lewis Craig—unauthorized preaching—refused to post bond—jailed.

1772—James Ware—unauthorized preaching—posted bond after 16 days in jail to keep the peace, but not to quit preaching.

1772—Benjamin Falkner, John and Walter Mackie, Presbyterians—disturbing the peace.

1772—James Pittman—allowing home to be used for unauthorized worship—posted bond after 16 days in jail to keep the peace—but refused to promise to stop unauthorized worship.

1772—Nathaniel Holloway—unauthorized preaching—refused to post 20 pound bond—went to jail.

1772—John Partlow—allowed unauthorized worship in home—refused to post bond—went to jail.

1772—John Waller—unauthorized preaching—refused to post 50 pound bond—went to jail.

1772—Henry Goodloe—allowed unauthorized worship in home—refused to post 20 pound bond—went to jail and declared insane.

1773—Stephan Fortson, Frederick Fortson, Sarah Young, John Harvie, Daniel Allen, Joseph DeJarnette, Sr., Stephan Fortson (2nd offense)—failed to frequent their parish church for two months—fined 5 shillings each.

1774—John Young—unauthorized preaching in an outhouse—case continued pending outcome of appeal on prior conviction appealed to the general court.

WELFARE

The church wardens did a certain amount of welfare work in spite of their preoccupation with the enforcement of the laws governing religious worship. Following are the cases they took charge of in Caroline from the records in the Order Books:

1735—George and Michael Yates, the sons of George Yates, bound to their uncle, Michael Guinney, because their father failed to instruct them in "Christian principles."(1)

1737—John and Charles Walton bound to Bryan Edmoundson.

1738—Children of Ann Blanton (ages 4 and 10), bound to William Morris.

1738—Bound the three children at John Terrell's, commonly known as the children of Elizabeth Harrison. (St. Margaret's Parish.)

1738—Ann and John Gough, poor orphans, bound to Thomas Oakley.

1741—Sussannah Brooks, a female of St. Mary's Parish, bound for immorality.

1741—Thomas Scott, the mulatto son of Mary Scott, a white woman, bound to Thomas Wild according to law.

1741—Elizabeth Dunn, a poor orphan, bound to Sussannah and William Hudson.

1742—Dorothy Kercheval prevented her son from being bound.

1743—John Jones, a poor orphan, bound to Stephan Johnston.

1744—Elizabeth Barnes, bound because immoral.(2)

1744—Catherine Jones, bound to Archibald and Elizabeth Macphearson.(3)

1744—Mary Hunt, bound because immoral.(2)

1745—Martha King placed under 10 pound bond because of her immorality.(2)

1745—Abraham, Mary, James and Jacob King, the children of Martha and Joseph King, bound by the wardens of St. Mary's Parish to Bennett Moore because their parents "failed to instruct them in religious principles and look after their education."

1746—Isabelle Gibbons, bound by the church wardens of St. Margaret's because of immorality.(2)

1746—Sarah Gibson, bound by the church wardens of St. Mary's because of immorality.(2)

1746—Isabelle Griffin, bound by the church wardens of St. Mary's because of immorality.(2)

1746—The children of Richard Jones, bound because their father did not take care of them.

1747—Reuben LaFoe, bound because his father, Daniel LaFoe, failed to take care of him.

1747—Thomas Burdette, mulatto bastard of a white mother, bound to Richard Step.

1747—Moses Anderson, a bastard child, bound to William Dyer.

1748—Sarah, Nicholas and James Scott, the mulatto bastards of Mary Scott, a white woman, bound according to law.

1748—Children of Thomas Martin bound because he neglected their education.

1748—Mary Stenard, a poor orphan, bound to Robert Robinson.

1748—Letitia (Lettis) Powell bound because of her immorality.

1748—The children of Letitia Powell bound because she neglected their education and to instruct them in the principles of Christianity.

1749—Hannah Trainham, bound because immoral.

1750—Bound Dinah, Cloe, Swaney and Doll Burdette, the mulatto children of a white mother to Hugh Noden, according to law.(4)

1750—Sarah King, bound because immoral.

1756—Bound Elizabeth, Ruth, Ambroise, John, Ann and Isiah Roberts, because their father, David Roberts, failed to take care of them. (Drysdale Parish.)

1756—Bound John Tarrent because his father, Henry Tarrent, did not take care of him.

1756—Bound Sarah Munday, a poor orphan, to Benjamin and Sarah Robinson.

1758—Liza Lawless bound to Griffin Jones because her father, Henry Lawless, "appears to neglect her education."(5)

1759—Bound the children of Jane Bearding.(6)

1759—Bound the children of Laurentia Salmon.

1759—Henry Lawless ordered to deliver his daughter, Eliza, to Christopher Dudley, because he negelcted her education.

1760—Children of Jean Sullivant bound to John Hoomes.

1760—John and Thomas Cooper Dickinson, orphans of John Dickinson, bound.

1760—James and John Choice, poor orphans, bound.

1761—Curtis and Peter Poe, the sons of John Blaikey Poe bound because their father neglected their education.

1761—The children of Thomas Hill bound. (St. Mary's Parish.)

1761—The children of Elizabeth Rains bound. (St. Mary's Parish.)

1761—George and John Watts, the sons of Shadrack Watts, bound. (St. Mary's.)(7)

1762—William Hewlett's orphans, bound. (St. Margaret's.)

1762—The children of James Minor, bound. (Drysdale.)

1762—Children of Dannis MacCarty, bound. (St. Mary's.)

1763—John Donahue, the son of Patrick Donahue, bound. (Drysdale.)

1763—The orphans of John Conner bound to Robert Tompkins. (St. Margaret's.)

1763—Reuben Brown, an orphan, bound. (St. Mary's.)

1763—Charles Conner, orphan son of John Conner, bound.

1763—Micajah Eaton discharged from Sarah Smith and church wardens of St. Margaret's ordered to bind him to a new master.

1763—Joshua Donahue, son of Patrick Donahue, bound. (Drysdale.)

1763—The children of John Cox bound because their father fails to take proper care of them.(8)

1763—Children of Sarah Smith bound.

1764—Children of William Eubank bound to Euclid Whitlock because their father did not take the proper care of them.

1764—Ann and Sussannah Tompkins, the orphans of Daniel Tompkins, bound because their guardian, Daniel Tompkins, absconded with the estate their father left for their support.

1764—John Simmons, the son of Henry Simmons, because his father did not take proper care of him and neglected his education.

1764—Elisha and Benjamin Estis, the children of Abraham Estis, bound to Joseph Reynolds.

1764—LaFoe Harper, a poor orphan, bound to Francis Conner.

1765—Thomas White, the son of William White, bound.

1765—Ann Salmon, daughter of Laurentia Salmon, bound because her former master gave her up.

1767—Lucy, Sally, Edmound and Hannah Putney, bound because their mother, Lucy Putney, neglected their education.

1768—Sussanah, Jean and Milly Pollet, because their father, Benjamin Pollet neglected their education.

1768—Martha and Mary Murray, orphans, bound according to law.

1770—Thomas Landrum, "a child who appears to be in the care of nobody," ordered bound.

1770—Thomas Livingston, an orphan, bound. (St. Mary's.)

1770—Thomas Lyon, the son of Andrew Lyon, bound because his father neglects his education.

1771—Douglas Oliver, the son of Richard Oliver, bound because his father failed to instruct him in the principles of Christianity.

1771—Henry and Peggy Hill, the children of James Hill, bound. (St. Mary's.)

1772—The children of James Powell, bound because their father neglected their education.

1772—John Whaling, Jr., the orphan of John Whaling, bound.

1772—The church wardens of St. Margaret's ordered to force John Sutton II to support his children born to his mulatto mistress, Sarah Mann.

1773—The children of Patrick Cuffey bound because their father failed to take care of them and instruct them in the principles of Christianity.

1774—The orphans of Ambroise Hutchinson transferred from Francis Baber to Mathew Crank.

1775—John Merryman, the son of Adam Merryman, bound.

1775—Lewis, Joseph and Abagail Murphey, the children of Ann Murphey, bound.

1775—William Hill, the son of James Hill, bound. (St. Mary's.)

---

(1) This was a fortunate move. Michael Yates became a celebrated Caroline physician.

(2) Caroline's only campaign to clean up prostitution during colonial days came during the great boom at Port Royal. It spread throughout the county.

(3) Catherine Jones was left an orphan with independent means. Archibald Macphearson, a magistrate, was her guardian. He ran through her estate, and after he squandered it had the court bind the girl to him and his wife. Similar cases happened frequently and caused numerous scandals. In 1770 Gawin Corbin, boldly told the Caroline Court that he did not want a guardian although he was under the age of 21.

(4) After Hugh Noden's death the custody of the Burdette children passed to his son, Charles Noden, who tried to remove them from Virginia in order to keep them slaves after they reached the age of 31.

(5) What happened to Liza Lawless at Griffin Jones is not of record.

(6) Jane Bearding's husband, Francis, was either hung or in prison for the theft of tobacco from Benjamin Hubbard.

(7) Three years before Shadrack Watt's was sent to the General Court for breaking into Conway's warehouse and stealing tobacco, which he sold in Fredericksburg. He was either in prison or had been hung.

(8) The Cox children's mother, Mary Cox, had been convicted of adultry with Isaac Baker.

EDUCATION

Primary education was a function of the Church but the clergy made a poor job of it in colonial Caroline. Rectors were paid to teach as well as preach but few performed the first duty. Many ministers hired an assistant to teach for them. The Rev. John Brunskill of St. Margaret's, first hired John Scott to do this work. Scott married his daughter Elizabeth, and he was able to keep the salary he paid in the family. But Scott turned out to be a drunkard, and Brunskill's parishioners forced him to hire a more competent teacher. He next em-

ployed Joseph DeJarnette. Although Brunskill refused to pay
DeJarnette, his reputation as a teacher was established, and he
easily secured all the pupils he was able to teach for substantial
fees. He acquired property and learned that it was more profitable to have apprentices, whom he could make till his land
while not in school, than pay pupils, who loafed during their
out of school hours. In time his classroom became about equal-
ly divided between apprentices and pay pupils, and many bright
and deserving boys of the county from modest but substantial
homes secured an excellent education. Joseph DeJarnette has
the distinction of training more apprentices than one other man
in the history of Caroline County.

The Rev. Johnathan Boucher took his duties as teacher
seriously. He came to Caroline originally to teach (for Edward Dixon) rather than to preach and after he became the
rector of St. Mary's Parish he kept on with his teaching. His
school was favorably known throughout the colony. But he
was interested in the education of the gentry rather than the
masses and his school became a school for young aristocrats.
George Washington's stepson was one of his pupils.

The attitude of Caroline rectors, other than Brunskill and
Boucher, is not known in detail, but it is of record that none
of them did much teaching. Only one schoolhouse is mentioned
in the Order Books. That was located on the land of "King"
Carter's heirs on Peumandsend between Port Royal and the
Bowling Green. The date of the entry is 1757. This apparently was a free school for the children of the overseer and other
freeholders nearby because the Carters never resided on their
Caroline plantation. There is no record of any other such
philanthropist and elsewhere in the county the poor were hard
put to find the means to educate their children although the
church wardens frequently bound the children out if they failed
in that duty.

With all the handicaps, however, literacy increased among
the free white masses during Caroline's colonial period. In
depositions in many chancery matters in the Order Books older
people made their marks while younger people signed their
names. For example in Abraham v. Taylor and Cowne tried

in 1759 one deponent, William Isbell, "aged 50 and upward" was illiterate while another, his son, Henry Isbell, "about 20 years" wrote his name with a flourish.

The well-to-do had private tutors. Some of these teachers were salaried men like Johnathan Boucher, who came from abroad to teach for Edward Dixon, and others were indentured servants. William Rigsby and Daniel Potter were the most celebrated indentured servants to serve as teachers. Thomas Catlett set Rigsby free and John Micou freed Potter for educating their children.

The upper crust sent their children to college. John Baylor I of New Market was educated at Caius College, Cambridge, and several, if not all, of his sons went to England to finish their schooling. The best evidence indicates that some of the Lomaxes and Beverleys attended college abroad. James Madison of Caroline stock graduated from Princeton and numerous residents of the county studied at William and Mary. The list compiled by William and Mary and corrected by this author to make it conform to the Caroline Order Books follows:

Year	Student	Year	Student
1775-76	Henry Ashton*	After 1720	Phillip Lightfoot‡
1759-60	William Buckner	1753-55	John Lomax
1770-72	John Dixon	After 1720	Benjamin Robinson
1736	Mathew Hubbard	1760-63	Henry Robinson
1753-56	Lawrence Battaile	1772-75	William Nelson
1770	William Buckner†	1762-68	Benjamin Robinson II
1771-	Beverley Fitzhugh	1770-71	John Taylor
1757-60	Rodham Kenner II	1753-55	William Taliaferro
1772-73	Robert Baylor	1761-64	Edmound Pendleton, Jr.
1720	Richard Corbin‡	1753-55	Richard Taliaferro
1738	Francis Fontaine§	1753-55	John Tennant

*Listed by the College of William and Mary as a resident of Caroline, but according to the Order Books of the Caroline Court no Ashtons lived in the county.
†There were two William Buckners.
‡Lived in Caroline part of the time.
§Son of the first rector of St. Margaret's Parish. His father died before he attended college, and his family may have moved from Caroline. Doubtless there were other students from Caroline during colonial times which have not yet been identified.

APPRENTICES

The most prevalent way for a youth to learn to read and write, and often learn to trade at the same time, was to serve as an apprentice. Apprenticeships had to be sanctioned by the court. They usually began when the youth was 13 or 14 and lasted until he was 21. But occasionally a grown man bound himself to learn a trade. The master agreed to train, clothe and feed the ward in exchange for his services and give him a limited amount of schooling, most often two years (13th to 15th year). One Caroline master, Thomas Griffin, managed to cut the schooling to six months. At the end of the apprenticeship the master contracted to give his apprentice certain dues. They consisted of a complete set of clothes, working tools, and a limited amount of money unless the terms of the apprenticeship provided otherwise.

Apprentices recorded in the Caroline Order Books follow:

Date	Apprentice	Master	Trade
1734	John Withers	William Woodcock	Shoemaker
1734	Edmound Pendleton	Benjamin Robinson	"all things about clerk's office"
1735	Robert Whitton	Robert Farish	Carpenter
1735	William Whitton	Robert Farish	Carpenter
1735	Jeremiah Whitton	Robert Farish	Carpenter
1736	Robert Rains	Edmound Graves	Carpenter
1736	George Merrill	John Potter	Education
1736	John Marsh	William Weller	Bricklayer
1737	Charles Walden	Robert Farish	Carpenter
1737	John Walden	Robert Farish	Carpenter
1737	Charles Merrill	Jason Potter	for schooling only
1738	William Spies	Thomas Durrum	for schooling only
1739	James Land	Mathew Brooks	Cooper
1740	John Cox	John Embrey	Cooper
1740	John Evins	Benjamin Duval	Carpenter
1742	John Ralls	Benjamin Duval	Carpenter
1744	Richard Anderson	Thomas Jones	Shoemaker
1744	Richard Rogers	Adam Lindsay	Carpenter & Millwright
1744	William Collawn	William Lindsay	Carpenter & Millwright

Date	Apprentice	Master	Trade
1744	Thomas Lewis	Joseph Minor	Schooling only
1744	Hannah Elmes	Thomas Berry	2 years—schooling
1744	Thomas Smith	Dr. Daniel Ferguson	Tailor
1744	Marmaduke Penny	John Montague	Carpenter
1745	John Frawner (Fraughnaugh)	Edmound Pendleton	Schooling only(1)
1745	James Carr	Adam Lindsay	Carpenter & Millwright
1745	Richard Stillman	John Montague	Carpenter
1746	Harrison Munday	Daniel Barksdale	Carpenter
1746	Anthony Lee	Francis James	Shoemaker
1746	William Lee	Sheerwood James	Cooper
1746	Lucy Lee	Francis James	Shoemaker
1746	Thomas Pannell	Thomas Griffin	Shoemaker
1747	Ambroise Long	Richard Elliott	Schooling only
1748	John Austin	John Evins	Carpenter
1748	Alexander Atkinson	Benjamin Duval	Carpenter
1748	Joseph Rogers (adult)	John Montague	Carpenter
1748	Augustine Vaughter	Adam Lindsay	Carpenter & Millwright
1749	William Pierce	Samuel Taliaferro	Schooling only
1749	John Chiles	Mourning Richards	Carpenter and house joiner
1749	William ohnston	Jacob Kendrick	Bricklayer
1750	James Sorrell	Daniel LaFoe	Weaver
1750	Mary Sorrell	Daniel LaFoe	Weaver
1750	William Sorrell	John Holloway	Carpenter
1750	William Brown	Jacob Johns	Tailor
1750	John Catlett	Robert Brooks	Surveyor
1750	Charles Beazley	Honorous Powell	(2)
1750	Zachery Coghill	Honorous Powell	(2)
1750	Edward Goode	John Lindsay	Carpenter & Millwright
1751	Martin Vaughan (adult)	Thomas Montague	Carpenter
1751	Phillip Ham	Richard Woolfolk Chandler	Schooling only
1751	John Rowe	Moses Sheets	Carpenter & house joiner
1752	Littleberry Dillion	Richard Woolfolk Chandler	Schooling only
1752	Edward Rolphe	John Watkins	Schooling only
1753	John Edwards	James Carden	Schooling only
1753	Joshua Grady	James Carden	Schooling only

Date	Apprentice	Master	Trade
1753	John Rowe	Robert Johnston	Store-keeping(3)
1753	Benjamin Sweeney	Samuel Burruss	Miller
1753	John Munday	William Shelton	Schooling only
1754	Peter Taliaferro	Jacob Lindsay	Carpenter & Millwright
1754	Joseph Sweeney	Samuel Hargrave	Merchant
1754	Thomas Norment	Joseph DeJarnette	Schooling only
1755	John Johnson	Michael Yates	Physician
1755	William Broaddus	Jacob Johns	Tailor
1755	John Woodford	John Catlett	Schooling only
1755	Lodowick O'Neal	James Pattie	Weaver & Carpenter
1756	Thomas Hailey	Benjamin Whitehead	Schooling only
1756	Richard Haynes	John Brown	Schooling only
1756	Thomas Haynes	John Brown	Schooling only
1756	John Peatross	Patrick Carey	Schooling only
1756	William Broaddus	Thomas Arthur	Blacksmith(4)
1756	Reuben Alestock	Thomas Roy	Tobacco Business
1756	Lewis Alestock	Thomas Roy	Tobacco Business
1756	Robert Clark	Richard Buckner	Schooling only
1756	James Fewell (?)	James Pattie	Carpenter & Weaver
1756	Samuel Duval	Gabriel Mitchell	Carpenter(5)
1756	John Norment	Joseph DeJarnette	Schooling only
1757	Phillip Hamm	Richard Woolfolk Chandler	Schooling only
1757	William Thomas	Samuel Daniels	Miller
1757	James Hall	John Mitchell	Carpenter
1757	Artemeneous Robinson	William Davis	Carpenter
1757	William Hall	James Pattie	Carpenter & Weaver
1758	William Rennolds	Phillip May	Schooling only
1758	St. Andrew McKenny	James Pattie	Carpenter & Weaver
1758	Oliver Towles, Jr.	Obediah Merriott	Lawyer
1759	Thomas Cooper	William White	Schooling only
1759	George Catlett	Humphrey Brooks	Surveyor
1760	Fox Hargrave	Benjamin Arthur	Blacksmith
1760	James Crutchfield	Absolom Devenport	Schooling only
1760	Thomas Collins	Mordicai Redd	Schooling only
1760	Elliott Emerson	George Wiley	Carpenter
1761	Chesley Schooler	Christopher Beck	Schooling only
1761	William Hall	Lawrence Catlett	Schooling only(6)
1762	James Wood	Walter Athey	(7)
1763	Minoah Stone	Robert Tompkins	Schooling only

Date	Apprentice	Master	Trade
1764	Lewis Bullard	William Owen	Schooling only
1764	James Rains	Joseph DeJarnette	(8)
1764	William Watts	Richard Boulware	Schooling only
1764	Humphrey Lucas	John Overstreet	Schooling only
1764	James Fletcher	David Stern	Carpenter & Builder
1764	Price Poe	John Beverley Roy	Schooling only
1765	Robert Smith	John Level	Schooling only
1765	James Pavey	Joseph DeJarnette	Schooling only
1765	James Taylor (son of (Francis Taylor)	Nathaniel Anderson	Shop & house joiner
1765	Burton Sulivan	Nathaniel Anderson	Shop & house joiner
1765	Benjamin Tompkins	Thomas Hurt	Schooling only
1766	Nicholas Cren (?)	John Harris	Schooling only
1766	Micajah Cren (?)	John Harris	Schooling only
1766	Charles Thomas	David Stern	Schooling only
1766	Joseph Norment	John Normen	Schooling only
1767	Thomas White	Record blurred	
1769	James Stokes	James Daniels	(9)
1769	William MacIntyre	Francis Tompkins	Schooling only
1770	John Allen	William Riggins	Schooling only
1770	Thomas Downer	James Dickinson	Schooling only
1770	Mary Carneal	Reynolds McKenney	(10)
1770	Benjamin Tompkins	——— Paisley	(11)
1770	John Brand	Robert Paul	Trader
1770	John Mills	Thomas Collins	Schooling only
1770	Charles Watts	James Munday	Schooling only
1771	Robert Scott	James Fletcher	Schooling only
1771	James Eubank	Joseph DeJarnette	Schooling only
1771	David Seal	James Whaley	Schooling only
1771	John George	Joseph DeJarnette	Schooling only
1771	Arthur Thomas	John Griffin	Shoemaker
1772	John Baynham	Marshall & Hart	Merchants
1772	Edmound Estis	Francis Tompkins	Schooling only
1772	Thomas Buckner, Jr.	Gawin Corbin	Schooling only
1772	Lawrence Gibbins	Thomas Nelson	Farmer(12)
1773	Thornton Taylor (son of Francis Taylor)	Anthony New	Chairmaker
1773	John Honey	Jasper Haynes	Schooling only
1773	William Blackburn	James Fletcher	Schooling only
1773	Benjamin Warren	Joseph DeJarnette	Schooling only

Date	Apprentice	Master	Trade
1773	Richard West	William Peatross	Farmer (12)
1773	William Merriman	Leonard Young	Schooling only
1773	Micajah Chapman	Nicholas Oliver	(13)
1774	Royal Eubank	Benjamin Kimbrough	Schooling only
1774	Joseph Stevens	Francis Tompkins	Schooling only
1775	Royal Eubank	Joseph DeJarnette	(14)
1775	George Doggett	James Pattie	Carpenter & Weaver
1777	Henry Mickleberry	Joseph DeJarnette	Schooling only
1777	William Glayson	John Harrison	Schooling only
1777	Peter Hutchinson	Joseph DeJarnette	Schooling only
1779	Timothy Chandler	Anthony New	Chairmaker
1780	John Mickleberry	Joseph DeJarnette	Schooling only
1780	William Parker II	William Parker	Schooling only

(1) Edmound Pendleton failed to teach Edward Fraughnaugh how to read and write until ordered by the court.

(2) Charles Beazley's and Zachery Coghill's indenture of apprenticeship is missing from the Order Books. The citation is from their suit for their dues at the end of their apprenticeship.

(3) The court transferred John Rowe's apprenticeship from Sheets to Johnston.

(4) The court transferred William Broaddus apprenticeship from Jacob Johns to Thomas Arthur. This William Broaddus appears to have been a son of William Broaddus, who was the first Broaddus to settle in Caroline County, and a brother of John, Shipley and Robert. Evidently he died in his youth or moved away because there are no other entries concerning him in the Order Books.

(5) Samuel Duval ran away to fight in the Virginia regiment in the French and Indian War.

(6) The court transferred William Hall's apprenticeship from James Pattie to Lawrence Catlett upon the complaint of Hall's mother that Pattie was not treating her son well.

(7) Wood complained against his master, complaint dismissed. Original articles of apprenticeship not in the Order Books.

(8) James Pavey, the first Pavey to live in Caroline, was brought into the county as an apprentice of the Rev. Robert Innis. When Innis died he sued for his freedom. But the court denied it and transferred his apprenticeship to Joseph DeJarnette.

(9) James Stokes sued James Daniel to terminate apprenticeship ahead of the indentures terms and won his suit.

(10) Mary Carneal, Sr., a widow, arranged the apprenticeship of his daughter, Mary Carneal, Jr. to Reynolds MacKenny. But after she became dissatisfied and tried to break it. The court denied her petition.

(11) The court transferred Benjamin Tompkins' apprenticeship from John Hurt to ———— Paisley.

(12) Lawrence Gibbins and Richard West were the only apprentices bound to learn to be farmers by the terms of their indentures, although that was actually what most apprentices bound for "schooling only" learned besides how to read and write.

(13) Nicholas Oliver was the only resident of Caroline to try to fake an apprenticeship. The court termed him the "pretended master" of Micajah Chapman.

(14) Royal Eubank transferred from Kimbrough to DeJarnette.

HEALTH

The residents of colonial Caroline appear to have been remarkably healthy for 18th century people. The diseases which gave them the most trouble were smallpox and fevers. When epidemics of these maladies developed there was little chance to control them until they burned themselves out. In 1745 Mary Taylor Powell lamented that her father and three sons all died within the space of two days and after they were ill only a few hours. (Chancery cause of Baylor v. Powell.)

Pest houses were commonplace and the court often committed the ill to them against their will. Around 1770 Dr. John Tennant began the innoculation of persons exposed to smallpox before they became ill with the disease. This innoculation was a crude form of vaccination and when it took effect was sometimes only slightly less virulent than the disease itself. Of the fevers malaria was the most prevalent. At an early date the more observant inhabitants decided that its spread was in some way connected with marshes and water but they failed to associate its spread with the mosquito. In 1773 Sarah Battaile asked the court's permission to move the site of her manor from the banks of the Rappahannock to a new location in the hills. She stated in her petition that the land was entailed and that she had lost, due to fever, her husband and all of her sons but one, and that she feared, that if her residence remained at the present site, she might lose her remaining son and that the whole line of her branch of the family become extinct. The court granted her request, the residence was moved and Lawrence Battaile, Jr. survived. This move led to others, and in time most families had moved their homesteads from the river banks to the hills.

1. THE PHYSICIANS

The following men practiced medicine in Caroline during colonial times. There may have been others but these are the only ones of record in the Order Books.

Dr. John Symmer lived and practiced in the vicinity of Roy's warehouse from before Caroline was organized as a county until after the founding of Port Royal. His most celebrated patient was Dorothy Roy. He attended her in her last illness and had trouble collecting his bill from her heirs.

Dr. Mirious, evidently of Dutch extraction, practiced at the first courthouse from the time the county seat was located in the Kidds Fork-Shumansville-Ideal triangle.

Dr. George Hoomes practiced at the Bowling Green until his death in 1733.

Dr. Daniel Farguson practiced at Roy's warehouse and Port Royal from about 1740 to around 1755. He was a tailor as well as a physician. The practice of medicine was not so lucrative in 1753 as it is in 1953 and most doctors had other sources of income besides their practice.

Dr. Hugh Noden practiced in St. Margaret's Parish during the 1730's, '40's and '50's. He was a magistrate as well as a physician.

Dr. George Todd was perhaps the most celebrated of all of Caroline's doctors of colonial times. He began his practice in Port Royal about 1745 and moved to Villborro on the Stage Road in 1749 where he continued to practice through the Revolution. Dr. Todd was a tavern-keeper as well as a physician. He ran taverns both at Port Royal and Villborro. A portion of his Villborro tavern still stands (1953). He was one of the two Caroline physicians whose age is definitely known. In a deposition recorded in the Order Books (Abraham v. Taylor and Cowne) he states that he was born in 1711.

Dr. John Sutherland practiced in Caroline during the French and Indian War. After 1760 he moved to Prince William County. In another deposition in Abraham v. Taylor and Cowne he states that he was born in 1727.

Dr. John Shores came directly to Caroline from Britain. He sold his headrights instead of pushing west and claiming his free crown land, and settled in the county. His period of residence was the 1750's. Afterwards he appears to have moved to the new city of Richmond where his sons became prominent. One of them was an early mayor.

Dr. William Johnston took over Dr. Todd's practice in Port Royal when the latter moved to Villborro. He continued to practice in Caroline through the Revolution.

Dr. John Baynham followed Dr. Hugh Noden in St. Margaret's Parish. Like Noden he was a magistrate as well as a physician. He died a short time before the outbreak of the Revolution and was buried on the farm which is the homestead of Tom Kay and his sisters, Cora and Lucy, in 1953. A tombstone marks his grave.

Dr. William Allison practiced in the vicinity of Port Royal from about the middle of the eighteenth century until after the end of the Revolution.

Dr. Michael Yates lived in upper Drysdale Parish near Guinney Bridge. He was born in Caroline and reared and educated by his uncle, Michael Guinney, the tavern-keeper, because his father failed to take care of him. He practiced from the French and Indian War through the Revolution.

Dr. John Tennant after Dr. George Todd was perhaps Caroline's most celebrated physician in colonial times. He attended William and Mary College in 1753-55 but where he got his medical education is not known. He practiced first at Port Royal and later at the Bowling Green. He was still actively engaged in practice at the end of the Revolution. He took a great interest in politics and was a member of the Caroline Committee of Safety. He also was interested in research and made an extensive study of means to control smallpox. His work did much to halt the ravages of this disease in Caroline.

Dr. Thomas Landrum was a young Port Royal physician at the outbreak of the Revolution. He promptly joined the Continental Navy and was surgeon's mate on the *Tartar* and the *Tempest*, two Continental privateers. After the war he practiced in Port Royal until 1812.

Dr. Robert Farish was a young physician practicing in St. Margaret's Parish at the outbreak of the Revolution. Like Landrum he joined the armed forces and served as a surgeon throughout the war.

Doctors from Nearby Counties: Dr. John Walker of Hanover, Dr. Campbell of King William and Dr. Hugh Mercer and Dr. George Gilmore of Fredericksburg also practiced in Caroline. Dr. Walker lived at Bullfield across the North Anna from the county. Dr. Mercer and Dr. Gilmore were frequently consulted when the members of the families of the great landowners along the Rappahannock and in upper Drysdale Parish were ill. Gilmore was a brother-in-law of some of the Thorntons.

2. INSANITY

Insanity was rare in colonial Caroline. Only six cases were reported in the Order Books. They concerned Thomas Hamm, Rachael Rogers, Mary Rennolds, William Catlett, Henry Goodloe and a nameless madman.

The Hamm, Rogers and Rennolds cases all arose over competence to make wills. The court held that while Hamm was insane when he died he was sane when he made his will and that it was a valid instrument, but it ruled that both Rachael

Rogers and Mary Rennolds were incompetent. The three cases arose in the 1740's, the 1750's and the 1770's, respectively.

The Catlett case grew out of a dispute over the Catlett fortune. Benjamin Catlett was in serious financial difficulties and he coveted the portion of his father's estate inherited by his brother, William, a bachelor and an eccentric. Benjamin Catlett had deserted the Caroline militia when it was stationed at Fort Mindenhall on the frontier during the French and Indian War and returned to his home in the county to attempt to recoup his finances before he went broke. Col. (later Gen.) William Woodford, commanding officer of the Caroline Militia, sent for him to stand court martial for desertion but the civil court in Caroline released him from the militia and ruled that he might remain in Caroline and look after his affairs much to the dismay of Woodford. This break did not save him, however, his finances went steadily from bad to worse. He looked covetously at the inheritance of his brother, William, and sought to gain control of it. To do this he moved the court to declare William insane and make him committee. Some of Caroline's most celebrated magistrates, Anthony Thornton, Lundsford Lomax and Robert Gilchrist, examined William Catlett and declared him unfit to manage his affairs. Benjamin Catlett became committee but other members of the Catlett family were dissatisfied and moved to have the appointment set aside. The court agreed with them and ordered William committed to the Public Hospital for the Insane in Williamsburg. Benjamin tried to nullify this order by hiding William. The court ordered him to produce the patient at once, and when he refused cited him for contempt. Rather than go to jail or abjectly surrender Benjamin tried to work out a compromise. He was successful. The court agreed to place the unfortunate William in the custody of one Francis Barbee, and convey to Barbee a portion of his estate to support him for the rest of his life. William lived out his life with Barbee and the Catletts shared the portion of his estate he did not need for his own use.

Henry Goodloe's trouble arose because he let John Waller preach at his residence in upper St. Margaret's Parish. His relatives decided that that Goodloe must be crazy to be taken in by a "new light" religion and moved the court to have him declared insane. The magistrates were no more in sympathy with the "new light" than the Goodloes, other than Henry, and readily agreed.

In the last case of insanity cited in the opening paragraph of this section the court paid a reward in 1771 to Andrew Leckie, the Port Royal merchant, "for preserving the clothes of a madman, who was taken up and placed in gaol."

LAW ENFORCEMENT

Colonial Caroline was remarkably free of major crime. The table below lists free (1) white persons tried or investigated for felonies:

1733—John Parlow—investigated for the killing of Thomas Downer— charges dismissed.

1740—Robert Baber—forgery—pillory 1 hr. & 50 pound bond for good behavior.

1742—Richard Munford—stole horse, bridle & sadle—to General Court.*

---

*Records of trials in the General Court of the Colony are lost. The fate of most of the accused from Caroline to stand trial in Williamsburg remains unknown. The Order Books indicate what happened to a few of them. Patrick Welch and John Kay were hung, Manus Fegan served a prison sentence and returned to Caroline, John Dugard was acquitted.

1742—John Lomax, Jr.—accessory to Munford—only 16 years of age —25 lashes at whipping-post.

1744—John Hoomes—stole bell from Thomas Buckner—10 lashes at whipping-post.

1744—Samuel Pryor—accused of rape by Ann Campbell—charges dismissed.

1744—Francis Bearding—stole tobacco from Benjamin Hubbard—to General Court.

1744—Shelton Raily — Bearding's accessory — charges dismissed upon payment of costs.

1745—Alexander Sweeney—sold base metal for gold—100 pound bond for good behavior.

1745—Peter Williams—a common runaway—expelled from Virginia.

1745—Thomas Pittman—accused of stealing Peter William's hogs— charges dismissed.

1745—John Harvie—stole goods from Robert Gilchrist—made restitution—charges dismissed.

1745—Patrick James—accused of theft of Henry Long's saddle—charges dismissed.

1747—Patrick Welch—stole church plate and counterfeited coinage—to General Court.

1747—Manus Fegan—accessory to Welch—to General Court.

1747—Patrick Roan—receiving stolen property and uttering counterfeit coinage—to General Court.

1747—Edward Dannerley—ruining church plate—charges dismissed.

1747—Catherine Roan—receiving stolen property and uttering counterfeit coinage—to General Court.

1747—Ann Dugan—receiving stolen property and uttering counterfeit coinage—charges dismissed.

1747—George Fox—counterfeiting and uttering coinage—to General Court.

1747—Bennett Beazley—possession of stolen property—50 pound bond for good behavior.

1748—Beaver Newby—theft of gun—50 pound bond for good behavior.

1748—James Stuart—stole hat from house in Port Royal—to General Court.

1748—John Noden—cutting up tobacco and burning houses of John Bowie—not proven—but placed under 20 pound bond for good behavior.

1748—Catherine Noden—accessory to John Noden—not proven—20 pound bond for good behavior.

1752—Henry Baites—robbed Edward Dixon and William Johnston (2 crimes) to General Court.

1752—Francis Sly—accessory of Baites in Dixon robbery—10 pound bond for good behavior.

1754—Benjamin Long—unlawfully entered home of widow Jane Cooper—fined 1 shilling and costs.

1754—John Powell—unlawfully entered home of widow Jane Cooper—fined 1 shilling and costs.

1756—Benjamin Catlett—desertion from militia at Ft. Mindenhall—case dismissed.

1757—Elizabeth Perrylake—suspicion of a felony—charges dismissed.

1758—William and Shadrack Watts—stole tobacco from Conway's warehouse and sold it in Fredericksburg—to General Court.

1758—John Harvie—raised colonial currency notes from one to ten pounds—to General Court.

1760—John Kay—killed wife, Mary Kay—to General Court.

1760—James Campbell & John Scott—attacked Edward Dixon, Robert Gilchrist, John Sneed and Robert Allen on streets of Port Royal —charges dismissed for lack of jurisdiction because they were seamen.

1760—Zachery & Errom Coghill—aggavated assault on Jacob King— 10 shillings fine each by jury.

1762—David Gordon—stole horse from Francis Fleming—to General Court.

1763—Rev. Robert Barrett—crime unknown—to General Court.

1763—Robert Burdette—forgery of bills of exchange and counterfeiting —to General Court.

1764—Joseph Baites—broke into store—to General Court.

1764—Mary Ann & Nancy Webster—assault and battery—charges dismissed.

1767—Joseph Abraham—true bill in blank—fled.

1769—Mace Pickett—forceable entry—50 pound bond to keep the peace.

1770—Harding Chewning—killed a Negro—not guilty.

1773—John & William Coleburn—indited for felonies—charges not stated—dismissed.

1773—John Dugard—bigamy—acquitted in General Court.

1774—William Reynolds—stole a Negro—charges dismissed.

1774—Robert Month—broke into home of Nathaniel Holloway— charges dismissed.

1774—Chillion White—rape—charges dismissed.

1775—Jacob Martin—accused of a felony—ran away.

1775—Edward Badrell—accused of a felony—ran away.

1777—John Hackett—stole 3 lambs from James Miller—to General Court.

2. Crimes Against the King, the Court and Public Officials

Caroline freeholders resented tyranny from the date of the organization of the county. When pushed they showed this resentment by overt acts. Cases of this type recorded in the Order Books are listed below. Some of them were inspired by justifiable resentment but others arose from plain "cussedness."

1732—John Jenkins—crime against the king—inditement only of record.

1733—George Willson—cursed King George—5 pound fine or 20 lashes at the whipping-post.

1736—John Boutwell, Nicholas Ware, Robert Kay, William Lawson, Richard Buckner, Oliver Towles, Joseph Rennolds, Charles Holloway, John Holloway, Benjamin Grubbs and John Miller refused to give evidence before grand jury investigating Johnathan Gibson's partisans during Gibson-Martin election contest —fined 100 lbs. of tobacco each.

1736—William Powell, John Hogg, Richard Hill, John Munday, John Robinson and John Goodwin—fined one penny each by jury for misconduct during Gibson-Martin election.

1736—John Henderson—drunk and struck sheriff during Gibson-Martin hearings—fined 5 shillings or 50 lbs. of tobacco.

1736—Thomas Roy—put under 100 pound bond to keep the peace during the second Gibson-Martin campaign.

1737—Thomas Buckner and John Catlett—refused to testify against Gabriel Long after buying punch from him when he was without a license to sell alcoholic beverages—350 lbs. of tobacco fine, each.

1737—John Plant—misbehaved in jury room—fined 200 lbs. to tobacco.

1738—John Bell—drunk and swearing in court—5 shillings fine.

1740—Thomas Lantor—misbehaved in court—stocks one hour.

1740—Thomas Buckner—failed to attend muster—fined 5 shillings.

1740—Thomas Blassingame—misbehaving in court—stocks one hour.

1741—Lawrence Battaile—failed to attend muster—5 shillings fine.

1742—Rev. John Brunskill—attempted to bribe jury—fined 10 shillings.

1742—Thomas Lantor—misbehaved in court—5 shillings fine.

1747—William Conner—failed to report for jury service—fined 300 lbs. of tobacco.

1748—Henry Ware—failed to report for jury service—fined 300 lbs. of tobacco.

1748—Thomas Bankes—refused to be deputized as a constable—fined 5 shillings.

1756—William Isbell, Dr. John Southerland and William Buckner— refused to testify in the case of Abraham v. Taylor & Cowne— fined according to law.

1758—George Wiley and John Goodall—broke out of debtors' prison— jury refused to convict.

1758—Charles Noden—contempt of court for removing mulattoes from Virginia—jailed until the mulattoes were returned.

1760—Peter Bullard—refused to serve as prison guard for John Kay— accused of murder—fined 20 shillings.

1763—James Farish, Jeremiah Pierce, John Mitchell—drunk in court—fined 5 shillings, each.

1763—James Farish—drunk in court—fined 5 shillings.

1763—James Farish—drunk in court—placed under 40 pound bond for his good behavior.

1765—Robert Woolfolk—insulted John Baynham, a magistrate—10 pound bond for his good behavior.

1768—David Hogan, Samuel Sale, William Knighton and James Watts refused to testify in Tignor v. DeJarnette—fined 350 lbs. of tobacco each.

1768—Nathaniel Dickinson, John Wiley, Reuben L. Brown and Lodowick George—refused to testify against tax evaders—fined 350 lbs. of tobacco each.

1769—John Hilton, sheriff of Chesterfield—failed to return an execution—fined 2 pounds, 10 shillings.

1769—Robert Mickleberry—refused to testify against tax evaders—fined 350 lbs. of tobacco.

1770—John Burk, William Dudley, James Riddle, James White, John Mason, Benjamin Hurt, Nicholas Ware, Thomas Allcock, Eusabious Stone and Maurice Knight—refused to serve on grand jury because of laws governing worship and taxes—fined 350 lbs. of tobacco each.

1770—Francis Fleming—refused to produce Sussannah Fleming's will—fined for contempt.

1772—John Penn—stirring up rebellion—fined one penny (jury verdict).

1772—Amy Taylor, Thomas Ditmar and John Montague—stirring up rebellion—acquitted, by jury.

1772—Michael Crenshaw and Robert Woolfolk—stirring up rebellion—court dismissed charges.

1772—Thomas Collins—stirring up rebellion—fined 5 pounds sterling.

1772—Betty Chewning and Samuel Daniel—refused to testify against John Waller and Henry Goodloe for holding unauthorized worship—fined 350 lbs. of tobacco, each.

1772—Andrew Ross, Thomas Kelley and Mathew Gayle—refused to obey the legal command of Anthony Thornton, the county lieutenant—fined 5 pounds sterling, each.

1773—William Sutton—insulted Anthony New, a magistrate—excused.

1777—Robert Woolfolk—insulted the court.

3. Disturbing the Peace and Disorderly Conduct in Cases Not Heretofore Reported

1732—Benjamin Rennolds—led mob which wrecked Robert Willis' tavern—acquitted by jury.

1733—George Tribble—drunk in public—fined 5 shillings or 50 lbs. of tobacco.

1733—George Bullard, Thomas Powell and John Scott—swearing— fined 5 shillings or 50 lbs. of tobacco per oath.

1734—Edward Rouse—swearing—fined 5 shillings, or 50 lbs. of tobacco per oath.

1734—John Scott—swearing and drunk in public—5 shillings or 50 lbs. of tobacco for being drunk fine and 5 shillings or 50 lbs. of tobacco fine for each oath.

1734—Zach Martin—disturbing the peace—20 ponnd bond for good behavior.

1735—Timothy Terrell and Zack Martin—swearing—fined 5 shillings or 50 lbs. of tobacco for each oath.

1735—John Scott—drunk in public and swearing—fined 5 shillings or 50 lbs. of tobacco for each oath and for being drunk.

1735—Andrew Phillips, Charles Lindsay, Robert Lindsay John Mic-kowla—swearing—5 shillings or 50 lbs. of tobacco per oath.

1736—John Scott—drunk in public and swearing—same punishment as before.

1737—John Scott—drunk in public and swearing—in court twice in 1737 for these crimes—same punishment as before.

1738—Robert Baber and William Crutchfield—disturbing the peace— 20 pound bond for good behavior for a year and a day.

1738—John Scott—drunk in public and swearing—same punishment as before.

1739—Joseph Herndon—breach of the peace—fined 1 shilling by jury.

1739—Edward Grady—petty larceny—5 pound bond for good behavior for one year and one day.

1739—John Scott—drunk in public and swearing—same punishment as before.

1740—John Brown Miller, William Mason and James Smith—swearing—5 shillings or 50 lbs. of tobacco per oath.

1740—William Harris—swearing—5 shillings or 50 lbs. of tobacco.

1741—John Buller—disturbing the peace—10 pound bond for good behavior for a year and a day.

1741—John Buller—assault—charges dismissed.

1742—Mace Pickett—disturbing the peace—complaint of Rev. John Brunskill—30 pound bond to keep the peace for a year and a day.

1742—Thomas Wilshire—swearing—5 shillings or 50 lbs. of tobacco per oath.

1744—Joseph Stevens—disturbing the peace—100 pound bond for good behavior—one year and one day.

1742—Thomas Rielly—disturbing the peace—20 pound bond for good behavior for one year and one day.

1747—John Long—swearing 2 oaths—5 shillings or 50 lbs. of tobacco an oath fine.

1747—Robert Lyon—disturbing the peace—5 shillings fine and 20 pound bond for good behavior for a year and a day.

1751—Mace Pickett—disturbing the peace—20 pound bond for good behavior for a year and a day.

1752—George Arnold—disturbing the peace—complaint of Peter Copeland—100 pound bond for good behavior for a year and a day.

1756—William Murray—disturbing the peace—complaint of Joseph DeJarnette—20 pound bond for good behavior for a year and a day.

1756—Joseph Buller and John Lewis—drunk in public—fined 5 shillings or 50 lbs. of tobacco each.

1757—Joseph Head, Henry Tarrent, Joseph Robinson—swearing—5 shillings or 50 lbs. of tobacco fine per oath.

1757—Francis Taliaferro, Michael Brown Roberts and Thomas Pittman—breach of the peace—20 pound bond each for good behavior for a year and a day.

1757—John Mitchell—drunk in public—5 shillings or 50 lbs. of tobacco fine.

1758—Mace Pickett—disturbing the peace—20 pound bond for good behavior for a year and a day.

1758—Samuel Burruss—swearing 2 oaths—10 shillings or 100 lbs. of tobacco fine.

1759—William Occletrie—disturbing the peace—20 pound bond for good behavior for a year and a day.

1759—John Powell—disturbing the peace—20 lb. bond for good behavior for year and a day.

1760—John Watkins—disturbing the peace—20 lb. bond for good behavior for year and a day.

1761—Mace Pickett—disturbing the peace—bound year and day.

1762—Silvanus Sanders—disturbing the peace—20 lb. bond for good behavior for year and a day.

1762—John Zachery and John Cole Lambert—bound to keep the peace for year and a day.

1763—John Powell—disturbing the peace—complaint of Mordicai Abraham—20 pound bond to keep the peace for a year and a day.

1763—William Clatterbuck—bound to keep the peace.

1763—Phillip May—drunk in public—fined 5 shillings or 50 lbs. of tobacco.

1763—James Farish—disturbing the peace—40 pound bond for good behavior for a year and a day.

1765—Mace Pickett—disturbing the peace—complaint of George Major—20 pound bond for good behavior for a year and a day.

1765—John Powell—drunk in public and swearing—5 shillings or 50 lbs. of tobacco fine for being drunk and each oath.

1768—John Brown—drunk on the Sabbath and swearing three oaths—fined 20 shillings or 200 lbs. of tobacco.

1773—Richard Sale, John Saunders and Joseph Craig—disturbing the peace—20 pound bond each to keep the peace for a year and a day.

1773—John Grady—disturbing the peace—complaint of James Taylor—20 pound bond to keep the peace for a year and a day.

1774—John Fergusan, Mace and William Pickett—bound.

1776—John Malear—disturbing the peace—20 pound bond for good behavior for a year and a day.

1776—James Munday and Thomas Pickett—disturbing the peace—10 pound bond, each, for good behavior a year and a day.

1777—George Tankersley—disturbing the peace—complaint of David Sterns—50 pound bond to keep the peace for a year and a day.

4. Slander and Assault and Battery

In spite of the list above the people of colonial Caroline were little concerned with criminal warrants. Instead they rebuked or fought people who offended them. Rebukes and fights led to scores of civil actions for slander and assault and battery. These suits clogged the docket of the Caroline court with suits for assault and battery by far the more prevalent. They are listed below with suits for slander designated by (Slander):

1732—William Burdette v. Robert Willis, John Terrell v. Robert Willis, John Bruce v. Robert Willis, Robert Willis v. Charles Durrett, Robert Willis v. William Smith and Moses Downer, Robert Powell v. Charles Durrett, Robert and Sarah Willis v. Benjamin Rennolds (all these suits arose out of the wrecking of

Willis' tavern by Benjamin Rennolds in Rennolds' attempt to get the contract to supply the court with small beer). Robert Bird v. John Stoghill, Gabriel Toombs v. Rodowick Gordon, Richard Green v. Peter Lantor, John Davis v. Thomas Fortune, Thomas White v. Thomas Warren (Slander).

1733—Thomas White v. Thomas Warren, Phillip Easton v. Jeremiah Pierce, Thomas Lantor v. Mungo Roy.

1734—William Watson v. John Powell, John Dodson v. William MacIllock (Slander).

1735—Henry Shaddock v. Thomas Dunwoody, John MacKolla v. Cornelius Rennolds.

1736—John Martin v. John Hudson, Henry Powell, John Smith, William Watson, Henry Wood, William Powell, William Pickett, Richard Long, Thomas Fox, John Jeter, John Hogg, Richard Hill, John Carter, John Gough, Andrew Harrison, Gabriel Long, Henry Samuel, John Robinson, John Munday, Ellis Griffin, William Daniels, John Lewis, William Bell, John Schooler, Thomas Royston and Samuel Robinson (John Martin sued these 26 freeholders after he lost the election for Burgess in 1735 to Johnathan Gibson for assault and battery because he claimed that they beat up and intimidated his supporters and kept them from voting on election day. Juries refused to award him damages). John Sexton v. Charles Goodall, John Brunskill v. John Pickett (jury verdict of 5 pounds), Walter Crawley v. Thomas Buckner (Slander), William Pugh v. John Baites, John Baites v. Silvanus Sanders, John Smith v. Benjamin Poe, Richard Straughn v. Henry Powell, Mathew Giles v. Michael Lawless, William Capoy (?) v. Roger Quarles, Joseph Carter v. Martin Hackett.

1737—William Crawford v. Benjamin Rennolds, John Fox v. John Ellis, Robert Farguson v. Thomas Morris, Francis Thornton v. Sarah Smith (Slander).

1738—Francis and Sarah Bearding v. Charles Walden, Thomas Smith v. James Atkins, John Jarrell v. William Emerson, Isaac Cecil v. John Pickett (false imprisonment added to the charge), John Williams v. Jacob Johns, Timothy Ellis v. Henry Burk, William Bradley v. William Buller, Anthony Samuel v. Thomas Samuel.

1739—John Long, Jr. v. Samuel James (Slander). John Smith v. John Pickett, Jr., Joseph King v. John Powell and Mace Pickett (false imprisonment added to charge). (50 shilling verdict by jury.)

1740—Thomas Powell v. Thomas Munday, Mary Jones v. James Young.

1741—David Griffin v. William Sutton, William Beazley v. John Rielly, James Boulware v. Michael Lawless, Richard Watkins, Jr., an Infant by Richard Watkins v. John Pickett, Joshua Longest v. James Herndon, John Rielly v. Richard Hampton and John Stevens.

1742—Joseph King v. John Brown, John Rielly v. Richard Powell and Thomas Powell, Robert French v. John Myler, Jeremiah Long v. Nicholas Ware, William Robinson v. Charles Goodall, Henry Powell v. Charles Beazley (verdict of 20 shillings), John Lindell v. John Howe. John Brunskill v. Mace Pickett (2nd suit).

1743—Robert Lyon v. John Hurt, William Gaines and Rebecca, his wife, v. Robert Byrd and Dinah, his wife, Thomas Howell v. John Waters, Mace Pickett v. Lewis Turner, William Powell v. William Daniel, David Stern v. John Waters, Edmound Badgett v. John MacGriffor, William Smith v. Henry Powell, John Jenkins v. Richard Roy, Samuel Fletcher v. Gabriel Long, Peter Holland v. William Holland. (The Brunskill v. Pickett suits resulted from fights over two women, Ann Oakley and Mary Rogers.) Mace Pickett v. John and Ann Beazley and Mary Vaughan, Thomas and Dorcas Wilshire v. Mace Pickett.

1744—Samuel George v. John Hipkins, John Adams v. Edward Young, Joseph and Martha King v. Joseph Mackie, Richard Straughn v. Dr. George Todd, Edward Coffee v. Elias Blackburn, Aaron Tarrent and Jane, his wife, v. James Turner, William Carter v. Thomas Fortune. Nicholas Lankford v. Robert Lyon (Slander), William Riddle v. Edward Herndon (Slander).

1745—Sarah Hart, an infant by Charles Hart, her next friend v. Joseph Wilshire, Thomas Estis v. Thomas Pickett, John Wallis Summers v. Jacob Kendrick, Sarah Walding, an infant, Charles Walding, her next friend, v. Ann Dillard, a widow, Isabell Walding v. Ann Dillard, Edmound Badgett v. Mace Pickett, William Woodford v. John Casey, Thomas Lantor v. Jeremiah Pierce, William Johnston v. Steven Johnston.

1746—William Goburn v. William Hatton, William Woodford v. John Mitchell.

1747—Daniel Barksdale v. Benjamin Grubbs, Christian Brand v. John Milear, William Watson v. John Terrell, William Marshall v. William Eubank, Robert Whitlock v. James Southworth, John Powell v. Thomas Eubank, Richard Blanton v. John Gillison, John Mourning v. Simon Miller.

1748—John Powell v. John Pierce, John Sorrell v. James Lewis Mourning Holeby v. Daniel Macpharlin, Manus Fegan v. Charles Beazley.

1749—Thomas Peatross v. Stephen Johnston, John Burton v. John Griffin, Christopher Acuss (Acors) v. John Estis, Christopher Acuss, Jr., an infant, who sues by his next friend, Christopher Acuss v. John Estis, Francis Long v. Charles Harrison.

1750—James Dismukes v. Thomas Johnston, Peter Copeland v. Samuel Pryor.

1751—Richard Straughn v. John Holloway, George Clark v. Richard Goode, verdict 40 shillings, Jacob Fewell v. Richard Bradford, Charles Noden v. John Whitton, verdict 7 pounds, 10 shillings.

1752—John Hipkins v. Samuel Jeter, 10 pound damages, Eleanor Cooper v. Richard Goode, one penny damages, Nicholas Mullins v. Martha King (Slander), 2 pounds damages.

1753—Henry Burk v. James and Edmound Taylor, 1 shilling damages, John Carden v. William Lewis (Slander), Jacob Johns v. Paul Thilman, John Milear v. William Plunkett, 40 shilling damages.

1754—Joseph DeJarnette v. Richard Corey, 2 pounds, 1 shilling, damages.

1755—Patrick Cockran v. Richard Blanton, 40 shillings damages, John Carter v. John Griffin, 40 shillings damages, John Griffin v. John Carter (Slander), 6 pounds damages (an unusual pair of verdicts), Thomas Pemberton v. John Griffin, 5 pounds damages, Robert Lyon v. Johnathan Gibson and John Pickett, James Gordon v. Thomas Pickett, John Miller v. John Gillison, Bartholomew Chewning v. Benjamin Williamson, 5 pounds damages.

1756—John Long v. John Gillison (Slander), 5 pounds damages, Alexander Legan v. John Gillison, 50 shillings damages, John Summers v. William Blanton, 1 penny damages, Thomas Watkins v. Paul Thilman, 5 pounds damages, William Young v. Rev. Musgrave Dawson, 4 pounds damages.

1757—William Boulware v. Thomas Johnston, John Sneed v. John Pickett, Gerald Davis v. Francis Taliaferro, 15 pounds damages, Richard Collins v. Phillip Jones (Slander), Oliver Towles v. Thomas Campbell, 55 pounds damages.

1758—Sarah Triplett v. Colin Reddock.

1759—Michael Brown Roberts v. Achilles Foster, John Fielding v. David Stern (Slander), 50 shillings damages, Mary Pye v. Charles Acuss (Acors) (Slander), James Hundley v. William and Mary Stevens (Slander), John Fielding v. Harry Beverley, Elizabeth Estis v. Phillip Estis, 20 shillings damages, James Herndon v. John Buller, John Royston v. John Buckner (Slander).

1761—Thomas Collawn v. James Powell, John Powell v. Thomas Collawn, John Puller v. Robert Garrett, John Cooper v. Thomas Jones, Richard Dickens v. James George, Thomas Pickett v. Jacob Tinsley, Reuben Shelton v. Garrett Hackett, James George v. William Whitlock and Ann, his wife (Slander).

1762—John Bowcock v. John Winterton, Elizabeth Chandler v. John Spearman, Robert Johnston v. Ambroise Fletcher, Phillip Brown v. Stephen Lowe, David Green v. Joseph Berry, Achilles Whitlock v. James George, Benjamin Lehon v. John Wynal Sanders, Mary Pickett by Mace Pickett, her next friend v. John Pickett and John Wiley, Ambroise Fletcher v. Achilles Foster, John Southworth v. Titus Hurt (Slander), 50 lbs. of tobacco damages. Bryan Fitzpatrick v. Silvanus Sanders, Isaac Spencer v. Richard Fortune, Henry Williams v. Achilles Whitlock, Mary Cooper v. James Farish (Slander), Francis Thorpe v. James Farish, Benjamin Hobbs v. Griffin Morris (Slander), 1 shilling damages.

1763—James Farish v. George Mitchell, Richard Dickens v. William Chick, John Pemberton v. William Whitlock, James Boulware v. John Evins, Nicholas Mullins v. George Alsop, Daniel, a free Negro, v. Jacob Tinsley, one penny damages.

1764—Francis Long v. William Brown, William Smith v. John Webster, John Bourne v. William Fortune, William Johnston v. James Farish, Elias Blackburn v. James Gant, Thomas Burk v. John Jones, Samuel Norment v. Duncan Graham.

1765—Aaron Service v. Thomas Burk, Thomas Burk v. James George, John Major v. Thomas Burk, Bryan Fitzpatrick v. Daniel Hughes, John Bourne v. Richard Fortune, Jane Harrihan v. James Farish, John Johnson v. James Terrell, Robert Dyer v. Thomas Coates.

1767—Francis Fleming v. Vincent Vass, James Horney v. John Fulcher.

1768—John Brooks v. Robert Woolfolk, Lodowick Jones Major v. John Sanders, Francis Long v. Joseph Cooper, Samuel Sale v. Richard Major, Reuben Wondrum v. William MacIntosh, John Parker v. John Brand, Joseph Rennolds v. William Arnold.

1769—William Dickinson v. Garrett Hackett, Achiles Whitlock v. William Whitlock (Slander), Edward Powers v. Thomas Daniel, James Gregory v. Garrett Hackett, 1 penny damages, John Grady v. Benjamin Alsop, James Southward v. Thomas Burk.

1770—Thomas Burk v. Richard Johnston, Benjamin Vaughan v. Thomas Brown, William Johnston v. Cosmo Meddice (?), Morris Spicer v. Jacob King, John Harringham v. John Smith, John Cummins v. James Pattie, Charles Alestock v. James Cash,

Anthony MacDonald v. John Cooper, John Carneal v. James Clark.

1771—William Pitts v. Jacob Daniel, James Walden v. Thomas Conduit, Benjamin Vaughan v. Thomas Burk, Dicey King v. William Beazley, Samuel Major v. Harry Beazley.

1772—Frederick Fortson v. James Gregory, Patty Mann v. John Sutton, Elizabeth Mackie v. John Milear, Jr., and John Sanders, James Wright v. John Bourne, George Mills v. Thomas Burk, George Major v. John Cooper, Benjamin Robinson, an infant, by his next friend, Joseph Robinson, v. Robert Parker, John Cummins v. James Pattie (Slander), John Hundley v. Robert Woolfolk, Moses Webster v. James Reynolds (Slander), Edward Phillips v. Jacob Daniel, John George v. Thomas Burk, Richard Dickens v. Thomas Collins.

1773—William Hewlett v. Euclid Whitlock, William Boulware v. James Farish and Thomas Hackett, John Milone v. Joseph Cooper, William Brown and William Crawley v. Thomas Hackett, Patrick Cuffey v. Federick Fortson, William Brown, Jr. v. Garrett Hackett, John Baynham v. Robert Woolfolk, William Crawley v. William Taylor, Nathaniel Bourne v. Gordon Glantor, Griffin Carter v. Charles Beazley, Walter Chiles v. Thomas Hackett, William Clark v. John Walden, John Dugard v. Rodham Kenner, William Goodall v. Thomas Hackett, Richard Goodall v. Thomas Hackett.

1774—John Alexander Still v. John Milear, Lodowick Janes Major v. Benjamin Alsop, Griffin Carter v. Charles Beazley, Nathaniel Bourne v. Gordon Glantor (Slander), John Sacrey v. Ambroise Jeter, Jesse Clark v. Thomas Sale, John Munday v. Robert Farish (Slander).

1775—Edward Brown v. Thomas Hackett.

No actions for slander or assault and battery were brought under the rule of the Committee of Safety, or during the early years of the Revolution.

1777—David Stern v. George Tankersley, James Pattie v. Rodham Kenner, Frederick Fortson v. John Alexander Still, William Southworth v. Thomas Burk.

1778—Henry Durrett v. Marshall Ellis, John Mitchell v. Richard Lewis, Micajah Johns v. John Oliver.

1781—Thomas Boulware v. Edward Munday.

THE LAWYERS

Lawyers were in demand due to the litigation arising from actions for slander and assault and battery and creditors' suits. Forty-nine men qualified to practice before the Caroline court. They included some of the ablest lawyers in Virginia, Edward Barradall, Edmound Pendleton, George Wythe, Obediah Merriott and Patrick Henry. But the Rev. Johnathan Boucher took a dim view of the lot. In his *Autobiography* published in *Notes and Quiries* he writes, "As for lawyers, they seemed to grow up spontaneously; many of the first name and note in their profession were men without any education and totally illiterate. Such a state of society was peculiar, and could not but have peculiar effects, for no other body of men, or all other bodies of men put together, had half so much influence as the lawyers."

But for all their influence lawyers were not particularly well paid. In 1742 William Waller took 40 gallons of cider for a fee in an important case, and Thomas Landrum wrote in his will made in 1764 before he began a trip to Europe and probated in the Caroline court in 1771 "I direct that the executors use what may be needed of the corpus of my estate to educate my sons to be doctors or parsons, I will not subject them to the drudgeries of the law."

Lawyers who Qualifiel to Practice in the Caroline Court (with the date of their qualification in the Order Books).

*Lived in Caroline.

Prior to 1732—William Robinson, Edward Barradall.

1732—Mark Wick.

1733—Benjamin Walker.*

1734—Zachery Lewis,* George Buckhannon.

1735—John Mercer(1)*

---

(1) John Mercer lived and practiced in Caroline while he was disbarred in Prince William. While in Caroline he compiled a code of the laws of the colony of Virginia which the General Court ruled was "fit to be printed." After the Prince William court removed his disabilities he returned to that county to practice. As an interesting side light John Mercer was the father of the Stampmaster of Virginia, George Mercer, during the period the Stamp Act was in force. The Stampmaster spent much of his youth in Caroline.

1736—William Waller,* Henry Barradall.

1738—John Martin, Jr.,* William Ballory.

1742—Edmound Pendleton.*

1743—Francis Gouldman, John Longman, Phillip Johnston.*

1746—George Wythe.

1748—William Munsel, Roger Dixon.

1749—Thomas Landrum.*

1750—Obediah Merriott.

1752—Alexander Ross (Rose),* Thomas Rogers.

1755—William Tate.

1757—John Lewis,* John Skinker,* John Buckner.*

1760—Charles Robinson.*

1762—John Penn,* Oliver Towles, Jr.,* Thomas Robinson.*

1765—Patrick Henry, John Semple,* William Underwood, William Boulware,* Edmound Pendleton, Jr.*

1766—Henry Robinson.*

1767—George Lyne.*

1768—John Aylett.

1769—Francis Coleman.*

1770—Charles Ross (Rose),* Harry Tompkins,* John Pendleton,* Thomas Lomax.*

1771—Thomas Claibourne.

1772—George Guy.*

1773—Andrew Buckhannon, John Taylor.*

1779—George Nicholas.

1780—Andrew Buckner.*

THE MASONS

Note: The minutes of Port Royal Kilminning Crosse Lodge No. 2 were stolen from Port Royal during the Civil War and carried north. Dr. Joseph W. Eggleston, the Grand Master of Masons in Virginia, in 1910 discovered them in Philadelphia and arranged for their purchase and return to Virginia. They were edited and printed in part, at least, as a supplement to the Grand Lodge Proceedings for 1910. These minutes cover the period from 1754-1859. They are among the oldest, if not the oldest, Masonic records in the United States. Only the portion through 1781 are used in this history.

As early as April 12, 1754, a group of men were meeting in Port Royal as Masons. This group included Patrick Coutts, Robert Gilchrist, John Cross, John Gray, James Miller, William Fox, Gideon Johnston, Alexander Rose (Ross), Andrew Crawford, John Crawford, Colin Riddick, Thomas Landrum and John Douglass. The organization was without either formal name or charter. In the late spring or early summer of 1755 David Cross of Scotland sent the lodge "proper Jewels and Aprons for the Master and Wardens," by William Fox, one of its original members, who was a mariner and made frequent voyages across the Atlantic. Reputedly David Cross was the father of John Cross, another original member, and Scottish agent for the celebrated trading house of Dunlop in which John Cross was a junior partner in Port Royal. In gratitude for the jewels and aprons the Port Royal Masons called their lodge the Port Royal Cross (not Crosse) Lodge. (Minutes June 8, 1754.)

On May 10, 1755, Robert Gilchrist, John Gray, James Miller and John Cross "for themselves and in the name of sundry other Brethern Free and Accepted Masons in Virginia" petitioned the Grand Lodge of Scotland for a charter. The new lodge to be called Kilwinning Port Royal Crosse. Kilwinning was added to the name in honor of Kilwinning, the seat of the Grand Lodge of Scotland. The Scottish Grand Lodge granted this charter on December 1, 1755 and Kilwinning Port Royal Crosse Lodge came into being. The original charter is still in existence, and in Masonic circles it is conceded to be the oldest charter now in possession of any Masonic lodge in America. Kilwinning Crosse, however, is not Virginia's oldest Masonic lodge. The Virginia Grand Lodge in 1786 granted that distinction to a lodge in Norfolk and rated the Port Royal lodge number two when it ranked the eight lodges in existence in Virginia before the organization of the Grand Lodge in 1778.

Kilwinning Port Royal Crosse Lodge took a leading part in the philanthropic, social and fraternal life of Port Royal, Caroline County, and the adjacent sections of Virginia throughout the colonial period. It helped organize the Grand Lodge of the Commonwealth (1777-78). James Kemp and Thomas Lomax were its representatives at these meetings, and James Kemp served as Provisional Grand Secretary.

Below are listed members of Kilwinning Crosse Lodge prior to 1781 with the dates of their initiations according to the records of the Grand Lodge of Virginia for 1785.

Robert Gilchrist, James Miller, John Gray (charter members— 1755), George Muse (1757), William Buckner (1761), Thomas Catlett (1761), Andrew Leckie (1767), James Dunlop (1767), Dr. John Tennant (1767), John Skinker (1767), William Lindsay (1767), Mungo Roy (1767), Gawin Corbin (1769), George Catlett (1770), Thomas Lomax (1770), Rev. Abner Waugh (1770), Richard Dixon (1770), Francis Conway III (1772), James Coates (1772), John Victor (1776), Peyton Stern (1776), John Timberlake (1777), Thomas Fitzhugh (1778), John Tankersley (1778), John Hipkins (1778), and Phillip Johnston (1779).

Other Caroline Masons whose names appear in the records of Kilwinning Crosse Lodge prior to 1781. These men were apparently all dead or had moved away before the makings of the roster of 1785 cited above.

John Cross, John Gray, William Fox, Alexander Ross, Andrew Crawford, John Crawford, Collin Riddick, John Miller, Thomas Landrum, William Scott, James Robb, James Taliaferro, Charles Mortimer, Thomas Cocke, John Hamilton, William Taliaferro, Mordicai Buckner, Harry Beverley, Joseph Smith, John Buckner, J. Monroe, James Semple, John Brown, Robert Bogle, Robert Chew, Peter Carne, Andrew Johnston, William Hudleston, John (Beverley?) Roy, George Weedon, Andrew Cranston, Lawrence Catlett, John Catlett, Lundsford Lomax, Jr., Lawrence Taliaferro, William Johnston, Hay Taliaferro, James Somerell, Archibald Clark, James Bowie, William Dickinson, Fleming Thomas, Charles Robinson, Catesby Woodford, John Carter, Thomas Robinson, William Lindsay, John Woodford, C. W. Carter, William Nelson, Jr., John Armistead, Augustine Moore, John Taliaferro, Hugh Stewart, George Gray, James Conduit, Ralph Lomax, LeRoy Hipkins, John Walsh, Harry Robinson, James Kemp (1770), Francis Thornton, Turner Dixon, Jacob Fox, Archibald McLean (1774), Thomas Bankhead, Harry Dixon (1776), Robert Paul, Thomas Paul, Lewis Hipkins, James Bowie, Jr.

The vast majority, but not all, of the above lived in Caroline County. George Weedon, who became the celebrated general, was never a resident. He subsequently transferred his lodge membership to Fredericksburg. Tradition holds that Robert and Thomas Paul were brothers of the naval hero, John Paul Jones.

ESTATES & EXECUTORS OR ADMINISTRATORS

1732

Decedent	Exec. or Adm.	Decedent	Exec. or Adm.
Sam Williams	William Oliver	Joseph Anderson	Robert Baber
Mary Jones	Edward Jones	Reuben Welch	Mary Welch
Joseph Andrews	Rogert Quarles		

1733

Decedent	Exec. or Adm.	Decedent	Exec. or Adm.
Francis Conway	Rebecca Conway	John Battaile	Sarah Battaile
James Gough	Ann Gough	Thomas Leftwitch	William Herndon
Robert Thomas	Owin Thomas	Davis Murray	Jane Murray
John Brooks	Phoebe Brooks	John Downer	John Downer, Jr.
Larkin Chew	Hannah Chew	George Hoomes	Christopher Hoomes
Isaac Allen	Henry Isbell		& George Hoomes, Jr.
Marcus Sanders	Humphrey Hill	James Gillison	Mary Gillison
Mary Buckner	Thomas Buckner	Richard Buckner	Elizabeth Buckner
Benj. Downer	Thomas Buckner	Robert Scrism(?)	William Taliaferro

1734

Decedent	Exec. or Adm.	Decedent	Exec. or Adm.
Richard Fowler	Francis Fowler	Isaac Hill	Clement Reed
John Morgan	Thomas Price	William Wafford	Mary Wafford
Ann Downer	George Downer	Thomas Dickinson	Griffin Dickinson
William Whitton	Robert Farish	John Roy	Dorothy & Thomas Roy
John May	Sussannah May	Abraham Brown	Mary Brown
Sandy Holeman	Anthony Thornton		

1735

Decedent	Exec. or Adm.	Decedent	Exec. or Adm.
Ralph Richards	Abel Sterns	Micajah Chiles	Henry Terrell
John Chisum	Lawrence Bradley	John Robinson	Sam & John Robinson
John Sanders	Charles Sanders	Rodham Kenner	Judith Beverley
John Brown	Mary Brown		Kenner
William Strother	Margaret Strother	John Watkins	Mary, William &
Charles Taliaferro	Mary Taliaferro		James Watkins
Baldwin Callawn	Mary Callawn	Jacob Vigon	John Micalle
John Plant	William Stapleton	John Ault	Michael Guinney
John Stone	Ralph Willson	William Singleton	James Terry
Dabney Anderson	James Trice		

1736

Decedent	Exec. or Adm.	Decedent	Exec. or Adm.
Evan Thomas	William Herndon	John Bourton	John Pickett
Elizabeth Stannard	William Stannard	John Foster	John Foster, Jr.
Thomas Terry	Stephen Terry	Amy Day	John Anderson
William Denis	Peter Marks	John Hogg	Sarah Hogg

Decedent	Exec. or Adm.	Decedent	Exec. or Adm.
1737			
John Eubank	Elizabeth Eubank	Abraham Allen	Edward Yarbrough
John Clark	Robert Dudley	Nicholas Lankford	William Burdette
Morris Clayton	James Bowie	John Stone	Mary Stone
Elias White	Henry Burk		
1738			
Robert Fleming	Elizabeth Fleming	Robert Campbell	Robert Tompkins
Henry Noland	John Goodall	John Hoster(?)	Richard Bradford
John Riddle	Ann Riddle	Mason Combs	Grace Butler
William Thomas	Mary Clark	Thomas Carr	William Carr, Sarah
Benjamin Walker	Ann & John Walker		Minor, Agnes Walker,
Randsome Dudley	Christopher		Mary Carr, John &
	Taliaferro		Thomas Carr
1739			
Isaac Franck	Mary Franck	George Morton	Sussannah Morton
Thomas Powell	Mary Powell	Thomas Catlett	Johnathan Gibson(1)
William Markham	(?)	Moses Chapman	Mary Chapman
John Hoy	Edward Scrimshaw	Philemon Hurt	Griggs Yarbrough
John Hurlock	William Carr		

(1) Martha Thornton Catlett, the widow of Thomas Catlett, persuaded the court to remove Johnathan Gibson as executor of her husband's estate, and make her the executrix. This was part of the Thornton-Catlett feud which arose over the Martin Gibson contest for Burgess.

Decedent	Exec. or Adm.	Decedent	Exec. or Adm.
1740			
Elizabeth Lomax	Lundsford Lomax	Henry Bell	Esther Bell
Thomas Buckner	Elizabeth Buckner	William Bunion	Rachael Bunion(2)
Robert Powell	James Powell	James Atkerson	Robert Hall
Thomas Durham	Frances Durham	Hipkins Moore	Henry Rains

(2) Rachael Bunion refused to serve as executor of her husband's estate, because she preferred her dower rather than her legacy under the will.

Decedent	Exec. or Adm.	Decedent	Exec. or Adm.
1741			
Mary Taliaferro	Thomas Slaughter	John Samuels	Sarah Samuels
Christopher Robinson	Benjamin	George Goodloe	Diannah Goodloe
	Robinson	Richard Turner	Elizabeth Turner
1742			
Benjamin Rennolds	Sarah Rennolds	Mary Tuck	Francis Stern
Thomas Norman	Timothy Chandler	Thomas Watkins	James Oliver
Michael Guinney	Arch Macphearson	Thomas Farson	Elizabeth Farson
George Tilley	Thomas Hoarde	William Turner	Thomas and
John Catlett	Mary Catlett		Mary Turner
John Keith	Jeremiah Keith	John Peatross	Ann Peatross
Betty Pendleton	Edmound Pendleton		
1743			
Robert Anderson	Oliver Towles	Ralph Beves	James Beves
Robert Smith	Elizabeth Smith	Elizabeth Cowing	John George

Decedent	Exec. or Adm.	Decedent	Exec. or Adm.
Head Lynch	Prudence Lynch	Henry Jeter	John Jeter
James Coghill	John George	Henry Bell	James Lindsay(3)

(3) The court removed Esther Bell and made James Lindsay the administrator of Henry Bell's estate.

1744

Decedent	Exec. or Adm.	Decedent	Exec. or Adm.
Thomas Catlett	John Bowie(4)	Thomas Hamm	Sarah & Thomas Hamm
James Stevens	John Stevens	Robert Woolfolk	Richard & Frances Woolfolk
John Bell	Elizabeth Bell		
William Sale	Hannah Sale	James Coghill	James Coghill, Jr. (5)
Elizabeth Pickerell	Walter Chiles	Ann Mayo	James Mayo
Catherine Jones	Arch Macphearson	Henry Harris	Ann Harris
Augustine Elmore	James Martin	Catlett Conway	Francis & Reuben Conway
William Partloe	Sarah Partloe		
Thomas Estis	Ann Estis	Nicholas Ware	Nicholas Ware, Jr.

(4) In 1744 the Catletts gained an advantage in the Catlett-Thornton feud and John Bowie, the husband of Thomas Catlett's sister, Judith, wrestled the executorship of Thomas Catlett's estate from his widow, Martha Thornton Catlett.

(5) James Coghill, Jr. was displeased with the way John George managed his father's estate, and persuaded the court to remove George and make him administrator.

1745

Decedent	Exec. or Adm.	Decedent	Exec. or Adm.
Daniel Gaines	Oliver Towles	Reuben Conway	Francis Conway
Benjamin Dickens	Mary Dickens	Mary Falkner	Benjamin Falkner
Moses Daniel	James Lindsay	William Durrett	Ann Durrett

1746

Decedent	Exec. or Adm.	Decedent	Exec. or Adm.
Sylvester Patty	Sarah Patty	Winney Gough	John Gough
Thomas Slaughter	Sarah Slaughter	Mary Mason	William Mason
Dorothy Roy	Richard Roy	Jeremiah Long	John Long(6)
Thomas Swinney	Jacob Burruss	Peter Mason	Peter & Thomas Mason
Sarah Boulton	Adam Lindsay	Thomas Harrison	Margaret Harrison

(6) John Long refused to serve and Judith Long, the widow, administered the estate.

1747

Decedent	Exec. or Adm.	Decedent	Exec. or Adm.
James Gillison	John Gillison	Samuel Coleman	Elizabeth Wyatt Coleman
William Baynham	John Baynham		
Joseph Young	Mary Young	James Sullinger	Martha, Peter and Thomas Sullinger
James Taylor	Elizabeth Cary and William Byrd Richards	William Higgins	Elizabeth & William Higgins, Jr.
Jane Butler	William Cammack	Robert Coleman	Spilsbey Coleman
Lewis Turner	John Turner	John Yarbrough	James Hurt

1748

Decedent	Exec. or Adm.	Decedent	Exec. or Adm.
George Eastham	John Rogers	Arch Chalmers	Elizabeth Chalmers
Joseph Dyer	John Dyer	Anthony Arnold	Isabell and George Arnold
Mary Carr	John Minor		
William MacGehee	John MacGehee	Richard Winn	Benjamin Winn

Decedent	Exec. or Adm.	Decedent	Exec. or Adm.
George Goodwin	Elizabeth Goodwin	Richard Taliaferro	Rose Taliaferro
William Pruitt	John Pruitt	Charles Holloway	Rachael Holloway
Thomas Schooler	William Schooler	Edward Ware	Lucy Ware
George Marsh	Elizabeth Marsh	John Oliver	Elinor Oliver
William Brown	Sarah Brown and Timothy Chandler	John Bell	Ann Bell and Ephriam Simmonds

1749

Decedent	Exec. or Adm.	Decedent	Exec. or Adm.
James Coghill	John Beazley(7)	George Penn	Ann Penn
Patrick Donahoe	Elizabeth & Edward Donahoe	John Miller	Sheriff Thomas Buckner
John Southworth	Hugh Noden	William Stuart	Joel, William & Ann Stuart
John Gregory	Thomas Johnston	Thomas Garnett	Guinian Garnett
George Campbell	James Campbell	John Bendell	John Jeter
William Weller	Sarah Weller	Thomas Jackson	Phobe Jackson
John Burt	Sheriff Thomas Buckner	Augustine Muse	George Muse
John Terrell	Sarah Terrell	Daniel Booth	Ruth Booth
Daniel Gaines	William Woodford	George Gibson	George Gibson, Jr.
William Arnold	John Mitchell	William Marlow	William Burdette
John Garnett	John Garnett		

(7) Other heirs of James Coghill forced the removal of James Coghill, Jr. as executor and the court substituted John Beazley.

1750

Decedent	Exec. or Adm.	Decedent	Exec. or Adm.
Silvanus Sanders	Ann Sanders	James Kay	John Watts
Kemp Taliaferro	Mary Taliaferro	John Thompson	Sussannah Thompson
Lawrence Battaile	Sarah Battaile(8)	John Young	Sarah Young
John Glanton	Ann Glanton(9)	Jeremiah Long	Nicholas & Jeremiah Long(10)
Thomas Dabyne	Frances Dabyne		
Michael Nailing	James Quarles	William Pannell	William Pannell, Jr.
William Mason	Thomas Wild	John Brown	William Fitzhugh
Sarah Battaile	Francis Thornton	William Rowe	Mary & Benjamin Rowe
William Bullard	Edward Brassfield		
James Fletcher	Mary Fletcher	John Potter	William Goodall
John Sorrell	Patrick Coutts	Thomas Harris	Sarah Harris

(8) Lawrence Battaile left two wills and a controversy developed. Before the court decided which was valid Sarah Battaile died and Francis Thornton took over the administration of his estate.

(9) Ann Glanton contested John Glanton's will and took over the administration of the estate.

(10) Judith Long failed as executor of Jeremiah Long's estate, and her sons, Nicholas and Jeremiah, Jr. took over.

1751

Decedent	Exec. or Adm.	Decedent	Exec. or Adm.
Roger Quarles	Jane & John Quarles	Benjamin Taliaferro	Edmound Pendleton
Richard Taliaferro	Edmound Pendleton(11)	William Evins	Jacob Garrett and Charles Blanton
Joseph Rennolds	Elizabeth Rennolds		
Thomas Hoard	Luke Burford	John Wyatt	John Pamplin

(11) Richard Taliaferro's estate was too involved for his widow, Rose, to handle and she turned it over to Edmound Pendleton to administer.

Decedent	Exec. or Adm.	Decedent	Exec. or Adm.
Sarah Campbell	William Campbell	Sarah Lucas	Ann Lindsay(12)
John Peatross	William Taliaferro	Anthony Minter	Elizabeth Minter
James Bailey	Elizabeth Bailey	James Carver Dickinson	John Griffin
Henry Bell	Edmound Pendleton(13)	John Dyer	James Dyer
Elizabeth Evins	John Evins	Richard Sanders	James Brown
Hugh Noden	Elizabeth Noden		

(12) Adam Lindsay resigned and Robert Brooks succeeded him.

(13) Edmound Pendleton was the third administrator for Henry Bell's estate. The estate had been in court for over 10 years when he took over. Henry Bell was father of Humphrey Bell of London and a merchant in his own right in Caroline. After his death his widow, Easter, tried to settle his affairs but they were too involved and she turned them over to James Lindsay, a sea captain, who made frequent trips to London and conferred with Humphrey. When Lindsay got tangled up the heirs engaged Pendleton to straighten out the estate.

1752

Decedent	Exec. or Adm.	Decedent	Exec. or Adm.
John Munday	Sarah Munday	Honorous Powell	William and Mary Powell
Mathew Cox	Richard Hodges		
David Griffin	Thomas Wild	William Wellbourne	Edmound Taylor
Samuel Bush	Abraham Bush	Daniel Triplett	John Triplett
Thomas White	Sussannah White	James Debusie	Bartholomew Durrett
Richard Mauldin	Peter Copeland	Joseph Norment	Abishie Norment
Richard Johns	Betty Johns	John Edmoundson	Sussannah Edmoundson
Ann Curtis	Rice Curtis		
Thomas Ship	Thomas Edward(14)	Richard Thilman	Richard Eubank
Benj. Martin	Elizabeth & Henry Martin	Johnathan Roberts	David Roberts
		Thomas Guittrey(15)	James Bowie & John Gray
William Sheet	Anthony Sheet		

(14) The court removed Thomas Edwards and made William Smith Adm.

(15) Guittrey was a French merchant who lived in Port Royal.

1753

Decedent	Exec. or Adm.	Decedent	Exec. or Adm.
Thomas Callawn	Daniel Triplett, Jr.	William Campbell	George Campbell, Jr.
John Stevens	Mary Stevens	Ann Hay	Benjamin Robinson & James Cooper(16)
John Mitchell	John Connor		
George Hoomes	Edmound Pendleton(17), John Baylor & Stephen Ferneau Hoomes	Richard Vaughan	William Goodall(18), Richard Wood & John Hackett
Jane Roy	Reuben Roy	Henry Long	John Long(18a)

(16) Francis Taliaferro succeeded Robinson and Cooper as executor.

(17) Baylor handled portion of estate in Culpeper and Orange, Stephen Ferneau Hoomes portion in Caroline, and Pendleton the legal angles.

(18) Divided estate rather than administered.

(18a) Resigned and sheriff administered estate.

1754

Decedent	Exec. or Adm.	Decedent	Exec. or Adm.
Joseph Hoomes	Sussannah Hoomes & Edmound Pendleton	Thomas Apperson	John Apperson
		John Allen	Mary Ship
Edward Crawley	The Sheriff	Mary Powell	Edward Ware and Millicent Powell
Richard Brunskill	The Sheriff		

Decedent	Exec. or Adm.	Decedent	Exec. or Adm.
Mathew Mills	Mary Mills (19)	John Boulware	Mary Boulware
Ambroise Blackburn	Thomas Blackburn	Jacob Burruss	Reuben Harris
Joshua Tinsley	Elizabeth Tinsley	Thomas Redd	Samuel Redd
John Rennolds	Elizabeth Rennolds (20)	William Pair (Parr)	James Miller
Thomas Peatross	Edward Dixon & Robert Gilchrist	William Henning	James Miller

(19) Mary Mills contested will of Mathew Mills. Court invalidated will and made her administratrix.

(20) Elizabeth died and Sarah Rennolds became administratrix.

1755

Decedent	Exec. or Adm.	Decedent	Exec. or Adm.
John Johnson	Johnathan Johnson	Arch Macphearson	Elizabeth Macphearson
Richard Billops	John Billops and James Kay	Ann Dillard	William Dillard
Thomas Key	Sheriff Richard Buckner	James Riddle	Elizabeth Riddle & James White
John Hubbard	George Carter		
Dorothy Stern	David Stern	Sarah Stone	Thomas Jett
Edward Leavill	Sarah Leavill	Francis Stern	Davis & Charles Stern
Benjamin Taliaferro (21)	Sheriff	Edward Tomlin	Catherine Tomlin
Thomas Buckner	John & Mary Buckner	Robert Kay	Robert Kay, Jr. & John Evins & Joseph Berry
Daniel Grant	Ellis Gravatt		
William Woodford	John Champ & Nicholas Battaile	William Powell	Edward Dixon & James Bowie

(21) Edmound Pendleton removed by the court.

1756

Decedent	Exec. or Adm.	Decedent	Exec. or Adm.
George Penn	Moses Penn	Robert Lyon	Robert Lyon, Jr.
Sarah Goodall	Charles Goodall	William Lawson	John Pendleton (23)
Joseph Crew	Agnes Crew	William Harris	Peter Copeland
Thomas Paine	John Elliott Paine	John Zachery	Elizabeth Zachery
John Long	John Jr. & Frances Long	Mary Bryan	James Chace
Merry Eastham	John Rogers & Robert Goodloe	James Taylor, the Younger	Edmound Pendleton & John Taylor
Thomas Dobbins	James Davis (22)	Francis Smith	Grancis Jr. and Sarah Smith
Thomas Jackson	Joshua Lindsay		

(22) Davis removed and Samuel Skinker, John Skinker and John Thornton adm. est.

(23) Benjamin Hubbard, John Sutton, Charles Storey and Francis Taylor.

1757

Decedent	Exec. or Adm.	Decedent	Exec. or Adm.
Richard Bradford	William Boulware	William Taliaferro	Ann and James Taliaferro
William Chewning	Jeannette Chewning	Thomas Turner	Mary Turner
Justinian Wills	Edmound Pendleton	John Major	Samuel Major
		Francis Durrett	John Durrett (24)

(24) Removed and Johnathan Gibson appointed.

1758

Decedent	Exec. or Adm.	Decedent	Exec. or Adm.
Daniel Gaines	Elizabeth Gaines	Edward Herndon	William and James Herndon
Luke Burford	Sarah Burford		

Decedent	Exec. or Adm.	Decedent	Exec. or Adm.
John Samuel	Josiah Samuel	William Southworth	Catherine and
John Hundley	Francis Hundley and		William Southworth, Jr.
	Francis Hundley, Jr.	Timothy Chandler	Justin & Richard
Thomas Fortune	Thomas Jr., Richard		Woolfolk Chandler
	& Alexander Fortune	James Lawson	John Pendleton
Mary Watkins	John Allmond	Thomas Smith	Sarah Smith
Mary Wyatt	Richard Wyatt	John Whitlock	Mary Whitlock
Francis Thornton	Reuben Thornton	John Pemberton	Ann Pemberton
William Allison	James Bowie and	George Chapman	Ann and George
	Robert Gilchrist		Jr. Chapman
Reuben Roy	William Fox		

1759

Decedent	Exec. or Adm.	Decedent	Exec. or Adm.
Henry Wyatt(25)	Henry Gilbert &	William Crutchfield	John Baughn,
	Richard Wyatt		Phillip Taylor, Wil-
Humphrey Tompkins	Charles Yar-		liam Boulware, Samuel
	brough & Christopher		Burruss(26)
	Tompkins, Robert	David Terrell	Agatha Terrell(28)
	Tompkins(26)	John Smith	Henry Dinwiddie
Charles Goodall	John Lewis(27)	John Emerson	Elizabeth & John
William Hunter	William Taliaferro		Emerson, Jr.
	and James Hunter	William Hewlett	William Holdman
Mary MacGehee	Carr MacGehee		and Jacob Burruss
Robert Hall	Robert Kay		

---

(25) A soldier killed in French and Indian War.

(26) Divided by.

(27) Named as executor in will, refused to serve. Charles Goodall, Jr. acted as executor.

(28) Agatha was unable to settle estate to suit heirs. It was divided by William Tyler, Charles Tompkins and Daniel Tompkins.

1760

Decedent	Exec. or Adm.	Decedent	Exec. or Adm.
Henry Terrell	John Minor, James	William Isbell	Henry Isbell
	Redd(29), Daniel and	Thomas Norment	John Taylor(29),
	Christopher Tompkins		John Wiley, William
Samuel Walden	William Walden,		Boulware, Martha Hampton,
	Charles Moulson Eubank,		John George
	John Elliott Payne,	Sarah Brown	Henry Burk, Samuel
	George Dillard(29)		Wortham, Robert Lowery
Thomas Samuel	Thomas Royston(29),		and Thomas Collins
	John Long, Robert Scott	Humphrey Bell of London	John
	and Abraham Mitchell		Maynard of London
Charles Moulson	Anthony Thornton,	William Taliaferro	Edward Dixon,
	Adam Merryman, Greensley		Robert Gilchrist & James
	Wagoner & John Hampton(29)		Miller(29) (30)

---

(29) Divided by.

(30) William Taliaferro's heirs were not satisfied with the division of his estate and the court appointed James Taliaferro and Charles Carter to settle it. They were unable to reach a settlement and the court appointed Walker Taliaferro.

Decedent	Exec. or Adm.	Decedent	Exec. or Adm.
Moses Penn	William Parker, Eusabius Stone, Charles Storey(29)	Monoah Chiles	Samuel Redd(29), Joseph Woolfolk, John Minor and Christopher Tompkins
George Yates	Thomas Garrett		
Thomas Hamm	William Pratt		
John Hutchinson	Richard George(29), Rickens Brayme, Henry Isbell and William Wyatt	Joseph Hoomes of Caroline	Joseph Homes of Dinwiddie
Abraham Estis	William Tyler, Anthony Thornton & Robert Taliaferro(29)	Thomas Richerson	John Johns, William Boulware, Jeremiah Rawlings, John Baynham, John Taylor(29), Benj. Robinson, Anthony Thornton, Nicholas Battaile and Francis Taliaferro
John Clark	Benjamin Winn(29), William Higgins, Roger Quarles & Robert Tompkins		

(29) Divided by.

1761

Decedent	Exec. or Adm.	Decedent	Exec. or Adm.
William Alsop	John Rowe, Peyton Smith(29) & Thomas Samuel	William Conner	Aquilla Johnson(29), John Estis, Michael Yates, Samuel Hawes
Hugh Mitchell	Daniel ???	Francis Conway II	John Taylor
Robert Farish	George Buckner, Samuel Hawes, Aquilla Johnson	Edward Baber	Robert Brame, John Wyatt, John Buller and William Boulware(29)
Jeremiah Long	James Coleman(29) (31), Samuel Hawes, James Coleman, Benjamin Tompkins, Michael Yates(32)	John Gillison	Edward Dixon(29, James Bowie & John Boutwell
James Lewis	Robert Lowry, David Herndon, John Collins & Samuel Wortham(32)		

(29) Divided by.

(31) Commission unable to divide satisfactorily, estate turned over to Edmound Pendleton to administer.

(32) Estate in court for over ten years. Numerous administrators.

1762

Decedent	Exec. or Adm.	Decedent	Exec. or Adm.
Mary Hutchinson	William Brunskill, William Chiles, Rickens Brame, William Wyatt(29)	George Penn	William Cabal, Moses(29) Higinbotham, Aaron Higinbotham
Benjamin Robinson	Edward Dixon, Robert Gilchrist and James Bowie(29)	John Brunskill	John Allmond, John Montague, Benjamin Falkner & John Sutton(29)
Thomas Cheadle	Thomas Bankes, John Allmond, John Thompson, William Holman(29)	William Terrell	John Taylor, John Baynham(29), William Boulware(29), Jeremiah Rawlings
Joel Halbert	Frances Halbert	William Terrell	John Taylor, John Baynham, William Boulware (29), Jeremiah Rawlings
Joel Conner	William Holman, John Thompson, Roger Kuarles and Robert Tompkins(29)	Jeremiah Long	Samuel Harris(33)
James Boulware	William Boulware	James Martin	Francis Coleman

(29) Divided by.

(33) A new administrator for Jeremiah Long.

Decedent	Exec. or Adm.
William Meredith	Wm. Jr. and Letitia Meredith
Charles Hutchinson	Ambroise and Charles Jr. Hutchinson
Stephan Haynes	Benjamin Hubbard
Thomas Hickman	William Hickman
William Tyler	John Clark, Samuel Redd, Roger Quarles (29)
Abraham Spencer	Lucy Spencer
John Beazley	Oliver Towles, Jr., James Lindsay, Richard Ship and William Beazley (29)
William Jones	Richard West, Daniel Isbell, Thomas Jones (29)
John Whitlock	John Baynham, William Parker, John Taylor (35)
William Hunter	William Taliaferro, James Hunter, Fielding Lewis, Charles Dick (36)
Bartholomew Durrett	Christopher Tompkins, Roger Quarles, Benjamin Winn & Henry White
Robert Berries	Andrew Kennedey

Decedent	Exec. or Adm.
Ann Phillips	Thomas Dudley, Abraham Martin, Christopher Long & John Pemberton (29)
John Kay	James Taliaferro, Sr.
John Micou	Catherine & Paul Micou
James Powell	Benjamin Hubbard
John Dixon	Ann & John Jr. Dixon
John Gouch	Edmound Pendleton, James Jameson & William Parker (29)
Thomas Robinson	Graham Frank
William Hampton	George Catlett
James Lewis	Judith, John and James Lewis
Robert Dudley	John Garrett, Robert Garrett, Henry Ware (29)
Charles Moulson	James Miller (34)
James Lawson	Benjamin Hubbard (38), Francis Taylor, William Parker
John Glanton	Robert Gilchrist, James Taylor, James Miller (37)
James Walker	John Brame, James Hill, & John Cunningham

(29) Divided by.
(34) James Miller replaced Adam Merryman and Anthony Thornton.
(35) Divided estate after Mary Whitlock was unable to effect a settlement.
(36) Fielding Lewis and Charles Dick added as administrators for William Hunter.
(37) Ann Glanton was unable to settle estate after twelve years.
(38) John Pendleton dismissed and estate divided by Hubbard, Taylor and Parker.

1763

Decedent	Exec. or Adm.
Joseph Norment	Chestley Cockran
George Robinson	Robert Gilchrist
John Waters	Thomas Reynolds, Charles Pemberton, William Hill (29)
Priscilla Norment	Chestley Cockran
Isaac Arnold	Mary Arnold
John Smith	Mary Smith
Joseph Herndon	James Herndon
Thomas Fortune	Elizabeth Fortune
Edward Goode	John Richards, Robert Woolfolk, Francis Leghton (29)
Robert Kay	John Boutwell, John Bowie, John Catlett, John Miller (29)

Decedent	Exec. or Adm.
Michael Brassfield (39)	Edward Strickland
Thomas Richerson	Richard George, John Buller, John George, Ambroise Hutchinson (29)
Abraham Estis	Anthony Thornton, Thomas Buckner, Robert Taliaferro, Walker Taliaferro (29)
William Conner	George Yates
John Taliaferro	Francis & Robert Taliaferro
Anthony Sale	Robert Sale
Richard Clatterbuck	John Epperson, John Benson, Zachery Benson, Christopher Dudley (29)

(29) Divided by.
(39) Thomas Brassfield succeeded Edward Strickland.

Decedent	Exec. or Adm.	Decedent	Exec. or Adm.
1764		Daniel Tompkins	Christopher and
Robert Call	James Bowie		James Tompkins
Nicholas Battaile	William Woodford	John Holloway	John Holloway, Jr.
John Martin	Isabell Martin	James Singleton	Mary Singleton
Mary Gouge	James Gouge	Caleb Lindsay	James Pattie and
James Buller	Ann Buller		John Miller
John Lucas	Ambroise Hutchinson	Farrell Hughes	Ann Hughes
Benjamin Allen	Erasmus Allen	William Doyle	Mary Doyle
Nicholas Battaile	Hannah Battaile	Elizabeth Zachery	Peter Zachery
Spilsby Coleman	Richard Woolfolk &	William Daniel, the elder	William
	Francis Coleman		Daniel, Jr.
Elizabeth Goulder	Thomas Loving	John Lewis	John Lewis, Jr.
William White	Edward Dixon		
John Scott	Thomas Scott		

Decedent	Exec. or Adm.	Decedent	Exec. or Adm.
1765		John Taliaferro	Francis & Robert
Samuel James	Elizabeth Macphearson		Taliaferro
Joseph Meacham	Joseph & Elizabeth	Richard Tankersley	Joseph Tankersley
	Meacham	George Dillard	Isabell Dillard
Martin Vaughan	Elinor Vaughan	John Champe	Jane, William and
William Whitlock	William Jr. and		John Champe
	Ann Whitlock	Oliver Charles	Elizabeth Charles
Francis Taylor	James and Edmound	Peter Mason	Isabell Mason, Melche-
	Taylor		sedeck Brame, Benjamin
Ann Collins	Robert Gilchrist		Faulkner and Mathew
Thomas Mason	James Mason		Abbott
Alexander Atkinson	John Mici(?)	Charles Beazley	William Beazley
Robert Innis, clerk	(?)		
Jacob Tinsley	William Tinsley		

Decedent	Exec. or Adm.	Decedent	Exec. or Adm.
1766		Waller Chiles	John Thilman and
John Hoomes	Anthony Thornton		George Guy
James Vaughan	Jane Vaughan	John Pickett	Henry Pickett
Joseph Stevens	Robert Farish	Christopher Acuss	Sarah Acuss
William Broaddus	John Broaddus,	Moses Sprallin	Daniel Sprallin
	James Garnett, John	Ambroise Hutcherson	Richard George
	Redd, Robert Chap-	Robert George	Robert George, Jr.
	man & John Puller	William DeShazo	Elinor DeShazo
Charles Beazley	Cornelius Reynolds	James Collins	John Collins
Elisah Estis	William Tompkins	John Hoomes	Walker Taliaferro
John Miller	Ambroise Hoard,	John Pickett	John Pickett, Jr.
	Abraham Wilson, John	Robert Innis	Benjamin Hubbard, John
	Boutwell, John Carter		Penn & Eusabious Stone
Edward Gradle	Daniel Barksdale,	Farrell Hughes	Jeremiah Rawlings
	Adam Merryman,		Benjamin Milward, John Burk
	John Benson	Richard Straughn	Reuben Straughn
William Young	Margaret Young,	Robert Powell	Richard Woolfolk
	William Crisp	Richard Mathews	Sussannah Cockran
Phillip Phillips	Stephan Phillips	John Downer (?)	
Thomas Eubank	John Taylor	John Woolfolk	Paul Thilman
John Isbell	Daniel Isbell	Robert Armistead	Walker Taliaferro
Agatha Terrell	Pleasant Terrell		

Decedent	Exec. or Adm.	Decedent	Exec. or Adm.

1767

Decedent	Exec. or Adm.
George Mitchell	John Yates, Michael Yates, Aquilla Johnston and John Estis
Robert Foster	Anthony Thornton, William Parker, Thomas Lowry, John Penn
William Reynolds	John Sneed, Jr., Richard Blanton, Thomas Dudley
John Redd	James Garnett, James Bell, Robert Houston
James Jameson	Thomas Lowry, Thomas Groucher, William Hoard, John Snead
Richard Satterwhite	Simon Miller, Richard Alcock, George Alsop
John Miller	Simon Miller
Sussannah Miller	Ambroise Hoard, John Carter, Abraham Wilson, James Pattie
Thomas Bullard	Mary & John Eubank
John Isbell	Henry Isbell
Thomas Cheadle	Car MacGehee
William Coleburne (?)	Edmound Pendleton
John Plant	John Williamson
Ann Long	John Long
Nicholas Battaile	William Woodford
William Whitlock	John Taylor, John Baynham, Jeremiah Rawlings George Guy

Decedent	Exec. or Adm.
Mary Catlett	Thomas Slaughter, Thomas Royston, John Jeter, Giles Samuel
John Tyler	William Mullins, James Rennolds, George Buckner, Peter Goodwin
Mary Lyon	Thomas Jones, Thomas Laughlin, William Broughill, Richard Woolfolk
Henry Rains	George Holloway, Joseph Dillard, George Todd, William Buckner
Ambroise Lipscombe	Richard West, John Young, Melchezdick Brame, Benjamin Faulkner
George Catlett	Richard Buckner, Francis Taliaferro, David Cheves, Aylett Buckner
Thomas Bullar	Mary & John Eubank
Benjamin Robinson, Jr.	Christopher Robinson, Jr.
Ivey (?) Smith	John Smith
Richard Allcock	Richard Jr. and Thomas Allcock
Robert Stanfield	Benjamin Tompkins
Jacob Lovell	Thomas Lovell
Yelverton Stern	(?)
William Tyler	William Tyler, Jr.
Elizabeth Golders	John Loving
John Martin	Edmound Pendleton and John Penn
Charles Holloway	William Buckner, George Todd, George Yates, George Buckner

1768

Decedent	Exec. or Adm.
John Butler	John Taylor, George Gray, Jeremiah Rawlings, William Dudley
James Terrell	John Jones, Joseph Campbell, Jacob Burruss, John Thompson
Jacob Lovell	Daniel Lovell
Mordicai Abraham	Nicholas Martin
Robert Dudley	Robert Garrett and James Taylor
John Gilloison	James Bowie
William Allcock	Henry Ware, Henry Ware, Jr. and Robert Garrett

Decedent	Exec. or Adm.
William Taliaferro	Robert Gilchrist, James Miller, John Miller, Seth Walker, James Taliaferro
Francis Taliaferro	William Woodford, John Buckner, Seth Thornton, Richard Buckner
Robert Hall	Charles Stern
Flower Mason	(?)
Robert Jackson	John Thornton
Thomas Fortune	Edmound Pendleton, Jr., Benjamin Hubbard John Penn
Charles Carter	Edmound Pendleton and William Parker

Decedent	Exec. or Adm.	Decedent	Exec. or Adm.
Mary Gouge	Simon Miller, Wm. Miller, John Ford and George Alsop	Reuben Thornton	Francis Thornton
		Mathew Peatross	Samuel Burruss, Melchezdeck Brame, George Guy, Richard West
Jeremiah Rawlings	George Guy, William Dudley, Nathaniel Norment, Thomas Pittman	William Foster	Charles Mason, Melchezdeck Brame, Benjamin Faulkner, Richard West
Francis Tompkins	Robert Tompkins, Roger Quarles, Francis Durrett & James Yarbrough	Elizabeth Rennolds	John Miller, John Micou, John and William Boutwell
Thomas Samuel	Elizabeth Samuel	Edward Murray	James Pattie, William Boulware, William Cammack, James Gouge
Henry Gooch	William Quarles, Samuel Redd, John Harris, William Sutton	Joseph Willis	Mary Willis Singleton
		Henry Gooch	Martha Gooch
Reuben Thornton	William Buckner, George Holloway, George Buckner, Robert Garrett	John Downer	Samuel Hawes, Robert Taliaferro, George Buckner, Aquilla Johnston
Sarah Battaile	William Woodford, John Thornton, Seth Thornton, James Stevens	John Davis	John Benson, Adam Merryman, Charles White, Thomas Doggett

1769

Decedent	Exec. or Adm.	Decedent	Exec. or Adm.
Johnathan Johnson	John Minor, William Quarles, John Harris, Samuel Redd	Robert George	Samuel Wortham, Thomas Dickinson, John Buller & George Guy
Ellien McClarren	John Minor, John John Harris, John Thilman, Benjamin Johnston	(?) Lipscombe	Jacob Burruss
		Daniel McClaren	Mary McClaren
William Martin	Carr MacGehee, John Minor, John Chiles, Samuel Redd	James Carson	John Boutwell, John Bowie, Richard Allcock, Benjamin Allcock
William Rennolds	Eusabious Stone, John Sneed, Robert Foster, James Bell	Thomas Clayton	Mathew Gale, Jr., John White, James Rennolds, George Buckner
Moza Hurt	Thomas Jones	John Glanton	John Holloway
George Turner	John Turner, Jr., Robert Sale, James Upshaw, John Spindle	Samuel Hawes	Isaac Hawes
		William Johnston	Benjamin Johnston (Mistake in will used)
John Baynham	Johnann Baynham	John Godby	William Dudley, William Chiles, John Buller, Richard Wyatt
William Conner	Anthony Thornton, Aquilla Johnston, John Estis	Margaret Terrell	John Hampton, Joseph Campbell, Benjamin Spicer, Robert Collins
Mathew Peatross	Amy Peatross, William Peatross, Joseph Campbell and Joseph DeJarnette	John Lyon	Nicholas Lankford John Smith, Richard & Robert Woolfolk
John Riddle	William Parker, Richard Woolfolk, Thomas Jones, Francis Coleman	Peyton Stern	Elizabeth, David & Peyton Jr. Stern
Henry Buchhannon	Josiah Samuel, William Marshall, Richard Stevens, Benjamin Winn	Bartholomew Durrett	William Taliaferro, Samuel Hawes, Christopher Tompkins, Benjamin Tompkins

Decedent	Exec. or Adm.	Decedent	Exec. or Adm.
Charles Goodall	Charles Goodall, Jr.	Abraham Estis	Walker Taliaferro & Anthony Thornton, Samuel Hawes, Robert Taliaferro
Robert Kay	John Bowie, John Boutwell, Thomas Buckner, John Catlett	John Rowe	Francis Coleman, Thomas Samuel, Ellis Gravatt, John Long
John Godby	John Taylor, Jeremiah Rawlings, George Guy, William Dudley	James Castarpen (?)	James Coleman, George Buckner, Nicholas Yates, Aquilla Johnston
John Gillison	Johnathan Gibson	James Sale	Thomas Lowery, Thomas Croutcher, James Upshaw, Leroy Hipkins
James Terrell	Robert Mickleberry, Samuel Wortham, Thomas Dickinson	Aquilla Johnson (?)	
Robert Hall	Thomas Buckner, John Bowie, John Catlett, Thomas Sullirge, Giles Newton		

1770

Decedent	Exec. or Adm.	Decedent	Exec. or Adm.
George Whitlock	Norman Dickens, William Watkins, Reuben George, Thomas Dickinson	William Goode	Francis Coleman, John Eubank, Christopher Blackburn, Ambroise Bullard
William Desmukes	Thomas Buckner, Peter Thornton, Francis Coleman, John Pickett	Abraham Swinney	John Minor
		Francis Taliaferro	Charles Robinson
William Hargrove	Benjamin Hubbard, Chillion White, William Eubank, Francis Fleming	Elias Blackburn	Thomas Croutcher, Benjamin, John & Isreal Snead
Joseph Woolfolk	Thomas Wortham, James Campbell, James Terrell	James Vaughan	William Mothley, Maurice Knight, William Kidd, James Lovell
John Emerson	James Taylor, Henry Ware, Robert Garrett, James Ware, Thomas Daniel	John Miller	Charles Lewis, Charles Robinson, Andrew Leckie, John Bowie, William Lindsay
Thomas Samuel	Elizabeth Samuel	Daniel Isbell	Ann Isbell
John Ashburn	George Yates, Aquilla Johnston, John Estis, Joseph Flippo	John Dudley	Phillip Johnston
		George Kennon	James Taylor, George Todd, Robert Garrett, Thomas Allcock
Mary Pomfert	Jeremiah Rawlings, George Guy, Mathew Arnold, John Butler	Robert Sale	John Broaddus, Benjamin Snead, John Spindle
Thomas Samuel	John Jeter, John Evins, William Graves, Ambroise Jeter	John Harris	Francis Coleman, Jeremiah Pierce, Thomas Gutridge, James Johnston
James Sale	John Broaddus, William Hoard, Benjamin Snead, John Spindle	John Holloway	Robert Garrett, Daniel Barksdale, Thomas Buckner, Francis Epperson
Robert George	John Taylor	Robert Robinson	William Buckner, William Buckner, Jr., Francis Coleman, Jeremiah Pierce, James Johnston
Massey (,) Ralls	Edward Powers, William Parker, Jr., Samuel Major, John Cummings		
Eames Dismukes	Abraham Wilson, John Hailey, Walker Taliaferro, Cornelius Vaughan	Edward Levell—will	John Sutton, Richard Edmoundson, Nathaniel Normen & Thomas Burk
Waller Chiles	Jeremiah Pierce, George Guy, John Butler, Cheadle Burch, Johnathan Faulkner	George Goodloe	Henry Goodloe, Benjamin Tompkins & Oliver Towles, Jr.

Decedent	Exec. or Adm.	Decedent	Exec. or Adm.
Agathy Terrell	Pleasant Terrell,	Henry Gooch	Martha Gooch
James Bowcock	Francis Coleman,	Mary Howle (?)	John Thompton,
	James Johnston, Thomas		William Hewlett, Phillip
	and Reuben Samuel		Estis, Robert Cobb
John Goodloe	William Tyler,	John Beazley	William Hoard,
	Walker Taliaferro, Samuel		Charles Beazley, John
	Hawes, John Minor		and Isreal Sneed
John Beazley	Thomas Inscoe	Charles Waldron, Jr.	John Penn,
William Tinsley	Richard Ship,		John Pendleton, Jr.,
	William Toombs,		Chillion White, Benjamin
	George Alsop		Hubbard, William Eubank

1771

Decedent	Exec. or Adm.	Decedent	Exec. or Adm.
John Brown	Thomas Dickinson,	Diannah Goodloe	George Chapman,
	Samuel Wortham,		William Marshall, John
	John Hayley		Marshall, George Durrett
John Miller, the younger	Robert	John Mitchell	Benjamin Sneed,
	Gilchrist		John Sneed, William
Samuel Mathews	Richard Roy,		and James Daniel
	John Catlett, James	James Ledford	William Kidd &
	& Thomas Conduit		Henry Stuart
John Brunskill	William Brunskill	Kemp Taliaferro	Mary Taliaferro
	& Thomas Terry	William Wisdom	Richard Micou &
Charles Noden	Richard Woolfolk		Walter Anderson
	& Samuel Hargrave	John Ashburn	Mary Ashburn
Thomas Downer	John Downer	Thomas Daniel	Thomas Croutcher,
Thomas Hewlett	William Tyler		Charles Beazley,
	& John Minor		Richard Ship &
William Brunskill	George, Guy,		William Hoard
	Robert Mickleberry, Thomas	Walter Ross	George Yates, John
	Dickinson, Samuel Wortham		Estis, Aquilla John-
Nathaniel Conduit	Benjamin Hub-		ston, William Arnold
	bard, John Pendleton, Eusa-	John Holloway	Elizabeth Holloway
	bous Stone, John Walden	William Wren	Mary Wren
Richard Satterwhite	Robert Gilchrist	Henry Langford	William Craddock
Elizabeth Powell	Edward Dixon	George Holloway	Thomas Slaughter
Robert Kay	John Apperson		& Betty Holloway
James Samuel	(?) Samuel	Sarah Farish	Robert Farish
James Bowcock	Betty and Anthony	Dr. William Allison	Robert Gilchrist
	Bowcock		& Johnathan Gibson
Mary Ralls	Norman Dickens	John Halloway	Henry Ware, Jr.
George Dillard	Isabella Dillard	Daniel Johnston	Elizabeth Johnston
	& John Walden	Phillip Easten	John Walden
Francis Coleman	Richard Johnston	Thomas Johnston	Phillip Johnston
Mary Stevens	Edward Stevens	Edward Boulware	Elizabeth Boulware
William Oliver	William Oliver, Jr.	James Taylor	James Taylor, Jr.,
William Pitts	(?)		Thomas Lowry &
Thomas Conduit	James Conduit		James Upshaw

1772

Decedent	Exec. or Adm.	Decedent	Exec. or Adm.
Jeremiah Long	Walker Taliaferro,	Henry Chiles	William Tyler,
	John Armistead,		John Minor, Richard
	Benjamin Tompkins		Chandler, Roger Quarles,
	Samuel Hawes,		Thomas Wortham

Decedent	Exec. or Adm.	Decedent	Exec. or Adm.
Richard Keeling (left property to the children of William Tyler)	William Tyler, John Minor, Roger Quarles & Car Macgehee	Robert George, Jr. William Wyatt	John Taylor Henry, Richard & Gilbert Wyatt
Charles Beazley	Nancy Beazley	Robert Kay	John Apperson
James Terrell	Rogert Quarles, William Tyler, Robert Tompkins, John Chiles	Ann Goodall William Watkins James Hurt	Richard Goodall Margaret Terrell Clara Hurt
James Sale	Thomas Lowry	John Baylor	Nathaniel Burwell & John Armistead
Thomas Buckner	Geo. & Elizabeth Buckner	John Milear Lotty (?) Davis	John Milear, Jr. Edmound Pendleton, Thomas Lowry, James
John Haley	Mary & Thomas Haley & Joseph Campbell		Upshaw, Thomas Roan
Joseph Reynolds	Elizabeth Reynolds	John Palmer	John Oliver
William Dismukes	John, William & Mary Dismukes	George Holloway Lundsford Lomax	Betty Holloway (w) Thomas Lomax
Charles Stern	David & Peyton Stern	Richard West	Charles West
John Hackett	Sussannah Hackett	John Conner	Robert Tompkins
John Ashburn	Mary Ashburn	John Hackett	The Sheriff
Larkin Garnett	Thomas Garnett	James Jameson	Mary Jameson
William Tompkins	John Minor, Benjamin Tompkins, Francis Taliaferro	Charles Lewis Augustine Ellis Ludowick Murrah	Lucy renounced will William Price James Jeter
William Snead	John Snead	William Fox	Ann Fox
Joseph Gaunt	Sarah Gaunt	Thomas Buckner div.	Anthony
James Singleton	George Guy, Anthony New, Jeremiah Rawlings, Melchezdeck Brame		Thornton, Charles Robinson, Harry Beverley, Anthony Thornton, Jr.
Richard Woolfolk	Joseph Richerson & Robert Chandler	James Sullinger	Robert Gilchrist & Andrew Leckie, Jr.
George Kenner	Robert Gilchrist, James Taylor, John Buckner	Elizabeth Walden Adam Merryman	John Walden Joseph Stoneham
William Croucher	Joseph Campbell, Hugh and Charles Rose and Daniel Gaines	Thomas Roy Titus Hurt	John Beverley Roy John Sutton, Nathaniel Norment & Samuel Burruss
		Elizabeth Johnston	Anthony Thornton
John Winterton	Elizabeth Atkins	John Baylor	John Baylor, Jr.

1773

James Goodall	William Goodall of the province of Georgia	William Tompkins	Catherine Tompkins
John Jones	Ann Jones	Caleb Walker	Elizabeth Walker
George Carter	Joseph Carter	Elizabeth Macphearson	Anthony Thornton
William Pitts	Younger Pitts		
John Sneed	John & Benjamin Sneed	Samuel Sutton	Tibitha Sutton
Francis Taliaferro	Charles Dick	James Vaughan	Thomas Lowry, James Upshaw, Leroy Hipkins
Moses Carneal	John Durrett, John Wright, Joseph Campbell, Robert Chandler	Felix Taliaferro Richard Buckner	(?) John Buckner & Nathaniel Washington
Sarah Lowry	Stephan Lowry	Benjamin Graves	Lucrece Graves
Francis Smith	Christopher Smith	Lawrence Battaile	Sarah Battaile
Benjamin Milward	John Penn		

Decedent	Exec. or Adm.	Decedent	Exec. or Adm.
John Downer, the Elder	Robert Dabney, Walker Taliaferro, Samuel Hawes, George Buckner, John Jones	Charles Robinson	Walker Taliaferro & Joseph Robinson
		Benjamin Robinson	Thomas Slaughter
William Buchell	Robert Broaddus	Easter Landrum	John Henshaw
William Murrah	Richard Buckner	William Herndon	Wm. Jr. & James Herndon

1774

Decedent	Exec. or Adm.	Decedent	Exec. or Adm.
Richard George	Henry Gains & Robert George	Harry Beverley	Dr. John Tennant
		Benjamin Harrison	Edwin Motley
Ann Hart	John Hart	Thomas Collins	Thomas Collins, Jr.
Elizabeth Rennolds	Benjamin Estis	Mary Buckley	Mary Buckley
John Hackett	so inconsiderable	George Kenner	John & Margaret* Dugart
John Boutwell	William Boutwell		
Thomas Fortune	Elizabeth Fortune	John Cheadle	Samuel Hargrave & Carr MacGehee
Thomas Cheadle	Elizabeth Cheadle		
James Wright	Elizabeth Wright	James Riddle	Elizabeth Riddle
Thadeus Pruitt	Mary Pruitt	William Coates	John Coates
Phillip Tinsley	William Tinsley	John Sneed	Richard Blanton
Easter (Esther) Bell	John Bell & Robert Wright	Henry White	John & Frances White
William Cammack	Mary Cammack	Benjamin Samuel	Reuben & Robert Samuel
Anthony Samuel	William Stevens		

*Transferred from Robert Gilchrist, James Taylor and John Buckner.

1775

Decedent	Exec. or Adm.	Decedent	Exec. or Adm.
Thomas Reynolds	Elizabeth Reynolds	Milley Buckley	Mary Buckley Phillips
Sarah Tyler	William Tyler		
James Isbell	Frances Isbell	Andrew Morrow	Joseph Jones
George Kenner	James Miller	Samuel Wortham	Margaret Wortham & Joseph Robinson
Richard Richards	John Clark		
John George	James George	Giles Samuel	Elizabeth, Giles & Jesse Samuel
Garrett Hackett	Frances Hackett		
Peter Thornton	Elizabeth renounced will	Josiah Tompkins	James Tompkins
		Joseph Flippo	Sarah Flippo
Thomas Doggett	John & Thomas Doggett	John Turner	John & James Turner
		Catherine Taliaferro	(?)
Robert George	Mary George	William Summerson	William Parker
James Garnett	James Garnett, Jr.	John Cummings	Peyton Stern

1776

Decedent	Exec. or Adm.	Decedent	Exec. or Adm.
John Watts	William Bernard	Peter Thornton	Anthony Thornton, James Bankhead, Sr.
Joseph Walston	William Adkinson		
Samuel Robinson	William Robinson & Joshua Tinsley	Judith Bankes	Sarah Battaile
		William Parker	John Parker
John Watts	John Ashton	Richard Devenport	David Devenport
Elizabeth B. Pea	(?)	George Spicer	James Dunlop
Gabriel Toombs	Edmound Toombs	Prettyman Saunders	Sarah Saunders
Redmond Coates	John Thompson & Melchezdeck Brame	Hannah Scott	Thomas Dogett
Ann MacGehee	Carr MacGehee	Charles Mason	David Mason
Charles Yarbrough	(?)	Elizabeth Chiswell	William Nelson

Decedent	Exec. or Adm.	Decedent	Exec. or Adm.
1777			
Humphrey Singleton	Joseph Willis	Daniel Duval	Henry & John Duval
William Hargrave	John Hargrave	Richard Boulware	John Boulware
Birkenhead Boutwell	Adam Boutwell	Ann Hambleton	Richard Hambleton
William Rouse	Simon Miller	John Buckner	Elizabeth Buckner
William Summerson	Ann Parker	Henry Burk	John Burk
William Samuel	James Kay	Benjamin Alsop	George Alsop
Joel Harris	Sarah Harris	Samuel Burruss	Samuel Burruss, Jr.
James Yarbrough	Mary Yarbrough	Barbara Davis	John Davis
Caleb Lindsay	Caleb Lindsay, Jr.	Thomas Ship	Richard & Gideon Ship
George Smith	Sussannah Smith	Richard Buckner	Richard Buckner, Jr.
John Baynham	John Peatross	Samuel Wortham	Joseph Richerson,
William Wyatt	Henry, Richard &		Samuel Temple, Anthony
	Gilbert Wyatt		New, George Guy
1778			
Thomas Downer	John Pickett	William Johnston	Ann Johnston
Daniel Tompkins	James Tompkins	David Devenport	David Mason
Elijah Samuel	James Samuel	William Chiles	John Chiles
William Beazley	Ann Beazley	Thomas Moore	James Moore
Jeter Samuel	Elizabeth Samuel	Sarah Eubank	James Eubank
Richard Young	Richard & Leonard	George Yates	(?)
	Young	John Baynham	Anthony New
William Samuel	John Samuel	John Estis	John Estis, Jr.
Reuben Royston	Sarah Royston	George Cheadle	Henry Chiles
Robert Tankersley	Henry Micou	John Estis	William Yates &
Minoah Chiles	Carr MacGehee		George Yates
	Samuel Hargrave	Jesse Samuel	(?)
John Burruss	Joseph Campbell &	John Samuel	William Samuel
	James Gatewood	William Hoard	James Upshaw &
Elizabeth Buckner	John Buckner		James Fletcher
James Bowie	John Skinker	Henry Cooper	Ann Mitchell
Sarah Harris	George Guy	John Davis	Sussannah Davis
William Wyatt	Richard & Henry	Jacob Burruss	William Tinsley
	Wyatt	Henry Burk	Thomas Burke
Phillip George	Reuben George	Richard Ship	William Murrah &
Humphrey Hubbard	William Yates		Richard Ship
John Eubank	John & George Eubank		
1779			
Martin Hollins	Benjamin Hollins	Samuel Boutwell	Adam Boutwell
John Samuel	Elizabeth Samuel	Thomas Samuel	Giles Samuel
Ann Chick	William & Shadrack	Thomas Buckner	Phillip & Eliza-
	Wisdom		beth Buckner
Joseph Flippo	Sarah Flippo	Waller Chiles	Johnston Faulkner
Christopher Tompkins	John Minor	William Burruss	Jemina Burruss
Benjamin Mason	Elizabeth & James	William Harrison	Thomas Beazley
	Mason		& Eusabious Stone
Edward Dixon	Henry & Turner	Benjamin Graves	George Guy
	Dixon	John Jones	Thomas Jones
James Beuden	Harry Beuden	Nicholas Page	John Page
Clark Trainham	Davis Trainham	Henry Pemberton	Richard Pemberton
Mary George	John Thilman		

Decedent	Exec. or Adm.	Decedent	Exec. or Adm.
1780			
William Graves	John Ashburn	Rebecca Bradley	Peyton Stern
	William Hill	Elizabeth Samuel	Giles Newton
John Burruss	William Burruss	Duncan Graham	Robert Graham
James Coleman	Thomas & Daniel	Mercy Rennolds	(?)
	Coleman	Sarah Baber	Francis Baber
William Dismukes	Frances Dismukes	Lawrence Anderson	(?)
John Carneal	Patrick Carneal		
1781			
Francis Durrett	William Durrett	Nathaniel Norment	Nathaniel
Robert Armistead	(?)		Norment, Jr.
James B. Meacham	Charles Mason	Joseph Hatton	James Hicks
Adam Boutwell	Abraham Wilson	John Boutwell	Abraham Wilson
Charles Beazley	Thomas & Benja-	William Martin	Elizabeth Martin
	min Beazley	William Woodford	Mary Woodford
Benjamin Hubbard	James Taylor	Thomas Collins	(?)
Ambroise Hoard	John Hoard	Reuben Saunders	(?)
Henry Martin	Mary Martin	Benjamin Sneed	Mary Sneed
George Green	Mary Ann Green	Alexander Fortune	Dacie Fortune
William Robinson	(?)	Elizabeth Buckner	Elizabeth Buckner
John Elliott Payne	William Payne	Thomas Lowry	William Richards
Joseph Saunderson	Thomas Allcock	John Brown	Henry Brown
Abraham Wilson	(?)	Nicholas Oliver	Richard & Nicholas
Euclid Whitlock	George Guy		Oliver
Charles Goodall	William Quarles	John Dickinson	Martha Dickinson
Achilles Durrett	John Durrett	Josiah Samuel	(?)
John Chenault	Sarah Chenault	John Dudley George	Lucy George
James Micou	Mungo Roy	Hugh Croucher	James Croucher
Thomas Sullinger	(?)	John Cliff	William Cliff
Reuben Bullard	Catherine Bullard	Thomas Adams	John Long
		William Page	James Page

GUARDIANS AND WARDS

Prior to 1750 few orphans had guardians in Caroline. The Order Books list those of record in 1740 when the court ordered all guardians to file their accounts in accordance with a new act of the General Assembly. These guardians with their wards were:

Richard Phillips, guardian of Ann Owins, dismissed because Ann had married.

Rev. John Brunskill, guardian of Marcina Livingston, failed to appear. The court ordered the sheriff to arrest him and bring him before it at its next session.

Richard Taliaferro, guardian of John Evins, exhibited his accounts and they were in order. Taliaferro had apprenticed Evins to Benjamin Duval, a carpenter.

Thomas Oakley, guardian of Ann and John Gough, was given until the next court to make up his accounts. Thomas married Ann, but the marriage was not successful and she sued for separate maintenance.

John Turner, guardian of John Townsing, dismissed because Townsing was of age.

Duncan Bohannon, guardian of Mary Burton, summoned from Orange County where he had moved after he qualified.

Mary Catlett, spinster, guardian of Elizabeth Evins, dismissed because Elizabeth had married.

Anthony Strother, guardian of Thomas Catlett II, account recorded.

Francis Poultney, guardian of Thommason Prince, account recorded.

Hausen Kenner, guardian of George Kenner, summoned from Prince William County.

Between 1740 and 1750 there were only six other qualifications. They follow:

Date	Ward	Guardian
1742—Elizabeth and Mathew Singleton		Robert Gilchrist
1743—Mary Evins		John Garnett
1743—Francis Stern, the son of David Stern		David Stern, Jr.
1744—Ann and Mary Stevens, daughters of James Stevens		Owin Thomas
1744—Richard Rogers, son of Robert Rogers		Adam Lindsay(1)
1744—William Collawn, son of Bawldin Collawn		William Lindsay(1)

(1) Rogers and Collawn became apprentices of the Lindsays.

The General Assembly passed another act to protect the estates of orphans in 1749 and after that date the record of guardians and wards in Caroline is complete. This list follows with date of qualification and names of parents in parenthesis after the names of the wards if the parents' names are revealed in the Order Books.

Date	Ward	Guardian
1750—Johnathan Gibson II (George) (4)		William Waller
	William and Machael Gibson (George) (1)	Robert Gilchrist
	Mary Gibson (George)	Jeremiah Pierce

Date	Ward	Guardian
	John, Mary and Sarah Rowe (William)	Benjamin Rowe
	Mary Ware	James Lindsay
	Rachael, Sussannah, Catherine and Mary Battaile (Lawrence and Sarah) (9)	Francis Thornton
	Lawrence Battaile, Jr. (Lawrence and Sarah) (2)	Thomas Buckner
	Robert Coleman (Samuel and Betty)	William Johnston
1751—	Tibitha Booth	James Trice
	Jane Pigg	Sarah Pigg
	William Yarbrough	Mathew Peatross
	William Quarles (Roger and Jane)	John Quarles
	Eleanor and Mary Marsh (5)	James Martin
	Philemon Caughland	Thomas Samuel
1752—	James Sale	William Sale
	Mary Sale	Giles Samuel
	Lawrence Catlett	Adam Lindsay
	John and Ann Harris	William Boulware
	Ann, Ursula and Jane White (Thomas)	Sussannah White
	Elizabeth Coleman (Samuel and Betty Wyatt)	William Green
	Cornelius Rennolds (Joseph)	Catherine Rennolds
	John, Elizabeth, Micajah and Jane Johns (Richard)	William Richerson
1753—	Thomas Collawn, Jr. (Thomas)	Robert Stuart
	Elizabeth Noden (Hugh)	Charles Noden
	Lucy Slaughter	Thomas Turner
	James Stevens (John)	Thomas Murray
	John Stevens, Jr. (John)	Owin Thomas
1754—	Spilsbey and Francis Coleman (Samuel Betty Wyatt)	Richard Woolfolk (7)
	Ann Hill	William Smith
	Charles Smith	David Stern
1755—	Thomas Rennolds (John)	John Picket, the Younger
	Lucy Terry (Thomas)	Thomas Terry, Jr.
	Thomas Apperson (Thomas Sr.)	Frances Apperson
	Daniel, Mary and Eusabious Hubbard (John)	George Carter
	Rose, Elizabeth, Mary and Frances Taliaferro (Richard)	William Taliaferro of King and Queen (6)
	William Guilliam	William Sale
	Mary and Rose Grant (Daniel) (11)	Ellis Gravatt

Date	*Ward*	*Guardian*
	Charles Taliaferro (Richard)	John Evins (8)
	Richard Taliaferro (Richard)	William Taliaferro of King and Queen
1756—	Margaret Grant (Daniel)	Ellis Gravatt
	James Riddle, Jr. (James)	Elizabeth Riddle
	John Hubbard, Jr. (John)	George Carter
	Joseph Hoomes (George)	Edmound Pendleton
	Thomas Jackson	Joshua Lindsay
	Ann and Sarah Lyon (Robert) (9)	Mary Lyon, their mother
1757—	John Turner	William Turner
	John and Priscilla Cockran	Chesley Cockran
	Henry Tandy	William Tandy
	Nellie, Molly, Joseph, Ann, John and William Cooper	Jane Cooper
	Daniel Grant, Jr. (Daniel)	Ellis Gravatt
	Harry, Mary and Sarah Taliaferro (Kemp)	Mary Taliaferro
	Benjamin, Edmound and Winnie Munday (John)	John Long
	John Jr., Reuben and Sarah Munday (John)	James Munday
	Sarah Ship (Joseph)	Arch Ship
	Mary and Mildred Lyon (Robert)	William Johnston
1758—	Arch Ship II (Joseph)	Mary Ship, his mother
	Michael Ship (Joseph)	William Toombs
	John Mason	Peter Mason
1759—	Robert Tompkins (Humphrey)	William Holdam
	James, Margaret, George and Thomas Crutchfield (William)	Richard West (13)
	Molly Triplett (Daniel)	Sarah Triplett
	Thomas Coleman II (Samuel and Betty Wyatt)	Thomas Soleman
	John Taylor (Elizabeth)	Ann Taylor
1760—	George Yates, Jr. (George)	Thomas Garrett
	Ann and Charles Terrell (Henry)	David Terrell
	Elizabeth, Lucy, Benjamin and Mary Estis (Abraham)	Elizabeth Estis, their mother (10)
	Benjamin Isbell (William)	Henry Isbell
1761—	Catherine and Martha Farish (Robert)	Sarah Farish, their mother
	John, Ann and Martha Chiles (Thomas)	Carr MacGehee
	Millie Norment	Nathaniel Norment
	George Marsh	John Oliver
	Sarah, Ann, Frances and William Burch (Birch)	Thomas Burch (Birch)

Date	*Ward*	*Guardian*

1762—Mary and Thomas Haynes (Stephen)   Benjamin Hubbard
    Benjamin Milear   John Milear
    Alben Mears, Jr. (Alben)   Jeremiah Rawlings
    John Woodford (William)   William Woodford, Jr.

1763—James Todd, Robert and Thomas Livingston
       (Thomas Sr.)   William Boulware
    Jane Thilman   Paul Thilman
    William Durrett (Bartholomew)   James Riddle
    Mary Durrett (Bartholomew)   Benjamin Winn
    Joel Durrett (Bartholomew)   Richard Durrett
    George, Frances, Elizabeth, John, Euclid (12)
       and Thomas Whitlock (John Sr.)   Norment Dickens
    William Thomas   John Watts

1764—Thomas Hewlett   John Watts
    Eleanor Baber (Edward)   Francis Baber
    Samuel Sale (Anthony)   William Hoard
    Dorothy Durrett (Bartholomew)   Benjamin Winn
    Robert Kay, Jr. (Robert)   Robert Gilchrist
    Josiah, Ann and Sussannah Tompkins
       (Daniel)   Daniel Tompkins, Jr. (14)
    William, John, Elizabeth, Martha, Frances
       and Joel Halbert (Joel Sr.)   Frances Halbert, their mother
    Joseph, Nicholas and Richard Bridges
       (Morgan)   Joseph Lankford
    Jane Chalmers (Sarah)   Benjamin Hubbard
    John Hoomes (Joseph)   Edmound Pendleton
    Priscilla Norment   Jeremiah Rawlings
    Mark and Sarah Ship (Joshua)   William Toombs
    Martin Crutchfield (William)   Ambroise Lipscombe

1765—Judith Martin   Abraham Martin
    John Jackson   William Daniels
    John, Peggy, Mary and Elizabeth
       Gillison (John)   Johnathan Gibson II
    Francis III, Catlett II, Mary and Sarah
       Conway (Francis II)   George Taylor
    Fanny Pemberton   William Pemberton (18)

1766—Elisha Estis, Jr. (Elisha)   William Tompkins
    Mark Boulware   Edward Vauter
    Sarah and James Chambers   Lawrence Battaile
    Robert, Ambroise and Rachael Pruitt   Thomas Laughlin
    Robert Stevens   Charles Todd
    Ann Downer (John)   Samuel Sterns

Date	*Ward*	*Guardian*
	Thomas and Molly Downer (John)	John Downer, Jr.
	Christopher Terrell (Agatha)	Pleasant Terrell
1767—	Hay Battaile (Nicholas)	William Woodford II
	John, Nicholas, Jr. and Lucy Battaile (Nicholas)	Joseph Jones(16)
1768—	Henry Turner	Walker Taliaferro
	Gawin Corbin	William Woodford II
	Elizabeth Ship (Joseph)	William Toombs
1769—	George, Thomas, Sarah, Ursula, Judy, Lucy, Betsy and Jacob Cheadle (Thomas)	John Minor(17)
	James Kay (Robert)	Robert Gilchrist
	John Conner (William)	Anthony Thornton
	William Conner, Jr. (William)	William Rogers
	Rice and Francis Conner (William)	George Yates
	Frances, Ann, Margaret and George(20) Conner (William)	Frances Conner (mother)
1770—	Terrell Hughes	George Guy
	Elizabeth and Mary (Fleming Chiles)	Robert Chandler
	John Mills (James)	Thomas Collins
	Thomas Hackett, the Younger	Robert Mickleberry
	William Lawson	Thomas Slaughter
1771—	Daniel Coleman, Jr. (Daniel)	James Coleman
	Edward Leavell	John Leavell
	Sally Daniels (Thomas)	Thomas Sale
	Gideon Coghill (Zachery)	William Penny
	Betty, Mary, Ann, Delphia and Lucy Daniels (Thomas)	Mary Daniels (mother)
	David, Elizabeth and Mary Jameson (James)	Edmound Pendleton
	Martha Hewlett (Thomas)	William Hewlett
	Russell and George Godby	Francis Baber
	James Leavell	William Pemberton
	Mary Sale	Samuel Sale
1772—	John Taylor	Edmound Pendleton
	John Long (Jeremiah)	Abraham Wilson
	John Russell, Jr. (John)	William Quarles
	John Yarbrough	Charles Yarbrough
	Elizabeth Davis	John Spindle
	Mary Conner (John)	William Tyler
	John Conner, Jr. (John)	Robert Tompkins
	Charles Holloway (George)	Betty Holloway (mother)

Date	*Ward*	*Guardian*
	Ignatius West (Richard)	Samuel Burruss
	John West (Richard)	William Peatross
	Joseph and Ann West (Richard)	William Young
	William and Alice West (Richard)	Charles West
	Rodham Kenner II (George)	James Miller
	Daniel and Clara Johnston (William)	Elizabeth Johnston (mother)
	William Buckner (Thomas)	John Buckner
	Elizabeth Buckner (Thomas)	George Buckner
	Elizabeth and Agnes Hurt (Titus)	James Ware
1773—	Caty Johnston (William)	Robert Coleman
	Ambroise Powell (Robert)	Robert Powell, Jr.
	James Garnett (Larkin)	Thomas Garnett
	John, Robert and Mary Ann Scott (Thomas)	————
1774—	Robert Gains Beverley (Harry)	Robert Brock(19)
	Charles Carter Robinson (Benjamin)	Thomas Slaughter
	Thomas Lowry (William)	John Collins
	Betty Daniel (Thomas)	William Rennolds
	Nelly Daniel (Thomas)	Phillip Buckner
	Augustine and John Taliaferro Lewis (Charles)	Joseph Jones
	Elizabeth, Richard and Francis Smith, Jr. (Francis)	William Richerson
	William Lowry, Jr. (William)	Thomas Collins
	Joseph Baynham (John)	Anthony New
	William Loving (Jacob)	William Robinson
	Mary Sale (James)	William Dunn
	William and Molly Coates (William)	Dianna Coates (mother)
	Ann Coleman (Francis)	James Johnston
	John Smith (Francis)	Christopher Smith
	William Samuel (Thomas)	Giles Newton
	Elizabeth Samuel (Thomas)	Elizabeth Samuel (mother)
	Joseph Stevens, Jr. (Joseph)	Robert Farish II
	Richard Roy and Jane Beverley Cammack (William)	Mary Cammack (mother)
	George, Robert, John and Christopher Cammack (William)	William Cammack, Jr.
	Thomas Terry, Jr. (Thomas)	George Guy
1775—	Thomas Lyon (Andrew)	Thomas Garnett)
	George Holloway (John)	James Newton
	Jane Chandler (Richard Woolfolk Chandler)	Joseph Richerson

Date	*Ward*	*Guardian*
	Richard, Samuel, John and Margaret Chandler (Richard Woolfolk Chandler)	Joseph Richerson and Robert Chandler
1776—	Ann and Richard Turner (John)	John Turner, Jr.
	George Doggett (Thomas)	George Turner
	Gawin Summerson (William)	William Parker
	Ann, William and Elizabeth Smith	Thomas Lowry
	Griffin and Abner George (John)	Reuben George
	Betty Hackett (Garrett, Sr.)	Frances Hackett (mother)
	Garrett Hackett, Jr. (Garrett)	Joseph Campbell
1777—	Molly and Richard Ship (Thomas)	Richard Ship
	Lucy and Samuel Ship (Thomas)	Robert Wright
	Charles and Fanny Wortham (Samuel)	Joseph Richerson
	Happy Turner	James Hambleton
	Stephen Mason (Charles)	David Mason
	Patty Gaunt	William Gaunt
	Benjamin Yarbrough (Charles)	Roger Quarles
1778—	Ann Douglass Chiles (Minoah)	James Samuel
	Reuben Eubank (Sarah)	John Eubank
	Lucy and Betsy Tankersley (Joseph)	John Tankersley
	Thornton Washington	Samuel Washington
	Mildred Lewis (Charles)	John Lewis
	Dabney Chiles (William)	Jemina Chiles
	Phoebe Royston (Reuben)	William Watkins
	Elizabeth and John Harris (John and Sarah)	George Guy
	Mary Stern (Charles)	Peyton Stern
	Samuel Coleman II (Francis)	Robert Johnston
	Francis, James and Mary Devenport (Daniel)	David Devenport
1779—	Robert and Bernard Rennolds (James)	William Rennolds
	Thomas Samuel, Jr. (Thomas Samuel)	Giles Samuel
	Robert, Polly, John, Molly and William Sale (Robert)	Ambroise Pitts
	Mary Estis (John)	Daniel Coleman
	Dangerfield and Phoebe Graves (Benjamin)	George Guy(24)
	Jennings Burruss (Samuel)	Samuel Burruss, Jr.
	Orphans of James Isbell	George Guy
1780—	Martha Harrison (William)	William Harrison, Jr.
	John Holloway (John)	Robert Ware
	William and Mary Pemberton (Harry)	William Harrison, Jr.
	Thomas Terry Cook (Henry)	George Guy

Date	*Ward*	*Guardian*
1781—Rejoice Hatton (Joseph)		David Wright
Mary and John Hatton (Joseph)		John Hogan
James Emerson (John)		David Stern
Richard, John, Catherine, Peter and Margaret Buckner (John)		John Washington
Sarah Samuel (Thomas)		William Beazley
Molly, George and Warren Yates (George)		Benjamin Winn
Martica, Milly, Caty, Achilles, Caleb, Ann, and Oliver Durrett (Achilles)		Benjamin Winn

(1) Transferred to Jeremiah Pierce—1751.

(2) Transferred to Joseph Hoomes—1751; to Benjamin Grymes—1752; to George Muse jointly with Benjamin Grymes in 1757.

(4) Transferred to William Boulware—1753.

(5) Transferred to John Oliver—1754.

(6) Transferred to Zachery Taliaferro of Caroline—1755.

(7) Transferred to William Johnston—1755.

(9) Transferred to William Boughill—1757.

(10) Transferred to Aquilla Johnston—1763.

(11) Rossannah, formerly called Rose. Grant transferred to William Samuel —1764.

(12) Transferred to Namoah Gibson—1754.

(13) George Crutchfield transferred to Ambroise Lipscombe—1764.
George and Thomas Crutchfield transferred to Stapleton Crutchfield—1767.

(14) Transferred to James Tompkins—1769.

(16) Transferred to James Taylor—1769.

(17) Transferred to Henry Chiles—1773.

(18) Transferred to Robert Foster—1774.

(19) Transferred to Richard Johnston—1777.

(20) Transferred to William Conner, Jr.—1778.

(21) Transferred to William Murray—1778.

(22) Transferred to William Murray—1778.

(24) Transferred to Joseph DeJarnette—1780.

INDEX

A

Abbott, Mathew, 479
Aberdeen, Alexander, 396
Aberdeen, Scotland, 396
Abraham, Joseph, 403, 455
  Mordicai, 133, 326, 384, 401, 402, 403, 408, 460, 480
Abraham v. Taylor & Cowne, 442, 450, 456
Accomac, 9, 21
Acors, Charles, 463
  family, xv
  See also Acres; Acuss.
Acres, Christopher, 367, 435, 463
  Christopher, Jr., 463
  See also Acors; Acuss
Actors, 420
Acuss, Christopher, 367, 435, 463, 479
  Christopher, Jr., 463
  Sarah, 479
  See also Acors; Acres
Adams, John, 380, 381, 382, 462
  Thomas, 487
Adkinson, William, 485
Administrators of Estates (1732-1781), 470-487
Adultery, 424-425
Adventure (ship), 270
Africa, slaves from, 30, 31, 33, 53, 72, 94, 142, 278, 332, 401
  See also Slaves
Albemarle, Earl of, 135
Albemarle County, 130
Alcock, Richard, 480
  See also Allcock
Alcoholic beverages, 139, 218
  See also Ale; Beer; Brandy; Liquors; Wines
Ale, 415
Alestock, Charles, 464
  Lewis, 446
  Reuben, 446
Alexandria, 143
Algonquian tribes, 4, 39
Algonquin Indians, 51
Allcock (Allcocke), Benjamin, 481
  Richard, 369, 480, 481
  Richard, Jr., 480
  Thomas, 164, 370, 388, 434, 457, 480, 482, 487
  William, 112, 146, 329, 331, 351, 365, 387, 388, 433, 480
  See also Alcock
Alleghaney Mountains, 4, 283

Allen, Abraham, 471
  Benjamin, 367, 479
  Daniel, 437
  Eleanor, 428
  Erasmus, 479
  Francis, 90
  Isaac, 315, 470
  James, 362, 376
  John, 373, 447, 474
  Robert, 174, 455
  Sussannah, 427
  Thomas, 311
  William, 373
Allison, William, 327, 476
  Dr. William, 450-451, 483
Allmond, John, 146, 333, 365, 412, 476, 477
Alps, 34
Alps-Sparta-Smoots Mill, 39
Alsop, Benjamin, 464, 465, 486
  Dolly, 366
  George, 464, 480, 481, 483, 486
  William, 477
Ambler, Richard, 396
Ambroise, Robert, 299
Amelia County, 288
American atlas, 290
American prisoners, 273
American ships, 279
  See also Ships
Amherst, Lord Jeffry, 205
Ammunition, 241, 242, 248, 255, 291
  See also Gunpowder
Amoroleck, 7
Anastrania, 3, 7
Anderson, Mr., 101
  Andrew, 397
  Charles, 373
  Dabney, 470
  James, 280, 376
  John, 96, 361, 373, 433, 470
  Joseph, 470
  Lawrence, 351, 367, 487
  Mary, 377, 428
  Moses, 438
  Nathaniel, 181, 406, 447
  Richard, 373, 444
  Robert, 471
  Walter, 483
  William, 307, 373
Anderson's Bridge, 291
Andirons, 379
Andrews, Henretta, 327
  Joseph, 470

www.ingramcontent.com/pod-product-compliance
Lightning Source LLC
Chambersburg PA
CBHW031934090426
42811CB00002B/178